Fundamentals of Mass Communication Law

Fundamentals of Mass Communication Law

DONALD M. GILLMOR
Silha Professor of Media Ethics and Law
University of Minnesota

JEROME A. BARRON
Lyle T. Alverson Professor of Law
National Law Center
The George Washington University

TODD F. SIMON
Professor of Journalism
Michigan State University

HERBERT A. TERRY
Professor of Telecommunications
Indiana University

West Publishing Company
Minneapolis/St. Paul
New York
Los Angeles
San Francisco

WEST'S COMMITMENT TO THE ENVIRONMENT

In 1906, West Publishing Company began recycling materials left over from the production of books. This began a tradition of efficient and responsible use of resources. Today, 100% of our legal bound volumes are printed on acid-free, recycled paper consisting of 50% new paper pulp and 50% paper that has undergone a de-inking process. We also use vegetable-based inks to print all of our books. West recycles nearly 22,650,000 pounds of scrap paper annually—the equivalent of 187,500 trees. Since the 1960s, West has devised ways to capture and recycle waste inks, solvents, oils, and vapors created in the printing process. We also recycle plastics of all kinds, wood, glass, corrugated cardboard, and batteries, and have eliminated the use of polystyrene book packaging. We at West are proud of the longevity and the scope of our commitment to the environment.

West pocket parts and advance sheets are printed on recyclable paper and can be collected and recycled with newspapers. Staples do not have to be removed. Bound volumes can be recycled after removing the cover.

Production, Prepress, Printing and Binding by West Publishing Company.

TEXT IS PRINTED ON 10% POST CONSUMER RECYCLED PAPER

Printed with Printwise
Environmentally Advanced Water Washable Ink

Copyediting: Pat Lewis
Interior and Cover Design: Jeanne Lee
Composition: Carlisle Communications
Index: Sonsie Carbonara Conroy
Photo Credits:
2 UPI/Bettmann; 44 © Robert Brenner/PhotoEdit; 82 Reuters/Bettmann; 120 © Robert Brenner/PhotoEdit; 142 © John Coletti/Tony Stone Worldwide, Ltd.; 158 AP/Wide World Photos; 186 © 1993, Mark Reinstein/FPG International; 216 © Robert Brenner/PhotoEdit; 242 Tony Stone Images; 256 © Jim Craigmyle, Masterfile; 270 © Michael Newman/PhotoEdit; 278 © E. Alan McGee/FPG; 340 © J.A. Kraulis/Masterfile.

03 02 01 00 99 98 97 96   8 7 6 5 4 3 2 1 0
Library of Congress Cataloging in Publication Data

ISBN: 0-314-06238-6 (Hard)

Contents in Brief

Contents

CHAPTER 3:
PRIVACY AND THE MASS MEDIA   **82**

CHAPTER 4:
JOURNALIST'S PRIVILEGE   120

CHAPTER 5:
OBSCENITY AND INDECENCY   142

CHAPTER 8:
PUBLIC ACCESS TO THE MEDIA

CHAPTER 9:
ADVERTISING: LAW AND REGULATION

CHAPTER 10:
MONOPOLY, DIVERSITY, AND ANTITRUST LAW   256

CHAPTER 11:
STUDENT PRESS RIGHTS   270

CHAPTER 12:
ELECTRONIC MEDIA LAW   278

CHAPTER 13:
INTELLECTUAL PROPERTY AND MEDIA BUSINESS ISSUES   340

APPENDIX: UNDERSTANDING THE AMERICAN LEGAL SYSTEM 376

Media and Law in Changing Times

I magine, if you can, a world without artificially mediated communication—no print, no photography, no video or audio recording, no broadcasting, no Internet. Such an oral society would move through a series of three-generation windows. There would always be an "active generation." That generation would have some memory of the generation preceding it and some ability to influence the next generation. History beyond a single generation, however, would be undependable and progress most likely constrained. Commerce would be limited, for money, after all, is a form of artifically mediated communication. Knowledge would be unorganized. Fields like the sciences, requiring systematic, long-term development, couldn't exist. Travel would be restricted, for without mediated communications it would be impossible to develop transportation technologies and coordinate travel systems. Individuals would lead stark, isolated, introspective lives in a primitive society.

Without mediated communication, formal law as we know it would disappear—no published or recorded law in print or electronic form. Oral law systems would have to serve as weak substitutes. An oral system would depend on the honesty and memory of individuals for what little law or custom a society might develop. Life would be much less predictable. Under formal law, individuals give up some personal autonomy and freedom to gain the benefits of collective and ordered society. The theory is that individuals can achieve more and have happier and more productive lives if they subject themselves to systematic, predictable, formal sets of recorded legal principles than if they try to live less formally. Without the order and predictability of recorded law and the ability to use it, rather than force, to resolve disputes through legal institutions, our imaginary society would be anarchic.

Fortunately, we do not live in primitive anarchy. The modern world has developed advanced means of mediated communication and formal, recorded, legal systems. Despite much popular bashing of both government and media over the last several decades, it is clear that we cannot do without law and mediated communications. Law, government, and media can be constantly refined and improved but appear indispensable if we wish to have a vibrant society. One inevitable part of a vibrant society, however, is change. This includes changes in institutions and technologies and, or course, in law.

Anthropologists have long distinguished humans from other intelligent creatures because of our tool-making abilities. Other animals use naturally occurring tools—a branch as a prybar for example—but humans design and build tools specifically for perceived tasks. Many of our tools are used for mediated communication. Printing presses, broadcast stations, word processors, and fax machines are all examples of tools created by humans to facilitate communication. Being intelligent creatures in a modern rather than primitive society, we constantly refine and at times replace our communications tools. With that, mass communications changes. So does mass communications law.

COMMUNICATIONS LAW: EVOLUTIONARY OR REVOLUTIONARY?

This book is largely about current mass communications law in the United States and the history of these laws. While we certainly will not ignore the future of communications law in the chapters to follow, we obviously can't describe it as we can describe communications law past and present. The future hasn't happened yet and anything we say about it is reasonable prediction at best and speculation at worst. The only sure thing is that continued change in communications technologies almost guarantees that future mass communications law, although derived from current law, will be quite different in many ways. An understanding of present and past law will help in working with and under future law.

Individuals and groups depend on legal predictability. Written, rather than oral, law increases that predictability. At the very least, when new problems arise, it becomes harder to ignore what the law has been in the past. People use knowledge of past and present law to predict consequences of their behaviors even if the precise facts underlying past law have changed somewhat. In a society ordered by law, others depend on us following the law as well. Suppose the chance arises to run a stoplight, but you know a police officer may be watching. Knowing the law, we predict that we're likely to get a ticket, if we run the light. Even if it is very early in the morning and no one else is in sight, we probably won't run the stoplight because we anticipate the adverse consequence of a ticket. In addition, even though we have looked around, and seen no one, other cars might appear and they would predict we will stop. Their predictions, combined with our violation of the law, could result in an accident. Stable legal systems tell us, and others, what is likely to happen, and we, in turn, take that into account in daily life.

Unlike some foreign systems, American law is heavily dependent on precedent. When new legal problems arise, we usually do not just invent totally new—unprecedented—laws to deal with them. Rather we examine previous similar problems and the law applied to them and then try to apply existing legal principles to new circumstances. If necessary, we may make minor modifications of precedent to deal with changed conditions. As a result of "following precedent," U.S. law is more often evolutionary than revolutionary. Applying this perspective, this book is not just a summary of current communications law. It's a summary of the precedent for future communications law. Knowing current law, then, is important even though it almost certainly will not be exactly the law of the future. Nor, most likely, would we want laws tailored for today's conditions to be rigorously imposed on the future if the means of communication have undergone fundamental change. Important as precedent is, it does not always provide all the answers—and may sometimes even provide incorrect answers—for legal problems related to communications during "communications revolutions."

COMMUNICATIONS REVOLUTIONS AND INFORMATION AGES

It's sometimes said that the late twentieth century has been a revolutionary period in communications. Alternatively, we are described as entering an "information age." These claims have some validity, but their uniqueness can be easily overstated. While mass communications is certainly changing, perhaps at a faster pace than ever before, depending on changing communications technologies and on information is nothing new. We have had periods of rapid technological change in communications before, exemplified by the invention of devices like printing presses, telegraphs and telephones, and broadcasting. We have been an information society for a long time.

Like most societies, ours began with an emphasis on subsistence agriculture. That agricultural society eventually became better organized, and some people—full time farmers—grew food for others rather than just to feed themselves. For much of our nation's history, most people who held jobs worked in agriculture or in jobs dependent upon it; it was the focus of working life. Farmers, however, read books (most likely the Bible), placed written orders, and produced bills of sale. As a sidelight, at least, they made and used information.

During the nineteenth and most of the twentieth centuries, we were a manufacturing society. Machines automated agriculture and fewer people were needed to produce our food. More people worked in manufacturing than in agriculture. With manufacturing came increased social organization and a less agrarian, more urbanized society. In the manufacturing age, however, information was machine made (by rotary presses and the like) and used (machines, after all, required instruction manuals!). Popular, free education proliferated. Information still mattered.

Sometime in the latter part of this century, however, information became less of a sidelight to social life and work. For the first time, a greater proportion of American workers held information jobs rather than manufacturing or agricultural jobs. Increased automation in manufacturing meant fewer people than ever before were needed to produce products our society needed. Foreign societies became industrialized and made many products we no longer made ourselves. Computers—information-processing machines—linked to robots replaced many manufacturing workers. Those who designed, programmed, or ran the computers that ran the robots became information workers rather than traditional manufacturing employees. They needed to be well-educated, thinking, information-processing individuals.

Today over half of those who hold jobs in the United States work intensively with information. University professors are clearly information workers. Professors produce, consume, process, and transmit information all the time. It is their primary product. Bank tellers, lawyers, secretaries, corporate executives, keyboard operators, politicians, and, of course, media employees are all information workers. People still work in agriculture, but those who do are tightly linked to the information society. Farmers watch commodities markets as closely as they watch the weather, and those markets trade in information more than they actually trade in commodities. People still work in manufacturing, but they too are closely tied to the information society. Products are now manufactured "just in time" to be delivered. That requires getting information about what to make and where to deliver it quickly. Order information often reaches manufacturing plants by satellite technology. Telecommunications networks coordinate the manufacturing and distribution process. Other networks handle payment. Few manufacturing workers today labor at just making products. What they make and how they make it are shaped by information and information technologies. Thus, the information age is not just in the future or over the horizon. It has been our past, it certainly is our present, and chances are that our society's focus on information as its primary product may become more pronounced in the foreseeable future.

SOME THINGS WILL CHANGE

More Source Diversity

Future media will differ from today's media in many ways. Many of these trends are already apparent. First, future means of communications will add to what can be called source diversity. There will simply be more places to go to get information—more sources—and, for that matter, more ways to move it around. Information users will have increased abilities to select the mode of communication that best suits their needs and communication style. Where print is the best way to do something, it will certainly remain available. If a wireless means of communication works best for a specific purpose, however, then it, rather than traditional print, will most likely be used. If a wired pathway is best, it will probably be both available and chosen. Our inventory of media outlets will grow. Newspapers, books, magazines, and broadcast stations will face new competition from CD-ROM and other, computer-based, electronic publishers. We are likely to have devices that allow financial life to become paperless, including even more digital cash. We may use the telephone network to receive a moving image from across the country or around the world. We may carry personal communications devices that can link us, wherever we may be, to a global communications network—a world-spanning system of highly advanced portable devices capable of handling voice, data, and video. Theoretically, all this technology should result in broader access to more information and, presumably, better lives. At least, this should be true for those who connect to these new technologies and have the knowledge and resources to use them fully.

Increased Interactivity

Second, our future information world will be more interactive than today. Today's newspaper publishers and editors and broadcast producers and directors decide what to include in a newspaper or broadcast and send it out to consumers in a largely blanket fashion. Although there is some consumer feedback in that newspapers and broadcast stations fail if nobody reads or watches, direct consumer feedback—actually asking for specific information—is rare. Thus far, mass media have delivered standardized packages of information designed for mass audiences. That is likely to change. In the future, instead of sitting back and waiting for information to be packaged and delivered by others, consumers with information needs will be more actively involved in seeking out information they decide they want and in having it delivered to them through preferred channels. That will change mass communications profoundly because, so far, our mass media have largely been one-way media systems.

  The current system certainly has some advantages. Standardized media products used by many citizens—from the Associated Press to network news—help unite the nation and give it cultural focus. Concern about whether a shared culture can persist in a world with information on demand is legitimate. If we aren't consuming fairly similar information, we may lose much of what we have in common with others with whom we live. In addition, standard mass media sometimes forced us to confront information we did not know we wanted or, in some cases, uncomfortably challenged our ideas and beliefs. In an information-on-demand society, those challenges may be avoided, and we may be less often unintentionally exposed to new ideas. That's not necessarily a positive development, however good it may be that we will have greater abilities to reach out and fulfill known information needs. For current communicators, coming communications technologies could result in a loss of power or control. The editorial decision making that previously went on in newsrooms will be, in some ways, transferred to information consumers. Editing may become not what "editors do" but, increasingly, what ultimate information consumers do. The journalist may become more of an indexer and less of a filter and interpreter of information.

Faster Access to Information

Third, information is likely to be available to us faster. Contrast fax service with the postal service or even "overnight" delivery services. Fax machines can transmit printed documents around the world in seconds. Letter carriers took days or weeks. E-mail (electronic mail) is replacing Snail-Mail (the post office). Digital audio and video faxes that can send sound and moving images almost instantaneously are not far away. Increased communications speed can have negative as well as positive consequences. Slow communications often allow reflection. Although you may write an intemperate letter, you may not, in the end, send it. Flaming—sending an intemperate electronic message—however, is frequent enough to have become part of our language. Pressing the "send" button does not entail the effort, reflection, or cost required to post a letter. Increased speed will affect mass communications, too. Communications workers who need information for their jobs should get it faster. A reporter, for example, may interactively browse in a government database and retrieve information that in the past might have come through the mails or required a trip to a government office. Faster access to information could improve the productivity of professional communicators, but speeding up the communications process could also lead to something like mass media flaming.

Consider the O. J. Simpson freeway pursuit in the summer of 1994. Millions of Americans connected with that event through modern communications technologies. Helicopters beamed signals to receivers for television networks that, in turn, transmitted pictures globally in real time. Telephone lines linked news sources, some reliable and some not, directly to network anchors. Raw information passed through media organizations to consumers. While journalists have always covered breaking news events and produced preliminary accounts that later turned out to be incomplete or incorrect, the O. J. Simpson chase was something else. Reporters were barely able to do their jobs, if that job includes processing raw information for consumers. The existence of rapid means of communications seemed to eliminate the opportunity for sifting and judging the information available.

Cost Implications

Fourth, the cost of information will become clearer and more important. For most of our recent history, mass information has been inexpensive. Newspapers, magazines, and broadcasters, mostly supported by advertising revenues, have consumed only a small part of family and business budgets. Not that long ago, nobody paid directly to receive video information. You bought a television, plugged it in, hooked up an antenna, turned the set on, and received programs and advertising without additional charge. Now more than half of all households with television get a monthly bill from a cable company for the fulfillment of their video needs. Millions also buy or rent tapes of recent movies to watch at home at their convenience. Some, however, can readily be left out of this new information- and payment-on-demand environment. The economically poor could become a disfranchised information-poor part of a society that places increased importance on information.

This is especially likely since information on demand can be readily accompanied by an instantaneous demand for payment. The forecast 500-channel cable systems of the future are not likely to offer 500 different networks like CNN or ESPN. Many of those channels are expected to be devoted to pay-per-view movies. Highly popular movies will be shown continuously on several channels with different starting times. When you want to see a movie, it will be available—but at a simultaneous special charge. Information-on-demand libraries could be very different than libraries today. Today, a library buys a copy of a book and, thereafter, lends it to many patrons at no additional cost. When a family buys a newspaper, that one newspaper can hang around the house for days and be read by many, again with no extra cost. Computer-based information data banks are different. Unlike a book publisher, the owner of that data bank, can charge, or at least attempt to charge, each time information is accessed. While there is always some ability to download information, copy it, and pass it on to others, in an interactive information world most people will probably browse in data banks for specific information, retrieve what they want, pay for it, and never share it with anyone. For information users, this could get expensive. On the other hand, added revenues might boost the production and distribution of even more information.

Information is clearly now a commodity. Its quantity can be measured, and more often than before, its value is also measurable. In the future, we are more likely than today to be charged for the value to us of the information we use. This could be a very positive development. Advertiser-supported mass media decide on content partly because certain kinds of content attract readers, listeners, and viewers that advertisers want to reach. This content, however, is not necessarily the information consumers would seek for themselves if they had control of the process. In the future, many will have that control and be able to obtain what they want and are willing to pay for. That's good. On the other hand, making the availability of information more dependent than at present on economics could result in widening what has been called a knowledge or information gap. The consequences of being information-poor today are slight compared to what they might be in the future when information is packaged in smaller, more personalized, more useful, and perhaps even essential units. Information has always been tied to power. If the wealthy have more access to information, or better access to especially valuable information, than the less fortunate, then we may well create a new lower class of the information-poor. That's probably not so good.

Every Computer Owner a Publisher

Fifth, those with something to say are likely to find it easier to reach people interested in their messages. Even on today's Internet, a system that is certain to look awfully primitive in just a few years, an individual with an idea and a modem can easily share that idea with untold people through electronic newsgroups and servers. Old arguments about who has access to the mass media to speak will be transformed into arguments about who has access to the "information superhighway"—both as a speaker and as an information user. Geography will become less important. Communities can already be created that are based only on access to common information. It is no longer necessary to live within the circulation area of a newspaper, for example, to be a part of an information community when you can be connected to a global information network instead, and can seek out people with common interests anywhere.

BUT OLD CONCERNS PERSIST

These changes, and more, have the potential to bring about substantial changes in all aspects of mass communication law. We may not, for long, continue to distinguish among mass communication law (media law), communication law (the law of speech), and information law (who owns information and who has access to it) as we do today. For the present, however, there is an established field of mass communication law having a generally agreed-upon structure. The thirteen chapters that follow discuss current laws and public policies. While details are likely to change, the major themes and concerns seem likely to persist through whatever changes in communications technologies come in future years.

Chapter 1: Freedom of Expression

The United States has a longer and stronger tradition of distancing government from legal control over communications than any other nation on earth. The most fundamental of all communications laws, the First Amendment to the U.S. Constitution with its protections for freedom of speech, press, religion, and assembly, has existed since 1791. This chapter reviews the philosophical and political history of freedom of expression in the United States. It explains why we are so skeptical about allowing law and government to control speech and press and reviews the social and individual benefits believed to be promoted by minimal government involvement in regulating communications. A few types of expression, courts have determined, do not qualify for First Amendment protection. The hows and whys of this are also explained. Finally, courts have developed a number of legal tests for setting the circumstances under which some regulation of communications can be justified. Understanding these tests, and the theories about expression underlying them, is crucial to making sense of communications law topics discussed in subsequent chapters.

As this chapter shows, our reverence for freedom of expression began in simpler times. New media developments, at the very least, will pose problems as we try to apply tests, principles, and boundaries worked out for print and broadcasting to faster, more interactive, personally tailored forms of communication. Should the government, for example, be able to crack coded messages on the Internet in order to prevent political fanatics from blowing up federal buildings? In perhaps old-fashioned terms, does that kind of speed pose a "clear and present danger" sufficient to justify government action? Can speech and press principles developed when we had relativley few publishers, filmmakers, and broadcasters be extended without modification to a time when more people can, through their computers, become widely distributed publishers?

Chapter 2: Libel and the Mass Media

Even though it's not expressly mentioned in the Bill of Rights, we presume Americans have a right to an accurate public reputation. If you are an upstanding individual, you have a right to a great reputation; if you're a gangster, you have a right to your well-deserved poor reputation. The law has also long recognized that media content can affect reputation. Libel law tries to balance interests in free expression and reputation. It tries to foster vigorous public debate while, at the same time, creating remedies for people whose reputations are unjustifiably harmed through irresponsible debate. This chapter explains how that balance is struck, discussing how far the press can go in publishing information affecting reputations and what can happen if reputations are damaged unjustifiably.

Changes in media systems are likely to create new dimensions of libel law. Like so much of media law, libel law largely assumed that individuals with damaged reputations could recover from relatively wealthy press institutions. It also presumed, for the most part, an established press that would generally be respectful of reputational rights. Libel law has tended to reduce the possibility for recovery of damages by libeled persons if normal professional standards of information gathering and dissemination are followed. Future media, however, may not be so careful or professional. New technologies may create numerous amateur publishers. The speed of networked communications increases the chance for damaging errors by reducing the opportunity to correct them. These libels can be distributed worldwide with a push of a button. In the past, libel law has varied from state to state and required some decisions about which state laws govern a particular alleged libel. Nationally and, for that matter, internationally networked media pay almost no attention to geography and state boundaries and are likely to complicate decisions about what libel laws should govern particular disputes. Should case be decided, for example, under the laws of a state where an allegedly libelous publication began, the states through which it passed, the state where a central computer processing the libel was located, the state of residence of the alleged libel victim, or someplace else? Or, perhaps, do libels now occur in a boundaryless cyberspace where state law or even federal law becomes conceptually inapplicable?

Chapter 3: Privacy and the Mass Media

Privacy is closely related to, but fundamentally different from, libel. In addition to presuming rights to accurate public reputations (libel), we also presume under privacy law that elements of people's lives exist that they have a right to keep to themselves—to keep private rather than make public. Mass media, obviously, can pierce that wall of privacy, disclosing matters to the public at large that others would prefer remain unknown. Privacy law establishes some circumstances under which disclosure of private information by media can be both unlawful and punishable. On the other hand, it also creates many circumstances allowing media to widely disseminate information that some would like to keep private. As with libel law, there is substantial diversity in privacy law among the fifty states.

Thus far, privacy has been one of the greatest concerns about emerging newer communications technologies. Computer data banks can store much private information so, in part, law has focused on what can be kept (usually by government) and what can't be. Privacy, of course, may be breached when information from such data banks gets beyond intended recipients. It can especially be compromised if computer systems are used to consolidate information from normally separate information systems. Combine someone's telephone and credit card records, for example, and much insight into the details of that person's life results. Mass media have long believed that it is sometimes necessary to disclose such private information, and media law often allows that. Enhanced abilities to store and correlate information, however, will surely raise new privacy concerns.

Chapter 4: Journalist's Privilege

Most media law protects the tail end of the communications process—the right to distribute information somehow gained. Journalists have long argued, however, that some legal protection of earlier stages in the process is necessary. This controversy has focused, primarily, on what should happen if, in the course of gathering information, journalists acquire information they choose not to disseminate but that would be highly useful in enforcing or implementing other areas of law. For example, should government have the power to compel a journalist who interviewed a criminal under a promise of confidentiality to fully disclose what that criminal said or should the choice about what to release and what to hold back be the journalist's alone to make? Journalists have argued that such a privilege against being compelled to release unpublished information by law is essential to gaining trust and being able to do their ultimate job of informing the public. While giving some recognition to these claims, courts have sometimes also concluded that the interests in having a fairly functioning and efficient legal system can outweigh the journalists' interests in maintaining confidences.

One problem in this area has always been in separating journalists who might have need of a privilege from nonjournalists who don't. If one establishes any journalist's privilege, one must define who is entitled to it. This has been hard enough when the varieties of journalists have been limited to regular newspaper, magazine, radio, and television reporters, for example. It may become infinitely more complex in the future. Is the "moderator" of a computer newsgroup, or a contributor to the group, for example, a new type of journalist who should be entitled to keep some confidences despite government interests in breaching them?

Chapter 5: Obscenity and Indecency

Despite our deep respect for freedom of expression, we have a long history of concern about sexual speech. This chapter explains how obscenity is defined and how it has become recognized as a type of speech not protected by the First Amendment and subject to government censorship and punishment. Also discussed here are related ideas such as indecency (sometimes unlawful in broadcasting but not in other forms of communication) and pornography (of great importance to feminists but difficult, so far, for courts to accept as another type of unprotected speech).

Obscenity law is already one of the hottest legal areas associated with the Internet. Under current law, obscenity is supposed to be determined in light of "contemporary community standards." In other words, nothing is always obscene everywhere. Networked communications, allowing nongeography-based communities to be created, have already spawned difficult cases and troubling proposed legislation relating to obscenity. Should government, for example, be able to prosecute operators of a sexually oriented electronic bulletin board in one state on the basis of allegedly obscene content originated in some other state and reflected, by their bulletin board, to a third jurisdiction? Since obscenity law has often been justified as necessary to protect minors from presumed harm, should the government be able to monitor the Internet for obscenity in order to protect kids? Should it require operators of computer services to know what is being transmitted through their services and to delete obscene content? Can government possibly oversee such vast amounts of information? Can anything be done given that children are such skilled computer hackers? Should any of these things be done?

Chapter 6: Access to the Judicial Process

For good or bad, through the O. J. Simpson trial, Americans have recently gained a great lesson in what happens when media have access to courts. That trial has brought to the forefront many long-standing concerns about how to square the rights of a free press to act as the public's representative and attend and monitor what courts do with the possibilities that press coverage may jeopardize an individual's right to a fair trial. This chapter is devoted to examining this long-standing free press/fair trial tension.

The proliferation of information sources in recent years seem to have accentuated free press/fair trial concerns. While the older, established press may work diligently to protect a defendant's rights, the tabloid press—both print and electronic—seems to some to be less careful about its reporting. There is room, in our expanded television universe, for Court TV and TV and radio talk shows devoted to wall-to-wall coverage of trials and speculation about them. Can people receive fair trials or, perhaps of even greater concern, fair retrials when so many of the details of judicial proceedings have been so much more widely distributed than was possible in a less diverse media world? Do old techniques for solving these tensions work in an era of electronic justice?

Chapter 7: Freedom of Information: Access to News of Government

This chapter, like Chapter 4 about journalist's privileges, deals with how the law can affect the communication process prior to public distribution of information. For much of our history, American journalism has emphasized reports about and criticisms of government. That kind of reporting requires getting information from government, a topic commonly known as Freedom of Information. In the United States, most laws guaranteeing that freedom are statutes written by the U.S. Congress and state legislatures. These statutes define what kinds of records and meetings of government are open and public and which, for various reasons, are not.

New media and information technologies suggest many new challenges and opportunities here. The very concept of a record, around which much of this law is built, may be obsolete. Government no longer necessarily compiles bits of information into routinely printed official reports and documents—the kinds of things these laws were written to cover. Rather, government now may collect information in computer files and sort and distribute it in all kinds of ways as needed for govenment use. When information is stored in computer files rather than records stystems, will the govenment claim that no traditional record exists for media or public access? Looking at things more positively, will laws governing access records to records and meetings evolve into more modern access-to-information laws that might actually expand media and public access to the operations of government?

Chapter 8: Public Access to the Media

Until very recently, you had to own a mass medium if you wanted to reach large segments of the public. Newspaper publishers and broadcast station owners had "access to the media"—and, hence, access to the public—but Jane Q. Public did not. Some argued that such monopolization of channels of mass communication by a small number of powerful entities was not contemplated by the authors of the First Amendment and that law, at least once in a while, should open up mass media to the public even if, occasionally, that meant government could force unwilling media owner's to distribute information against their will.

Developments in contemporary communication seem likely to alter this debate. A computer and modem can give almost anyone very inexpensive access to large numbers of information consumers. Perhaps the Internet is the democratized mass communication system that access advocates have so long promoted. Will laws and policies be needed to protect or enhance public access to these newer means of information distribution? How should much of our communications law, created for an environment with limited public access to the means of mass communication, change if public publication becomes much easier for so many persons?

Chapter 9: Advertising: Law and Regulation

Advertising has long been important in at least two ways. It is an important way of alerting consumers to possible purchases and their attributes. It has also been a primary means of generating revenue supporting the distribution of other less commercial information such as the news and editorial content of newspapers or the entertainment content of broadcasting. Despite its importance, however, advertising has never been treated by the law exactly like other less commercial forms of speech. It has been subject to much regulation, some of it discussed here, mostly intended to protect consumers from presumed harms.

Many old advertising law problems will clearly continue in new media, but new forms of advertising are likely to emerge that will call for new law. A set-top printer, for example, may one day allow a television broadcaster to send a fax-like supplement to a TV ad or a coupon that can be exchanged at a local store. The possibilities for new types of public harm, as well as the opportunities for enhanced public participation in economic life, are substantial and will require adjustments of current advertising law.

Chapter 10: Monopoly, Diversity, and Antitrust Law

For the most part, our communications media are businesses. They gain money from business practices such as selling advertising or subscriptions and, in turn, provide commercial and noncommercial information. Since the direct control government can exert on communications content is limited, we have long used business law—especially antitrust law—to structure and police the business of communication. The goal, at least sometimes, has been to promote First Amendment values. We have believed, for example, that the public benefits in information terms when it gets its information from diverse, competitive sources. Antitrust law has been applied to media companies to protect and enhance such competition.

Today, however, many old industry boundaries are shifting or even collapsing. We have used antitrust law, for example, to break up one huge communications company—AT&T and create increased competition in local and long-distance telephony. Attempts have been made to apply antitrust law to the computer software industry to prevent it from being dominated by a single software provider. We have tried, and will continue to try, to use antitrust law to shape the communications marketplace. In electronic media, especially, antitrust law has been used to enhance and promote competition; as a consequence, arguments for reduced government regulation are being heard as electronic media become more influenced than in the past by the competitive forces of the marketplace. Antitrust law is already in some significant ways a substitute for communications laws and policies of old, and that trend seems likely to continue.

Chapter 11: Student Press Rights

This may seem to be a sidelight to the main thrust of this book—laws governing broad and mature forms of public communication. Communication organizations, however, need a constant source of new employees, and those employees often gain experience through student media. In addition, student communities have information needs that perhaps are not well served by the adult press. American law, however, has not always equated press rights of students with press rights of adults. Sometimes these distinctions have been justified on the basis of lack of maturity. At other times, special government control over student communication in school settings has been justified in the name of education. This chapter reviews why student press rights and adult press rights sometimes differ. The future of these problems is also affected by developments in communication technologies since students, like many other subgroups of Amercian society, now have much enhanced access to means of information distribution. Many students, today, ask "why publish, when you can network?"

Chapter 12: Electronic Media Law

Electronic media in the United States have long been treated differently than almost all other forms of communication. Among the media, only radio and television broadcasters require federal licenses and are subject to some review by an administrative agency (the Federal Communications Commission). Cable TV systems and telephone companies have also been subject for years to state and federal government review quite unlike government regulation of print. A broadcast station, for example, can still be forced by government to provide some access to its facilities for the use of federal candidates. Newspapers, however, are free to ignore federal elections if they want to do so. This chapter reviews the historical justifications for treating electronic media uniquely and discusses the details of regulation affecting current electronic mass media.

These distinctions, however, may not persist for long. Electronic and print media are converging: radio and TV stations can transmit text while newspaper companies now often produce local news for cable systems. The telephone network, once simply a point-to-point conduit for voice and data, may become a replacement for cable television and video rental stores, capable of providing movies, news, and sporting events on demand. Long-standing core principles of electronic media law, described in this chapter, appear ripe for reconsideration.

Chapter 13: Intellectual Property and Media Business Issues

We conclude with a chapter about special problems. Copyright is a part of intellectual property law. It says that those with ideas that can be converted to a fixed form such as a newspaper article, an audio or video recording, or a computer program should "own" those fixed ideas like any other property and, accordingly, have control over their use. Under copyright law, creators of such intellectual property can control who uses it and under what conditions. They can charge for it, theoretically being compensated for their labor and encouraged to create still more intellectual property. Changes in our ways of creating and preserving information—in copying technologies, for example—have always required adjustments of intellectual property law. In our new, largely digital world, intellectual property law must be revised as it becomes easier to manipulate someone's intellectual property into new forms, harder to detect such manipulations, and harder still to recover money when unauthorized uses occur.

We have long taxed mass media, but only in the same ways we tax other businesses. When government has targeted special taxes at the media out of distaste for content, courts have overturned such taxation systems. Current developments in communications technology open the prospect of new media taxes—a media consumption tax, for example, could be possible, and in some electronic media, such as cable television, franchise fees take the form of somewhat hidden taxes on the public upon which government has become increasingly reliant. All sorts of new varieties of government "revenue enhancement" may become possible. For example, a meaningful dent has been made in the federal debt by auctioning spectrum space for things like personal communications services. Careful attention will have to be paid, however, to the effects on communication of all these new efforts to enhance government revenues.

Finally, there is the consequence of government efforts to both check and profit from Americans' appetite to gamble. For many years, advertising and news about gambling, including government and private lotteries, were severely restricted. Many of those laws have been relaxed in recent years, making it easier for government and private business to make money from lotteries and less risky for the media to promote or report on them. Few things, however, appear to be more readily adaptable to a nationwide or global electronic communications network than gaming activites. Huge pots of money could be created, and betting at home could be easy. Future law will have to address these possibilities.

Clearly, communications law is a moving target. Its specifics are subject to constant change. At least some of the laws and principles described in detail here will have changed by the time this book reaches your hands. It would be foolish to rely on knowledge of mass communication law gained from this book very many years into the future because law will have moved on and been much affected by changes in forms of communication. With an understanding of the current fundamentals of mass communication law, however, the future should be more intelligible. While new ways of communicating will pose new problems and result in new law, whatever comes about in the future will almost certainly have its roots in communications law past and present.

ACKNOWLEDGMENTS

Our deep appreciation to our Acquiring Editor Elizabeth Hannan for her patient insistence upon excellence, and to our skillful and perceptive Production

Editor Michelle McAnelly for moving this through the various stages of the production process. Thanks, also, go to Stephen Rockwell of the class of 1996 for his excellent research assistance and to the staff at the Library of the Indiana University, Bloomington School of Law for all their help. We also appreciate the superb preliminary edit by Pat Lewis, the best we have so far experienced, and the innumerable suggestions made by colleagues in the field who were asked by West to review the original manuscript.

Freedom of Expression

THE FIRST AMENDMENT

The words of the First Amendment, enacted in 1791, are short and direct:

The First Amendment. Congress shall make no law respecting an establishment of religion, or prohibiting the free exercise thereof; or abridging the freedom of speech, or of the press; or the right of the people peaceably to assemble, and to petition the government for a redress of grievances.

A literal reading of these words discloses a number of things immediately. First, the guarantee of freedom of expression within the First Amendment has two components: a Free Speech Clause and a Free Press Clause. In addition, unlike the constitutions of many other countries, the **U.S. Constitution** does not provide any further definition or elaboration for either freedom of speech or freedom of the press. The Framers left definition to the future.

In terms of its precise language, the First Amendment is directed only to Congress. The Framers of the amendment feared the new federal government they had created, not the states. They wished from the outset to prevent

● **Constitution**
The fundamental law of the United States. Under Article VI, the Supremacy Clause, state or federal laws that conflict with the Constitution are invalid. Since *Marbury v. Madison* (1803), state and federal courts exercise judicial review—the power to set aside government action that is inconsistent with the Constitution.

Congress from interfering with freedom of speech or press. Colonial newspaper editors, however, had not infrequently become embroiled in conflicts with the royal governors of the colonies. If the state governments that succeeded the colonial regimes also attempted to muzzle newspapers, the press would have to look to the state constitutions for relief.

The years since 1791 have greatly broadened the scope of the First Amendment and extended its reach far beyond the specific warning to Congress that its language provides. In 1925, in a case that would otherwise be unremembered, Supreme Court Justice Edward Sanford, who would likewise be forgotten by history, uttered a casual observation in the course of an opinion. The observation involved the free expression rights of a subsequently repentant Communist named Benjamin Gitlow, who had run afoul of a New York state law. Since Gitlow was being prosecuted by the state rather than the federal government, he could not, under the strict text of the First Amendment, claim its protection. Justice Sanford declared that "we may and do assume that freedom of speech and of the press—which are protected by the First Amendment—are among the fundamental personal rights and 'liberties' protected by the due process clause of the Fourteenth Amendment from impairment by the states."[1]

> **● Fourteenth Amendment**
>
> Provides that no state shall "deprive any person of life, liberty or property without due process of law." Liberty has been interpreted to include freedom of expression, so the Fourteenth Amendment protects against state restraints on freedom of expression in the same manner as the First Amendment protects against restraints by the federal government.

The **Fourteenth Amendment** was enacted in 1868. Its purpose was to endow the newly emancipated slaves with legal equality and constitutional rights. Perhaps the most famous language in the Fourteenth Amendment is its provision that no state shall "deprive any person of life, liberty, or property, without due process of law."

Almost seventy years ago, Justice Sanford declared on behalf of the Supreme Court that the Due Process Clause of the Fourteenth Amendment included within it fundamental rights such as freedom of speech and freedom of the press. These guarantees bind the state governments no less than the First Amendment binds the federal government. Today it is accepted that the First Amendment is binding on the states through the Due Process Clause of the Fourteenth Amendment.

Although the state constitutions guarantee freedom of expression, they sometimes do so in words less protective and more qualified than the simple guarantees of freedom of speech and freedom of the press found in the First Amendment. The extension of the guarantees of free speech and free press in the federal constitution to the state governments has, therefore, been of enormous importance.

Interpretation of the Fourteenth Amendment—a part of the federal constitution—is a responsibility of the U.S. Supreme Court. The Supreme Court is the highest federal court. On federal constitutional matters, its decisions bind both the state courts and the lower federal courts. The nine justices of the Supreme Court essentially have life tenure. Given their authority and independence, they are in a much better position to announce unpopular decisions than are many state court judges who serve only for limited terms and thus must face the electorate periodically.

The U.S. Supreme Court has come to play a crucial role in the interpretation of free expression for both the state and federal governments. Indeed, the

Supreme Court's role in defining the meaning of free expression *vis-à-vis* the states is a critical one. In fact, the Supreme Court has invalidated a far greater number of state statutes on free expression grounds than it has federal statutes.

A further matter should be mentioned. As was indicated earlier, the First Amendment speaks directly only to one branch of the federal government—the Congress. But today it is understood that the First Amendment applies to all three branches of the federal government. For example, in the Pentagon Papers case, the U.S. Department of Justice tried to prevent leading newspapers including the *New York Times* and the *Washington Post* from publishing classified material involving the Vietnam War. The Justice Department asked the federal courts to enjoin or prevent the newspapers from publishing the papers. The Justice Department made this request even though no law of Congress authorized such an **injunction**. The newspapers complained that the injunction violated the First Amendment. Note that it was an arm of the executive branch of the federal government—the U.S. Department of Justice—that sought the injunction. The Supreme Court held that injunctive relief here—judicial orders directing the newspapers not to publish—would violate the First Amendment.[2] In short, the First Amendment applied not only to congressional action but to federal judicial and executive action as well. See exhibit one for the Bill of Rights.

- **Three branches of the federal government**
  The legislative, executive, and judicial branches. The legislative branch makes laws and appropriates funds. The executive branch enforces and administers the laws. The judicial branch interprets the laws in the course of deciding particular cases.

- **Injunction**
  A judicial order that prevents a party from doing something or orders it to perform a specific act.

LICENSING, CENSORSHIP, AND SEDITIOUS LIBEL

The First Amendment did not arise in a vacuum. It had its origins in the desire of the Framers to make sure that the unhappy experiences with censorship in English history and, later, in the colonies would not be repeated. One of the formative documents in the development of the Anglo-American tradition of a free press was *The Areopagitica,* written by the great English poet John Milton. Milton wrote *The Areopagitica* in the context of seventeenth-century England's experience with censorship. On June 14, 1643, the Lords and Commons [in Parliament] decreed that no publication could be published or imported without first being registered by the Stationer's Company. The Stationer's Company, founded in 1557, thus became a means for establishing a system of censorship. One scholar has described the system as follows:

> The exclusive privilege of printing and publishing in the English dominions was given to 97 London stationers and their successors by regular apprenticeship. All printing was thus centralized in London under the immediate inspection of the Government. No one could legally print, without special license, who did not belong to the Stationer's Company. The Company had power to search for and to seize publicationswhich infringed their privilege.[3]

Milton wrote *The Areopagitica* in 1644 to protest Parliament's order. In this pamphlet, Milton made a lasting contribution to the history of ideas with his passionate defense of free expression. The law or Order of 1643 was

Exhibit 1: The Bill of Rights

Amendment I

Congress shall make no law respecting an establishment of religion, or prohibiting the free exercise thereof, or abridging the freedom of speech, or of the press; or the right of the people peaceably to assemble, and to petition the government for a redress of grievances.

Amendment II

A well regulated Militia, being necessary to the security of a free State, the right of the people to keep and bear Arms shall not be infringed.

Amendment III

No Soldier shall, in time of peace be quartered in any house, without the consent of the Owner, nor in time of war, but in a manner to be prescribed by law.

Amendment IV

The right of the people to be secure in their persons, houses, papers, and effects, against unreasonable searches and seizures, shall not be violated, and no Warrants shall issue, but upon probable cause, supported by Oath or affirmation, and particularly describing the place to be searched, and the persons or things to be seized.

Amendment V

No person shall be held to answer for a capital, or otherwise infamous crime, unless on a presentment or indictment of a Grand Jury, except in cases arising in the land or naval forces, or in the Militia, when in actual service in time of War or public danger; nor shall any person be subject for the same offence to be twice put in jeopardy of life or limb; nor shall be compelled in any criminal case to be a witness against himself, nor be deprived of life, liberty, or property, without due process of law; nor shall private property be taken for public use, without just compensation.

Amendment VI

In all criminal prosecutions, the accused shall enjoy the right to a speedy and public trial, by an impartial jury of the State and district wherein the crime shall have been committed, which district shall have been previously ascertained by law, and to be informed of the nature and cause of the accusation; to be confronted with the witnesses aginst him; to have compulsory process for obtaining witnesses in his favor, and to have the Assistance of Counsel for his defence.

Amendment VII

In suits at common law, where the value in controversy shall exceed twenty dollars, the right of trial by jury shall be preserved, and no fact tried by jury shall be otherwise re-examined in any Court of the United States, than according to the rules of common law.

Amendment VIII

Excessive bail shall not be required, nor excessive fines imposed, nor cruel and unusual punishments inflicted.

Amendment IX

The enumeration in the Constitution, of certain rights, shall not be construed to deny or disparage others retained by the people.

Amendment X

The powers not delegated to the United States by the Constitution, nor prohibited by it to the States, are reserved to the States respectively, or to the people.

intended, according to its terms, to prevent "the defamation of Religion and Government." Ultimately, Justice William Brennan made clear in the *New York Times v. Sullivan*[4] decision in 1964 that the very purpose of freedom of expression is to encourage criticism of government officials.

Milton's pamphlet began the long road that led to the acceptance of that position. In addition, Milton insisted that warring ideas should be allowed to contend with each other freely. The state should not attempt to sponsor some ideas and banish others.

Licensing ended in England in 1695 but continued in America for a brief time thereafter. Prosecutions for **seditious libel** or criminal libel soon supplanted licensing as a means of government censorship of the press in the years prior to the American Revolution. The law of seditious libel made criticism of government officials a crime punishable by fines and imprisonment. Happily, such prosecutions were uncommon, but nevertheless they did occur.

A famous seditious libel case involving freedom of the press was that of colonial editor John Peter Zenger. Zenger's paper, the *New York Weekly Journal*, was a bitter critic of William Cosby, colonial governor of New York. Because of his and his patrons' criticisms of Cosby, Zenger was arrested in 1734 for publishing seditious libels and jailed for eight months before trial. But in August 1735 in a famous verdict, the jury determined that Zenger was not guilty, even though the judge had instructed them otherwise. It was a hard-won victory for Zenger's lawyer, Andrew Hamilton. Prosecutions for seditious libel were particularly hard to combat because even if what a defendant had said about a government official was true, the truth of the utterance was considered irrelevant.

Today we think of the Zenger case as a milestone in the history of freedom of the press. But legal historians tell us that Andrew Hamilton won his case by insisting on the wisdom of local juries and on the rights of a free people to criticize those who govern them. Hamilton won his victory for Zenger by appealing to the free speech rights of a free people rather than to freedom of the press.[5]

In a trial for the **common law** crime of seditious libel, the judge had a very large role, and the jury theoretically at least had only a small one. The judge was responsible for deciding whether the publication in question was or was

● **Seditious libel**
Laws originating in England that made criticism of government officials criminal offenses.

● **Common law**
The body of law, originating in England and continued in the United States, whereby principles of law are shaped by judges in decisions. It is judge-made law, in contrast to statutory law, which is enacted by legislatures.

not seditious libel. The jury's task was simply to decide whether the defendant had in fact published the offending material. As this description indicates, seditious libel gave precious little scope to free expression. That is why the English Parliament's enactment of Fox's Libel Act in 1792 was considered a triumph for free expression. Fox's Libel Act made truth a defense and allowed the jury rather than the judge to decide whether the offending publication constituted seditious libel.

Seditious Libel and the First Amendment

Journalists and lawyers have long argued about what the Framers intended by the guarantees of freedom of speech and freedom of the press. Many of those who participated in drafting, discussing, and enacting the Constitution generally, and the First Amendment specifically, were lawyers trained in English law. Did they intend, for example, that freedom of the press should mean what it meant in English law and no more? Sir William Blackstone wrote that liberty of the press meant there could be no "*previous* restraint upon publication" but that there was no "freedom from censure" if criminal matters were published.[6] Blackstone was distinguishing between what is called freedom from prior restraint versus freedom from subsequent punishment. In this view, the state may not prevent something from being published, but it may punish the publisher after the publication has appeared.

In 1960 the American constitutional historian Leonard Levy in an influential book contended that all the Framers intended to do in the First Amendment was to prevent the state from imposing prior restraints. In Levy's view, they did not intend to prohibit punishment for speech after the fact, such as was involved in the crime of seditious libel.

In 1798—seven years after the ratification of the First Amendment—the Federalist Party, out of fear of the radicals who sympathized with the revolutionaries in France and out of hostility toward their Republican critics, succeeded in getting Congress to pass the Alien and Sedition Laws. One of these laws was the Sedition Act, which declared that publication of false, scandalous, or malicious writings designed to bring the government, Congress, or the President into contempt or disrepute or to excite popular hostility toward them would constitute a crime.

Editors who supported Thomas Jefferson's Republican or Anti-Federalist Party were among those convicted under the Sedition Act. Not surprisingly, the Republicans contended that the Sedition Act was being used as a weapon to silence Republican criticism of the Federalists who were in power. The First Amendment states that "Congress shall make no law. . . . abridging the freedom of speech, or of the press." Could it be constitutional for Congress to forbid criticism of itself? Jefferson thought the Sedition Act was a clear violation of the First Amendment. Some members of the Congress that enacted the Sedition Act had also participated in the framing of the First Amendment. How is this explainable? Leonard Levy's research served to rationalize this historical paradox. The Congress that enacted the Sedition Act did so because it understood the First Amendment only to reach prior restraints.[7]

● **Fox's Libel Act**
A statute enacted by Parliament in 1792 that made truth a defense in seditious libel actions and allowed the jury rather than the judge to decide whether a challenged publication constituted seditious libel.

● **Sedition Act**
One of the Alien and Sedition Laws enacted by Congress in 1798, which made criticism of the president, Congress, or government a crime. The act was never tested by the Supreme Court and simply expired.

Ultimately, Professor Levy came to take a richer view of the eighteenth century's understanding of freedom of expression. As a practical matter, he concluded, eighteenth-century printers and editors functioned as if their freedom included freedom from seditious libel.[8] The Sedition Act expired and was not reenacted, and the Supreme Court never had occasion to pass on its First Amendment validity. In 1964 in *New York Times v. Sullivan*, the long debate came to an end. Justice Brennan said for the Court: "Although the Sedition Act was never tested in this Court, the attack upon its validity has carried the day in the court of history."[9]

First Amendment scholar Harry Kalven said the repugnance expressed in the *Times* case toward the concept of seditious libel illuminated the central meaning of the First Amendment: Criticism of government and government officials cannot be punished by government.[10] Not only is criticism of government a right of citizenship, it is a duty of citizenship.

THE RATIONALE OF FIRST AMENDMENT PROTECTION

Our society in its fundamental law—the Constitution—has given freedom of expression a special and protected place. Why? Not surprisingly, a number of competing theories have been offered as the rationale for the First Amendment. Each theory basically posits a particular model of what the First Amendment is designed to accomplish.

The Marketplace of Ideas Theory

A theory that has had great influence as a rationale for special protection for free expression is the **marketplace of ideas theory.** In a widely quoted passage in *The Areopagitica*, Milton wrote:

> And though all the winds of doctrine were let loose upon the earth, so Truth be in the field, we do injuriously by licensing and prohibiting to misdoubt her strength. Let her and Falsehood grapple; who ever knew truth put to the worse, in a free and open encounter?[11]

John Stuart Mill in his essay *On Liberty of Thought and Discussion* wrote that "the peculiar veil of silencing the expression of an opinion" is that it robs the human race.[12] Writers like Mill and Milton asked government and society to refrain from silencing expression even if the idea espoused was wrong—even if it was evil. In a similar vein, Justice **Oliver Wendell Holmes** wrote: "[T]he best test of truth is the power of the thought to get itself accepted in the competition of the market."

A particularly persuasive statement of the marketplace of ideas theory was provided by Justice William O. Douglas when he challenged the anti-Communist prosecutions of the 1950s as a form of political repression:

> When ideas compete in the market for acceptance, full and free discussion [exposes] the false and they gain few adherents. Full and free

● **Marketplace of ideas theory**
Ideas should be allowed to compete freely without government censorship or intervention. Proponents contend that out of this competition the best or truest ideas will emerge.

● **Oliver Wendell Holmes**
Supreme Court justice from 1902 to 1932; appointed by President Theodore Roosevelt. Holmes's influence on First Amendment law was considerable both because of the power of his thought and the quotability of his decisions.

discussion even of ideas we hate encourages the testing of our own prejudices and preconceptions. Full and free discussion keeps a society from being stagnant and unprepared for the stress and strains that work to tear all civilizations apart.[13]

The marketplace of ideas theorists assign government a passive role. Government should simply stay out of the marketplace of ideas. If government neither censors nor interferes, these theorists believe, a kind of Darwinism will operate in the life of competing ideas. Out of this combat, the best or truest ideas will emerge.

By the middle of the twentieth century, a more critical approach to the marketplace of ideas theory began to develop. One of the hallmarks of the marketplace of ideas theory is a certain tolerance, a willingness to let ideas enter the marketplace. Writing in the 1960s, New Left philosopher, Herbert Marcuse took aim at the tolerance aspect of the marketplace theory. Influenced by Marx, Marcuse contended that although society professed a formal tolerance, the economic and political structure made that tolerance meaningless:

> The tolerance which was the great achievement of the liberal era is still professed and (with strongqualifications) practiced, while the economic and political process is subjected [to domination to an ubiquitous and effective administration] in accordance with predominant interests. The result is an objective contradiction between the economic and political structure on the one side, and the theory and practice of toleration on the other.[14]

Marcuse simply did not believe in one of the major premises of the marketplace of ideas theory. This premise is that if individuals are given full and free information, they will make the rational decisions that a democratic self-governing society requires. On the contrary, Marcuse thought individuals in contemporary mass society were completely susceptible to manipulation by big government, big business, and big media. The marketplace of ideas in his view was neither free nor open.

Jerome Barron, one of the authors of this book, has argued that the marketplace of ideas theory no longer describes the opinion process: "Our constitutional theory is in the grip of a romantic conception of free expression, a belief that the 'marketplace of ideas' is freely accessible. But if ever there were a self operating marketplace of ideas, it has long ceased to exist."[15] In this view, any theory of protection for expression has to grapple with a central fact: "There is inequality in the power to communicate ideas just as there is inequality in economic bargaining power; to recognize the latter and deny the former is quixotic."[16] This theory calls for the creation of legal mechanisms to stimulate public access to and participation in the media.

Professor Edwin Baker says that Barron's view takes a "**market failure**" perspective of the First Amendment. Proponents of access to the media are really saying: The marketplace of ideas is not working; how can we repair it? Baker replies that the proposed remedy may be as harmful as the problem

● **Market failure theory**

Argues that the marketplace of ideas does not work because even if entry to the marketplace is not restricted by government, entry is still restricted because the marketplace is dominated by large business interests.

that inspired it. If government is going to decide what access to the media is adequate, this allows the government to decide "the correct resolution of the marketplace debates." Government is, thereby, allowed "to define truth."[17]

Owen Fiss has argued that those like Edwin Baker who advocate absolute noninterference by government tend to take a fungible approach to individual autonomy, which embraces corporations as well as individuals. The result is a "public debate that is dominated [by] the same forces that dominate social, structure, not a debate that is 'uninhibited, robust and wide open.' "[18]

Students may wish to reserve judgment about which side they find more persuasive in this debate. At present, the marketplace of ideas metaphor still endures as an explanation of the rationale of First Amendment protection. Perhaps it endures not so much because we believe it adequately portrays the reality of modern communications as because we are at a loss to know what to use as its replacement.

The Liberty Model or Individual Autonomy Theory of Free Expression

In his treatise on the First Amendment, Professor Thomas I. Emerson stated that individual self-fulfillment is one of the premises on which the system of free expression is grounded: "[F]reedom of expression is essential as a means of assuring individual self-fulfillment. The proper end of man is the realization of his character and potentialities as a human being."[19]

For Professor Emerson, individual self-fulfillment is one of the justifications for protecting expression. For Edwin Baker this rationale is *the* purpose of the First Amendment. In Baker's view, a system of free expression does not exist just to protect the marketplace of ideas: "The liberty theory holds that the free speech clause protects not a marketplace but rather an arena of individual liberty from certain types of governmental restrictions. Speech is protected not as a means to a collective good but because of the value of speech conduct to the individual."[20]

Critics of the **individual autonomy theory** say that it proves too much. If free expression is protected because of its relationship to the larger values of individual self-fulfillment and realization, then why is free speech more important than other means of self-expression such as portrait painting, sculpture, or soccer? From this vantage point, the individual liberty model may trivialize the importance of free expression since it is but one of the ways whereby individuals express themselves.[21] This theory is also criticized because it tends to portray the state as the only menace to individual autonomy. Private power centers and their ability to limit, and even destroy, individual self-autonomy are ignored. But Edwin Baker defends the liberty or individual autonomy model of the First Amendment as preferable to rival rationales in view of "the inadequacy of both the classic marketplace of ideas theory and the market failure theory."

● **Individual autonomy theory**
Sometimes called the individual liberty model of the First Amendment. Holds that freedom of expression is protected because of its relationship to the protection of individual autonomy and individual self-fulfillment.

The Self-Governance Rationale of First Amendment Protection

Political philosopher Alexander Meiklejohn has had a powerful influence on the wide currency that the self-government rationale has had in First Amendment thinking. Meiklejohn distinguished between two kinds of expression—public speech and private speech. Public or political speech was accorded absolute protection by the First Amendment.[22] No **balancing tests** were permissible. Private speech—discussion that did not deal with the political process or individual decision making in a democracy—was under the protection of the more flexible Due Process Clause of the Fifth Amendment. Regulation of private speech would be valid so long as it was reasonable. Absolute protection was necessary for political speech because a self-governing society demands that its citizens have the fullest information in order to make their decisions.

Taken literally, the Meiklejohn self-governance rationale of First Amendment protection is far less inclusive than, say, the liberty model. The self-governance theory basically extends full protection only to what is called core political speech, speech that affects the governance of the society. Commercial speech, for example, would not be protected.

In contemporary mass society, can we say that government is still the result of the sum of the decisions of individual citizens? Vincent Blasi suggests that we cannot: "[T]he Meiklejohn vision of active, continued involvement by citizens fails to describe not only the reality but also the shared ideal of American politics."[23] The mass media rather than individuals are the effective antagonists of government. Or, as Blasi puts it, the press has a **checking function** to prevent government abuse. In this view, protection of the press rather than of the individual citizen speaker becomes the primary objective of First Amendment protection. The media have the power and the influence in the opinion process to monitor government; the individual no longer does.

Does Blasi's theory of the First Amendment make citizenship a spectator sport? Blasi contends that the press is the appropriate countervailing force to government. This makes it possible "for citizens, in most, but not all, periods to have the luxury to concern themselves almost exclusively with private pursuits." For Meiklejohn, of course, the individual citizen is at the heart of First Amendment theory. Despite its critics, Meiklejohn's idea that the First Amendment is concerned with protection of public speech continues to influence First Amendment thinking.

Contemporary alternatives to Meiklejohn's emphasis on individual decision making and political self-governance have emerged. By way of illustration, Robert Post has argued that public discourse is the proper focus for First Amendment protection. Public discourse is essential to the creation and preservation of community. But Post's conception of public discourse is broader than just political speech: "Public discourse lies at the heart of democratic self-governance. [T]he first amendment preserves the independence of public discourse so that a democratic will within a culturally heterogenous state can emerge under conditions of neutrality, and so that individuals can use the medium of public discourse to persuade others to new forms of community life."[24]

- **Balancing test**
  Courts using the balancing test weigh the strength of the government interest in curbing expression against the First Amendment interest in allowing it.

- **Checking function**
  Theory that the contemporary role of the press is to check or curb abuses by government. In this view, press scrutiny of government is likely to be more effective than anything individual citizens can provide.

Strengthening the community and community self-governance rather than the individual and individual self-governance is the focus of attention.

THE FIRST AMENDMENT AND WHAT IT PROTECTS

The Categorical Approach

The First Amendment does not say that all speech and all publication are protected. Instead, it protects freedom of speech and freedom of the press. In short, First Amendment law recognizes that some forms of expression are and should be unprotected. Indeed, First Amendment law is to a large degree an effort to distinguish what is protected from what is not.

To accomplish this task, the Supreme Court has used a categorical approach. Some categories of expression are absolutely protected. An example of a fully protected category of speech is speech dealing with the political process. Other categories of speech are absolutely unprotected. Unprotected categories of speech include obscenity, fighting words, child pornography, and illegal incitement to violence or lawless action.

What causes expression to be placed in an unprotected category? Usually, the courts have made this decision because they have concluded that a particular form of expression has no social or political value or importance. In 1957, the famous case *Roth v. United States* defined obscenity as an unprotected category of speech. Obscene expression, the Court said, was without "redeeming social importance."[25]

The Supreme Court altered the *Roth* test for obscenity in 1973 in *Miller v. California*.[26] But once again the Court included as an element of the definition of obscenity the fact that the work under review, taken as a whole, lacked "serious literary, artistic, political, or scientific value."[27] The rationale, then, for denying a category of expression full First Amendment protection, or any protection at all, is that it is "low value" or, indeed, "no value" speech. In short, these categories are deemed to be areas of expression with which the First Amendment is not concerned.

If a court uses a categorical approach to resolve First Amendment problems, identification of the category becomes all important. If the material under consideration is defined as obscene, for example, the government may subject it to reasonable regulation. Some forms of expression fall somewhere in between. They are accorded neither full protection nor no protection. Examples of expression that are given some but not full First Amendment expression are commercial speech and libelous speech.

For those who favor the maximum amount of freedom for expression, the categorical approach has much to offer. Under the categorical approach, expression that is clearly not in an unprotected or partly protected category is assumed to be absolutely protected. Today, however, there is a considerable movement toward broadening the categories of unprotected expression. Social critics have proposed several candidates for inclusion in the unprotected category, including offensive and sexist speech, racist or hate speech, and pornography that exploits and degrades women.

● **Unprotected speech**
If expression is unprotected by the First Amendment, legislatures and government officials may more easily regulate it. Usually includes obscenity, fighting words, child pornography, and illegal incitement to lawless action, among other categories.

The Special Status of the Electronic Media

The electronic media have been treated by the courts as presenting unique free expression problems that merit a particularized First Amendment approach. Broadcast journalists are subjected to a regulatory regime that is not applied to print media journalists. Former Chief Justice Warren Burger once both described and explained this situation: "A broadcaster seeks and is granted the free and exclusive use of a limited and valuable part of the public domain; when he accepts that franchise it is burdened by enforceable public obligations. A newspaper can be operated at the whim or caprice of its owners; a broadcaster cannot."[28]

The Supreme Court has offered many reasons for the special First Amendment status of the electronic media. In the case of broadcasting, the inherent scarcity of the electronic spectrum has been offered as a justification for regulation.[29] In *FCC v. Pacifica Foundation,*[30] the Court also offered a social impact theory—the pervasiveness of broadcasting and its unique accessibility to children—as justification for regulation. Indeed, in this connection, the Court concluded in *Pacifica*: "And of all forms of communication, it is broadcasting that has received the most limited First Amendment protection."[31]

Today as new electronic media emerge all around us, the future First Amendment status of the electronic media is unclear. For example, how should cable systems be treated for First Amendment purposes? Should cable systems—with their abundant channels—be analogized to newspapers or to broadcasters? The Supreme Court, when presented with this question for the first time, declined to decide, saying it needed additional information.[32]

In 1994, in *Turner Broadcasting System, Inc. v. FCC,*[33] the Court revisited this issue in connection with a First Amendment attack on the must-carry provisions of the 1992 Cable Act (see the discussion of *Turner* in Chapter 8). Justice Anthony Kennedy declined to treat cable systems like newspapers for all purposes. The Court viewed the must-carry provisions as **content-neutral** and applied the mid-level standard of review set forth in the *O'Brien* case. If, however, cable regulations were deemed to be **content-based,** then the strict standard of review would be used (see the discussion of strict scrutiny and content controls later in this chapter).

Whatever the future holds, it is clear that at the present time First Amendment parity does not exist between the print media and the electronic media. The electronic media are still subject to a greater degree of regulation than the print media.

Balancing

In dealing with First Amendment problems, the Supreme Court has developed various doctrinal tools and tests. In recent years, as discussed earlier, the Court has increasingly used the categorical approach to deal with some First Amendment issues. In the immediate post-World War II era, the Court used a balancing test to resolve many First Amendment problems. It balanced the gov-

● **Content-neutral**
Regulation that is content-neutral limits expression regardless of its content. Such regulation is usually evaluated by a standard of review less demanding than strict scrutiny.

● **Content-based**
Regulation that limits expression on the basis of harm flowing from its content. Such laws are subjected to strict scrutiny by courts.

ernmental interest in regulation against the free expression rights of the person asserting them. The trouble with balancing is that its predictive quality is quite weak. The weighing of the competing interests—the process of balancing—seems to give too much authority to judges. There is a danger that the balancing of interests may follow the subjective social and political preferences of the judges who decide the cases. Further, it is also the judges who decide into which category the speech at issue should fall.

Strict Scrutiny Review

Balancing has not been abandoned, although today the Supreme Court uses it in a different way. Instead of balancing the interests on a case-by-case basis, the Court may use a form of *weighted* balancing in which the scales may be weighted in favor of free expression and against the validity of a regulation. For example, the Court may conclude that a regulation falls in a core area of protected speech. In that event, the regulation does not automatically fall. The Court subjects the regulation to strict review, which means that the regulation will be evaluated with the strictest scrutiny. Strict scrutiny review usually, but not always, means that the regulation is likely to be invalidated.

A rare example of a situation where a law regulating protected speech was *upheld* under the strict scrutiny standard was the 1992 case of *Burson v. Freeman*.[34] A Tennessee law prohibited the dissemination of campaign materials and the solicitation of votes within one hundred feet of a polling place. Clearly, the law was directed at protected political speech. It was also clear that the law was content-based. Accordingly, the Court applied the strict scrutiny standard to the law, but, surprisingly, the Court *upheld* the law. The state had a **compelling interest** in protecting a fundamental right, the right to vote, and in securing that right against fraud and intimidation.

When strict scrutiny is used, the Court will sustain the regulation only if it is necessary to achieve a compelling governmental interest and if the means used have been narrowly tailored to accomplish that interest. In other words, if some means less destructive of First Amendment rights are available where core protected expression is involved, the regulation will be struck down.

Content Controls

An important distinction in First Amendment law is the difference between regulations that are content-based and those that are content-neutral. A content-based regulation is one where the reason for the regulation is the content or message of the speech. Content-based regulations of speech are generally invalid unless the regulation involves expression that falls into one of the unprotected or partially protected categories of expression. If a content-based regulation affects a protected category of expression, it will be upheld only if it can survive the strict scrutiny test. A content-neutral regulation, on the other hand, is one where the basis for the regulation is unconnected to the content of the speech. Such regulations are more easily upheld against First Amendment attack.

● **Strict scrutiny**
The most demanding standard of review applied by courts to regulation infringing fundamental rights such as freedom of expression. Thus, these rights are not absolute, but regulations that limit them must both serve a compelling governmental interest and be narrowly tailored to do so.

● **Compelling interest**
Regulation that infringes upon fundamental constitutional rights such as freedom of expression must further a compelling governmental interest and be narrowly tailored to do so. The governmental interest must be so compelling that the free expression interest should be subordinated.

The decision in *Texas v. Johnson*,[35] the flag desecration case, is an example of a content-based regulation being struck down precisely because it aimed at "expressive conduct on the basis of the content of its message." In that case, Texas criminalized the conduct of anyone who mutilated, defaced, or defiled an American flag. Certain individuals demonstrating in front of the Republican convention in Dallas, Texas, set fire to the American flag and were prosecuted under the statute. The U.S. Supreme Court held, 5–4, that the prosecutions were inconsistent with the First Amendment and must be set aside. Justice Brennan said for the Court: "If there is a **bedrock principle** underlying the First Amendment, it is that the Government may not prohibit the expression of an idea simply because society finds the idea offensive or disagreeable."[36]

A content-based statute cannot be defended on the ground that the state is regulating or prohibiting expression because of particular harms that it wishes to avoid. Texas, for example, defended its flag desecration statute on the ground that it served important societal and governmental interests—the flag's significance as a symbol of unity and of the nation. But that argument cemented the case for the statute's invalidity; the argument simply underscored that suppressing free expression was the reason for the prosecutions.

An intense but short-lived controversy greeted the Supreme Court's flag protection decision in 1989. President George Bush called for a constitutional amendment to reverse the decision. To obviate the necessity for such an amendment, Congress enacted a federal flag protection law. That law was soon tested in the Supreme Court, and once again a flag protection law was struck down. In *United States v Eichman*,[37] the government argued that expressive conduct such as flag burning should be considered an unprotected category of expression like obscenity or "fighting words." Justice Brennan refused to accept this contention. After all, he observed, what the Court was dealing with here was "concededly political speech."[38]

The *O'Brien* Test and Content-Neutral Laws

As we have seen, content-based regulations of fully protected expression are subject to the severest kind of scrutiny by the courts. What about a law that **on its face** is neutral but whose detractors assert was really enacted because of government's hostility to some message or idea? A case illustrating this problem generated a now widely used test for resolving it.

The case is *United States v. O'Brien*.[39] In the spring of 1966, when U.S. troops were fighting in Vietnam, the war and the draft were becoming increasingly unpopular at home. Anti–Vietnam War activist David O'Brien and three companions burned their draft cards on the steps of the courthouse in South Boston. O'Brien was indicted for violating a 1965 amendment to the Selective Service Act prohibiting the willful mutilation or destruction of a draft card. The government contended that the law was designed to improve the administration and operation of the Selective Service System—an important and content-neutral objective.

O'Brien vigorously contended that the real purpose behind the 1965 amendment was to punish the protected political expression of those, such as

---

• First Amendment bedrock principle
Government may not prohibit the expression of an idea simply because society finds the idea to be offensive.

• On its face
Refers to the actual words set forth in a law.

O'Brien, who had demonstrated their opposition to the Vietnam War by burning their draft cards. Chief Justice Earl Warren for the Court refused to probe the motive of Congress in enacting the amendment. Courts do not like to probe motive. For one thing, if a law is invalidated because it was passed for a bad motive, then all the legislature has to do to revive the law is simply to reenact it for a good motive. Furthermore, a legislature has many members. Some may vote for a law for a permissible reason and some for an impermissible reason. It is hard to say, therefore, that the legislature as a whole voted for a law for an impermissible reason.

Instead, the Court devised a test for situations such as *O'Brien:* If a regulation affects conduct that has both speech and nonspeech components, and the regulation incidentally restricts expression, the regulation will be held valid if it meets four criteria. First, did Congress have constitutional authority to enact the regulation? Second, does the regulation further a substantial governmental interest? Third, is the governmental interest served by the regulation unrelated to the suppression of free expression? Fourth, is the incidental restriction on free expression no greater than what is essential to the furtherance of that interest? If all these questions are answered in the affirmative, the regulation is deemed to be valid.

To see how this test works, it is helpful to go down this list and see how the Court applied each criterion in the *O'Brien* case. First, the Court held that Congress, under its war powers and other constitutional powers, had the authority to enact the law punishing the destruction of draft cards. Second, the regulation *did* further the efficient and smooth functioning of the Selective Service System. Third, these governmental interests were not related to the suppression of free expression. Fourth, the incidental restriction on free expression that was a consequence of punishing draft card burning was no greater than what was required to accomplish the governmental interests in maintaining the integrity of draft cards.

The *O'Brien* test has been criticized by some, including the late First Amendment scholar Professor Thomas Emerson, as giving insufficient protection to First Amendment values. One may also argue that it too easily provides comfortable camouflage for a legislature's censorious purpose. Nevertheless, the test is often used when conduct has speech and nonspeech elements and when a regulation, at least on its face, is content-neutral.

The *O'Brien* test can be understood as a kind of balancing test. But it indicates the factors that are to be balanced and weighs them more heavily in favor of the government than, say, the strict scrutiny standard discussed above.

Symbolic Speech

One aspect of the *O'Brien* case merits separate discussion. This is the so-called **symbolic speech** problem. For example, is draft card burning speech or action? A generation ago, a First Amendment approach championed by Professor Emerson argued for a distinction between speech and action. Speech under this theory is fully protected from governmental restraint. Action, on the other

● *O'Brien test*
If regulation of conduct incidentally restricts expression, the regulation will be upheld only if (1) there was constitutional authority to enact the regulation, (2) the regulation furthers a substantial governmental interest, (3) the governmental interest is unrelated to the suppression of free expression, and (4) the restriction on free expression is no greater than necessary to further the governmental interest.

● **Symbolic speech**
Expressive activity that is not verbal or written, e.g., burning the flag to express hostility to the government. The purpose of describing such expressive activity as symbolic speech is to try to elevate it to the status of protected speech.

hand, is subject to reasonable regulation by government. The difficulty, of course, is that sometimes actions *speak.*

Emerson contended that if activity is predominantly communicative in nature, it should be given First Amendment protection. From a civil libertarian point of view, this approach is desirable since it broadens the reach of what is protected in the name of free expression. But it also presents problems.

Suppose someone shoots the secretary of state to attract attention to the movement for independence for Hawaii. Or a demonstrator burns the flag to convey disrespect for the policies of the government that the flag symbolizes. Or, as in *O'Brien,* a Vietnam War protester burns his draft card in front of a crowd at the federal courthouse to show his opposition to the war and the draft. Should these activities be given full First Amendment protection as symbolic speech? In *O'Brien,* Chief Justice Warren declined to use the Emerson approach to symbolic speech: "We cannot accept the view that an apparently limitless variety of conduct can be labelled 'speech' whenever the person engaging in the conduct intends thereby to express an idea."[40]

Instead of giving full protection to symbolic speech, the Court used the four-part test, which has come to be known as the *O'Brien* test, and upheld the congressional ban on draft card burning. Similarly, the burning of the flag at the Republican convention in Dallas to protest government policies might have been deemed protected expressive activity under a symbolic speech analysis. Instead, the Court chose to view the statute punishing flag burning as content-based legislation that should be struck down using the strict scrutiny standard of review.

Today the symbolic speech concept reminds us that conduct such as draft card burning or flag desecration may be undertaken as a way to communicate ideas. But use of the symbolic speech test as a tool to protect communicative activity has little currency today. Instead, legislation regulating such activity is analyzed either under the *O'Brien* test if it is deemed content-neutral or under the strict scrutiny standard if it is deemed content-based.

Overbreadth and Vagueness

- **Void for vagueness doctrine**
  A law that does not provide notice to people as to the conduct that they must take or not take to avoid the sanction of the law is void for vagueness.

- **Procedural due process**
  The idea that government should at a minimum afford notice and hearing to people before it attempts to affect their interests adversely.

Sometimes, in a First Amendment case, a party challenging the validity of a law under the First Amendment may contend that the law is either vague or overbroad. Objection to vagueness in a law has deep roots in Western civilization. A maxim of Roman law taught: *Nulla poena sine lege* (There should be no punishment without a law). This idea is at the root of the modern concept of vagueness.

If people do not know the meaning of a law, they are likely to have difficulty obeying it. The doctrine that a law is **void for vagueness,** therefore, is a **procedural due process** concept. The idea is that a law should give people notice of the conduct that they must take, or not take, in order to avoid the sanction of the law. If the law fails to do this, then the law should be struck down as void for vagueness.

But the doctrine of void for vagueness also has an important First Amendment dimension. In the First Amendment area, the idea that law should be clear is particularly important. Laws affecting expression must be clear; otherwise expression that is protected may be chilled because people will be uncertain whether the law affects the expression they wish to undertake.

The doctrine of **overbreadth** in First Amendment law is directed at regulation that proscribes both protected and unprotected expression. Vagueness and overbreadth are not different names for the same thing. A law can be quite clear and thus not be vague. Yet, at the same time, it may be overbroad because it reaches not only expression that is not protected under the First Amendment but also expression that is protected.

The overbreadth doctrine permits litigants to challenge a law even though the law as applied to them is valid. Similarly, the overbreadth doctrine can be raised even though a far narrower law applied to the particular expressive activity of the litigant would indeed be invalid. Overbreadth finds a particular application in so-called gatekeeper cases. Where government appoints a gatekeeper to make decisions, say, to grant permits or licenses for parades or demonstrations, and yet provides no standards for those decisions, the overbreadth doctrine may be used to strike down the entire regulatory scheme.

For example, an Ohio city ordinance placed discretion in the mayor to grant or deny licenses to coin-operated newspaper machines on city streets. But the ordinance provided no standards or guidelines to inform the mayor's decision making. In such circumstances, the opportunity for the government official to discriminate based on the content or viewpoint of the publication seeking a license clearly existed. In *City of Lakewood v. Plain Dealer Publishing Co.*, this licensing scheme was, therefore, struck down as overbroad even though the mayor in fact had not discriminated against any particular publication.[41] The possibility that the mayor could discriminate against protected expression was enough to invoke the overbreadth doctrine and invalidate the scheme.

● **Overbreadth**
A law that proscribes both protected and unprotected expressive activity is overbroad and, therefore, invalid. The problem is that an individual may forego protected expression for fear of being sanctioned for engaging in unprotected expression.

The Public Forum Doctrine

An important concept in First Amendment law is the idea that there are some public places where the citizenry has a right to assemble, demonstrate, and debate ideas as of right. At common law the village green served this function. Today this common law tradition endures in the Mall in Washington, D.C., as demonstrated by the crowds that still assemble to support causes such as peace, anti-abortion, the war on poverty, and civil rights. First Amendment scholar Harry Kalven described such public places as public forums. The generosity with which these public sites are made available for the communication of ideas is a continuing measure of the status of liberty in the society.[42]

Central to the public forum doctrine is the idea that access to public forums cannot be selective on the basis of content: "[G]overnment may not grant the use of a forum to people whose views it finds acceptable, but deny use to those wishing to express less favored or more controversial views."[43]

Certain public places such as parks are long-recognized sites for the discussion of ideas. What about public buildings whose primary function is not for discussion of controversial ideas? For example, the statehouse? Or the public library? The civil rights movement of the 1960s witnessed the use of public facilities to protest segregation. Could they be used for this purpose? The Supreme Court ruled that they could as long as the expressive activity to be undertaken did not obstruct the primary purpose for which the facility existed.[44]

Eventually, however, the Court began to distinguish between two kinds of public forums—the **traditional public forum** and the **limited public forum**. Courts apply the strict scrutiny standard of review if government denies access on a content basis to either type of forum. On the other hand, government is given more latitude in the case of content-neutral regulations.

In one case, the Minnesota state fairgrounds were ruled to be a limited public forum. The Hare Krishnas wanted to go up to people at the fairgrounds and offer their literature. The state fair had a regulation that printed materials could be distributed only from fixed locations on the grounds. The regulation was upheld because it was content-neutral.[45] The regulation applied no matter what the content of the literature. It was evenhanded in that it applied to all distributors. Moreover, it was narrowly tailored to serve a significant governmental interest—maintaining the smooth and efficient movement of the crowds at the fair. Finally, the regulation did not preclude the Hare Krishnas from speaking to individuals and proselytizing as they wished. They were still free to do that outside the fairgrounds.

How does one distinguish a traditional public forum from a limited public forum? The distinction seems to depend on whether the government intended to open or dedicate the public site in question for expressive activity. A limited public forum can exclude expressive activity from its premises altogether if it chooses. A traditional public forum cannot. Thus, the limited public forum is open for the discussion of ideas or as a site for protest at the sufferance of the state. The traditional public forum, on the other hand, is open for such discussion and protest subject to reasonable regulation as a matter of right.

Not all public property is open to some degree for First Amendment purposes. During the civil rights struggles of the 1960s, when so many public facilities were the sites for protest, the Court decided *Adderley v. Florida*,[46] a case that is still a landmark **nonpublic forum** decision. The Supreme Court refused to recognize a First Amendment right to use prison premises to protest the imprisonment of civil rights demonstrators confined there. A prison was simply not a public forum. This conclusion, of course, is debatable. Remember the role the Bastille played in the French Revolution, for example.

In *Adderley*, the Court held, 5–4, through Justice Hugo Black, that the state could limit the uses to which its property was put. A jail existed for the confinement of prisoners: "The State, no less than a private owner of property, has power to preserve the property under its control for the use to which it is lawfully dedicated."[47] Justice Douglas, writing for the dissenters, responded: "And when [a jail] houses political prisoners or those who many think are unjustly held, it is an obvious center for protest."[48]

- **Traditional public forum**
  A public area such as parks and streets that has long been opened or dedicated for expressive activity by government. Discussion and protest are available in such areas as a matter of right, subject to reasonable regulation.

- **Limited public forum**
  A public area that, while it may be used for expression for ideas, was not opened or dedicated for that purpose. The government can eliminate all expressive activity in a limited public forum if it wishes. A content-based restriction on expression will be subject to strict scrutiny.

- **Nonpublic forum**
  Public areas such as airports that are not intended to be used as sites for expressive activity. Government may subject expressive activity in such forums to reasonable regulation.

Deciding whether a public facility should be categorized as a traditional public forum, a limited public forum, or a nonpublic forum is a difficult question. Yet, as we have seen, whether First Amendment rights exist with respect to a public facility very much depends on how we characterize the site. The village green is clearly a traditional public forum. But what about an airport terminal?

In *International Society for Krishna Consciousness, Inc. v. Lee*,[49] the Court, through Chief Justice William Rehnquist, held, 5–4, that an airport was not a traditional public forum. The airport terminal had only recently made its appearance. Only more recently still had it come to be used as a forum for the dissemination of literature for all manner of proselytization. Unlike the village green, it could not be said that the airport terminal had " 'immemorially . . . time out of mind' been held in the public trust and used for purposes of expressive activity."[50]

Further, the airport terminal was not a limited public forum either. Certainly, there had been no dedication to speech activity. Otherwise, why would airport authorities and operators continually litigate to exclude those who sought to use airport terminals for expressive activity? The airport terminal was a nonpublic forum owned and controlled by the airport authority. Where government is a proprietor managing its own facility, regulations of expressive activity need not meet a strict standard of review.

In dissent, four justices, led by Justice Kennedy, challenged Rehnquist's static conception of the public forum. The Supreme Court should encourage rather than limit the recognition of new public forums: "In a country where most citizens travel by automobile, and parks all too often become locales for crime rather than social intercourse, our failure to recognize that new types of government property may be appropriate forums for speech will lead to a serious curtailment of our expressive activity."[51]

In short, Kennedy and the other dissenters wanted a dynamic definition of the public forum: "One of the places left in our mobile society that is suitable for discourse is a metropolitan airport. It is of particular importance that such spaces are public forums because in these days an airport is one of the few government-owned spaces where many persons have extensive contact with other members of the public. In my view, our public forum doctrine must recognize this reality, and allow the creation of public forums which do not fit within the narrow tradition of streets, sidewalks, and parks."[52]

In summary, the public forum doctrine began with the idea that public property could be used by citizens for the purpose of exercising First Amendment rights. Public facilities could also serve as public forums. Today the public forum has been divided into traditional public forums, limited public forums, and nonpublic forums. Only in the case of the traditional public forum is the right to engage in expressive activity relatively untrammeled. And in the case of the nonpublic forum, foreclosure is self-evident. The critical factor thus becomes one of characterization. As we have seen, the calculus for making this determination is currently a matter of bitter division on the Supreme Court.

THE PRIOR RESTRAINT DOCTRINE

- **Prior restraint**
A requirement that a publication be presented to an official for review and approval before it is disseminated to the public. At common law, freedom of the press was understood to mean freedom from prior restraint.

Historically speaking, in the Anglo-American world, freedom of the press meant freedom from **prior restraint.** This is the idea that publication must proceed even though ultimately the law may impose some sanction for its having been published. In *Near v. Minnesota*,[53] still the Supreme Court's most influential prior restraint case, Chief Justice Charles Evans Hughes quoted the definition of prior restraint advanced by the eighteenth-century English jurist Sir William Blackstone. That definition is still worth quoting:

> The liberty [of the press] deemed to be established was thus described by Blackstone: "The liberty of the press is indeed essential to the nature of a free state; but this consists in laying no *previous* restraints upon publications, and not in freedom from censure for criminal matter when published. Every free man has an undoubted right to lay what sentiments he pleases before the public, to forbid this, is to destroy the freedom of the press; but if he publishes what is improper, mischievous or illegal, he must take the consequences of his own temerity." 4 Bl. Com. 151, 152.[54]

- **Subsequent punishment**
Differs from prior restraint in that although subsequent punishment may befall an editor who publishes what has been prohibited, nonetheless, the publication has been disseminated. The idea has been communicated.

In this passage Blackstone is making a distinction between freedom from prior restraint and freedom from **subsequent punishment.** Blackstone's conception of freedom of the press is limited to freedom from prior restraint. Freedom from prior restraint precludes a state official from demanding that an editor furnish a copy of a publication before it can be published. Of course, this does not preclude the state from punishing the editor *after* publication.

Blackstone's definition of freedom of the press has been rightly criticized as too narrow. Today in the United States we define freedom of the press and freedom as expression as embracing both freedom from prior restraint and freedom from subsequent punishment. Nevertheless, Blackstone's conception of freedom of the press demonstrates that in English law freedom from prior restraint was considered the essential condition of freedom of the press.

Why was freedom from prior restraint considered so important? The late First Amendment scholar Thomas Emerson offered an explanation. Prior restraint is more inhibiting of free expression than subsequent punishment because it subjects a far broader range of expression to government supervision:

> [Prior restraint] shuts off communication before it takes place; suppression by a stroke of the pen is more likely to be applied than suppression through a criminal process; the procedures do not require attention to the safeguards of the criminal process; the system allows less opportunity for public appraisal and criticism; the dynamics of the system drive toward excesses, as the history of all censorship shows.[55]

With freedom from prior restraint, the idea or the publication can circulate. It is not snuffed out at birth. The speaker or the publisher may be punished thereafter, but society has received the idea.

Freedom from prior restraint is a fundamental component of the freedom of the press protected by the First Amendment and applied to the states through the Due Process Clause of the Fourteenth Amendment. Although, as we have seen, prior restraint had its origins in administrative censorship, a prior restraint regime that requires judicial approval in advance of publication is also impermissible. This principle was set forth in *Near v. Minnesota*.

The *Near* case involved a Minnesota law authorizing the state to stop the public nuisance of "malicious, scandalous, and defamatory" newspapers and publications. The county attorney in Minneapolis enforced this law against a scandal sheet known as *The Saturday Press,* which had published articles accusing Minneapolis law enforcement authorities of failing to punish illegal gambling, bootlegging, and racketeering. The publication alleged that these activities were in control of a "Jewish gangster." The state trial court found that *The Saturday Press* had violated the statute and perpetually enjoined future publications of such a nuisance. The U.S. Supreme Court held, 5–4, that the Minnesota law violated freedom of the press. The law made it possible to suppress a newspaper and preclude future publication. This, Chief Justice Hughes said, constituted the "essence of censorship."[56]

The *Near* case did not establish absolute freedom from prior restraint in the United States, but it did create a presumption against the validity of prior restraints. Chief Justice Hughes set forth three exceptions to the general freedom from prior restraint. The first exception dealt with situations where publication might imperil the national security in time of war. The second exception involved obscene publications—cases involving, as Hughes put it, the "primary requirements of decency."[57] The third exception involved situations where the public order would be endangered by incitements to violence and the overthrow by force of orderly government.

One of the most famous cases invoking the doctrine of prior restraint was the **Pentagon Papers** case, *New York Times v. United States.*[58] Daniel Ellsberg, a former Pentagon employee, made available to the *New York Times* a classified government report on American involvement in the Vietnam War. The government had not authorized Ellsberg's action. After much anguish over the matter, the *Times* decided to publish excerpts from the report. The U.S. Department of Justice then sought a temporary restraining order to prevent the publication of the remaining Pentagon Papers.

Curiously enough, there was no specific federal statute prohibiting the publication of these papers by the press. The government based its request to prevent publication on national security interests. Other newspapers in other parts of the country such as the *Washington Post* and the *Boston Globe* soon joined the fray. The press contended that the government's attempt to suppress publication of a government report was a clear violation of the First Amendment. The executive branch contended that it had inherent authority to protect the national security. A major conflict between the government and the press had arisen. The U.S. Supreme Court took the rare step of expediting review of the matter.

The Court, 6–3, flatly rejected the government's request to enjoin the further publication of the Pentagon Papers by the press. Although only a cursory

● **Pentagon Papers**
Classified papers that a former Department of Defense (Pentagon) employee made available to the press and whose publication government sought unsuccessfully to prevent.

statement, the Court's opinion reaffirmed the First Amendment's hostility to prior restraint:

> *"Any system of prior restraints of expression comes to this Court bearing a heavy presumption against its constitutional validity."* The Government *"thus carries a heavy burden of showing justification for the imposition of such a restraint."* The federal [d]istrict Court [in] the *New York Times* case and [the federal courts in the District of Columbia] in the *Washington Post* case held that the Government had not met that burden. We agree.[59] (Emphasis added.)

Each of the nine justices wrote an opinion in the Pentagon Papers case. The dissenters—Warren Burger, Harry Blackmun, and John Marshall Harlan—could not accept the doctrine that prior restraint is never permissible. A grave threat to the nation's security as perceived by the executive was in their view an exception to the general presumption against the validity of prior restraints. As Justice Blackmun put it, "The First Amendment, after all, is only one part of an entire Constitution. First Amendment absolutism has never commanded a majority of this Court. [E]ven the newspapers concede that there are situations where restraint is in order and is constitutional."[60] The members of the majority placed much greater weight on the traditional presumption against the validity of prior restraints. For Justices Black and Douglas, the First Amendment *was* a near absolute. Since the government was asking for the imposition of a prior restraint against the press, the case was a simple one: The First Amendment forbade it. Justice Brennan also felt that the government was asking for an impermissible prior restraint. But, in his view, the absolutist First Amendment position went too far. For example, the press might be restrained from publishing the departure date of a troop ship during wartime.

The other three members of the majority—Byron White, Potter Stewart, and Thurgood Marshall—took an even more middle-of-the-road position than Justice Brennan. Justices Marshall and Stewart saw it as critical that Congress had not authorized the issuance of an injunction in these circumstances. Furthermore, Justice White hinted that if Congress had enacted a statute authorizing what the government had requested, he might have supported the government position. Nevertheless, he concurred in the result rejecting the government's request for an injunction "because of the concededly extraordinary protection against prior restraints enjoyed by the press under our constitutional system."[61] In retrospect, the Pentagon Papers case has to be seen as a victory for the doctrine that prior restraints are presumptively invalid under the First Amendment.

The Supreme Court continues to reaffirm the doctrine that there is a heavy presumption against the validity of prior restraints. In *Nebraska Press Association v. Stuart,*[62] the Supreme Court, per Chief Justice Warren Burger, held that there was a heavy presumption against the validity of "gag" orders. Gag orders are prior restraints directed at the press by trial judges seeking to guard against undue publicity. Under *Nebraska Press,* a prior restraint such as a gag order is permissible only when there is a clear and present danger to the administration of justice and no alternatives less destructive of First

● Gag orders
Court orders to journalists prohibiting dissemination of court proceedings to protect the defendant from prejudicial publicity. Gag orders are prior restraints and are presumptively invalid unless there is a clear and present danger to the administration of justice and no less drastic alternatives are available.

Amendment rights exist. But the Court left the door slightly ajar by declining to say that *all* gag orders are invalid prior restraints. In a concurring opinion, Justice Brennan argued that the Court should have done precisely that. As a practical matter, however, this is the effect of the decision. After *Nebraska Press,* a judge issuing a gag order against the press must meet an extremely stringent standard. As a result, gag orders against the press that withstand appeal are increasingly rare.

Not all prior restraints are invalid. The validity of prior restraints, like so many other issues in First Amendment law, depends very much on the context in which the question arises. Illustrative is a case in Forsyth County, Georgia, where an ordinance allowed the county administrator to grant permits for private demonstrations using public property. Under the ordinance, the county administrator could adjust the fee for assembling or parading to reflect the cost of law enforcement at such demonstrations. The ordinance provided that an applicant would not have to pay more than $1,000 for a permit.

A racist group, the Nationalist Movement, applied for a permit for a demonstration on the county courthouse steps on a Saturday afternoon to protest making Martin Luther King, Jr.'s birthday a federal holiday. The county imposed a $100 fee. The Nationalist Movement challenged the ordinance. In 1992, the Supreme Court held, 5–4, that the ordinance violated the First Amendment by, among other things, imposing an invalid prior restraint.[63]

The Supreme Court has long recognized that in order to regulate competing demands for use of public forums, government may impose a **permit requirement** for parades or demonstrations.[64] But this did not mean that a government official could be authorized to decide what the fee should be. The ordinance offered no guidance in the way of standards, allowing content and viewpoint discrimination. Groups sponsoring parades for causes that the administrator favored might be charged only a small fee; groups espousing disfavored causes might be charged high fees. As Justice Blackmun put it for the Court in the *Forsyth* case: "The Forsyth County ordinance requiring a permit and a fee before authorizing public speaking, parades, or assemblies in 'the archetype of a traditional public forum,' is a prior restraint on speech."[65] Although some licensing schemes were valid prior restraints, a law that delegated "overly broad licensing discretion to a public official" was invalid.[66]

THE CLEAR AND PRESENT DANGER DOCTRINE

Origins and Evolution

A surprising fact about First Amendment law is that the Supreme Court did not begin generating significant and substantial First Amendment interpretation until well into the first quarter of the twentieth century. A doctrinal tool developed in this period that has greatly influenced First Amendment law is the clear and present danger doctrine. This doctrine was first most closely identified with Justice Oliver Wendell Holmes and later with Justice Louis Brandeis. Holmes formulated it to deal with prosecutions under the **Federal Espionage Act**

● **Demonstration permit requirements**
Permit requirements for access to public forums are permissible as long as standards for awarding permits are clear and do not allow content and viewpoint discrimination by administrative officials.

● **Federal Espionage Act**
Legislation enacted by Congress in 1917 during World War I under which many anti-war and pro–Russian Revolution dissidents were prosecuted. The Supreme Court opinions considering these prosecutions laid the foundation for modern First Amendment law and the clear and present danger doctrine.

against radical pamphleteers and anti-war activists during World War I. Holmes devised the clear and present danger doctrine as a way to limit the incursions a repressive legislature might seek to make on free expression in a time of crisis.

In 1919, in *Schenck v. United States*,[67] the government claimed that the defendants had published and circulated a pamphlet that was calculated to cause insubordination in the armed forces and obstruction of the draft. This publication could be the basis for a conviction under the Espionage Act, said the Court, if "the words used are used in such circumstances and are of such a nature as to create a clear and present danger that they will bring about the substantive evils that Congress has a right to prevent."[68] Whether or not the publication presented such a clear and present danger, Holmes said, was a "question of proximity and degree."[69]

In its beginnings, the clear and present danger test did not always provide much latitude for free expression. Indeed, in *Schenck* Holmes wrote the opinion for the Court affirming the convictions. However, in another case in 1919, *Abrams v. United States*,[70] which also involved leaflets distributed by radicals, Holmes dissented. His statement of the clear and present danger doctrine in *Abrams* was more protective of free expression: "It is only the present danger of immediate evil or an intent to bring it about that warrants Congress in setting a limit to the expression of opinion where private rights are not concerned."[71] Holmes emphasized the significance of the immediacy of the danger: "Only the emergency that makes it immediately dangerous to leave the correction of evil counsels to time warrants making any exception to the [First Amendment's] sweeping command."[72]

The most influential formulation of the clear and present danger doctrine during its formative period came not from Justice Holmes, however, but from Justice Brandeis. Brandeis wrote a concurring opinion in *Whitney v. California*[73] that was designed to wrench as much protection for free expression from the clear and present danger doctrine as possible. Like Holmes in the *Abrams* case, Brandeis stressed that there must be "probability of serious danger to the State" before government could lawfully suppress speech.[74] But in *Whitney* Brandeis expanded on the meaning of an *imminent* danger. Expression would be protected if "the advocacy falls short of incitement and there is nothing to indicate that the advocacy would be acted upon."[75]

In *Whitney,* Brandeis said: "Only an emergency can justify repression."[76] Free exchange of ideas, no matter how noxious, is the norm. The remedy for hateful or dangerous speech is counterspeech. Or, as Brandeis put it, "[T]he fitting remedy for evil counsels is good ones."[77] Only when an emergency makes it impossible for the curative work of counter speech to take place is government intervention justified. In addition, Justice Brandeis made clear that even

● **Role of judge in clear and present danger** Courts and not the legislature have the task of deciding whether the clear and present danger test is met.

if the legislature stated in the law that a particular danger was serious and imminent, that did not dispose of the matter. It was for the **courts,** *and* not the legislature, to decide whether the **clear and present danger** test was satisfied.

During the McCarthy era, the officers of the Communist Party in the United States were prosecuted under a federal antisubversive law, the Smith Act. The prosecution was challenged as a violation of the First Amendment.

The Supreme Court considered the matter in *Dennis v. United States*,[78] which affirmed the conviction against the Communist Party officials and upheld the Smith Act against the First Amendment challenge.

The *Dennis* Court professed to follow the Holmes-Brandeis version of the clear and present danger doctrine, but critics said it did no such thing. Chief Justice Fred Vinson seemed to excise the factor of immediacy from the clear and present danger test. Government did not have to wait before acting "until the *putsch* is about to be executed."[79] The probability of a plan to overthrow the government could not be the decisive factor. Neither could the imminence of the danger. Instead, courts should weigh the seriousness or the gravity of the evil with which the legislature was concerned against its improbability.

For Chief Justice Vinson, the ultimate constitutional value for a society was its self-preservation. For Justices Black and Douglas who dissented in *Dennis*, the First Amendment's prohibition against government restraint of free speech was the fundamental value. In 1957, six years after the *Dennis* case, *Yates v. United States*[80] removed some of the sting from *Dennis*. The Smith Act's provision against advocacy of violent overthrow of the government was interpreted to reach "advocacy of action" but not "advocacy of abstract doctrine or ideas." The distinction was important. A teacher in a class on comparative political ideas could talk about Marxism or even support it without fear of prosecution.

The clear and present danger doctrine was not returned to its Holmes-Brandeis understanding until *Brandenburg v. Ohio* in 1969.[81] The *Brandenburg* case involved the application of a state law prohibiting the advocacy of terrorism or violence to achieve industrial or political reform. The law was applied against some speakers at a Ku Klux Klan rally. Because the statute punished "mere advocacy," the Court struck down the statute as inconsistent with the First and Fourteenth Amendments.

Brandenburg set forth a **test** for dealing with the advocacy of illegal conduct that owes much to the Brandeis statement of the clear and present danger set forth in *Whitney*: Advocacy of illegal conduct can be punished only "where such advocacy is directed to inciting or producing imminent lawless action and is likely to incite or produce such actions."[82] *Brandenburg* is a much tighter test than the one Vinson set forth in *Dennis*. The *Brandenburg* test focuses on whether there has been incitement to lawless action. But it looks at the context. Was there an imminent likelihood of the lawless action? Was it probable that the incitement to lawless action would be successful? Although *Brandenburg* did not actually refer to the clear and present danger doctrine in so many words, it has been understood to state the contemporary understanding of that doctrine.

The Clear and Present Danger Doctrine—Useful or Not?

The clear and present danger doctrine has been subjected to severe and continuous criticism since its inception. The nature of the debate reveals a great deal about the fundamental issues involved when a society seeks to protect freedom of expression. Such questions include the following: Which is more important,

● ***Brandenburg*** **approach to the clear and present danger doctrine** The approach currently in force was set forth in *Brandenburg v. Ohio* (1969): Advocacy of illegal action can only be prohibited "where such advocacy is directed to inciting or producing imminent lawless action and is likely to incite or produce such action."

a society's self-preservation or free expression? Is it possible for a constitution to protect free expression if the society's elected representatives don't really value free expression?

● **Meiklejohn critique of clear and present danger**

Meiklejohn criticized the clear and present danger doctrine for offering less protection than the Framers intended. In his view, the First Amendment provides absolute protection for core political speech.

Political philosopher Alexander **Meiklejohn** thought that by permitting government to suppress expression, in some circumstances, the clear and present danger doctrine simply ended up permitting what the First Amendment forbade—the abridgment of free expression.[83] Did Meiklejohn believe then that all expression was protected under the First Amendment? The answer is that he did not.

Clearly, both Holmes and Meiklejohn were interested in giving freedom of expression the fullest scope possible. Meiklejohn insisted that an absolutist position would do this. Holmes believed his clear and present danger test was more likely to do it. Professor Zechariah Chafee, reviewing Meiklejohn's book on *Free Speech and Its Relation to Self-Government*, remarked dryly that it was apparent that Professor Meiklejohn was not a pragmatist. In Chafee's view, the issue was not the abstract question of how much speech *should* be protected from suppression by government, but rather how much expression *could* be protected when society was in a mood to suppress it. Chafee wrote that the alternative to the clear and present danger doctrine was not Meiklejohn's absolute protection for all public or political speech but instead "no immunity at all in the face of legislation."[84]

In short, Chafee simply assumed that in a time of emergency and crisis society was going to be intolerant and pass repressive laws. The task, then, of First Amendment theory was to devise tests that would confront that reality and at the same time try to provide as much protection as possible for freedom of expression.

Finally, it should be noted that attempts to salvage the clear and present doctrine such as occurred in *Brandenburg* have had their critics on the Supreme Court itself. Justice Douglas concurred in *Brandenburg* and bitterly criticized the doctrine:

> Though I doubt the "clear and present danger" test is congenial to the First Amendment in time of a declared war, I am certain it is not reconcilable with the First Amendment in days of peace. I see no place in the regime of the First Amendment for any "clear and present danger" test, whether strict and tight as some would have it, or free-wheeling, as the Court in *Dennis* rephrased it.[85]

The Clear and Present Danger Doctrine Today

Today the clear and present danger doctrine is less widely used than it once was. Indeed, it may be argued that once it can be shown that government is restraining protected expression, the court will simply invoke the strict scrutiny test. But the clear and present danger test may prove useful in the future if new conflicts between the security of the state and political expression arise. But it is important to recognize that the Court has used the clear and present danger test in contexts far removed from advocacy of political revolution where it was developed. As we have seen, the First Amendment validity of gag orders against the press are evaluated under a clear and present danger standard.[86] Similarly,

Virginia was prevented on the basis of the First Amendment from punishing a newspaper reporter for publishing confidential information about the proceedings of a state judicial disciplinary commission. The Court concluded that Virginia's interest in protecting the reputation of its judiciary did not constitute a clear and present danger to the administration of justice.[87]

CATEGORIES OF EXPRESSION

At an earlier point in this chapter, we observed that in solving First Amendment problems the courts distinguish among categories of expression. Some are fully protected, some have less than full protection, and some have no protection. One could argue, for example, that the clear and present danger doctrine deals with a category of expression—advocacy of subversive activity—that receives less than full protection. This would explain why problems arising in this category of expression were evaluated using the clear and present danger test rather than the strict scrutiny standard used for fully protected expression.

Fighting Words

One of the earliest categories of expression identified by the Supreme Court for less than full protection deals with so-called **fighting words**. The case originated in a small New Hampshire town. A Jehovah's Witness called a local police officer a "God-damned racketeer and a damned fascist." These words were said to be likely to cause acts of violence by the person to whom they were addressed. Just by their utterance, said the Court, such words inflicted or incited immediate breaches of the peace.

In *Chaplinsky v. New Hampshire*,[88] the conviction of the Jehovah's Witness was upheld. The Supreme Court reasoned that some categories of expression such as "fighting words" are not protected. Why not? They were of "such slight social value as a step to truth that any benefit that may be derived is too clearly outweighed by the social interest in order and morality."[89] Fighting words then did not contribute to the life of ideas; they were not relevant to the purposes with which the First Amendment was concerned.

In the years since the enunciation of the fighting words doctrine, the Court has been very careful to take a narrow view of the reach of the fighting words category. If a breach of the peace or disorderly conduct is based on a statute that in its own terms, or as construed by a court, reaches clearly protected expression, the Court will not affirm the conviction even though the words that gave rise to the arrest may have been fighting words. In these circumstances, the Court uses the overbreadth doctrine, and thus the scope of the fighting words concept has been quite limited.[90]

The greatest challenge to the traditional understanding of the fighting words concept came in 1992 with Justice Antonin Scalia's decision for the Court in *R.A.V. v. City of St. Paul.*[91] *R.A.V.* considered the First Amendment validity of the Bias-Motivated Crime Ordinance of St. Paul, Minnesota; the

● **Fighting words**
Words that have a direct tendency to cause acts of violence by the individuals to whom they are addressed. Traditionally considered an unprotected category of expression and, therefore, subject to sanction. The rationale for regulation is that fighting words do not contribute to the life of ideas.

ordinance punished fighting words based on race, color, creed, religion, or gender. The case arose when several teenagers assembled a crude cross and burned it inside the fenced yard of a black family. The Minnesota Supreme Court interpreted the statute under which the youths were convicted to be limited to "fighting words."

Justice Scalia, however, held that the St. Paul ordinance, as construed by the Minnesota court, was unconstitutional. Speaking for a majority of the Court, Justice Scalia said that the St. Paul ordinance was impermissibly under-inclusive. The law permitted restrictions on the content of speech in limited areas such as obscenity, defamation, and fighting words. But that did not mean, he said, that government could practice viewpoint discrimination within these limited areas:

> We have sometimes said that these categories of expression are "not within the area of constitutionally protected speech," or that the "protection of the First Amendment does not extend" to them. Such statements must be taken in context, however, and are no more literally true than is the occasionally repeated shorthand characterizing obscenity "as not being speech, at all." What they mean is that these areas of speech can consistently with the First Amendment, be regulated because of their constitutionally proscribable content (obscenity, defamation, etc.)—*not that they are categories of speech entirely invisible to the Constitution, so that they may be made the vehicles for content discrimination unrelated to their distinctively proscribable content.* [Emphasis added] Thus, the government may proscribe libel; but it may not make the further content discrimination of proscribing only libel critical of the government.[92]

Scalia pointed out that the St. Paul ordinance constituted viewpoint discrimination. The ordinance did not prohibit fighting words condemning people because of their politics or sexual preference. Only certain kinds of hate speech were proscribed. Justice White joined by three other justices contended that the view expressed by Scalia and four other justices was startling and wrong. It had been assumed that fighting words were simply a category of unprotected expression. Therefore, any government regulation of it was permissible.

Does the Scalia decision for the majority in *R.A.V.* mean that fighting words will no longer be subject to sanction? No. But it does mean that only a general ban on fighting words would be acceptable. Selectivity among subcategories of fighting words would not be acceptable. Critics of the *R.A.V.* decision say it shrinks the domain of free expression. In order to proscribe *some* fighting words, legislatures will now have to proscribe *all* fighting words.

The Hostile Audience Problem

A variation on the fighting words theme is the hostile audience problem. If a racist demagogue so offends an audience that people move toward him to silence him and, perhaps, to beat him, what should the police do? Arrest the speaker? Or arrest the crowd? Should the First Amendment tolerate a heckler's veto? If the speaker is convicted of disorderly conduct in such circumstances,

● **R.A.V. limitation on fighting words doctrine**
In *R.A.V. v. St. Paul* (1992), the Court held that even fighting words are not invisible to the First Amendment. Fighting words may be regulated for their proscribable content but may not be used as vehicles for content discrimination.

such a conviction should not stand unless the demands of the clear and present danger standard are met. The Supreme Court so ruled in *Terminiello v. Chicago*.[93] In language that has been much quoted ever since, Justice Douglas said for the Court in *Terminiello* that free speech may "best serve its high purpose" when it "creates dissatisfaction" or "even stirs people to anger."[94] If *Terminiello* were the Supreme Court's only statement on the **hostile audience** problem, the law on this point would be clearer than it is. Two years later a case arose involving a radical speaker who invited himself to an American Legion picnic in a public park and proceeded to insult the town's mayor. When the crowd moved on the speaker, the police arrested him, and he was convicted for disorderly conduct. Unlike the *Terminiello* decision, however, the Supreme Court in *Feiner v. New York*[95] affirmed the speaker's conviction. Chief Justice Vinson said the arrest was proper because the speaker had incited the crowd to a riot. The clear and present danger standard was met. The dissenters led by Justice Black didn't see it that way at all. They thought there was no clear and present danger of a riot. As one can see, the threat to the public order and the likelihood of a riot appear to be in the eye of the beholder.

Which approach then will the Court take today to the hostile audience problem? Is *Terminiello* the law? Or is *Feiner* the law? This is a difficult question to answer definitively. But subsequent Supreme Court cases have rejected the notion that the possibility of civil disorder permits the arrest of the speakers or demonstrators. The Court's position has been that it is the duty of law officers to enforce constitutional rights, not to surrender to those who are hostile to the exercise of those rights. When Arkansas Governor Orval Faubus used the threat of social unrest as an argument to prevent the integration of a public high school in Little Rock, Arkansas, a unanimous Supreme Court said it was his duty nevertheless to enforce the Constitution and follow court orders to desegregate the school.[96] In the absence of intentional incitement to violence by the speaker,[97] the police must also protect the speaker no matter how much he or she may annoy the onlookers.[98]

● **Hostile audience**
The fact that a speaker arouses a hostile reaction does not justify the speaker's arrest, unless the speaker intentionally incites to violence. One of the purposes of the First Amendment is to invite dispute and stimulate unrest.

Offensive Speech

Suppose speech doesn't provoke an immediate physical response or a breach of the peace? But suppose also that it engenders feelings of distaste or even disgust by the public? Should offensive speech be treated as just another category of low-value speech? Indeed, should the courts conclude that offensive speech has no value as far as the goals of the First Amendment are concerned? The famous Supreme Court case raising and disposing of this issue is *Cohen v. California*.[99]

The facts of the case certainly raised the offensive speech problem. During the Vietnam era, a young man sat in a Los Angeles courtroom wearing a jacket emblazoned with the words "Fuck the Draft." The young man was arrested on the ground that his conduct had been offensive, and he was convicted of disturbing the peace. Justice John Marshall Harlan, speaking for the Supreme Court, reversed the conviction.

The basis for Cohen's arrest, Harlan declared, was the message on his jacket, not conduct on his part. His conviction rested upon **offensive speech**.

● **Offensive speech**
Speech that provokes reactions of disgust or distaste. It is protected speech and is not subject to regulation absent some compelling governmental interest.

This offensive speech was not obscene nor did it constitute fighting words. In short, the speech did not fall in any category of expression to which anything less than full protection should be granted. California could not create a new category of offensive speech that would be removed from First Amendment protection: "The State has no right to cleanse public debate to the point where it is grammatically palatable to the most squeamish among us. [W]hile the particular four-letter word being litigated here is perhaps more distasteful than most others of its genre, it is nevertheless often true that one man's vulgarity is another's lyric."[100]

Government cannot be permitted to punish words because they are offensive or vulgar. Even vulgarity can contribute to the message intended to be communicated: "[W]ords are often chosen as much for their emotive as their cognitive force."[101] The problem with trying to excise certain words from the public vocabulary is that it is impossible to do so without suppressing ideas. In the absence of some compelling governmental interest, the state could not punish the use of the offending word. The *Cohen* case continues to stand as an eloquent and definitive statement against censorship based on the offensiveness of the speech.

Hate Speech

- **Hate speech**
  Expression that denigrates a racial, ethnic, or religious group. Some have contended that it should be treated as unprotected low-value speech, but so far, the Court has not made it a new, unprotected category of expression.

Hate speech—called group defamation at an earlier time—has long been a volatile First Amendment issue. In 1952, the Supreme Court in *Beauharnais v. Illinois*[102] upheld, 5–4, an Illinois criminal libel law that criminalized such expression. The Illinois law punished publications or exhibitions that exposed citizens of any race, color, or creed to contempt or derision or led to breaches of the peace or to riots.

Speaking for the Court, Justice Felix Frankfurter offered a defense of the Illinois law. If the low-value speech category of fighting words could be subject to the sanction of the state, so could such words directed to defined groups. Furthermore, the state had an interest in countering the harmful effects continued denigration of particular racial or religious groups had on the position of members of those groups in the larger society. Clearly, it was reasonable for the legislature to conclude that "a man's job and his educational opportunities and the dignity accorded him may depend as much on the reputation of the racial and religious group to which he willy-nilly belongs, as on his own merits."[103]

Beauharnais's precedential effect is difficult to gauge, as it has neither been followed nor reversed by the Supreme Court. The statute that it upheld has long since been repealed. As for the case itself, it has been treated as discredited in subsequent Supreme Court decisions. In the early 1960s, Justice Douglas delivered an extremely negative but influential estimate of *Beauharnais:* "*Beauharnais v. Illinois* [s]hould be overruled as a misfit in our constitutional system and as out of line with the dictates of the First Amendment."[104] Many First Amendment scholars thought these comments accurately described the status of the case and the group defamation law that it upheld.

Recently, however, the hate speech problem has been analyzed from a different perspective than the classic libertarian position represented by Justice Douglas and many others. The harmful effects hate speech has on members of minority groups has emerged in recent First Amendment literature as providing a **basis for regulation,** but in a somewhat different form. Today proponents of punishing hate speech argue that such expression tends to reinforce existing power relationships and to freeze the subordinate position of the vilified group. The dynamic that propels the fighting words theory is transformed when applied to racial groups. Professor Charles Lawrence has explained this dynamic: "The fighting words doctrine anticipates that the verbal 'slap in the face' of insulting words will provoke a violent response with a resulting breach of the peace. When racial insults are hurled at minorities, the response may be silence or flight rather than a fight, but the preemptive effect on further speech is just as complete as with fighting words."[105]

Because of the subordinate position of members of minority groups, silence rather than response is the likely reaction of the victim. Presumably, in such circumstances, the low-value nature of the speech is particularly highlighted. Professor Lawrence has written: "Women and minorities often report that they find themselves speechless in the face of discriminatory verbal attacks. Words like 'nigger,' 'kike,' 'faggot' produce physical symptoms that temporarily disable the victim."[106] Lawrence argues that since racist speech puts an end to dialogue, there is no First Amendment interest in protecting it.

Not all writers on this topic are convinced that hate speech has no value. Lee Bollinger has pointed to the benefits society can obtain from tolerating hate speech. Extending the guarantee of free speech even to hate speech requires that the society be possessed of "extraordinary self-restraint": "The purpose of this [principle of self-restraint] is to develop and demonstrate a special capacity to control feelings evoked by a host of social encounters."[107] This theory is, of course, open to the criticism that it makes the victims of hate speech—not the society at large—martyrs to free expression; the victims of hate speech have no choice but to "tolerate" racial epithets. Their toleration serves only to illustrate their general powerlessness, a status hate speech only serves to perpetuate.

These developments as well as the enactment of "hate speech codes" on many university campuses have focused attention on *R.A.V. v. City of St. Paul,* the Supreme Court's 1992 hate speech case. The *R.A.V.* decision did not directly discuss the merits of characterizing hate speech as a category of unprotected expression like obscenity. But the case did make clear that future hate speech laws would have to confront serious First Amendment problems.

The facts of *R.A.V.* were discussed in the section on fighting words. The St. Paul ordinance punishing hate speech had been limited by the Minnesota courts to fighting words. But the Supreme Court declared that the ordinance, even as limited, was a violation of free expression. The St. Paul ordinance punished only those fighting words that caused anger, fear, or resentment in others because "of race, color, creed, religion or gender."

Such selectivity in choosing only to punish fighting words on certain disfavored topics, Justice Scalia declared, violated the First Amendment. Fighting words could also refer to one's political affiliation or sexual preference or union

> ● **Rationale for hate speech regulation**
> The argument that toleration of hate speech serves to reinforce the general powerlessness and subordinate status of minority groups. Protecting hate speech tends to strengthen existing patterns of inequality.

membership. Yet fighting words about those topics were not punished. The St. Paul ordinance was intolerably underinclusive. The ordinance represented viewpoint discrimination by government.

The city of St. Paul might prohibit all fighting words, but it could not permit some and punish others. It was no excuse that fighting words had been thought to be an unprotected category of expression. Statements to that effect in prior Supreme Court cases, said Justice Scalia, "must be taken in context, however, and are no more literally true than is the occasionally repeated short-hand characterizing obscenity 'as not being speech, at all.' "[108] Such statements provided no justification for government suppression of expression within such a category solely on the basis of viewpoint.

Viewpoint-based government regulation of speech can be upheld if it meets the strict scrutiny standard. If the interest that government is trying to serve is a compelling one, it will override the normal protection given to free expression. The governmental interest in seeking to provide protection for minorities who have historically been discriminated against was a compelling one. But that interest, the *R.A.V.* majority declared, could not override the free speech concerns presented by the ordinance. Why not? The reason was that content-neutral alternatives for dealing with the hate speech problem were open to government. The city, for example, could proscribe all fighting words.

Four justices in *R.A.V.*, in an opinion by Justice White, concurred with the result in the case—that the ordinance as interpreted should be invalidated. But they disagreed with the reasoning of the majority. They believed the St. Paul ordinance was invalid because it was overbroad. They also adhered to the doctrine that fighting words are an unprotected category of expression. Therefore, hate speech as a subcategory within fighting words could be proscribed by government. The majority's theory, Justice White argued, would encourage legislatures to suppress more speech than they really wished to reach. The result would be to contract rather than expand the domain of free expression.

What is the First Amendment **future for government efforts to deal with hate speech** after *R.A.V.*? In 1993, the Court decided a case that indicated that *R.A.V.* may not be the last word on the subject. In *Wisconsin v. Mitchell,*[109] the Court upheld a Wisconsin law that provided for enhanced criminal penalties when a victim is selected because of race. A group of black men and teenagers attacked and beat a white youth. One of the perpetrators who had been convicted for the crime received an enhanced penalty because the victim had been selected because of his race. The perpetrator, who normally would have been sentenced to two years for the crime, was sentenced instead to seven years.

Was Wisconsin selectively punishing the motive behind certain crimes and making the disfavored ones subject to enhanced criminal penalties? If so, the defendant argued, then Wisconsin was punishing his thoughts and beliefs, a realm protected by the First Amendment. Chief Justice William Rehnquist, speaking for the Court, said that the law was valid. The sentencing decision could take into account the motive for a crime. Motive, after all, was considered in other areas of the law such as antidiscrimination laws. Such laws are directed to conduct that is not protected by the First Amendment.

● **Future of hate speech regulation**
Although *R.A.V.* presents problems for future hate speech regulation unless *all* fighting words are regulated, enhanced penalties for bias-motivated crimes are valid. Such laws are directed to conduct rather than expression and are not protected by the First Amendment.

Did *R.A.V.* require the invalidation of the Wisconsin law? No. *R.A.V.* raised a different issue. The St. Paul ordinance in *R.A.V.* punished expression whereas the Wisconsin law punished conduct. Chief Justice Rehnquist explained that the Wisconsin law singled out for "enhancement bias-inspired conduct because the conduct is thought to inflict greater individual and societal harm."[110] Crimes motivated by bias were "more likely to provoke retaliatory crimes, inflict distinct emotional harms on their victims, and incite community unrest."[111] The state was not simply disagreeing with the beliefs or biases of offenders by its penalty-enhancement law. Instead, it was acting to redress the perceived harms that flowed from their conduct.

How persuasive is the Court's attempt to distinguish *Wisconsin v. Mitchell* from *R.A.V.*? Justice Frankfurter insisted in *Beauharnais* that racial epithets—hate speech—inflict emotional harms and lead to serious and undesirable social and economic consequences. Harmful effects may flow from hate speech as well as from hate-inspired conduct. The new attention being focused on the harms experienced by the victims of hate speech may yet call into question the approach adopted by the Court in *R.A.V.*

Commercial Speech

Alexander Meiklejohn taught that the purpose of the First Amendment was to provide protection for political speech. What, then, is the First Amendment status of speech that is commercial rather than political in nature? Is commercial speech, such as speech that is dedicated to persuading someone to buy something, protected by the First Amendment? The Supreme Court has not followed a steady course in answering this question.

In 1942, in *Valentine v. Chrestensen*,[112] the Supreme Court reviewed a municipal antilitter ordinance and declared that the Constitution precluded government from unduly burdening freedom of communication on the public streets. Yet it was equally clear that there was no such constitutional barrier to regulation of commercial advertising. The Supreme Court did not explain why commercial speech was unprotected speech. We may speculate that commercial speech like fighting words—a category of expression also designated as unprotected in 1942[113]—was deemed of such "low value" that it made no contribution to the exposition of ideas. This view harmonizes with some of the rationales of the First Amendment that we have studied. Commercial speech, it can be argued, contributes neither to individual self-realization nor to political self-governance.

The development of a rigid distinction between commercial and noncommercial speech drew criticism. Slowly, it began to be rethought. In 1971, Professor Martin Redish wrote that commercial speech was, in fact, related to the individual autonomy rationale for First Amendment protection. Commercial speech had a First Amendment dimension: "When the individual is presented with rational grounds for preferring one product or brand over another, he is encouraged to consider the competing information, weigh it mentally in the light of the goals of personal satisfaction he has set for himself, counter-balance his conclusions with possible price differentials, and in so

● **Commercial speech**
Defined in *Virginia Pharmacy* as speech that does nothing more than propose a commercial transaction. Defined more broadly in *Central Hudson* as expression that relates entirely to the economic interests of the speaker and the audience.

● **Rationale for protection of commercial speech**
In a free enterprise society, the free flow of commercial information and democratic decision-making is directly related. Although commercial speech does not receive full First Amendment protection, it is entitled to some protection.

doing exercise his abilities to reason and think; this aids him towards the intangible goal of rational self-fulfillment."[114]

The sharp bifurcation between unprotected commercial speech and fully protected speech collapsed in 1976 with the decision in *Virginia State Board of Pharmacy v. Virginia Citizens Consumer Council, Inc.*[115] A Virginia statute prohibiting pharmacists from advertising the price of prescription drugs was struck down on First Amendment grounds. The question presented in *Virginia Pharmacy* was this: Was speech that did nothing more than propose a commercial transaction so removed from the exposition of ideas that it was denied all First Amendment protection? The answer to the question was "No."

The advertiser's interest in the free flow of commercial information did not lose all claim to First Amendment protection simply because the interest was an economic one. Labor disputes between employees and employers have long enjoyed First Amendment protection. The consumer's interest in the "free flow of commercial information" was particularly intense.[116] Indeed, the aged, the poor, and the sick may be more interested in the price of drugs than "in the day's most urgent political debate."[117]

Society also has a strong interest in the free flow of commercial information. Advertising that is commercial may still have significance for the public interest. For example, a manufacturer of artificial furs may promote its product over those of competitors by pointing out that its product does not depend on the destruction of furry animals. In a free enterprise economy, allocation of resources is necessarily the sum of many "private economic decisions."[118] In such circumstances, the public interest lies in the free flow of commercial information. Moreover, given the nature of our free enterprise society, commercial information is directly related to democratic decision making: "And if [commercial information] is indispensable to the proper allocation of resources in a free enterprise system, it is also indispensable to the formation of intelligent opinions as to how that system ought to be regulated or altered. Therefore, even if the First Amendment were thought to be primarily an instrument to enlighten public decision making in a democracy, we could not say that the free flow of information does not serve that goal."[119]

As a result of the foregoing developments, some important conclusions about commercial speech emerged. First, commercial speech was defined as speech that did nothing more than propose a commercial transaction. Second, commercial speech was deemed to merit some First Amendment protection. Indeed, Justice Blackmun who wrote the opinion in *Virginia Pharmacy* related the particular commercial speech involved in the case—advertising the price of pharmaceuticals—to both the self-governance and individual autonomy rationales of First Amendment protection.

- **Critique of protection for commercial speech**
Commercial speech should not merit First Amendment protection since it does not contribute to self-government or to individual self-fulfillment or autonomy.

Academic critics Thomas Jackson and John Jeffries, Jr., rejected Justice Blackmun's attempt to rationalize a new First Amendment status for commercial speech: "[C]ommercial speech is remarkable for its insignificance. It neither contributes to self-government nor nurtures the realization of the individual personality."[120]

Virginia Pharmacy gave commercial speech a new First Amendment status, but it did not elevate such speech to full First Amendment protection. For example, commercial speech does not enjoy the same level of protection accorded to political speech. Commercial speech is subject to some state regulation. Why is this? Commercial speech is hardier and more objective than political speech. The commercial claims of advertisers are more easily verified than are the claims of political candidates. Further, given the profit motive at the heart of commercial advertising, it is unlikely that regulation of commercial speech will chill it to the extent such regulation might chill political speech.

What does it mean to say that commercial speech enjoys some protection but not full protection? Regulation of fully protected expression such as political speech is usually evaluated by the strict scrutiny standard of review, which usually means that the regulation will fall. Commercial speech regulation, however, is not subjected to such searching review. Instead, the Court has developed a special test for commercial speech. This test is called the *Central Hudson* test after the case where it was set forth. The case arose when the New York state public utility commission imposed a complete ban on promotional advertising by an electric utility company in an effort to further the conservation of energy. The Supreme Court held that the ban violated the constitutional guarantee of free expression.[121]

In *Central Hudson,* the Court set forth a four-part **test**. To be valid, a regulation must be evaluated under four criteria. First, the speech at issue might be misleading or connected to an illegal activity. Illegal or misleading commercial speech is not protected by the First Amendment. Second, the government's interest in the regulation must be substantial. Third, the regulation before the court must directly advance the government's interest in it. Fourth, the regulation must be no more extensive than necessary to meet the governmental interest that is to be served.

The Court's application of this four-part test illustrates its use. First, the electric company's promotional advertising was neither illegal nor misleading. Consequently, it was commercial speech meriting First Amendment protection. Second, the government's interest in the regulation must be substantial. The interest of the public utility commission in conserving energy and in maintaining a fair rate structure obviously constituted a substantial governmental interest. Third, the commission's interest in conserving energy was directly advanced by the regulatory ban. There was a connection between the ban on promotional advertising and the demand for electricity. However, the ban failed to meet the fourth part of the *Central Hudson* test—that the regulation must be no more extensive than necessary to implement the governmental interest. The ban extended to *all* the utility's promotional advertising even if such advertising did not affect the conservation of energy. Nor had the commission shown that some more limited ban could not have satisfied the governmental interest in energy conservation. Simply put, the ban was not the least restrictive way of handling the problem. The promotional advertising ban failed to meet the fourth prong of the four-part *Central Hudson* test.

Central Hudson has since been refined further to provide even less protection to commercial speech. *Board of Trustees of State University of New York (SUNY) v. Fox,*[122] which was decided almost a decade after *Central Hudson,* softened the fourth prong of the test. *Fox* held that a narrowly

● *Central Hudson* **test**
Commercial speech may be regulated only if (1) the speech at issue is not misleading or illegal, (2) the government interest served by the regulation is substantial, (3) the regulation directly advances the governmental interest, and (4) the regulation is no more extensive than necessary to advance the governmental interest being served.

● *Fox* **limitation on** *Central Hudson* **test**
Board of Trustees of State University of New York v. Fox (1989), softened the fourth part of the *Central Hudson* test. Even though a regulation is not the least restrictive way of dealing with a problem, it may still satisfy the no more extensive than necessary requirement. The fit between legislative objectives and the means to accomplish those objectives needs only to be reasonable, not perfect.

tailored regulation could meet this prong even though it was not the least re-strictive way of dealing with the problem. A flexible approach was needed in the commercial speech area. What was really required was a fit between the legislature's objectives and the means used to secure those objectives. The fit need not necessarily be perfect, said Justice Scalia, but it should be reason-able. Thus, the substantial protection under the First Amendment that the Supreme Court seemed to promise for commercial speech has been signifi-cantly modified.

The *Central Hudson* test has received mixed reviews from First Amendment scholars. Some think it undoes some of what *Virginia Pharmacy* tried to accomplish. Aspects of the four-part test trouble these critics. The sub-stantiality of a governmental interest is hardly an objective standard. As a re-sult, the critics fear, the *Central Hudson* test may be so malleable that expres-sion that should be protected will be subjected to regulation.

The *Central Hudson* test expanded the definition of commercial speech from speech that does nothing more than propose a commercial transaction to "expression [which is] related solely to the economic interests of the speaker and its audience."[123] This broader definition of commercial speech raises a new problem. What is the line between commercial and noncommercial speech? For example, a cigarette company may advertise that there is no irrefutable scien-tific evidence linking cancer to smoking. An oil company may advertise on the editorial page of a newspaper about the dangers presented by nuclear power as an alternative source of energy. These are advertisements, but they are also more than that. They constitute "expression relating to important public issues, but on behalf of entities with an economic interest in one side of the debate."[124] Whether such expression should be characterized as commercial speech is a tough issue. Broadening the definition of commercial speech poses the risk that expression that might otherwise get full protection will receive something less than that under the *Central Hudson* test.

The basic point, however, is that the Supreme Court's current approach to commercial speech—the *Central Hudson–Fox* test—does provide significant protection for commercial speech. Certainly, the protection is greater than was provided when the Court confronted the commercial speech problem in 1942.[125] Illustrative is a 1993 case, *Cincinnati v. Discovery Network, Inc.,*[126] which struck down a Cincinnati, Ohio, ban on newsracks that distributed com-mercial publications. No ban was imposed on newspaper newsracks, however. Cincinnati justified its ban on commercial newsracks because of its interests in promoting safety and esthetics on city streets. The reasonable fit that *Fox* had required between the means used and the governmental objective behind the regulation was lacking, however. A ban on commercial newsracks would re-move a mere 62 commercial newsracks from Cincinnati streets, while leaving 1,500 to 2,000 newspaper newsracks in place. In such circumstances, the safety and aesthetic interests asserted by the city in favor of its commercial newsrack ban seemed trivial indeed. Newsracks had been selected for the ban, Justice John Paul Stevens surmised, because the city assumed that commercial speech was low-value speech and, therefore, more susceptible to regulation. Such an assumption was wrong and seriously underestimated the value of commercial speech.

SUMMARY

Our society has placed great weight on a constitutional guarantee of freedom of the press and freedom of speech for a number of reasons. These reasons include protection for a marketplace of ideas, a desire to protect the autonomy of the individual and to encourage individual creativity and self-expression, and, finally, an effort to protect self-governance and to encourage citizen participation in the political process.

Although the **First Amendment** protects freedom of the press and freedom of speech, not every utterance or every printed word receives **protection**. The Supreme Court has developed a number of doctrinal tools to aid it in the task of separating what is protected under the First Amendment from what is not. For example, government regulation of political speech that is content-based is subject to the strictest judicial scrutiny and will only be upheld if it is justified by some overriding or compelling reason or if the speech falls into an unprotected category such as obscenity. Content-neutral regulation, on the other hand, is subject to less exacting review.

Other tools that have been developed to protect freedom of expression include the concepts of overbreadth and vagueness. If a law reaches both a substantial body of expression that is protected as well as expression that is not, it is deemed overbroad and is invalid. If a law is so vague that those affected by it cannot understand its meaning and are afraid to express themselves for fear they may be covered by the law, the courts may say that the law is void for vagueness.

A judicially created weapon used to protect freedom of the press is the doctrine of prior restraint. If a government official, or even a court, were to demand to see the text of a newspaper story, or the script of a television news broadcast, as a condition for its publication or communication, under First Amendment law such a prior restraint carries a heavy presumption of invalidity. The vice of the prior restraint, as Professor Thomas Emerson pointed out, is that it shuts off communication before it takes place. A primary tenet of First Amendment law is that the story should be published. Whether those who published the story broke the law in some way by doing so can be determined later.

Once communication has taken place, the communication or publication may nevertheless be prohibited by government. One way of dealing with a government prohibition on speech is to balance the free speech interest against the governmental interest served by the prohibition. First Amendment absolutists like Professor Alexander Meiklejohn reject such a balancing approach. In Meiklejohn's view, such prohibitions are invalid if they affect political speech. But civil libertarians like Meiklejohn do not abound in legislatures. In times of crisis, the legislative urge to censor is strong. To deal with this reality, the Supreme Court has developed the clear and present danger doctrine to measure

● **Nature of First Amendment protection**
The First Amendment protects freedom of speech and press, but this does not mean that it protects every spoken utterance or every printed word. Unprotected categories of expression may be regulated.

conflicts between the security of the state and freedom of expression. In an effort to explain the philosophy of the clear and present danger doctrine, Justice Brandeis said that "[o]nly an emergency justifies repression."[127] This approach gives expression great scope, but it does permit some repression of speech in an emergency.

● **Categorical approach**
Expression is divided among various categories. Some like political speech receive full First Amendment protection. Others like commercial speech receive different levels of protection. False and misleading commercial speech, for example, receives no protection. Other kinds of commercial speech are evaluated under the *Central Hudson* test.

Another way the Supreme Court has dealt with problems of freedom of expression is to take a **categorical approach.** Under this approach, expression is divided among various categories. Some categories such as political speech merit full First Amendment protection. Regulation directed at such speech will only be upheld if it survives the strictest judicial scrutiny. Other speech like commercial speech receives gradations of protection. Commercial speech is not protected at all if it is false or illegal. If commercial speech is neither false nor illegal, it is still subject to some government regulation. Such regulation is not evaluated under the strict scrutiny standard but under the less exacting *Central Hudson* test.

Still other categories of expression like fighting words have not been granted First Amendment protection. Fighting words have been deemed of such "slight value as a step to truth that any benefit that may be derived is too clearly outweighed by the social interest in order and morality."[128] A significant limitation on the fighting words doctrine was established in the *R.A.V.* case in 1992 when Justice Scalia pointed out for the Court that no category of expression is "entirely invisible" to the First Amendment.[129] Government cannot practice viewpoint discrimination by punishing only a certain subcategory of fighting words such as hate speech.

Occasionally, efforts are made to create new categories of unprotected or less protected expression. In 1971, in *Cohen v. California*, Justice Harlan for the Court refused to recognize offensive speech as a new category of unprotected expression. A memorable line captures the Court's reason for refusing to deprive offensive speech of full First Amendment protection: "[O]ne man's vulgarity is another's lyric."[130]

The Supreme Court has been reluctant to expand the categories of unprotected expression. After all, when a new category of unprotected expression is created, the domain of free expression granted full protection by the First Amendment is necessarily diminished. The *R.A.V.* case can be seen as a rebuff to an attempt to create a category of unprotected hate speech.

Often controversies about whether new categories of unprotected expression should be created rest on arguments about the harm caused to individuals and groups from the exercise of unrestrained expression. Opponents of hate speech contend that racist attacks on members of minority groups further weaken their already subordinate and marginal status in society.

● **No general theory of the First Amendment**
Different tests, doctrines, and standards of review are applied in different contexts in First Amendment law.

The law of freedom of expression can best be understood if it is recognized that the law in this area is like speech itself—volatile and dynamic. Different tests and doctrines apply in different contexts. There is **no general theory of the First Amendment.** But this should be expected in an area of law that deals with the fundamental issues and controversies that beset society. This is an area where certainty should be neither sought nor expected. Yet the fact that in the American polity, freedom of the press and freedom of speech are guaranteed in the society's fundamental law—the constitution—assures that these freedoms will have a special status in the courts and in the society.

KEY TERMS

Constitution
Fourteenth Amendment
Three branches of the federal government
Injunction
Seditious libel
Common law
Fox's Libel Act
Sedition Act
Marketplace of ideas theory
Oliver Wendell Holmes
Market failure theory
Individual autonomy theory
Balancing test
Checking function
Unprotected speech
Content-neutral
Content-based
Strict scrutiny
Compelling interest
First Amendment bedrock principle
On its face
O'Brien test
Symbolic speech
Void for vagueness doctrine
Procedural due process
Overbreadth
Traditional public forum

Limited public forum
Nonpublic forum
Prior restraint
Subsequent punishment
Pentagon Papers
Gag orders
Demonstration permit requirements
Federal Espionage Act
Role of judge in clear and present danger
Brandenburg approach to the clear and present danger doctrine
Meiklejohn critique of clear and present danger
Fighting words
R.A.V. limitation on fighting words doctrine
Hostile audience
Offensive speech
Hate speech
Rationale for hate speech regulation
Future of hate speech regulation
Commercial speech
Rationale for protection of commercial speech
Critique of protection for commercial speech
Central Hudson test
Fox limitation on *Central Hudson* test
Nature of First Amendment protection
Categorical approach
No general theory of the First Amendment

CASE PROBLEMS

1. New York City officials decide that recent St. Patrick's Day parades have become too rowdy, causing trouble and expense for the city. The city passes a regulation setting up a new commission that will issue licenses to groups wishing to participate in the parade. The regulation states that a license will be given to any applying group that can show the commission that they have a valid and strong connection to the Irish holiday. The city hopes that this process will eliminate the participation of groups interested only in activities that tend to disturb the peace. Is this licensing regulation valid?

2. A small western town makes much of its revenue during the autumn hunting season. Lately, an ani-

mal rights group based in Washington, D.C., has come to town. This group protests against hunting and is generally causing major harm to this crucial source of revenue in the town. The town is considering an ordinance that would prohibit antihunting protests outside local stores within the town. Is the activity of the animal rights group protected, unprotected, or partially protected expression? Under what standard of review would a regulation controlling it be evaluated?

3. Radio talk show host G. Gordon Liddy is a strong advocate of a citizen's right to own a gun under the Second Amendment. He has suggested to callers that if agents of the Department of Alcohol,

Tobacco, and Firearms come to their homes to confiscate their firearms, the callers are justified in resisting with deadly force. He has also said that if you do resist the agents, it is best to aim for their heads, as they wear body armor. Can this speech be sanctioned under the clear and present danger doctrine?

4. A victims' rights group in Los Angeles, California, is angry about the attitude of many Americans toward O. J. Simpson. The group feels the rights of Simpson's murdered wife and her companion have been ignored. On the day that the verdict is to be handed down, the group demonstrates at the courthouse. They know that the press and many individuals who support Simpson will be there; indeed, that is why they have chosen that day. During their demonstration, they hang an O. J. Simpson effigy, which greatly angers others present. The Los Angeles police fear that violence will result. Under the Supreme Court's decisions, especially *Terminiello,* should the police arrest or otherwise remove the victims' rights demonstrators?

5. A great many advertising billboards have been erected alongside highways and roads in Houston, Texas. Suppose the Houston city council decides that these billboards, taken cumulatively, present a safety hazard to motorists. Accordingly, the council passes an ordinance outlawing any new billboards and preventing contracts for current ones from being renewed. Will this regulation pass the four-part test set up in both *Central Hudson* and *Fox* for judging the validity of regulations of commercial speech?

ENDNOTES

1. *Gitlow v. New York,* 268 U.S. 652, 45 S.Ct. 625 (1925). Some of the discussion in this chapter is based on material in Chapter 1 of Donald M. Gillmor, Jerome A. Barron, Todd F. Simon, and Herbert A. Terry, *Mass Communication Law: Cases and Comment,* 5th ed. (St. Paul: West Publishing, 1990).

2. *New York Times Co. v. United States,* 403 U.S. 713, 91 S.Ct. 2140 (1971).

3. Richard C. Jebb, ed., Introduction to Milton, *Areopagitica* (Cambridge: Cambridge University Press, 1918), p. xxiii.

4. 376 U.S. 254, 84 S.Ct. 710 (1964).

5. See Norman L. Rosenberg, *Protecting the Best Men: An Interpretive History of the Law of Libel* (Chapel Hill: University of North Carolina Press, 1986), pp. 38–39.

6. William Blackstone, *Commentaries,* (1769).

7. See Leonard Levy, *Legacy of Suppression: Freedom of Speech and Press in Early American History* (New York: Oxford University Press, 1960), pp. 247–48.

8. See Leonard Levy, *Emergence of a Free Press* (New York: Oxford University Press, 1985), p. x.

9. 376 U.S. 254, 84 S.Ct. 710 (1964).

10. Harry Kalven, "The New York Times Case: A Note on 'The Central Meaning of the First Amendment'" *Supreme Court Review* 191: 205 (1964).

11. Jebb, Introduction to Milton, *Areopagitica,* p. 58.

12. John Stuart Mill, *Three Essays,* (New York: Oxford University Press, 1975), p. 24.

13. *Dennis v. United States,* 341 U.S. 494, 584, 71 S.Ct. 857, 904 (1951).

14. Herbert Marcuse, *Repressive Tolerance in Wolff, Moore, and Marcuse: A Critique of Pure Tolerance* (Boston: Beacon Press, 1965), p. 110.

15. Jerome Barron, "Access to the Press—A New First Amendment Right," *Harvard Law Review* 80:1641 (1967).

16. *Id.* at 1647.

17. C. Edwin Baker, "*Scope of the First Amendment Freedom of Speech,*" *U.C.L.A. Law Review* 25:964, 986 (1978).

18. Owen Fiss, "Why the State?" *Harvard Law Review* 100:781, 786 (1987).

19. Thomas I. Emerson, *The System of Freedom of Expression* (New York: Random House, 1970), p. 6.

20. Baker, "Scope of the First Amendment Freedom of Speech," 964.

21. Robert Bork, "Neutral Principles and Some First Amendment Problems," *Indiana Law Journal* 47:1 (1971).

22. Alexander Meiklejohn, *Free Speech and Its Relation to Self-Government* (New York: Harper Brothers, 1948).

23. Vincent Blasi, "The Checking Value in First Amendment Theory," A.B.F. Res. J. 521, 561 (1977).

24. Robert C. Post, "The Constitutional Concept of Public Discourse: Outrageous Opinion, Democratic Deliberation and *Hustler Magazine v. Falwell*," *Harvard Law Review* 103:601, 684 (1990).

25. 354 U.S. 476, 77 S.Ct. 1304 (1957).

26. 413 U.S. 15, 93 S.Ct. 2607 (1973).

27. *Id.* at 24, 93 S.Ct. at 2615.

28. *Office of Communication of United Church of Christ v. FCC,* 359 F.2d 994, 1003 (D.C. Cir. 1966).

29. *NBC v. United States,* 319 U.S. 190, 63 S.Ct. 997 (1943); see also *Red Lion Broadcasting v. FCC,* 395 U.S. 367, 89 S.Ct. 1794 (1969).

30. 438 U.S. 726, 98 S.Ct. 3026 (1978)

31. *Id.* at 748, 98 S.Ct. at 3039.

32. *City of Los Angeles v. Preferred Communications, Inc.,* 476 U.S. 488, 106 S.Ct. 2034 (1988).

33. ____ U.S. ____, 114 S. Ct. 2445 (1994).

34. *Burson v. Freeman,* 504 U.S. 191, 112 S.Ct. 1846 (1992).

35. 491 U.S. 397, 109 S.Ct. 2533 (1989).

36. *Id.* at 414, 109 S.Ct. at 2545.

37. 496 U.S. 310, 110 S.Ct. 2404 (1990).

38. *Id.* at 315 fn. 4, 110 S.Ct. at 2408 fn. 4.

39. 391 U.S. 367, 88 S.Ct. 1673 (1968).

40. *Id.* at 376, 88 S.Ct. at 1678.

41. 486 U.S. 750, 108 S.Ct. 2138 (1988).

42. Harry Kalven, "The Concept of the Public Forum: *Cox v. Louisiana*," *Supreme Court Review* 1 (1965).

43. *Police Dept. of the City of Chicago v. Mosley,* 408 U.S. 92, 92 S.Ct. 2286 (1972).

44. See *Edwards v. South Carolina,* 372 U.S. 229, 83 S.Ct. 680 (1963) (state house); *Brown v. Louisiana,* 383 U.S. 131, 86 S.Ct. 719 (1966).

45. *Heffron v. International Society for Krishna Consciousness, Inc.,* 452 U.S. 640, 101 S.Ct. 2559 (1981).

46. 385 U.S. 39, 87 S.Ct. 242 (1966).

47. *Id.* at 47, 87 S.Ct. at 246.

48. *Id.* at 49, 87 S.Ct. at 248.

49. ____ U.S. ____, 112 S. Ct. 2701 (1992).

50. *Id.* at ____, 112 S.Ct. at 2706.

51. *Id.* at ____, 112 S.Ct. at 2717.

52. *Id.* at ____, 112 S.Ct. at 2717-2718.

53. 283 U.S. 697, 51 S.Ct. 625 (1931).

54. *Id.* at 713-714, 51 S.Ct. at 630.

55. Emerson, *The System of Freedom of Expression,* p. 506.

56. *Near,* 283 U.S. at 713, 51 S.Ct. at 630 (1931).

57. *Id.* at 716, 51 S.Ct. at 631.

58. 403 U.S. 713, 91 S.Ct. 2140 (1971).

59. *Id.* at 714, 91 S.Ct. at 2141.

60. *Id.* at 761, 91 S.Ct. at 2164.

61. *Id.* at 730-731, 91 S.Ct. at 2149-2150.

62. 427 U.S. 539, 96 S.Ct. 2791 (1976).

63. *Forsyth County, Ga. v. Nationalist Movement,* 505 U.S. 123, 112 S.Ct. 2395 (1992).

64. *Cox v. New Hampshire,* 312 U.S. 569, 61 S.Ct. 762 (1941).

65. *Forsyth County, Ga.,* ____ U.S. at ____, 112 S.Ct. at 2401.

66. *Id.*

67. 249 U.S. 47, 39 S.Ct. 247 (1919).

68. *Id.* at 52, 39 S.Ct. at 249.

69. *Id.*

70. 250 U.S. 616, 40 S.Ct. 17 (1919).

71. *Id.* at 628, 40 S.Ct. at 21.

72. *Id.* at 630–631 40 S.Ct. at 22.

73. 274 U.S. 357, 47 S.Ct. 641 (1927).

74. *Id.* at 378, 47 S.Ct. at 649.

75. *Id.*

76. *Id.* at 377, 47 S.Ct. at 648-649.

77. *Id.* at 375, 47 S.Ct. at 648.

78. 341 U.S. 494, 71 S.Ct. 857 (1951).

79. *Id.* at 509, 71 S.Ct. at 867.

80. 354 U.S. 298, 77 S.Ct. 1064 (1957).

81. 395 U.S. 444, 89 S.Ct. 1827 (1969).

82. *Id.* at 447, 89 S.Ct. at 1829.

83. See Meiklejohn, *Free Speech and Its Relation to Self-Government,* p. 29.

84. See Zechariah Chafee, "Book Review," *Harvard Law Review* 62:891, 898 (1949).

85. *Brandenburg,* 395 U.S. at 452–454, 89 S.Ct. at 1832-1833.

86. *Nebraska Press Association v. Stuart,* 427 U.S. 539, 96 S.Ct. 2791 (1976).

87. *Landmark Communications, Inc. v. Virginia,* 435 U.S. 829, 98 S.Ct. 1535 (1978).

88. 315 U.S. 568, 62 S.Ct. 766 (1942).

89. *Id.* at 572, 62 S.Ct. at 769.

90. *Houston v. Hill,* 482 U.S. 451, 107 S.Ct. 2502 (1987).

91. ____ U.S. ____, 112 S.Ct. 2538 (1992).

92. *Id.* at ____, 112 S.Ct. at 2543.

93. 337 U.S. 1, 69 S.Ct. 894 (1949).

94. *Id.* at 4, 69 S.Ct. at 895.

95. 340 U.S. 315, 71 S.Ct. 303 (1951).

96. *Cooper v. Aaron,* 358 U.S. 1, 78 S.Ct. 1401 (1958).

97. *Cohen v. California,* 403 U.S. 15, 91 S.Ct. 1780 (1971).

98. *Gregory v. Chicago,* 394 U.S. 111, 89 S.Ct. 946 (1969).

99. 403 U.S. 15, 91 S.Ct. 1780 (1971).

100. *Id.* at 25, 91 S.Ct. at 1788.

101. *Id.* at 26, 91 S.Ct. at 1788-1789.

102. 343 U.S. 250, 72 S.Ct. 725 (1952).

103. *Id.* at 263, 72 S.Ct. at 733-734.

104. Justice Douglas made these observations in a concurring opinion in *Garrison v. Louisiana,* 379 U.S. 64, 85 S.Ct. 209 (1964), a case that applied the actual malice test of *New York Times Co. v. Sullivan,* 376 U.S. 254, 85 S.Ct. 710 (1964) to criminal libel.

105. Charles R. Lawrence III, "If He Hollers Let Him Go: Regulating Racist Speech on Campus," *Duke Law Journal* 1990:431 (1990).

106. *Id.*

107. Lee Bollinger, *The Tolerant Society: Freedom of Speech and Extremist Speech in America* (New York: Oxford University Press, 1986), p. 107.

108. *R.A.V.,* ____ U.S. at ____, 112 S. Ct. at 2543.

109. ____ U.S. ____, 113 S. Ct. 2194 (1993).

110. *Id.* at ____, 113 S.Ct. at 2201.

111. *Id.*

112. 316 U.S. 52, 62 S.Ct. 920 (1942).

113. *Chaplinsky v. New Hampshire,* 315 U.S. 568, 62 S.Ct. 766 (1942).

114. Martin H. Redish, "The First Amendment in the Marketplace: Commercial Speech and the Values of Free Expression," *George Washington Law Review* 39:429 (1971).

115. 425 U.S. 748, 96 S.Ct. 1817 (1976).

116. *Id.* at 764, 96 S.Ct. at 1827.

117. *Id.* at 763, 96 S.Ct. at 1826.

118. *Id.* at 765, 96 S.Ct. at 1827.

119. *Id.*

120. Thomas Jackson and John Jeffries, Jr., "Commercial Speech: Economic Due Process and the First Amendment," *Virginia Law Review* 65:1 (1979).

121. *Central Hudson Gas & Elec. Corp. v. Public Serv. Comm'n,* 447 U.S. 557, 100 S.Ct. 2343 (1980).

122. 492 U.S. 469, 109 S.Ct. 3028 (1989).

123. *Central Hudson,* 447 U.S. at 561, 100 S.Ct. at 2348-2349.

124. Alex Kozinski and Stuart Banner, "Who's Afraid of Commercial Speech?" *Virginia Law Review* 76:627 (1990).

125. See *Valentine v. Chrestensen,* 316 U.S. 52, 62 S.Ct. 920 (1942).

126. ___ U.S. ___, 113 S.Ct. 1505 (1993).

127. *Whitney,* 274 U.S. at 377, 47 S.Ct. at 648-649.

128. *Chaplinsky,* 315 U.S. at 572, 62 S.Ct. at 769.

129. *R.A.V.,* ___ U.S. at ___, 112 S.Ct. at 2543.

130. *Cohen,* 403 U.S. at 25, 91 S.Ct. at 1788.

Libel and the Mass Media

WHAT IS LIBEL?

● Defamation
An attack on a person's reputation or character by false, malicious, or negligent statements.

Libel, the bane of communicators and perhaps the most complex area of media law, is print or broadcast defamation. **Defamation** is technically a false attack on someone's reputation that supports a claim of loss of one's good name, humiliation, disgrace, shame, ridicule, mental suffering, embarrassment, or exposure to public hatred. When defamation is published or broadcast, it is called libel. Words alleging the commission of a crime, charges of professional incompetence, unethical practices, or other moral failures resulting in injury to reputation and business standing account for nearly all libel cases.

A report that a police chief was accepting bribes by assigning town towing work to a particular towing company was said by an Illinois appeals court to be defamatory on its face (**libel** *per se*) because it imputed the commission of a criminal offense that is indictable and punishable by a prison term. It also suggests moral turpitude or failure.[1]

● Libel *per se*
Libel on its face. An obvious libel.

Although there are broad disagreements among legal writers, researchers, and courts as to definitions, a third of all libel suits are brought by public officials of varying degrees of status and by celebrities or those whom some courts call "public personalities." Business and professional people account for at least another third of plaintiffs—those who bring the lawsuit. Private persons account for yet another 20 or 30 percent. More than 70 percent of all libel suits are brought against the mass media. Newspapers bear the brunt of these suits, accounting for at least two-thirds of all media libel cases and far outstripping broadcasters, magazines, and other media as libel defendants—those who are sued.[2]

To call a person dishonest, corrupt, cruel, perverted, or a drug abuser, whether seriously or in jest, may also be defamatory. When the *National Enquirer* falsely accused comedienne Carol Burnett of being drunk and disorderly in a posh Washington, D.C., restaurant, she successfully sued for libel.[3] When presidential candidate Barry Goldwater was alleged to be mentally ill on the basis of a phony medical survey run by *Fact* magazine, the magazine's publisher, Ralph Ginzburg, lost a libel suit to Goldwater. While mental incompetency does not normally carry with it any sense of moral fault, jurors and subsequent appeals courts agreed that the context of the charge made it especially damaging to a candidate for the nation's highest office.[4]

Although there may be disagreement as to whether highly visible and powerful public people ought to be allowed to abuse libel law by bringing unwinnable suits, they do bring suit often and with devastating consequences in time and money for those they sue. These futile but punishing suits are usually unwinnable because the courts have over time drafted an incredibly complex set of rules favoring the press and designed to recognize and protect a First Amendment interest in public speech. The D.C. Circuit Court of Appeals put the problem succinctly when it wrote, "Libel suits, if not carefully handled, can threaten journalistic independence. Even if many actions fail, the risks and high costs of litigation may lead to undesirable forms of self-censorship."[5] The *Burnett* and *Goldwater* suits, as we shall see, are among the few examples of plaintiffs of such prominence winning libel suits against the media.

WHAT A PLAINTIFF HAS TO PROVE

Defamation

Words can be insulting but still not defamatory. In a Vermont case, a political opponent had characterized the plaintiff as a "horse's ass," a "jerk," an "idiot," and "paranoid." Words used in the heat of a political campaign, said the state supreme court, would not be read in their literal sense and were clearly not intended to destroy the plaintiff in his profession as an accountant. Such words may be insulting, abusive, and objectionable, but they are not defamatory in and of themselves, and they reflect more on the character of the user than on the person at whom they were directed.[6]

The U.S. Supreme Court in 1970 held that the term "blackmail" when used to characterize the negotiating position of a real estate developer was not slander (spoken defamation) when uttered in the emotional atmosphere of a city council meeting. Nor was it libel when reported accurately in the local newspaper.[7]

A few states, Alabama, Mississippi and Virginia, for example, have passed "insulting words" statutes, which are meant to punish insults before they reach the level of defamation.

So how does a reporter or an editor know when unpleasant words have crossed the line into actionable libel? He or she doesn't. There is no general guideline. Every state has compiled its own record in libel law in state statutes and their interpretation by state courts in actual cases. This is where the cautious communicator should begin.

State rulings, of course, must comply with the constitutional standard established by the U.S. Supreme Court in the great 1964 case of *New York Times v. Sullivan*,[8] a case arising out of the civil rights movement. *New York Times* partially took libel out of tort law (a wrong done to another person) and made it a matter of the Constitution's First Amendment. It will become clear how this constitutionalizing of libel law fashioned the rules that govern libel today. At the same time the Rehnquist Supreme Court in the 1980s and 1990s seemed to be enouraging state courts to depend more upon their own precedents, laws, and constitutions in deciding libel cases.

● *New York Times v. Sullivan*
The landmark 1964 case that constitutionalized the law of libel by making it a First Amendment matter and by shifting the burden of proof for showing fault from defendant to plaintiff.

It can be said with some assurance, however, that words imputing crime, gross immorality, criminal associations, or financial chicanery must be handled with great care in every jurisdiction. Who makes the charge? What are the circumstances? How is it likely to be interpreted? By whom?

Several states, New York, Massachusetts, Colorado, Connecticut, and Georgia among them, subscribe to what is called the *single instance* rule. That is, you may charge a professional person with a mistake on a single occasion and be safe from a libel suit as long as you don't imply overall incompetence or give that person a reason to plead special damages (actual money loss).[9] This rule is not without problems. You could find yourself a defendant in a libel suit after an initial reference to a person prepared to sue, even in a jurisdiction where the rule is in effect. The rule lends itself to contradictory interpretations.

Several other states follow the innocent construction rule. This means simply that language will be construed in its ordinary, commonly accepted meanings. Unfamiliar or strained interpretations will be rejected. This is also a tricky rule to live by. In one Illinois case, a newspaper, editorializing in behalf of higher salaries for village trustees, declared that good government had to be paid for. A trustee chose to interpret that as meaning bribery, but failed in his libel suit. In another Illinois case, however, no innocent construction could be made of the statement that "I think 240 pieces of silver changed hands—30 for each alderman."[10] In most states judges decide whether a statement could be defamatory; juries decide in what sense it was read by its audience.

● **Libel** *per quod*
Indirect libel. A libel by innuendo, implication, or inference.

Another hazard in libel law is that some states recognize libel by implication, inference, or innuendo (**libel** *per quod)*, a libel that is not obviously damaging on its face. The question often is did the communicator anticipate a defamatory inference? Courts are divided on whether to permit liability for inferences drawn by readers, listeners, or viewers from accurate reports. Two Minnesota appeals courts recently held that accurate newspaper reports and opinions on a county attorney's lackluster performance in prosecuting domestic abuse cases could not support a suit for defamation by implication (libel *per quod)*. Nor could a second county attorney succeed in a suit for defamation by innuendo unless he could show that unreported facts would change the whole tenor of stories suggesting his lack of enthusiasm in investigating a murder case.[11]

Other jurisdictions allow suits for defamatory inferences drawn from factually accurate news reports.[12] In a case brought against the *Washington Post* and NBC for reports on irregularities in routine drug testing procedures required for a police lieutenant's promotion to captain and his later elevation to head of the police narcotics squad in Washington, D.C., a federal appeals court noted that if style or language suggests that a reporter intends or endorses a defamatory inference from even a true report, she may be liable.[13] Here the police captain failed in his suit because such a defamatory inference could not be made.

The *Post* was also protected by having published a fair and accurate report of a governmental proceeding. NBC would have enjoyed the same privilege had it attributed its story to an official investigation or to the documents the investigation had generated. It had failed to do so, but, as with the newspaper, no defamatory inference could be drawn from NBC's report and that protected it from the libel claim.

Defamatory innuendo may be drawn from headlines, illustrations, and photographs as well. The important point is that those bringing libel suits must demonstrate that the offending language carries a defamatory meaning.

The danger of misquotes, especially where they change the meaning of what someone said to a reporter, was dramatically brought home by a U.S. Supreme Court ruling in June 1991. Former psychoanalyst Jeffrey Masson accused writer Janet Malcolm of deliberately misrepresenting what he had said to her in an interview for a *New Yorker* article that later became a book. In reinstating Masson's $10 million libel case against Malcolm, the Court said a jury would have to decide whether discrepancies between the writer's notes and tape recordings and the published references to Masson describing himself as an "intellectual gigolo" and promising to turn Anna Freud's home into a place of "sex, women and fun" constituted actual malice and damaged him. And were these deliberate or reckless falsehoods on Malcolm's part? Actual malice, the linchpin of libel law, will be discussed below. In a trial noted for its theatrics as much as its legal lessons, a federal court jury found in favor of the psychoanalyst, but disagreed on what amount of money damages he should receive. Malcolm, said the jury, had shown reckless disregard for the truth in publishing two quotations attributed to Masson. At the same time, *The New Yorker* was dropped from the suit as a defendant since it had depended upon a usually reliable contributor, a freelance writer rather than an employee.

While the outcome for publishers could have been worse, at the very least the case warns writers and their publishers against fabricating quotations or condoning the practice. Nevertheless, the line between fabrication and a fair rendering of what was said in a long and complex dialogue between the parties to the lawsuit may often be indistinct.[14] In a second trial, a federal jury found in favor of Janet Malcolm: Masson had not proven actual malice.

Publication

The offense in publication is the spreading of the defamation to the four winds by air, wire, paper, gravestone inscription, or skywriting, in big and powerful or weak and humble media. All these forms of dissemination have led to libel suits in the past. Anyone taking part in the crafting of a libel or in its distribution may be liable for damages.

For there to be a libel suit, there must be a publication, whatever the mode of communication. In some jurisdictions this means that a report must have reached a substantial portion of the audience for which it was intended, no matter what the date on the cover page. In other jurisdictions a single person may constitute an audience sufficient for there to have been publication.

And this gives rise to another rule, the **single publication rule.** A significant number of states subscribe to the rule either by statute or by court decision. The initial publication of a newspaper or magazine is one libel, one cause of action, regardless of how many people read it, when they read it, or how often they read it. The rule protects publishers from the perpetual harassment of multiple and never-ending libel suits. The **statute of limitations** also begins to run at the point of publication, setting a date of one, two, or three years from publication after which a libel suit cannot be brought.

Most media and their messages cross state lines, and therefore plaintiff and defendant may reside in different states. In such circumstances, federal courts assume jurisdiction in what is known as a **diversity suit.** The federal court may apply the law of the state in which the greatest injury to the plaintiff occurred. In single publication rule states, the libel suit may be brought where publication first took place, and that will usually be the place of greatest circulation. Where there is no single publication rule, some federal courts have allowed a separate lawsuit in each state where the publication circulated.

If there is a conscious republication of a libel, the statute of limitations will begin running from the date of that second publication. The original

● **Single publication rule**
Only one suit can be maintained for one libel, regardless of how many individual newspapers have been printed and circulated.

● **Statute of limitations**
The period in which a libel suit can be brought: one, two, or three years, depending upon the state.

● **Diversity suit**
A lawsuit in which plaintiff and defendant reside in different states. In such situations a federal court will generally take jurisdiction.

authors will not be legally liable for a republication, however, unless they have given their permission for it. The republisher, of course, will be.

A hard lesson in publication was learned when reporters for the *Alton* (Illinois) *Telegraph* sent a memo to the Justice Department summarizing the findings—not quite substantial enough for publication in the newspaper—of their year-long investigation of possible links between a real estate developer and organized crime. No one at Justice seemed interested, but the memo found its way to the Federal Home Loan Bank Board. The developer, his credit sullied before the board, sued the *Telegraph* for $9.2 million, forcing it into bankruptcy.[15] The plaintiff later tried to take over the newspaper in payment of a money judgment awarded him by a jury. Note that the newspaper had never published the story. Nevertheless, publication was held to have taken place when the memo was mailed to the Justice Department.

The case highlights another legal point. Clearly, in this case the corporate employer was responsible for libel committed by an employee. A majority of states hold the employer responsible for damages incurred by an employee committing a "malicious tort." Designed to encourage employers to know what their employees are doing, the rule is known as **respondeat superior**.

A minority of states, but a significant minority because it includes New York, California, and the District of Columbia, subscribes to what is called the **complicity rule**: employers are not liable, at least for punitive damages, unless they authorize or participate in employee misconduct.

Identification

Identification must be precise. Whom does the libel damage? Is it a person identifiable by name or nickname, initials, physical peculiarities, photograph, dress, address, or professional reputation? Patterns of behaviors that by their sheer uniqueness identify a particular person in fiction or docudrama could establish identification.

Kimberly Pring, a former Miss Wyoming, claimed she was identified in a salacious and phantasmagorial *Penthouse* magazine short story by the color of her costume and her baton-twirling ability. Her name was never mentioned.[16] No evidence was presented to support the allegation that the author had her in mind when he wrote his story. Her costume and talent alone were not enough to constitute identification.

Identification can be lost in a crowd. If a group is too large, individual identification is impossible, and a libel suit cannot proceed. Group libel has not found favor in Anglo-American law, partly because of its resemblance to criminal or seditious libel. **Criminal libel** is criticism of the government or words that disrupt public peace and good order. In a criminal libel case, the state is the plaintiff. Such laws, said Justice William O. Douglas, make someone a criminal because an audience can't hold its temper.[17] They turn a tort into a crime. He was thinking of pamphlets critical of law enforcement and a newspaper publisher during a Kentucky miners' strike.

Nevertheless, much interest has been shown recently in protecting minority groups from the wrath of bigots and their sexist, racist, and homopho-

- **Respondeat superior**
  An employer in most states is responsible for defamatory statements made, written, published, or broadcast by an employee.

- **Complicity rule**
  In other states, an employer may not be responsible for the statements of an employee, at least not for punitive damages.

- **Criminal libel**
  A suit in which the state is the plaintiff. Also called seditious libel, now generally discouraged in American jurisdictions.

bic speech. Some refer to these efforts, pejoratively, as "political correctness." An interesting and important question is to what extent, if at all, the "politically correct" speech movement would reinstate criminal libel, a crime that, as we shall see, the Supreme Court did away with in *New York Times v. Sullivan,* the first great *New York Times* case?

The question remains: how big is too big for individual identification? Under current law there is no way political parties, racial, religious, or gender groups, or occupational or interest groups can successfully sue for libel. Even a group of twenty-nine teachers, clearly identifiable in their own community, was said by a federal district court not to be "so small" that a newspaper article investigating possible sexual misconduct "may reasonably be understood to have personal reference to any member of the group."[18] But as a group gets smaller, the danger increases.

Someone other than the plaintiff must reasonably infer from a publication that the defamatory reference is to that person. A single person may suffice to make identification. If a name is not used or identification is otherwise obscured, the plaintiff must show, by what lawyers call **colloquium,** that the defamatory reference is to her or him.

Until recently, the dead took their reputations with them. In a number of states, the dead are rising to smite those who would defame them. New Jersey, Pennsylvania, perhaps New York, and a number of other states now recognize libel of the dead either by statute or common law. The assumption, of course, is that a libel of the deceased reflects adversely on his or her survivors.

Falsity

A central concept in libel has always been falsehood. Before *New York Times v. Sullivan,* the falsity of a defamatory statement was presumed. Now the plaintiff must prove it. Moreover, the core of the Supreme Court's holding in *New York Times* was that any public official from that day forward would have to prove actual malice as well as falsity to win a libel suit. **Actual malice,** as we shall see, would be given a constitutional definition—knowing falsehood or reckless disregard as to truth or falsity. Any doubts about who carries the burden of proof of falsity were dispelled by the Supreme Court in an important 1986 case, *Philadelphia Newspapers v. Hepps.*[19] At least where speech of public concern is involved, said the Court, all plaintiffs, whether private or public people, have the burden of proving falsity. This burden requires the plaintiff to prove a negative, that is, that a libelous allegation is *not* true.

"To ensure that true speech on matters of public concern is not deterred," wrote Justice Sandra Day O'Connor for the Court, "we hold that the common-law presumption that defamatory speech is false cannot stand when a plaintiff seeks damages against a media defendant for speech of public concern." She did not say what rule would apply to private plaintiffs who were not involved in matters of public concern, nor did she address herself to the standing of non-media defendants.

Hepps also holds that falsity has to be established by **clear and convincing evidence,** at least where the plaintiff is a public person. This standard of

---

● **Colloquium**
A plea that, although a plaintiff is not named in a publication, facts in the context of the publication, often called extrinsic facts, serve to identify that person.

● **Actual malice**
Knowing falsehood or reckless disregard as to whether a statement is true or false. The level of fault that has to be met by a public official or public figure suing for libel.

● **Clear and convincing evidence**
A standard of proof between "a preponderance of evidence" and "beyond a reasonable doubt," required in proving actual malice in a libel suit.

evidence or proof, as shall be noted, is required in other areas of libel law as well. It is an intermediate standard between the lesser standard of fair preponderance and the higher standard of beyond a reasonable doubt.

While one might not be as sanguine as the courts in drawing a line between truth and falsehood, it is clearly incumbent upon editors to check the accuracy of every story they handle. Truth, however it is measured and assessed, is an absolute defense against libel suits.

Israeli General Ariel Sharon's $50 million libel suit against *Time* provides a dramatic illustration of the falsity step in a libel suit. The magazine, in a report on the massacre of Palestinian refugees in Lebanon, intimated that the general had discussed "revenge" with Phalangist assassins. The magazine's correspondent admitted that his information was no more than an inference from Israeli documents.

The presiding federal judge, Abraham Sofaer, instructed the jury to consider falsity and fault separately. The jury decided that the *Time* report was false. Before jurors could get to the question of fault, Sharon dropped the case and went home claiming victory. He was probably correct in anticipating that actual malice would be difficult to prove and that he should quit while he was ahead. No damages were paid.[20]

Fault

The **New York Times** *Doctrine* • Having proved defamation, publication, identification, and falsity, a plaintiff still has to prove fault on the part of the publisher to succeed in a libel suit. Fault may be the central concept of libel law.

Recall that *New York Times v. Sullivan* was the case that constitutionalized libel law. Prior to 1964, publishers were held to what lawyers call a rule of strict liability for what was published. A libel was presumed to be false and injurious, and the burden of proof in presenting an affirmative defense was on the defendant. A defendant's purpose or motive in publishing—for public good or personal profit—had nothing to do with the case.

Reversing the Alabama Supreme Court, the decision in *New York Times* changed all that. The *New York Times* had published an editorial advertisement proffered by a civil rights organization that contained inaccuracies as to the actions of an Alabama county commissioner in dealing with demonstrating black students in the civil rights movement that was sweeping the country. In their written briefs to the Supreme Court, the newspaper's lawyers argued that:

> Under the doctrine of *libel per se* . . . a public official is entitled to recover "presumed" and punitive damages for a publication found to be critical of the official conduct of a governmental agency under his general supervision if a jury thinks the publication "tends" to "injure" him "in his reputation" to "bring" him "into public contempt" as an official. The publisher has no defense unless he can persuade the jury that the publication is entirely true in all its factual, material particulars. The doctrine not only dispenses with proof of injury by the complaining official, but presumes malice and falsity as well. Such a rule of liability works an abridgement of the freedom of the press.[21]

Justice William Brennan agreed and in unforgettable language wrote for the Court that ". . . we consider this case against the background of a profound national commitment to the principle that debate on public issues should be uninhibited, robust, and wide-open, and that it may well include vehement, caustic, and sometimes unpleasantly sharp attacks on government and public officials." Erroneous statement is inevitable in free debate, he added, and it must be protected if freedom of expression is to have the breathing space that it needs to survive.

The federal rule that emerged from the case was that public officials could not recover damages for a defamatory falsehood relating to their official conduct unless they could prove with convincing clarity that the statement was made with "*actual malice*"—*that is, with knowledge that it was false or with reckless disregard of whether it was false or not.* (emphasis added)

The actual malice test of *New York Times* thus became and remains the central precept of a constitutionalized defamation law. A public-official plaintiff must prove fault on the part of the publisher before an award of damages can be made.

From Public Officials to Public Issues • In cases sometimes referred to as the progeny of *New York Times,* the actual malice rule would first be stretched to cover criminal libel. Jim Garrison, a Louisiana district attorney—memorialized by Kennedy assassination conspiracy theorists—had taken it upon himself to criticize eight New Orleans judges by calling them lazy. They represented the judicial branch of government, and you could say that Garrison was being sued by the government. His conviction for criminal defamation was overturned by the U.S. Supreme Court. "(O)nly those false statements made with the *high degree of awareness of their probable falsity* demanded by New York Times may be the subject of either civil or criminal sanctions," said Justice Brennan, again writing for the Court. "For speech concerning public affairs is more than self-expression; it is the essence of self-government"[22] (emphasis added).

Next the actual malice rule would reach *public figures*. In two cases decided together, one involving a state university athletic director and the other a retired army general, Justice John Marshall Harlan wrote for the Court:

> We consider and would hold that a "public figure" who is not a public official may also recover damages for a defamatory falsehood whose substance makes substantial danger to reputation apparent, *on a showing of highly unreasonable conduct constituting an extreme departure from the standards of investigation ordinarily adhered to by responsible publishers.*[23] (emphasis added)

Equivalent to actual malice, this would become the **prudent publisher test.**

More was yet to come. In 1971 the actual malice rule would be stretched to the breaking point in order to cover private-person plaintiffs if they were involved in matters of public interest or in a public issue. The case was *Rosenbloom v. Metromedia,*[24] and it involved a magazine distributor who was referred to in a radio broadcast as a "smut distributor" and a "girlie-book

● **Prudent publisher test**
One of a number of variations of the definition of *actual malice;* here "a showing of highly unreasonable conduct constituting an extreme departure from the standards of investigation ordinarily adhered to by responsible publishers."

peddler." Justice Brennan, this time writing for a plurality (the result receiving the greater number of votes, but not a majority of the Court), said:

> If a matter is a subject of public or general interest, it cannot suddenly become less so merely because a private individual is involved, or because in some sense the individual did not "voluntarily" choose to become involved. The public's primary interest is in the event; the public focus is on the conduct of the participant and the content, effect, and significance of the conduct, not the participant's prior anonymity or notoriety.

This would be known as the *public issue* test.

The stretch from public official to public figure to public issue would prove to be more than a by-now-badly-divided Court could bear. Looking for a case to pick up the broken pieces of the shattered rule, the Court found it in *Gertz v. Robert Welch, Inc.*[25] *Gertz* essentially provides the crux of today's libel rules and is therefore worth extended treatment.

Gertz v. Robert Welch (1974) • The family of a youth shot by a policeman had retained Elmer Gertz, nationally known in legal circles, to represent them in a civil suit for damages against the policeman. The policeman had already been convicted of second-degree murder. In the meantime, the editor of the John Birch Society magazine, *American Opinion*, saw it as his patriotic duty to publish an article discrediting Gertz by identifying him with a "conspiracy" to undermine law enforcement in order to ensure a communist takeover of the United States.

To heap opprobrium upon Gertz, the article falsely accused him of having a criminal record, of planning the 1968 Chicago convention riots, and of being a longtime Leninist. What he was in fact was one of Chicago's best-known lawyers, an expert on libel, free speech, civil rights, the death penalty, and housing law. He was the author of books, pamphlets, magazine articles, book reviews, and radio plays. He was a professor of law, a civil rights leader, and a founder and charter member of organizations ranging from the Civil War Roundtable to the Henry Miller Literary Society and the George Bernard Shaw Society.

Hardly a private person, Gertz played a leading role in rewriting the Illinois Constitution. He won a parole for Nathan Leopold, co-defendant in the infamous Bobby Franks murder case in Chicago. He engineered a death sentence commutation for Jack Ruby, the killer of Lee Harvey Oswald.

Gertz sued *American Opinion*. A sympathetic jury who had never heard of Gertz awarded him $50,000. A federal district court disallowed the award on the authority of *Rosenbloom's* public issue test, and the federal circuit court of appeals affirmed. Gertz sought review in the Supreme Court.

Speaking through Justice Lewis Powell, the Supreme Court reversed, declaring the very public Mr. Gertz to be a private person in the circumstances of the case: simply a lawyer serving a client. This provided the Court with an opportunity to discard the public issue test and bring the idea of the private person back into libel law. Private people, even those involved in public events, would henceforth have only to prove negligence to win money damages from

● **Negligence**
A level of fault below actual malice that private or nonpublic plaintiffs have to prove in libel suits.

those who had defamed them. This was the essential holding of *Gertz*, but there was more:

1. There could be, as we have noted, *no liability without fault.* The plaintiff would have to demonstrate at least negligence on the part of the defendant.

2. A plaintiff, whether a private or public person, seeking **punitive damages** would have to prove actual malice. The purpose here seemed to be to discourage punitive damages.

3. Jury awards in the future would be restricted to **actual damages** for demonstrated *injury,* whatever form that injury might take, e.g., humiliation, shame, mental anguish, loss of standing in the community.

4. There could be no punishment for the expression of opinion, or as the Court put it, "there is no such thing as a false idea."

Gertz was eventually awarded $100,000 in compensatory (actual) damages and $300,000 in punitive damages.

This may an appropriate point at which to unravel some of the semantic confusion that surrounds the courts' various definitions of *damages.*

Damages • At least in the absence of a showing of actual malice, *presumed* damages have not survived *Gertz. Nominal* damages, token awards of a dollar, for example, symbolizing a moral victory rather than compensation for injury to reputation, may also have disappeared with *Gertz,* since that case requires a showing of actual injury in all cases.

Compensatory damages in libel cases, which are meant to compensate for damage to one's reputation, take two forms: *actual* damages, which make amends for reputational injury and the mental distress that follows; and **special damages,** designed to pay back proven out-of-pocket money losses, say, medical expenses or documented loss of business. Confusion has resulted from the fact that some authorities in the past have used the terms "actual" and "special" interchangeably. In some jurisdictions special damages have to be proven before awards can be made in slander (spoken defamation), libel *per quod* (libel by implication or innuendo), and **trade libel** (disparagement of someone's service or product) cases. Compensatory damages are sometimes called general damages or are considered a subset of general damages.

Punitive or *exemplary* damages, featured in what have come to be called "megaverdicts," often seem to be aimed more at putting a publication out of business than at punishing it or making it an example for others. Punitive damages may also be a surviving form of presumed damages because there are no clear limits on the sums juries can award and on what grounds. Lawyers call them "smart money" because their gargantuan amounts sting defendants. The *Gertz* Court tied punitive damages to a showing of actual malice, but at the same time encouraged state courts to go their own way in fashioning their libel rules. And state courts have done just that.

● Punitive damages
Payment of money to an aggrieved party designed to punish or make an example of so as to discourage similar behavior in the future. Sometimes called exemplary damages.

● Actual damages
Compensation for demonstrated injury, whatever form that injury might take. Sometimes referred to as general damages.

● Special damages
Compensation for out-of-pocket money losses.

● Trade libel
Disparagement of someone's product or services. Generally, special damages have to be proven in such cases.

● **Common law malice**
Ill will, spite, hostility, a desire for revenge. An older,
common law form of malice;
still required to be shown in
some states to support a
claim of punitive damages.

Washington, Oregon, Massachusetts, and Michigan generally disallow punitive damages under any circumstances. In other states **common law malice** (ill will, spite, a desire for revenge) must be shown, as well as actual malice, to support a claim for punitive damages. Some states prohibit punitive damages when a request for a retraction is honored. And some consider a preponderance of the evidence rather than clear and convincing evidence a sufficient level of evidence for punitive damages. In some jurisdictions common law malice must also be demonstrated in claiming damages for slander, libel *per quod,* and trade libel.

A development obviously distressing to defendants and their attorneys has been the propensity of some courts to assign damages according to a defendant's net worth, the stated purpose being to punish and deter reprehensible conduct, not destroy. So in *Brown & Williamson v. Jacobson,*[26] a case that dramatically illustrates the concept of actual malice and for that reason will be discussed below, the court measured damages against CBS's net worth of $1 billion and the commentator's assets of $5 million. And in Wayne Newton's suit against NBC, the network's net worth of $2 billion was computed by a federal district court in Nevada in constructing appropriate damages. The case against NBC was later reversed on the grounds that the network was not responsible for negative inferences concerning Newton that audience members may have drawn from its reports. In such judicial maneuvers, the purposes of the First Amendment sometimes become secondary. The result may be what Justice Powell in *Gertz* called "intolerable self-censorship."

Traditionally, courts have been instructed to make certain that punitive damages bear some relationship to the actual harm done or some relationship to the amount of actual damages awarded. Media lawyers argue that punitive damages thwart the central purpose of the First Amendment, while plaintiff attorneys argue that they discourage irresponsible journalism. Excessive awards in punitive damages are often reduced by appeals courts—but not always. In 1993 the U.S. Supreme Court affirmed an award of $19,000 in compensatory damages and $10 million in punitive damages.[27]

In 1985 in the case *Dun & Bradstreet v. Greenmoss Builders,*[28] the Supreme Court seemed to be endorsing a return to the discarded rule of presumed damages when it held that presumed and punitive damages, to use the Court's language, could be awarded "even absent a showing of actual malice" where *no* matters of public concern were involved. Perhaps contradicting its own holding in *Gertz,* the Court said that private plaintiffs in nonpublic situations might recover punitive damages *without* a showing of actual malice. The decision upheld an award of $300,000 in punitive damages to a builder who had been mistakenly referred to as bankrupt in a credit reporting agency's newsletter that was sent to five subscribers.

The Elements of Libel in Summary

The courts have recognized that in fulfilling the public interest goals of American journalism, libel will be committed, either directly or by implication, in the course of covering and analyzing the news. Accordingly, the constitutionalized law of libel puts heavy burdens on those bringing suit. Furthermore, an appreciation for differences among the states in defining and applying the elements of libel is the beginning of wisdom in this area of media law. To be successful, plaintiffs must prove:

1. Defamation

2. Publication

3. Identification

4. Falsity

5. Fault

Various forms of damages are awarded according to the level of *injury* inflicted on the plaintiff by the publication and the degree of fault the judge and jury ascribe to the defendant.

PUBLIC OR PRIVATE PLAINTIFF?

Courts have provided no sure way of distinguishing between public and private plaintiffs. Context is important. Mary Alice Firestone, a wealthy Palm Beach socialite, may have been a public figure in Palm Beach, even in Florida, and may have had to prove actual malice had she brought suit against the *Miami Herald*. But in a national arena, she was a nobody and entitled to private-plaintiff status in her libel suit against *Time*, a national news magazine.

Justice William Rehnquist, writing for the Court in 1976, defined her as a private person who had "not thrust herself into the forefront of any particular public controversy" but who "was compelled to go to court by the state in order to obtain legal release from the bonds of matrimony."[29] Extramarital affairs that would have made Dr. Freud's hair curl, according to a Florida circuit court, indicated that neither Mrs. Firestone nor her spouse, scion of one of America's wealthiest industrial families, was susceptible to domestication. *Time* magazine had erroneously quoted the Florida court's complicated order as citing "adultery" on the part of Mrs. Firestone as the grounds for divorce.

Nevertheless, context determined her status, making her a private person. The journalist, then, should pose these questions in trying to determine a plaintiff's legal status:

1. Is there a public controversy and what is its context?

2. Did the plaintiff voluntarily participate in the controversy?

3. And, if so, did the plaintiff try to affect the outcome of the controversy?

4. Did the plaintiff have access to communication media?

- **Vortex or limited-purpose public figure**
  A person who momentarily or for a limited period becomes visible, controversial, or newsworthy.

If the answer to all of these questions is yes, then the plaintiff is what the courts call a **vortex** or **limited-purpose public figure:** people who get involved in political, social or literary controversies, or loudly and prominently express their opinions, or play the role of product promoters, or are political hopefuls.

If the answer to these questions is no, then the plaintiff is probably a *private* person. The difference is important because public figures, like public officials, must prove *actual malice* to win libel suits. Private persons need only show *negligence* to achieve the same result.

"A private individual," wrote Justice Rehnquist for the Court in a 1979 case, "is not automatically transformed into a public figure by becoming involved in or associated with a matter that attracts public attention. To accept such reasoning would in effect re-establish the doctrine advanced by the plurality opinion in *Rosenbloom v. Metromedia.*"[30] In other words, media coverage alone does not create public figures.

A state court made the same point when it held that general public concern about recruiting violations in college athletics does not in itself make an assistant basketball coach a public figure. Public interest alone does not create a public controversy, nor does it create a public figure. The same court ruled that arrest on a murder charge does not in itself raise a plaintiff to the status of public figure.[31]

- **Pervasive or all-purpose public figure**
  A person who is constantly in the public eye or has gained the status of celebrity or what some courts call a "public personality."

Some public figures, however, are public figures for all time. They are called **pervasive** or **all-purpose public figures** by the courts. Some reach the status of *public personalities* or celebrities. Nothing changes their status. They are recognized by substantial segments of the mass audience as public people forever. They include the stars of stage and screen, the great athletes of our time, the prize winners, the creators of our fads and fashions, the great corporations, and the movers and shakers.

- **Involuntary public figure**
  A person who becomes newsworthy but would just as soon remain anonymous. Most criminals and accident victims would fit this definition.

The category of **involuntary public figure,** rare at best, may apply only to criminals, political power brokers, or other prominent people and their relatives who unexpectedly find themselves embroiled in public controversies, that is, topics upon which sizable segments of society have different, strongly held views.[32] For obvious reasons some of these people thrive in the shadows; publicity would spoil their games. But here also there are differences among the state courts.

The passage of time can also affect court-designated status to the surprise and consternation of reporters. Public people can fade back into anonymity. A plaintiff who served as head of a U.S. Department of Justice Organized Crime Strike Force, said a federal district court, was not a public official in his libel suit against an Arizona newspaper for reporting on his activities after he left office.[33] Time and context had made him someone else.

And speaking of public officials, it is important to remember that not all public employees are public officials. To qualify as a public official, an elected or appointed official should have control over the conduct of governmental affairs to the extent that the public has an interest in scrutinizing and discussing the person's qualifications and performance. He or she should have some policy-making power and enjoy significantly greater access to the mass media than private persons and therefore have a genuine opportunity to contradict false statements.[34] What about the private lives of public officials? Do they affect the body politic? Of course they do.

Whether through disdain for the peccadilloes of the press or concern for its power, courts seem reluctant to bestow public figure status on even some of the most publicly involved plaintiffs. Corporate officers, consultants, teachers, attorneys, physicians, drug dealers, appointees to governmental committees and commissions, and litigants are often classified as private persons. This makes the all-important distinction between private and public plaintiffs—all important because of the different standards of fault that apply—a crap shoot for reporters and editors. In making these distinctions, the courts are often ambiguous and even arbitrary. Again the context or the circumstances of the case may be the determining factor. Remember Elmer Gertz!

STANDARDS OF FAULT

Negligence

The Supreme Court in *Gertz* invited states to fashion their own standards of fault for private persons. Would it be a reasonably prudent person[35] standard or the standard of the communication industry—what the Court in *Curtis Publishing Co. v. Butts*[36] called "standards of investigation and reporting ordinarily adhered to by responsible publishers"? State courts have gone both ways, but most prefer the reasonable person standard, even though that term is itself without dependable definition.

In 1990 some thirty-two states, the District of Columbia, and Puerto Rico had adopted *Gertz*'s negligence test for private plaintiffs, although the term has no precise or generally agreed-upon definition. New York has a higher standard: gross irresponsibility. Another five states apply other standards, which, like New York's, fall somewhere between actual malice and negligence. Four states, Alaska, Colorado, Indiana, and New Jersey, require private plaintiffs to meet a public issue or *Rosenbloom* standard if they are involved in matters of public concern. Other states have not taken the opportunity to adopt a standard.

What is negligence? The dictionary defines it as failure to exercise the care that the circumstances justly demand. Some courts would appear to be defining negligence as a kind of journalistic malpractice. In news terms one might ask the questions:

1. How many identifiable sources did I have for my allegedly defamatory report? Hopefully, more than one source.

2. Were those sources credible and did I listen carefully enough to have understood what they said? And do I have readable notes or a tape recording to document any claims I might make regarding an interview?

3. Did I give the defamed an opportunity to respond to the allegations made by my sources?

4. Was I reasonably accurate in reporting what was in a document or a transcript?

5. Did I check and recheck incriminating facts or statements?

If the answer to all or any of these questions is no, the communicator should prepare for a lawsuit.[37]

Actual Malice

Knowing falsehood or reckless disregard as to truth or falsity is a single federal standard applied to all public-official and public-figure plaintiffs. Actual malice has been called negligence raised to a higher power. A federal appeals court in the *Wayne Newton* case[38] distinguished negligence and actual malice by characterizing the former as an objective test and the latter as deliberately subjective.

Note that the definition of actual malice, first framed in *New York Times v. Sullivan,* appears to include two standards. Knowing falsehood is akin to a deliberate lie and implies the necessity for a plaintiff to read the defendant's mind to prove it; reckless disregard is the act of publishing with wild abandon, of not caring for the consequences a publication may have for its victim. For obvious reasons, reckless disregard, the seemingly lower level of fault, but one still sufficient to constitute actual malice, is what plaintiff attorneys prefer to pursue. And under the second part of the test, there is less need to probe the mind of the journalist—the chink in the test's First Amendment armor—although some probing may still be necessary. Yet, any such pursuit can lead to hundreds of pages of depositions and considerable legal expense for both sides.

It is fair to say that courts do not find actual malice very often, at least in the absence of evidence of gross moral or professional failure. But showing a failure to follow accepted journalistic practices or to be objective is not enough to prove actual malice; neither is showing signs of past or present hostility toward a plaintiff.[39] What would constitute actual malice?

1. A fabricated story, a product of a reporter's imagination, with no warning to readers or viewers.

2. Evidence that a publisher knew a story was false or had serious doubts about its truthfulness before it was published.

3. Evidence that the reporter had no credible sources and did not investigate the charges made.

4. A story so farfetched that reasonable people would not believe it, although, as we shall see, this could be a defense.

For actual malice these factors should be cumulative. Failure to investigate, the rejection of a contradictory story, a reliance on biased sources, a reporter's antagonistic or abrasive investigative techniques, inaccurate reporting, misleading headlines, sloppy writing, a breach of professional ethics, a refusal to retract—none of these alone necessarily proves actual malice. There are no assurances, however, that state courts are going to agree. And where actual malice has been found, appeals courts are expected to review the factual record carefully to make certain that free expression will not be constrained in the future.[40] Efforts to investigate, editorial review, balance, and efforts to dig out relevant material are useful in disputing actual malice.[41] But let us look at a case in which actual malice was found.

A CBS news report, presented as a commentary, accused a cigarette manufacturer of linking smoking to "pot, wine, beer, and sex" in order to attract young people to the habit. Chicago's WBBM-TV anchorman, Walter Jacobson, called the tobacco company "liars." In fact, the company had rejected an advertising agency's proposal that would have followed such a line in promoting its products. Moreover, Jacobson's research assistant had uncovered information showing that what Jacobson was prepared to broadcast was false.

The most compelling evidence of actual malice, however, was the research assistant's intentional destruction of documents critical to the case, contrary to CBS's own policy, while the case was pending. The result was a $3.05 million judgment against CBS and Jacobson, the largest libel award in history at that time.[42] The Supreme Court declined to review the case. In an unreported case in 1991, a Texas jury awarded $58 million in damages to a plaintiff, who was alleged by a Dallas broadcast station to have accepted a bribe. A few days later, the case was settled out of court for an undisclosed amount, and no appeal was taken.[43]

Routing reporters' notes to media attorneys would establish a lawyer-client privilege to protect those notes against subpoenas. The downside might be that it would inject lawyers and the judiciary into the norms and patterns of investigative reporting.

Standards of Fault in Summary

The earlier discussions of fault and plaintiff categories described in a nutshell the *New York Times* doctrine that in 1964 constitutionalized the tort of libel by making it a First Amendment question. Public plaintiffs now must prove actual malice by clear and convincing evidence to collect damages. Private plaintiffs must prove negligence by at least a preponderance of the evidence to collect damages, but there are significant variations from state to state. As the Supreme Court said in *Gertz*, however, there can be no liability without fault.

Although few public plaintiffs succeed in proving actual malice, this does not discourage them from bringing lawsuits that punish, not through jury awards, but through court costs and lawyers' fees. A 1990 study by the author and a research assistant found that only 10 of 164 public-official plaintiffs and 5 of 44 public-personality plaintiffs ultimately won money judgments in court cases that cumulatively took years and years to resolve.[44]

While the *New York Times* or constitutional defense is the first defense that comes to a good media lawyer's mind when a lawsuit is threatened, others are available, and they will now be discussed.

THE COMMON LAW OR STATUTORY DEFENSES

Truth

In putting together a defense, a libel attorney needs all the help he or she can get from the journalist. Where did you get the story? Did you check it out? Is there anything about it you should tell me that you haven't? Do you have documentation that will help prove the truth of your report?

The traditional common law defenses were all journalists had before 1964. The major drawback to these defenses, both then and now, is that they put the burden of proof on those raising them—on the defendant publication.

Truth or justification as a defense, however, has been largely absorbed by the *New York Times* doctrine. It has become part of the constitutional fabric in that a plaintiff has to prove falsity at the threshold. In the law, if something's not false, it's true. And under the doctrine, the initial burden of proof is on the plaintiff.

If truth is used as a separate or supplementary defense, however, the burden of proof would be on the defendant publisher. Where truth alone is pleaded as a defense, the proof must be at least as broad as the charge. Literal truth is not required if what is published is substantially true. In one case a plaintiff, testifying before a congressional committee, had attacked "political Zionist planners for absolute rule via a one-world government." A newspaper report charging that the plaintiff had attacked "Jews" was held to be substantially true and therefore not actionable.[45]

It is not a defense, however, to say that you accurately reported a false accusation made by someone else, unless, as we shall see, you are quoting from a trial transcript or some other governmental document or proceeding. Under a truth defense, you must be prepared to prove the charge itself. Remember that the chief offense in libel is the spreading of the defamation to the four winds.

Truth is a difficult defense because reporters seldom possess the kind of evidence that would "prove" truth in a court of law. Witnesses upon whom they have been counting often evaporate. Sources may disappear or change their stories. A reporter's sincerity or depth of feeling about the truth is not enough. Detailed documentation is usually a necessity for a truth defense.

The Opinion Defense (Fair Comment and Criticism)

Also part of the constitutional fabric is the opinion defense or what traditionally was referred to in the common law as **fair comment and criticism**. Recall in *Gertz* that Justice Powell said, "there is no such thing as a false idea. However pernicious an opinion may seem, we depend for its correction not on the conscience of judges and juries but on the competition of other ideas."[46]

Under fair comment and criticism, one was permitted to go to the utmost lengths of denunciation, condemnation, and satirization when criticizing people and institutions seeking public attention and approval. At the same time, common law malice (ill will, spite, demonstrated hostility) could destroy the defense. So could an opinion based on false facts.

In 1984 a D.C. Circuit Court of Appeals ruling gave structure to the opinion defense.[47] Columnists Rowland Evans and Robert Novak criticized the ap-

---

• Truth

A traditional or common law defense in libel suits. Where it is used as a separate defense, the burden of proving truth would be on the defendant.

• Fair comment and criticism

A traditional or common law defense in libel suits, now more generally referred to as the "opinion" defense. It is qualified by the requirement that opinions not be based on demonstrably false facts. It is meant to protect those who criticize persons, such as actors and authors, who seek public approval for their work. The more disconnected to fact, or the more outrageous, incredible, or unverifiable, the less the chance of a successful suit.

pointment of professed Marxist Bertell Ollman to head the University of Maryland's department of politics and government because, they said, he would use the classroom as an instrument for preparing for "revolution." They belittled his academic standing and challenged his pedagogic motives. Ollman asked for a retraction. It was refused, but a letter from Ollman was published in the *Washington Post*. Ollman sued, and a federal district court granted summary judgment to the columnists. Ollman appealed.

In a carefully crafted opinion, the federal appeals court upheld the summary judgment, affirming a long tradition of judges deciding what was fact and what was opinion; the result was a four-part test for making the distinction:

1. *Common usage.* Does the language have a precise meaning in ordinary usage or is it indefinite and ambiguous?

2. *Verifiability.* Can the language be objectively characterized as true or false? The assumption is that facts can be so designated while opinions can only be called fair or unfair.

3. *Context and setting.* Where does the statement appear? In a column or on an op-ed page, or in a news story? What kind of language surrounds it? How would the intended audience take the statement?

4. *Cautionary language.* Is the reader tipped off in any way that the statement is an opinion through the use of metaphor, hyperbole, or other figurative forms of speech?

The difficulty in distinguishing fact and opinion is still the central problem with this test.

Former Judge Robert Bork, concurring in the same case with a ringing defense of freedom of the press, added a fifth factor to *Ollman: political or public speech.* Those "who choose the pleasures and distractions of controversy," he wrote, "must be willing to bear criticism, disparagement, and even wounding assessments."

One of the first to feel the punch of *Ollman* was William Janklow, former governor of South Dakota. His libel claims were rejected first by a federal appeals court and later by the highest court of South Dakota on the grounds that assertions that he went "from raping an Indian teen-ager to raping Mother Earth" were words "imprecise, unverifiable" and "presented in a forum where spirited writing is expected and involves criticism of the motives and intentions of a public official. . . ."[48]

And so with impunity people began to call other people, "unscrupulous charlatans," "cancer con artists," "Al Capone," "neo-Nazis" "a sleazebag" who "kind of slimed up from the bayou," and "an ignorant spineless politician." All of these expressions led to libel suits, and all were held in 1987 to be protected expressions of opinion.

Judge Antonin Scalia's dissent in the *Ollman* case may have been a harbinger. Scalia reviled the press for descending from discussion of public issues to destruction of private reputations and called for solutions.

A partial solution may have arrived with the Supreme Court's 1990 holding in *Milkovich v. Lorain Journal Co.*[49] A high school wrestling coach sued when the Willoughby (Ohio) *News-Herald* alleged that he had lied under oath about a fight at a wrestling match. There is no separate constitutional privilege, said the Court again in contradiction of *Gertz,* for anything called opinion, especially when based on false statements of fact, facts that cannot be supported, or facts that are simply implied. To write "in my opinion, Jones is a liar," is no defense. The charge implies a knowledge of facts.

The Court seemed to be making verifiability the only consequential part of the now five-part opinion test for actionable libel. If a statement could be proven, it was a fact not an opinion. And the Court reversed the long-held rule that separating fact from opinion was a task for the judge rather than the jury.

The media world was stunned. The 55,000-circulation newspaper paid Milkovich $116,000 in settlement of his suit and estimated that its legal costs over a sixteen-year period amounted to $500,000

The only redeeming feature of *Milkovich* for the media was that the Court affirmed the rule laid down in *Hepps* that the plaintiff has to prove *falsity.* This constitutional requirement may be more protective of the media in the long run than a defendant having to convince a jury that what was written was opinion rather than fact. And, of course, pure opinion is still protected. The more fantastic, hyperbolic, unbelievable, implausible, and exaggerated a statement, the more likely it is to fall into the protected opinion category.

An example of such "rhetorical hyperbole"[50] was a suit brought by the Reverend Jerry Falwell against Larry Flynt and *Hustler* magazine. In a parody of an advertisement for a liqueur, Flynt had Falwell testify that his first sexual experience was with his mother in an outhouse when both were drunk. In small print at the bottom of the page was a disclaimer. A horrified Falwell sued for "intentional infliction of emotional distress."

A unanimous Court led by Chief Justice William Rehnquist, the same justice who would seriously weaken the opinion defense two years later in *Milkovich,* using the analogy of the political cartoon,[51] held that Flynt's effort to "assassinate Jerry Falwell" was sufficiently outrageous to be classified as clearly protected opinion.[52] In *Falwell* the Court may also have discouraged the bringing of suits for "intentional infliction of emotional distress," although there is disagreement on that point.[53]

Charting the Supreme Court's course on the opinion defense since *Milkovich* is risky, but it appears, in part at least, to be returning to earlier common law rules and the traditional defense of fair comment and criticism. A fact is a fact; an opinion an opinion. And you can't get away with calling a fact an opinion. Let juries struggle with the vast gray wasteland in the heart of this false dichotomy, one of many in the law. Or let state laws and constitutions help juries find their own way out of the wilderness. And state courts, in spite of *Milkovich,* still grant summary judgments (to be explained below) on the grounds that the offending language is protected opinion.

For example, in 1991, New York's highest court, in a case remanded by the U.S. Supreme Court, held that a letter to the editor of a scientific journal complaining about the handling of laboratory chimpanzees qualified as opinion under the state's constitution and common law. The content, tone, and apparent purpose of the letter when viewed in *context,* said the New York court, made it an expression of opinion on matters of public interest. While seeming to criticize the Supreme Court's narrow focus on the fact-opinion distinction in *Milkovich*, the New York court nevertheless recognized its reponsibility to that body by noting that nothing in the letter had been proven false by the plaintiff, as the federal Constitution (presumably the First Amendment) and *Hepps* would require in a libel suit involving public matters.[54]

In an even more dramatic case, a three-judge panel of the influential D.C. Circuit Court of Appeals voted 2–1 to reverse a decision by a federal trial court granting a newspaper's motion for summary judgment.[55] Judge Harry Edwards, who wrote the opinion for the panel, would, within ten weeks, reverse himself and admit making an error in judgment in his earlier holding.

The facts of the case were these. Dan Moldea, author of the book, *Interference: How Organized Crime Influences Professional Football,* sued the *New York Times* for a review that accused him of "sloppy journalism" and thus, said the court, depicted him as an incompetent practitioner in his field. In its initial opinion, known as *Moldea I,* the appeals court majority said the newspaper would have to support its opinion with "true facts" to win a summary judgment. In response, the newspaper argued that the majority's reliance on *Milkovich's* verifiability requirement was misplaced because "sloppy journalism," a subjective evaluation of a writer's work, is not verifiable. Recall that in *Milkovich* the Supreme Court pulled back from the *Ollman* guidelines, where context was one of a number of necessary considerations. Here again, the opinion defense appeared to be losing ground.

Then Judge Edwards changed his mind and in *Moldea II* adopted what had been the minority position in *Moldea I.* Context, he said, as *Ollman* held, is important. Here the criticism appeared in a book review, "a genre in which readers expect to find spirited critiques of literary works. . . ." Still, there would be no wholesale exemption from liability in defamation for statements of opinion "if they imply a provable false fact or rely upon stated facts that are provably false."[56] While not rejecting *Milkovich's* holding that allegations of crime are not usually defensible as opinion (in that case perjury), the appeals court seemed to be moving back toward *Ollman.*

The difficulty with the fact-opinion dichotomy is suggested in the following paragraph of *Moldea II:*

> There is simply no way to distinguish between reviews written by those who honestly believe a book is bad, and those prompted solely by mischievous intent. To allow a plaintiff to base a lawsuit on claims of mischief, without some indication that the reviewer's interpretations are unsupportable, would wreak havoc on the law of defamation."[57]

Qualified Privilege (Fair Report)

Also known as the fair report, the public eye, or public record privilege, the **qualified privilege** defense is rooted in the common law theory that in some situations the public interest in full disclosure of official public business overrides harm to individual reputation. "A report of any meeting, assembly or gathering

● **Qualified privilege**
A traditional or common law defense in libel suits that protects the reporting of governmental proceedings in any form, if that reporting is reasonably accurate. Negligence will defeat a defense of qualified or conditional privilege. Sometimes called the fair report or public eye defense.

that is open to the general public and is held for the purpose of discussing or otherwise dealing with matters of public concern"[58] may be privileged. Although the purpose of the privilege was historically to expose citizens to the process of self-government, non-governmental or private meetings may be covered when their agendas are largely political.

Here again state law may be determinative. Generally a news organization may publish with impunity a fair and accurate report of any judicial, quasi-judicial, legislative, executive, or administrative proceeding at any level of government. Reports and documents relating to such proceedings are also protected. In some states common law malice will destroy the defense. In most states actual malice will do the same. In others, only the formal, official record of the proceedings is privileged. In a few states cloakroom and corridor discussions may also be protected if they are related to the issues of the official process. A New York court ruled that anything pertinent to a case, whether part of the record or not, would be privileged. "To be outside of the privilege," it held, "a statement made in open court must be so outrageously out of context as to permit one to conclude from the mere fact that the statement was uttered that it was motivated by no other desire than to defame."[59]

California's rule does not even require pertinence. Any publication that has a reasonable connection to a judicial proceeding, including even reports of what was said outside the courtoom and reports of closed grand jury hearings, may be privileged. The report need only have some relationship to what is going on in the courtroom.[60] But be careful. Few jurisdictions are as permissive as California.

In every instance, the news story should clearly indicate the source of the privileged material.[61] The story need not be anything close to a verbatim report of what was said or documented, as long as it is a fair representation.

Unofficial police sources, police radios, and off-the-cuff remarks by police officers, witnesses, and attorneys have been held not privileged. The media can safely report that a crime has been committed and that a particular person is being held for questioning. An arrest should not be reported until a suspect is booked. A police blotter or log book is usually an official public record. Although some states have statutes extending privilege to reports of arresting officers, police chiefs, county prosecutors, and coroners, collateral details on investigations and speculation on evidence from such sources are generally not privileged.[62]

Michigan newspapers found themselves in trouble when they reported that a man arrested for sexual assault had been "charged" when in fact he had never been arraigned. An official-proceedings privilege did not apply since, under Michigan law, arrest is not part of the judicial process.[63] But Michigan's supreme court later vacated a $1 million libel award to the plaintiff on other grounds.

In a minority of states, a pleading or a complaint is also not privileged until some official action has been taken by a judge or other officer of the court. The assumption is that documents containing possibly false, defamatory, and uncontradicted charges are addressed initially to the courts and not to the public at large. For example, before divulging the contents of a legal document, a reporter must be certain that it has been served on the party named as defendant. Otherwise no legal proceeding has begun. In a majority of states, however, pleadings or complaints once filed are privileged whether or not a judge has acted upon them.

Separating the official from the unofficial can be a daunting task, although the constitutional or *New York Times* defense may now cover many doubtful situations. Some records and proceedings are sealed and closed by state statute—for example, juvenile, divorce, and sexual assault matters. Yet in *Cox Broadcasting Corp. v. Cohn*,[64] the Supreme Court held that where an accurate report from a judicial record broadcast the name of a rape-murder victim, contrary to Georgia law, the report was privileged.

Accuracy need not be perfect. Even errors in fact may be overlooked where complex technical language is involved.[65] An oft-cited case is *Time, Inc. v. Pape*.[66] A deputy chief of detectives sued *Time* magazine when it implied in a story about a civil rights commission report that the police officer was guilty of brutality. Although the news magazine had confused a complainant's testimony with the independent findings of the commission itself, the Supreme Court ruled that in the circumstances of the case the magazine had not engaged in "falsification" sufficient in itself to sustain a jury finding of "actual malice."

"These considerations apply with even greater force," the Court added, "to the situation where the alleged libel consists in the claimed misinterpretation of the gist of a lengthy government document. Where the document reported on is so ambiguous as this one was, it is hard to imagine a test of 'truth' that would not put the publisher virtually at the mercy of the unguided discretion of a jury." Substantial accuracy seems to be the rule.

But the purposeful distortion of a record will negate the privilege. Not everything a public official does is part of his or her official duties. Senator William Proxmire learned that lesson when making one of his often mindless Golden Fleece awards. This activity was outside the perimeters of his official Senate duties and therefore not subject to absolute protection by the Constitution's Speech or Debate Clause, said the U.S. Supreme Court. A behavioral scientist, one of a number of such researchers ridiculed by the senator, settled his libel suit for $10,000, and the U.S. Senate paid $25,000 out of public funds for Proxmire's costs.[67]

Common Law Defenses against Libel in Summary

You are now familiar with the three traditional common law defenses against libel—*truth, fair comment,* and *qualified privilege (fair report)*—all of which to some degree have been folded into the *New York Times* or constitutional defense. Remember that if these defenses are used standing alone, the burden of proof will be on the publisher. Truth requires evidence and documentation and is often more difficult to prove than a defendant expects. Fair comment or what has come to be called the opinion defense was curtailed by *Milkovich* and revived to a degree by *Moldea II*. False facts still must not be inferred or used as the basis for an opinion.

Qualified privilege or the fair report defense has been least affected by *New York Times* and remains a useful defense where relevant. But in using it one must be sure that anything defamatory in the report comes from an official proceeding. Or one has to know the exceptions for unofficial proceedings allowed by state law. A news report need not be a verbatim account of a document or a governmental proceeding, but it should be substantially true.

All of these defenses may be used—and are most often used—as backup to the *New York Times* doctrine, the primary defense against libel. And to a degree all have become part of that defense in that only *actual malice* will put in jeopardy a report on public business regardless of its truth, its fairness, and its source.

SECONDARY AND TECHNICAL DEFENSES

Major secondary defenses are *neutral reportage, consent,* and the *community of interests privileges and "right of reply"* defense.

Neutral Reportage

Court interpretations of the "reckless disregard" language of the *New York Times* defense have greatly limited the reporter's liability for communicating someone's libelous charges against public persons. "While verification of the facts remains an important reporting standard," the Fifth Circuit Court of Appeals said in 1966, "a reporter, without a 'high degree of awareness of their probable falsity, may rely on statements made by a single source even though they reflect only one side of the story without fear of libel prosecution. . . ."[68] Five years later came the constitutional rule of *Medina v. Time, Inc.*:[69] News media reports—these particular reports on the infamous My Lai massacre—of statements made by participants in a public controversy are protected, where the fact that one participant levels charges against another is itself a newsworthy event.

It is even better when both sides or all sides of a controversial issue of public importance can be reported with a modicum of detachment. The defense of **neutral reportage** was first articulated by the Second Circuit Court of Appeals in a case involving a heated controversy between opponents and proponents of the use of the pesticide DDT. On one side was the National Audubon Society; on the other were a number of chemical companies and their scientific consultants, some of whom were prominent in the scientific community. In the middle was John Devlin, a science reporter for the *New York Times*.

The scientists were accused by their detractors of being "paid to lie." The reporter, contacting as many of the scientists as would talk to him, incorporated their angry responses into his stories. Nevertheless, three of the scientists sued his newspaper, and a jury awarded them $20,000 in damages. The federal ap-

● **Neutral reportage**
A secondary defense based on the argument that the reporter, without malice or bias, is simply reporting both sides of a controversial issue of public importance. Courts are divided on its acceptability.

peals court reversed, holding that "the First Amendment protects the accurate and disinterested reporting of those charges, regardless of the reporter's private views regarding their validity. What is newsworthy about such accusations is that they were made. . . . The public interest in being fully informed about controversies that often rage around sensitive issues demands that the press be afforded the freedom to report such charges without assuming responsibility for them."[70]

This defense is in only moderately good standing. At last count, a few federal district courts, the Eighth Circuit, and state courts in Ohio, Vermont, Florida, Wyoming, and Arizona have recognized it. Many more reject it, including the Third Circuit Court of Appeals and appellate courts in New York, Kentucky, Rhode Island, South Dakota, and Michigan. Courts within a state, New York, for example, have disagreed on its validity. Justice Harry Blackmun gave the defense a mere moment of respectability in a concurring opinion in a 1989 Supreme Court case.[71]

Under the defense, a reporter must not have initiated an investigation leading to defamatory allegations. The controversy must have existed prior to the reporter's involvement. Nor should the reporter have taken sides at any point in the coverage. The reporter is no more than a disinterested communication channel, an honest broker, for the responsible representatives of the two sides of a public controversy involving public figures.

The defense of neutral reportage ought to be approached cautiously, and because its requirements are high in those jurisdictions that recognize it,[72] it should never be substituted for a fair report defense.

Consent

Another shaky defense is the implied **consent** a news source gives when publicly disputing charges someone else has made against her or him. A denial requires republication of the original charge, of course, since a denial alone would be meaningless. The very act of talking to a reporter indicates consent to publication. As the Fourth Circuit Court of Appeals put it in an oft-cited case:

> In view of the fact that [the plaintiff] gave this statement to the press in an interview to be published, he is hardly in a position to complain of the publication with it of the charge to which it was an answer, even if the latter were otherwise objectionable.[73]

The Reverend Jerry Falwell was unsuccessful in a suit against *Penthouse* magazine following publication of a concededly accurate account of an interview he had willingly granted. Violations of conditions imposed by the cleric did not negate his *consent* nor constitute publication with malice.[74]

Since consent can be a secondary defense, it is good practice for a reporter to contact all potential libel plaintiffs, to get all sides of a controversy, and to tell readers when relevant sources are unavailable for comment.

● **Consent**
Implicit or explicit consent to publication. Those talking to reporters, unless there is an agreement to the contrary, ought to assume they are speaking for publication. A secondary defense against libel.

Community of Interests Privilege and "Right" of Reply

There is a qualified privilege to publish defamatory matter in defense of one's own reputation, that is, to answer back. There is also a qualified privilege to circulate defamation among those with whom one is associated in pursuit of mutual property, business, or fraternal or professional interests; among one's own family; or, for example, to fulfill one's social obligations to law enforcement. The trick in using this defense is to stay within the boundaries of those areas of mutual interest and to make certain that a reply is measured and, as a counterattack, does not exceed in vitriol the original verbal assault. In most jurisdictions, common law and/or actual malice will defeat the privilege.

Generally speaking, these situations do not involve the press, although the Kansas Supreme Court recently held that the community of interests privilege covered a meeting between *Kansas City Star* editors and power company officials who were concerned about a freelancer's investigative article on lack of recreational access to a nuclear generating station's cooling lake. The freelancer unsuccessfully sued the power company for defamatory remarks that were made about him at the meeting.[75]

Credit reports, letters of recommendation, and correspondence with criminal justice agencies are more likely to invoke this defense. Recall the Alton, Illinois, newspaper libel case where the community of interests privilege was raised in posttrial motions and on appeal but was rejected.

Statutes of Limitations and Equal Time

One *technical* defense has already been mentioned. *Statutes of limitations* are designed to protect alleged wrongdoers against stale claims. They are an absolute bar to libel actions after they have run.

In 1977 Kathy Keeton, associate publisher of *Penthouse*, sued Larry Flynt and *Hustler* magazine for libel and invasion of privacy. Both claims were dismissed because Ohio's statute of limitations had run. Keeton then filed in New Hampshire where there was still time left because the state then had a six-year statute.

A federal district court dismissed the suit on the ground that the Due Process Clause of the Fourteenth Amendment forbade use of New Hampshire's long-arm statute (a state law that allows the courts of one state to claim jurisdiction over persons or property in another) to claim jurisdiction over *Hustler*. The court of appeals affirmed, largely because of Keeton's lack of contact with New Hampshire.

Keeton appealed and a unanimous Supreme Court reversed, much to the distress of media attorneys. Justice Rehnquist, writing for the Court, found no problem in a plaintiff shopping for a jurisdiction with a stretched-out statute or more favorable rules. *Hustler* had chosen to enter the New Hampshire market and therefore had to cope with that state's laws.[76]

A second absolute bar to a libel suit protects a broadcaster who is required by the Federal Communications Act to give **equal time** or *equal opportunity* to federal candidates running for the same public office in either a primary or a general election. Before 1959, broadcasters did not enjoy this

● **Equal time**
A defense applicable to broadcasters who are required by law to provide equal opportunities (paid or unpaid) to candidates competing for the same federal elective office. They are immunized against libel suits resulting from this use of their facilities.

immunity from libel suits brought as a consequence of a candidate's defamatory speech.[77] Now they do.

MITIGATION

To mitigate in libel law is essentially to lessen the damages that might otherwise be assessed. One might plead that the character and reputation of the plaintiff are so bad that they cannot be further impaired by a fresh accusation. In *Brooks v. American Broadcasting Companies, Inc.,*[78] a federal district court held that the plaintiff's reputation had been so severely tarnished by his much-publicized criminal history that he was **libel-proof**. This is better than mitigation, but a plaintiff could be only partly libel-proof, so be careful.

It may also be argued in mitigation that you had a *usually reliable source.* This is sometimes called the **wire service defense.** A federal district court in Kentucky ruled that a newspaper's failure to conduct an independent investigation before republishing a wire service article concerning allegations of sexual misconduct of high school teachers did not constitute negligence.[79] Nor would it constitute actual malice. Not all sources, of course, are as reliable as the wire services or reputable publications.

The most reliable mitigating factor is the *retraction*. At least thirty states have retraction statutes, some of them 150 years old. Few are the same. Some allow no punitive damages if the plaintiff has requested a retraction within a certain period of time and the publisher has complied according to state law. Some permit only special damages under similar circumstances.

A **retraction** is a full, fair, and timely apology that can and should be made where appropriate in the absence of a statute. A retraction should not be equivocal or partial. It goes beyond a mere correction. Unlike the right-of-reply statute struck down in the *Tornillo* case (see p. 000), a retraction is always voluntary. And a failure to retract is not evidence of either negligence or actual malice. In fact, such a failure may suggest that the newspaper reasonably believed that the plaintiff had not been defamed,[80] or that the defamatory statement was true.

A plaintiff's refusal to accept a retraction may also serve to mitigate, as will an honored policy of correcting mistakes and using ombudsmen, preferably independent of newspaper management, to intercede for readers or viewers. Any evidence of good faith and caring on the part of the communicator may serve to mitigate damages.

Retraction statutes can be idiosyncratic. Know what your state's retraction law covers. Some specify type size, headline, and placement. Some fail to cover certain categories of publications, magazines in California, for example. Never use a retraction to repeat or amplify the original libel, even though the libel may have to be referred to in the course of apologizing; the offended person should be aware of this.

A lawyer should be involved when a retraction is part of a *settlement*. When properly executed, a settlement will bar a suit for damages. It is therefore

● **Libel-proof**
A reputation so tarnished that it cannot be further impaired by a fresh accusation.

● **Wire service defense**
An argument in mitigation of damages that your publication had a usually reliable source.

● **Retraction**
A full and fair correction and apology for a defamatory publication. A majority of states provide for retraction by statute, that is, by a retraction law.

something more than mitigation. Too many settlements by a particular publication, however, could attract suits.

The most practical way to mitigate or ease damages is to carry an *insurance policy* covering libel as well as other categories of media litigation. While most libel suits now end in settlements, reaching that point can cost $50,000. Gaining a **summary judgment** to end a case at its earliest stage can also cost $50,000. The costs of suits that go through the judicial process can be astronomical. Wayne Newton's unsuccessful suit against NBC cost the defendant's insurance company at least $9 million. And even without appeals, a case that goes to trial can run up costs in the hundreds of thousands of dollars.

Four major companies dominate the field, and premiums and deductibles have held fairly steady, although the trends for both are upward. No responsible publication or broadcast operation can afford to be without insurance. At the very least, lawyers' fees and court costs in the pretrial period and punitive damages should be covered. Acceptable policics will ensure that editors and publishers remain in control of the lawsuit so that appropriate journalistic and First Amendment values will be protected.

• **Summary judgment**
A motion designed to prevent a case from going to trial, there being no dispute as to facts and the law being clearly on the side of the defendant.

Summary of Secondary and Technical Defenses and Mitigation

Secondary and *technical* defenses, as well as *mitigating* factors, follow the *New York Times* defense and its encapsulated common law concepts of truth, fair comment, and qualified privilege (fair report) in constructing a total libel defense.

Neutral reportage, where it is recognized, may be added to the *New York Times* and common law defenses; but it is a defense requiring a kind of pure detachment not often found in real-life journalists. Its requirements, for example, are much higher than those expected in a fair report or qualified privilege defense.

Consent as a secondary defense is little more than a reminder that it may be helpful and that it is always good journalism to get both sides of the story by making every effort to contact those against whom charges have been made.

Community of interests and "right" of reply defenses do not often involve reporters and editors, but one such example involving the *Kansas City Star* is cited above.

Statutes of limitations and *equal time* immunity are *absolute* bars to libel actions and are therefore the only unconditional defenses available. They are technical in the sense that when they apply, no libel suit can succeed, whatever its merits. But they are available only in special circumstances involving either the passage of time or the words of competing political candidates.

Mitigation is doing whatever one can to lessen the damages in a lawsuit that may already be lost. To argue that a plaintiff is *libel-proof* or that your story came from a *usually reliable source* will help in mitigation. Even more helpful will be a *retraction* where you realize that an honest mistake has been made. Thirty states have legal rules for making a retraction, and these ought to be paid close attention.

Finally, a publisher or broadcaster may avoid disaster by shifting the financial burdens of a libel suit from itself to an *insurance* company. One should no more publish or broadcast without insurance coverage than one would drive a car or buy a house without it.

LEGAL PROCESS

A defendant's initial goal in a libel suit is to win a *summary judgment,* that is, to get the judge to decide that the plaintiff has no case under prevailing legal rules. This usually means that the plaintiff is unable to meet some or all of the threshold factors necessary for a suit to proceed, namely, defamation, publication, identification, falsity, and fault (negligence or actual malice). The awarding of summary judgment is the rule rather than the exception.

"Summary judgment must be awarded," said the Supreme Court in 1962, "where (1) there is no genuine issue of material fact and (2) such judgment is required as a matter of law. When considering motions for summary judgment, courts must view the facts and inferences to be drawn from them in the light most favorable to the opposing party."[81] The opposing party would be the plaintiff.

Judge Skelly Wright made a First Amendment argument for summary judgment in a 1966 case involving the *Washington Post:*

> In the First Amendment area, summary procedures are even more essential. For the stake here, if harassment succeeds, is free debate. One of the purposes of the *Times* principle, in addition to protecting persons from being cast in damages in libel suits filed by public officials, is to prevent persons from being discouraged in the full and free exercise of First Amendment rights with respect to the conduct of their government. The threat of being put to the defense of a lawsuit brought by a popular public official may be as chilling to the exercise of First Amendment freedoms as fear of the outcome of the lawsuit itself, especially to advocates of unpopular causes.[82]

In 1984 Justice John Paul Stevens recommended summary judgment and directed courts to "make an independent examination of the whole record" to make sure "that the judgment [presumably that of lower courts] does not constitute a forbidden intrusion on the field of free expression."[83] That is, has actual malice been proven by clear and convincing evidence? More recently, the Supreme Court has suggested that independent appellate review should focus primarily on the question of actual malice.[84]

These declarations also serve to reaffirm the *New York Times* doctrine. Although neither CBS nor *Time* magazine was granted summary judgment in the cases of the generals Westmoreland and Sharon, the suits were foreshortened in part by the plaintiffs' discouraging prospect of having to prove actual malice.

If a case is not dismissed summarily, the parties to the suit appear in court and present arguments for and against motions to dismiss. If these are denied, the case moves on to the jury. In the interim, both summary judgments and dismissals can be appealed, although this is rare. These can be affirmed, reversed, or reversed and remanded (sent back to the judge for reshaping). Before a case goes to a jury but after the evidence has been presented, it is possible for the judge to take the case out of the jury's hands and announce a directed verdict for the defense. Evidence for the defense must be compelling for a directed verdict, so it is rare.

In a *trial by jury,* plaintiffs able to sustain the burden of proof usually receive a verdict in their favor and are awarded money damages. If not, the case is dismissed. The defendant is not given a judgment, but does essentially "win" the case. Trial court decisions can also be appealed. A money judgment resulting from a trial by jury could be affirmed, completely reversed, reversed and remanded, reduced in size (remittur), or enlarged (additur), although the latter is rare.

In a study by the author and a research assistant covering libel cases against the media in the period 1982 to 1988, more than 90 percent of filed cases resulted in summary judgments or dismissals. In 30 percent of these cases, the court found no defamation. In 20 percent there was no evidence or insufficient evidence of actual malice, and in 30 percent the allegedly defamatory publications were privileged either as opinion (fair comment) or as fair reports of privileged material.

More than half of these summary judgments or dismissals were appealed, resulting in decisions favorable to the defendants in 77 percent of cases. Of the small number of cases going to a second stage of appeal, 76 percent were decided in favor of the defendants. Third and final appeals are rare and were won by defendants in our study only 33 percent of the time.

Summary judgments and dismissals are crucial to the media because once a case goes to trial, the chance of media success drops to about 25 percent. When trial verdicts are appealed, however, defendants win 64 percent of the cases at the first stage, 50 percent at the second stage and 50 percent at the third stage. Most trial verdicts get at least to the first stage of appeal.[85]

Actual malice is rarely found in libel cases, but the search for it, both in the discovery period when both sides gather their evidence and in the courtroom, can be frighteningly expensive in terms of time, energy, and money. Findings of negligence are also rare because private persons bring a relatively small number of libel suits.

ALTERNATIVES TO LIBEL SUITS

Partly because libel suits can have such damaging consequences for free expression, especially when those suits are brought—and most often lost—by highly visible public officials or public personalities, many recommendations have been made in recent years for modifications in the law or for alternatives to it. Most of these proposals would end a suit with a **declaratory judgment** (a judicial action that answers a legal question without awarding any damages or ordering that anything be done). The most notable was the *Annenberg* Washington Program Proposal for the Reform of Libel Law. It would work as follows:

● **Declaratory judgment**
A declaration by a court of the rights of the parties to a lawsuit without ordering anything to be done. A suit would end at that point.

1. A complainant would seek specifically either a retraction or an opportunity to reply; failure to do so within thirty days of publication of the libel would bar any future legal action.

2. If either party elected to try the suit as an action for declaratory judgment, the suit would conclude with the court making a judgment as to truth or falsity.

3. Having chosen this process, the losing party would pay the winner's attorneys' fees in what is known as **fee shifting.**

● **Fee shifting**
The losing party in a suit pays the winner's attorney costs.

If this procedure were rejected, under the Annenberg proposal only actual damages would be considered in an ensuing libel action. Both plaintiffs' and defendants' attorneys have criticized this no-money, no-fault proposal, one side because constitutional protections under *New York Times* would be lost, the other because just compensation in dollar amounts would no longer be available to those wronged by the media. No jurisdiction has adopted this proposal.

A similarly comprehensive alternative has been proposed by the National Conference of Commissioners on Uniform State Laws. It is called the Uniform Correction or Clarification of Defamation Act and is dated August 1993. The American Bar Association's House of Delegates approved it in February 1994 in a divided vote, and its proponents are now seeking to have the act introduced into state legislatures.

Essentially, it would require a timely and written request for a correction to precede a libel action (time limits are specified in the act). Subsequent damages would be limited to provable economic loss (special damages) if the request is made within ninety days of knowledge of publication. The request would specify with particularity the alleged false and defamatory statement. The publisher could request disclosure of any information bearing on falsity. If that were unreasonably refused, again the plaintiff could later recover only provable economic loss.

A correction or clarification would be timely and sufficient if published within forty-five days of its receipt and request; given prominence equal to the original publication; and clearly corrected, asserted the truth, or disclaimed any intent to communicate a defamatory meaning. If a timely correction were no longer possible, a publisher could avoid a trial by offering to publish a correction and to pay reasonable litigation expenses, including attorneys' fees incurred prior to the publication of the correction. Clearly, the act revolves around the concept of correction and seeks to avoid expensive and extended litigation, while controlling damages. Its wording is complex enough to have evoked a cautious response from press organizations.

A Philadelphia judge, Lois Forer, has recommended a uniform federal libel statute to clear up the mess created by differing state laws.[86] Other proposals for reform include mandatory retractions and rights of reply or rights of repair (correction).[87] Others would go on the offensive and file countersuits to ward off and discourage prospective plaintiffs. Many argue for an end to or a limit on punitive damages, although one of the authors of this text and many others see punitive damages as having the salutary effect of leveling the playing field for the relatively defenseless plaintiff.[88] One writer recommends that policy-making public officials and celebrities, whatever their cultural, artistic, or athletic niche, should have no remedy in libel, but that those media that attack them should provide voluntary opportunities for reply.[89]

The Iowa Libel Project recommends circumventing the judicial process altogether. A system of arbitration or alternative dispute resolution is currently being tested in that state.[90]

The American Civil Liberties Union (ACLU) has in effect opted for Justice Brennan's *Rosenbloom* test. Defamation suits, the ACLU believes, violate the First Amendment when brought by public officials on matters relating to their public position, by public figures on matters relating to their public status, and by private or public figures on matters of public concern.

In the meantime, the courts continue to enforce the libel laws as they stand.

HOW TO AVOID LIBEL SUITS

No responsible or professional publication can avoid libel altogether. It goes with the territory. But journalists can at least begin to help themselves stay out of court by doing the following:

1. Acknowledge mistakes generously and sympathetically. Always be prepared to check your facts and to clarify, correct, and retract where appropriate. None of these will keep you out of court, but they will help once you're there.

2. Confirm and verify to whatever extent deadlines and resources permit. Have attributions for all quotations. Make certain photographs, headlines, captions, cutlines, and promotional spots conform to the facts of stories. Good editing is a must.

3. What's true and what you can prove to be true are two different things. Having a source is not proof of truth. And don't make promises to sources if you are not prepared to keep those promises. Unidentified sources can be dangerous.

4. Make sure opinions do not infer or are not based upon false facts.

5. Always indicate the source of a story resulting from governmental proceedings or documents.

6. Avoid unofficial statements from law enforcement officers.

7. Get the other side of the story, especially that of the defamed person. Don't leave critical notes and tapes laying around the newsroom.

8. Keep up to date on what is happening in media law in state and federal courts, especially those in your circulation or coverage area.

9. Finally, don't talk to a complainant's lawyer directly. Refer him or her to your lawyer.[91]

SUMMARY

Since *New York Times v. Sullivan* in 1964 constitutionalized libel by making it a First Amendment matter, libel laws have made it difficult for public people—officials and celebrities—to win libel suits. The laws do not, however, discourage these same people from bringing libel suits. Libel plaintiffs at the threshold must prove defamation, publication, identification, falsity, and fault. Fault must be proven at one of two levels: a public-person plaintiff must prove actual malice (knowing falsehood or reckless disregard as to truth or falsity) by clear and convincing evidence; a private-person plaintiff must prove negligence, a lesser standard of fault, by at least a preponderance of the evidence, a lesser standard of evidence. On the issue of negligence, especially, there are variations from state to state. And courts have provided insufficient guidelines for distinguishing private from public plaintiffs.

Other defenses are also available. Truth, fair comment (the opinion defense), and qualified privilege are common law defenses that to a degree have been folded into the *New York Times* doctrine. Where they are used alone, the burden of proof shifts to the defendant. Generally, defendants in libel suits mount as many defenses as possible.

Technical and secondary defenses are also available. A plea of neutral reportage will work in some jurisdictions. Consent of the plaintiff to publication is another secondary defense. A more technical defense is the statute of limitations; when it has run or the time has expired, no libel suit can be brought.

In addition, mitigating factors may lessen damages in a losing suit. The explanation that you received your information from a usually reliable source (the wire service defense) is one example. Another is to run a retraction when you realize that an unintended inaccuracy has occurred. Few mass communicators, large or small, should operate without libel insurance.

KEY TERMS

Defamation	Colloquium
Libel *per se*	Actual malice
New York Times v. Sullivan	Clear and convincing evidence
Libel *per quod*	Prudent publisher test
Single publication rule	Negligence
Statute of limitations	Punitive damages
Diversity suit	Actual damages
Respondeat superior	Special damages
Complicity rule	Trade libel
Criminal libel	Common law malice

Vortex or limited-purpose public figure
Pervasive or all-purpose public figure
Involuntary public figure
Truth
Fair comment and criticism
Qualified privilege
Neutral reportage
Consent

Equal time
Libel-proof
Wire service defense
Retraction
Summary judgment
Declaratory judgment
Fee shifting

CASE PROBLEMS

1. When faced with the question of whether or not to print a story, or a portion of a story, that may be actionably libelous, it may be useful to go through a subset of questions or a sequence of points that track with the textbook. What might these be?

2. The police chief of Yourtown sues a local television station for what he claims was a false and defamatory news story about his alleged connections with organized crime. Assume that the story was indeed false and defamatory with respect to the chief. The city attorney is prepared to argue in behalf of the chief that the television station and its reporter were negligent because they failed to interview two obvious sources who would have denied the allegation and been sympathetic to the chief. Will this argument win the case for the chief?

3. *Gertz v. Robert Welch, Inc.* remains one of the central cases in libel law. It contains both negatives and positives for the press. What are they?

4. In a "Hard Copy" story on the lifestyles of Hollywood's rich and famous, a television reporter states that "most people in show business live a de-

praved life and have serious alcohol and drug problems." One well-known actor becomes very upset at these general allegations and files a libel suit. What would be the outcome? Explain.

5. In a story for her newspaper, a reporter quotes a source, the ex-wife of the city treasurer, as saying that her former husband is a "known adulterer." In a discussion over whether the story is actionable, the reporter argues that truth is her defense. She says she has a tape recording of the wife making the allegation that proves the truth of the statement. Will that defense work against a libel suit?

6. Evaluate the libel suit brought by psychoanalyst Jeffrey Masson against writer Janet Malcolm. Were the parties public figures? Were the alleged misquotes defamatory? Did Malcolm's information gathering and presentation procedures constitute actual malice—reckless disregard for the truth? Was *The New Yorker's* reliance on Malcolm—a usually reliable source—evidence of a lack of malice, justifying the court's dropping the magazine as a defendant in the suit?

ENDNOTES

1. *Moore v. Streit,* 181 Ill.App.3d 587, 130 Ill.Dec.341, 537 N.E.2d 408, 17 Med.L.Rptr. 1144 (1989).

2. Marc Franklin, "Suing Media for Libel: A Litigational Study," 1981 *American Bar Foundation Res. Journal.* 797–831; Randall P. Bezanson, Gilbert Cranberg and John Soloski, *Libel Law and the Press.* (New York: Free Press, 1987); Donald M. Gillmor, *Power, Publicity and the Abuse of Libel Law* (New York: Oxford University Press, 1992).

3. *Burnett v. National Enquirer,* 7 Med.L.Rptr. 1321 (Calif.Super.1981), 144 Cal.App. 3d 991, 193 Cal.Rptr. 206 (1983).

4. *Goldwater v. Ginzburg,* 414 F.2d 324 (2d Cir. 1969).

5. *McBride v. Merrell Dow & Pharmaceuticals, Inc.,* 717 F.2d 1460, 1466 (D.C.Cir. 1983).

6. *Blouin v. Anton,* 139 Vt. 618, 431 A.2d 489 (Vt. 1981).

7. *Greenbelt Co-op Publishing Association v. Bresler,* 398 U.S. 6, 90 S.Ct. 1537 (1970).

8. 376 U.S. 254, 84 S.Ct. 710 (1964).

9. *Bowes v. Magna Concepts, Inc.,* 561 N.Y.S.2d 16, 166 A.D.2d 347, 18 Med.L.Rptr. 1303 (1990).

10. *Kaplan v. Greater Niles Township Publishing Corp.,* 2 Ill. App.3d 109 278 N.E.2d 437 (1971); *Catalano v. Pechous,* 69 Ill.App.3d 797, 25 Ill.Dec. 838, 387 N.E.2d 714 (1978), *affirmed* 83 Ill.2d 146, 50 Ill.Dec. 242, 419 N.E.2d 350 (1980).

11. *Diesen v. Hessburg,* 455 N.W.2d 446, 17 Med.L.Rptr. 1849 (Minn. 1990); *Foley v. WCCO-TV Inc.,* 449 N.W.2d 497, 17 Med.L.Rptr. 1233 (Minn.App. 1989).

12. *Southern Air Transport, Inc. v. American Broadcasting Companies, Inc.,* 877 F.2d 1010, 1014 (D.C.Cir. 1989).

13. *White v. Fraternal Order of Police,* 909 F.2d 512, 17 Med.L.Rptr. 2137 (D.C.Cir. 1990).

14. *Masson v. New Yorker Magazine, Inc.,* 501 U.S. 496, 111 S.Ct. 2419, 18 Med.L.Rptr. 2241 (1991).

15. *Green v. Alton Telegraph Printing Co.,* 107 Ill.App.3d 755, 63 Ill.Dec. 465, 438 N.E.2d 203 (Ill. 1982). Thomas B. Littlewood, *Coals of Fire: The Alton Telegraph Libel Case* (Carbondale: Southern Illinois University Press, 1986).

16. *Pring v. Penthouse International,* 695 F.2d 438 (10th Cir. 1982).

17. *Ashton v. Kentucky,* 384 U.S. 195, 86 S.Ct. 1407 (1966).

18. *O'Brien v. Williamson Daily News,* 735 F.Supp. 218, 18 Med.L.Rptr. 1037 (E.D.Ky. 1990)

19. 475 U.S. 767, 106 S.Ct. 1558 (1986)

20. *Sharon v. Time, Inc.,* 609 F.Supp. 1291 (S.D.N.Y. 1984). In an amusing case involving satirist Andy Rooney of "60 Minutes" fame, the Ninth Circuit Court of Appeals held that Rooney's remark that a windshield product didn't work was a trade libel or disparagment, not a protected opinion. But the plaintiff, failing to prove falsity, was denied redress. *Unelko Corp. v. Rooney,* 912 F.2d 1049, 17 Med.L.Rptr. 2317 (1990).

21. *Brief for the Petitioner,* 376 United States Supreme Court Records and Briefs 254–314 (Vol. 12), pp. 28–29.

22. *Garrison v. State of Louisiana,* 379 U.S. 64, 85 S.Ct. 209 (1964).

23. *Curtis Publishing Co. v. Butts* and *Associated Press v. Walker,* 388 U.S. 130, 87 S.Ct. 1975 (1967).

24. 403 U.S. 29, 91 S.Ct. 1811 (1971).

25. 418 U.S. 323, 94 S.Ct. 2997 (1974).

26. 827 F.2d 1119 (7th Cir. 1987).

27. *TXO Production Corp. v. Alliance Resources Corp.,* ____ U.S. ____, 113 S.Ct. 2711 (1993).

28. 472 U.S. 749, 105 S.Ct. 2939 (1985).

29. *Time, Inc. v. Firestone,* 424 U.S. 448, 96 S.Ct. 958 (1976).

30. *Wolston v. Reader's Digest Association, Inc.,* 443 U.S. 157, 99 S.Ct. 2701 (1979).

31. *Warford v. Lexington Herald-Leader,* 789 S.W.2d 758, 17 Med.L.Rptr. 1785 (Ky. 1990); *Yancey v. Hamilton,* 786 S.W.2d 854, 17 Med.L.Rptr. 1012 (Ky. 1989).

32. *Lerman v. Flynt Distributing Co.,* 745 F.2d 123, 137–138 (2d Cir. 1984).

33. *Crane v. Arizona Republic,* 729 F.Supp. 698, 17 Med.L.Rptr. 1353 (C.D. Cal. 1989).

34. *Mosesian v. McClatchy Newspapers,* 205 Cal.App.3d 597, 252 Cal.Rptr. 586 (1989), *cert. denied* 490 U.S. 1066, 109 S.Ct. 2065 (1989).

35. *McCall v. Courier-Journal,* 623 S.W.2d 882 (Ky. 1981), *cert. denied,* 456 U.S. 975, 102 S.Ct. 2239 (1982).

36. 388 U.S. 130, 155, 87 S.Ct. 1975, 1991 (1967).

37. For an extended discussion on "negligence," see W. Wat Hopkins, "Negligence 10 Years after *Gertz v. Welch,*" *Journalism Monographs* 93 (August 1985).

38. *Newton v. National Broadcasting Co.,* 913 F.2d 652, 18 Med.L.Rptr. 1001 (9th Cir. 1990).

39. *Fletcher v. San Jose Mercury News,* 216 Cal.App.3d 172, 264 Cal.Rptr. 699, 17 Med.L.Rptr. 1321 (1989).

40. *Bose Corp. v. Consumers Union,* 466 U.S. 485, 104 S.Ct. 1949 (1984).

41. *Janklow v. Viking Press,* 459 N.W.2d 415, 17 Med.L.Rptr. 2220 (S.D. 1990).

42. *Brown & Williamson v. Jacobson,* 827 F.2d 1119 (7th Cir. 1987).

43. *Feazell v. Belo Broadcasting Corporation,* No. 86–227–11 (McLennan County Texas District Court, April 19, 1991).

44. Gillmor, *Power, Publicity and the Abuse of Libel Law.*

45. *Dall v. Pearson,* 246 F.Supp. 812 (D.D.C. 1963).

46. *Gertz v. Robert Welch, Inc.,* 418 U.S. 323, 339, 94 S.Ct. 2997, 3006 (1974).

47. *Ollman v. Evans,* 750 F.2d 970 (D.C.Cir. 1984), *cert. denied* 471 U.S. 1127, ____ S.Ct. ____ (1985).

48. *Janklow v. Newsweek,* 788 F.2d 1300 (8th Cir. 1986); *Janklow v. Viking Press,* 459 N.W.2d 415, 17 Med.L.Rptr. 2220 (S.D. 1990).

49. 497 U.S. 1, 110 S.Ct. 2695, 17 Med.L.Rptr. 2009 (1990).

50. The Supreme Court first referred to "rhetorical hyperbole" in *Greenbelt Co-op Publishing Association v. Bresler,* 398 U.S. 6, 90 S.Ct. 1537 (1970).

51. See, for example, *King v. Globe Newspaper Co.,* 400 Mass. 705, 512 N.E.2d 241 (1987), *cert. denied* 485 U.S. 940, 108 S.Ct. 448 (1988).

52. *Hustler Magazine v. Falwell,* 485 U.S. 46, 108 S.Ct. 876 (1988).

53. Robert Drechsel, "The Survival of 'End-Run' Theories of Tort Liability after *Hustler v. Falwell,*" *Journalism Quarterly* 67:4, 1062 (Winter 1990).

54. *Immuno A.G. v. Moor-Jankowski,* 77 N.Y.2d 235, 566 N.Y.S.2d 906, 567 N.E.2d 1270, 18 Med.L.Rptr. 1625 (1991).

55. *Moldea v. New York Times Co., Inc.,* 15 F.3d 1137, 22 Med.L.Rptr. 1321 (D.C.Cir. 1994).

56. *Moldea v. New York Times Co., Inc.,* 22 F.3d 310, 22 Med.L.Rptr. 1673 (D.C.Cir. 1994).

57. *Id.* at 1681.

58. Restatement (Second) of Torts, § 611 comment (1977).

59. *Martirano v. Frost,* 25 N.Y.2d 505, 307 N.Y.S.2d 425, 255 N.E.2d 693 (1969).

60. *Ascherman v. Natanson,* 23 Cal.App.3d 861, 100 Cal.Rptr. 656 (1972). See also, *Dorsey a/k/a Engelbert Humperdinck v. National Enquirer, Inc.,* 973 F.3d 1431, 20 Med.L.Rptr. 1745 (9th Cir. 1992).

61. *White v. Fraternal Order of Police,* 909 F.2d 512, 17 Med.L.Rptr. 2137 (D.C.Cir. 1990).

62. See David A. Elder, *The Fair Report Privilege* (Stoneham, MA: Butterworth, 1988) for a detailed review of the status of press releases, news conferences, speeches, and private meetings at all levels of all branches of government.

63. *Rouch v. Enquirer & News of Battle Creek,* 184 Mich.App. 19, 457 N.W.2d 74, 17 Med.L.Rptr. 2305 (Mich.App. 1990).

64. 420 U.S. 469, 95 S.Ct. 1029 (1975).

65. *Jennings v. Telegram-Tribune Co.,* 164 Cal.App.3d 119, 210 Cal.Rptr. 485 (1985).

66. 401 U.S. 279, 91 S.Ct. 633 (1971).

67. *Hutchinson v. Proxmire,* 443 U.S. 111, 99 S.Ct. 2675 (1979).

68. *New York Times v. Connor,* 365 F.2d 567, 576 (5th Cir. 1966).

69. 439 F.2d 1129 (1st Cir. 1971).

70. *Edwards v. National Audubon Society,* 556 F.2d 113 (2d Cir. 1977).

71. *Harte-Hanks Communication, Inc. v. Connaughton,* 491 U.S. 657, 109 S.Ct. 2678 (1989).

72. *Crane v. Arizona Republic,* 729 F.Supp. 698, 17 Med.L.Rptr. 1353 (C.D.Calif. 1989).

73. *Pulvermann v. A. S. Abell Co.,* 228 F.2d 797 (4th Cir. 1956).

74. *Falwell v. Penthouse International Limited,* 521 F.Supp. 1204 (D.Va. 1981).

75. *Knudsen v. Kansas Gas and Electric Co.,* 248 Kan. 469, 807 P.2d 71, 18 Med.L.Rptr. 1900 (1991).

76. *Keeton v. Hustler,* 465 U.S. 770, 104 S.Ct. 1473 (1984).

77. *Farmers Educational and Cooperative Union of America v. WDAY, Inc.,* 360 U.S. 525, 79 S.Ct. 1302 (1959).

78. 737 F.Supp. 431, 17 Med.L.Rptr. 2041 (N.D. Ohio 1990). The concept may have originated in *Cardillo v. Doubleday & Co.*, 518 F.2d 638 (2d Cir. 1975). It has been recognized in a few appellate state courts and a number of federal appeals courts.

79. *O'Brien v. Williamson Daily News*, 735 F.Supp. 218, 18 Med.L.Rptr. 1037 (E.D.Ky. 1990).

80. *Connelly v. Northwest Publications, Inc.*, 448 N.W.2d 901, 17 Med.L.Rptr. 1204 (Minn.App. 1989).

81. *United States v. Diebold, Inc.*, 369 U.S. 654, 82 S.Ct. 993 (1962).

82. *Washington Post Co. v. Keogh*, 365 F.2d 965 (D.C.Cir. 1966).

83. *Bose Corporation v. Consumers Union*, 466 U.S. 485, 104 S.Ct. 1949 (1984).

84. *Harte-Hanks Communication, Inc. v. Connaughton*, 491 U.S. 657, 109 S.Ct. 2678 (1989).

85. Gillmor, *Power, Publicity and the Abuse of Libel Law.*

86. Lois G. Forer, *A Chilling Effect* (New York: W. W. Norton & Company, 1987).

87. Rodney A. Smolla, *Suing the Press* (New York: Oxford University Press, 1986). See also Paul LeBel, "Defamation and the First Amendment: The End of the Affair," *William and Mary Law Review* 25:779, 788–790 (1984).

88. Jerome A. Barron, "Punitive Damages in Libel Cases—First Amendment Equalizer?" *Washington and Law Review* 47:105 (Winter 1990).

89. Gillmor, *Power, Publicity and the Abuse of Libel Law*, fn. 78.

90. Bezanson, Cranberg, and Soloski, *Libel Law and the Press*. For a broad critical evaluation of the *New York Times* doctrine see Murchison, Brian, Solski, Bezanson, Cranberg, and Roselle Wissler, "*Sullivan's* Paradox: The Emergence of Judicial Standards of Journalism," 73 *North Carolina L. Rev.* 7 (November 1994).

91. These suggestions are based partly on a list published by the Pennsylvania Newspaper Publishers Association and excerpted from a booklet, *Synopsis of the Law of Libel and the Right of Privacy*, distributed by the First Amendment Coalition's *Media Survival Kit*.

Privacy and the Mass Media

PRIVACY AND THE MEDIA: AN OVERVIEW

The risk of being found liable for money damages for an **invasion of privacy** is probably a newsroom's second greatest legal worry after libel. Unlike libel, however, very few invasion of privacy cases are decided against the media even at the trial level. The defenses available to thwart a privacy claim are both broad and numerous, and as a result, successful privacy lawsuits are extremely rare.

Another major difference between privacy and libel is that privacy consists of at least four separate tort actions. While libel is a single cause of action in tort law with many rules, privacy is a set of causes of action, each with a fairly simple set of elements and a fairly simple list of defenses.

The four major privacy actions are disclosure of private facts, intrusion upon seclusion, portrayal in a false light, and appropriation for commercial purposes. In addition, three other causes of action are closely linked to privacy. The right of publicity protects the commercial value of the names and likenesses of celebrities. The action developed as an offshoot of appropriation law. Actions for infliction of emotional distress and for negligence are aimed at making the media responsible when they report on or portray individuals in a way that was either calculated to cause mental or physical harm or could have been predicted to cause harm. Many emotional distress and negligence cases appear to be attempts to avoid the strong defenses available to the media in privacy and libel suits. In most of these cases, the plaintiffs have lost.

● **Invasion of privacy** Interference with any legally recognized interest in protecting personal information or behavior, based on constitutional, common law, statutory, or data grounds. For the mass media, common law invasion of privacy is the greatest concern.

One major similarity between privacy and libel is that the U.S. Supreme Court has introduced First Amendment–based defenses in privacy. To date the Court has imported defenses in disclosure of private facts cases and portrayal in false light cases.

Of the various privacy and related actions, only disclosure of private facts, intrusion upon seclusion, portrayal in a false light, infliction of emotional distress, and negligence should be of concern to journalists. Appropriation and right of publicity actions almost by definition apply in the fields of advertising and public relations rather than journalism. When suits are filed based on news accounts, plaintiffs must overcome a news defense. Both types of lawsuits in advertising and public relations can be avoided in a fairly commonsense way: permission is usually expected when the media look to exploit someone for profit. Defenses are available—although not always successful—when a celebrity is used humorously.

Knowing one's own state law is more important in privacy than in most areas of communication law. All of the actions are not recognized in every state. A few states allow no privacy actions. Although most states have adopted privacy law by common law through court decisions, in some states, the most important being New York, the action is based entirely on statutes.

By the time this chapter is read, the student should have in mind a good outline of the major elements and defenses that apply in invasion of privacy actions. As will be seen as the chapter progresses, the courts do not address many things that we might consider invasions of privacy.

WHAT IS PRIVACY LAW?

In privacy, a large gulf exists between what public opinion would allow and what the law allows. Most Americans place a very high value on privacy. But what one person may consider press insensitivity, another may deem newsworthy and important. So, while the public has often indicated it would prefer to see some restraint on the media,[1] the courts have been reluctant to impose restraints in the form of civil invasion of privacy suits for damages. As a result, most privacy issues involving the media turn on ethical rather than legal decisions.

When we speak of privacy and the media, we primarily mean that part of privacy law informally referred to as "common law" invasion of privacy. This type of privacy was first formally proposed by Louis Brandeis and his Boston law partner Samuel Warren in an 1890 law review article,[2] although the law had been concerned with protecting privacy for many years.[3] Early judicial attempts to protect privacy were based on the laws of property and contract for the most part. The 1890 article was the first to urge a separate legal claim for invasion of privacy. The article was enormously influential in the creation and adoption of privacy law by most of the states. The most dramatic change Brandeis and Warren proposed was that the media should be held liable for publishing truthful information.

The development of privacy law in the twentieth century would probably have surprised Brandeis and Warren. They were most concerned with protecting "intimate" information from publication by the rapidly growing high-circulation newspapers of the day. Instead, by 1960 legal scholar William Prosser found that there were four distinct common law invasion of privacy actions.[4] One of the four was for **disclosure of private facts,** but the others had been developed using rationales different from those presented by Warren and Brandeis. Although these causes of action continue to be called common law privacy, they may be and have been adopted either by court opinion or by statute. Forty-seven states recognize one or more of the four causes of action.

The action first adopted by courts and legislatures was **appropriation.** In this action, private individuals may recover when their names or pictures are used without consent for commercial purposes. A closely related fifth cause of action, the **right of publicity,** has developed over the last forty years to protect the famous against unauthorized commercial exploitation.

Another claim, **intrusion upon seclusion,** was developed to prevent the press from unauthorized entry when gathering news. It protects the right of individuals to enjoy privacy in their homes, offices, and other spaces.

The last action is **false light** invasion of privacy. The idea behind false light is very similar to that behind libel, but with two important differences. First, damages are based on how the false light portrayal affects the individual rather than on what third parties might think. Second, the message about an individual need not be defamatory to support a false light action. Indeed, the action is specifically aimed at preventing erroneous portrayals that are not necessarily defamatory. In practice, though, false light and libel have gotten thoroughly entwined.

The bulk of this chapter addresses the four—or five, if right of publicity is counted as separate—privacy actions identified by Prosser in 1960. Each of the four actions is distinct, so it is necessary to study their elements separately. The defenses available to the media also vary from one action to another. Only two defenses, consent and "plain view," apply in every action, and they are not always interpreted similarly in different types of privacy claims.

The four privacy actions all have one critical element in common. Like libel, they are considered personal rights. In other words, they protect only the person or persons directly affected. When family members or those close to someone who has been reported on complain about an invasion of "relational" privacy, the courts generally will not allow the case to continue.[5] Since the action is considered purely personal, an action normally may not be maintained to vindicate the rights of someone who is dead.

With the exception of appropriation and right of publicity cases, plaintiffs suing the mass media for privacy invasion have usually lost their cases, especially in recent years. Often they bring multiple claims in a single privacy case, hoping that one of the claims will work. It is not unusual to find two or three privacy claims raised in a single case; but, if there is no proof of any one of the types of privacy invasion, multiple claims seldom help. Consequently, plaintiffs and their lawyers have turned to alternative causes of action in an attempt to get around the difficult privacy law. These cases include claims for

- **Disclosure (unreasonable) of private facts**
  An action based upon the publication of embarrassing, sensitive personal information; sometimes called "pure privacy."

- **Appropriation**
  An action to compensate private figures whose names or pictures have been used without consent in advertising or promotional materials.

- **Right of publicity**
  An action designed to protect the ability of celebrities and other famous people to profit from and control the use of their names, photos, or attributes in advertising and promotional materials.

- **Intrusion upon seclusion**
  An action designed to protect the privacy of individuals in their homes and other spaces by preventing the press from unauthorized entry when gathering news.

- **False light**
  An action based upon inaccurate representation rather than assertion of fact, regardless of whether or not the information is defamatory.

infliction of mental distress, incitement (provoking harmful behaviors), outrage, and warranty, all causes of action with long histories but not as applied against the media. Plaintiffs have lost almost all of these cases involving alternative causes of action. Some courts, however, have at least established the precedent that plaintiffs may bring these kinds of claims.

This chapter does not address two important types of privacy: constitutional privacy and data privacy. The U.S. Supreme Court has long interpreted the Fourth Amendment's guarantee against unreasonable searches and seizures involving criminal suspects to provide a right of privacy in one's home, office, or automobile.[6] The connection with the common law privacy action for intrusion is obvious. Another constitutional privacy right protects one's right to physical or bodily independence. This is the right from which a woman's freedom to have an abortion is derived.[7] The constitutional protections apply to privacy invasions by the government, not private parties, and have therefore not involved the mass media.

Data privacy is becoming increasingly important in the United States. As technology makes both record keeping and dissemination of private information more complete and easier than ever before, citizens worry that details about their banking, credit, and other personal matters will fall into the wrong hands. Data privacy is meant to prevent unauthorized dissemination of personal information held by banks, schools, the government, and other record keepers. This type of privacy is usually protected by statute. An example is the Federal Privacy Act of 1974,[8] which among other things prohibits distribution of most information about student records held by colleges and universities. Data privacy has not been of much concern to the news media for the simple reason that the statutes normally do not apply to the media. On occasion journalists receive material protected by data privacy legislation, but the party responsible for infractions is the record keeper, not the journalist.

This chapter addresses common law invasion of privacy as it applies in the majority of jurisdictions. Students should be aware that the precise rules may differ somewhat from one state to another. Interpretations may differ depending upon whether the privacy law is based on court opinions or statutes. When a statute has been enacted, courts are reluctant to interpret the statute beyond its text or the judicially perceived intention of the state legislature. Court-made rules are always open to reinterpretation on a case-by-case basis. Like libel and journalist's privilege, privacy is an issue where it is necessary to know each state's law.

The elements of the four privacy causes of action discussed here largely match those suggested in the Second Restatement of Torts.[9] Tort law refers to civil wrongs between individuals. In addition to privacy and libel, tort law includes fraud, assault, trespass, and negligence. The restatement is a summary of an area of common law recommended by a panel of experts, most of them law school professors. Its purpose is to help make the laws of the various states more uniform. Judges often rely on the second restatement, which was published in 1965. It explicitly recognized the four privacy actions recommended by Prosser, not surprising since he was the chief author of the restatement. The first restatement had fueled the adoption of privacy some thirty years earlier.

● **Tort**
A legal action providing redress for wrongs between individuals. Tort law includes fraud, trespass, negligence, libel, and invasion of privacy.

DISCLOSURE OF PRIVATE FACTS

The action most people think of when privacy law is mentioned is the one preventing unreasonable disclosures of embarrassing private facts. This claim is what Brandeis and Warren had in mind in 1890. It is the lawsuit that the news media fear most in privacy—even though they almost always win. The exact name of this cause of action varies from one author to another, but the basic rules are the same everywhere.

Elements of the Cause of Action for Private Facts

When a person's private life is publicized, the person responsible for the publicity may be liable for an invasion of privacy when the private information is something that would be "highly offensive to a reasonable person" and "not of legitimate public concern."[10] Some courts also include a community standards test, which requires proof that the disclosure would outrage the community's notions of decency. A plaintiff, then, must show the following elements:

1. Publication or dissemination

2. Privacy of information

3. Highly offensive to a reasonable person

4. Not of public concern

5. Outrage to community decency

Publication or Dissemination • Normally, publication is not an issue since the appearance of a news story in the mass media is what usually triggers a lawsuit. Publication can be important for other reasons, though. The date of publication will start the clock for any statute of limitations on privacy actions. A **statute of limitations** prescribes the length of time a plaintiff has to file suit. In most states the general tort statute of limitations will be one or two years. Publication is also occasionally an issue where a privacy invasion claim is based upon previously published material. When *Penthouse* magazine decided to use a previously published Associated Press story about an obese woman who did not know she was pregnant, the magazine prevailed in part because the information had already been widely publicized.[11]

Privacy of Information • The plaintiff must show that the facts are indeed private ones. This task sounds easier than it has been in practice. If information is widely known to third parties, the courts are likely to dismiss a privacy claim when the information is obtained and reported by journalists. A leading case interpreting this principle is Sipple v. Chronicle Publishing Co.[12] Oliver Sipple became a hero in 1975 when he prevented a would-be assassin from aiming a handgun at President Gerald Ford in San Francisco. Sipple, a former Marine, sued after he was identified as gay in news stories. The court could not consider his sexual orientation a private fact since Sipple was a well-known and active

● **Statute of limitations**
A statute that specifies a limited period of time in which a plaintiff may file an action.

member of San Francisco's large gay community. Sipple had not wanted his family in another part of the country to know.

Courts appear more willing to find that facts are private in two circumstances. One is when the case involves minors. When a teenage mother charged in a newspaper story that Craig Hawkins, also a minor, was the father of her child, the South Carolina Supreme Court allowed a jury verdict for Hawkins to stand.[13] Hawkins had even granted an interview to the reporter who wrote the story. It seems that the scope of private information may be interpreted more broadly for minors. This would be consistent with the law's concern for minors in other areas, but is inconsistent with private facts cases generally.

Medical information, the second circumstance where courts may more easily find facts to be private, may be considered inherently more private than other types of information. Details of operations, including plastic surgery[14] and sex-change surgery,[15] have been determined to be private facts. The traditional legal privilege against disclosure of medical information by physicians may play a role in these and similar cases.

The Supreme Court has twice indicated that information obtained from public records and published by the media will generally not be considered private facts no matter how sensitive the information. In *Cox Broadcasting v. Cohn*,[16] a father whose teenage daughter was raped and murdered filed suit against a television station that had identified her. Identification of rape victims was banned by a Georgia statute. The father also claimed a disclosure of private facts violation. The Court did not establish an absolute rule that information taken from court records cannot be a private fact, but came close, indicating that a state must show a compelling interest to uphold such a statute or to allow a privacy action. In a key paragraph of the majority opinion, Justice Byron White noted:

> We are reluctant to embark on a course that would make public records generally available to the media but forbid their publication if offensive to the sensitivities of the supposed reasonable man. Such a rule would make it very difficult for the media to inform citizens about the public business. . . . The rule would invite timidity and self-censorship. . . .

In 1989 the Supreme Court revisited the issue of a statutory ban on identification of a rape victim. In *Florida Star v. B.J.F.*,[17] the Court reversed a trial decision awarding damages to a rape victim who was named in a newspaper story. A reporter had seen a report left on a counter in the police station and had written a verbatim account of the crime from it. The trial court determined that the newspaper, by violating the statute that prohibited publication of names of rape victims "in any instrument of mass communication," had been negligent *per se*. In other words, the judge ordered the jury to assume the newspaper was at fault. The Florida appeals court upheld the trial judge.

In reversing, the Supreme Court said that punishment for publishing information provided by the government, even if the government's disclosure was an accident, would be allowed only upon proof that it was necessary to uphold a "state interest of the highest order." The Court was troubled as well by the

fact that the statute applied only to the mass media, allowing gossipers and letter writers to disclose the same information without liability. Most scholars
have interpreted the decision as having used a compelling interest test, since
compelling interests are considered interests of the highest order. In practice,
application of a compelling interest test almost always means that government
or a plaintiff will lose.

In a different case in 1993, the Florida Court of Appeals found the statute
itself unconstitutional on its face.[18] The court held that the statute violated
both the federal and Florida constitutions. It also determined that the statute
could not be interpreted narrowly enough to make it constitutional. Also in
1993, the Georgia Court of Appeals upheld a civil damage award against a
newspaper based upon that state's statute barring identification of sexual assault victims,[19] even though police officers had disclosed the name orally to reporters. In the case, a woman who was being sexually assaulted shot and killed
an intruder. The court hinted that the statute would be found constitutional in
cases where no government records were used by the press, thereby distinguishing it from the *Florida Star* case. On appeal, the Georgia Supreme Court
reversed, holding that the woman's name was newsworthy and that newsworthiness was protected under the state and federal constitutions.[20]

Few cases are decided solely upon the privacy of information issue. In
practice, most potential plaintiffs are probably talked out of bringing suit if
their lawyers conclude that the information at issue is not private. Once the
case is filed, the media defendant is free to attempt to show that the facts were
not private, as in the *Sipple* case. The *Cox* and *Florida Star* cases make it clear
that the press may always use public records as a defense.

Highly Offensive to a Reasonable Person • The courts have been unable to define precisely what sorts of disclosures would be highly offensive to a reasonable person. Even Prosser was forced to rely on examples rather than a formal
definition.[21] The sorts of examples that are usually offered include a person's
sex life or physical characteristics. In one of the earliest cases, *Barber v. Time,*[22]
the Missouri Supreme Court determined that *Time* magazine violated the privacy of a woman who was undergoing treatment for an overeating disorder
when it published a story that portrayed her as a glutton. The story was accompanied by a photograph of her lying in a hospital bed. The plaintiff had objected to having a photo taken. The court adopted the restatement's view that
liability was allowed

> [I]f the defendant's conduct was such that he should have realized that it
> would be offensive to a person of ordinary sensibilities. It is only where
> the intrusion goes beyond the limits of decency that liability accrues.

In *Barber,* it was easy to decide that the plaintiff would have been offended because she had said so to a reporter and photographer. The court questioned the
news judgment of *Time,* suggesting that the story would have been just as newsworthy if it had been run without the plaintiff's name. When a trial judge tried
the same thing in the 1980s, a court of appeals reversed and scolded the judge:

Plaintiff's proposed rule—that a published report of embarrassing but newsworthy private facts is actionable unless the report omits the name of its subject—would overhaul journalism as we know it. The press could not without consent reveal the name of anyone other than a public official or a public figure.[23]

A peculiar case involving a man who had been famous as a genius and prodigy while a teenager is widely considered the leading case on what material might be highly offensive. In *Sidis v. F-R Publishing Corp.*,[24] the U.S. Court of Appeals for the Second Circuit denied the plaintiff's privacy claim for an article in *The New Yorker.* A reporter had looked up William Sidis to see what had become of him more than twenty years after he received extensive coverage for his intellectual exploits. The reporter found Sidis working as a clerk and living in a shabby room in a poor part of Boston. The reporter wrote a sympathetic article about the eccentric genius who had sought solitude and anonymity. The court indicated that the story would likely have been offensive to a reasonable person, but determined that Sidis was a "public person" by virtue of his past publicity. As a result, an examination of his present private life to compare it with his prior public one was not a privacy violation because ". . . the answer to whether or not he had fulfilled his early promise, was still a matter of public concern." The *Sidis* court in addition posed the test requiring that a disclosure must outrage the community and also adopted an expansive defense for newsworthy information.

For journalists, unfortunately, the *Sidis* case is more useful for explaining one type of information that will be considered neither private nor highly offensive if disclosed than it is for identifying what sorts of disclosures might lead to lawsuits. Perhaps because of this vagueness, successful private facts lawsuits have been scant since the mid-1960s. Either plaintiffs cannot prove all the required elements of the cause of action, or, more likely, one of the strong defenses available to the media proves applicable. The natural debate over the value of privacy interests and the press's role of informing the public has largely been decided in favor of the press. The highest courts in two states, North Carolina and Oregon, have explicitly rejected a private facts cause of action in recent years.[25] New York's highest court has repeatedly refused to recognize any common law privacy actions, including private facts;[26] it has left privacy to the legislature, which has created a claim only for appropriation.

Not of Public Concern • The restatement calls for the plaintiff to prove that the private information is not a matter of public concern. This approach puts a plaintiff in the difficult position of having to prove a negative—that there cannot be any public value in the material published. In practice, the analysis is often reversed, with media defendants producing evidence to establish that a particular story is newsworthy.

A court is free to decide this question based solely upon the evidence presented by a plaintiff. When the media coverage that led to a lawsuit involves any of the most traditional types of news, judges may assume that the story covered a matter of public concern. Stories about crime, official corruption, the qualifications of persons for public office, and even the habits of celebrities are so common and accepted in journalism circles that they are usually condoned if not approved by the judiciary.

Outrage to Community Decency • In Sidis, the court noted that "revelations may be so intimate and so unwarranted . . . as to outrage the community's notions of decency." Analysis of a community's standard of decency appears to be slightly different from analysis of what would offend a reasonable person. In *Fry v. Ionia Sentinel-Standard*,[27] Peggy Jo Fry surely was reasonably offended when the local newspaper published her name and her children's names in a story about the death by fire of her husband and his lover in a lakeside cabin. The court asserted that the story was not offensive to a reasonable person, but the person the court had in mind was a newspaper reader who would be familiar with rather than outraged by such coverage. A community standards rather than an individual offensiveness test appears to have been applied.

Virgil v. Time, Inc.[28] is probably the most cited case on the outrage issue. *Sports Illustrated* ran a personality profile on Mike Virgil, who was well-known as a body surfer in part of California. Virgil was boastful and his behavior was often strange, including eating spiders and claiming to have bitten someone's cheek off. When he disliked the article, he sued for private facts. The magazine claimed a newsworthiness defense, but the appeals court would agree only that the topic of surfing, not Virgil, was newsworthy. The court did decide that the newsworthiness defense was required by the First Amendment. Whether personal details of weird behavior were newsworthy should be decided by a jury, the court said, and sent the case back for trial with the following advice:

> The line is to be drawn when the publicity ceases to be the giving of information to which the public is entitled, and becomes a morbid and sensational prying into private lives for its own sake, which a reasonable member of the public, with decent standards, would say he had no concern. . . ."

It is easy to conclude that the court disliked the article almost as much as Mike Virgil did. But the standard it announced is open-ended. When the case returned to the district court, the judge issued summary judgment against Virgil using the standard called for by the appeals court. The judge argued that the personal details were "included as a legitimate journalistic attempt to explain Virgil's extremely daring and dangerous style of body surfing. . . ."[29] No jury ever heard the case.

Working journalists may take comfort in knowing that types of news coverage acceptable to audience members in the community in the past will normally be immune to a claim that they outrage the community. Standard journalism practices also define, although vaguely, the boundaries that should not be crossed. In one notorious case, a television station passed the line of community outrage. It broadcast videotape of the skull of a six-year-old who had been abducted and killed. In deciding to air the tape, the news director overrode objections from everyone in the newsroom. Among the at-home viewers was the family. In court, however, the child's parents were not able to prevail on privacy grounds because the crime story was newsworthy. They were, however, allowed to prevail on the independent tort of "outrage," which punishes extreme and outrageous conduct.[30] The tort is similar to infliction of emotional distress.

Defenses against the Action for Private Facts

Although virtually all of the scholarly writings focus on newsworthiness as the primary defense to a private facts lawsuit, the decided cases indicate that at least five distinct arguments may be used as defenses. The most important continues to be newsworthiness. Four additional defenses may also be available: the plaintiff consented to the disclosure of the information, the material obtained by the media was in plain view, the information concerned a public official or public figure, and the material was taken from a public record or official proceeding. The defense also always has the option of arguing that the facts were known to others and were no longer private.

● **Newsworthiness**
A defense that prevents privacy plaintiffs from winning cases when traditional standards of journalistic judgment have been used in publishing.

Newsworthiness • The defense of **newsworthiness** was proposed by Brandeis and Warren in 1890 and appears to have been universally adopted by states recognizing the private facts action. Application of the defense normally calls for a review of the journalistic values that led to publication of the story. The news media have for the most part been able to persuade the courts to accept their standards of what is newsworthy. If the story fits within one of the traditional areas of news coverage or matches one of the traditional news values, a finding of newsworthiness is almost automatic. In *Sanchez Duran v. The Detroit News, Inc.*,[31] the plaintiff was a former Colombian judge who had resigned after presiding over the indictment of a drug lord and receiving death threats. She had subsequently moved to Detroit, where she shunned publicity. She had not, however, kept her identity completely secret. After the newspaper published an article exposing her presence in Detroit, she brought multiple claims, including private facts. She reasonably suspected the death threats from Colombia might follow her to Detroit. The court effectively extended the newsworthiness defense by announcing that *past* news coverage served as proof that her story was "a matter of public record."

Since almost every kind of news coverage has been deemed newsworthy, it is perhaps more useful to look at some rare cases where stories were not found to be newsworthy. In one case, a trade publication published a letter of reprimand taken from the personnel file of the plaintiff. The letter had been sent anonymously. It accused the plaintiff, a research pathologist, of professional misconduct. A jury found that the public interest in the plaintiff's cancer research was offset by the expectation of privacy of personnel files. In other words, the story was not quite newsworthy enough to fit the defense.[32]

In another case, a newspaper's story that featured a self-styled psychic was declared not newsworthy. The court considered the story less important than traditional crime or accident stories; instead the court emphasized that the story dealt mainly with the plaintiff's private business concerns and was not something the public was "validly" interested in.[33] This type of judicial evaluation is rare, and it may be best to look at the case as an isolated example.

A continuing problem in assessing newsworthiness has been follow-up stories. Plaintiffs have claimed that their stories should no longer be considered newsworthy after a large amount of time has passed. Usually, this passage of time argument fails. The leading case again is *Sidis v. F-R Publishing Corp.,*[34] in which William Sidis was considered newsworthy even though he had avoided the public eye for twenty years. When the person or event was famous or infamous, the courts will usually conclude that the story remains newsworthy.[35]

Consent • Cases decided on the basis of **consent** are fairly rare. This is not surprising, since anyone who consented to disclosure of facts would be unlikely to sue in the first place. Consent operates directly as a defense. All the defendant needs to show is that the plaintiff consented and that the material publicized was covered by the consent. Although the *Virgil v. Sports Illustrated* case discussed above was decided on newsworthiness grounds, Virgil's consent undoubtedly influenced the court's analysis. Virgil had consented to interviews, cooperated by providing material, and spent considerable time with the reporter.

In general, anyone who speaks with a reporter has consented to publication of information obtained in the interview. Unless a third person is present, this kind of oral consent may be difficult to prove. When a news organization publishes a news story with quotations attributed to the plaintiff, the news organization is in effect asserting that the plaintiff consented to an interview. Quotes are fairly good evidence that the plaintiff talked voluntarily with a reporter, unless, of course, the comments were obtained by covert means, which would likely fall under intrusion on seclusion. The burden of proof to show that limits were placed on the consent is usually on the plaintiff. When Jerry Falwell sued for privacy, libel, and copyright infringement because an interview a freelance writer conducted with him appeared in *Penthouse* magazine, he lost because he had failed to limit his consent to specific publications.[36]

Formal, written consent is seldom an issue in private facts cases because these cases most often arise from routine news-gathering situations. The same is true in false light and intrusion privacy cases. In contrast, formal consent is sometimes the only possible defense in appropriation and right of publicity cases. If written consent is sought, it should specify the information to be obtained, the intended use of the information, and any limitations agreed to by the parties. News organizations, advertising agencies, public relations firms, and other media-related organizations often use standard consent forms. The forms are usually written by lawyers and can be difficult to understand. Both the person giving consent to publication of information and the person obtaining the information must be sure that they understand the language of the form. Ambiguity in the form will normally be interpreted against the party that drafted the form.[37]

Plain View • This defense operates on a simple premise: whatever occurs in a public place is fair game for use by whoever observes it. The term **plain view** seldom appears in the written court opinions. It has been developed extensively in criminal law, however, where it is said that a police search that finds evidence

● **Consent**
In privacy law, consent generally refers to an explicit agreement between an individual and a representative of the media. Consent is occasionally inferred when public officials or public figures have been interviewed for news stories.

● **Plain view**
A defense that provides that anything that could have been seen or heard from a public place, or a private place with consent, may be freely reported on.

of criminal activity lying in plain view does not violate a defendant's Fourth Amendment right against unreasonable searches and seizures.[38]

Although the court in *Cape Publications v. Bridges*[39] appeared to decide the case on newsworthiness grounds, it seems to have been influenced by plain view notions. A woman who was held at gunpoint and forced to remove her clothes escaped when police stormed her apartment building. Accompanied by a police officer, she rushed into the street, clutching a dish towel to cover herself. The newspaper published one of the least revealing photos taken. It is important that the photographed event occurred in a public place. In reaching its decision, the court compared the case to those involving disasters or accidents, events that normally occur in plain view. Another plain view case was *McNamara v. Freedom Newspapers, Inc.*,[40] where a photograph of the plaintiff with his genitals exposed was published. Since he was a voluntary spectator at a public event, a high school soccer match, his private facts claim failed.

The heart of the defense was summarized in a recent California case. Senior citizen surfer Mickey Dora sued over a documentary, "The Legends of Malibu." The program contained video footage of Dora surfing and also included recorded interviews with him. Referring to the surfing video, the court said, "One's voluntary action in a public place waives one's right of privacy. . . ."[41] Accident and crime victims have not voluntarily become victims, but they have typically voluntarily placed themselves in a public area,[42] making the plain view defense applicable.

Public Official/Public Figure • No separate defense has been created to protect the media when they report on public officials and public figures. When public officials and public figures are plaintiffs in private facts cases, however, the courts have all but borrowed the First Amendment defense from libel law. In privacy law, the public status of a plaintiff relates directly to the newsworthiness defense. The basic idea is similar to the analysis of public officials and public figures developed in libel law. A person who has accepted public office or sought public notoriety will almost always be a legitimate subject of public concern and therefore considered newsworthy for private facts cases. In other words, many courts have assumed newsworthiness when public officials or public figures sue, but the newsworthiness defense must be established by the media when a private person sues.

The *Dora* case referred to above also includes this element. Mickey Dora had gained notoriety as a surfer in the 1950s, when the lifestyle associated with surfing was just starting to develop, but by the time of the documentary, he had avoided publicity for twenty years. The court indicated, however, that he remained a "public personage" by the "force of circumstances." He was part of history.

A **public figure** defense can be applied when a defendant is able to show that a person was the subject of considerable publicity in the past or in the present. This would include having been caught up in an event of historical importance.[43] People who otherwise might be considered private may be treated as public and newsworthy figures if they get close enough to another person who is the subject of extensive publicity.[44] The burden of proof to establish

● **Public figure**
A person who has either achieved general fame or who has actively sought notoriety; the definition is the same in privacy law as in libel law.

public figure status is on the defendant. Once that is established, however, a newsworthiness decision for the defense is almost automatic.

Public Record/Public Proceeding • It is virtually impossible for a private facts plaintiff to win if the publicized information came from **public records** held by government or from a **public meeting** of a governmental body. In general, the courts assume that coverage of the public's business as revealed in government documents is either newsworthy in itself or inherently public in any event. The leading case is the Supreme Court's *Cox Broadcasting v. Cohn*,[45] discussed earlier. The Sixth Circuit has interpreted the case as creating a First Amendment privilege to report on public records and court proceedings.[46] Under that privilege, there can never be liability for truthful information obtained from formal public sources.

Other courts describe the privilege as qualified rather than absolute, but apply it as if it were absolute anyway.[47] The common law privilege to report on official public matters is also very strong and virtually automatic. In a 1992 case, *Jenkins v. Bolla*,[48] the news stories drew upon criminal records dating to the 1940s. The court said that "a public record can fade into a private fact," but not when the story presented in the record remains of public concern.

INTRUSION UPON SECLUSION

Trespass is the principle underlying the privacy action for intrusion upon seclusion. The claim protects individuals against unconsented and offensive entries into private space. Since the action is based upon the way news is gathered rather than upon the information the news contains, it is possible for a plaintiff to bring a lawsuit without anything having ever been published. It is likely, though, that plaintiffs will not know of an intrusion until the news that was obtained as a result of the intrusion is published. Once material has been published, a plaintiff may claim damages for distress caused by publication as well as for distress caused by the intrusion itself.

Intrusion protects one's right of spatial privacy. It applies to places. Most of the decided cases have involved claims that a journalist invaded the sanctity of a home or office. A plaintiff is generally required to prove only two elements to make an initial case for intrusion. The plaintiff must show that the place intruded upon was one where the plaintiff had a "reasonable expectation" of spatial privacy. In other words, the plaintiff must prove that the area was a private place. Then the plaintiff must also show that an act of intrusion occurred.[49]

Three major defenses are available: consent or permission, plain view, and newsworthiness. Newsworthiness or good motives are less relevant to this action. The public or private status of the plaintiff is also of less importance.

Early cases indicated that nonphysical intrusions could be actionable. These included looking through windows, examining bank accounts, and prying in general. The only modern cases allowing an action for nonphysical intrusions appear to be those involving surreptitious recording by telephone or wiretapping.[50] Many states make it illegal for one party to a telephone

- **Public record**
  Any record generated by a government body. The term includes but is not limited to records specified in freedom of information statutes.

- **Public meeting**
  A gathering of a quorum of a public body, such as a city council, at which government business may be conducted.

- **Trespass**
  Entering onto or affecting the property of another person without permission.

conversation to record the conversation without the consent of the other party. Despite the efforts of plaintiffs, the federal wiretap law has not been applied to reporters.[51] It is assumed that when parties enter into telephone conversations, they recognize the risk that anything they say may be repeated.

The Federal Communications Commission sets various requirements regarding use of police and fire broadcasts. It also prohibits private use of radio devices to listen to conversations without consent. Telephone callers whose comments will be aired by broadcasters must be informed and give consent. In general, interception of the communications of other parties when the message is in any electronic form is prohibited.[52] The prohibition extends to digital and satellite communications as well as to those by telephone. A phone call initiated by a reporter is, of course, not an interception. The rationale behind the recording and interception rules is somewhat different from the reasoning in the common law privacy intrusion claim, however. In intrusion, the claim is for solitude, while in recording cases the claim typically is that the plaintiff was deceived by the reporter or other person doing the recording.[53]

Private Place

An individual must normally have control over a space for it to be considered a private place for intrusion claims. It is not enough to argue that a journalist entered a nonpublic place. In *Barger v. Courier-Journal*, the family of a man who was photographed as he was dying was not allowed to make a claim based upon trespass or intrusion. The man was the victim of a shooting rampage by a fellow employee, and his photograph was taken at his workplace.[54]

Dietemann v. Time, Inc.[55] is considered the leading intrusion case, although the intrusion occurred as a result of misrepresentation or fraud. A reporter and photographer for *Life* magazine gained access to the home of a person who practiced healing with clay, minerals, and herbs, described by the court as "simple quackery." The journalists pretended to have been referred by friends. They took photographs without consent or knowledge and also relayed conversations through a radio device to law enforcement officers outside. The court recognized that "one who invites another to his home or office takes the risk that the visitor may not be what he seems. . . . But he does not and should not be required to take the risk that what is heard and seen will be transmitted by photograph or recording. . . ." The court determined that the First Amendment offered no defense against "calculated misdeeds." The case really turns on the misrepesentation rather than the entry, however, and is perhaps better viewed as an example of journalists exceeding consent than as intrusion.

Act of Intrusion

Classic intrusions are difficult to find in the reported cases. The clearest examples are found in "ambush" journalism. When CBS went into a fancy restaurant with lights on and cameras running, the restaurant was allowed to pursue a trespass claim.[56] The patrons, had they desired, could have likely pursued an intrusion claim.

That journalists have received the products of an intrusion is normally not sufficient to allow an action against them. If, for example, stolen documents are delivered to a newsroom, liability for intrusion will be allowed only if reporters instigated the intrusion or knew the material was stolen.[57] When newspapers received copies of recordings of conversations made without consent, however, one court indicated that a trial on the issue based on violation of federal statutes might be appropriate.[58] It mattered that reporters knew the people recorded had not consented.

Persistence by reporters attempting to gather news, even if they repeatedly telephone, drive by a person's home, and follow the person, usually does not rise to the level of an act of intrusion.[59] But full-time harassment can.

Photographer Ron Galella made a career out of following Jacqueline Onassis. His news-gathering rights were limited after Onassis demonstrated that his behavior was intrusive, offensive, and emotionally draining for her personally and for her family. Galella would pop out of bushes, appear around corners, and finagle his way into restaurants and hotels to get his photos. In court, Onassis was able to get a restraining order requiring Galella to photograph from a distance.[60] He was later found in contempt of court for repeatedly violating the order.[61] In framing its order, the court emphasized how emotionally disturbing Galella's behavior had been to Onassis. The case in effect recognized that people carry a small zone of privacy with them wherever they go. Today, though, a case such as this would more likely be brought under an infliction of emotional distress claim than under intrusion.

Consent and Permission

When people invite a reporter into their home or office, they have consented to reporting about their private space. Anything heard or, more important, seen is fair game for publication. The person interviewed usually recognizes that any documents or objects left in view may be reported upon. Many reporters become expert at reading documents upside down, a practice that is within the scope of consent, although it annoys sources if noticed. Consent is exceeded only if the reporter takes extra steps such as looking in desk or file drawers when the source leaves the room momentarily.

Technically, consent may be given only by the person who has the right to control access to the property. It is sometimes said that reporters who accompany police to crime scenes have received consent. The argument is that official actions involving the police or fire departments create an implied consent on the part of a property owner. But the person who controls the property can apparently object to the entry of newspeople if he or she is on hand.[62] When an official such as a police officer or safety inspector has apparent authority to allow entry, the cases usually allow the permission to serve as a defense, based upon the customs and practices that have developed between officials and journalists. The burden to establish the custom and practice will likely fall on the media defendant.[63] In one case, the court indicated that accompanying police on a raid would serve as a partial defense, a factor mitigating the offensiveness of the entry.[64]

Plain View

The plain view principle applies most strongly in intrusion cases. Anything that can be seen in or from a public place can be reported upon because no extra steps are necessary to obtain the information. The analysis is more complicated if extraordinary means are used to obtain information. The courts have said that the use of telephoto lenses to take photographs through an open window is allowed under this analysis.[65] The rationale appears to be that anyone could have seen the events that were photographed. Flyover reporting from helicopters, popular with the supermarket tabloids, apparently falls within this line of analysis since no cases have yet been reported against these often-sued media.

Remote sensing devices, satellite photographs, and eavesdropping equipment raise a different issue, however. The courts have not yet had occasion to address the use of high technology to go through or beyond walls and closed windows. The argument for imposing liability is that any information obtained in this fashion would not have been physically detectable or observable by others using only their senses. The argument against imposing liability is that sophisticated spying equipment is just an extension of the senses as telephoto lenses are.

State laws regulating the recording of private conversations are also apparently limited by the plain view analysis. If the conversation occurred where anyone might have heard it, the participants would appear to have no reasonable expectation of privacy under any circumstances, no matter how strictly the state statute was written.[66]

Newsworthiness

The *Dietemann* case argues that newsworthiness should not be a defense against bad behavior. It has nevertheless been applied as a defense in some cases.[67] The reported cases are almost all from trial-level courts, however, and the strength of the defense as precedent must be doubted. When the intrusion is on purely private property, such as a home or individual office, a newsworthiness defense is weakest.[68] When the intrusion occurs in a privately owned but generally accessible place, the defense will likely be rather strong.[69]

PORTRAYAL IN A FALSE LIGHT

Preventing individuals from being publicized in an erroneous and offensive fashion is the principle at the heart of the common law action of invasion of privacy for portrayal in a false light, according to the restatement. The similarity to libel is obvious, and the action and its defenses are almost identical to those in libel.

The primary differences between false light and libel are that the publicity complained of need not be defamatory, only "highly offensive to a reasonable person,"[70] and the harm to be redressed is based on personal or emotional distress stemming from the publicity rather than on damage to reputation. In outlining the cause of action in 1960, William Prosser clearly envisioned an action that was an alternative to libel rather than something of a twin. As a practical matter, however, most false light litigation involves publicity that the plaintiff also considers libelous, and it is common to find both claims fused in the same lawsuit. Courts will not allow recovery for both in the same suit, however. Assuming that both harm to reputation in libel and harm to emotional well-being are proved, the plaintiff will have to choose.

Another difference between most false light and libel cases is that successful false light cases almost always are based on a story where the plaintiff was "portrayed," often visually, in an inaccurate and embarrassing situation. In these cases, the falsehood is usually implied rather than explicit. It must be interpreted by the audience. By comparison, an explicit factual assertion, if false, is better suited to a libel action. One of the early false light cases turned on the misinterpretation caused by a news use of a photograph. In *Gill v. Curtis Publishing Co.,*[71] a photo of an affectionate, long-married couple, taken in a public place, was used to accompany an article about the dangers of love at first sight. The article said the attraction was based entirely on sex. The court agreed that the couple would find the portrayal humiliating.

False light is probably the most controversial and unpredictable of the common law privacy actions.[72] A number of state courts have refused to recognize the cause of action,[73] usually because they consider it duplicative of libel or unnecessary in general. Courts in Minnesota, Mississippi, Missouri, North Carolina, Ohio, and Texas have reached this conclusion. New York courts have not adopted the cause of action, insisting that creation of privacy rights is a matter for the legislature. Thus, familiarity with state law is essential.

Knowing state false light law is also important because the tests and standards vary widely among those states that have recognized the action. The major debate has been over the application of **fault** standards following the Supreme Court opinion in *Gertz v. Robert Welch, Inc.*[74] That decision requires plaintiffs to prove fault, usually negligence or actual malice depending upon whether the plaintiff is a private or public person,[75] to win a libel suit. The restatement had said that a plaintiff must show that a defendant either knew the publicity was false or acted with reckless disregard; this is the actual malice requirement of libel law. Following *Gertz,* though, some states have determined that a private figure need only prove negligence in false light cases.[76] A number of others apply an actual malice fault standard when publicity is considered newsworthy.

The Supreme Court has decided two cases involving false light claims. One of those cases, *Time, Inc. v. Hill,*[77] involved a family that had been held hostage by escaped convicts. The event inspired a play, which became the subject of a *Life* magazine story. The story portrayed the family as heroic in the face of atrocious mistreatment by the convicts, which was wrong. The U.S. Supreme Court held that the plaintiffs must prove actual malice because they were caught up in a newsworthy event.

In the second case, *Cantrell v. Forest City Publishing Co.,*[78] the Court held that proof of intentional falsification by a reporter was sufficient to

● **Fault**
In tort law, fault usually refers to some type of negligence. When proof of fault is required, a plaintiff must show at least negligence on the part of a defendant.

establish actual malice. A writer for the Cleveland *Plain Dealer* had purported to interview the widow of a man who had died months earlier in a bridge collapse. Instead, the reporter talked with her children, then wrote a story "quoting" her. The Court determined that the bridge story was still newsworthy, bringing the actual malice test into play.

As a result of the *Gertz* and *Hill* cases, false light, like libel, is now a hybrid tort with both common law and constitutional elements. It is uncertain whether *Hill's* newsworthiness rule survives the more-recent *Gertz* case and its emphasis on public or private figure status, however.

The elements of the cause of action, then, include (1) a false portrayal, (2) that is offensive to a reasonable person, (3) that causes emotional or other damage, and (4) that was caused by the fault, measured by negligence or actual malice, of the defendant. Proof of "mass" publication is also required in most states, but is seldom an issue since reported cases are brought against media defendants who always hope to publish or broadcast to a vast audience.

The defenses include most of those available in libel actions: truth, opinion and fair comment, qualified privilege, and consent. Newsworthiness can be argued to raise the burden of proof to actual malice, as in the *Hill* case. A defense based on a plain view argument may also sometimes be useful.
The discussion of the libel defenses in Chapter 2 should be reviewed since the actions have become so similar. Discussion of the defenses here will review only those aspects specific to false light claims.

False Portrayal/Offensive to a Reasonable Person

Proof of a false portrayal appears to follow two lines of analysis. The first concerns reports that are somehow distorted. The second concerns claims arising from works of fiction or from other creative works.

Distortion is well illustrated by the case of Linda Duncan, who was walking down a Washington, D.C., sidewalk when a live WJLA-TV camera showed her passing by. Duncan would normally have no complaint since she was in plain view. In a later broadcast, though, the station aired the footage of Duncan while introducing a story on "[T]he twenty million Americans who have herpes. . . ."[79] Duncan argued that viewers would conclude she had the disease. The case apparently never went to trial after the court, suggesting the station should be more careful in its news-gathering methods, said that the issue of audience interpretation should be left to a jury.

The *Duncan* case, along with the *Gill* case discussed earlier, are virtual blueprints for what journalists should not do. Almost all of the successful distortion cases result from the media inaccurately joining words and pictures.

Not all mismatching of words and photos will result in liability, though. In *Arrington v. New York Times,* the plaintiff could not show that the portrayal would be inaccurately interpreted by the audience. When a middle-class African American was used to illustrate a *New York Times Magazine* cover story about upwardly mobile African Americans, the court found little merit in the plaintiff's claim that readers would associate him with persons mentioned in the article who had turned their backs on African Americans who were less well-off.[80]

A similar fate befell actress Robyn Douglass's claim against *Hustler* magazine when it published unauthorized nude photos of her with another woman. Douglass claimed that it was humiliating to be portrayed as a woman who would appear nude in *Hustler*. The court found the claim weak, in part because she had willingly appeared nude in print on many other occasions.[81] *Hustler*'s practice of using unauthorized photographs cost the magazine in *Braun v. Flynt*, however, when it failed to obtain consent from a woman whose photo was run along with a distorted caption that poked fun at her.[82] Like Douglas, Braun argued that simply appearing in the magazine placed her in a false light as an unchaste woman, and the jury agreed.

Fictionalized accounts are analyzed differently. The two major U.S. Supreme Court cases on false light both involved claims of fictionalization. In *Time, Inc. v. Hill*,[83] the plaintiff complained about a magazine story describing how he and his family were held hostage by escaped convicts. The authors were accused of having created incidents of violence and verbal sexual assault. Hill also appeared to complain that he was shown as more heroic than he actually was. The incident became the basis of a play and two motion pictures. The Court opinion was devoted to analysis of the fault issue, so the falsity of the portrayal was not addressed. The Court appeared to accept the notion that false nondefamatory portrayals could be actionable, however.

In the second case, *Cantrell v. Forest City Publishing Co.*,[84] the plaintiff was able to prove that a published "interview" with her was fictional because she never met the reporter. In addition, the newspaper story exaggerated the plight of the plaintiff and her children, left to fend for themselves after her husband died in a bridge collapse. The case was brought for false light because it made them appear ridiculous and pathetic, causing mental distress and personal shame.

Other successful fictionalization cases have occurred in two situations. In one, a creative work uses a person's actual name and portrays the character in an accurate way.[85] It would seem obvious that the author of an account deemed fictional should be careful not to use real people in the work. In the second, although a fictional name is used, the description may be precise enough to allow audience members to identify an individual, creating the false light portrayal.[86] Film and broadcast docudramas present special false light dangers because they are typically based on historical material, but must by necessity use fictional dialogue. On occasion, docudramas also find it necessary to create events. The issue has arisen infrequently, but the courts appear willing to allow some artistic license in these circumstances as long as the portrayals are reasonable interpretations and would not be offensive.[87] Where the falsehood complained of is clearly fiction and no reasonable person could believe it, the plaintiff will be unable to establish a false interpretation of fact.[88]

The case of a ninety-seven-year-old woman who was portrayed as being forced to quit her newspaper sales and delivery work after becoming pregnant stretches the concept of what an audience might believe. An appeals court upheld a jury verdict imposing both compensatory and punitive damages against the defendant, a supermarket tabloid. The paper had taken a photograph of the plaintiff from its files and labeled her a "pregnant granny." The paper assumed that she had died since she had been very old when her photograph had originally appeared. On appeal, the defense argued that no reasonable person could believe the story, which the paper freely admitted was pure fiction. The court agreed that the pregnancy claim was dubious, but that related portrayals about sexual activity and quitting work were capable of belief and had been spread throughout the community.[89] The U.S. Supreme Court refused to review the case. In its brief to the Court, the newspaper argued that it was simply being punished for being an unpopular publication.

While the element of inaccuracy or falsity has been addressed frequently by the courts, the offensiveness of a portrayal has seldom been a major issue in the reported cases. Once the plaintiff proves that the portrayal is false, the issue of offensiveness will usually be for a jury to decide. In all likelihood, most defendants probably settle before trial if their legal defenses fail and a plaintiff proves falsity. In general, it would be reasonable to expect that normal people are offended if they are inaccurately portrayed in the mass media, and equally reasonable to expect that most juries would agree. A mere inaccurate quotation, or even a debatable portrayal as in the *Arrington* case, likely will not be enough to prove a portrayal offensive. The portrayal must be understood by the audience as the plaintiff claims it was understood. Where reasonable minds may differ, there is little basis for a lawsuit. In one case, plaintiffs argued that they were placed in a false light when a photo taken of them at a greyhound track was used in an advertising brochure. They apparently thought others would wrongly think they had endorsed the brochure. The court could not find portraying someone as a customer at a racetrack offensive.[90] A substantially accurate historical account that portrays a person as less honorable than they later became also is unlikely to be considered offensive.[91]

Fault

Fault analysis in false light cases tracks fault analysis in libel cases. Many of the successful cases involve situations where the defendant either knew the portrayals were false, as in the "pregnant granny" and *Cantrell* cases, or acted recklessly by not noticing how unflatteringly a portrayal would be interpreted by the audience, as in the *Duncan* and *Braun* cases. The Arizona Supreme Court has declared that public officers may never bring false light claims on any fault standard.[92] The best advice here is to practice good journalism. Do not fabricate stories. When using visuals, always be sure that people portrayed are shown for what they really are.

● **Negligence**
Injury or harm resulting from a failure by a defendant to behave as a reasonable person would have behaved under similar circumstances.

Proof of **negligence** may operate a bit differently in false light cases. The general standard of care requires proof of a failure to act as a reasonable person would have acted under similar circumstances. In libel, that means proof that the reporter failed to gather the story in a fairly diligent fashion. In false light, since the plaintiff's argument often is that the portrayal was embarrassing, it may be sufficient for a private-figure plaintiff to convince a jury that a reasonable person would have noticed the undesirable false implication.[93]

The majority of states appear to adhere to the restatement view that proof of actual malice is necessary regardless of the plaintiff's status as a private or public figure. Since the restatement was drafted before *Gertz*, the strength of this protection must be doubted. False light cases rarely reach the state supreme courts, but when they do, those courts might consider *Gertz* controlling and apply actual malice only to public-figure and public-official plaintiffs.

Truth and Consent

The most potent defenses are either that the portrayals complained of are accurate or, if inaccurate, that the plaintiff consented to the portrayal. What often happens is that a person, having agreed to an interview, dislikes the result when the story is printed or broadcast. That was the situation in *Morganroth v. Whitall*.[94] Shila Morganroth objected to her portrayal in the *Detroit News* as a person who dressed suggestively, used a blowtorch to style hair, and performed hair styling on dogs. The Michigan Court of Appeals found the story true. Although it did not address consent, the court apparently was influenced by evidence that the plaintiff acted flamboyantly during the interview and photo session. The court applied the usual test for a truth defense, substantial truth. The defendant is not required to prove that everything in a story is correct—only that the basic claims are accurate.

When Mike Virgil, the surfer whose case was discussed under private facts, complained that the *Sports Illustrated* story made him look like a buffoon, his voluntary cooperation with the reporter allowed a consent argument. In cases such as *Morganroth* and *Virgil,* the courts appear to recognize that feature stories are more interpretive and creative than traditional news stories, and allowance is made for the writer's impressions as long as they are based upon direct observation during an interview. Consent therefore includes permission to characterize appearance, mannerisms, and surroundings of people reported upon.

Opinion and Fair Comment

The opinion and fair comment defenses are seldom raised in false light cases, but when they are, they operate just as they do in libel. The information must be understood by reasonable members of the audience as an assertion of opinion or evaluation. If a portrayal was intended as commentary but was understood by the audience as a fact, the defense will not apply. Obvious parody will be protected under this defense,[95] although the defense may not apply when the assertions go beyond comment and become abusive.[96]

Qualified Privilege

The qualified privileges available in libel for public records and official proceedings should apply just the same in false light cases.[97] In most states, when a defendant can show that a report described a public meeting or proceeding, was based upon a public record, or concerned a matter in the public interest that might affect people, qualified privilege raises the burden of proof from negligence to actual malice for private figures. When the claim is that the portrayal was taken from a meeting, proceeding, or record, the defense should prevail as long as the media portrayal is a substantially accurate depiction of the proceeding or an accurate summary of the document. Only a few cases address this issue. In most cases involving stories based upon official proceedings or public records, the plantiff cannot establish falsity in the first place, and the suit will end there.

A qualified privilege to report upon matters in the public interest operates very differently from a meeting or records privilege. Here the key question is whether the subject of the portrayal was one that might have an effect on the public. Once a court decides that a subject is a matter in the public interest, negligent inaccuracies in news coverage will be excused.

Plain View

In general, plaintiffs cannot complain if they are photographed or reported upon when they were in a place where anyone could have seen them, as long as the report contains no distortion.[98] In one case, plaintiffs were revelers in a Mardi Gras parade on a city street when they were filmed. When the footage later appeared in a soft-core sex movie, the court would not allow a false light action.[99]

APPROPRIATION AND THE RIGHT OF PUBLICITY

The tort of appropriation for commercial purposes is the simplest of the four original common law actions. It was also the first to be recognized either by statute or by court decision. The New York legislature in 1903 was the first to create a right against appropriation.[100] The legislature was reacting to a court's refusal to grant relief in a case where the photograph of a woman who was a private figure had been used in an advertisement for flour.[101] Georgia adopted appropriation as a common law action in 1905 in a case where a photograph of a man who was a private figure had been used in insurance advertising.[102]

As originally proposed by Brandeis and Warren, and as interpreted by courts in the earliest cases, the action was designed to protect the integrity of one's identity by preventing others from using it for their own financial gain. The rationale was that ordinary people would be mortified and distressed by finding themselves used to advance the financial interests of others. Preventing appropriation was seen as a personal right. Like other privacy actions, appropriation varies somewhat from state to state, so familiarity with the local statute or common law is necessary. Appropriation is the most widely accepted of the privacy torts, apparently being recognized in almost every state where the issue has arisen. Two exceptions are Texas and Virginia. A federal court in Texas determined that Texas has not recognized the action, and Virginia's statute protects only names and likenesses with monetary value.

The action as originally proposed obviously did not anticipate the vast amount of celebrity endorsement that would develop in the last half of this century. Beginning in the 1950s, courts developed a separate common law action, the right of publicity.[103] This action is designed to protect the value of identity, rather than to protect peace of mind, and has been applied almost exclusively to celebrities and other public figures.[104] The right of publicity has been adopted in many states, both by statute and by common law. Only about half of the state supreme courts have heard right of publicity cases, however. Usually, the right of publicity has been adopted, but media personnel would be wise to find out if the cause of action has been adopted in their states. The rules vary widely in those states that already recognize the action in any event, so checking on each state's law is important.

Appropriation and right of publicity are often treated as if they were identical because each seeks to prevent unauthorized commercial uses of identity, but there are important differences. The private action for appropriation does not survive death, while in most states a right of publicity is considered a form of property right that can be transferred while a person is alive and remains descendible after death.[105] In appropriation, damages are typically based upon the intangible personal suffering of the plaintiff,[106] although the value of the commercial use may also be claimed. Punitive damages are rare. By comparison, in publicity cases the damages are based upon the value of the use. The rationale for recovering damages is more like that in contract law—the plaintiff will be allowed to get the benefit of the bargain that the defendant should have offered. Celebrities who have not previously sold their names, faces, or voices for endorsements have received higher damages when they are used without permission. In one such case, musician Tom Waits received punitive damages after showing that the defendant had behaved atrociously. Waits had repeatedly declined the defendant's offer, so the defendant used a singer who imitated Waits.[107] A celebrity who has not previously endorsed products in advertising will in effect argue that his or her good name has been tarnished.

Lawsuits on both appropriation and right of publicity grounds are most likely to arise as a result of advertising in the mass media. A valid news use provides a powerful defense against liability. Consent is available as a defense against either action as well. In right of publicity cases, some courts have recognized a fair use or fair comment type of defense, drawn from copyright and libel principles.

Appropriation

To state a case for appropriation, plaintiffs must prove that (1) their name or likeness was taken, (2) that the name or likeness was used for commercial purposes, and (3) that damages resulted from the use. Where there is no consent or news use, the plaintiff is almost sure to win. When a medical center used a doctor's name, photograph, and title on a calendar that was widely distributed to patients and various organizations, the court agreed that appropriation had occurred.[108]

In recent years private-figure appropriation plaintiffs have won very vew reported cases. There are two reasonable explanations for these results. First, good appropriation cases are cut-and-dried, and perhaps most of the viable ones are settled out of court. Second, as a practical matter, advertisers normally do not find much value in using unknown people to promote a product or service. Where ordinary consumers are featured as endorsers in an advertising campaign, agencies routinely obtain consent. Most of the appropriation cases arise because the advertising was prepared by amateurs, as in the medical center case, or because the defendant did not think the use was commercial in nature. When Anheuser-Busch used the plaintiff's image in a documentary about Hispanic Congressional Medal of Honor recipients that the company produced as a public relations project to be viewed in schools, veterans organizations, and Hispanic organizations, the court agreed that the use was not commercial.[109] Any incidental increase in corporate goodwill was thought to be too indirect to be considered gain for the defendant.

Consent • Consent must be clear, unequivocal, and preferably in writing. Courts will not infer consent in appropriation and right of publicity cases as they will in other privacy claims that result from news coverage. Some states may allow only written consent when consent is used as a defense for advertising uses. When consent was obtained orally, the court places the burden of proof on the party claiming consent. In any event, ambiguity will be interpreted against the party claiming consent. Normally, consent will only be valid for the purposes specified in the document. For example, if consent is obtained to use someone's photo for one specific type of use, any subsequent uses will exceed consent.[110] The time that the consent will be valid is also usually specified. A representative of the person whose name or likeness is used may grant consent, which will be binding, but a publication may have a duty to independently check the authority of agents.[111] Consent granted by parents for use of their children's names or images is normally valid, but only as long as the children cannot legally enter a contract.

News Use/Newsworthiness • The courts have universally recognized that news coverage can operate as a defense against appropriation lawsuits. There are two reasons for creating this defense. First, even though news organizations are in business for profit, news has never been considered a commercial use for direct profit. Ordinarily, profit cannot be traced to a specific news story. Second, a strong public policy favoring news coverage is embodied in both the First Amendment and the common law.[112] Some courts consider a news defense required under the First Amendment.

Proof that the plaintiff's name or picture appeared in a news story as a result of news gathering is sufficient to prove the defense. The courts generally refuse to second-guess a bona fide news judgment. The defense is successful against both private-figure and public-figure plaintiffs.[113] Coverage of public figures is almost absolutely protected, as is coverage drawn from public records or obtained in a public area.[114] Placing the plaintiff on the cover of a publication does not change the news use. Neither does using the plaintiff to promote a story in a newscast.

Occasionally, plaintiffs have argued that appropriation occurred when material originally used for news purposes is later used to promote a publication or broadcast. Reasoning that what was once news is always news, the courts have concluded that the news use defense still apllies, and that promotional material simply provides potential consumers with a sample of the product.[115]

Right of Publicity

The right of publicity has almost as much in common with intellectual property law as with privacy law. Many states, notably California and Tennessee, treat the right of celebrities to commercially exploit their fame as similar to copyright. In some cases plaintiffs have brought claims of trademark or service mark infringement along with a right of publicity charge. In at least one case, the claim was based solely on trademark.[116] A trademark is a symbol protected under federal and state laws from use by others when it represents a specific product or service and has a specific, strong meaning to the public.

The early decisions creating right of publicity as an extension of appropriation recognized that famous plaintiffs were more concerned with getting paid for the use of their identities than with emotional or personal suffering.[117] It is generally accepted now that the right of publicity is designed to protect the business interests of celebrities, and the action is most often interpreted as one involving property.

The harm in right of publicity violations is twofold. First, by taking aspects of a celebrity's identity, an infringer profits (or tries to) from the selling power of the celebrity without paying compensation to the celebrity. Second, the public is deceived by the use into thinking that the celebrity has endorsed the product or service advertised. Only the first of these applies in appropriation cases, and even then the compensation value is quite low. In cases where a celebrity has never endorsed products or services, the cases recognize a sort of "moral right" to avoid commercial exploitation.[118]

A key rationale for accepting a right of publicity is that, like copyright or trademark law, it creates an incentive for people to be creative. The most influential case is *Zacchini v. Scripps-Howard* from 1977,[119] in which the U.S. Supreme Court seemed to embrace the intellectual property argument. The case is more notable, however, for giving prominence to the right of publicity issue then arising in the state courts than for its legal analysis or precedent.

The facts of *Zacchini* read more like a copyright case than a publicity case. Hugo Zacchini, a human cannonball, sued when the local 11 o'clock television news show ran film of his entire act. Since the act took only fifteen seconds, showing less would have been difficult. The station had also promoted the story during its evening entertainment programming. The Court majority appeared to admit that Zacchini would have had no claim if less had been used. The dissenters thought the use was routine news coverage of an unusual story. The case is often misread as rejecting a news defense. All the majority said was that a constitutional news defense would not be required. The state courts remained free to apply a news defense using state law if they wished—and they did.

The real issue in *Zacchini* was whether a state's right of publicity law conflicted with the First Amendment, not whether the Court approved of the cause of action for right of publicity itself. The Court said there was not necessarily a conflict between the First Amendment and the right of publicity and declined to create a First Amendment–based defense. The Ohio courts had relied upon the *Time, Inc. v. Hill* decision. State legislatures and courts have recognized a newsworthiness defense since *Zacchini*, however. It operates in the same way as the newsworthiness defense in appropriation cases.

Following *Zacchini*, right of publicity litigation exploded.[120] Since the right of publicity is considered like property, it differs from appropriation in several ways. The first is that it is transferrable and descendible. A celebrity may, in effect, license her or his identity for any variety of uses, from T-shirts to shoes. Business agents typically handle transfers and licenses. A private figure has no comparable market. Allowing the right to descend to heirs after a celebrity's death provides an additional motivation to produce creative materials, it is argued. If the right of publicity is descendible, the full value of the asset may then be exploited.[121] When a nationwide ad campaign is planned, it should be assumed that even the dead have publicity rights. Caution is best even with local promotions. Most states have not decided the descendibility issue, but it is best to err on the side of caution and assume the right will be descendible. A subindustry has sprung up to license rights to the famous, dead or alive.

A second major difference from appropriation is scope of protection. The right of publicity protects all identifiable aspects of a celebrity, while appropriation has been applied only to names and pictures.[122] As a result, virtually any use that an audience can recognize as naming or referring to a celebrity may be the basis of a publicity claim. In one case, a plaintiff was allowed to go to trial based on the use of a photograph of his distinctive motorcycle helmet.[123] The Ninth Circuit upheld the right of game show host Vanna White to go to trial when an advertisement used an image of a robot that resembled her.[124] The dissenters argued that the protection had gone too far; they claimed that no audience member would have thought White endorsed the product, especially since the advertisement at issue was spoofing White. The case is also important for its analysis of the fair use and fair comment defenses in right of publicity claims.

The basic elements of the cause of action include (1) the unauthorized use of a celebrity's identity; (2) proof that the plaintiff's identity has value; (3) proof that the use was commercial; and (4) proof of damages based upon the value of the use or upon the harm caused by the use. In some cases, a fifth requirement has applied: plaintiffs must show that the use would lead a reasonable audience member to think that the plaintiff was affiliated with the advertised product or service. The consent and news defenses available in appropriation are also available here and operate in the same fashion. In addition, defendants in right of publicity cases have successfully raised defenses based upon fair use and fair comment.

Proving the elements is relatively simple. Most of the reported decisions focus on defenses against the action rather than on the elements of the action. Media professionals have little basis to complain of an action that prevents them from stealing value from celebrities, but many scholars are concerned that celebrities are going too far. They argue that celebrities have started bringing cases less to protect the value of their identities than to squelch use of their identities. A case that provides a good example supporting scholarly criticism is *Carson v. Here's Johnny Portable Toilets.*[125] Former *Tonight Show* host Johnny Carson sued over the use of the phrase "here's Johnny," with which the show had introduced Carson each night from 1962 to 1992. The portable toilet company placed the phrase on its portable toilets, which could be read from roadways, and added the line, "the world's foremost commodian." Carson was not amused. The defendant admitted that he used the line because of its association with Carson, but there was no evidence that anyone thought Carson was connected with the company. Nor was there a showing of monetary harm. Since Carson sought an injunction rather than a fee for the use, it seems that his real goal was to distance himself from a less-than-tasteful promotion.

Similarly, Ginger Rogers sued because she disliked the association with the Federico Fellini film *Ginger and Fred*, although the film was not about her and apparently derived no profit from referring to her and her famous film dance partner Fred Astaire in the title.[126] Rogers claimed false advertising under federal law, right of publicity violation under the law of her home state, Oregon, and false light invasion of privacy. The court denied all the claims.

The right of a celebrity to be free from unwanted exploitation includes a right not to be associated with a product or service. Singers Bette Midler and Tom Waits both sued after sound-alike substitutes were used in commercial advertising. In both cases, the plaintiff had been contacted about appearing in the ads and refused.[127] Neither entertainer had ever licensed his or her name for advertising purposes. The facts of these cases contrast sharply with the *Carson* and *Rogers* cases because the defendants were trying to confuse the public into thinking that the substitute singers were the real thing. A general rule has been developed regarding look-alike and sound-alike uses. When the use is so close to the real thing that an audience is unlikely to be able to tell the difference, the use is actionable. Disclaimers warning that the advertisement is using celebrity stand-ins can be sufficient to prevent liability if the disclaimer is prominent enough to be noticed by audience members.[128]

Consent • Consent is a complete defense. It can take two forms. The first is an explicit contractual release specifying the use or uses of a celebrity's identity in advertising and promotion. The consent should note whether the celebrity has the right to review material prior to publication. If it does not, chances are that a court might interpret a publication that the celebrity has consented to but not approved as exceeding consent.[129] The written consent should stipulate the amount to be paid the celebrity, the duration of the use, and any limits placed upon the celebrity's right to endorse other products or services.

The second type of consent is implied when a celebrity grants an interview to a journalist or otherwise allows access for news purposes. Although subsequent uses of the material have been the basis for lawsuits, they will fail unless the defendant has altered the use into a commercial one.[130] In these cases, it is better to think of the media as having been given something rather than having taken something.

News Use/Newsworthiness • A celebrity's appearance in a bona fide piece of news will defeat a right of publicity claim. The defense may exist under statute, common law, state constitutional law, or the First Amendment. In any event, courts agree that the First Amendment principle of a marketplace of ideas requires a news defense of some type.[131] The concepts of newsworthiness as applied in private facts, false light, and appropriation cases apply to right of publicity. If the story is presented in typical journalistic fashion, the defense should apply almost automatically. One area of much-publicized dispute has concerned depictions of celebrities in biography and history. Elizabeth Taylor and Frank Sinatra both raged against author Kitty Kelley over unauthorized biographies. The general rule appears to be that people cannot "own" their life stories,[132] although a celebrity is always free to make life difficult for unauthorized biographers simply by filing suit.

Fair Use and Fair Comment • These defenses protect derivative uses of celebrity identities when they appear in new creative works. In libel law, the **fair comment** and opinion defenses work to protect comment on a wide variety of topics and people. In copyright law, the fair use doctrine allows a limited use of protected material for news and other public purposes. In right of publicity cases, the courts do not always recognize that they are applying a fair comment or **fair use** analysis; instead, they rely upon the principle of "breathing space" for discussion of public figures under the First Amendment.[133] Ironically, the most articulate argument for a fair use privilege is found in Judge Alex Kozinski's dissenting opinion in the *Vanna White* case.[134] He argues that the famous open themselves to comment simply by being famous and asserts that making fun of celebrities is an important part of popular culture.

The advertising community was alarmed at the Ninth Circuit's refusal to recognize a defense in the case because lampooning the famous is a staple advertising tactic. Kozinski provides an impressive list, including films, song titles, and books, that could result in trademark or right of publicity suits because they spoof famous people or well-known products. Media lawyers were surprised that the Supreme Court agreed to hear a copyright parody case involving the song "Oh, Pretty Woman," but declined to review the *Vanna White* decision. In the "Pretty Woman" case, the Court said that digital sampling of the original recording by the group 2 Live Crew was probably a fair use because it was used for parody.[135] The issues are very similar.

The leading case on the right to comment on, use, or parody the famous is probably *Hustler Magazine, Inc. v. Falwell*.[136] The magazine had run an extremely distasteful advertising parody purporting to be about minister Jerry Falwell's first sexual experience. The U.S. Supreme Court's opinion focused upon Falwell's claim of infliction of mental distress, but the broad protection announced for parody, humor, and comment affects other areas of law. The Court said an actual malice standard is required when a public figure alleges emotional distress. For all practical purposes, the Court said that celebrities and public figures have no recourse when the media poke fun at them. In a majority opinion tracing the history of political humor in the United States, Chief Justice William Rehnquist endorsed the notion that public debate using even malicious humor must be protected.

> ● **Fair comment**
> A defense that protects statements that appear in the form of opinion, criticism, or commentary.
>
> ● **Fair use**
> A doctrine in copyright law that provides a limited legal right for others to use copyrighted materials. The fair use defense has had influence in right of publicity and trademark infringement cases.

In most cases involving these defenses, the courts have looked at factors similar to those assessed in fair use cases in copyright: amount of use, nature of the use, and effect, if any, upon marketability. A similar defense is available in actions brought for trademark infringement, and the analysis is comparable as well.[137] In an earlier decision in the *Falwell* case, the Fourth Circuit had explicitly rejected an appropriation-type claim because no audience would believe the parody was true.[138] This analysis also protects comment, but on statutory or common law grounds.

EMOTIONAL DISTRESS AND NEGLIGENCE

Plaintiffs have found it difficult to win libel suits and invasion of privacy suits against the media. Accordingly, they have sought alternative causes of action to remedy harms caused by media portrayals or media content. In addition to emotional distress and negligence, claims have been brought based upon incitement, warranty, outrage, and justifiable reliance.[139] In incitement, the plaintiff claims that media content resulted directly in harm. This claim requires proving cause-and-effect, which is extremely difficult. A warranty claim is based on the notion that there is an enforceable promise between a media company and the plaintiff. Since the plaintiff and the company have not directly contracted with one another, this claim almost always fails. The tort of outrage allows recovery for behavior so outlandish that a civilized society should not countenance it. At the same time, the tort is so ambiguous that courts are reluctant to allow recovery for it. Justifiable reliance is essentially the same as warranty. The plaintiff argues that the defendant knew or should have known that audience members would rely on specific media content. Of the "alternative" claims, emotional distress and negligence have been raised most often.

Emotional Distress

There are two types of actions for emotional distress, negligent infliction of emotional distress and intentional infliction of emotional distress. Each is a separate tort. In the *Falwell* case, Jerry Falwell argued that *Hustler* and its publisher Larry Flynt had intentionally inflicted distress. The Supreme Court added an actual malice test to the common law rules when a public figure sues. The common law elements of the tort, which is recognized in most states, include proof of extreme and outrageous conduct, intent or recklessness, and severe distress. The plaintiff must also show that the defendant's behavior caused the distress.[140] To date, plaintiffs have failed to win cases against the media. However dubious their ethics and tasteless their stories, journalists seldom intend to cause harm.[141] A court will look at the content of the coverage as well as the behavior of journalists. If the content is not "beyond the bounds of decency," it cannot be the basis of an intentional infliction claim.[142]

A plaintiff whose claim is too weak to support intentional infliction might file for negligent infliction of emotional distress. Three key issues are common

- ● **Negligent infliction of emotional distress** Occurs where a reasonable person should have anticipated that his or her actions would cause anguish or distress to an identifiable third person.

- ● **Intentional infliction of emotional distress** Occurs when a defendant, through a pattern of behavior aimed directly at an identified third party, intends to cause anguish or distress.

to all negligence actions: the existence of a duty to another person, a failure by the defendant to act reasonably, and foreseeability.[143] Proof of foreseeability requires showing that the defendant was aware or should have been aware of the harmful results of its actions. In the case where a television news show aired videotape of a murdered child's skull, the court found an outrage claim, but stressed that the station should have foreseen the harmful effects.[144] The only other negligent infliction case in which a plaintiff prevailed—both were settled out of court—was *Hyde v. City of Columbia*.[145] A woman who had been abducted and threatened with rape escaped from her attacker. Like a good citizen, she filed a report with the police. The report, against department policy, was left where a reporter saw it. The reporter and editors, against newspaper policy, ran her name and address. She began to get threatening phone calls. The court refused to grant a public records or public interest defense to the newspaper and announced Hyde was entitled to try to prove negligence to a jury at trial.

So few cases involving negligent infliction of emotional distress have been reported that posing general rules is risky. It seems likely that the courts will not find a duty unless the foreseeable risk of danger is extremely high. In the *Hyde* case, it takes little review to conclude that the newspaper should have foreseen the risk to Hyde from an attacker still at large.

Negligence

The only practical difference between a pure negligence action and a negligent infliction of emotional distress action is that the claim is based solely on assessing risk and foreseeable harm, but not to a specific individual. A leading case is *Braun v. Soldier of Fortune Magazine, Inc.*[146] The magazine published an advertisement from a self-styled mercenary that promised "all jobs considered." He was hired to murder Richard Braun by a business partner of Braun's. After the killing, Braun's family sued. The Eleventh Circuit declared that the ad presented an obvious risk that any citizen would be under a duty to prevent. The court emphasized that its decision was narrow. A publisher may be held liable for an advertisement only if the danger is obvious from reading the ad copy.

Claims that liability should be imposed for acts inspired by media content have often been raised, but the courts have usually found no liability. In *Walt Disney Productions, Inc. v. Shannon*,[147] the plaintiff was an eleven-year-old boy who imitated a trick from the "Mickey Mouse Club" that called for putting a BB pellet in a balloon. The balloon exploded, partially blinding him. The court said that the risk was foreseeable, but not obviously so, and was reluctant to impose liability unless risk of danger was apparent. The rationale has also been applied when the plaintiff was injured by someone imitating media content. In *Olivia N. v. NBC*,[148] the nine-year-old plaintiff was raped with a bottle by assailants who had seen a similar scene involving a plunger handle in a television movie.

Another group of negligence claims arises when someone uses a guidebook, cookbook, or other media content that gives explicit instructions about how to do something. The courts have almost universally decided for media defendants, although they often note that plaintiffs may seek recovery against authors. An example is *Winter v. G. P. Putnam's Sons.*[149] Putnam published the American edition of *The Encyclopedia of Mushrooms,* which the plaintiffs used while hunting for edible mushrooms. The book erroneously identified a poisonous mushroom as edible; the plaintiffs ate it, fell ill, and ultimately suffered liver failure. The court held that negligence could not be shown because the law to date did not recognize a duty for publishers to investigate the accuracy of book contents. The court said that it was guided by First Amendment principles as well. The extension from libel law of avoiding a chilling effect on "robust debate" seems awkward when the publication is expressly designed to be relied upon, but that is the position of the majority of courts.[150]

SUMMARY

Privacy law is a twentieth century creation, devised by Warren and Brandeis to reduce the intrusive effects of modern mass media. Ironically, they have for the most part won the battle theoretically but not practically; almost all the states recognize privacy actions, but judges have been reluctant to substitute their judgment about what is suitable for audiences in place of judgments by media professionals. We have a large body of privacy law that protects very little that is private.

The actions for disclosure of private facts, intrusion upon seclusion, portrayal in a false light, and appropriation for commercial purposes were all designed to protect the mental and emotional well-being of individuals when the press goes too far. But because courts have such difficulty determining what is beyond the pale, only appropriation actions are successful, and they succeed because appropriation is concerned with unauthorized use rather than with using inappropriate information.

Right of publicity actions are often successful. Yet that cause of action, like appropriation, is really designed to protect against unauthorized uses rather than tacky or painful ones. Right of publicity cases and appropriation cases seldom deal with mental or emotional suffering.

The alternative actions of infliction of mental distress and negligence attempt to recover some of the ground privacy has lost by focusing on the likelihood of a media portrayal causing harm rather than upon whether the portrayal includes sensitive personal information. These actions look to punish media defendants for their actions or inactions rather than for the content of the publication. So far plaintiffs have not been persuasive.

In the 1980s and 1990s, invasion of privacy law has begun to wither. Several state supreme courts have reconsidered privacy and have dropped it. Even when it remains on the books, it seldom works to protect privacy. As a result, invasion of privacy has become far more a matter of professional ethics in the media than of legal rules in court.

KEY TERMS

Invasion of privacy
Disclosure of private facts
Appropriation
Right of publicity
Intrusion upon seclusion
False light
Tort
Statute of limitations
Newsworthiness
Consent
Plain view

Public figure
Public record
Public meeting
Trespass
Fault
Negligence
Fair comment
Fair use
Negligent infliction of emotional distress
Intentional infliction of emotional distress

[handwritten margin note, left side: reasonable expectation of privacy — consent — plain view — newsworthiness]

CASE PROBLEMS

1. You are a reporter for the *World-Globe*. It's a slow Saturday, and you get a call from a local minister, Herbert Figgs, who asks you to stop by to discuss the decay of moral values in the metro area. Figgs is the head of a local antipornography group. You agree to stop over at 2:30. Running ahead of schedule, you show up at Figgs's house at 2 o'clock. When no one answers at the front door, you go around back. On the way you see Figgs's car in the driveway and notice a number of books-on-cassette tapes on the front seat, bearing titles such as "Sadomasochism Made Easy." After finding Figgs and conducting the interview, you ask to use the bathroom. The door to the medicine cabinet is slightly open; you open it a bit further and discover credit card receipts from a dial-a-porn service. You also see a plastic bag with powder that looks like cocaine.

   You head to the office and write a story based on the interview. When you tell the editor about the other items you found, she insists that you include them in the story, which then runs on the front page. Figgs calls you and is livid. He claims that the material was all for research on moral decay and concludes, "I'll see you in court." How will you defend yourself?

2. James Earl Ray, convicted of murdering Dr. Martin Luther King, Jr., in 1968, has been released from prison in Tennessee on parole. He has assumed a new name under a federal government parolee relocation program and has been placed in a new community. Glenn Schmertz, ace reporter for WYME-TV, has learned that Ray, under the new

[handwritten margin note, center: public figure defense]

name James Warren, is working as a brake repairman at a national chain muffler repair shop on the southside of your city. Schmertz obtained a copy of the parole report from a friend at federal district court. The report concluded that "James Earl Ray has been completely rehabilitated and is ready to assume a role of responsibility in society." The parole was widely covered in the national press, but Ray's new name was never reported. You are the news director of WYME. Do you see any legal risk in running the story? *[handwritten: highly offensive, outrage to comm. decency, private]*

3. Marna Carnes works part-time as a nude model for figure studies classes in the art department at the university. *World-Globe* photographer Jamie Nance was walking down a hallway adjacent to classrooms in which figure studies classes were held, and noticed Carnes and the students in the room. Nance figured that, with the soft late-afternoon light, the picture would work best if taken from outside the room through the window. Nance presents the editors with a photo that shows Carnes's bare backside and a number of students sketching. Carnes's face is not visible, but several students are easily recognizable. The professor is seen standing off to the side. A reporter calls the professor to ask for more information and is told that the class was taking advantage of the natural light to learn figure sketching in deep shadow. The professor also says that Carnes's family is not aware of her part-time work. Nance strongly desires to have the photo run as "wild" art for its aesthetic value. You are the managing editor. Are you at risk if you run this photograph?

[handwritten margin note, bottom: No. Not identifiable, plain view, no false light]

[handwritten annotation near "such as": generally accessible]

[handwritten annotation in top margin: emotional & monetary harm could show reckless disregard]

4. It is a slow news day at WNOZ-TV, when a source who has been reliable in the past calls with a tip. Frank McTeague, a local dentist, has allegedly been molesting women patients when they are under anesthetic. The source insists on anonymity, which you grant. You are news director Walter Burns. You convince Linda Grant, a new reporter just out of college, to get the story. She goes to McTeague's office for an appointment with a remote microphone hidden in her skirt pocket. Camera operator Nestor Nyquist hides in some bushes just outside; he will attempt to videotape what happens inside. He also has a tape recorder that is capturing dialogue and sound from Grant's microphone. As Grant's voice fades from the effects of the anesthetic, Nyquist sees McTeague lean closely over her. He leaves his post and bursts into the office, camera running. McTeague looks up and his leer changes to a frown. All videotape clips, both from outside and inside, are used on the evening news, with Grant doing the story. The police arrest McTeague the next morning. McTeague publicly threatens to sue you, but does not specify any grounds. Are you in any kind of trouble?

[handwritten: plain view → not necessarily truth]

5. You are the legal adviser to the governor. She has a bill on her desk called the "Physical Privacy Act," which the legislature passed last week. Similar bills were introduced in other states following tabloid TV news coverage of videotapes of skater Tonya Harding half-naked at a Halloween party. Comparable incidents involving Michael Jackson, Paula Jones, and Princess Diana are also cited by the legislature as examples. In Jones's case, photos had been taken by a former boyfriend, who sold them to *Penthouse* magazine without her consent. The tapes of Harding had been shot by her ex-husband and were made available to the media without her consent. The bill would make it a civil infraction for "any person or news organization to publish to the general public nude or partially nude photographs, videotapes, or motion picture films without the subject's consent." Under the bill, the only defense is consent by the person depicted or consent by that person's legally authorized agent. Will you tell the governor to sign or veto the bill? Why?

[handwritten: Veto.]

6. You are an attorney in private practice. You have been asked for a legal opinion by the president of the university chess club. As a fundraising project, the club published a calendar called "University Faces" The project was approved in writing by the assistant vice president for student affairs. Among the faces on the calendar are the university president, the head football coach, and the star of the men's basketball team. The basketball player sent a letter complaining that he had never consented to the use and was upset that he appeared to be endorsing the calendar and the chess club. He said that endorsements may threaten an athlete's eligibility under National Collegiate Athletic Association rules. All the photos were provided by the university's public relations office. How will you advise the chess club?

[handwritten: using it for financial gain they have a case- get permis.]

7. On Sunday morning at 9 A.M., someone pulled the fire alarm in the Alhambra Apartments building downtown. Hundreds of residents came rushing out of the building, many having been roused from sleep by the alarm. Two of these people were Paul Davis and Karen Bigelow. They were naked, and it was cold. Police officers passed out blankets to many of the residents, and Davis and Bigelow took a blanket and shared it. Just as Bigelow was wrapping the blanket around them, a *World-Globe* photographer came by and took their picture. The photo appeared in the next day's paper. Davis's buttocks and Bigelow's breasts were plainly visible in the photo. Davis was identified as a resident of the Alhambra, Bigelow as a visitor. The photographer obtained their names during a brief conversation. The residence information was obtained from the building manager. Davis and Bigelow each call to complain and threaten legal action; they get you on the phone. You're the metro editor. What will you tell them?

[handwritten: must show neglig]

[handwritten: plain view false light -inaccurate & embarrassing]

8. You are Don Farley, president of the Farley Advertising Agency. As part of your campaign for the nationwide Good Value Hardware chain, you ran an ad that focused on the "down-home" nature of the chain's 384 stores. These ads featured old photos and film from the 1950s and 1960s—designed to evoke nostalgia in the minds of customers in their 30s and 40s, the greatest market for hardware. One of those photos was of a high school senior class from 1968. There were 106 students in the photo. One of the students, Linda Milton, called and told you that "you'll be hearing from my attorney for using my photo." Milton is a social worker in town. A lawyer for musician Ted Nugent, who was also a member of the class, calls to announce that "we are going to sue the socks off you for using Ted's photo." Based on these facts, are you in any trouble?

[handwritten: no]

[handwritten: yes no]

[handwritten: using for $ gain   not thought to endorse the product]

ENDNOTES

1. See generally Robert O. Wyatt, *Free Expression and the American Public* (Murfreesboro, Tenn.: American Society of Newspapers Editors, 1991).

2. "The Right to Privacy," *Harvard Law Review* 4:193 (1890).

3. Arthur B. Hanson, *Libel and Related Torts* (New York: American Newspaper Publishers Association Foundation, 1969), pp. 197–213.

4. William L. Prosser, "Privacy," *California Law Review* 48:383 (1960).

5. *Fitch v. Voit*, 624 So.2d 542 (Ala. 1993).

6. *California v. Greenwood*, 486 U.S. 35, 108 S.Ct. 1625 (1988).

7. *Roe v. Wade*, 410 U.S. 113, 93 S.Ct. 705 (1973).

8. 5 U.S.C.A. § 552a.

9. *Restatement of the Law (Second) Torts* (St. Paul, Minn.: American Law Institute, 1965).

10. *Restatement of the Law (Second) Torts*, § 652D.

11. *Grimsley v. Guccione*, 703 F.Supp. 903 (M.D.Ala. 1988).

12. 154 Cal.App.3d 1040, 201 Cal.Rptr. 665 (1984).

13. *Hawkins v. Metromedia*, 288 S.C. 569, 344 S.E.2d 145 (1986).

14. *Vassiliades v. Garfinckel's*, 492 A.2d 580 (D.C.App. 1985).

15. *Diaz v. Oakland Tribune*, 139 Cal.App.3d 118, 188 Cal.Rptr. 762 (1983).

16. 420 U.S. 469, 95 S.Ct. 1029 (1975).

17. 491 U.S. 524, 109 S.Ct. 2603 (1989).

18. *Florida v. Globe Communications Corp.*, 622 So.2d 1066 (Fla.App. 1993).

19. *Macon Telegraph Publishing Co. v. Tatum*, 208 Ga.App.III, 430 S.E.2d 18 (1993), vacated 213 Ga.App. 536, 446 S.E.2d 797 (1994).

20. *Macon Telegraph Pubg. Co. v. Tatum*, 263 Ga. 678, 436 S.E.2d 655 (1993).

21. *Prosser and Keeton on Torts*, 5th ed. (St. Paul, Minn.: West Publishing Co., 1984), pp. 856–63.

22. 348 Mo. 1199, 159 S.W.2d 291 (1942).

23. *Pasadena Star-News v. Los Angeles Superior Court*, 203 Cal.App.3d 131, 249 Cal.Rptr. 729 (1988).

24. 113 F.2d 806 (2d Cir. 1940).

25. *Hall v. Post*, 323 N.C. 259, 372 S.E.2d 711 (1988); *Anderson v. Fisher Broadcasting Cos.* 300 Or. 452, 712 P.2d 803 (1986).

26. *Howell v. New York Post Co.*, 81 N.Y.2d 115, 596 N.Y.S.2d 350, 612 N.E.2d 699 (1993).

27. 101 Mich.App. 725, 300 N.W.2d 687 (1980).

28. 527 F.2d 1122 (9th Cir. 1975).

29. *Virgil v. Sports Illustrated*, 424 F.Supp. 1286 (S.D.Cal. 1976).

30. *Armstrong v. H&C Communications, Inc.*, 575 So.2d 280 (Fla.App. 1991).

31. 200 Mich.App. 622, 504 N.W.2d 715 (1993).

32. *Reuber v. Food Chemical News*, 899 F.2d 271 (4th Cir. 1990).

33. *Buller v. Pulitzer Publishing Co.*, 684 S.W.2d 473 (Mo.App. 1984).

34. 113 F.2d 806 (2d Cir. 1940).

35. *Romaine v. Kallinger*, 109 N.J. 282, 537 A.2d 284 (1988).

36. *Falwell v. Penthouse International*, 521 F.Supp. 1204 (W.D.Va. 1981).

37. *Cory v. Nintendo of America, Inc.* 185 A.D.2d 70, 592 N.Y.S.2d 6 (App.Div. 1993).

38. *California v. Greenwood*, 486 U.S. 35, 108 S.Ct. 1625 (1988).

39. 423 So.2d 426 (Fla.App. 1982).

40. 802 S.W.2d 901 (Tex.App. 1991).

41. *Dora v. Frontline Video, Inc.*, 15 Cal.App.4th 536, 18 Cal.Rptr.2d 790 (1993).

42. *Anderson v. Fisher Broadcasting Cos.* 300 Or. 452, 712 P.2d 803 (1986).

43. *Street v. NBC*, 645 F.2d 1227 (6th Cir. 1981); *Haynes v. Alfred A. Knopf, Inc.*, 8 F.3d 1222 (6th Cir. 1993).

44. *Campbell v. Seabury Press*, 614 F.2d 395 (5th Cir. 1980).

45. 420 U.S. 469, 95 S.Ct. 1029 (1975).

46. *Lusby v. Cincinnati Monthly Publishing Corp.* 904 F.2d 707, 17 Med.L.Rptr. 1962 (6th Cir. 1990).

47. *Wolf v. Regardie*, 553 A.2d 1213 (D.C.App. 1989).

48. 411 Pa.Super. 119, 600 A.2d 1293 (1992).

49. *Prosser and Keeton on Torts*, pp. 854–856.

50. Kent R. Middleton, "Journalists and Tape Recorders: Does Participant Monitoring Invade Privacy?" *Hastings Communication and Entertainment Law Journal* 2:287 (1979–1980).

51. *United States v. Turk*, 526 F.2d 654 (5th Cir. 1976).

52. Electronic Communications Privacy Act of 1986, 18 U.S.C.A. § 2510.

53. *McCall v. Courier-Journal*, 6 Med.L.Rptr. 1112, unpub., No. 79–CA–1011–MR (Ky.App. 1980).

54. 20 Med.L.Rptr. 1189, unpub., No. 90–CA–473–MR (Ky.App. 1991).

55. 449 F.2d 245 (9th Cir. 1971).

56. *LeMistral, Inc. v. CBS*, 61 A.D.2d 491, 402 N.Y.S.2d 815 (App.Div. 1978).

57. *Bilney v. Evening Star Newspaper Co.* 43 Md.App. 560, 406 A.2d 652 (1979); *Pearson v. Dodd*, 410 F.2d 701 (D.C.Cir. 1969).

58. *Natoli v. Sullivan*, 159 Misc.2d 681, 606 N.Y.S.2d 504, 21 Med.L.Rptr. 2097 (1993).

59. *Dempsey v. National Enquirer*, 702 F.Supp. 927 (D.Me. 1988).

60. *Galella v. Onassis*, 487 F.2d 986 (2d Cir. 1973).

61. *Galella v. Onassis*, 533 F.Supp. 1076 (S.D.N.Y. 1982).

62. *Florida Publishing Co. v. Fletcher*, 340 So.2d 914 (Fla. 1976).

63. *Prahl v. Brosamle*, 98 Wis.2d 130, 295 N.W.2d 768 (App. 1980).

64. *Magenis v. Fisher Broadcasting, Inc.* 103 Or.App. 555, 798 P.2d 1106 (1990).

65. *Mark v. KING Broadcastintg*, 27 Wash.App. 344, 618 P.2d 512 (1980).

66. *Fordyce v. Seattle*, 840 F.Supp. 784, 21 Med.L.Rptr. 2177 (W.D.Wash. 1993).

67. See, for example, *Cassidy v. ABC*, 60 Ill.App.3d 831, 17 Ill.Dec. 936, 377 N.E.2d 126 (1978); *McLin v. Dayton Newspapers*, 17 Med.L.Rptr., 1074, unpub., No. 88-CVE-7528 (Ohio Mun. Ct. 1989).

68. *Miller v. NBC*, 187 Cal.App.3d 1463, 232 Cal.Rptr. 668 (1986).

69. *Barger v. Courier-Journal*, 20 Med.L.Rptr. 1189, unpub., No. 90-CA-473-MR (Ky.App. 1991).

70. *Restatement of the Law (Second) Torts* § 652D, Comment c.

71. 38 Cal.2d 273, 239 P.2d 630 (Cal. 1952).

72. Ruth Walden and Emile Netzhammer, "False Light Invasion of Privacy: Untangling the Web of Uncertainty," *Hastings Communications and Entertainment Law Journal* 9:347 (1987); Diane Zimmerman, "False Light Invasion of Privacy: The Light That Failed," *New York University Law Review* 64:364 (1989).

73. See, for example, *Waring v. William Morrow & Co., Inc.*, 821 F.Supp. 1188 (S.D.Tex. 1993); *Renwick v. News & Observer Publishing Co.* 310 N.C. 312, 312 S.E.2d 405 (1984); *Angelotta v. ABC*, 820 F.2d 806 (6th Cir. 1987)(applying Ohio Law).

74. 418 U.S. 323, 94 S.Ct. 2997 (1974).

75. Lackland H. Bloom, Jr., "Proof of Fault in Media Defamation Litigation," *Vanderbilt Law Review* 38:247 (1985).

76. Walden and Netzhammer, "False Light Invasion of Privacy," pp. 364–373.

77. 385 U.S. 374, 87 S.Ct. 534 (1967).

78. 419 U.S. 245, 95 S.Ct. 465 (1974).

79. *Duncan v. WJLA-TV, Inc.*, 106 F.R.D. 4 (D.D.C. 1984).

80. *Arrington v. New York Times*, 55 N.Y.2d 433, 449 N.Y.S.2d 941, 434 N.E.2d 1319 (1982).

81. *Douglass v. Hustler Magazine, Inc.*, 769 F.2d 1128 (7th Cir. 1985).

82. *Braun v. Flynt*, 726 F.2d 245 (5th Cir. 1984).

83. 385 U.S. 374, 87 S.Ct. 534 (1967).

84. 419 U.S. 245, 95 S.Ct. 465 (1974).

85. See, for example, *Marcinkus v. NAL Publishing*, 522 N.Y.S.2d 1009, 14 Med.L.Rptr. 2094 (1987); *Polakoff v. Harcourt Brace Jovanovich, Inc.* 67 A.D.2d 871, 413 N.Y.S.2d 537 (1979).

86. *Bindrim v. Mitchell*, 92 Cal.App.3d 61, 155 Cal.Rptr. 29 (1979), *cert. denied*, 444 U.S. 984, 100 S.Ct. 490 (1979); *Ali v. Playgirl*, 447 F.Supp. 723 (S.D.N.Y. 1978)(false light claim brought on right of publicity grounds).

87. *Hicks v. Casablanca Records*, 464 F.Supp. 426 (S.D.N.Y. 1978).

88. *Falwell v. Flynt*, 805 F.2d 484 (4th Cir. 1986), *reversed in part* 485 U.S. 46, 108 S.Ct. 876 (1988); *Pring v. Penthouse International, Ltd.*, 695 F.2d 438 (10th Cir. 1982).

89. *People's Bank and Trust Co. v. Globe International Publishing, Inc.*, 978 F.2d 1065 (8th Cir. 1992).

90. *Schifano v. Greene County Greyhound Park, Inc.*, 624 So.2d 178 (Ala. 1993).

91. *Haynes v. Alfred A. Knopf, Inc.*, 21 Med.L.Rptr. 1314 (N.D.Ill. 1993), *affirmed*, 8 F.3d 1222 (7th Cir. 1993).

92. *Godbehere v. Phoenix Newspapers, Inc.*, 162 Ariz. 335, 783 P.2d 781 (1989).

93. *Kelson v. Spin Publications, Inc.*, 16 Med.L.Rptr. 1130, unpub., No. HAR 87-16 (D.Md. 1988).

94. 161 Mich.App. 785, 411 N.W.2d 859 (1987).

95. *Salek v. Passaic Collegiate School*, 255 N.J.Super. 355, 605 A.2d 276 (App.Div. 1992).

96. *Kolengas v. Heftel Broadcasting Corp.* 217 Ill.App.3d 803, 161 Ill.Dec. 172, 578 N.E.2d 299 (1991).

97. *Sallomi v. Phoenix Newspapers, Inc*, 160 Ariz. 144, 771 P.2d 469 (App. 1989).

98. *Aisenson v. ABC*, 220 Cal.App.3d 146, 269 Cal.Rptr. 379 (1990).

99. *Easter Seal Society v. Playboy Enterprises, Inc.*, 530 So.2d 643 (La.App. 1988).

100. N.Y. Civil Rights Law §§ 50–51 (McKinney 1976).

101. *Roberson v. Rochester Folding-Box Co.* 171 N.Y. 538, 64 N.E. 442 (1902).

102. *Pavesich v. New England Life Insurance Co.* 122 Ga. 190, 50 S.E. 68 (1905).

103. *Haelan Laboratories v. Topps Chewing Gum, Inc.*, 202 F.2d 866 (2d Cir. 1953).

104. Michael M. Madow, "Private Ownership of Public Image: Popular Culture and Publicity Rights," *California Law Review* 81:125 (1993).

105. *State ex rel. Presley v. Crowell*, 733 S.W.2d 89 (Tenn.App. 1987).

106. *Bowling v. Missionary Servants of the Most Holy Trinity*, 972 F.2d 346 (6th Cir. 1992).

107. *Waits v. Frito-Lay, Inc.*, 978 F.2d 1093 (9th Cir. 1992), *cert. denied*, _____ U.S. _____, 113 S.Ct. 1047 (1993).

108. *Beverley v. Choices Women's Medical Center*, 78 N.Y.2d 745, 579 N.Y.S.2d 637, 587 N.E.2d 275 (1991).

109. *Benavidez v. Anheuser-Busch, Inc.*, 873 F.2d 102 (5th Cir. 1989).

110. *Canessa v. J. I. Kislak, Inc.* 97 N.J.Super. 327, 235 A.2d 62 (1967).

111. *Cory v. Nintendo of America, Inc.* 187 A.D.2d 70, 592 N.Y.S.2d 6 (1993); *Wood v. Hustler*, 736 F.2d 1084 (5th Cir. 1984).

112. *Brooks v. ABC*, 737 F.Supp. 431 (N.D.Ohio 1990).

113. *Eastwood v. Superior Court*, 149 Cal.App.3d 409, 198 Cal.Rptr. 342 (1983); *Booth v. Curtis Publishing Co.*, 15 A.D.2d 343, 223 N.Y.S.2d 737 (1962).

114. *Cox v. Hatch*, 761 P.2d 556 (Utah 1988); *Powell v. Toledo Blade Co.*, 19 Med.L.Rptr. 1727 (Ohio Common Pleas 1991).

115. *Anderson v. Fisher Broadcasting Cos.* 300 Or. 452, 712 P.2d 803 (1986); *Lawrence v. A. S. Abell Co.* 299 Md. 697, 475 A.2d 448 (Md.App. 1984).

116. *Prudhomme v. Procter & Gamble Co.*, 800 F.Supp. 390 (E.D.La. 1992).

117. *Paulsen v. Personality Posters, Inc.*, 299 N.Y.S.2d 501 (Sup. 1968).

118. *Waits v. Frito-Lay, Inc.*, 978 F.2d 1093 (9th Cir. 1992), *cert. denied*, _____ U.S. _____, 113 S.Ct.

1047 (1993); *Grant v. Esquire*, 367 F.Supp. 876 (S.D.N.Y. 1973).

119. 433 U.S. 562, 97 S.Ct. 2849 (1977).

120. See Frank G. Houdek, "Researching the Right of Publicity: A Revised and Comprehensive Bibliography of Law-Related Materials," *Hastings Communications and Entertainment Law Journal* 16:385–423 (Winter 1994).

121. *Lugosi v. Universal Pictures*, 25 Cal.3d 813, 160 Cal.Rptr. 323, 603 P.2d 425 (Cal. 1979)(rejecting descendability).

122. Todd F. Simon, "Right of Publicity Reified: Fame as Business Asset," *New York Law School Law Review* 30:699 (1985).

123. *Int-Elect Engineering, Inc. v. Clinton Harley Corp.*, 21 Med.L.Rptr. 1762 (N.D.Cal. 1993).

124. *White v. Samsung Electronics America, Inc.*, 971 F.2d 1395 (9th Cir. 1992), *rehearing denied* 989 F.2d 1512 (1993).

125. 698 F.2d 831 (6th Cir. 1983).

126. *Rogers v. Grimaldi*, 875 F.2d 994 (2d Cir. 1989).

127. *Midler v. Ford Motor Co.*, 849 F.2d 460 (9th Cir. 1988).

128. *Allen v. National Video, Inc.*, 610 F.Supp. 612 (S.D.N.Y. 1985).

129. *Cher v. Forum International*, 692 F.2d 634 (9th Cir. 1982).

130. *Namath v. Sports Illustrated*, 48 A.D.2d 487, 371 N.Y.S.2d 10 (1975).

131. *New Kids on the Block v. New America Publishing, Inc.*, 971 F.2d 302 (9th Cir. 1992); *Maheu v. CBS*, 201 Cal.App.3d 662, 247 Cal.Rptr. 304 (1988).

132. *Matthews v. Wozencraft*, 21 Med.L.Rptr. 1848 (E.D.Tex. 1993).

133. *Frosch v. Grosset & Dunlap, Inc.* 75 A.D.2d 768, 427 N.Y.S.2d 828 (1980).

134. *White v. Samsung Electronics America, Inc.*, 989 F.2d 1512 (9th Cir. 1993).

135. *Campbell a/k/a Skyywalker v. Acuff-Rose Music, Inc.*, ____ U.S. ____, 114 S.Ct. 1164 (1994).

136. 485 U.S. 46, 108 S.Ct. 876 (1988).

137. *L. L. Bean, Inc. v. Drake Publishers, Inc.*, 811 F.2d 26 (1st Cir. 1987); *Mutual of Omaha Insurance Co. v. Novak*, 836 F.2d 397 (8th Cir. 1987).

138. *Falwell v. Flynt*, 797 F.2d 1270 (4th Cir. 1986).

139. Todd F. Simon and Mary M. Cronin, "Searching for Media Liability: The Law's Response to Perceived Changes in Harms Caused by Mass Media," paper presented at the annual convention, Association for Education in Journalism and Mass Communication, Boston, Mass., August 1990.

140. *Restatement of the Law (Second) Torts*, § 46(1).

141. *Howell v. New York Post Co., Inc.*, 81 N.Y.2d 115 (1993).

142. *Holtzscheiter v. Thomson Newspapers, Inc.*, 306 S.C. 297, 411 S.E.2d 664 (1991).

143. *Prosser and Keeton on Torts*, pp. 359–65.

144. *Armstrong v. H&C Communications, Inc.*, 575 So.2d 280 (Fla.App. 1991).

145. 637 S.W.2d 251 (Mo.App. 1982).

146. 968 F.2d 1110 (11th Cir. 1992), *cert. denied* ____ U.S. ____, 113 S.Ct. 1028 (1993).

147. 247 Ga. 402, 276 S.E.2d 580 (1981).

148. 126 Cal.App.3d 488, 178 Cal.Rptr. 888 (1981), *cert. denied* 458 U.S. 1108, 102 S.Ct. 3487 (1982).

149. 938 F.2d 1033 (9th Cir. 1991).

150. *Demuth Development Corp. v. Merck & Co., Inc.*, 432 F.Supp. 990 (E.D.N.Y. 1977).

Journalist's Privilege

THE RATIONALE FOR THE PRIVILEGE

An inevitable and natural tension exists between parties to litigation in court, who are seeking information to help their cases, and journalists, who are in the business of collecting and disseminating information. Not surprisingly, reporters are more likely than other persons to have information litigants think will be useful. For one thing, most news stories rely on standard news values such as conflict, crime, or impropriety; often the result is stories where sources accuse one another of wicked or illegal behavior. When the subject of the story also becomes the subject of a lawsuit, reporters likely hold information that appears relevant to one or more of the parties.

In this chapter we will examine the development of evidentiary privileges for journalists. An evidentiary privilege allows the person covered by the privilege to refuse to testify when called to court, so long as the information sought is within the scope of the privilege. An **evidentiary privilege** recognizes and respects the confidentiality of a particular relationship by letting those who hold the privilege refuse to testify. The best-known evidentiary privileges are those between physicians and patients and those between attorneys and clients.

What began as a fairly simple request by journalists that courts honor reporters' promises to anonymous sources has expanded greatly in the last thirty years. The "journalist's privilege" recognized in most states and in the majority of federal courts of appeal is actually several types of privilege bundled together.

To understand the privilege, it is necessary first to know what kinds of information litigants seek from journalists. Demands for information fall into three major types. In one, reporters are asked to reveal the identities of anonymous sources who supplied information for news stories. In the second, the demand is for materials such as notes, film, or videotape. The third type is a request for the testimony of reporters who were eyewitnesses to events. Journalists claim they should be protected by a privilege not to testify or not to submit materials.

● **Evidentiary privilege**

The right to refuse to testify in court about certain confidential relationships. Attorney-client and physician-patient relationships are covered by evidentiary privilege.

● **Subpoena**
An order requiring someone to appear in court as a witness or provide materials to the court.

● **Discovery**
A pretrial phase in which parties seek information from each other.

● **Quash**
To vacate or nullify.

When a litigant seeks information for a lawsuit, a **subpoena** is issued. A subpoena is an order for someone to either appear in court as a witness or provide materials to the court. Failure to respond to a subpoena normally results in the person to whom the subpoena was issued being found in contempt of court. A subpoena may also be sought by prosecutors during grand jury investigations conducted to decide whether criminal charges should be brought. In civil litigation, journalists are often subpoenaed during **discovery**, a pretrial phase in which parties seek information from one another. Occasionally, prosecutors investigating crime without a grand jury or legislative committees and other government bodies may subpoena a journalist to testify or submit materials, but such summons are rarer than the other types.

Most reporters and news organizations think that any order to provide information in court interferes with news gathering and discourages confidential sources from coming forward with news. When a subpoena is issued, news organizations frequently respond with a motion to **quash,** or vacate, the subpoena. Many news organizations choose to comply with routine requests, but demands for the names of sources or for notes and similar background material are more likely to be challenged.

The news media have had many opportunities to oppose subpoenas in recent years. A survey by the Reporters Committee for Freedom of the Press that included only a small portion of news organizations nationwide found that more than 3,200 subpoenas were issued in 1991.[1] In a similar survey in 1989, more than 4,400 subpoenas were reported. Less than half the news organizations surveyed were subpoenaed, but those that were got seven or eight subpoenas. A reporter has a much greater chance of facing a judicial or governmental request for information than of being sued for libel.

Honoring promises of anonymity has long been an accepted ethical principle among journalists. Throughout the 1970s and 1980s, journalists sought—and largely obtained—formal legal protection against forced disclosure of confidential sources. They stressed that unless the guarantee of anonymity was solid, sources would stop talking to reporters, leading to a "chilling effect" on news gathering. The journalist's privilege that resulted varies considerably from state to state and court to court. As you will see throughout the chapter, though, the differences often involve procedure and definition rather than principles. The major reason for so much variety is that the U.S. Supreme Court has repeatedly declined to craft a nationwide privilege based upon the First Amendment.

Many jurisdictions have recognized a privilege for notes, film, videotape, and even eyewitnesses. Journalists have simply extended the chilling effect argument: any intrusion into the editorial process to obtain information reduces the boldness of both news sources and journalists themselves, especially if the material is sought by government prosecutors rather than by private litigants. Without a privilege, reporters might be less likely to pursue the kinds of important stories that eventually lead to criminal investigations and court actions, press advocates have argued. In practice, subpoenas have been issued following publication of almost any type of news story, but the press's argument has centered on investigative work.

The privileges adopted over the last two decades come in many forms. Although the Supreme Court has not directly recognized a First Amendment privilege, every United States circuit court of appeals but one has recognized such a privilege when the issue arose. Twenty-nine states have passed shield laws, statutes adopting the privilege in some form. One of these states, California, has also included the shield in the state constitution after a voter referendum. The courts in another seventeen states and the District of Columbia have adopted a privilege based on the First Amendment, the state constitution, or common law. Thus, some type of journalist's privilege exists in almost all jurisdictions in the United States.

Two decades of journalist's privilege law does not easily overcome two centuries of evidence law, however. There are two rules of evidence that reporters must understand. First, it is assumed that every citizen is obliged to come forward when called to testify. This means the courts will usually make every effort to find a reason to require that subpoenas be obeyed. Second, even where an evidentiary privilege exists, the privilege will be interpreted as narrowly as possible to allow as much testimony and evidence as possible. This means that journalists (and their lawyers) must know the specific rules that apply in their states or regions. The judicial rule that privileges be read narrowly has often meant that the formal protection provided in the text of statutes or court decisions is weaker than it appears to be.

BACKGROUND OF THE PRIVILEGE

Journalists have resisted attempts to force disclosure of the sources for their articles since before the country was founded. In the early years, refusal to disclose was apparently a natural reaction to perceived judicial or government coercion. But by the late 1800s and early 1900s, pledges of confidentiality began to appear in the codes of ethics of news organizations and professional societies. Reporters throughout the twentieth century have been taught in journalism school or told on the job that honoring promises of confidentiality is both a professional and an employment obligation. The importance of protecting anonymous sources is stressed in all the major textbooks on reporting and editing.

Journalists' first attempts to claim privilege were based on the common law, but state courts usually said that only a statutory privilege would be accepted. In 1896 Maryland became the first state to adopt a reporter privilege by statute. Few other states addressed the issue until the 1960s and 1970s, when demands by courts, criminal defendants, prosecutors, and civil litigants for information from journalists began to increase rapidly, in part because of an increase in investigative reporting. Journalists first pressed a claim for privilege based on the First Amendment in 1958,[2] but the U.S. Supreme Court did not hear a reporter privilege case until *Branzburg v. Hayes* in 1972. The number of cases involving both constitutional and common law claims for privilege grew after 1972. Thus, although working journalists tend to think of the privilege as having existed for a long time, its legal history is actually rather brief.

The classic argument for a privilege is based on the need to protect anonymous sources who provide information for stories. A surprising amount of the material in news stories comes either directly or indirectly from anonymous sources.[3] Persons with background information about criminal wrongdoing or political misdeeds are typical anonymous sources. They are often employees who do not want to be identified for fear of losing their jobs or other reprisals. Without a promise of confidentiality, they may never approach a reporter and the story may never get done. In other words, the sources may be deterred from coming forward—the "chilling effect."

The argument for privileging notes, documents, photographs, and video-tape is based on the institutional role of the press in society. It is argued that the press's ability to do its news-gathering job is inhibited when outsiders can interfere by demanding reporters provide information.[4] Journalists are extremely sensitive to the possible effects of serving as involuntary investigators for the police and courts. Not only would doing so take time away from their primary job, but any impression they are in league with the authorities might by itself scare away news sources.

The "chilling effect" on news gathering is less clear when reporters are asked for documentary evidence, though, and legislatures and courts have been more doubtful about this privilege claim than about the confidential source claim. Nevertheless, some level of protection is provided in most jursidictions.

The rationale for protecting journalists from testifying to events that they have personally seen is also based on the institutional role of the press in society. But this argument is considered weaker because reporters are being asked only to use their memories rather than to turn over work products such as notes or tapes. As an eyewitness, a reporter has usually seen only what any passerby might have, although perhaps with better-trained powers of observation. The courts consider requiring eyewitness testimony less intrusive than ordering names of sources. Even those that have adopted a privilege have been more ready to say that it has been overcome by the need for every person's evidence in observation cases.

The professed similarity between journalist's privilege and other types of privileges is deceptive. In the traditional lawyer-client or physician-patient privilege, the privilege is for the benefit of the client or patient, not the professional, and the client or patient controls the privilege. Only the client or patient can waive the privilege and disclose information or allow it to be disclosed. The professional is duty-bound not to disclose.

By contrast, the journalist's privilege is considered to operate for the benefit of society, which relies on the news media as its agent for gathering and disseminating news. The differences between journalist's privilege and other professional privileges have made interpretation more difficult for the courts. The privilege is controlled by the reporter, not the news source. Since the privilege benefits society as a whole, there is no direct, special personal relationship between the professional and those receiving the benefit of the privilege. Journalists nevertheless continue to be dismayed that the courts do not consider their privilege comparable to those applied to other professions.

Although the privilege has been accepted in some form almost everywhere, even statutes that appear to offer absolute protection probably only provide a **qualified privilege**.[5] A privilege is considered qualified when it can be overcome by a stronger interest presented by the person seeking disclosure. For example, the qualified First Amendment privilege adopted in most federal courts of appeal can be overcome by proof that the requester's constitutional interests are greater than the journalist's. Therefore, a reporter who promises anonymity to a source may be ordered to identify the source even though a privilege applies. If the reporter refuses to obey the court order, the reporter will likely be found in **contempt of court** for directly disobeying the order. Contempt may be enforced with jail time, fines, or both. Although jailing of reporters is rare, it still occurs.[6] Often when a case approaches this extreme result, sources voluntarily come forward to save the reporter from "doing time."

Journalists must be cautious in using confidential sources and claiming privilege for materials. Many news organizations require reporters to clear any use of anonymous sources with their supervising news director or editor. Even when using anonymous sources, most journalists prefer sources who can lead them to additional sources who may be willing to talk on the record. In deciding to claim a privilege, either for sources or materials, reporters need to be familiar with the state or federal circuit rules that apply where they work.

Although the law affecting journalist's privilege has become well-established and settled in most of the United States, it remains one of the most complex areas of communication law because it differs slightly from state to state and from one federal circuit to another. The only rule that applies everywhere concerns **due process**. Due process requires that courts follow specified procedures when making decisions that will affect any person's rights. The principles of due process require that a court provide the journalist with a hearing to present arguments whenever a privilege claim is made.

- **Qualified privilege**
  A privilege that can be overcome by a stronger interest. In communications law, a journalist's privilege not to identify a source is qualified in that it can be overcome by greater constitutional interests.

- **Contempt of court**
  A type of punishment for violation of a court order. It will typically include fines, but may also include jail time.

- **Due process**
  The requirement that courts must follow specified procedures when making decisions that affect a person's rights.

FIRST AMENDMENT PROTECTION

A First Amendment or federal common law privilege protecting journalists has been adopted in every federal circuit court of appeals that has considered the matter but one. The exception is the Sixth Circuit, which has expressed judicial hostility to the privilege.[7] The Sixth Circuit has indicated it will not adopt the privilege unless commanded to do so by the Supreme Court. Journalists in the Sixth Circuit, which includes Kentucky, Michigan, Ohio, and Tennessee, must therefore rely upon state law alone.

All the rest of the federal courts of appeal have adopted the privilege to cover both confidential sources and materials. The protection is strong, except in the Fourth Circuit, which includes Maryland, North Carolina, South Carolina, Virginia, and West Virginia. That circuit uses a case-by-case ad hoc balancing test.[8] In ad hoc balancing, a court uses a "preponderance of the evidence" standard to assess a list of factors to decide which side should prevail. By contrast, where the privilege is strong, a heightened burden of proof is placed upon the party seeking disclosure.

The formula used most frequently nationwide protects against disclosure of sources or documents unless the party seeking the information can meet a three-part test that requires the following proof:

1. That the information is critical to the decision in the case.

2. That there are no reasonable alternative sources for the information.

3. That there is a compelling or overriding public or personal interest in disclosure of the information.

The test is derived from Justice Potter Stewart's dissent in *Branzburg v. Hayes*, discussed in the next section. The test is a good example of how a dissenting opinion can influence the development of an area of law. Under this test, journalists will be forced to testify only if there is no other way to get information, and then only if the information is central to the case. The last part of the test is the most difficult to apply. The Supreme Court has never provided a strict definition of "compelling" or "overriding" interests, although the Court has often indicated that a compelling interest must be grounded in the Constitution.

Because the last part of the test is somewhat unclear, what may be considered compelling or overriding in a criminal prosecution may not be in a civil lawsuit. In general, though, the three-part test is a useful guideline. The Third Circuit uses a slightly different formula. That circuit, covering Delaware, New Jersey, and Pennsylvania, adopted the privilege as part of the federal common law of evidence rather than as part of constitutional law; it does not use the compelling or overriding interest language in its test,[9] but considers the strength of the interests anyhow.

The status of an eyewitness privilege is less certain. Some courts have required eyewitness testimony about nonconfidential events based on the argument that a journalist is essentially no different from any other eyewitness.[10] Others have said that the testimony should not be compelled unless the journalist is the only potential witness able to provide the desired information, but these courts may not require proof of a compelling interest or proof that the information is critical to the decision in the case.[11] Where it is recognized, then, the eyewitness privilege is weaker than the confidential source or materials privilege.

The *Branzburg* Case

The lower federal courts have adopted the privilege in the wake of the Supreme Court's 1972 decision in *Branzburg v. Hayes*,[12] which remains the most important journalist's privilege case more than twenty years after it was decided. Some familiarity with *Branzburg* is necessary to understand the privilege developments that followed. The case is a genuine puzzle, requiring extended direct study to unravel all of its threads of argument. It provides ammunition for both advocates and opponents of a journalist's privilege. It provides a framework for the creation of a privilege by state and lower federal courts and by legislatures, but does not explicitly recognize any privilege—and certainly not one based upon the First Amendment. The case expresses serious doubts about the ability of judges to make distinctions among news gatherers in applying a journalist's privilege, but at the same time a majority of the justices appeared willing to apply one.

To understand *Branzburg*, it is important to remember that the Court was severely divided. Legal writers usually describe it as a 5–4 decision, but the vote was actually 4–1–4. Justice Byron White wrote the majority opinion, but Justice Lewis Powell concurred so narrowly that he robbed the majority opinion of much of its persuasive force. Some lower courts have decided that *Branzburg* operates as precedent only for the narrow points where Powell agreed with White. Justice Stewart led the four dissenters. Since Powell agreed with much of what was said on both sides, his short individual opinion is the key to the case.

The facts that gave rise to the Supreme Court's *Branzburg* decision were most undesirable from the news media's point of view. Actually a consolidation of three separate appeals, *Branzburg* involved claims by three reporters that the First Amendment should provide them with a privilege to refuse to appear before a **grand jury** investigating crimes. A grand jury is an investigative body that reviews information and accusations in criminal cases to determine if there is sufficient evidence to bring indictments.

● **Grand jury**
An investigative body that reviews information and accusations in criminal cases to determine if there is sufficient evidence to bring an indictment.

The crimes and the times were of no help in these cases. In one case, reporter Paul Branzburg of the Louisville *Courier-Journal* had been invited to observe marijuana being transformed into hashish, but only after making a pledge of confidentiality. In the other two cases, reporters Paul Pappas and Earl Caldwell both had confidential sources within the Black Panther Party. The militant Panthers were believed by many officials to be planning guerrilla warfare against white society. Pappas was allowed entry to the group's Massachusetts headquarters upon promising secrecy. Caldwell had been covering the Panthers in the San Francisco area for the *New York Times* on a continuing basis. Social concern over the drug trade and radical politics was at its height in the late 1960s and early 1970s, a period in which President Richard Nixon had reporters spied upon as potential threats to national security.

All three reporters were called by grand juries—Branzburg and Pappas by state grand juries, Caldwell by a federal grand jury. Branzburg and Pappas both appeared but refused to answer questions about the individuals they had observed. Caldwell, who suspected he would be asked about his Panther contacts in general, refused to appear and would have landed in jail if the lower courts had not accepted his privilege argument.[13]

All three journalists argued that the mere requirement of appearing before a grand jury, which conducts its proceedings in secret, would erode their ability to function as news gatherers because sources would dry up in fear that reporters would be forced to disclose their names. Sources would have good reason to worry. Once before a grand jury, the only privilege a witness can routinely claim is the Fifth Amendment guarantee against self-incrimination.

A footnote in Powell's concurring opinion states the one point where he unequivocally agrees with White: the reporter must at least appear before the grand jury, then invoke the privilege. Powell considered it inappropriate to allow journalists to contest the very authority of government to call them as witnesses. Once the privilege is invoked, however, Powell called for courts to consider the needs of journalists—and to protect journalists if they are harassed or if the grand jury has no legitimate need for their information.

Justice White's lengthy opinion concluded that a journalist's privilege is not required under the First Amendment and would be impractical and too complicated to apply even if it were adopted. White raised several issues that continue to haunt analysis of the privilege. Who is entitled to claim the privilege? White did not want the courts determining who is a legitimate journalist. What is protected by the privilege? White anticipated that the privilege would not remain limited to protection of confidential sources. White also doubted the claim that lack of a privilege would have a chilling effect on reporting, noting that no studies proved the claim.

Perhaps most important to White, however, was the constitutional status of the grand jury. The Fifth Amendment calls for a grand jury to be convened "for a capital, or otherwise infamous crime," at least in the federal legal system. Many states have similar provisions. Even if White's opinion had explicitly adopted the privilege, he apparently would have sided with the function of the grand jury in this battle of competing constitutional interests. As he noted, the journalists' claim of privilege was not directly based upon the language of the First Amendment, and he added that journalists could seek relief in court if grand juries began hindering news gathering.

Despite his misgivings, White emphasized that Congress, state courts, and state legislatures were free to enact a journalist's privilege. His encouragement played a major role in the widespread adoption of the privilege in the 1970s and 1980s.

Justice Stewart's dissent accepted the chilling effect argument presented by the journalists, concluding that failure to protect confidential sources would reduce the flow of information to the public. His three-part test was designed to put the burden of proof on government to show that a reporter's information was inescapably necessary in a legal dispute. In effect, he created a presumption against disclosure, whereas White had accepted the traditional presumption in favor of disclosure.

The Aftermath of *Branzburg*

It probably came as a surprise to Justice White and the majority when the lower federal courts began interpreting *Branzburg* in the narrowest ways possible. The courts determined that the arguments favoring the privilege were stronger in other types of cases, and soon *Branzburg* was being read as applying only to subpoenas before grand juries, and perhaps only to refusals by reporters to obey subpoenas and appear.

One of the first cases to distinguish *Branzburg* was *Baker v. F&F Investment*,[14] which involved a civil suit alleging discrimination in housing sales. The plaintiffs sought names of sources from Alfred Balk, then editor of the *Columbia Journalism Review*, for a magazine story he had written ten years earlier. Balk offered to cooperate but would not reveal sources. The Second Circuit determined that the purely private interests of plaintiffs in civil litigation were not as strong as the constitutional interest in the function of grand juries. The privilege claim was upheld, but the court did not adopt a specific test.

The privilege was soon accepted in criminal matters as well. In *Bursey v. United States*,[15] the Ninth Circuit had followed its analysis in the earlier *Caldwell* case by conditionally protecting journalists who had been called to testify before a grand jury. The court rejected a petition to rehear the case when *Branzburg* was decided shortly thereafter. Instead, the court added a separate opinion about why it felt the case was different from *Branzburg*. Since the journalists in *Bursey* had appeared and testified, the case was different. When a radio station manager refused even to appear before a grand jury two years later, the Ninth Circuit said that *Branzburg* did apply.[16] Within a short time, almost all jurisdictions had limited *Branzburg* to apply only to virtually identical fact situations.

Applying a journalist's privilege in criminal trials is a bit more awkward for two reasons. First, a criminal defendant has an explicit right to a fair trial under the Sixth Amendment. A defendant is normally entitled to all material that may be relevant in presenting a defense. Courts have repeatedly noted that the right to a fair trial is a compelling interest, but they have also noted that the other parts of the test apply.[17] Unless information held by a journalist cannot be obtained elsewhere, the interest in a fair trial is not endangered. Even if information is available only from a journalist, it must go to the "heart of the claim," a test stricter than looking to see whether the information is merely relevant.

The second problem in criminal trials is that sometimes the prosecution rather than the defense seeks information. The prosecution in effect argues that society has a compelling interest in deterring, discovering, and punishing crime, a point argued by Justice White in his *Branzburg* opinion. Since a trial differs from a grand jury hearing, the courts have upheld claims of privilege when journalists are subpoenaed to testify by the prosecution. To keep the government from taking off on "fishing expeditions" at the expense of the news media, some courts require evidence that success or failure of the prosecution will likely depend upon the information sought.[18]

The privilege was also quickly applied in libel cases, where journalists are involved parties rather than third parties. In *Cervantes v. Time, Inc.*,[19] the Eighth Circuit distinguished *Branzburg* and upheld a privilege claim in a libel suit brought by the mayor of St. Louis against *Life* magazine. The mayor argued that identification of anonymous sources was necessary to meet the actual malice test public officials must prove in libel cases. The court said that the mayor must prove that the sources would prove highly relevant on the issue of actual malice before disclosure would be ordered. Later cases directly applied versions of the three-part test.

The scope of the privilege also expanded quickly to include notes and materials as well as confidential sources. Courts accepting the privilege usually apply it to protect both unpublished and nonconfidential materials.[20]

Problems with the First Amendment Privilege

Journalists' greatest concern about the First Amendment privilege is that it has not been adopted by the Supreme Court despite its wide acceptance by the lower courts. In a number of cases, the Court has indicated its awareness of the privilege and its widespread adoption,[21] but has consistently refused to hear journalist privilege cases. As long as it is not ratified by the Court, the privilege remains a bit shaky. While the privilege exists in most federal circuits, the variations in rules, especially in the Third, Fourth, and Sixth Circuits, invite a clarifying decision from the Supreme Court.

Another difficulty with the First Amendment–based privilege is its relative vagueness. Any judge-made rule is fine-tuned as additional cases are decided. If a privilege claim arises from facts that are significantly different from those in past cases, the courts may find it more difficult to apply the privilege. This problem also exists whenever a state or federal court adopts the privilege as a matter of common law. With a judge-made rule, courts are constantly having to address original issues and craft responses. Examples include whether the privilege covered a newspaper librarian (it did not),[22] whether to prevent disclosure of previously broadcast videotape because disclosure would also release portions that had not been broadcast (the tape was protected),[23] and whether an investment analyst who wrote on a public issue is covered by the privilege (he was).[24] Statutory privileges in the form of shield laws provide more specific rules for deciding cases; the major problem with shield laws, however, is that they may be too narrow. Either approach involves a trade-off from the press's point of view.

The Supreme Court's only case directly involving journalist's privilege since *Branzburg* was *Cohen v. Cowles Media Co.*[25] in 1991. But *Cohen* was about the legal consequences of the news media breaking confidentiality promises, not the protection of source identities. The source, Dan Cohen, worked for the Republican candidates for governor and lieutenant governor in Minnesota. After securing a promise of anonymity from reporters at both the Minneapolis and the St. Paul daily newspapers, Cohen delivered documents showing that the Democratic candidate for lieutenant governor had years before been charged with unlawful assembly and convicted of petty theft. After the reporters returned to their newsrooms with the material, their editors decided to ignore the promises made by the reporters and identified Cohen as the source. He was fired the day of publication from his permanent job as a public relations specialist in an advertising agency.

Cohen filed suit claiming that the pledge of anonymity was an enforceable contract. There was no written contract, of course, so Cohen tried to show that the oral promise should be enforced just the same as a written promise. The Minnesota Supreme Court said applying contract law would violate the First Amendment by interfering with the editorial independence of the news media.[26]

The U.S. Supreme Court reversed the state court and sent the case back to the Minnesota courts. The Court urged Cohen to consider the state common law doctrine of promissory estoppel as the basis of his claim rather than contract. The five-member majority, again led by Justice White, said that no First

Amendment violation had occurred because promissory estoppel is a "law of general application" that applies to everyone and is not aimed at the press in particular. Four dissenters argued for the use of a compelling interest test or a comparable test that would make suits such as Cohen's more difficult.

Following the Supreme Court decision, Cohen prevailed in state court under **promissory estoppel**. This flexible doctrine exists to prevent injustice when someone relies and acts upon the promise of someone else, even if there is no written agreement and no money changes hands. Cohen claimed that the information had value, making it the basis of the deal in the absence of money. He was helped by testimony from the reporters, who said that they fully expected the newspapers to honor their promises of anonymity. After reconsidering the case, the Minnesota Supreme Court decided a new trial was unnecessary and upheld a $200,000 damage award against the newspapers.[27]

The *Cohen* case caused a stir in publishing circles. Journalists have reason to worry that the Court has opened the door to alternative theories of liability, and the decision is likely to encourage other sources who have been "burned" to consider suing. The Court's opinion has been criticized as being out of step with the Court's own approach to press cases.[28] The decision does not directly affect the legal status of journalist's privilege, however. It only emphasizes that promises may be enforced. Lower courts may limit the effect of *Cohen* by applying the law of promissory estoppel strictly.[29] In many ways, however, the newspapers have no one but themselves to blame in *Cohen*. If the editors had honored the promises of confidentiality and chided the reporters later in private, there would have been no case.

● **Promissory estoppel**
The doctrine that requires a promise to be enforced when someone has relied upon and acted (or refrained from acting) upon it and injustice can be avoided only by enforcement of the promise.

STATE LAW PRIVILEGE

Following the Supreme Court's refusal in *Branzburg* to create a nationwide journalist's privilege grounded in the First Amendment, there was a modest rush to seek protection at the state level. At the time *Branzburg* was decided, seventeen states had laws protecting journalists from disclosing information. Today twenty-nine have statutes. These statutes are normally referred to as **"shield laws"** because they shield journalists from forced disclosure. They are typically passed explicitly to protect journalists. An exception is Michigan's statute, which was passed to prevent abuse of grand juries by prosecutors. The states with statutes are Alabama, Alaska, Arizona, Arkansas, California, Colorado, Delaware, Georgia, Illinois, Indiana, Kentucky, Louisiana, Maryland, Michigan, Minnesota, Montana, Nebraska, Nevada, New Jersey, New Mexico, New York, North Dakota, Ohio, Oklahoma, Oregon, Pennsylvania, Rhode Island, and Tennessee.

The press also sought protection under state constitutions and under state common law. Seventeen additional states and the District of Columbia have recognized a privilege this way. The states are Connecticut, Florida, Idaho, Iowa, Kansas, Louisiana, Maine, Massachusetts, New Hampshire, North Carolina, South Carolina, Texas, Vermont, Virginia, Washington, West Virginia, and Wisconsin. In addition, court opinions in eight states with shield

● **Shield laws**
State statutes that protect journalists from being forced to disclose information or materials in court.

laws—Alabama, Alaska, California, Delaware, Indiana, New York, Ohio, and Oklahoma—have hinted that there may be common law or constitutional protection beyond that provided by statute.

Only Hawaii, Mississippi, Missouri, South Dakota, Utah, and Wyoming do not explicitly provide protection from disclosure. Journalists in these states must rely upon the federal privilege recognized by the U.S. circuit courts of appeal.

In the event that a journalist is called upon to provide information or materials in court, the forum is more likely to be a state court than a federal court because far more actions are filed at the state level than at the federal level. For this reason alone, familiarity with state privilege law is important for journalists. It is also important because the state courts typically prefer to decide privilege disputes using their own law rather than federal law, even if both state and federal law might apply to the case. When the state has a shield law, courts will almost always consider how it applies before moving to any common law or constitutional arguments. If the shield law resolves the issue, the case normally ends.

Common Law and Constitutional Law Protection

For the most part, state courts adopting a privilege by judicial decision mirror the federal decisions. The three-part test advanced by Justice Stewart in *Branzburg* is fairly standard. Coverage is not standard, however. Since this method of creating privilege is analyzed on a case-by-case basis, a journalist cannot be certain protection will apply unless the circumstances are similar to those previously addressed by the state court. For example, a court may accept that a reporter has a privilege not to disclose sources in a civil case where the reporter is not a party to the case. The decision is little help to a reporter trying to determine the protection available in a criminal case, where the defendant's fair trial right is likely to be seen as a compelling interest.[30] Similarly, if the reporter is a defendant, as in a libel action, the court may squeeze the privilege to avoid letting the press use its protection for self-interested purposes.[31]

Cataloging the judge-made protections is difficult. In most of the states, only a handful of cases have been decided, and they cover a limited range of situations. Protection appears strongest when a reporter claims privilege to protect the identities of informants or to prevent release of confidential documents. Protection is weaker for published materials or for eyewitness testimony. To qualify for the privilege, a showing that one is a regularly employed journalist or an active freelancer is typically required.

Of the states with judicially created privileges, Florida has traditionally provided the strongest protection, but the protection applies almost exclusively to confidential sources and does not include eyewitness testimony or requested materials.[32] Florida also has the largest number of decided cases. Until recently, the state followed the three-part test, but has apparently now adopted an ad hoc, case-by-case balancing test.[33] Such a test offers no predictable level of protection.

Ironically, Florida has also been the site for a recent widely publicized conflict that ended with reporter Tim Roche serving eighteen days in jail. Roche had published a judge's order in a child custody case despite state law requiring that parental rights hearings be closed and sealed. The state's attorney then began an investigation of the closure violation and issued a subpoena for Roche to identify the source, undoubtedly a court employee, who had given Roche the judge's order. The court of appeals determined that the secrecy of child custody hearings was a compelling interest and upheld a criminal contempt order against Roche entered by the judge who originally oversaw the child custody hearing. The U.S. Supreme Court declined review.[34] The Roche case highlights the hazards of a case-by-case approach. In its opinion, the court of appeals distinguished Roche's situation from two earlier cases where reporters had violated closure rules and remained protected.

While a constitutional or common law privilege is subject to modification by its very nature, the modification is not always in the direction of less protection for journalists. In the case *In re Ridenhour*,[35] the Louisiana Supreme Court adopted a constitutional privilege based on the state constitution and the First Amendment when the state shield law would not prevent a reporter from forced disclosure before a grand jury. The shield law allowed forced disclosure whenever "disclosure is essential to the protection of the public interest," an ambiguous balancing test to be applied initially by trial court judges. The court in *Ridenhour* adopted a constitutional test—less protective of journalists than Stewart's, however.

For the most part, states using common law or state constitutional law have followed Stewart's three-part test in applying privileges. A major advantage of relying upon state law is that when privilege is based on "**independent state grounds,**" the decision cannot be reconsidered by the federal courts.[36] This can also be a major disadvantage if the privilege recognized in the federal circuit court of appeals is actually stronger. The inevitable conflict among jurisdictions is the greatest argument for having the U.S. Supreme Court permanently resolve the issue.[37] Many journalists, though, would prefer no Supreme Court resolution because the justices could decide against the privilege.

● **Independent state grounds**
A privilege based on a state constitution or state statute cannot be reconsidered by the federal courts.

State Shield Laws

For many journalists, statutory protection will be the initial line of defense against forced disclosures. As statutes, shield laws have two major advantages. First, their provisions are reasonably clear and therefore easy to follow. Second, statutes can be amended to accommodate situations that were not foreseen when the original version of a law was adopted. Legislatures in many of the shield law states have passed amendments, most of which have broadened protection for journalists. To many journalists, the ability to amend readily is also the greatest argument against shield laws: what the legislature grants one term, it can always take away the next. The history of state shield laws indicates that this has not been a real danger, however.

Journalists should become familiar with the shield laws in their individual states. Statutory provisions vary widely from one state to another. More important, when there is a shield law, state courts will normally apply the statute before considering any common law or constitutional arguments. If the shield law's application is especially clear in a particular situation, the shield law will be the shortest route to a journalist prevailing in court. Since shield laws constitute changes from the common law of evidence, it is important to remember that the courts tend to interpret them narrowly, granting no more protection than the language of the statute indicates the legislature intended.[38] If the statute provides sweeping protection for journalists, though, the court will normally follow the language and intent of the legislature.[39]

Although proposed federal statutes have been introduced repeatedly, no federal shield law has been enacted or seems likely to be enacted. The U.S. Department of Justice has established guidelines for government lawyers to follow when seeking to subpoena journalists or when seeking telephone records from news organizations. By their own terms, however, the guidelines do not provide for judicial enforcement.[40] The guidelines do at least caution against interfering with news organizations. Journalists may also rely to a limited extent on the federal courts to apply federal rules of evidence and procedure to prevent unduly broad inquiry into the editorial process.[41]

The protection provided by state shields varies from virtually absolute to virtually nonexistent. Among the strongest on paper are those in Nebraska[42] and Alabama.[43] Alabama's applies only to the disclosure of sources used by a person "connected with or employed by" media, but it applies to every sort of legal and political proceeding. Nebraska's is just as strong and much broader. It applies to all persons who intend to communicate with the public and protects against disclosures in all proceedings, state or federal. It also applies to information as well as to sources.

The weakest shield law is undoubtedly Michigan's.[44] The law applies only to disclosure of sources before grand juries, and even then contains an exception for cases where a grand jury is considering a capital crime such as murder. Until it was amended in 1986, the law protected only print journalists. The Michigan courts have always read the statute narrowly.[45] The Michigan Court of Appeals has recognized a limited First Amendment privilege to protect the identities of anonymous sources in civil cases,[46] but there is reason to suspect the state supreme court might not agree.

In assessing the scope of protection under a shield law, one must look at three areas of protection. Who is covered by the statute? What information or material is protected? In what proceedings is the privilege effective? It is also necessary to look for specific exceptions to the privilege.

Who is Protected? • To be protected by a shield law, an individual must be within the classification of persons listed. All the shield laws cover journalists who are regularly employed by news organizations. But the statute may not cover freelancers, book authors, and those not regularly engaged in news media activities.[47] In a nonstatutory case, a Florida trial court ruled that a newspaper librarian was not covered by a privilege because a librarian is not engaged in the gathering of news.[48] A New York state trial court determined that students working on a college newspaper were not "professionals" as intended by the shield law.[49] Another twist on qualifying for the privilege concerns intent. Since the statutes are passed to help ensure a free flow of information to the public, a journalist may still not qualify for protection if the information gathered was not intended to be distributed publicly.[50]

Despite some limitations, qualifying for protection is simple for most journalists. Most are employees. Freelancers may need to show a past record of publication or, in some cases, a contract with a publisher. Fledgling journalists who are not employees are left out of most shield laws.

Information and Materials Protected • A handful of shield laws apply only when a news organization has published a story, while the others apply without regard to publication.[51] A publication requirement could have an obvious chilling effect upon ongoing investigative reporting.

The identity of confidential sources is the information most frequently protected, which is not surprising since source identity has been the classic privilege issue. The courts may find it difficult to accept a reporter's claim that a subpoena seeks the identity of an anonymous source if the reporter's testimony is the only support for the confidential relationship. The statute recently debated in South Carolina calls for a written memorandum between a journalist and an editor or other supervisor.[52] The memo would serve as proof that a confidential source relationship existed. Most states do not require proof of a confidential relationship.

The status of notes, records, video outtakes, and unused negatives varies greatly from statute to statute. The best rule for a journalist to follow is to assume these materials are not protected unless the local law explicitly includes them. On occasion state courts have extended a source privilege to other materials, reasoning that notes and similar items may lead to identification of a source.[53] Given the tendency of courts to read these laws narrowly, one should not expect other state courts to be persuaded to judicially broaden a shield law. Many states protect unpublished materials only if a source would be implicated. In general, the trial judge decides whether the material would identify a source.[54] Sometimes the judge conducts an **in camera review**—personal observation of materials in the judge's chambers—of the materials to decide if the privilege applies. *In camera* review is also frequently used when a judge must decide whether an exception to the shield law, such as proof of the three-part test, applies.[55]

States with very broad protection follow a different rationale—that the courts and government should not interfere with the practice of journalism unless absolutely necessary. For example, Tennessee protects any information, while Nebraska's statute even specifies the forms in which information may appear. One sure way to make the protection strong as well as broad is for the statute not to allow *in camera* review by judges in the privacy of their chambers.[56] That way no one except the journalist sees the material.

Proceedings Covered by Shield Laws • The majority of statutes are written very broadly to apply to all judicial, administrative, legislative, and investigative proceedings, including grand juries. That does not mean the shields apply

● **In camera review**
A personal examination of materials by the judge in his or her chambers.

uniformly. The type of proceeding makes a great difference, with privilege strongest in civil suits where a journalist is not a party and weakest in libel suits. Protection is also weaker in criminal trials than civil trials, due to the conflict between the constitutional interests of the defendant and the privilege claims of journalists. When the statute conflicts with state or federal constitutional rights, constitutional law prevails.

Exceptions to Shield Laws • Journalists should watch for three major exceptions to the shield laws. First is the use of a balancing test that a party seeking disclosure must meet to overcome the privilege. The majority of states use Stewart's three-part test for this purpose. This test provides fairly strong protection, as most parties seeking disclosure cannot meet the three elements of a compelling interest, lack of alternative sources, and proof that the evidence may make or break the case. Other states use a less-focused balancing test along the lines of assuring that the interests of justice are served. This type of ad hoc, ambiguous balancing in effect leaves protection to the discretion of the trial judge.[57]

The second major exception is for entire classes of court actions. The most typical is for libel. Under any of the privileges—statutory, common law, or constitutional—a libel suit in which the journalist is a defendant poses difficulties. Although there is no general rule weakening privilege in libel cases, that has been the overall tendency.[58] Some states modify the three-part test for libel. For example, Minnesota does not require proof of a compelling interest to force source disclosure in libel cases.[59]

The third major statutory exception concerns eyewitness testimony. In almost all cases, the courts have said that a journalist who personally witnesses an event must testify.[60] Courts applying constitutional and common law privileges usually reach the same result.[61] Some states will protect eyewitness testimony because of the disruption of the news process caused by a subpoena. New Jersey, for example, requires proof that the journalist will likely have relevant evidence, and additionally requires a showing that other witnesses just as appropriate were not available.[62] In other circumstances, however, a journalist is treated just like any other citizen who may have witnessed an event.

SUMMARY

The law of journalist's privilege is among the most confusing in mass communication law. Libel and privacy also feature a mixture of federal and state law, but in libel the federal law is nationwide, and most states follow the same common law tort rules for libel and privacy. The Supreme Court's offhand encouragement of experimentation in *Branzburg* has led to the creation of privileges based upon six distinct areas of law—federal constitutional law, federal common law, federal statutes and rules, state constitutional law, state common law, and state statutes. The Court's position that privilege can be a matter for the states to decide has led to two decades of jurisdictional ambiguity. When a reporter's work crosses state lines, any subsequent subpoena may be complicated by competing privileges from different jurisdictions. A journalist needs to know what the law is in each jurisdiction where news gathering occurs. Under present law only a court can decide with authority what privilege applies and how strongly.[63]

All is not confusion, however. Protection for the names of confidential sources is almost universal. Almost as universal is the use of Justice Stewart's three-part test to assess any demand for disclosure. Although the press has long sought absolute privileges, it has gained them in only a few states. As in many other areas of mass communication law, the interests of the mass media are weighed against other interests. The weighing heavily favors journalists, but on occasion the privilege is overcome.

KEY TERMS

Evidentiary privilege
Subpoena
Discovery
Quash
Qualified privilege
Contempt of court

Due process
Grand jury
Promissory estoppel
Shield laws
Independent state grounds
In camera review

[handwritten: info. is critical / no other sources / public/personal int]

CASE PROBLEMS

[handwritten: info. central to case]

1. You are Nancy Sellers, a reporter at WELP-TV. A few months ago, you ran a story on drug dealing in your community. As part of the story, you aired clips from an interview with a major local drug dealer. By agreement, the dealer's face was obscured, and his voice was disguised on the videotape. Anonymity was promised, and obtained, since no one apparently could identify the dealer from what was broadcast. Only portions that were broadcast obscured the dealer's face and disguised his voice. In the portion broadcast, the dealer announced he is "the biggest cocaine dealer in the city." He credited his success in part to "lousy work by the police department."

In early July, a large shipment of impure cocaine hit the market. Twelve cocaine users died after using the drug. Police efforts to locate the source of the adulterated drug have failed. Now the county prosecutor has asked you to identify the dealer you talked to so that investigators might get a lead on the bad cocaine; he assures you that no prosecution of your source is anticipated, but says that he may convene a grand jury and subpoena you and all your videotapes if you do not help voluntarily. You answer that you will check with your news director and with the station's lawyer and get back to him.

Will you be able to uphold your promise of confidentiality? *[handwritten: yes – if they could prove he was it – no]*

2. The state legislature has just passed a reporter privilege statute. The statute defines "persons covered" under its provisions as follows:

> [T]hose who are employed by recognized news organizations in this state or in the United States. Ordinarily, proof of membership in a professional journalism organization or of employment will be considered sufficient evidence for application of the privilege.

The statute provides an absolute privilege and applies to all court, administrative, and legislative proceedings in state or federal bodies. There is no exception that allows for forced disclosure of the names of sources or of materials. You are the governor's legal adviser. He tells you he generally supports this kind of protection for reporters, but wants your opinion on the likelihood of later troubles with the law. Advise him.

3. Doctors and lawyers have traditionally been granted a common law exemption from being compelled

to testify in court about anything said between themselves and their patients or clients. Yet courts were slow in recognizing a similar privilege to protect the relationship between journalists and their sources. What *theoretical* rationales and justifications do judges have for not according the same privilege to journalists that other professionals have?

4. *World-Globe* reporter Jo Beets is in trouble again. Beets was sent to jail this morning by federal district court judge Alice Williams. Beets refused to testify or turn over notes, photocopies, and tapes of interviews despite a subpoena in the case *United States v. Northern Airways*. A little background is necessary.

Beets had been assigned by the managing editor to prepare an investigative series on the airline industry. Northern Airways, Canada's third largest privately owned airline, was the focus of three of the twelve stories in the series. The company has had three serious crashes in the last two years—including one last month in Burlington, Vermont, that killed eighty-six people. According to the U.S. attorney prosecuting the case, all three crashes were a result of improper maintenance. The federal government has brought criminal charges against Northern as a company and against its president, Norbert Duncan, individually.

Beets got to know several sources within Northern. Those sources told her how maintenance records had sometimes been falsified to look as though required safety checks and maintenance work had been performed when no work had taken place. Beets promised the sources anonymity after clearing the promise with her editor. The sources gave Beets photocopies of the records.

Beets also learned that several of the sources, including at least three members of the maintenance crew at the local City Airport, had drug problems that might impair the quality of their work. Beets taped all interviews and made extra copies of all documents. One document, a memo labeled "confidential," ordered the maintenance department to "cut maintenance costs by 20 percent by whatever means necessary." The memo bore Norbert Duncan's signature. It was reprinted in part in the *World-Globe*.

At least three of Beets's sources said they would talk to the federal prosecutor if they were guaranteed immunity from prosecution themselves. The prosecutor refused to grant immunity, but said that those who cooperate might get a reduced sentence.

The sources decided not to identify themselves to authorities.

The prosecutor wants Beets's notes, photocopies, and tapes to prove that Northern and Duncan falsified repair reports. The prosecutor wants to know the names of sources for the same reason—and also perhaps to file drug charges against them.

Beets is sure there must be some legal protection for her. She uses her quarter to call you, the managing editor, for advice. What do you say?

5. You are reporter Luis Martinez of the *World-Globe*. Last year you wrote a story that accused Mark Talbot, the local director of the Community Campaign (formerly United Way), of embezzling more than $400,000 in funds donated to the agency by members of the public. The story originated with a call from Mary Stone, who had been Talbot's administrative assistant. Stone agreed to talk with you only if she was promised anonymity, which you promised. Following newspaper policy, you informed the managing editor of Stone's identity. Stone provided you with more than a hundred pages of photocopies of financial and accounting records, which showed that funds were shifted from agency accounts to private bank accounts in the names of members of Talbot's immediate family. No documents proved that Talbot himself ever had control of transferred funds. Talbot is being prosecuted on the embezzlement charge by the county prosecutor; the case has not come to trial. Talbot was fired without a hearing by the agency board of directors. After a nationwide search, Stone was hired as director. She has repeatedly said in news coverage that she "knows nothing" about Talbot's handling of funds while he was director. She said she would sue you if you ever disclosed that she was the main source for the article.

The prosecutor has filed for a subpoena that would require you to identify your source and would also require "disclosure of any records" in your possession relating to the case. A hearing on the subpoena is scheduled for tomorrow. The judge tells you in court to bring the records with you. It appears that Talbot ran the financial records through a shredder the day after the story appeared. You tell the managing editor that both the subpoena and the order to bring documents should be challenged. She asks you how they should be challenged. Tell her.

6. Assume all the facts given in Question 5 above. Now Talbot has sued the *World-Globe* for libel. His

lawyer has filed a motion for an order to disclose the "sources consulted in the story" and to disclose "all records used in the preparation of the story." In addition to Stone, there were twelve human sources for the article, all named. You also used twenty-seven documents in addition to those provided by Stone. All of the documents were publicly available, but none indicated embezzlement by Talbot. The lawyer cites the state constitution's explicit provision for a cause of action for libel as proof that reputation is a fundamental right. Again you tell the managing editor that the disclosure request should be challenged. Again she asks you how. Tell her.

Talbot should prove it's not true & negligence — burden of proof on plaintiff

ENDNOTES

1. "Report Finds Increased Reliance on Shield Laws to Quash Subpoenas," *The News Media and the Law*, Winter 1993, p. 49.

2. *Garland v. Torre*, 259 F.2d 545 (2d Cir. 1958).

3. John L. Hulteng, *The Messenger's Motives: Ethical Problems of the News Media* (Englewood Cliffs, N.J.: Prentice-Hall, 1985), pp. 89–95.

4. Timothy L. Alger, "Promises Not to Be Kept: The Illusory Newsgatherer's Privilege in California," *Loyola of Los Angeles Law Review* 25:1:155–228 (November 1991).

5. Todd F. Simon, "Reporter Privilege: Can Nebraska Pass a Shield Law to Bind the Whole World?" *Nebraska Law Review* 61:2:446–498 (1982).

6. "Florida Reporter Begins Jail Sentence," News Notes No. 4, *Media Law Reporter*, March 23, 1993.

7. *Storer Communications v. Giovan*, 810 F.2d 580 (6th Cir. 1987).

8. *In re Grand Jury Subpoena*, 955 F.2d 229 (4th Cir. 1992).

9. *Riley v. City of Chester*, 612 F.2d 708 (3d Cir. 1979).

10. *In re Shain*, 978 F.2d 850 (4th Cir. 1992).

11. *Parsons v. Watson*, 778 F.Supp. 214 (D.Del. 1991).

12. 408 U.S. 665, 92 S.Ct. 2646 (1972).

13. *Caldwell v. United States*, 434 F.2d 1081 (9th Cir. 1970).

14. 470 F.2d 778 (2d Cir. 1972).

15. 466 F.2d 1059 (9th Cir. 1972).

16. *Lewis v. United States*, 501 F.2d 418 (9th Cir. 1974).

17. *United States v. Burke*, 700 F.2d 70 (2d Cir. 1983).

18. *United States v. Marcos*, 17 Media L. Rep. 2005 (S.D.N.Y. 1990).

19. 464 F.2d 986 (8th Cir. 1972).

20. *United States v. Cuthbertson*, 630 F.2d 139 (3d Cir. 1980).

21. *Philadelphia Newspapers v. Hepps*, 475 U.S. 767, 106 S.Ct. 1558 (1986).

22. *Florida v. Funches*, 20 Med.L.Rptr. 1200 (Fla.Cir.Ct. 1992).

23. *Hatch v. Marsh*, 134 F.R.D. 300, 18 Med.L.Rptr. 1686 (M.D.Fla. 1990).

24. *Summit Technology v. Healthcare Capital Group*, 19 Med.L.Rptr. 2180 (D.Mass. 1992).

25. 501 U.S. 663, 111 S.Ct. 2513 (1991).

26. 457 N.W.2d 199 (Minn. 1990).

27. 479 N.W.2d 387 (Minn. 1992).

28. Patrick M. Garry, "The Trouble with Confidential Sources: A Criticism of the Supreme Court's Interest-Group View of the First Amendment in *Cohen v. Cowles Media Co.*," *Hasting Communications and Entertainment Law Journal* 14:3:403–421 (Spring 1992).

29. *Ruzicka v. Conde Nast Publications, Inc.*, 794 F.Supp. 303 (D.Minn. 1992), vacated 999 F.2d 1319 (8th Cir. 1993).

30. *In re John Doe Grand Jury Investigation*, 410 Mass. 596, 574 N.E.2d 373 (1991).

31. *Downing v. Monitor Publishing Co.*, 120 N.H. 383, 415 A.2d 683 (1980).

32. *CBS v. Jackson*, 578 So.2d 698 (Fla. 1991).

33. *Id.*

34. *Roche v. Florida*, 589 So.2d 978 (Fla.App. 1991), *cert. denied* ___U.S.___, 113 S.Ct. 1027 (1993).

35. 520 So.2d 372 (La. 1988).

36. *Pruneyard Shopping Center v. Robins*, 447 U.S. 74, 100 S.Ct. 2035 (1980).

37. Bruce N. Sanford, "Twenty Years after *Branzburg*: Echoes for Justice White in Philadelphia," *Communications Lawyer* 11:1:1, 18–20 (Spring 1993).

38. *New Jersey v. Boiardo*, 83 N.J. 350, 416 A.2d 793 (1980).

39. *Maressa v. New Jersey Monthly*, 89 N.J. 176, 445 A.2d 376 (1982).

40. Policy with Regard to the Issuance of Subpoenas to Members of the News Media, Subpoenas for Telephone Toll Records of Members of the News Media, and the Interrogation, Indictment, or Arrest of, Members of the News Media, 28 C.F.R. § 50.10 (1980).

41. Donald M. Gillmor, Jerome A. Barron, Todd F. Simon, and Herbert A. Terry, *Mass Communication Law,* 5th ed. (St. Paul, Minn.: West Publishing Co., 1990), pp. 371–375.

42. Neb. Rev. Stat. §§ 20–144–20 to 20–146 (1987).

43. Ala. Code § 12–21–142 (1978).

44. Mich. Comp. Laws Ann. § 767.5a.

45. *Marketos v. American Employers Insurance Co.*, 185 Mich.App. 179, 460 N.W.2d 272 (1990).

46. *In re Photo Marketing*, 120 Mich.App. 527, 327 N.W.2d 515 (1982).

47. *Matera v. Maricopa County Superior Court*, 170 Ariz. 446, 825 P.2d 971 (Ariz. App. 1992).

48. *Florida v. Funches*, 20 Med.L.Rptr. 1200 (Fla.Cir.Ct. 1992).

49. *New York v. Hennessey*, 13 Med.L.Rptr. 1109 (N.Y.Dist.Ct. 1986).

50. *Sands v. News America Publishing Co.*, 15 Med.L.Rptr. 2326 (N.Y.Sup. 1988).

51. Carl C. Monk, "Evidentiary Privilege for Journalists' Sources: Theory and Statutory Protection," *Missouri Law Review* 51:1, 49–54 (1986).

52. "Shield Law Passes in Florida; S.C. Assembly Weighs Bill," *The News Media & the Law*, Spring 1993, pp. 5–6.

53. *In re Taylor*, 412 Pa. 32, 193 A.2d 181 (1963).

54. *Cinel v. Connick*, 792 F.Supp. 492 (E.D.La. 1992).

55. *Minnesota v. Brenner*, 488 N.W.2d 339 (Minn.App. 1992), vacated 497 N.W.2d 262 (Minn. 1993).

56. Tenn. Code Ann. § 24–1–208; *State v. Shaffer,* 17 Med.L.Rptr. 1489 (Tenn.App. 1990).

57. Monk, "Evidentiary Privilege," pp. 54–58.

58. *Mitchell v. Superior Court*, 37 Cal. 3d 268, 208 Cal. Rptr. 152, 690 P.2d 625 (1984).

59. Minn. Stat. Ann. § 595.025 (West Supp. 1988).

60. *Outlet Communications, Inc. v. Rhode Island*, 588 A.2d 1050 (R.I. 1991).

61. *Dillon v. San Francisco*, 748 F.Supp. 722 (N.D.Cal. 1990).

62. *New Jersey v. Santiago*, 250 N.J. Super. 30, 593 A.2d 357 (App.Div. 1991).

63. *Miller v. Transamerican Press*, 628 F.2d 932 (5th Cir. 1980).

Obscenity and Indecency

JUDICIAL STANDARDS

"This is a case between two ancient enemies: Anything Goes and Enough Already."

These whimsical yet telling words opened the opinion of a federal district judge in a 1990 civil suit brought by a record store owner against a Florida sheriff who had confiscated all his copies of recordings by the rap music group 2 Live Crew. While the judge found lyrics in the record "As Nasty As They Wanna Be" obscene, he held that the actions of the police and another judge in confiscating the recordings before there had been a judicial determination of obscenity and in intimidating the record store proprietor constituted a denial of due process and an impermissible **prior restraint**.[1]

A jury later acquitted the group of violating obscenity laws. The lyrics were nasty but not obscene. An award-winning Duke University professor of black art and culture described the lyrics as "signifying," a rhythmic teasing and cajoling, parody peppered with lewd remarks that can be meant as insult or compliment; it was, he said, a genre with its roots in slavery. Opponents of rapping, however, had learned how to use what they saw as obscene about it to get headlines, cancel concerts, and scare recordings off the shelves.

A second federal district court jury found a record store owner guilty of obscenity for selling the album, but was reversed by a federal appeals court. In an indication of the confusion surrounding obscenity law, an Alabama jury had come to the opposite conclusion in the criminal prosecution of a record store owner a few months earlier.

Also in 1990, Cincinnati's Contemporary Art Center and its director Dennis Barrie were found not guilty by a jury of pandering-obscenity and child nudity charges after exhibiting the photographic works of Robert Mapplethorpe. Jurors were convinced by expert witnesses that the works on trial, however offensive or prurient, possessed some artistic value.

Amid a continuing national debate on whether controversial art should be publicly funded, jurors in the Mapplethorpe case seemed indignant that prosecutors had underestimated them by presenting no credible evidence. The

● **Prior restraint**
Censorship, prohibition of publication by government.

weight of expert testimony on the defense side had forced them to concede that the works at issue were art.

The "artistic-value" test derives from the 1973 case of *Miller v. State of California*[2] in which the U.S. Supreme Court held that to warrant First Amendment protection, erotic expression would have to possess "serious literary, artistic, political or scientific value." It would also have to be free of any appeal to "prurient interest" and anything "patently offensive" to the average person. These not easily definable concepts would be measured against "community standards," said Chief Justice Warren Burger for the Court, because "people in different states vary in their tastes and attitudes."

Burger went on to describe the **patently offensive** as "ultimate sexual acts, normal or perverted, actual or simulated" as well as "masturbation, excretory functions, and lewd exhibition of the genitals." To restate the *Miller* **test** for identifying obscenity in a single paragraph:

> (a) Whether the average person applying contemporary community standards would find that the work taken as a whole appeals to prurient interest, (b) whether the work depicts or describes in a patently offensive way sexual conduct specifically defined by the applicable state law, and (c) and whether the work taken as a whole lacks serious literary, artistic, political, or scientific value.

As might be expected, the Court has had trouble applying these standards to the cases it has reviewed. For example, in *Jenkins v. Georgia*,[3] the Court said the movie *Carnal Knowledge* was not "hard core" because the camera did not focus on the genitals of actors Candice Bergen and Jack Nicholson during scenes of "ultimate sexual acts."

On the same day, the Court ruled in another case that expert testimony of any kind as to what was obscene to an average person could be barred from trial and that jurors, as average persons, could exercise their own judgments. The average person, however, would be neither the most prudish nor the most tolerant in the community.[4] Some years later, the Court, in a vain effort to clarify, said that "community standards" did not mean a majority view and that an "average" or ordinary person had to be "reasonable."[5]

In any case, said the Court, only "prurient interest" and "patent offensiveness" should be decided with reference to "community standards." "Serious value," the Court seemed to be saying, would be a fixed or intrinsic characteristic of any disputed work. It would not vary from community to community.[6] Note that judges tend to use the word *obscenity* in their opinions.

It is safe to say that the words *obscenity* and *pornography* are generally used interchangeably. The dictionary defines *pornography* as obscene or licentious writing or painting, and *obscenity* as that which is offensive to chastity or to modesty, the lewd, foul, and disgusting. The only difference is that *pornography*, to some ears, may be a stronger word and may denote something worse than obscenity. To add to this definitional imprecision, the Supreme Court itself has in the past referred to "hard core" pornography and "soft core" pornography. The law, however, has made no particular distinction between the terms *obscenity* and *pornography*. **Indecency,** however, does suggest a lesser

---

● **Patently offensive**
As defined by the U.S. Supreme Court: "ultimate sexual acts, normal or perverted, actual or simulated," as well as "masturbation, excretory functions, and lewd exhibition of the genitals."

problem for society, but still something contrary to public morality. "Indecency" has also been the legal threshold for broadcasters in both judicial and regulatory doctrine, as have "dirty words," or what the courts often refer to as "profanity."

Pamphlets making hateful attacks on the Roman Catholic church in England brought obscenity into the common law in *Curl's* case in 1727. A century and a half later, the lord chief justice of England laid down a test for obscenity in the *Hicklin* case designed to protect the feebleminded: "Whether the tendency of the matter charged as obscenity is to deprave and corrupt those whose minds are open to such immoral influence and into whose hands a publication of this sort should fall."

Hicklin was adopted in America and was the law until John Woolsey, the federal district judge in a 1933 case involving James Joyce's literary masterpiece, *Ulysses*, wrote an opinion for normal people. A better test, said the judge, would be the impact or the dominant effect of the whole book on the average person of normal sensual responses and an evaluation of the writer's intent or purpose. Judge Woolsey had read the book.

Ulysses led directly to the 1957 Supreme Court ruling in *Roth v. United States* in which Justice William Brennan for the Court defined the test of obscenity as: "Whether to the average person, applying contemporary community standards, the dominant theme of the material taken as a whole appeals to prurient interest."[7]

Between 1957 and the present, the concept of community standards has swung between local and national definitions. Commercial exploitation can be punished. There should be no assaults on personal privacy. And children will be protected. But the definition of obscenity remains elusive. *Roth* led to *Miller* and today's vain efforts to define obscenity.

ZONING LAWS

If you think judicial definitions of obscenity and standards for punishment are unclear, consider what legislative bodies have tried to do. Courts have been permissive in letting a city's compelling interest in regulating the use of its commercial property override allegations of prior restraint.

A major issue for local authorities has been whether adult bookstores and theaters ought to be scattered through a community or clustered in what sometimes comes to be called a "**combat zone.**" While zoning ordinances must not be vague or overbroad, they do seem to win judicial approval when they are carefully drafted and allow for timely adjudication. But the absurd enters into this realm of control also.

In 1972, Detroit adopted ordinances requiring that adult theaters, those that dealt with "specific sexual activities or anatomical areas," be dispersed. In addition, an adult theater could not be located within 1,000 feet of any *two* other "regulated uses." Regulated uses referred to other adult theaters or bookstores, cabarets, bars, pawnshops, hotels or motels, pool halls, public lodging houses, secondhand stores, shoeshine parlors, and taxi dance halls. And an

● **Indecency**
Something less offensive than obscenity and the standard government generally applies to broadcasters in regulating content; defined by the U.S. Supreme Court in 1978 as "nonconformance with accepted standards of morality."

● **Combat zone**
In the context of obscenity law, an area in which "sin" businesses such as adult bookstores are clustered or concentrated.

adult theater had to be at least 500 feet from any residential area. That would assure isolation!

The ordinances survived a constitutional challenge because, said the Supreme Court, the content affected was less important than ideas having social or political significance.[8] Ten years later, the Court relied on its opinion in the Detroit case to uphold a Renton, Washington, zoning ordinance as a time, place, and manner regulation designed to preserve the quality of urban life.[9] Unlike Detroit's "dispersal" ordinance, the Renton law "concentrated" adult theaters, but similar ordinances have been struck down.

An Ann Arbor, Michigan, law didn't make it. There a geographer testified that only 0.23 percent of the city's space could lawfully contain an adult bookstore under the law. Also flawed was the law's requirement that no more than 20 percent of a bookstore's total stock be adult in nature, the assumption being that everything "adult" is obscene. "It is clearly quite restrictive," said the Sixth Circuit Court of Appeals, "to permit a business to engage in . . . protected expression only 20 percent of the time."[10]

A New Jersey ordinance aimed at live nude dancing prohibited all live entertainment including plays, concerts, musicals, and dance. Such a law, said the Supreme Court, violated the First and Fourteenth Amendments.[11]

EVIDENCE OF HARM

Forty years of empirical study of the effects of erotic expression on attitudes and behavior have not satisfied large segments of society. The first Presidential Commission on Obscenity (the 1970 **Lockhart Commission**) found no evidence of a causal connection between obscenity and antisocial conduct. Sixteen years later, the **Meese Commission** came to the opposite conclusion, blaming obscenity or pornography (two concepts inadequately distinguished by the commission) for many of society's ills.

Clearly, legislators do not have to wait for hard evidence before enacting laws to punish obscenity, nor, as has been noted, do jurors and judges have to give weight to so-called expert witnesses. Jurors can determine whether something is obscene simply by listening to it or looking at it. And community standards are often whatever a judge or jury says they are.

Courts are ambivalent about how to assess comparative evidence of obscenity's effects, expert testimony, and attitude surveys. At the federal level, comparative evidence has been discouraged because it may confuse the jurors more than they are already confused by subjective responses to obscenity. Chief Justice Burger reflected this subjectivity when he wrote in a companion case to *Miller* that the films in the case "are the best evidence of what they represent." So did Justice Potter Stewart's famous line that while he couldn't define obscenity—"I know it when I see it."[12]

The highest court of Massachusetts held that a properly conducted public opinion survey would be admissible if it addressed itself to state obscenity standards.[13] An Illinois appellate court held that a trial court erred in not admitting into the record evidence from a public opinion poll. The survey results,

- **Lockhart Commission**
  The first Presidential Commission on Obscenity (1970), headed by then University of Minnesota Law School Dean William Lockhart.

- **Meese Commission**
  The second Presidential Commission on Obscenity (1986), chaired by then Attorney General Edwin Meese.

it said, were strong evidence that community standards would not reject the portrayal of sexually explicit material in movies when access to the movies was limited to adult viewers.[14]

A Georgia court, however, held that survey evidence concerning Larry Flynt's *Hustler* and other magazines was inadmissible where "there was no attempt in the survey itself to determine whether respondents were of the opinion that the content of the . . . magazines would or would not exceed the limits of permissible candor in the depiction of 'nudity and sex.' "[15]

Even more confusion would result from efforts to test the limits of the public with respect to "prurient interest" and "patent offensiveness." Evidence on these two elements of the definition of obscenity is hard to come by. To obtain a scientifically sound estimate of community standards for these two elusive concepts, researchers might have to expose scores of citizens to psychologically traumatizing words and pictures. How to avoid this without biasing the sample by using only "tolerant" members of the community would be a methodological challenge. Interviewer effects involving differences in age and gender would also pose problems, as would noncooperation rates.

For many, evidence of this kind is irrelevant anyway. As one writer puts it: "For **Frederick Schauer** and the Meese Commission, pornography is something more than speech. For (**Catharine**) **MacKinnon**, pornography is reality. Both views ascribe extraordinary powers to expression. Words and images take on fearsome attributes. They can literally drive history, by 'constructing' entire political, economic, and social structures."[16] Schauer and MacKinnon are both law professors. Schauer worked with the Meese Commission, named for then Attorney General Edwin Meese.

This is not to suggest that communities should reject the use of social surveys as a means of gaining a deeper and more complete understanding of community sentiment. Such studies may be the only way to reflect accurately the limits of community tolerance and the delicate balance between constitutional rights and governmental responsibilities.

- **Frederick Schauer**
A Harvard law professor who assisted in the writing of the Meese Report.

- **Catharine MacKinnon**
A University of Michigan law professor and leading opponent in articles, books, and speeches of obscenity and its consequences.

THE POLITICS OF PORNOGRAPHY

Pornography lends itself to politicization. While the Meese Report may have engaged in the selective use of social evidence to support its moral assumptions, and in overkill in its prescriptions, its major recommendation was that state legislatures amend their obscenity statutes to incorporate provisions of the federal Racketeer Influenced Corrupt Organization (RICO) law, a subsection of the federal Organized Crime Control Act of 1970. At least half the states have since complied.

Criminal penalties under the act include fines of up to $25,000 or imprisonment for up to 20 years, or both, and forfeiture of any and all assets acquired or maintained through a violation of the law. The purpose of forfeiture is to confiscate material gains made through racketeering activities. Attached to the criminal penalties are civil penalties, including divestment and treble damages. The federal statute has been applied with telling effect even in states without RICO laws.

- **RICO**
The Racketeer Influenced Corrupt Organization law, a 1984 amendment to the federal Organized Crime Control Act of 1978, which allows the forfeiture of all assets acquired or maintained through a violation of law.

It should not be surprising that the constitutionality of laws as draconian as these has been challenged. In 1989, the U.S. Supreme Court upheld the constitutionality of Indiana's RICO statute when it was applied to obscene material. The Court objected only to the seizure of the contents of a bookstore before an adversarial hearing had been held.[17]

Under state and federal RICO laws, there has been a huge increase in federal obscenity indictments. These have been accompanied by a nationwide crackdown, known as Project PostPorn, on firms that produce and mail obscene materials across state lines. The Department of Justice has encouraged federal prosecutors to charge obscenity producers and distributors in several jurisdictions at the same time, making their cases expensive to defend.

Reactions to the project have included charges of harassment, intimidation, and violation of First Amendment principles. Support for the laws has come from conservatives playing the role of moral arbiters and feminists arguing with some force that pornography is an attack on the civil rights of women. The most prominent of the latter has been Professor Catharine MacKinnon of the University of Michigan Law School. She proposes what some have called "progressive censorship."

MacKinnon argues that pornography leads to the terrorization of women by men in such a way that the free speech accorded men silences the free speech of women. Pornography, she contends, is ultimately not speech but action leading to the submission of women.[18]

City councils in both Minneapolis and Indianapolis approved ordinances written by MacKinnon and feminist author **Andrea Dworkin** incorporating these ideas. The mayor of Minneapolis vetoed the statute. The Indianapolis law did not survive its first federal court test of constitutionality.[19]

A problem with this kind of moral maternalism, or paternalism, depending upon where it originates, is that it depends upon moral arbiters outside the judicial structure, and it poses the danger of spreading to all forms of deviant expression. It makes a crime out of what for many is a sin. And it is essentially reactionary because it would permit the state "to certify a realm of moral certainty in the face of a constitutional structure that denies the state that very power."[20]

Many feminists disagree with MacKinnon on evidence of harm, questions of consent, and the consequences for feminism of feminists joining with the Far Right to forbid forms of expression by the application of governmental power. Nevertheless, MacKinnon's work has altered the terms and the focus of the debate over what to do about obscenity, and it has had a direct effect upon the law in Canada where Parliament has enacted a statute very similar to what she has proposed. What little consensus there is on this matter in the United States may revolve around the need to protect children.

● **Andrea Dworkin**

A feminist author who with Catharine MacKinnon drafted an ordinance in both Minneapolis and Indianapolis that would make obscenity an attack on the civil rights of women.

PROTECTION OF CHILDREN

Courts as well as national commissions on obscenity have shown a keen interest in protecting children from viewing sexual materials and being involved in its manufacture. That interest was emphasized in a 1968 Supreme Court decision upholding the constitutionality of a New York statute prohibiting the sale of "girlie" magazines to anyone under seventeen.

The New York law prohibited the sale to a minor of any depiction of nudity that included "the showing of . . . female buttocks with less than a full opaque covering, or the showing of the female breast with less than a fully opaque covering of any portion thereof below the top of the nipple. . . ."

Speaking for the Court, liberal Justice William Brennan held that the power of the state to control the conduct of children reached beyond the scope of its authority over adults. And there was a strong presumption that parents supported the law.[21]

The case illustrates the idea of variable obscenity: material that would not have been obscene if sold to adults was obscene when sold to juveniles. The First Amendment rights of children are not equivalent to the First Amendment rights of adults. A 1982 New York case permitted the Court to go even farther.

In *New York v. Ferber*,[22] the Court supported an outright ban on the exhibition of films that visually depict sexual conduct by children under sixteen whether such presentations are obscene under the *Miller* guidelines or not. The Court seemed unwilling to take any chances where children were concerned. It noted that forty-seven states and the Congress had passed laws specifically directed at child pornography. Half of these did not require that the banned material be legally obscene. While admitting its own struggle with "the intractable obscenity problem," notably the definition of obscenity, the Court remained firm in its position that "the states have a legitimate interest in prohibiting dissemination of obscene material when the mode of dissemination carries with it a significant danger of offending the sensibilities of unwilling recipients or of exposure to juveniles."

Lower federal courts have upheld the constitutionality of ordinances requiring stores to cover portions of some adult magazines by "blinder racks" or opaque covers. In 1986, however, the Fourth Circuit Court of Appeals overturned a Virginia statute prohibiting the display of sexually explicit materials to juveniles. The court feared that the law would lead vendors to restrict adult access to protected, nonobscene materials. Blinder racks, covers, adults-only sales areas, and similar devices, the court said, were either unconstitutional or ineffective.

The Supreme Court later sent two factual questions back to the Virginia Supreme Court, which subsequently ruled that the sixteen books in question were not harmful to juveniles and that the bookseller had made reasonable efforts to prevent juveniles from perusing potentionally harmful material. The U.S. Supreme Court then vacated the Fourth Circuit's decision, and the constitutional questions originally raised by the case were left unresolved.[23]

Prosecution of those who view child pornography in their homes was upheld by a 1990 Supreme Court decision. Reversing a decision it had made in 1969, the Court ruled that it was reasonable for a state to conclude that the production of child pornography would be reduced if those who possess and view it were subject to penalties.[24]

● *New York v. Ferber*
The 1982 Supreme Court ruling that, in effect, upheld the constitutionality of laws in forty-seven states that seek to protect children from viewing obscenity or being involved in its making.

ELECTRONIC INDECENCY

A desire to protect children has also been the primary motivation behind broadcast regulations and court decisions allowing a stricter standard for broadcasting than for other media. The federal criminal code provides that "whoever utters any obscene, indecent, or profane language by means of radio communication shall be fined not more than $10,000 or imprisoned not more than two years, or both."

The Federal Communications Commission (FCC) is charged with punishing infractions. It has often done so hesitantly, preferring to admonish licensees rather than revoke their licenses. One problem has been, again, lack of definition. Are obscenity and indecency synonymous, or is indecency a less serious infraction? It would seem that profanity is even less serious and that its use on the air is no longer punished. Obscenity is another matter.

Sonderling Broadcasting Corp., WGLD-FM[25] was the first significant broadcast obscenity case decided by the FCC. It came about in 1973 after several stations adopted what was called a "topless radio" format. Basically a talk or call-in format, topless radio featured hosts (usually male) who encouraged members of the audience (usually female) to call in and discuss a topic of the day, nearly always sexual in nature. The format generated complaints to the FCC. Applying the Supreme Court obscenity standard of the day, the commission concluded that Sonderling's broadcasts were obscene and in violation of federal law. They were also indecent. But upon whose community standards were these decisions based?

A citizens group and the Illinois Civil Liberties Union petitioned the D.C. Circuit Court of Appeals for a review. That court upheld the FCC, partly on the bases that the station's approach had been one of conscious commercial exploitation and that the broadcasts were made at times when children would be in the audience.[26]

A year later, a student station at the University of Pennsylvania, WXPN-FM, got in serious trouble for what the FCC called indecent and obscene broadcasts, including use on the air of a conversation with a three-year-old boy who was asked whether he could say "fuck" after his mother had agreed to put him on the phone. The university's license renewal was made conditional on a housecleaning of the station by the university's trustees.

Indecency may have become the standard for broadcasting earlier. In 1970, WUHY-FM, a noncommercial radio station, interviewed Jerry Garcia ("Crazy Max") of the Grateful Dead in a hotel room. Garcia used four-letter words with remarkable frequency in the interview, and they were left in for broadcast.

Noting a difference between radio and other media, the FCC said "no" to Garcia. Large numbers of children would be in the audience, and indecency, not obscenity, should be the applicable standard, said the commission. The station was fined $100.[27]

The FCC, using elements from Supreme Court definitions of obscenity, defined indecency as that which is patently offensive by contemporary community standards and utterly without redeeming social value. But "contempo-

● **Federal Communications Commission (FCC)**
The administrative agency responsible for the regulation of broadcasting and most other forms of electronic communication.

rary community standards" here were standards for the broadcast media alone. Different media were not to be considered together as a single, uniform entity. Not until a 1978 decision by the Supreme Court would the indecency standard be nailed down.

The case was *FCC v. Pacifica Foundation*,[28] and it involved the Pacifica Foundation's New York station, WBAI-FM. In a decision that surprised broadcasters and disappointed civil libertarians, the Supreme Court agreed that the FCC's authority to regulate "indecent" programming was not limited by the constitutional requirements associated with its authority to regulate "obscene" programming.

At issue were satirist George Carlin's now famous "Filthy Words" monologue and the "seven dirty words" that were repeated time and again in the broadcast. "(T)he concept of 'indecent,' " said the Court, relying on the FCC, "is intimately connected with the exposure of children to language that describes in terms patently offensive as measured by contemporary community standards for the broadcast medium, sexual or excretory activities and organs at times of the day when there is a reasonable risk that children may be in the audience."

"Obscene" and "indecent," the Court added, were meant to have different meanings, and indecent was defined as "nonconformance with accepted standards of morality." "Prurient appeal," a component of the Supreme Court's definition of obscenity, would not be necessary in defining what is indecent. But the Court did something else as well. Noting that "the broadcast media have established a uniquely pervasive presence in the lives of all Americans," and that they are "uniquely accessible to children, even those too young to read," the Court seemed to suggest that broadcasting has an impact on its audiences that other media may not have. Therefore, a more stringent level of regulatory and judicial supervision was warranted.

The Cable Communications Policy Act of 1984 also dealt with indecency. Cablecasters did not have to provide leased access channels if any of the programming was judged to be obscene, lewd, lascivious, filthy, or indecent. Cable system operators were also required to provide "lock boxes" for sale or lease that cable subscribers could use to block viewing of particular cable channels when children were home alone.

State and local laws aimed at indecent cable programming usually did not survive constitutional challenge, even though they tried to incorporate the *Pacifica* standard. No First Amendment theory for cable emerged from a number of federal cases, and the courts said *Pacifica* did not apply to cable.

Meanwhile the FCC remained cautious. It found no other broadcasters guilty of indecent utterances between *Pacifica* in 1975 and April 1987. In that month, however, the FCC issued four decisions that indicated it was taking a renewed interest in indecency as a general term and in the protection of children against it.

A "get tough" policy was outlined in an FCC order titled, "New Indecency Enforcement Standards to be Applied to All Broadcast and Amateur Radio Licensees." In determining what was patently offensive, the commission said it would consider whether language was "vulgar" or "shocking." It would also consider the manner in which the language was used and whether the language was "concentrated" or "repeated" or "fleeting" or "isolated." The overall merit of the work would be important, the FCC said, as would the question of whether the medium had some way of separating children and adults. Finally, contemporary community standards would refer to average broadcast listeners and viewers rather than to any specific local community.

The D.C. Circuit Court of Appeals later upheld these standards. Although the court thought the commission's definition of indecency was still inadequate, it felt that the Supreme Court had foreclosed further discussion on that question for the moment. The court noted that children's access to indecent material may be regulated because even where there is an invasion of protected freedoms, the state's power to control the conduct of children reaches beyond the scope of its authority over adults. The court, however, asked the commission to justify its time restraints on the broadcast of indecent material (midnight to 6 A.M.). It also questioned the commission's age limits of twelve to seventeen, when earlier its concern had been with children under twelve.[29]

Seventeen news media organizations had told the court that the FCC's indecency standard was unconstitutional and inconsistent with *Pacifica*, which did not mandate a total ban on broadcasting indecent material but tried to protect children against surprise broadcasts. Moreover, the news media saw indecency as a vague and "boundless" standard that would bar material from large segments of the adult audience and reduce adults to seeing and hearing only what was fit for children. In June 1988, Kansas City station KZKC-TV was fined $2,000 for violating the indecency rule in a movie aired before midnight.

Any softness of resolve on the part of the FCC in enforcing the indecency standard was hardened in the fall of 1988 when President Reagan signed fiscal 1989 appropriations for the FCC and other agencies. Senator Jesse Helms's amendment to the bill ordered the FCC to enforce its indecency standards around the clock—twenty-four hours per day.

The FCC chose to comply with what it considered a congressional mandate. Its compliance, however, was stayed by the court of appeals to give the commission time to hold hearings, build a record, and justify its twenty-four-hour ban.

In 1990, a ban was put into effect that the commission said was "narrowly tailored" to protect children from indecency as ordered in the *Sable* case. In *Sable Communications of California v. FCC*,[30] the Supreme Court had invalidated legislation outlawing telephone indecency or dial-a-porn. The FCC Authorization Act of 1983 made it a crime to use telephone facilities to make "obscene or indecent" interstate telephone communications "for commercial purposes to any person under eighteen years of age or to any other person without that person's consent." The law violated the First Amendment, said the Court, because it was not sufficiently narrowly drawn to serve the government's legitimate interest in protecting children from exposure to indecent messages.

The Court, quoting Justice Felix Frankfurter in a 1957 case, was not about to burn the house down to roast the pig, and it reminded lawmakers and

- **Sable Communications of California v. FCC**
  A 1990 Supreme Court case invalidating legislation outlawing telephone indecency or dial-a-porn.

regulators that "deference to Congress' legislative findings cannot limit judicial inquiry where First Amendment rights are at stake." But it would still expect dial-a-porn to adjust its messages to the standards of thousands of different communities. Another protection for most children, the Court felt, was provided by FCC rules that required the "dial-it" medium, unlike radio or television, to be safeguarded by credit card screening, access codes, and scrambling.

In the meantime, the twenty-four-hour broadcast ban continued to be strictly enforced. Broadcasters challenged the ban, and in 1991 the D.C. Circuit Court of Appeals declared it unconstitutional. "(A)ny curtailment of 'safe harbor' periods during which indecent material can be broadcast intrudes upon constitutionally protected interests," said the court.[31] The Supreme Court declined to review the decision. In 1992, Congress responded by passing legislation channeling most indecent programming into a midnight to 6 A.M. time period, but this policy was again stayed by the D.C. Circuit Court of Appeals, pending further arguments, and later held to be a violation of the First Amendment.[32]

UNCERTAINTIES

The purely rhetorical distinction between obscenity and indecency remains a part of the law. Obscenity can be censored; indecency cannot, at least not where adults are concerned. Yet the former is used to define the latter. Two 1994 cases reflect these difficulties.

A Tennessee listener invoked the federal law imposing fines of up to $10,000 and prison terms of up to two years against National Public Radio (NPR). In its news program "All Things Considered," NPR had broadcast excerpts from wiretapped telephone conversations between convicted Mafia boss John Gotti and his underworld associates. Gotti's mode of communication depended upon an almost continuous stream of profanities that the listener found indecent. Much of the argumentation in the case revolved around the question of whether the irate listener had standing to sue. The FCC and the D.C. Circuit Court of Appeals decided that he did not. Furthermore, the listener's injury, said the court, was an isolated instance.[33] In amici briefs opposing the listener's request for review by the U.S. Supreme Court, it was further argued that the listener did not regularly tune in to "All Things Considered" and that he was making no effort through his litigation to protect a child from exposure to indecent material. The same groups, however, in order to protect the rights of radio and television audiences in the future, would have granted the listener standing to sue in the first place.

At about the same time, the FCC went way beyond the federal law's $10,000 limit when it fined Infinity Broadcasting $200,000 for each of its three stations carrying indecent broadcasts by Howard Stern, the syndicated "shock-jock" radio talk show personality. Infinity must feel that Stern is worth the penalties. His purple prose has led to $1.9 million in fines to Infinity and other broadcasters (although most of them have not yet been paid) and aroused opposition from minority groups to Infinity being granted additional broadcast licenses. The African American Business Association, for example, accused Stern of racism, but dropped its opposition to Infinity's acquisition of a Washington, D.C., AM-FM station in exchange for Infinity's promise to pay the association's legal expenses, to contribute $750,000 to the training of minority business advertisers, and to allow them discounted advertising spots.[34] Infinity is not the only broadcaster or cablecaster that has problems with material judged indecent by some. Renewal problems remain a constant threat for many broadcasters and cablecasters.

In the realm of obscenity and indecency, there's little agreement on what we're really talking about. In cultural studies, pornography has been compared to a black mass, to science fiction, to a computer program, to the obliteration of privacy, to shamelessness and thereby inhumaneness in public life, and to various forms of political repression. These diverse reactions are testimony to the subjective responses it evokes.

Social science, on the other hand, has had great difficulty demonstrating a connection between pornography and rape. There is a connection between pornography and sexual fantasy, but sexual fantasy is a poor predictor of behavior. Whether pornography harms adolescent boys or girls depends on prior sex education, sex roles, and the availability of alternative imagery.

● **Pornoviolence**
A mixture of pornography and violence in visual communications.

Certainly, a society that always portrays women as sex objects contributes to the devaluation of women. And what about **pornoviolence,** that mixture of sex and violence so readily available to television audiences? A University of Wisconsin researcher in a comprehensive review of effects studies, including his own, concludes, "If you take out the sex and leave in the violence, you get increased violent behavior in the laboratory setting . . . if you take out the violence and leave the sex, nothing happens."[35] Violence ought to be a component of any communication deemed censorable.

In 1987, the Oregon Supreme Court rejected the punishment of obscenity as contrary to Article 1, Section 8 of the Oregon Constitution.[36] The relevant language follows:

> No law shall be passed restraining the free expression of opinion, or restricting the right to speak, write or print freely on any subject whatever, but every person shall be responsible for the abuse of this right.

As for state or local community standards, the court declared:

> In a law censoring speech, writing or publication, such an indeterminate test is intolerable. It means that anyone who publishes or distributes arguably "obscene" words or pictures does so at the peril of punishment for making a wrong guess about a future jury's estimate of "contemporary state standards" of prurience.

The Oregon Constitution would permit the regulation of expression only where negative effects could be demonstrated. Thus, Oregon confidently found its constitutional protection of expression broader than that provided by the U.S. Supreme Court's interpretation of the First Amendment.

But even the Oregon judges would protect youth and the privacy of unwilling viewers, as would the comparatively permissive report of the 1970 Lockhart Commission and Justice William Brennan's comprehensive dissent from the *Miller* formula, an opinion in which the liberal justice abandoned a legal structure he had hammered together in the preceding sixteen years.[37] Both Brennan and the commission called for the repeal of all obscenity laws as applied to adults. But children and personal privacy remained outside the limits of tolerance.

When a judge or a jury must decide what is obscene or indecent, they still have no precise constitutional guidelines to follow. Community standards are pretty much what judges and juries say they are, as long as they act as reasonable people. But reasonable people often disagree. This places great pressure on the jury system.

No one knows what kind of evidence of prurient interest, patent offensiveness, and community standards will be admissible from one court to another. Expert witnesses can make a difference, as in the Mapplethorpe case, but in the final analysis, it will be jurors, however unrepresentative of the public they may be, who will decide what is obscene and not obscene under the standards of *Miller v. California*. And it will be the evolving norms of society, or perhaps its myriad publics, that will ultimately, if ever, decide what is to be outside the bounds of tolerance.

SUMMARY

Much confusion surrounds the law of obscenity, pornography, and indecency. The major problem is that these terms have not found acceptable definitions. Nor have terms related to them such as "prurient interest," "patent offensiveness," "average person," and "community standards." The Supreme Court, however, has dedicated itself to the protection of children and to personal privacy, sometimes through zoning laws. Evidence of harm from this kind of communication, whether from social science or cultural studies, has had little effect on the law. Rhetoric about pornography has been useful to political movements, both liberal and conservative.

Conservatives who see pornography as evidence of moral decay use racketeering laws to put adult bookstores out of business. Radical feminists propose laws that would punish pornography as an assault on the civil rights of women.

Courts have decided that because broadcasting and cable have more pervasive effects than other media, the electronic media will be subject to an indecency standard that is more restrictive than an obscenity standard. But adults are not to be governed by an indecency test. Perhaps sexual violence ought to be an element of obscenity if this type of communication is not to have First Amendment protection. In the final analysis, the public will decide where society's limits of tolerance are.

KEY TERMS

Prior restraint
Patently offensive
Indecency
Combat zone
Lockhart Commission
Meese Commission
Frederick Schauer

Catharine MacKinnon
RICO
Andrea Dworkin
New York v. Ferber
Federal Communications Commission (FCC)
Sable Communications of California v. FCC
Pornoviolence

CASE PROBLEMS

1. Definition has always been a problem in the law of obscenity. The Supreme Court's definition, however, is the operable one. What is that definition and where does it come from? Do you discern any problems with it?

2. How does Catharine MacKinnon's approach to the regulation of obscenity differ from that of the U.S. Supreme Court?

3. Why do the broadcast media have to comply with an "indecency" ban as well as an "obscenity" ban?

ENDNOTES

1. *Skywalker Records, Inc. v. Navarro,* 739 F.Supp. 578, 17 Med.L.Rptr. 2073 (S.D. Fla. 1990), reversed by *Luke Records, Inc. v. Navarro* 960 F.2d 134, 20 Med.L.Rptr. 1114, (11th Cir. 1992).

2. 413 U.S. 15, 93 S.Ct. 2607 (1973).

3. 418 U.S. 153, 94 S.Ct. 2750 (1974).

4. *Hamling v. United States,* 418 U.S. 87, 94 S.Ct. 2887 (1974).

5. *Pinkus v. United States,* 436 U.S. 293, 98 S.Ct. 1808 (1978).

6. *Pope v. Illinois,* 481 U.S. 497, 107 S.Ct. 1918 (1987).

7. 354 U.S. 476, 77 S.Ct. 1304 (1957).

8. *Young v. American Mini Theatres,* 427 U.S. 50, 96 S.Ct. 2440 (1976).

9. *City of Renton v. Playtime Theatres, Inc.,* 475 U.S. 41, 106 S.Ct. 925 (1986).

10. *Christy v. Ann Arbor,* 824 F.2d 489, 14 Med.L.Rptr. 1483 (6th Cir. 1987).

11. *Schad v. Mont Ephraim,* 452 U.S. 61, 101 S.Ct. 2176 (1981).

12. *Jacobellis v. State of Ohio,* 378 U.S. 184, 84 S.Ct. 1676 (1964).

13. *Commonwealth v. Trainor,* 374 Mass. 796, 374 N.E.2d 1216 (1978).

14. *People v. Nelson,* 88 Ill.App.3d 196, 43 Ill.Dec. 476, 410 N.E.2d 476 (1980).

15. *Flynt v. State,* 153 Ga.App. 232, 264 S.E.2d 669 (1980).

16. Steven G. Gey, "The Apologetics of Suppression: The Regulation of Pornography as Act and Idea," *Michigan Law Review* 86:1564, 1606 (June 1988).

17. *Fort Wayne Books, Inc. v. Indiana,* 489 U.S. 46, 109 S.Ct. 916 (1989).

18. Catharine A. MacKinnon, *Feminism Unmodified.* Cambridge: Harvard University Press, 1987.

19. *American Booksellers Association v. Hudnut,* 771 F.2d 323 (7th Cir. 1985).

20. Gey, "Apologetics of Suppression," p. 1613.

21. *Ginsberg v. State of New York,* 390 U.S. 629, 88 S.Ct. 1274 (1968).

22. 458 U.S. 747, 102 S.Ct. 3348 (1982).

23. *American Booksellers Ass'n v. Virginia*, 792 F.2d 1261 (4th Cir. 1986); *Commonwealth of Virginia v. American Booksellers Ass'n*, 236 Va. 168, 372 S.E.2d 618 (1988).

24. *Osborne v. Ohio*, 495 U.S. 103, 110 S.Ct. 1691 (1990).

25. 41 FCC 2d 777 (1973).

26. *Illinois Citizens Committee for Broadcasting v. FCC*, 515 F.2d 397 (D.C.Cir. 1974).

27. *In Re WUHY-FM Eastern Education Radio*, 24 FCC 2d 408 (1970).

28. 438 U.S. 726, 98 S.Ct. 3026 (1978).

29. *Action for Children's Television v. FCC*, 852 F.2d 1332 (D.C.Cir. 1988).

30. 492 U.S. 115, 109 S.Ct. 2829 (1989).

31. *Action for Children's Television v. FCC*, 932 F.2d 1504 (D.C.Cir. 1991).

32. *Action for Children's Television v. FCC*, 11 F.3d 170, 21 Med.L.Rptr. 2289 (D.C.Cir. 1993), Vacated in banc by 15F.3d 186 (C.A.D.C. 1994).

33. *Branton v. FCC*, 993 F.2d 906, 21 Med.L.Rptr. 1532 (D.C.Cir. 1993).

34. *Broadcasting & Cable*, May 30, 1994, p. 44.

35. Edward Donnerstein, Daniel Linz, and Steven Penrod, *The Question of Pornography: Research Findings and Policy Implications* (New York: Free Press, 1987).

36. *Oregon v. Henry*, 302 Or. 510, 732 P.2d 9, 14 Med.L.Rptr. 1011 (1987).

37. *Paris Adult Theatre 1 v. Slaton*, 413 U.S. 49, 93 S.Ct. 2628 (1973).

Access to the Judicial Process

AN OVERVIEW OF THE ISSUE

Getting access to information, meetings, and proceedings goes to the heart of a journalist's vocation. More access cases appear in the official court reports than any other types of communication law disputes.

This chapter will examine the nonstatutory reasons the courts have relied upon to assure that the public and the press have access to pretrial judicial proceedings, documents introduced at court, and trials themselves (Chapter 7 is devoted to statutory access rights). Since the founding of the republic, there has been a common law right to attend court, a right that also guaranteed the right to look at court records.

Beginning in the 1970s, the courts, led by the U.S. Supreme Court, crafted a First Amendment right of access to the judicial process in addition to the traditional common law right. The constitutional right of access is much stronger than a common law right because it in effect requires anyone trying to keep out the public or press to show that the interests in denying access are constitutionally stronger than those of the public or press in obtaining it.

The Court's cases assuring access recognize the importance of legal news in late twentieth-century America. One need only look at the biggest story of 1994 and 1995 in terms of coverage—the arrest, pretrial proceedings, and trial of O. J. Simpson on murder charges—to see how important the news media think courtroom news is. One need only look at the television ratings for extended coverage of the Simpson case to see that audiences seem to agree.

The Simpson case also highlights the enduring issues surrounding free press–fair trial debates. Will extensive pretrial publicity weaken the defendant's constitutional right to a fair trial? May a judge close parts of pretrial proceedings and jury selection to protect the defendant's rights? If so, when: how much evidence is required to justify full or partial closure? And may the trial itself *ever* be closed, fully or partly?

Each community replays the issues raised in the Simpson case. Every notorious criminal investigation, charge, and trial attracts heavy local news coverage—and with it worries that the media may have an effect on the outcome. Defense lawyers routinely seek closure in notorious cases, probably knowing that the odds of getting it are small. Journalists must remain alert to ethical guidelines, but report in the heat of competition. And judges must walk a tightrope to respect constitutional rights on both sides.

BACKGROUND OF THE FREE PRESS–FAIR TRIAL DEBATE

Coverage of law enforcement and criminal trials has traditionally been a major emphasis of local newspapers and television news. Along with stories on local government and schools, crime coverage helps make up the preponderance of local news. Although crime stories are numerous, few individual crimes receive extensive coverage. To attract heavy media attention, a case generally must be unusual, important, or sensational.

Over the last twenty years, news organizations have increased their coverage of civil lawsuits as well. The expansion of business reporting in special newspaper sections and in local television news has also resulted in more attention being paid to disputes between private parties.

In both criminal and civil cases, the press argues that it acts as an agent of the public, providing citizens with access to information that they would never get on their own. Increasingly, the courts have agreed, opening the judicial system to greater press scrutiny than at any time in U.S. history.

Under present legal rules, journalists have a presumed right to attend virtually any court proceeding, be it pretrial, trial, or posttrial. They also have rights of access to persons involved in court cases, materials introduced as evidence for trials, and jurors after trials. Often access is required for pretrial documents as well. In addition, there is an almost absolute prohibition on judges issuing formal "gag orders" preventing publication of information. **Gag orders,** a form of prior restraint, have occasionally been issued to prevent dissemination of information considered prejudicial. Violation of a gag order is enforced with a **contempt of court** citation.

The unprecedented flood of access rights stems from a series of cases decided by the Supreme Court starting in the mid-1970s. The First Amendment, the Court has said repeatedly, ensures a right to attend criminal proceedings.

● **Gag order**
An order by a judge prohibiting news organizations from publishing information they have in their possession.

● **Contempt of court**
A type of punishment for violation of a court order. It will typically include fines, but may also include jail time.

The lower courts have expanded access rights to civil cases as well. Media access to judicial documents and materials has not been addressed by the Supreme Court, but the state and lower federal courts have wrestled with the issue. Access to documents and materials is provided, depending upon the court case, on common law, statutory, or constitutional grounds. But a presumption in favor of access has been universally recognized.

None of the access rights is absolute. Each can be defeated by a showing that other interests are in peril. Press access cannot be restrained, however, without clear evidence that a highly valued interest is imperiled. In most cases, the interest must be of constitutional status. A judge who has been asked to limit media access must apply a multipart test before issuing any limiting order.

For most of this century, the courts and the press have been engaged in a dispute about news coverage of criminal cases. Judges, defense lawyers, and criminal defendants have contended that widespread media coverage often results in prejudicial publicity—stories that impair a defendant's chances of getting a fair trial.

The criminal defendant's claim is based on the Sixth Amendment's guarantee of a **fair trial**. Under the amendment, a criminal defendant is entitled to a "speedy and public trial, by an impartial jury of the State and district wherein the crime shall have been committed. . . ." Since most news coverage will also be centered in the community where the crime occurred, conflict between the rights of the defendant and the rights of the press is almost inevitable.

● **Fair trial**
A right guaranteed by the Sixth Amendment. It requires that a defendant be tried by an unbiased jury.

PREJUDICIAL OR HARMFUL PUBLICITY

The central idea behind a claim of **prejudicial publicity** is that at some point news coverage will saturate the community, making it impossible to assemble an impartial jury. The courts define an impartial jury as one that is able to decide a case solely on the basis of the evidence presented.[1] Jurors need not be totally ignorant of a case, but they must not have already reached an opinion as a result of news coverage.[2] On occasion, appellate courts have overturned convictions because they were convinced that publicity had prejudiced potential jurors. In those cases, the saturation news coverage was considered so pervasive that bias seemed inevitable.[3]

The decision on limiting the press is difficult for trial judges, who must attempt to predict when coverage will begin to have a prejudicial effect. Judges historically erred on the side of caution when they first dealt with extensive news coverage early in the century. Relying more often on intuition and common sense than on evidence, they tended to overestimate the likelihood that news coverage would have a prejudicial effect. Since it is a judge's job to protect the rights of defendants, the caution was understandable.

There is little evidence to support the widely held view that news coverage has an effect, however. Many years of research on the effects of publicity on potential jurors have failed to provide clear answers on when the courts should step in to restrain the press.[4] In the meantime, research on how audiences process and retain information from news indicates that the media are far less influential than they would probably hope.[5]

● **Prejudicial publicity**
News coverage of a criminal case that due to its style, amount, or prominence has the capacity to influence potential jurors in the case.

Courts have implied recognition of a second category of publicity that may on occasion result in restraints upon news media. In general, the claim is that publicity will be harmful to an important personal interest, such as privacy,[6] or a business interest, such as protecting trade secrets or other confidential information.[7] Often the claim is raised by a witness or on behalf of potential jurors who may be asked sensitive personal questions. Because these harmful publicity cases are relatively new, making generalizations about them is difficult. Restraints on the press are assessed on a case-by-case basis. The only universal requirement is that the person seeking the restraint has the burden of proving that a restraint is justified, which is also true for criminal defendants. No uniform test to assess privacy or other interests has been adopted nationally.

Defense attorneys now routinely raise prejudicial publicity arguments in high-profile cases. They are trying to get their clients tried in a more sedate atmosphere. Requests for media restraints are almost as routinely rejected by the courts because the primary rule today is that the news media may be acted against directly only as a last resort. Accommodating the media can be difficult—even annoying—for judges and for lawyers on both sides, but accommodation must be made. Defendants may prove inconvenience and embarrassment, but they seldom prove prejudice to a fair trial.

Proving a prejudicial effect from publicity may be nearly impossible. Any support that may have existed for powerful, immediate effects has dwindled. The local newspaper no longer serves as the sole, or even primary, news source for many people. Much of the writing about media effects on trials seems to assume that everyone in a community is getting exactly the same news. It also seems to assume that every reader or viewer is affected in exactly the same way. Yet, with more media choices available to the public than ever before, some people choose to avoid news altogether.[8] The chances that a potential juror has no information about a case appear greater than ever before. The notorious 1980 Abscam case received unusually heavy local and national coverage. Nevertheless, when television reporters asked to copy videotapes that were introduced in evidence at a criminal trial, the judge observed:

> Defendants, as well as the news media, frequently overestimate the extent of the public's awareness of news. In this very case . . . about half of those summoned had no knowledge of Abscam. . . ."[9]

CONTEMPT OF COURT AND ENFORCEMENT OF RESTRICTIVE ORDERS

A trial judge who issues a restrictive order against the press or against trial participants may enforce an order through the contempt power. The authority to find someone in contempt of court is considered necessary to assure that orders are obeyed. It is an inherent power, long recognized as a matter of common law. It is also provided for by statutes. Contempt citations can come in two forms, civil contempt and crimi-

nal contempt. In general, criminal contempt applies when the court is punishing someone, usually for disrupting proceedings, while civil contempt applies
when the court is enforcing orders designed to protect parties to a trial or to
protect the integrity of the trial itself.[10] The distinction is probably academic to
the reporter facing a contempt citation, since fines and jail time are sanctions
allowed under either civil or criminal contempt. If the activities of journalists
seriously interfere with a proceeding, increasing costs to the public, the costs
may be part of the fine.[11]

There is some dispute about the authority of judges to hold journalists
and news organizations in contempt for violating an order. The leading case is
United States v. Dickinson,[12] in which reporters covering an open pretrial hearing in a murder case were ordered by the trial judge to publish nothing from
the hearing. The reporters published anyway, thinking the order was an invalid
prior restraint that violated the First Amendment. The Fifth Circuit agreed that
the order was invalid, but held that the reporters were still obliged to obey it.
The trial judge's criminal contempt order fining the reporters was upheld.

One problematical aspect of *Dickinson* was the delay between the time
the trial judge's order was entered and the time the appeals court declared the
order invalid. The news story had become history. The Fifth Circuit urged in its
opinion that review of restrictive orders be speedy in the future. A handful of
courts have applied the practice of accelerated review, apparently taken from
the Supreme Court's prior restraint cases,[13] to assure that issues involving time-
critical news will be resolved while the news is still fresh.[14]

Since the Supreme Court declined to review it, the lower courts assumed
the *Dickinson* rule was applicable nationwide. In 1986, however, the First
Circuit decided that the *Providence Journal* was entitled to disregard an order
prohibiting publication of information from FBI wiretaps.[15] The material was
about Raymond Patriarca, who had died in 1985, but at one time was thought
to be the organized crime boss of New England. The rule announced by the
court said that the news media could ignore an order when the order on its face
failed to satisfy Supreme Court tests for restraining the media. Judge Wisdom
accepted the newspaper's argument that delay was inconsistent with the role of
journalism:

> [I]t is misleading in the context of daily newspaper publishing to argue
> that a temporary restraining order merely preserves the status quo. The
> status quo of daily newspapers is to publish news promptly that editors
> decide to publish.

The appeals court later modified its decision, but only to advise the news media that seeking reversal of an invalid order in a court of appeals was the preferred first refuge. "If timely access to the appellate court is not available or if
timely decision is not forthcoming, the publisher may then proceed to
publish. . . ."[16] The Supreme Court first agreed to review the case, then decided
to dismiss it on procedural grounds. The Court said nothing about the First
Amendment issues.

In the meantime, journalists are caught in the middle. The *Providence*
case invites them to guess that the trial judge was wrong. But what if they guess

wrong? Then they are still liable for the original contempt citation. Furthermore, the rule formally applies only in the First Circuit. Journalists everywhere, including the First Circuit, have been reluctant to take the potentially disastrous step of willfully violating judicial orders. Unless the Supreme Court chooses between the *Dickinson* and *Providence* rules, news organizations will play it safe and follow the traditional Fifth Circuit rule that orders must be obeyed even if invalid.

PROCEDURAL SAFEGUARDS AGAINST PREJUDICIAL PUBLICITY

The last thing appellate courts want to do is reverse a criminal conviction because of media publicity, but they have done so on rare occasions. The most famous example came in *Sheppard v. Maxwell*,[17] which was decided by the Supreme Court in 1966. By the time the case reached the high court, Sam Sheppard had already served twelve years in prison for the murder of his wife. The Court decided that the conviction must be reversed because the trial judge had allowed the press and the public to create a "carnival atmosphere" during the trial. The Court blamed the judge for failing to control the courtroom. *Sheppard* established, if there had been any doubt, that under the First Amendment the press is free to report whatever occurs at trial. But a judge should consider taking steps to reduce potential influence on jurors.

The case, which originated near Cleveland, Ohio, received sensational coverage from the time the murder was reported on July 4, 1954. The coverage remained sensational through investigation, pretrial, and trial. Newspapers reported that Sheppard refused a lie detector test. An inquest was held in a gym; it lasted three days, with parts being broadcast live. Newspapers reported details of the investigation, apparently leaked by the police, that were never introduced at trial. The judge made the list of potential jurors, all seventy-five of them, available to reporters, along with their addresses. The court set up a table for reporters *inside* the bar, a spot normally reserved for court personnel. Photographers were allowed to roam and shoot at will. Jurors' photographs were run on the front page. A radio station set up a temporary studio and broadcast live from the courthouse. The judge agreed to a television interview during trial. Sheppard was escorted into the courtroom early each day for a photo session. Given all this, it was little surprise that the Court felt Sheppard had been denied his right to a fair trial.

Sheppard had asked for a continuance, a change of venue, and a mistrial. All were denied by the trial judge. The Supreme Court said the trial judge should have considered not only these requests, but also other means to assure a fair trial. In admonishing the trial judge, the Court created a checklist of procedural devices for judges to use in the future to assure fair trials. Almost three decades later, the *Sheppard* "laundry list" continues to be the first line of analysis for a trial judge faced with claims that publicity may bias a trial. The items on the list are all matters that a judge must consider short of placing direct restrictions on the media. Direct restrictions are allowed only if the judge concludes, based on evidence, that the alternative measures specified in *Sheppard* will not work. Although the list was compiled with criminal trials in mind, many of the items may also be considered in civil cases.

The behavior of journalists in *Sheppard* and in the case of *Irvin v. Dowd*,[18] where the defendant faced a "barrage" of publicity including improper reporting of a confession, created an antagonistic relationship between the press and the judiciary that lasted into the 1970s. Even today judges and lawyers are dubious about the press, despite obvious improvements in crime reporting. Contemporary journalists still pay a price for long-past deeds.

Time, Place, and Manner Regulations

The first step urged by the Court majority in *Sheppard* is for judges to control the behavior of journalists and members of the public. Reasonable time, place, and manner regulations will be upheld. Among the most typical actions are limitations on the use of courtroom space. For example, in a trial with extensive news coverage, a judge may establish a first-come, first-seated policy for reporters when there are not expected to be enough seats. As long as the judge does not favor some news organizations over others, such regulations will likely be upheld. It is not unusual for a judge to reserve space for reporters close to the front of the courtroom. As long as the allocation is evenhanded, the practice is probably safe.

Two cases have decided that news-gathering limits are reasonable time, place, and manner regulations. The most important concerned a claim that the First Amendment requires that reporters be allowed to make sound tapes at trials. The Second Circuit said that the First Amendment right of access, then applied only to protect reporters' right to attend trials, did not apply under the circumstances. Unless otherwise required by the Supreme Court, the appeals court would consider court rules prohibiting recording to be time, place, and manner regulations allowed under *Sheppard*.[19] A federal district court relied on the same analysis in prohibiting sketches that would identify jurors in a murder trial.[20]

The single largest group of time, place, and manner regulations today is made up of those placed on broadcast and photographic coverage. Cameras and photographers are usually required to stay in specific spots without moving. Often television stations are required to share a single feed. Since these requirements affect the manner of reporting only, they are routinely upheld.

Admonishing Jurors and Reporters

The *Sheppard* opinion suggested that, at least in some cases, it would be sufficient to advise jurors to avoid news coverage of the trial on which they were serving. Perhaps no one really expects admonishment to prevent news exposure, but a warning can serve to keep jurors focused on the evidence presented in court rather than what appears in the news.

Admonishing reporters is not directly suggested in *Sheppard*, but some lawyers and judges have considered talking with reporters about the delicate aspects of the case a good way of alerting journalists about potential ethical issues. Reporters covering criminal trials are often surprisingly inexperienced[21] and rely heavily upon information from lawyers for stories.[22]

Insulating Witnesses

A judge has inherent authority to order that witnesses be kept away from the press. Since witnesses have the same First Amendment rights as anyone else, it follows that insulating witnesses works only if the witnesses agree. The most common form of insulation is physical—keeping witnesses in separate rooms until they are called to testify, and providing protected entry and exit away from the main entrances. It is less common for a judge to order that reporters stay away from witnesses, and such an order will almost certainly be challenged.

Proscribing Out-of-Court Statements

Although a judge generally may not prohibit news organizations from reporting what they obtain, the *Sheppard* Court appeared to approve of placing proscriptions on those involved in the case. As a result, attorneys on both sides, defendants, and witnesss have been told to not talk to members of the news media. In addition, bar association guidelines in most states warn lawyers against using the media to influence the outcome of a case. Enforcement of such a "gag order" is accomplished with a contempt of court citation. In a handful of cases, judges have argued that reporters who talked to gagged trial participants were also in contempt because they abetted violation of a court order. Usually, a court lacks proper jurisdiction to enforce a third-party order against the press, since reporters are not under the direct supervision of the judge as lawyers, plaintiffs, or defendants are.

Limits on out-of-court contact with reporters have been challenged both by the gagged parties and by the news media whose news gathering has been hindered. The rules that prevent gag orders against the press are slowly being applied to gag orders against trial participants. The most important case is *Gentile v. State Bar of Nevada*, which involved a lawyer who held an interview with reporters and found himself the object of state bar disciplinary proceedings. The Supreme Court said a state may restrain the speech of lawyers under a substantial probability test,[23] a test easier to meet than the compelling interest test used to assess media gags. Under the compelling interest test, a gag can only be justified if a constitutional right is at risk. Under a substantial interest test, an order may be allowed to protect an interest that is considered strong but not overriding.

Witnesses and defendants, who are not considered "officers of the court" as lawyers are, may have greater speech rights. In addition, many courts have recognized that news organizations have standing—a legal right to pursue a claim in court—because any limitation on news gathering affects the First

Amendment rights of the press. The lower courts have not agreed on a test, and the Supreme Court has not resolved the issue.[24]

The *Sheppard* majority also recommended that judges consider ordering court employees and law enforcement personnel to refrain from leaking non-public information to the press.

Change of Venue

Venue refers to the place where a trial will be held. When a criminal defendant thinks that publicity may prejudice the trial, a motion for change of venue may be sought. The defendant is then in effect waiving the Sixth Amendment right to have the trial held in the "district," or community, where the crime was committed. A change of venue is assumed to assure that an impartial jury may be drawn because people in the second community were not exposed to the same news coverage.

Most motions for change of venue fail for two major reasons. First, truly notorious cases often attract statewide and even national news coverage. As a result, no community in the state will have been immune. Second, a large amount of news coverage, standing alone, does not prove a prejudicial effect. It proves only that news organizations thought their audiences had an interest in the case. In all likelihood, a defendant will be required to prove a "substantial probability" of a prejudicial effect. Most cannot prove a cause-and-effect relationship.

A practical argument against changes of venue is the inconvenience for everyone involved and the expense for the court. Travel and housing costs are typically borne by the court or another local government body.

- **Venue**
  The geographic location where a trial is held. The Sixth Amendment calls for criminals to be held in the community where the crime was committed.

Continuance

A defendant may seek a **continuance**, a delay in the beginning of the trial, in hopes that publicity will die down prior to jury selection. By filing a motion for continuance, the defendant in effect waives the Sixth Amendment right to a speedy trial. When there is evidence to support a continuance, the trial judge may order one without a motion from the defense, but it is rare for judges to order a continuance on their own without a motion.

Continuance sounds more useful than it probably is. News coverage will likely spring up again as the delayed trial date draws near. If anything, a continuance enables the press to be better prepared to cover the trial thoroughly.

- **Continuance**
  A delay in the time a trial is scheduled to begin. It is occasionally sought in hopes that news coverage will diminish over time.

Intense Voir Dire

Conducting an intense voir dire is the most widely used of all the procedural safeguards recommended in *Sheppard*. **Voir dire** is the portion of a trial in which the jury is selected. During the voir dire, citizens whose names have been drawn for jury duty are called into court for questioning by the judge and by the lawyers on both sides. If any potential jurors show signs of being biased, or otherwise being unable to decide solely on the evidence to be presented, they

- **Voir dire**
  The portion of a trial in which a jury is selected.

will likely either be excused by the judge or subjected to a challenge for cause by one of the lawyers. To challenge a juror for cause, all a lawyer must do is convince the judge that there is a basis for the lawyer's concern. Additional challenges called peremptory challenges allow either side to disqualify jurors for any or no reason. The number of peremptory challenges varies from state to state.

In a case that has attracted news coverage, much of the questioning in the voir dire will focus on whether potential jurors have been exposed to the news. In a case with saturation coverage, the number of potential jurors quizzed can run very high.[25] Even if they have been exposed to coverage, the test for jurors is whether they have the ability to independently analyze the evidence, not whether they are completely ignorant about the case. Voir dire cannot weed out every biased juror, but lawyers and judges think it is quite successful overall.

Sequestering Juries

- **Sequestration**
  The practice of isolating members of a jury from the potential of outside influences; it may result in jurors living in hotels and having limited access to the news media.

Sequestration formally refers to the practice of placing an item in dispute into the hands of a third party until the dispute is settled.[26] In cases where it is feared that news coverage might affect the outcome of the trial, jurors are placed into the hands of a third party, usually guards, and kept away from family and friends until the case is over. They are not allowed to see news stories about the case, and their telephone calls and movements may be monitored.

Sequestering a jury is an extreme remedy, reserved for only the most extreme cases. It is very effective at preventing access to news coverage, so it is safe to say that any prejudicial effect is avoided. But the cost in time and money is vast. Some sequestered juries have been kept in isolation for six months or more. The government bears the costs of housing and feeding the jurors for the duration of the trial.

Ordering a New Trial

A trial judge may order a new trial based on evidence that a verdict was based on prejudice resulting from news coverage, but it is more likely that a reversal would be ordered by an appellate court. An order for a new trial in effect means that none of the procedural safeguards worked, or perhaps were not used. The record supports the conclusion that the *Sheppard* laundry list works well, though. In one study of appeals of verdicts in criminal cases, reversals due to publicity accounted for less than one three-hundredth of 1 percent (0.00028) of all appeals and less than 5 percent of appeals based on prejudicial publicity.[27]

- **Bar-press guidelines**
  Voluntary statements, adopted in many states, that have been developed by journalists, lawyers, and judges regarding kinds of information that are appropriate for news coverage of criminal cases.

Bar-Press Guidelines

The Supreme Court did not recommend that journalists, lawyers, and judges gather together to discuss coverage of the judicial system, but they did in many states during the 1960s and 1970s. The goal was to reach agreement on what constituted ethical reporting in the context of trials. The result often took the form of **bar-press guidelines**.

In general, the guidelines recommend against publishing potentially inflammatory information about prior criminal records of defendants and about inadmissible evidence. They urge against editorials and opinions concerning guilt or innocence. Rules of courtesy for photography are also usually included. Any objective information directly related to the trial is usually assumed to be fit for ethical publication. If a state has guidelines, copies may normally be obtained from either the state bar association or the state press association.

Bar-press guidelines appeared to many to offer the advantage of allowing the two sides to work out their differences voluntarily. Since the state bar-press committees often held regular meetings, the two groups could also become more familiar with each other. But the goodwill promised by the bar-press guidelines swiftly disappeared after two cases in which trial judges issued orders imposing the guidelines as binding.[28]

GAG ORDERS

Gag Orders against the Media

Some lower court judges read the *Sheppard* and *Dickinson* cases as approving orders that prevented news organizations from publishing news in their possession. That viewpoint became more widespread after a 1972 reporter privilege case in which the Supreme Court made an offhand reference that implied that there is no constitutional prohibition against restraints on publication about trials.[29] In any event, the use of "gag orders," so named because they are direct commands that prevent someone from speaking or publishing, became much more common in the early 1970s. An order barring a lawyer or defendant from talking to the press would be a direct gag order as to the person named, but an indirect gag order so far as press rights were concerned.

The use of direct gag orders against the press came to an abrupt end with the decision in *Nebraska Press Association v. Stuart*.[30] In its opinion, the Supreme Court declared gag orders to be a form of prior restraint, presumptively unconstitutional. The Court established a test so difficult to meet that Justice Byron White doubted a trial judge would ever be able to issue a valid gag order.[31] The test requires proof that:

> 1) the nature and extent of pretrial publicity would impair the defendant's right to a fair trial; 2) there were no alternative measures which could mitigate the effects of the publicity; and 3) a prior restraint would effectively prevent the harm.[32]

The rule is equivalent to the clear and present danger test in the prior restraint cases. Under *Nebraska Press*, the danger to a criminal defendant's Sixth Amendment fair trial right is not "clear" until a cause-and-effect relationship between news stories and likely juror bias is proved. The danger to the fair trial right is not "present" until all alternatives to gagging the press have been considered and found useless. Three justices would have dispensed with the issue permanently by creating an absolute rule against gag orders.

The Court also required that any gag order must be based on more than the intuitive conclusions of a trial judge. There was little doubt where the Court stood when Chief Justice Warren Burger's majority opinion called the trial judge's analysis "speculative." The expectation that the judge must explain the order has become the rule that a trial judge must make specific, written findings to support an order restraining the news media. Trial judges must also give notice before issuing a gag order and must hold a hearing to give news organizations an opportunity to argue against any order.[33]

If the facts in the *Nebraska Press* case cannot support an inference of prejudicial effect from news coverage, it is difficult to imagine what facts would. In October 1975, Erwin Simants had murdered an entire family of six in Sutherland, Nebraska, a town with 850 residents. The case understandably attracted the press, for whom the murder of the Cutter family in nearby Kansas[34] and the murder rampage of Charles Starkweather through Nebraska and Wyoming[35] were still fresh memories. The judges who drew the assignment believed, reasonably the Court thought, that a prejudicial effect would be inevitable in such a small town. But, Burger noted, rumor was just as inevitable, and professional news coverage would be preferable to rumor.

Two state judges issued orders against the press, among them a requirement that reporters adhere to the Nebraska Bar-Press Guidelines. Judge Hugh Stuart also announced that he would screen reporters to determine their fitness to cover the case. Finally, both judges issued an order that information taken from public pretrial hearings not be published. By the time the Supreme Court heard the case, only the gag order remained at issue. In the end, just as in *Sheppard*, the Court said that media effects were a problem for the judge to deal with, not a reason to curb the media.

The *Nebraska Press* case also highlights a nonjudicial fact that those who might wish to restrain the press should keep in mind. Issuing a prior restraint always results in more, not less, publicity. Before the judges' orders, only reporters from the region were covering the case. After the order, the case attracted national coverage.

Since *Nebraska Press*, valid gag orders have been rare. News organizations can safely assume that they have the right to publish any information they obtain lawfully about a court proceeding, even if the information would normally be confidential. The rules requiring that a judge's order be obeyed are still in effect, but trial judges who issue invalid orders normally are quickly reversed. In *Oklahoma Publishing Co. v. District Court,*[36] the Court said that protecting the identities of juvenile defendants could not justify a gag order. The rule against gag orders applies not only to information, but to specific forms of media, such as photos or videotape.[37]

Gag orders have been upheld in three notable cases since 1976, but only one concerned normal news gathering. In *KUTV v. Wilkinson,*[38] the Utah Supreme Court upheld a trial judge's order that news organizations not publish allegations that a defendant in a theft trial had organized crime connections. The judge had followed all the steps required under *Nebraska Press*, the court said. More important, the trial judge had evidence of actual juror exposure to publicity and also had evidence of testified-to effects from the publicity.

The other two cases are clear exceptions to the normal gag order rules. In *Seattle Times v. Rhinehart*,[39] the Supreme Court let stand a trial court order barring a newspaper from publishing information taken from discovery documents in a civil suit. Discovery is a pretrial stage during which the parties in a case exchange information through documents, depositions, and interrogatories. An interrogatory is a set of written questions the other side is obliged to answer or face a contempt charge. In *Rhinehart*, though, the lawsuit was a libel case in which the *Seattle Times* was the defendant. It seems untoward for a member of the media to benefit from news coverage of the compelled evidence of its adversary. The newspaper remained free to report whatever it could obtain from other sources, however.

In the second case, *United States v. Noriega*,[40] Cable News Network (CNN) had received tapes of conversations between Manuel Noriega and his defense attorneys, recorded in prison. Noriega, former president of Panama, was awaiting trial for drug trafficking. He argued that the recordings violated the traditional attorney-client privilege and sought a temporary restraining order to prevent them from being aired. According to the trial judge, who seemed rankled by CNN's mysterious possession of tapes that clearly intruded on Noriega's privacy, the tapes might also disclose defense strategy, thereby affecting Noriega's right to a fair trial. The next day, CNN filed an "emergency motion" with the court of appeals, which upheld the order. Both courts chided CNN for refusing to disclose the tapes. Eight days later, the Supreme Court declined to review the case. CNN then handed over the tapes. After reviewing them, the trial judge lifted the order, concluding there was no threat to a fair trial.[41]

The last two cases have apparently had little influence on the lower courts, which have relied instead upon other precedents in deciding gag order cases.[42] It is noteworthy that most of the recent gag order cases have concerned orders prohibiting trial participants from talking with journalists. Gag orders directly against the press seem virtually extinct. The *Rhinehart* and *Noriega* cases should remain exceptions that do not weaken the general rule against gag orders.

Traditionally, an exception has been made for cases involving juveniles. In many states, statutes prohibit identification of juveniles charged with crimes, unless they are charged as adults. The courts in most states have begun applying the principles of *Nebraska Press* even to juvenile cases.[43] Some states continue to view juvenile cases as completely different, however, and allow gags on juvenile names without applying any test.[44] Even then, the press is free to report names if they are obtained out of court.

Punishment after Publication

Courts may not attempt to impose indirect gags by punishing publication. The general rule that the courts have adopted is that truthful information that was acquired in open court or by other legal means cannot be the basis for a liability action against the press after the information is published. This rule holds even if a statute prohibits publication of the type of information involved.[45]

The rule applies whether the state brings an action for violation of a statute or a private person brings a civil liability action based upon the statute.

Gag Orders against Trial Participants

As noted earlier in the chapter, the imposition of gag orders on trial participants is an area of law that is still developing. The *Gentile* case indicates that it may be easier to impose gag orders against lawyers and others who fall directly under the court's supervisory authority. It is doubtful that witnesses and defendants fit that mold, however, and limits on them are likely to be difficult to uphold. In the absence of directions from the Supreme Court, the safest course is to find out what the standards are in each state and federal circuit. The tests vary widely. Hawaii, for example, has a test similar to that in *Nebraska Press,* which makes it extremely difficult to gag anybody.[46] The Fourth Circuit makes it slightly easier to gag trial participants, requiring only a "substantial probability" of prejudice test.[47] The trend has been for courts to increase the burden of proof required to justify these orders.

A few general rules have been established. Just as with gag orders against media, a judge must provide written findings that support the order. Alternatives must have been considered and rejected as impractical or useless. An order will normally become invalid once the proceeding has ended,[48] unless an additional interest such as privacy is at stake.[49]

Gag Orders in Civil Cases

Because a party seeking a gag order must show a threat to a compelling or overriding interest, gag orders are seldom granted in civil lawsuits. A compelling interest is normally based on federal or state constitutional grounds—the Sixth Amendment right to a fair trial is the classic example. In civil suits, by contrast, money is usually at issue, and constitutional interests appear only on rare occasions. The *Rhinehart* case is perhaps the best example. In that case, the newspaper was prohibited from publishing information obtained during discovery in a libel suit. The plaintiff, a charitable organization, had been asked to disclose the names of all donors. The organization argued that publication of the names would violate the privacy interests and rights of the donors under the First Amendment's guarantee of freedom of association.[50]

ACCESS TO LEGAL PROCEEDINGS

Unable to try to ensure a fair trial by issuing gag orders against the press, judges countered by closing trials and other court proceedings, a logical although ultimately unacceptable response. The Supreme Court had appeared to approve of closure as an alternative in the *Sheppard* and *Nebraska Press* cases. Accordingly, the number of closures began rising in the late 1970s.

To the press, a First Amendment right to publish what it learned in court was of little use if the courtroom was closed. It was inevitable that the media and the judiciary would clash on this issue too. After all, the cases most likely to draw closure motions from defendants are the very ones that generate the most news coverage.

The *DePasquale* Pretrial Proceedings Case

When the issue first arose, it was not at all clear that the news media would prevail and that access to proceedings of all types would be protected by either the First Amendment or the common law, or both. Indeed, quite the opposite was true initially. The first decision by the U.S. Supreme Court, *Gannett v. DePasquale*,[51] led many to believe that the Court supported closure in general. The case arose when a pretrial hearing on admissibility of evidence in a murder case was closed. The court granted a closure motion from the defendants. No hearing was held on the motion. A reporter in attendance did not object until the next day.

The Supreme Court, divided 5–4, held that the Sixth Amendment's guarantee of a public trial was a personal guarantee for defendants, who could waive it, as had been done. The majority opinion refused to decide whether the press and the public had a separate right of access based on the First Amendment.

Following the decision, motions to close proceedings mushroomed. At least 270 closure motions were filed in a year; half of them were thought to have been successful. Although most of the closures were of pretrial proceedings, many were of actual trials. News organizations became alarmed.

First Amendment Access Guaranteed in the *Richmond* Case

The next year the Supreme Court reversed its course. In *Richmond Newspapers v. Virginia*,[52] the Court decided 7–1 that the First Amendment guarantees the press and public the right to attend criminal trials. The case arose when an exasperated judge was beginning the fourth trial of a defendant after a series of reversed verdicts and mistrials. With the acquiescence of the prosecutor, he closed the trial upon the request of the defendant.

There was no majority opinion. Chief Justice Burger's plurality opinion used many of the arguments that Justice Harry Blackmun had used in dissent the year before in *DePasquale*. Burger attempted to explain that the two cases could coexist.

Burger announced that "[a]bsent an overriding interest articulated in findings, the trial of a criminal case must be open to the public," a test apparently as strict as the test that bars gag orders. He noted in a footnote that the right of access was assumed to apply to civil trials as well. Three justices, William Brennan, Thurgood Marshall, and John Paul Stevens, argued that the case recognized a more general First Amendment right of access to information held or controlled by government. The various opinions recognized the idea that the press acts as the agent of the public in covering judicial news. Access to such news, Burger said, serves a "core purpose of assuring freedom of communication on matters relating to the functioning of government."

Burger outlined the steps that a trial judge must follow to close a trial without violating the Constitution: prepare written findings and try alternatives less drastic than closure. It followed that the trial judge must also provide notice to the press and allow a hearing before granting a closure motion.

First Amendment Right of Access Extended

In 1982, 1984, 1986, and 1993, *Richmond* was followed by Supreme Court cases that firmly establish a right to attend and report on proceedings of almost all types. The two most important cases were *Globe Newspaper Co. v. Superior Court*[53] in 1982 and *Press-Enterprise v. Riverside County Superior Court*[54] in 1986. In *Globe*, the trial judge had closed part of a rape trial. A Massachusetts statute required closure during the testimony of a rape victim under eighteen years of age. In the majority opinion, Justice Brennan clearly adopted a compelling interest test for closing trials. He said the statute violated the First Amendment because the compelling interest test requires that each case be considered on its own merits. Ever since, automatic closure of proceedings has been presumptively unconstitutional. Brennan did not argue that the state interest in protecting rape victims was unimportant, but said that the interest could not be advanced by an automatic rule.

The *Press-Enterprise* case expanded the access right to pretrial proceedings. Access had already been applied to voir dire, which is considered part of the trial itself, in an earlier case involving the same newspaper.[55] The Court said that the right of access is applied in light of a two-part analysis. First, have the place and the type of proceeding historically been open? Second, does public access play a "significantly positive role in the functioning of the particular process in question"? The Court did not say that both must be shown. Obviously, though, press coverage of a proceeding will typically be thought to play a positive role in the process. *Richmond* assumes as much.

The *Press-Enterprise* case involved the **preliminary hearing** of Robert Diaz, a nurse accused of murdering twelve patients with massive doses of a heart drug. The bizarre case drew heavy news coverage. In California the preliminary hearing assesses the evidence to determine whether charges will be brought, much like an **arraignment** in many other states. Unlike pretrial hearings in other states, though, preliminary hearings in California review at length almost all the evidence that will appear at trial. This one took forty-one days, and almost all of it had been closed following a motion from Diaz. The newspaper was also denied transcripts of the hearing.

The U.S. Supreme Court announced that the "reasonable likelihood" test applied by the California courts to uphold closure was too generous to defendants and too restrictive against the press. Unfortunately, the majority opinion by Burger was ambiguous. He cited the compelling interest test from *Globe*, but claimed that a "substantial probability" test was called for. The Court formally endorsed the substantial probability test for pretrial matters in 1993.[56]

● **Preliminary hearing**
An examination of a person charged with a crime and a review of the evidence against that person. It is conducted by a judge or magistrate.

● **Arraignment**
A hearing to examine evidence to determine if formal charges of criminal wrongdoing will be made against a suspect.

The *Press-Enterprise* case was important in another way. Most criminal cases do not go to trial. They are either plea-bargained or dismissed near or after the preliminary hearing/arraignment stage. As the Court noted, if the public is to know about this large portion of judicial and law enforcement activity, access is essential.

The net result of the *Globe* and *Press-Enterprise* cases is that a compelling interest test is constitutionally required only when closure of the trial itself is attempted. The Court did not attempt to explain the difference in treatment for pretrial proceedings in *Press-Enterprise*. Many lower courts have chosen to interpret the case more strictly. New York, for example, has rejected a "possibility" standard and applied something like the compelling interest test.[57] North Dakota follows the substantial likelihood formula.[58] Some states interpret the issue in light of their state constitutions. Usually, that means stronger protection for press access.[59] Several states have interpreted their state constitutions to require access to juvenile proceedings as well, since the protections for access are stated in absolute terms.[60] There have been few reported closures of either trials or pretrial proceedings since the late 1980s, indicating that the line of cases beginning with *Richmond* has succeeded for the most part in keeping courts open at every stage of the legal process.

Under the *Press-Enterprise* rationale, an argument may be made to open virtually any type of proceeding. Access has been argued for and gained in various types of criminal proceedings, including plea hearings, sentencing hearings, motion hearings, and bail hearings.

A right of access has also generally been recognized for civil actions[61] and applies even to divorce actions, once thought to be mainly private in nature. The right includes protection for access to pretrial hearings, such as on motions to dismiss and motions for summary judgment, in addition to trials. The scope of the right of access has not been litigated in every state, however, and access to divorce or juvenile matters may be contested.[62]

Closure is occasionally allowed, but reviewing courts make sure that trial judges follow all the steps outlined in either *Richmond* or *Press-Enterprise*.[63] If closure is ordered, it must be as limited as possible. For example, testimony from an undercover police officer[64] or a witness guaranteed anonymity might justify a limited closure. A closure must be narrowly tailored to protect the interest that justified closure. If it goes further than necessary, it may be reversed.

ACCESS TO DOCUMENTS AND EVIDENCE

The logical next step for news organizations was to attempt to extend the First Amendment right of access to documents and evidence filed with courts and law enforcement agencies. There has long been a common law right to inspect and copy court records, including evidence, but a constitutional right is thought to provide stronger protection.[65] A common law right, in general, may be overridden if a court is convinced that the party opposing access has the stronger argument.[66] By contrast, a constitutional right will trigger a stricter test; a party opposing disclosure must satisfy a substantial interest test or something higher, although the courts cannot seem to agree on a test.[67] At this time, a First Amendment right of access to documentary evidence introduced in court has been clearly established in almost every jurisdiction that has considered the question, for both civil and criminal cases.[68] The access right also applies to all written orders by the courts themselves, including plea agreements and sentencing.[69]

Often the press is able to obtain the same material even with the common law right of access,[70] and some states apply a common law or statutory presumption of access almost as strictly as a constitutional one.[71] Nevertheless, there is simply less wiggle room to allow nondisclosure under a constitutional test.[72]

The general rules, still developing, appear to provide access to any materials introduced for trial or otherwise under the control of the court. The rationale is that the public has an interest in the materials once they are filed with the court. The right can have a constitutional, statutory, or common law basis.

Access to pretrial materials, especially discovery documents, is more troublesome. Historically, there was no common law right to inspect discovery materials.[73] Although states have been reluctant to apply a First Amendment access rule to discovery, some will apply the common law rule.[74] A number of courts have also allowed access to such pretrial materials as affidavits supporting search warrants, either on First Amendment[75] or common law[76] grounds. Materials that are created early in the criminal judicial process, such as videotapes of police searches[77] or of police station lineups,[78] have generally not been disclosed. The courts said the materials were still part of an ongoing investigation and therefore not available.

The courts generally recognize only a common law right to inspect and copy nondocumentary materials.[79] As a result, it is easier for a party to prevent news organizations from using actual videotape or audiotape that has been introduced as evidence. Requests to copy have been denied both on the basis of privacy or dignity and on the basis of risk to a fair trial. Most courts apply a balancing of factors approach when the access right is based on common law.[80]

In recent years, news organizations have sought to force disclosure of sealed records, especially settlement agreements. In civil cases, the parties often reach a settlement before going to trial; sometimes they even settle after trial but before the verdict is formally entered by the judge. Most courts have treated sealed settlements the same as other records. A presumption of access applies.[81] In one case, decided under a public records statute, the settlement file was released, and the newspaper seeking disclosure was awarded attorney fees.[82]

The issue of access to documents and materials created in or introduced during law enforcement activity or filed with courts for trials has produced a torrent of cases in recent years. Although a right of access has been generally accepted, the right is uncertain. It may be based on constitutional, common law, or statutory grounds. The tests applied vary as well. In one recent case, a trial court determined that the First Amendment provided a right of access to records that were exempt from disclosure under a state freedom of information act.[83] If the lower courts continue to disagree on how to treat the matter, review will undoubtedly be sought in the Supreme Court.

BROADCAST AND PHOTOGRAPHIC COVERAGE

W hether cameras should be allowed in the courtroom was a major media law issue of the 1970s and 1980s. Broadcasters argued that banning television coverage hindered their ability to gather news and favored print media. They also argued that broadcast coverage would serve to better inform the public. By 1994, all but three states allowed television and still cameras in court, and the federal system was conducting a test with cameras in selected federal district courts. The major issues today concern fine-tuning the rules allowing camera access in court.

For most of this century, cameras were not allowed in courts. The decision to ban or allow cameras is considered to be part of the inherent authority of the various state supreme courts to supervise their states' judicial systems. The American Bar Association's code of judicial ethics recommended against allowing cameras, and most jurisdictions banned them. The cause of the broadcasters was slowed by a 1965 case, *Estes v. State of Texas*,[84] in which the Supreme Court decided that allowing television coverage of a criminal trial had violated due process of law. The Court appeared to be saying that televising trials was unacceptable whether the defendant suffered from prejudicial publicity or not. The intrusiveness of early 1960s television equipment was thought to change the tone of the proceeding itself. Critics expected that witnesses, lawyers, jurors, and even judges would change their behavior if trials were televised. In a concurring opinion, Justice John Marshall Harlan suggested that one day television would be so commonplace that it would have little or no potential negative effect.

Most states followed *Estes*, but by 1980 a number of states had begun allowing cameras. One was Florida. Its rules allowing broadcast coverage were challenged in *Chandler v. Florida*.[85] In this case, the Supreme Court backed away from the presumptions of *Estes*. Chief Justice Burger said the concern that the equipment would be disruptive was weaker than in 1965. The cameras were smaller and did not require extra bright lights. The Court said that a criminal defendant must establish that televising the trial actually had a prejudicial effect on its outcome. The Court did not create a First Amendment right for camera access, but said that the states were free to allow or not allow cameras without violating due process.

Today only Indiana, Mississippi, and South Dakota fail to provide some courtroom access to cameras. In the other states, the supreme courts have adopted various rules allowing access. In most states, the supreme court has appointed a committee of judges, lawyers, and journalists to advise it on setting camera rules. Rules are implemented first on an experimental basis, then usually become permanent.

In the states allowing cameras, two issues are still not fully resolved. First, many of the rules require that the judge and/or the parties consent to broadcast coverage. When consent of the parties is required, the proceedings are almost never broadcast. Judges are more likely to grant consent, but access is greater in states requiring no consent of any kind. Second, a few states allow access only for arguments in appellate courts. Those proceedings may interest law school students, but journalists seldom cover oral arguments on appeal.

Delaware, Idaho, Illinois, and Louisiana allow only coverage of appeals courts. For television stations and newspaper photographers, such access is a slight blessing.

The rules in many states specify that jurors or witnesses may ask that they not be shown or that they be visually obscured. The trial judge has discretionary authority to impose limits on broadcast coverage as well. Limitations on airing breaks during trial, such as bench conferences, are typical. Similarly, conversations between lawyers and clients usually may not be broadcast. Most courts allow only a single television camera, which is put in a fixed location. All stations interested in carrying video of a trial normally share a common feed. The same rules apply for sound-only recording. Many courthouses are being fitted with permanent cameras and sound systems. Newspeople in many instances can now take their feed right from the court's equipment. Courts have found audio and video records quite useful for judicial purposes apart from their news uses.

Written court opinions regarding broadcast access are rather rare. News organizations usually try to work with judges to resolve differences of opinion about what is acceptable in a given case. Since the right of access is conditional and the judge has tremendous discretion in interpreting the rules, in the final analysis the judge's opinion will almost certainly prevail. Under the rules in most states, a judge's order to deny access in part or in whole is assessed using a "best interests of justice" test, which almost always upholds the trial judge.[86] A few states apply a stricter "substantial likelihood" test.[87]

The federal courts have refused to allow camera access. The Supreme Court has refused to allow cameras to broadcast its proceedings. This position is hard to justify since there are no witnesses or jurors to affect. Several justices have said they would be willing to give television coverage a try. The Judicial Conference of the United States, which proposes rules for the federal courts, established a three-year experimental program to allow broadcast, photographic, and sound coverage in two circuit courts of appeal and six federal district courts.[88] Only civil cases and appeals could be covered, though. After reviewing the experimental program, the judicial conference decided against creating a general rule allowing camera coverage in the federal courts. A curious result developed in early 1995 when two infamous cases were tried and received extensive news coverage. Under California's rules, audiences could watch the entire O. J. Simpson trial, but could see only sketches drawn at the federal court trial of defendants in the World Trade Center bombing. Nevertheless, it seems only a matter of time until camera coverage is made permanent in the federal courts and extended to criminal trials, just as in the state courts.

SUMMARY

The rights of reporters to cover judicial news have been affirmed repeatedly and strongly. The trend for two decades has been to strengthen the constitutional tests guaranteeing right of access while simultaneously extending the right to documents, parties in court, and even witnesses. Although the precise test varies for each type of material or proceeding, the basic rule is clear: the press and public may not be kept from judicial news unless an unusually strong justification is given.

Judicial orders to block coverage of legal news almost always fail to meet the constitutional tests. But the media's rights are often not vindicated until appeal, long after the news event has ended. It is crucial for reporters to know their rights, and at least the general constitutional tests, so that they can press their case in court if need be when a motion for closure is filed. They should at a minimum be able to get a judge to wait until a lawyer can appear and a proper hearing can be scheduled.

The tendency of many judges and lawyers to approve of closures was rooted in the belief that news reports and unfair trials were connected by a cause-and-effect relationship. The scientific evidence does not support this view. Unbiased juries can be found. Nor is there any solid evidence that broadcast coverage leads to unfair trials. Although broadcast access has no constitutional protection, it is clearly here to stay. In both instances, the courts have followed the rationale drawn from prior restraint cases—news gathering and dissemination cannot be restrained on the basis of speculation.

Paradoxically, freeing journalists to report legal news creates new ethical burdens. Now the media must make almost all the decisions about what is appropriate to publish or broadcast about legal issues, just as in libel, invasion of privacy, and prior restraint. That a legal right allows publication does not mean that publication is desirable. Access increases the availability of material that may be prejudicial to defendants or may exceed the bounds of taste of the audience.

KEY TERMS

Gag order
Contempt of court
Fair trial
Prejudicial publicity
Venue
Continuance

Voir dire
Sequestration
Bar-press guidelines
Preliminary hearing
Arraignment

CASE PROBLEMS

1. You are a reporter for the daily *World-Globe*, covering the murder trial of Laura Gates, who is charged with having bludgeoned her husband and three children to death with a garden shovel while they slept. The case has attracted considerable media attention. Gates's lawyer submitted statements from three potential character witnesses asserting that the presence of the media frightens them, and that they will not testify if media representatives are present during their testimony. The lawyer files a motion to close the trial during the testimony. The motion also requests that TV cameras, which are presumptively allowed under state court rules, be turned off during the testimony. A character witness is normally useful in helping a jury decide if a defendant was capable of committing the acts he or she is charged with. Often evidence of good character may help to reduce a sentence even if it does not persuade a jury to find a defendant not guilty. The trial judge asks you to meet in the judge's chambers

to discuss the issue—off the record, of course. What will you tell the judge?

2. You are the court reporter for the daily *World-Globe*. For the last two weeks, you have been covering the case of Lloyd Binns, who has been arrested and charged with having assassinated state senator Florence Aldiss on the steps of the state capitol last February 14. Aldiss, who was single, had been dating Binns for several months. She cut off the relationship February 13. You have covered the crime and the arrest in a total of eight separate stories. Today Binns comes up for preliminary examination in county circuit superior court. You have been informed by attorneys from the prosecutor's office that Binns plans to raise two major points at the hearing.

    First, Binns plans to move that a suicide note found at his apartment be ruled inadmissible. The note said, "If I can't be with you, no one can." It then detailed a plan to kill Aldiss and himself outside her home. The note, though stamped and addressed, was never mailed. It was dated February 13. City police obtained the letter when they went to search Binn's apartment after the murder. It was found, however, by the building superintendent who accompanied the police into the apartment. It had been hidden in a partly full box of cereal—a place the building superintendent "knew" was used for hiding things. Binns thinks this constituted an unlawful search and seizure.

    Second, Binns plans to plead temporary insanity to avoid having a trial at all. He is scheduled to introduce affidavits and/or testimony from five psychiatrists, including a personal psychiatrist he has been seeing for more than eight years. Binns argues that the publication of material would impinge on his privacy and on the doctor-patient relationship. This second claim is related to the first, since the apparent premeditation inferable from the suicide note tends to contradict Binns's insanity claim.

    At the hearing, Binn's lawyer moves to close the proceedings. She introduces a file containing the following evidence: (1) Since the murder of Senator Aldiss, newspapers and TV stations in the state have carried more than 1,420 stories about the case. (2) The stories, analyzed for inflammatory language by a state university professor, show "372 instances of inflammatory language." (3) Examples of inflammatory terms used include "lovesick," "long history of mental illness," and "Valentine's Day Murderer." (4) The story has been covered by every daily newspaper and every TV news operation in the state and has also been covered to some extent in all forty-nine other states. (5) A survey of 100 county residents showed that 82 percent knew who Binns was and already thought he was guilty. In light of this evidence, the lawyer asserts that Binns's fair trial rights are in danger.

    Judge Jane Boyd announces that "based on this body of substantial evidence, I am inclined to close this proceeding, unless the prosecution objects." The prosecution does not object. "There being no objection, I hereby. . . ."

    At this point, you rise and declare, "Your honor, I object. As a reporter, I have a legal right to attend this proceeding. I request that the closure order be delayed until our lawyers can argue this issue."

    Boyd responds, "I'll give you fifteen minutes. I want to get on with this. The hearing on closure will start then." You frantically call the newsroom, then the paper's lawyer. The lawyer who represents the paper is out of town. The city editor tells you, "Well, Beets, it looks like you're on your own with this hearing." You head back to the courtroom, wondering what to say.

    What arguments will you make to the judge?

3. You are the lawyer for TV station WYME-TV, Channel 48. The station recently asked you to help it obtain and copy materials to be introduced in evidence by the prosecution in the bank robbery and murder trial of Roto Barnes. In October 1991, a man who has been identified as Barnes robbed a Third National Bank branch at the intersection of Maple and Sycamore Streets. Two customers were shot in the head as the robber left the bank. Both the robbery and the shootings were caught on videotape by mounted cameras in the bank. Judge Lesley Waller of the county circuit superior court has ordered a hearing on the issue of admitting the videotape after the defendant and relatives of the deceased customers objected to having the videotapes made available for copying. In addition, the defendant argues that showing the tapes would hinder his chances of getting a fair trial, while the relatives argue that release would violate the privacy of the deceased. How will you argue for the station?

4. TO: New Junior Lawyer
    FROM: Senior Lawyer
    RE: WOLD-TV—Access to Court Materials
    I met with E. D. Murrow, news director of WOLD-TV here in Rock Falls, this morning. WOLD would like to attend the trial and also copy materials introduced into evidence at the Kane divorce trial in county court.

In the divorce trial, Laura Kane has sued for divorce from Charles Foster Kane on the grounds of extreme cruelty and adultery. Charles Kane has countersued on the same grounds. Mr. Kane is heir to the Xanadu Newspaper chain fortune. The newspaper chain was founded by his father, Charles Foster Kane I.

The trial has attracted a great deal of attention from the media at both the local and national level. Not only are the two parties involved well-known and wealthy, but the evidence heard in the case so far "is enough to make your hair curl," according to at least one news report in the *World-Globe*. The Kanes are considered members of high society in Rock Falls.

WOLD would like to obtain access to two particular items that were scheduled to be introduced in evidence at the trial yesterday morning. At the time the evidence was introduced, WOLD's in-house counsel, Larry Snelling, moved that WOLD be granted access to the materials. Judge Mary Foley denied the motion, but has recessed the trial until arguments on the motion can be made next week. Snelling suggested that Murrow stop over to discuss the matter with us.

At the same time, Foley granted a motion filed jointly by the Kanes that portions of the trial be closed to the press and the public. Foley granted the motion for closure, but only for those portions of the trial in which the evidence listed below will be shown or played. Arguments challenging the motion will also be heard next week.

The two particular items of evidence detail the curious personal lives of the Kanes. Both Kanes, according to testimony already given at trial, have unusual sexual habits. Apparently, both are also fond of remembering them, because the couple's sexual encounters have been preserved on both audio and visual recording tapes. The first tape sought by WOLD is a videotape made by Mr. Kane of an "orgy" in the Kane home; the event was attended by the Kanes and six other married couples who are their friends. The tape was made through a camera with a wide-angle lens mounted on the ceiling of the living room, where the event took place. No guests have as yet been identified. Mr. Kane testified that one guest asked about the camera and was told it was part of the security system. Indeed, the camera is linked to the security system.

The second item sought by WOLD is a sound tape recording of Mrs. Kane. The tape was recorded over several months by means of a hidden microphone in her private bedroom. The tape contains the audible interactions of Mrs. Kane and a series of sexual partners. These encounters occurred during late morning and early afternoon, when Mr. Kane was at his office. The tape ran continuously while Mr. Kane was away. It was edited by one of Mr. Kane's employees to delete soundless portions.

Both Mr. and Mrs. Kane have opposed release of the materials to WOLD. They contend that release would violate both their personal rights and the personal rights of the third parties involved in the events. Judge Foley agreed on the privacy interest. The Kanes additionally contend that a divorce is "almost strictly a private matter between two people," and that the media have fewer rights to documents and other material in divorce proceedings. With this, Foley disagreed. The Kanes have also filed complementary motions to have the rest of the trial closed to the press and the public.

I called Mr. Snelling after talking with Murrow. Snelling said that this problem has never arisen for the television station before, and that WOLD wants our advice on how to proceed. They also plan to use the memo I've asked you to prepare as a future reference. Snelling said that WOLD does not plan to broadcast any material "that may offend a significant portion of our audience." The station refuses, however, to allow anyone to approve or disapprove of materials used prior to the broadcast on which they are aired.

I'd like you to prepare a memo that outlines the current state of the law and also suggests how this case will be decided.

5. Six defendants are on trial in county circuit superior court. They are charged with having beaten a jogger nearly to the point of death in Pylon Park. The jogger, whose identity has been withheld throughout pretrial proceedings, will be the key witness at the trial. All that is known is that she is a lawyer in one of the large law firms in town, and that she suffered forty-two broken bones in the attack and lost a lung and one eye. The three defendants, all age eighteen, have been identified as members of gangs. Their names are known. Each has an unusually lengthy criminal record for an eighteen-year-old. Their names and their criminal histories have been reported widely in newspapers, on television, and on radio—local, state, national, and international. Two hundred news organizations have indicated that they will have reporters on hand to cover the trial. The courtroom only seats 175 observers.

Upon a motion by lawyers for the six defendants, judge Gary Ebbett has issued an order allowing only reporters who have previous experience in covering trials to attend the proceedings. Ebbett's order also requires that reporters submit photocopies of news stories on trials they have done previously. He announced that he would review them to see "if any reporter has a habit of violating the state bar-press guidelines." Ebbett's order relied upon evidence submitted by the defense. It showed that the story had received saturation coverage both in the city and also nationally, and that 98 percent of area residents were familiar with the case. The defense also introduced a study by a journalism professor that showed that inexperienced reporters are far more likely to write one-sided, biased stories. Ebbett said that the evidence was enough to establish a "substantial likelihood of an unfair trial due to influence upon jurors and potential jurors arising from well-meaning but skewed news coverage."

The judge also announced that the trial will be closed in part. The victim has requested that the trial be closed during her testimony. She asserts that an open trial would, in effect, amount to victimizing her a second time. She also wants to keep her identity private. Her request is joined by the prosecuting attorney. Lawyers for the defendants opposed the motion. They argued that the order violated their clients' Sixth Amendment rights. Reporters present also opposed the motion, arguing that the order would violate First Amendment rights. Ebbett said that since the order "was not directed at the press," the First Amendment issue was not relevant. He ruled that the witness-victim's "privacy rights, at least in this context, clearly outweigh the defendants' interests." In addition, Ebbett ordered that transcripts of the victim's testimony not be released during trial, and that they be permanently sealed following trial, because "it is

the only way to assure that her identity will not become known."

Following the judge's orders, a group of reporters come to you, a newly licensed lawyer, for advice on how to proceed. They tell you their main goal is to assure that they are able to continue covering the trial without delay. The trial itself is scheduled to begin in two weeks. Judge Ebbett has asked that reporters submit photocopies of news stories in one week. What legal options and strategies are available to the journalists? How will the case likely be decided?

6. You are the attorney for the daily *World-Globe.* The paper was covering the case of *Watson v. Davis,* a county circuit court case that involved a suit by Watson, who had advanced $5,000 for a mink farm franchise, against Davis, who had advertised in the *Penny Pincher,* a free-circulation advertising circular, that "there is a fortune to be made in mink farming." During the first day of the trial, Watson had outlined the case he would present to the jury. Watson planned to show that Davis never intended to live up to the deal, that Davis knew the county was unsuited to mink farming, and that Watson had tried to "make a go of" mink farming. On the second day, reporter Jo Beets arrived at court but was refused entry. Watson's attorney showed Beets an order from the judge closing the trial based on the consent of the parties. "Unlike the criminal context, in which the public is necessarily an interested party, there is no inherent public need for attendance at or press coverage of a civil trial," the judge wrote. The state court of appeals and the state supreme court affirmed. Now the case is before the U.S. Supreme Court, and you are the lawyer arguing it. Argue.

ENDNOTES

1. *Murphy v. Florida,* 421 U.S. 794, 95 S.Ct. 2031 (1975).

2. *Patton v. Yount,* 467 U.S. 1025, 104 S.Ct. 2885 (1984).

3. See, for example, *Irvin v. Dowd,* 366 U.S. 717, 81 S.Ct. 1639 (1961).

4. Newton M. Minow and Fred H. Cate, "Who Is an Impartial Juror in an Age of Mass Media?" *American University Law Review* 40:631 (1991).

5. Ellen M. Bennett, Jill Dianne Swenson, and Jeff S. Wilkinson, "Is the Medium the Message?: An

Experimental Test with Morbid News," *Journalism Quarterly* 69:921 (Winter 1992); Melvin L. DeFleur, Lucinda Davenport, Mary Cronin, and Margaret DeFleur, "Audience Recall of News Stories Presented by Newspaper, Computer, Television and Radio," *Journalism Quarterly* 69:1010 (Winter 1992).

6. *New York v. Gross,* 179 A.D.2d 138, 583 N.Y.S.2d 832 (1992).

7. *Woven Electronics Corp. v. The Advance Group, Inc.,* 930 F.2d 913, 19 Med.L.Rptr. 1019 (4th Cir. 1991).

8. Stephen Lacy and Todd F. Simon, *The Economics and Regulation of United States Newspapers* (Norwood, N.J.: Ablex Publishing Corp., 1993), pp. 26–40, 119–120.

9. *United States v. Myers,* 635 F.2d 945 (2d Cir. 1980).

10. *Williams v. Florida,* 399 U.S. 78, 90 S.Ct. 1893 (1970); *Bloom v. Illinois,* 391 U.S. 194, 88 S.Ct. 1477 (1968).

11. *In re Stone,* 703 P.2d 1319 (Colo.App. 1985).

12. 476 F.2d 373 (5th Cir.), *cert. denied* 414 U.S. 979, 94 S.Ct. 270 (1973).

13. *New York Times v. United States,* 403 U.S. 713, 91 S.Ct. 2140 (1971).

14. *In re U.S. ex rel. Pulitzer Publishing Co.,* 635 F.2d 676 (8th Cir. 1980); *Goldblum v. NBC,* 584 F.2d 904 (9th Cir. 1978).

15. *In re Providence Journal,* 820 F.2d 1342 (1st Cir. 1986).

16. *In re Providence Journal,* 820 F.2d 1354 (1st Cir. 1987), *cert. dismissed* 485 U.S. 693, 108 S.Ct. 1502 (1988).

17. 384 U.S. 333, 86 S.Ct. 1507 (1966).

18. 366 U.S. 717, 81 S.Ct. 1639 (1961).

19. *United States v. Yonkers Board of Education,* 747 F.2d 111 (2d Cir. 1984).

20. *Tsokalas v. Purtill,* 756 F.Supp. 89 (D.Conn. 1991).

21. Elinor Kelley Grusin, "Shotgun Marriage: A Study of Tennessee Law Enforcement, Reporters and Sources," *Journalism Quarterly* 67:514 (Autumn 1990).

22. Jeremy Harris Lipschultz, "A Comparison of Trial Lawyer and News Reporter Attitudes about Courthouse Communication," *Journalism Quarterly* 68:750 (Winter 1991).

23. *Gentile v. State Bar of Nevada,* 501 U.S. 1030, 111 S.Ct. 2720 (1991).

24. *In re Dow Jones & Co.,* 842 F.2d 603 (2d Cir. 1988), *cert. denied* 488 U.S. 946, 109 S.Ct. 1094 (1988).

25. *Press-Enterprise Co. v. Riverside County Superior Court,* 464 U.S. 501, 104 S.Ct. 819 (1984).

26. *Black's Law Dictionary,* 4th rev. ed. (St. Paul, Minn.: West Publishing Co., 1968), p. 1531.

27. Dale R. Spencer, "The So-Called Problem of Prejudicial Publicity Is a Red Herring," *Communications Lawyer* 2: 11–12 (Spring 1984).

28. *Nebraska Press Association v. Stuart,* 427 U.S. 539, 96 S.Ct. 2791 (1976); *Federated Publications v. Swedberg,* 96. Wash. 2d 13, 633 P.2d 74 (1981), *cert. denied* 456 U.S. 984, 102 S.Ct. 2257 (1982).

29. *Branzburg v. Hayes,* 408 U.S. 665, 92 S.Ct. 2646 (1972).

30. 427 U.S. 539, 96 S.Ct. 2791 (1976).

31. 427 U.S. at 570, 96 S.Ct. At 2808.

32. *In re Providence Journal,* 820 F.2d 1342 (1st Cir. 1986).

33. *KUTV v. Conder,* 668 P.2d 513 (Utah 1983).

34. Truman Capote, *In Cold Blood* (New York: Random House, 1965).

35. William Allen, *Starkweather* (Boston: Houghton Mifflin, 1976).

36. 430 U.S. 308, 97 S.Ct. 1045 (1977).

37. *CBS v. U.S. District Court,* 729 F.2d 1174 (9th Cir. 1984).

38. 686 P.2d 456 (Utah 1984).

39. 467 U.S. 20, 104 S.Ct. 2199 (1984).

40. 752 F.Supp. 1032 (S.D.Fla. 1990), affirmed *In re Cable News Network, Inc.,* 917 F.2d 1543 (11th Cir. 1990), *cert. denied* 498 U.S. 976, 111 S.Ct. 451 (1990).

41. *United States v. Noriega,* 752 F.Supp. 1045 (S.D.Fla. 1990).

42. See, for example, *Vermont v. Schaefer,* 157 Vt. 339, 599 A.2d 337 (1991); *United States v. Salameh,* 992 F.2d 445 (2d Cir. 1993).

43. See, for example, *Florida Publishing Co. v. Brooke,* 576 So.2d 842 (Fla.App. 1991).

44. *Illinois v. The Champaign News-Gazette,* 205 Ill. App.3d 480, 150 Ill. Dec. 942, 563 N.E.2d 1069 (1990).

45. *Florida Star v. B.J.F.,* 491 U.S. 524, 109 S.Ct. 2603 (1989); *Smith v. Daily Mail Publishing Co.,* 443 U.S. 97, 99 S.Ct. 2667 (1979); *Landmark Communications, Inc. v. Virginia,* 435 U.S. 829, 98 S.Ct. 1535 (1978).

46. *Breiner v. Takao,* 73 Hawaii 995, 835 P.2d 637 (1992).

47. *In re the State-Record Co., Inc.,* 917 F.2d 124 (4th Cir. 1990).

48. *Butterworth v. Smith,* 494 U.S. 624, 110 S.Ct. 1376 (1990).

49. *Ohio ex rel. Cincinnati Post v. Hamilton County Court of Common Pleas,* 59 Ohio St.3d 103, 570 N.E.2d 1101 (1991).

50. *Seattle Times v. Rhinehart,* 467 U.S. 20, 104 S.Ct. 2199 (1984).

51. 443 U.S. 368, 99 S.Ct. 2898 (1979).

52. 448 U.S. 555, 100 S.Ct. 2814 (1980).

53. 457 ____ U.S. ____ 596, 102 S.Ct. 2613 (1982).

54. 478 ____ U.S. ____ 1, 106 S.Ct. 2735 (1986).

55. *Press-Enterprise v. Riverside County Superior Court,* 464 ____ U.S. ____ 501, 104 S.Ct. 819 (1984).

56. *El Vocero de Puerto Rico v. Puerto Rico,* ____ U.S. ____, 113 S.Ct. 2004 (1993).

57. *Gannett Westchester Rockland Newspapers v. Lacava,* 158 A.D. 2d 495, 551 N.Y.S.2d 261 (1990).

58. *Minot Daily News v. Holum,* 380 N.W.2d 347 (N.D. 1986).

59. See, for example, *Pennsylvania v. Murray,* 348 Pa. Super. 439, 502 A.2d 624 (1985).

60. See, for example, *Allied Daily Newspapers v. Eikenberry,* 121 Wash. 2d 205, 848 P.2d 1258 (1993).

61. See, for example, *Anderson v. Cryovac,* 805 F.2d 1 (1st Cir. 1986).

62. James F. Brelsford and Rachel A. Silvers, "Juvenile Courts: Part I, The Battle for Access," *Communications Lawyer,* Summer 1994, at 7–11.

63. *New York v. Clemons,* 78 N.Y. 2d 48, 571 N.Y.S. 2d 433, 574 N.E.2d 1039 (1991).

64. *New York v. Gross,* 179 A.D. 2d 138, 583 N.Y.S.2d 832 (1992).

65. Sherrie L. Wilson, "Journalists' Right to Copy Audio and Video Tapes Presented as Evidence During Trials," paper presented to the Law Division, annual convention, Association for Education in Journalism and Mass Communication, Kansas City, Missouri, August 1993.

66. *United States v. Edwards,* 672 F.2d 1289 (7th Cir. 1982).

67. *In re Continental Illinois Securities Litigation,* 732 F.2d 1302 (7th Cir. 1984).

68. *The Baltimore Sun v. Thanos,* 92 Md. App. 227, 607 A.2d 565 (1992).

69. See, for example, *Washington v. Campbell,* unpub., No. 92–1–002221–6, 21 Med.L.Rptr. 1895 (Wash.Super. 1993).

70. *SEC v. Van Waeyenberghe,* 990 F.2d 845 (5th Cir. 1993).

71. *Holland v. Eads,* 614 So.2d 1012 (Ala. 1993).

72. *In re Keene Sentinel,* 136 N.H. 121, 612 A.2d 911 (1992).

73. *Leucadia, Inc. v. Applied Extrusion Technologies, Inc.,* 998 F.2d 157 (3d Cir. 1993).

74. *Doe v. Florida,* 587 So.2d 526 (Fla.App. 1991).

75. *In re Search Warrants,* 18 Media.L.Rptr. 2106 (Ariz.Super. 1991).

76. *In re Flower Aviation of Kansas, Inc.,* 789 F.Supp. 366 (D.Kan. 1992).

77. *U.S. v. Thomas,* 745 F.Supp. 499 (M.D.Tenn. 1990).

78. *WBZ-TV 4 v. District Attorney,* 408 Mass. 595, 562 N.E.2d 817 (1990).

79. Wilson, "Journalists' Rights," 11–18.

80. *United States v. Beckham,* 789 F.2d 401 (6th Cir. 1986).

81. *Brown v. Advantage Engineering, Inc.,* 960 F.2d 1013 (11th Cir. 1992).

82. *Lesher Communications, Inc. v. Contra Costa County,* 21 Med.L.Rptr. 1879 (Cal.Super. 1992).

83. *Chicago Sun-Times, Inc. v. Chicago Board of Education,* 22 Med.L.Rptr. 2469 (Ill.Cir.Ct. 1994).

84. 381 U.S. 532, 85 S.Ct. 1628 (1965).

85. 449 U.S. 560, 101 S.Ct. 802 (1981).

86. *Iowa v. Douglas,* 485 N.W.2d 619 (Iowa 1992).

87. *Massachusetts v. Cross,* 33 Mass. App. Ct. 761, 605 N.E. 2d 298, 20 Med.L.Rptr. 2261 (1992); *Florida v. Green,* 395 So.2d 532 (Fla. 1981).

88. *In re Judicial Conference Guidelines,* 18 Med.L.Rptr. 1270 (U.S. Judicial Conf. 1990).

CHAPTER 7

Freedom of Information: Access to News of Government

THE GOVERNMENT VERSUS THE PRESS AND THE PUBLIC?

It can be said that access to information and privacy/secrecy are interdependent: whatever is added to one must be taken from the other. Privacy and secrecy, however, are not synonymous. Privacy is personal: one's private space is intruded upon, or an intimate detail of one's persona is published without consent. Secrecy is institutional: an agency of government chooses to conduct its business in secret, to make its work product inaccessible to the public, or to close the nation's eyes and ears and its ports of entry to ideas.

While recognizing the weaknesses and excesses of the American press, this chapter is written with an acknowledged bias in favor of public access to the public's business, with reasonable and adequately supported exceptions. It is assumed that democracy requires an informed public. Democratic societies have paid a high price for unnecessary government secrecy. The Gulf of Tonkin Resolution of August 10, 1964,[1] for example, based as it was on faulty and much-disputed factual assertions by the White House, led Congress and the public more deeply into the Vietnam War quagmire and may have changed the course of American history.

The 1983 invasion of Grenada, another example of government business conducted in secret, seemed at the time like the culmination of a tug-of-war between press and government, between those accustomed to hiding information and those committed to uncovering it, however mixed the motives of both may be. Outcries from the press against a government decision to exclude all eyewitness media coverage led to a post-invasion compromise: a pool of reporters would be allowed access to combat zones in the future.

This arrangement was applied with negative results to the Panama incursion on December 20, 1989. Representative Charles Rangel (D-NY), for example, had to file a formal Freedom of Information Act (FOIA) request with Defense Secretary Dick Cheney to get Panama invasion footage. (FOIA, the federal freedom of information or open records statute, and open meetings laws, will be discussed in detail below. Access laws, of course, are written not for the press but for the public.)

Then came the Gulf War in January 1991, and the most draconian restrictions on press coverage of military actions in American history. Again pooling was imposed for coverage of specific military events. The mobility of journalists was strictly controlled, interviews could be conducted only in the presence of commanding or public affairs officers, and press copy, including photographs and videotapes, was subjected to prepublication review by military censors. The daily military briefings reminded some veteran reporters of what used to be called the "Five O'Clock Follies" in the Vietnam War—military information officers in Saigon would provide reporters with cautious answers to questions and carefully worded handouts.

To avoid charges that the Gulf War procedures constituted "prior restraint," an exhaustive appeals process was written into the military's press guidelines. News organizations were permitted to make final judgments as to publication, but delays meant that much news would no longer be news. "In the end," said a detailed Freedom Forum report on tension between media and military in the Gulf, "media coverage of the Gulf War was shaped far more by the military's concern for achieving a decisive victory than the media's paramount goals of comprehensive and accurate coverage."[2]

A legal challenge to these rules brought by *Harper's, Nation* magazine, the *Village Voice, Mother Jones,* and others was dismissed more than a year later by a federal district judge in New York as lacking specificity and as being moot because the war had ended. A subsequent challenge to the military's barring of press and public access to Dover Air Force Base in Delaware, a receiving center for war fatalities, also failed.[3] One of the government's arguments was the "privacy" of grieving survivors, even though military family support groups joined the media as plaintiffs.

One might have expected a major confrontation between press and government over Somalia, especially after television cameras met U.S. troops as they waded ashore. It didn't happen, but the Department of Defense still controls the deployment and composition of press pools in potential combat areas.

All governments deal in disinformation and secrecy for what they claim are reasons of national security. Although some of the facts eventually emerged, the American public was for a time denied information about the Pan American Airline bombing over Lockerbie, Scotland, American hostages in Lebanon, Soviet defense spending, the savings and loan scandals, the drug wars, and General Manuel Noriega's overthrow by American forces with its attendant

Panamanian civilian casualties, to name only a few highly visible examples. The purpose of secrecy may be to control the directions of public debate. The government does this frequently, successfully, and sometimes necessarily with the forbearance of the mainstream American press.

For the sake of "national security," large segments of the federal budget are secret. As many as 20 million documents are classified annually. Foreign policy is often conducted undercover as, on occasion, it must be. Another argument for nondisclosure, as has been noted, is privacy, as when the Farmers Home Administration refused to provide the names of thirty-one borrowers whose $1 million debts had been stricken from the records under new federal credit procedures. When the government argues "privacy," is it really making a case for secrecy—for removing itself from public scrutiny?

On a more mundane level, federal documents are said by some record keepers to be packed away so thoroughly that it would cost tens of thousands of dollars to unpack them. Or they've been transferred to another agency. Or they've simply been misplaced. Or there's a terrible backlog in an agency. These kinds of excuses led one wag to call the FOIA the "Freedom to Delay" Act. The government certainly has the initial advantage when disclosure is requested. Most federal agencies try to meet the FOIA time limits. The FBI and CIA, however, can stretch a delay into years; others give the impression that they wait until an appeal is made before taking a request seriously.[4]

There are probably more court cases involving access to federal and state records and meetings than in any other area of media law. An estimated 500,000 FOIA requests are filed annually by the public and the press. Some reporters file requests merely as a means of protesting government secrecy: the information they need never gets to them on time through the FOIA anyway.

Nevertheless, Congress has done for the public, press, and other communicators such as public relations practitioners and advertisers what they could not have done for themselves. Although President Lyndon Johnson signed the bill reluctantly, Congress passed the FOIA in 1966. It went into effect in 1967. Congress has since leaned on presidents to limit secret classifications of documents. The Reagan and Bush administrations did much to counter that pressure, and the Clinton administration has still to deliver on campaign promises. In 1982, President Reagan told officials through an executive order to favor the highest level of classification for national security materials and to avoid automatic declassification. Various presidents have also attempted to muzzle for life all government employees with access to classified information and have favored using espionage laws to punish unauthorized leakers, whistle-blowers, and deviant reporters.

One former CIA agent was forced to forgo all royalties from a book on America's panicked flight from Saigon as American involvement in the Vietnam War concluded. Frank Snepp had violated an executive order that required those handling sensitive CIA material to sign an enforceable order that they would write nothing without governmental clearance. The Supreme Court upheld the punishment.[5] Hundreds of manuscripts have since been reviewed by the CIA, including one by its former head, Stansfield Turner. Even he now

- **Intelligence Identities Protection Act**
A 1982 federal law making it a crime to expose covert American agents.

complains about the reduced flow of unclassified material to the American public because of the CIA review process.

Also in 1982, Congress passed the **Intelligence Identities Protection Act,** making it a crime to engage in a "pattern of activities . . . intending to expose covert agents." A U.S. agent had been assassinated in Athens after exposure by an American writer. The writer's passport was revoked and the Supreme Court let the decision stand.[6]

Samuel Loring Morison, an employee at the Naval Intelligence Support Center in Maryland, was sentenced in 1984 to two years in prison for theft and espionage after he sent spy satellite photographs of a partly built Soviet nuclear aircraft carrier to a British military magazine for which he fancied working. His prison conviction was affirmed on appeal.[7]

- **Computer tapes**
May be records under the FOIA, but the software needed to retrieve them may not be.

Technology, of course, has played an independent role in making records less accessible, more easily obscured or destroyed, and more expensive. Complex technology complicates the request process.[8] **Computer tapes** are records under the FOIA, but computer software used in manipulating file data may not be, depending on the agency. Some agencies have gone so far as to claim that the computer programming required to retrieve computer records constitutes record creation, and that they are not required to create records under the FOIA. If no programming is available, certain kinds of information may never be disclosed. Other agencies use private companies to computerize their records; this takes the records out of the agency and gives FOI officers the librarian's old excuse of the "book is in the bindery." Processing FOIA requests can sometimes take years as a result.

- **Reporters Committee for Freedom of the Press**
A Washington-based watchdog organization that is especially sensitive to freedom of information and access to government records and meetings claims.

The **Reporters Committee for Freedom of the Press,** one of the vanguard freedom of information organizations, outlines in a readily available booklet, *Access to Electronic Records,* how to approach and examine electronically stored information.[9] The Society of Professional Journalists and the Sigma Delta Chi Foundation (SPJ-SDX) publish annual freedom of information reports, and a number of other media, legal, and public interest groups will provide access assistance in special circumstances.

After eleven years of litigation, the Reporters Committee and most of the public suffered a setback in March 1989 when the Supreme Court, though recognizing that computerization would make official data less accessible, ruled that the FBI did not have to disclose "rap sheets," computerized compilations of individual criminal records, because they were compiled for law enforcement purposes and were therefore exempt under the FOIA, at least during the lifetimes of their subjects. The FOIA, said the Court, was meant to monitor governmental, not private, affairs. The record sought in this case was that of an organized crime figure implicated in a scandal involving a Pennsylvania congressman who had pleaded guilty to soliciting campaign funds from government contractors. Personal privacy and agency discretion and convenience simply outweighed the public interest in this case.[10] The government saw "a great potential for mischief" in the reporter's request. The Reporters Committee saw a distinct public interest in the criminal record of a person selling missile and tank parts to the federal government.

As a result of this ruling, privacy has been weighted more heavily in the balance in subsequent cases. Also, courts are condoning what Justice John Paul Stevens, in his opinion for the Court, called a "practical obscurity"—information buried in computer databases that if retrieved would violate personal privacy.

One example from scores of federal court cases illustrates this change in favor of privacy. In *Gannett Satellite Information Network, Inc. v. U.S. Department of Education*,[11] the D.C. Circuit Court of Appeals in 1990 denied *USA Today*'s request for computerized data held by the department in its administration of the Guaranteed Student Loan Program. "The purpose of FOIA is not furthered," said the court, "by the disclosure of information about private citizens that is accumulated in various governmental files but that reveals little or nothing about an agency's own conduct."

Federal court rulings also suggest that agencies may not have to go to the trouble of segregating nonexempt from exempt information held in computer files. For example, the Occupational Safety and Health Administration turned down a request for electronic data, claiming the request would require a significant computer reprogramming effort. Format is another sticking point. Sometimes computer printouts are impossible to read, and agencies are under no compulsion to provide information in a more readable form. Bills pending in Congress perennially seek to overcome these problems.

Until recently, the First Amendment has not helped communicators gain access to public documents or places. "There is no constitutional right to have access to particular government information, or to require openness from bureaucracy . . . ," said Justice Potter Stewart in a Yale University address. "The Constitution itself is neither a Freedom of Information Act nor an Official Secrets Act."[12] Yet in the Pentagon Papers case, he had said, wisely, that "when everything is classified, then nothing is classified." And his colleague Byron White observed in his opinion for the Court in *Branzburg v. Hayes* that "without some protection for seeking out the news, freedom of the press would be eviscerated."[13]

A series of cases having to do with press access to prisons followed. In a case marking the first such effort by San Francisco television station KQED, Chief Justice Warren Burger said, "This Court has never intimated a First Amendment guarantee of a right of access to all sources of information within government control."[14]

Thirteen years later, in 1991 KQED was again rebuffed when it sought camera access to prison execution chambers. The case set off a widespread debate on the ethics of photographing executions, with sometimes surprising arguments on both sides.[15] For example, those in favor thought photographing would make murderers think twice; others speculated that it would demonstrate to society the horrors of capital punishment. Those opposed were largely concerned about security and the media "spectaculars" that would result. But a federal district court said that though the warden of San Quentin could not bar all media representatives, who by tradition have been present with their pencils, paper, and sketch pads, he could under California law impose clear limits on who could or could not attend executions for reasons of prison security. "Prohibition of cameras, still or television, from the execution witness area," the court added, "is a reasonable and lawful regulation."[16]

Another federal court allowed the Bureau of Prisons to reach far outside the prison and prohibit an inmate from writing for the *San Francisco Chronicle*. He had a First Amendment right to send what he wrote out of the prison with its content undisturbed, but he could not be a bylined reporter for the newspaper. When a prison regulation impinges upon an inmate's constitutional rights, said the court, "the regulation is valid if it is reasonably related to legitimate penological interests." The concern here was that the published articles could lead to violence and threaten prison security.[17]

The only chink in this judicial armor has been the Supreme Court's 1980 decision in *Richmond Newspapers v. Virginia,* which made access to a place traditionally open to press and public a matter of First Amendment law. The place was the criminal trial courtroom. "(F)or the first time," said Justice John Paul Stevens in what he called a "watershed" case, "the Court unequivocally holds that an arbitrary interference with access to important information is an abridgement of the freedom of speech and of the press protected by the First Amendment."[18]

Two years later, a federal appeals court permitted the General Services Administration to segregate private from public material in the Nixon tapes to allow public access to "presidential historical material."[19]

In their time, these were heartening victories for the press and public. But the fact remains that the right to gather information is by no means as sweeping as the right to publish information once in hand, although the Freedom of Information Act has sought to remedy that.

- **Richmond Newspapers v. Virginia**
The 1980 case that first made traditional access of press and public to criminal trial courts a First Amendment right.

The Government versus the Press and Public in Summary

The relentless struggle between press and public on the one hand and the government on the other over what information should be accessible and what should be kept private or secret seems never to end. Those seeking information must run after it as fast as they can just to keep even. The most recent confrontation between press and Pentagon began with Grenada and ended with the Gulf War. A First Amendment lawsuit on the issue was simply postponed. Classification for national security reasons or to protect personal privacy often invokes a cynical response. Excuses for nondisclosure are legion. The positive benefits of the FOIA have been offset by increasing White House appeals for classification and the use of espionage laws and the Intelligence Identities Protections Act to punish those who leak information to the media. Arrayed against secrecy are the Reporters Committee for Freedom of the Press, SPJ-SDX, and a number of other media, legal, and public interest groups. The First Amendment has been of little help in opening up the system, although the 1980 *Richmond Newspapers* case did for the first time give powerful judicial support to the First Amendment arguments in favor of access. Still, the First Amendment claim to publish remains much stronger than the right to gather information.

THE FREEDOM OF INFORMATION ACT

Section 3 of the Administrative Procedures Act of 1946 was amended in 1966 to incorporate the **Freedom of Information Act.** The act became law on July 4, 1967, a symbolic date one might note. It was based on a simple premise: unless specifically exempt under the act, public records are now available to the public. No longer can a government agency deny access on the grounds that the information seeker has no "personal" interest in the material sought or that its release would be contrary to a broad, undefined public interest.

Bureaucrats still insist on substituting their definitions of the "public interest" and "news" for those of reporters and editors, and they often prefer interpretations of the law that lead to backlogs and unbearable delays in releasing information, especially when releasable and nonreleasable segments of documents have to be segregated. Or fees for search and duplication are so high that weaker publications and ordinary citizens are discouraged from appealing adverse responses to their requests.

Nine exemptions in the act make the protection against disclosure of some categories of information "discretionary" either with the executive branch itself or with the federal courts. The act does not prohibit the disclosure of exempt material but leaves that question up to the record keeper or the federal appeals court. Too often that discretion is exercised in favor of the government.

But the FOIA has opened federal files to investigative reporters, scholars, and public interest groups (notably consumer advocate Ralph Nader who in the early days of the act taught the press how to use it) looking into government wrongdoing, unsafe working conditions and consumer products, nuclear power plants, toxic chemicals, drug trafficking, airport security, noncompliance with antidiscrimination laws, violations of the law by the CIA and FBI, and a host of other urgent public matters. Freelancers without publishing contracts and anyone seeking information for personal profit or for purposes of litigation, however, may be viewed suspiciously by record keepers.

Various amendments to the FOIA have sought either to improve or restrict it. Examples of improvement in the act were 1974 amendments that led to lower search and duplication costs or, in cases of substantial public interest, fee waivers, indexes of information held, and payment of court costs and lawyers' fees where appeals from agency decisions were found to be justified. A contrary result was legislation giving Justice Department lawyers discretion to decide what was or was not in the public interest. The FOIA Reform Act of 1986 amended the FOIA by authorizing the FBI to refuse to acknowledge the existence of records pertaining to foreign intelligence, counterintelligence, or international terrorism for "as long as the existence of records remains classified information."

The 1986 amendments standardized fee schedules and made fee waivers easier to obtain, especially for those whose purpose was scholarly, scientific, or in the public interest.

● **Freedom of Information Act (FOIA)**
The 1967 federal law making government documents available to the public unless they fit one or more of nine exemptions.

What Are Records?

The FOIA applies to agencies, departments, and government-controlled corporations of the executive branch of the *federal* government. This includes cabinet-level departments such as State, Defense, Transportation, Interior, Justice, and Treasury. Independent regulatory agencies such as the Federal Communications Commission (FCC), the Federal Trade Commission (FTC), and the Security and Exchange Commission (SEC) are also included, as are the U.S. Postal Service, the National Aeronautics and Space Administration (NASA), the Civil Service Commission, and executive offices such as the Office of Management and Budget (OMB). Their functions and rules are published in the *Federal Register.*

> ● *Federal Register*
> The first place to look for the rules and regulations of U.S. administrative agencies such as the Federal Communications Commission and the Federal Trade Commission.

The FOIA does not apply to the president, his immediate staff, or consultants such as the president's Council of Economic Advisers. A federal appeals court held in 1990 that neither the FOIA nor the Federal Advisory Committee Act (first passed in 1972 to open to public scrutiny the advising of government agencies by private persons) required the Office of Administration of the Executive Office of the President or White House counsel to produce documents relating to the Tower Commission, which was investigating the Iran-contra scandal. The Office of the President, said the court, is not an "agency" subject to the FOIA.[20] Nor does the act apply to Congress, the federal courts, or private corporations, unless their documents are filed with a federal agency.

The FOIA is a federal law. It does not apply to state or municipal records. They are covered only by state law.

Only records generated by a federal agency and in its possession are available from that agency under the FOIA. The Supreme Court held in *Forsham v. Harris*[21] that records of a federally funded university research project were not records subject to disclosure under the FOIA until a government agency had assumed exclusive control of them for its own review or use. An agency is not responsible for documents that have escaped its control, and it has no obligation to retrieve them once gone.[22] Generally speaking, the FOIA makes no distinction between manual and computer storage systems.[23]

Using the FOIA

> ● *Vaughn* Index
> A motion for a Vaughn Index is a motion asking a court to order a government agency to provide a complete accounting of all the documents in its possession that it is withholding and its reasons for withholding each piece that has been requested.

A first step in using the act is to buy the Washington-based Reporters Committee for Freedom of the Press handbook, *How to Use the Federal FOI Act* (the FOI Service Center, 800 18th Street N.W., Washington, D.C. 20006). It includes sample letters for formal requests, appeals, waivers of fee, and the making of indexes (called a *Vaughn* motion after a case requiring that refusals to release records be based on complete indexes of agency records).[24] A federal district court complaint is also illustrated in the handbook.

The handbook also explains how to use the federal Privacy Act of 1974,[25] which, as we shall see, is interconnected with the FOIA.

Once you are familiar with the act, the first step is to make an informal request by telephone. Be specific about who you are and what you want. Each agency, bureau, or department of government will have an FOI officer to assist you. Some will be helpful; others will not. If a written request is asked for, send it by certified mail marked FOIA request. Fax, of course, is a faster method of communication.

Technically, an agency has a legal duty to reply within ten working days. The FBI, CIA, and State and Justice Departments may argue "backlog" to avoid that duty. If a delay seems unreasonable, you may appeal in writing to the agency head who—again technically—is supposed to respond within twenty working days. If that doesn't work, you may ask the Office of Information Law and Policy of the Department of Justice, a federal agency responsible for overall administration of the FOIA, to review your case. In spite of what may appear to be a built-in conflict of interests, that office can pressure a recalcitrant agency to comply. Going directly to your federal representative or senators may be yet another step.

If nothing works, you are entitled under the act to bring suit in the most convenient federal district court, that is, the one closest to home. You should expect an expedited hearing, meaning that your case goes to the top of the docket and gets immediate attention. The burden of proof for nondisclosure is on the government; the government must justify its need for secrecy.

Agencies are authorized to charge reasonable fees for searching and copying. Ask for estimates of the cost before you order anything. Fee schedules for the various agencies are published in the *Federal Register*. If costs are prohibitive, you may request a waiver on the ground that you are serving a public benefit as an author, journalist, or scholar. Don't expect a uniform response across agencies to such an appeal. A trip to inspect documents may be more in line with your financial resources and research needs. Many agencies have reading rooms.

Exemptions to the FOIA

Nondisclosure under nine exemptions to the FOIA has led to hundreds of lawsuits. Though it is impossible to summarize all of this litigation in any meaningful way, each exemption will be discussed briefly, and a few representative cases will be mentioned.

1. *National security.* Exemption 1 is the most difficult to dispute. Under the act, federal judges are authorized to examine in their chambers material that, if released, would cause, according to record keepers, identifiable damage to the national security or the foreign policy of the United States. "Expertise" and initiative remain with the government. All it has to show is that the material sought has been properly classified "top secret, secret, or confidential."

   The difficulty of beating the national security exemption was dramatically demonstrated by the "Glomar Project," which was jointly financed by the CIA and the late Howard Hughes. The object was to raise an obsolete Russian submarine from the ocean

In camera
An examination of material in a judge's chambers, out of sight and hearing of the courtroom.

De novo
New, over again from the beginning.

Glomarization
A term invented out of the Glomar case that has come to represent the right of an agency neither to deny nor to confirm the existence of a document.

Housekeeping
The right of a governmental agency generally to manage its own affairs.

floor. The public was told it was a deep-sea mining project. When more information was sought on the project, the D.C. Circuit Court of Appeals said, "It is well established that summary judgment is properly granted in Exemption 1 cases without an *in camera* [in the judge's chambers] inspection or discovery by the plaintiffs [the public] when the affidavits submitted by the agency are adequate to the task."[26]

Earlier the same federal court had laid a foundation for that holding by ruling that in making a *de novo* (completely new) determination, the court must first "accord substantial weight to an agency's affidavit concerning the details of the classified status of the disputed record."[27] Two years later, the court said it again: ". . . Congress intended reviewing courts to respect the expertise of an agency; for us to insist that the agency's rationale . . . is implausible would be to overstep the proper limits of the judicial role in FOIA review."[28] In other words, courts will seldom second-guess agency decisions.

The Glomar case gave rise to the term "Glomarization," meaning that an agency is permitted to "neither confirm nor deny" the existence of a document, although an agency may have to justify such a response.[29] Documents are sometimes reclassified after an FOIA request is made, as the government is alerted by the request to needless classification.

2. *Internal rules and practices.* Exemption 2 is a "housekeeping" claim. Matters "related solely to the *internal personnel rules and practices* of an agency" may be exempt. Courts are divided on the extent to which Exemption 2 authorizes the withholding of portions of agency manuals where disclosure would risk divulging the agency's investigative or prosecutorial strategies. A complete draft manuscript of the Air Force's official history of the Vietnam War was held exempt from disclosure so as to protect the agency's deliberative process in editing and reviewing manuscripts.[30]

A more credible case involved the manual of the Bureau of Alcohol, Tobacco and Firearms, "Raids and Searches (Special Agent Basic Training—Criminal Enforcement)". The section of the manual dealing with the surveillance of premises and persons was held not to be exempt under Exemption 2. "There can be little doubt," said the court, "that citizens have an interest in the manner in which they may be observed by federal agents. . . . Neither exemption (b)(2) nor any other exemption prevents a citizen from satisfying his curiosity on these matters. The contents of this document . . . pertaining to surveillance of the public cannot possibly be assimilated to mere 'internal housekeeping' concerns."[31]

Agencies have gone so far as to claim exemptions for vacation schedules and parking lot assignments. Courts must balance the genuine needs of government agencies with a legitimate public interest.

3. *Statutory exemptions.* Exemption 3 refers to federal statutes that already exempt certain classes of information. And they are myriad. More than a hundred statutes have been cited to justify withholding information. Courts in such cases must weigh the purposes of the FOIA against the statute cited as an exception, one federal statute against another.

In a case that reached the Supreme Court, a plaintiff sought Federal Aviation Administration (FAA) reports analyzing the operation and maintenance performance of commercial airlines. Section 1104 of the Federal Aviation Act permitted the administrator to withhold reports if disclosure was not in the public interest and if a person contributing information to the reports objected. The Air Transport Association objected, arguing that without confidentiality the whole performance program would be endangered.

The plaintiff won at the district and appeals court levels, but the Supreme Court reversed in the case *Administrator, FAA v. Robertson.*[32] The information sought was expressly exempt by statute, wrote Chief Justice Warren Burger for the Court, and the statute, because it ensured a flow of information to the agency, was not inconsistent with the disclosure policy of the FOIA.

Congress reacted to *Robertson* a year later by amending the FOIA to narrow the scope of the information it shielded. As amended, Exemption 3 requires the government to show (1) that the requested information falls within the scope of the statute cited, and (2) that the statute either vests no discretion to disclose (that is, it mandates secrecy), or that the information fits criteria delineated to authorize withholding.[33]

Congress also has gone the other way. A 1984 amendment to the National Security Act removed from the ordinary search and review requirements of the FOIA all sensitive CIA "operational files" dealing mainly with foreign and counterintelligence operations. A year later, the Supreme Court certified that the CIA has broad authority under the National Security Act to protect all its sources of information.[34] Exempt are files related to operations that Congress or other executive agencies might be investigating for possible CIA wrongdoing. That exception was relevant to the Walsh committee investigation of the Iran-contra affair.

The **Family Education Rights and Privacy Act** of 1974,[35] sometimes referred to as the Buckley Amendment, gives students, within limits, a right of access to their own educational records maintained by institutions that receive federal funds, and it also protects those files from public disclosure. Parents have access to these files until their postsecondary school children have reached the age of eighteen; at that point the consent of the student is required. School administrators, who under certain conditions also have access to such files, sometimes use the act for purposes Congress never intended. For example, a Missouri federal judge

● **Family Education Rights and Privacy Act**
Also referred to as the Buckley Amendment, a 1974 federal law that gives students the right to examine their own academic files. Parents need the consent of their children to see the files after the children reach age eighteen.

ruled in 1991 that campus crime records were *not* exempt from disclosure by the act.[36]

4. *Trade secrets.* Exemption 4 is designed to protect "trade secrets and commercial or financial information obtained from a person (that are) privileged or confidential." Trade secrets might include profit and loss statements, market share information, secret formulas, product innovations, and customer lists. This is information supplied to the government by private firms, not information about private firms generated by the government itself. Federal agencies are expected to prove that materials sought through the FOIA are indeed trade secrets; that is, that they are confidential and that their release would cause considerable business loss, lead to competitive harm, or make it difficult for an agency to collect similar information in the future.

Before 1979, persons supplying information to the government would frequently sue to block disclosure to third parties. These were called **reverse FOIA suits.** In *Chrysler Corporation v. Brown,*[37] the U.S. Supreme Court held that the FOIA does not create a private right of action to prevent an agency from releasing documents covered by one or more of the nine exemptions. To release or not is within an agency's discretion as long as that discretion is not abused. Under Exemption 3, of course, it would be an abuse of discretion to release documents covered by the federal Trade Secrets Act.

Justice William Rehnquist's opinion for the Court in *Chrysler,* while acknowledging the difficulty of balancing secrecy against disclosure, seemed to opt for disclosure. Because corporations do not like to disclose, they have successfully exerted pressure on Congress to exempt documents relating to pricing policies, product safety, truth-in-advertising, and warranty data. A 1986 presidential executive order instructed agency heads to notify record submitters when confidential commercial information is requested.

● **Reverse FOIA suit**
A suit to require an agency to keep information secret.

● **Executive privilege**
In one sense the right of an executive agency to protect its deliberative process.

5. *Executive privilege.* Exemption 5, **executive privilege,** prevents disclosure of "interagency or intra-agency memoranda or letters which would not be available by law to a party other than an agency in litigation with the agency." Nothing that is part of or defined as discovery (two sides in a civil case looking at one another's evidence) is available under the FOIA. The act was not intended to be used to circumvent discovery proceedings. Thus, confidential, unsworn statements made to Air Force crash investigators did not have to be disclosed because they were part of pretrial discovery.[38]

Generally speaking, predecisional documents (material generated prior to a decision) are not disclosable; postdecisional documents are. Final reports must be disclosed; working papers may be withheld. Memos, recommendations, opinions, policy statements, and staff comments that go into a final decision or report may be released, but only if they constitute the basis for that decision. More likely they are supplemental to the decision and not releasable.

A Watergate Special Prosecution Force memorandum, for example, created as an integral part of that body's required report to Congress recommending that Richard Nixon not be indicted, was held disclosable. It was part of the final decision. Standing alone, it would have been exempt as a "predecisional intra-agency legal memorandum."[39]

Purely factual information, such as names and addresses of unsuccessful applicants for federal funds, is not exempt from disclosure if it can be segregated from exempt material. Nor are factual portions of predecisional documents unless their disclosure would breach a promise of confidentiality and diminish an agency's ability to obtain similar information in the future. Also, a compilation of facts, if complete enough, could expose an agency's deliberative process.[40] Government-generated commercial information, the disclosure of which would disadvantage the government in awarding contracts, may also be withheld.[41]

"Executive privilege" was first asserted early in American history by the Jefferson administration. Its purpose then and now is said to be to encourage frank discussion among agency personnel prior to a decision. For example, a Justice Department staff attorney prepared legal analyses and conclusions to aid his superiors in responding to criticisms of legislation they had proposed to amend the FOIA. The analyses were held to be exempt from disclosure under Exemption 5.[42]

Well-established privileges such as those between lawyer and client or between an agency and its lawyer are covered by Exemption 5. National Public Radio reporter Barbara Newman found herself blocked by Exemption 5 when she tried to get information from the Justice Department on its investigation into the mysterious death of Karen Silkwood, an employee of a plutonium manufacturer. Silkwood, who was suspected of being contaminated by plutonium, died in a car accident while on her way to conduct business on behalf of her labor union and to talk with a *New York Times* reporter. There were suspicions that her car had been forced off the highway. A file of documents she was carrying was never recovered.

Portions of a "death investigation" file held by Justice contained working papers analyzing evidence and legal issues in the case. They fell under Exemption 5 as "memoranda prepared by an attorney in contemplation of litigation which set forth the attorney's theory of the case, his litigation strategy."[43]

6. *Personal privacy.* Next to national security, privacy may be the most persuasive argument for secrecy. Exempt under 6 are "personnel and medical files and similar files the disclosure of which would

constitute a clearly unwarranted invasion of personal privacy." Much litigation has focused on the meaning of the words "similar files." Courts will have to decide when the proper balance has been struck between individual privacy and the basic purpose of the FOIA to open government to public scrutiny. It is no easy task.

Courts have tried to balance these values by considering how the information being sought will be used. It may be important to explain to the record keeper why you are seeking the information and how it concerns the public interest. Courts also have considered levels of intimacy and personal detail in files. Names and other identifying data can be deleted (blacked out or what lawyers call "redacted") before documents are released. Promises of confidentiality add weight to claims of exemption. Even where the lives of two former Iranian officials might have been in jeopardy, the Supreme Court opted for disclosure, observing that the balance generally is heavily in favor of disclosure. The public had a right to know whether the Immigration and Naturalization Service had failed to enforce the law.[44]

This bias was reinforced when a federal appeals court observed, "The balance struck under FOIA Exemption six overwhelmingly favors the disclosure of information relating to a violation of the public trust by a governmental official, which certainly includes the situation of misuse of public funds and facilities by a Major General of the United States Army."[45] The U.S. Supreme Court may have shifted the balance from public to private in *Reporters Committee,* discussed earlier in this chapter.

Information having to do with medical conditions, job evaluations, welfare payments, and the legitimacy of children generally will be protected by Exemption 6. A recent and tragic example of protected thoughts and feelings was the words of the astronauts moments before their deaths in the *Challenger* explosion. The tapes could be withheld, said a federal appeals court, if disclosure would constitute a clearly unwarranted invasion of personal privacy.[46] That, of course, would depend on what the astronauts said in those final moments. Personal privacy, of course, is waived when one applies for federal grants or contracts.

Because the "clearly unwarranted invasion of personal privacy" language of Exemption 6 is also found in the Federal Privacy Act of 1974 and in the language of Exemption 7 (except for the word "clearly"), we are not done with it yet. It can be argued that the absence of the word "clearly" in Exemption 7 makes that exemption a better protector of privacy than Exemption 6.

7. *Law enforcement investigations.* Exemption 7 protects records or information compiled for law enforcement purposes, but only to the extent that the production of such records could reasonably be expected to (a) interfere with enforcement proceedings, (b) deprive a

person of a right to a fair trial or an impartial adjudication, (c) constitute an unwarranted invasion of personal privacy, (d) disclose the identity of a confidential source, or the information itself in the case of a record compiled by a criminal law enforcement authority in the course of a criminal investigation, or by an agency conducting a lawful national security investigation, (e) disclose guidelines for law enforcement and prosecutions, or (f) endanger the life or physical safety of any individual. When an investigation or enforcement proceeding has concluded after trial, conviction, and sentencing, Exemption 7 no longer applies.

More public information is probably kept secret by interpretations of this exemption than by any other. Technically, to qualify under Exemption 7, the government must first show that the record is both "investigatory" and contained in a file "compiled for law enforcement and prosecutions" purposes. Then it must fall within one of the six exempt categories enumerated above under Exemption 7.

Until recently rap sheets, arrest and conviction records, department manuals, personnel rosters, and other routine compilations and records were not exempt. This is no longer the case. In addition, documents no longer need to have been originally compiled for law enforcement purposes in order to be exempt from disclosure under the FOIA. In other words, documents not expressly gathered for law enforcement purposes may be withheld under Exemption 7 if they are subsequently combined with material gathered for that purpose. The word "originally" is key. Nonexempt records, as Justice John Paul Stevens noted in a dissenting opinion in a Supreme Court case, may now be transferred from a civilian agency to the FBI and constitute an exempt compilation.[47]

All FBI investigatory records are, for purposes of satisfying Exemption 7, compiled for law enforcement purposes. The legality of a particular investigation is not relevant. In 1982, the Supreme Court upheld Exemption 7(c) claims against the request of an independent journalist that FBI documents on the Nixon administration's "enemies list" be made public. The list included such prominent citizens as Harvard economist John Kenneth Galbraith, political philosopher and theologian Reinhold Niebuhr, baby doctor Benjamin Spock, and farm worker organizer Cesar Chavez.

The crux of the Court's ruling was that material originally exempt under 7(c) does not lose that exemption simply because it is transmitted to a second agency in a slightly different form. The Court was assuming, of course, that the original list was compiled for law enforcement purposes. In justifying his opinion for the Court, Justice Byron White argued that the kind of people who had voiced suspicions about the loyalty of the celebrities on the list might be discouraged from informing in the future if disclosure were to occur. And he rebuked Justice Sandra Day O'Connor for observing in her dissent that the Court had ignored the plain language of the FOIA and that the documents in question had been compiled for "political" not "law enforcement" purposes.[48]

On occasion, the exemption does not work. When *Playboy* sued the Justice Department for release of a task force report on an FBI informer within the Ku Klux Klan, the department cited five FOIA exemptions. None applied, said a federal district court. When it came to Exemption 7, the department had failed to show that the report was an investigatory record compiled for law enforcement purposes.[49]

Congress reinforced Exemption 7 in the Anti-Drug Abuse Act of 1986 by substituting the words "could reasonably be expected" to occur for "would" occur with reference to the enumerated harms that might follow from disclosure. As far as the amended Exemption 7 is concerned, an agency need not acknowledge that records exist if they are part of an investigation, would identify informants, or have to do with intelligence or terrorists.[50] Then, too, some records simply are not covered by the FOIA. This supports numerous refusals to provide access.

Even FBI informants in a 1931 murder investigation were still confidential sources in a 1990 case.[51] The personnel file of an FBI agent containing a letter of reprimand was exempt.[52] U.S. Postal Service records containing the statements of identified persons interviewed during an investigation into the shooting of postal workers by a deranged fellow employee are records compiled for law enforcement purposes. Their disclosure, said a federal appeals court, would also constitute an invasion of privacy. Moreover, those interviewed had been given implied promises of confidentiality.[53] However, the U.S. Supreme Court in 1993 held that Exemption 7(d) did not protect the confidentiality of all sources supplying information to the FBI during the course of a criminal investigation. The agency had presumed erroneously that diverse sources, individual or institutional and with or without a promise or an inference of confidentiality, were confidential. The Court said they were not.[54]

8. *Banks.* Exemption 8 protects federal agency reports about the condition of banks and other federally regulated financial institutions. Considering the number of bank, brokerage house, and savings and loan scandals that have rocked the nation in the past few years, this exemption has taken on new significance. If there was ever a need for public accountability and an alert press, it was in the years immediately preceding the S&L disaster, when millions of dollars of customer funds were lost in collapsed savings institutions.

9. *Oil wells.* To discourage speculation based on information about the location of private oil and gas wells and to protect competition, Exemption 9 covers geological and geophysical data and maps concerning wells. The implications for oil supplies of the Gulf War may in time bring the light of public scrutiny to this exemption also.

The FOIA in Summary

The FOIA assumes that all public documents are open to the public unless they fall into one or more of nine specifically exempt categories. Hundreds of court cases have sought to interpret Congress's intentions in establishing the exemptions. Congress itself has frequently amended the act. Whatever its use or misuse, the FOIA has opened thousands of otherwise closed files to public scrutiny. The act covers executive agencies of the federal government, but does not include the president's staff and advisers. Only records generated by and in the possession of a federal agency are covered by the FOIA. A Reporters Committee handbook explains in detail how to use the act. The following are the FOIA exemptions:

1. National security

2. Internal rules and practices

3. Statutory exemptions

4. Trade secrets

5. Executive privilege

6. Personal privacy

7. Law enforcement investigations

8. Banks

9. Oil wells

THE FEDERAL PRIVACY ACT

In 1974, Congress passed a comprehensive federal law to protect the privacy of government data on individuals created and stored by federal agencies. Under the law an individual has access to his or her files. After clearly identifying yourself, you can learn what information about you is on record, and you can correct it if it is inaccurate. The Reporters Committee includes a sample **Privacy Act** letter in its FOIA handbook.

Under this law you pay for duplication but not for search time. The Office of Management and Budget, which supervises the act, expects federal agencies to acknowledge receipt of a request within ten working days and provide access, if it is granted, within thirty.

An important section of the act prohibits the government from creating any record having to do with the exercise of a First Amendment right—lawfully demonstrating, leafleting, placarding, street-corner speaking. The rule prevented the Internal Revenue Service from keeping records of its surveillance of speeches made by nuclear weapon and nuclear policy protesters.[55] Only a statute, a legitimate law enforcement activity, or your consent can change this rule.

● **Federal Privacy Act**
A 1974 law that is meant to protect the privacy of information held in federal government files. People named in those files have access to them, subject to the act's exemptions and the requirements of the FOIA. An FOIA for the individual.

Unless a record is open to public inspection under one of the Privacy Act's exemptions or the FOIA, a government agency must have your personal written consent for disclosure. You can win damages, attorney's fees, and court costs if an agency "acted in a manner which was intentionally willful" in violating this rule.

The Privacy Act might be thought of as an FOIA for the individual. Any disclosure of a record about an individual to any member of the public other than the individual to whom the record pertains is forbidden under the Privacy Act, if the disclosure would constitute a "clearly unwarranted invasion of personal privacy." General exemptions apply to entire systems of records rather than to specific documents, as is the case with the FOIA. CIA records, FBI rap sheets, and some other criminal records would be examples. Specific exemptions deal with particular records that are part of a larger system of records, for example, "information compiled for the purposes of a criminal investigation" and "testing or examination material used solely to determine individual qualifications for appointment or promotion in the Federal service the disclosure of which would compromise the objectivity or fairness of the testing or examination process."

Exemption 2 of the Privacy Act, for instance, provides that a record may be disclosed without the written consent of the person about whom the record is kept if disclosure is required under the FOIA. In other words, *if a document is required to be made public by the FOIA, it cannot be kept secret by the Privacy Act*. What is exempt from disclosure to an individual under the Privacy Act is not necessarily exempt from disclosure to the same person under the FOIA. In a sense privacy defers to publicity.[56]

At the same time, the FOIA's Exemption 6 states that documents need not be disclosed if they are "personnel and medical files and similar files the disclosure of which would constitute *a clearly unwarranted invasion of personal privacy*." Under the Privacy Act, an agency is *not* permitted to cite an FOIA exemption to withhold from an individual a record available through the Privacy Act. Requests for disclosures to third parties are made under the FOIA rather than the Privacy Act.

An understanding of the articulation of the two acts does not come without effort. Making privacy and openness work together is a challenge; they pull in opposite directions. Record keepers sometimes exploit the confusion by arguing that they cannot risk penalties under the Privacy Act, even though the FOIA gives them clear discretion to decide whether to disclose.

The Privacy Act in Summary

The Federal Privacy Act of 1974 is an FOIA for persons wanting to know what information about them is held in government files. No disclosure without a person's consent is allowed under the act if that disclosure would constitute a "clearly unwarranted invasion of personal privacy." No First Amendment activities are to be recorded in one's government files. There are numerous exemptions to the Privacy Act, and the FOIA takes precedence when it comes to the release or the protection of information. The two acts interrelate in a somewhat complex fashion, and record keepers often exploit this confusion by citing the Privacy Act as a reason for refusing to disclose under the FOIA.

THE FEDERAL OPEN MEETINGS LAW

A Government-in-Sunshine Act was passed in March 1977 requiring fifty federal agencies, commissions, boards, and councils to hold their deliberative, policy-making meetings in public. Any meeting, formal, regular, or bare quorum, in which business is discussed, is presumed to be open. Communications to an agency from public interest groups or corporations must be made part of the public record. Public notice of a meeting is to be made at least a week in advance, preferably with an agenda included.

● **Government-in-Sunshine Act**
The 1977 federal open meetings law.

There are almost as many ways for getting around the federal open meetings law as there are for getting around the FOIA. Business is still conducted informally between meetings by telephone or at social gatherings.

Ten exemptions, the first nine of which parallel FOIA exemptions, allow closed meetings. Exemption 10 applies to agency litigation, arbitration, or adjudication. It is often invoked to save a case—or a reputation.

When the Nuclear Regulatory Commission sought to close its budget preparation meeting, the Washington-based public interest group Common Cause went to court. In deciding for Common Cause, a federal appeals court noted that, unlike the FOIA, the Sunshine Act was designed to open, not close, predecisional deliberations. The commission had cited Exemption 9, an exemption generally closing meetings where openness could lead to significant financial speculation, endanger the stability of a financial institution, or interfere with a proposed agency action.[57] Deliberations on the reopening of the Three Mile Island nuclear power plant, however, were permitted to be closed.

The law has not helped reporters cover international conferences attended by bureaucrats[58] or get into meetings of correctional institutions or public hospitals. Nor has it accommodated demonstrators—or reporters—on private property, even private property regulated by government.

Rules granting press passes and establishing press access to scenes of crime and disaster ought to define "press" liberally. Otherwise law enforcement officers will be in the position of certifying "legitimate" news media, a role government should not play, although it does just that in granting postal subsidies. When denied a press pass, you should insist upon an explanation.

When the secretary of labor excluded press and public from meetings of the Mine Safety and Health Administration looking into the cause of a fatal mine fire, the Society of Professional Journalists brought suit and won. A federal district court ruled that the press and public had a constitutional right of access to such hearings subject to reasonable rules of conduct set forth by the secretary.[59] In another case, a federal district court's posttrial order prohibiting press interviews with jurors in a civil case was said to be impermissibly overbroad by an appeals court because it included no time or scope limitations and was not supported by compelling reasons.[60]

Laws prohibiting exit polling at voting places have been struck down in a number of states, including Florida, Minnesota, and Washington. Although voting places are not meetings in the usual sense of that term, they are places where news traditionally has been gathered and where people have a right to speak.

ACCESS TO LEGISLATURES

Access to legislative bodies and their committees should never be presumed. Legislators, after all, write the laws, and they are in a perfect position to exempt themselves from the irritations of press and public. Access to legislatures is governed by custom and practice; state and federal House and Senate rules; open meetings laws in some states; state constitutions; and well-formed First and Fourteenth Amendment arguments encased in the state's common law. For example, an Alaska court ruled in 1986 that the press and the public had an implied right under the Alaska Constitution to attend meetings of members of the state legislature so as to observe "every step" of the deliberative process.[61]

Periodically, the Reporters Committee publication, *The News Media & the Law,* summarizes the status of access to state legislatures. Protocols must be observed as to dress, positioning (coverage from the floor, galleries, or press boxes), cameras, and credentials when covering a legislative body.

Questions of due process and equal protection have arisen when particular reporters have been discriminated against in covering state lawmaking bodies and city councils.[62] A state court upheld both houses of the Maryland legislature when they excluded tape recorders from their sessions. While recognizing some First Amendment protection for news gathering, the court held that the legislative rule did not interfere with the usual pencil-and-pad duties of reporters. There was no violation of due process in a rule intended to preserve order and decorum, even at the expense of news-gathering efficiency. As to equal protection, the court held that the tape recorder ban was directed against equipment, not a class of citizens.[63] This case and others illustrate the sensitivity of one branch of government toward the prerogatives of another.

Federal Open Meetings and Legislative Access in Summary

The Government-in-Sunshine Act is a federal open meetings law applying to approximately fifty federal agencies, boards, commissions, and councils. Ten exemptions, the first nine of which track with the FOIA exemptions, allow closed meetings. Many meetings, especially those involving personnel discipline and attorney-client strategies, are exempt. And much business is conducted and policy made by informal means, out of sight of press and public.

Access to legislative bodies is governed by custom, practice, the rules of the assembly, state constitutions, and open meeting laws in some states. Protocols as to dress, credentials, and observation points must be observed.

OPEN RECORDS AND MEETINGS IN THE STATES

Open Records

All states, the District of Columbia, and the territories have open records laws. They vary widely, change frequently, and do not lend themselves to generalization. Know the law of your state, how it has been applied, and its loopholes. No state has an ideal **open records or open meetings law.**

A *model* statute, from a press perspective at least, would define "records" broadly, by both physical format and origin or source, and make as few exceptions as possible. As with the FOIA, state agencies are not required to create or acquire records in response to a request. They are responsible only for existing and identifiable records in their possession that are subject to the state open records law. Unfortunately, few state laws require indexes. A state-created agency that is federally funded and performs federal functions could be subject to *both* state and federal open records laws.

You will find quirks in many of these laws. In a few states, you must be a resident of the state to benefit from its open records laws. On the positive side, some states have set up FOI commissions or compliance committees, such as New York's Committee on Public Access to Records, and deputy attorneys general to assist aggrieved record seekers and assure judicial review of denials.

Many of these open records laws have the same kinds of exemptions that are found in the FOIA. Know what they are. And know how state courts have interpreted them. Legal language can be troublesome. A number of state laws refer to "all official records *required by law* to be kept shall be open. . . ." Records kept by tradition rather than by law, even if necessary for the functioning of a public body, may be claimed exempt from the law. As with the federal law, there are statutory exemptions often relating to welfare, medical, child adoption or abuse, unemployment compensation, tax, bank, criminal history, and other kinds of law enforcement information. Some records are closed for reasons no one can remember.

And there can be egregious delays. Any survey of recent cases will show increasing evidence of bureaucrats, legislative bodies, including public school boards and university boards of regents, and law enforcement agencies circumventing state open records laws by erasing tapes,[64] making "computer" excuses,[65] and concocting strained interpretations of state law.[66] Some bureaucrats will interpret state law as prohibiting publication even after information is in the hands of reporters and editors.[67] It is like playing a never-ending game of cat and mouse.

For an advanced reporting course project, a teaching assistant at the University of Minnesota asked the Minneapolis Police Department for access to ten years of inactive internal affairs complaint forms and other records stemming from alleged criminal misconduct by police officers. After a lengthy correspondence with the police chief and city attorney, he was told the records were not available except where disciplinary action had been taken. It would be unfair to a public employee who is the subject of a baseless complaint, said the police chief, to have that information made public. But the forms with all

> ● **Open records and open meetings laws** All states now have their own open meetings and open records laws.

nonpublic data deleted, including the identity of complainants, would be available upon receipt of a certified check for $2,322.50.

Minnesota has buried its open records law in a seventy-page Data Practices Act that encourages multifarious interpretations. Privacy appears to be the main concern of this law and laws like it in about half of the states. The Minneapolis city attorney used the Data Practices Act to affirm the police chief's decision. The instructor went to court, and a district judge ruled that the complaint forms, including information about complainants, were public data. The Minnesota Court of Appeals and the Minnesota Supreme Court both upheld that decision, on the bases of the "plain language of the act and by strong public policy considerations."[68]

After a second wave of desultory correspondence, the city still refused to comply, arguing that other kinds of information on the complaint form were exempt from disclosure under the same Data Practices Act. Two years later, the by now frustrated and somewhat cynical journalism instructor filed a second lawsuit against Minneapolis, contending that the city had violated the district court's ruling in the first suit. This time he asked for punitive damages against the city and the police chief for waging "a campaign of obfuscation and distortion." And he argued in his brief that citizens who are wrongly accused of committing a crime have no right to privacy under the Data Practices Act. Why then should the police, the only group allowed by society to use deadly force, be exempt? He lost. A second district court judge ruled that the complaint forms were personal rather than criminal records, until it had been determined that a crime had been committed. An appeals court upheld that determination. In yet a third lawsuit, this time to gain access to research data involving a University of Minnesota research center and the Minneapolis police Civilian Review Board, a district court held that the information generated was not public until the study was completed. An appeals court upheld that decision as well. The instructor by this time was psychologically and financially exhausted.

If arguments for privacy and the imposition of excessive costs do not discourage requests for records disclosure, then time will, and time is always on the side of the public institution. Most state laws say little or nothing about time limits for responding to requests. And few provide penalties for violations of the law. Litigation continues over access to police blotters, investigative files, wiretap records, prison and hospital records, autopsy reports, and documents developed by personnel search committees.

Illegal-appearing denials of access to records should be challenged. Ask a record keeper for written authority for a denial. Ask to speak to supervisors. Indicate that you know your rights under the law. Keep editors posted on what is happening.

Recent examples of state records that have been opened by a liberal interpretation of open records laws include a California governor's appointment schedule, records having to do with the pensions of former legislators, a correctional department's videotapes of a prison uprising, police department records of the police shooting of a suspect, names and addresses of replacement teachers hired during a strike, legal memoranda prepared by a city's outside attorney for litigation purposes, a state university's response to National

Collegiate Athletic Association charges, and department of health records concerning an investigation of nursing homes.

Examples of records closed to public inspection by interpretation of state open records laws include an assistant state's attorney's personnel file regarding matters of race, videotapes of the execution of a search warrant, names of state university students employed by the university's police department, mental health records of a person charged in a shooting, telephone billing records of county board members, records of a corporate-administered local development program for small businesses, and reports evaluating the performance of a state's attorney. It is difficult to predict how such cases will be decided.

Open Meetings

All states, the District of Columbia, and the territories have open meetings laws or constitutional provisions guaranteeing some level of access to public meetings. Here again the laws differ substantially from state to state and are frequently amended. These laws are generally easier to understand and apply than are open records laws.

An ideal open meetings law from the viewpoint of the press would apply to both houses and the committees of the state legislature, state boards, commissions, county boards, city councils, and all executive branch agencies. Some laws use a public "funds" or "functions" test in deciding the applicability of the law to a governmental body.

Executive sessions (special closed meetings of an organization's officers or committees) and other evasive devices for avoiding public scrutiny would not be permitted in an ideal law. A quorum would not be a condition of access. Advisory committees to public bodies would also be required to have open meetings. Minutes would have to be kept and all votes recorded. If exemptions must be written into the law, they should be precise and severely limited. Any business transacted in a secret meeting would be null and void. Enforcement procedures ought to be practicable and available to ordinary citizens. There should be penalties for noncompliance, although penalties are not generally enforced in the few state statutes that contain them. One exception was Minnesota. In 1994, a unanimous Minnesota Supreme Court ruled that the mayor of Hibbing, Minnesota, and two members of the city council should be removed from office for repeated violations of the state's open meeting law. Although this penalty for three violations of the law had been on the books for twenty-one years, it had never been enforced. The law was invoked, not by the press, but by four irate citizens.[69] The state legislature thereafter changed the law so that removal from office would no longer be an option. Instead, attorneys fees of up to $13,000 would be available to those alleging intentional violation of the open meetings law by public officials, and violation would more likely be considered "intentional" when a public official had been to open-meeting training sessions or had been in office for some length of time.

Where intent to violate an open meeting law can be proven, criminal or civil penalties, usually in the form of fines, can be assessed and attorneys' fees awarded plaintiffs in a number of states. In thirty-eight states, some business transacted in a secret meeting is null and void.[70] Other remedies for so-called sunshine law violations are writs of mandamus (a judge orders something done to restore a right that has been illegally deprived) or injunctive relief (a judge prevents something from happening or permits it to happen).

Unannounced, irregular, or informal (telephone) meetings and social gatherings are still a major means of circumventing these laws. Parole and pardon boards are often closed by statute, although this can have disastrous consequences for society as when unrehabilitated prisoners are released or reformed prisoners are unjustly kept in prison. Law enforcement, state National Guard, and hospital board affairs are nearly always conducted in secret. Legislative bodies routinely go into executive session to discuss personnel matters, particularly where disciplinary action is involved. Attorney-client privilege will apply where a council or an agency is planning its strategy for litigation or labor negotiations. Inquests are held in secret in some states, although state laws have been used to open them. State laws have also opened municipal library advisory boards. Public university and other governmental selection and search committees and in-house disciplinary hearings are closed in most states, although meetings of public university trustees or regents are generally open to the public. Reporters still have problems gaining access to law enforcement boards, jails, and accident scenes.

When wrongfully denied attendance at a meeting of a public body, ask for reasons and a vote of the membership. Ask also that a record of your exclusion be entered in the minutes of the meeting. Do not leave a meeting until ordered to do so. If possible, photograph public officials escorting you out of a meeting. As with record keepers, of course, be respectful even when you are convinced that a public body is acting illegally. And keep in touch with the state press association; they have done an excellent job of monitoring open records and open meetings situations.

In cases of both records and meetings, state and federal, litigation opens more than it closes the system. Nevertheless, in many states the long-range prospects for both openness and personal privacy are not good. The long-range prospects for government secrecy, on the other hand, are very good.

Open Records and Open Meetings in Summary

All states have open records and meetings laws. They vary widely both in their drafting and in their interpretation by state courts. Some are idiosyncratic and known more for their loopholes than for their overall effectivness. Know the laws of your state. Delay, here also, is the main obstacle to the record seeker. Denials of both records and the right to attend meetings must be challenged. Open meetings laws can be used to confront evasive tactics such as executive sessions and policy making over cocktails. All of the enforcement procedures referred to above must be imposed in appropriate situations if public officials are to take access laws seriously. Open meetings and open records laws ought to be written so clearly and precisely that judicial discretion in applying them is at a minimum.[71]

SUMMARY

Obtaining access to government information is a long-standing challenge to the media. This is particularly true in wartime where national security may be at stake. National security, however, is also an argument against openness in peacetime. While the 1967 federal Freedom of Information Act (FOIA) attempted, and largely succeeded, in making government records more accessible to the public, national security is still the srongest argument for secrecy. In spite of the *Richmond Newspapers* line of cases that opened the judicial process in general to the public on First Amendment grounds, the press has a much stronger constitutional claim to publish information in hand than to gather information.

The FOIA contains nine exemptions that have led to hundreds of cases interpreting the act. Only records generated by and in the possession of federal agencies are covered. The president and his staff are not included.

The Federal Privacy Act of 1974 is an FOIA for individuals who wish to know what information about them is contained in federal government files. The content of those files cannot be disclosed without the individual's consent. This act also contains exemptions and is interconnected with the FOIA in a complex way.

There is also a federal open meetings law called the Government-in-Sunshine Act. It applies to approximaely fifty federal agencies, boards, commissions, and councils. Nine of the ten exemptions in this act parallel the FOIA exemptions. Meetings involving the discipline of personnel and the discussion of attorney-client strategies, for example, are exempt. In spite of the act, many decisions continue to be made privately, informally, or secretly. Access to legislative bodies is governed by custom, practice, the rules of the assembly, state constitutions, and, in a few states, open meetings laws.

At present, all fifty states have their own open records and open meetings laws, many of which preceded the FOIA. These laws vary from state to state. It is important to know the laws of the state or states in which you report or gather information. This advice applies equally to libel, privacy, and journalist's privilege statutes.

KEY TERMS

Intelligence Identities Protection Act
Computer tapes
Reporters Committee for Freedom of the Press
Richmond Newspapers v. Virginia
Freedom of Information Act (FOIA)
Federal Register
Vaughn Index
In camera
De novo

Glomarization
Housekeeping
Family Education Rights and Privacy Act
Reverse FOIA suit
Executive privilege
Federal Privacy Act
Government-in-Sunshine Act
Open records and open meetings laws

CASE PROBLEMS

1. Why is the FOIA's exemption for national security (Exemption 1) the most difficult for the press and the public to get around?

2. What steps would you take in making an FOIA request?

3. You are a reporter for *Yourtown Sun*. You learn that the federal Food and Drug Administration (FDA) has been studying the possibility of banning the use of a powerful drug used in AIDS therapy because of its potential harmful side effects. The final decision has been delayed several times. You decide to file an FOIA request with the FDA asking for copies of several advisory recommendations on the proposed ban. What response from the FDA might you expect?

4. Get copies of your state's open records and open meetings laws from a law library, from a news or-

ganization, or from reference materials. Measure them against the model or ideal laws that are suggested in this text. Do they measure up? Do they have unusual elements that serve as booby traps for the unwary reporter or citizen? How would you improve them? Finally, how have the courts interpreted your state's open records and open meetings laws? In favor of the press and public? In favor of the record keeper or presiding officers of meetings? *Brief* the two or three most important state court rulings in each of these areas of access to information.

5. You have reason to believe that your photograph and other identification are in Defense Department or FBI files because some time ago you took part in lawful anti–nuclear war demonstrations in Washington, D.C. What can you do about it?

ENDNOTES

1. P.L. 88–408, House Joint Resolution 1145.

2. David Stebenne, Gannett Foundation Report, *The Media at War: The Press and the Persian Gulf Conflict* (New York: Gannett Foundation Media Center, 1991).

3. *JB Pictures, Inc. v. Defense Department,* 21 Med.L.Rptr. 1564 (D.D.C. 1993).

4. Allan R. Adler, ed., *Litigation under the Federal Open Government Laws,* 16th ed. (Washington, D.C.: ACLU Foundation, 1991), p. 22.

5. *Snepp v. United States,* 444 U.S. 507, 100 S.Ct. 763 (1980) (1981).

6. *Haig v. Agee,* 453 U.S. 280, 101 S.Ct. 2766 (1981).

7. *United States v. Morison,* 604 F.Supp. 655 (D.Md. 1985); *United States v. Morison,* 844 F.2d 1057 (4th Cir. 1988).

8. An excellent treatment of this subject in five Western democracies, including the United States, is David H. Flaherty's *Protecting Privacy in Surveillance Societies* (Chapel Hill: University of North Carolina Press, 1989). In the United States,

the Justice Department's Office of Information and Privacy oversees FOIA compliance.

9. Reporters Committee for Freedom of the Press, *Access to Electronic Records: A Guide to Reporting on State and Local Government in the Computer Age* (Washington, D.C.: 1990 [Suite 504, Eye St. N.W. 20006]).

10. *U.S. Department of Justice v. Reporters Committee for Freedom of the Press,* 489 U.S. 749, 109 S.Ct. 1468 (1989). See also *Department of Defense v. FLRA,* ____ U.S. ____, 114 S.Ct. 1006 (1994).

11. Unreported case.

12. Potter Stewart, "Or of the Press," *Hastings Law Review* 26:631, 636 (1976).

13. 408 U.S. 665, 92 S.Ct. 2646 (1972).

14. *Houchins v. KQED,* 438 U.S. 1, 98 S.Ct. 2588 (1978).

15. Walter Goodman, "Executions on Television: Defining the Issues," *New York Times,* May 30, 1991, p. B6.

16. *KQED v. Vasquez,* 18 Med.L.Rptr. 2323 (N.D. Cal. 1991). The Fifth Circuit reached the same conclusion in the 1977 case of *Garrett v. Estelle,* 556 F.2d 1274 (5th Cir. 1977).

17. *Martin v. Rison,* 741 F.Supp. 1406 (N.D.Cal. 1990).

18. 448 U.S. 555, 100 S.Ct. 2814 (1980). *Publicker Industries v. Cohen,* 733 F.2d 1059 (3d Cir. 1984), extended the First Amendment right of attendance to civil trials.

19. *Nixon v. Freeman,* 670 F.2d 346 (D.C.Cir. 1982), opinion vacated by 962 F.2d 959 (1992).

20. *National Security Archive v. U.S. Archivist,* 909 F.2d 541, 17 Med.L.Rptr. 2265 (D.C.Cir. 1990).

21. 445 U.S. 169, 185–186, 100 S.Ct. 977, 986–987 (1980).

22. *Kissinger v. Reporters Committee for Freedom of the Press,* 445 U.S. 136, 100 S.Ct. 960 (1980).

23. *Yeager v. Drug Enforcement Administration,* 678 F.2d 315, 321 (D.C.Cir. 1982).

24. *Vaughn v. Rosen,* 484 F.2d 820 (D.C.Cir. 1973), *cert. denied* 415 U.S. 977, 94 S.Ct. 1564 (1974).

25. 5 U.S.C.A. § 552a.

26. *Military Audit Project v. Casey,* 656 F.2d 724 (D.C.Cir. 1981).

27. *Ray v. Turner,* 587 F.2d 1187 (D.C.Cir. 1978).

28. *Hayden v. National Security Agency,* 608 F.2d 1381 (D.C.Cir. 1979).

29. *Marrera v. U.S. Department of Justice,* 622 F.Supp. 51 (D.D.C. 1985).

30. *Dudman Communications Corp. v. Department of Air Force,* 815 F.2d 1565 (D.C.Cir. 1987).

31. *Crooker v. Bureau of Alcohol, Tobacco and Firearms,* 670 F.2d 1051 (D.C.Cir. 1981).

32. *Administrator, FAA v. Robertson,* 422 U.S. 255, 95 S.Ct. 2140 (1975).

33. For an application of the amendment, see *Lessner v. U.S. Department of Commerce,* 827 F.2d 1333 (9th Cir. 1987).

34. *CIA v. Sims,* 471 U.S. 159, 105 S.Ct. 1881 (1985).

35. 20 U.S.C.A. Sec. 1233g.

36. *Bauer v. Kincaid,* 759 F.Supp. 575 (W.D.Mo. 1991).

37. 441 U.S. 281, 99 S.Ct. 1705 (1979).

38. *United States v. Weber Aircraft,* 465 U.S. 792, 104 S.Ct. 1488 (1984).

39. *Niemeier v. Watergate Special Prosecution Force,* 565 F.2d 967 (7th Cir. 1977).

40. *Wolfe v. HHS,* 630 F.Supp. 546 (D.D.C. 1985), revd 839 F.2d 768 (C.A.D.C. 1988).

41. *Federal Open Market Committee v. Merrill,* 443 U.S. 340 (1979).

42. *Access Reports v. Justice Department,* 926 F.2d 1192, 18 Med.L.Rptr. 1840 (D.C.Cir. 1991).

43. *National Public Radio v. Bell,* 431 F.Supp. 509 (D.D.C. 1977).

44. *Department of State v. Washington Post,* 456 U.S. 595, 102 S.Ct. 1957 (1982).

45. *Cochrane v. United States,* 770 F.2d 949 (11th Cir. 1985).

46. *New York Times v. NASA,* 920 F.2d 1002, 18 Med.L.Rptr. 1465 (D.C.Cir. 1990).

47. *John Doe Agency v. John Doe Corp.,* 493 U.S. 146, 110 S.Ct. 471, 17 Med.L.Rptr. 1225 (1989).

48. *FBI v. Abramson,* 456 U.S. 615, 102 S.Ct. 2054 (1982).

49. *Playboy v. U.S. Department of Justice,* 516 F.Supp. 233 (D.D.C. 1981).

50. *Freedom of Information Reform Act of 1986,* P.L. 99–570 §§ 1801–1804, 100 Stat. 3248 (1986).

51. *Schmerler v. FBI,* 900 F.2d 333, 17 Med.L.Rptr. 1709 (D.C.Cir. 1990).

52. *Dunkelberger v. Justice Department,* 906 F.2d 779, 17 Med.L.Rptr. 2298 (D.C.Cir. 1990).

53. *KTVY–TV v. U.S. Postal Service,* 919 F.2d 1465, 18 Med.L.Rptr. 1479 (10th Cir. 1990).

54. *Justice Department v. Landano,* ____ U.S. ____, 113 S.Ct. 2014, 21 Med.L.Rptr. 1531 (1993).

55. *Clarkson v. IRS,* 678 F.2d 1368 (11th Cir. 1982).

56. *Greentree v. Customs Service,* 674 F.2d 74 (D.C.Cir. 1982). See also *Department of Justice v. Provenzano,* 469 U.S. 14, 105 S.Ct. 413 (1984).

57. *Common Cause v. Nuclear Regulatory Commission,* 674 F. 2d 921 (D.C.Cir. 1982).

58. *ITT World Communications v. FCC,* 725 F.2d 732 (D.C.Cir. 1984).

59. *Society of Professional Journalists v. Secretary of Labor,* 616 F.Supp. 569 (D.Utah 1985).

60. *Journal Publishing v. Mechem,* 801 F.2d 1233, 13 Med.L.Rptr. 1391 (10th Cir. 1986).

61. *League of Women Voters v. Adams,* 13 Med.L.Rptr. 1433 (Alaska Super. 1986).

62. *Kovach v. Maddux,* 238 F.Supp. 835 (D.Tenn. 1965); *Westinghouse Broadcasting Co. v. Dukakis,* 409 F.Supp. 895 (D.Mass. 1976); *Borreca v. Fasi,* 369 F.Supp. 906 (D.Haw. 1974).

63. *Sigma Delta Chi v. Speaker, Maryland House of Delegates,* 270 Md. 1, 310 A.2d 156 (1973).

64. *Globe Newspaper Co. v. Pokaski,* 17 Med.L.Rptr. 1223 (D.Mass. 1989).

65. *Brownstone Publishers, Inc. v. New York City Department of Buildings,* 146 Misc.2d 376, 550 N.Y.S.2d 564, 17 Med.L.Rptr. 2237 (1990).

66. *Buffalo News v. Commissioners of Buffalo Municipal Housing Authority,* 163 A.D.2d 830, 558 N.Y.S.2d 364, 17 Med.L.Rptr. 2167 (1990); *Indianapolis Convention & Visitor Association, Inc. v. Indianapolis Newspapers, Inc.,* 17 Med.L.Rptr. 1215 (Ind.Cir.Ct. 1989); *Board of Regents of University System of Georgia v. Atlanta Journal,* 259 Ga. 214, 378 S.E.2d 305, 17 Med.L.Rptr. 1670 (1989); *Brouillet v. Cowles Publishing Co.,* 114 Wash.2d 788, 791 P.2d 526, 17 Med.L.Rptr. 1982 (1990).

67. *Doe v. Florida Supreme Court,* 734 F.Supp. 981, 17 Med.L.Rptr. 1405 (S.D. Fla. 1990); *Providence Journal Co. v. Newton,* 723 F.Supp. 846, 17 Med.L.Rptr. 1033 (D.C. R.I. 1989).

68. *Demers v. City of Minneapolis,* 458 N.W.2d 151 (Minn.App. 1990).

69. *Claude v. Collins,* 518 N.W.2d 836 (Minn. 1994).

70. Charles N. Davis and Milagros Rivera-Sanchez, University of Florida, "If You Do the Crime, Will You Do the Time? A Proposal for Reform of State Sunshine Law Enforcement Provisions" (unpublished AEJMC paper, Atlanta, 1994).

71. Ibid., fn. 136 ff.

Public Access to the Media

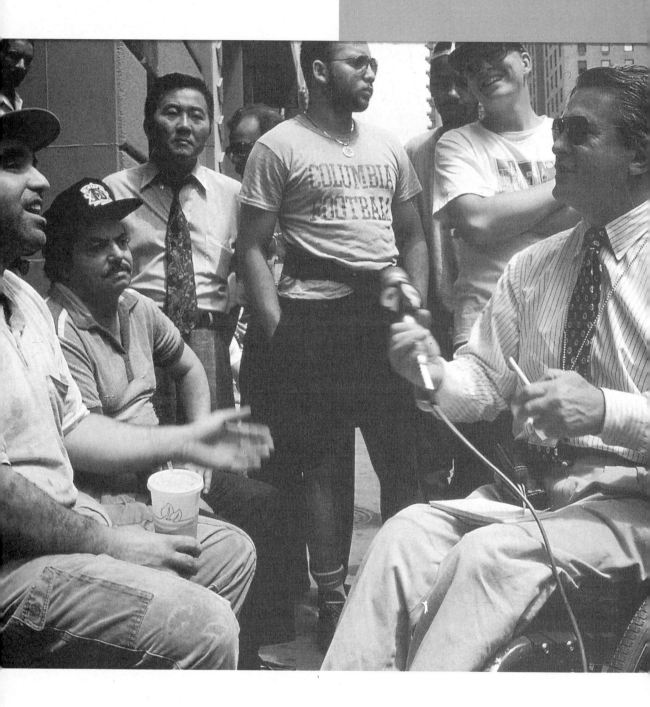

ACCESS FOR IDEAS?

In the previous chapter, we examined access *for* the media. In this chapter, we will examine access *to* the media. Journalists fear government and rightly so. The media now, and in the past, have experienced government efforts to prevent them from publishing what they wished to publish. But put the shoe on the other foot for a minute. Are the media themselves guilty of censorship on occasion? Do the media keep out, or shy away from, ideas that may be opposed by their owners or editorial staffs? What obligation, if any, do the media have to provide the full spectrum of opinion in a community to their audience or readers?

Prohibiting government from censorship does not in itself result in access for ideas. Ideas must enter the marketplace in the first place. Admission is not necessarily automatic. "There is inequality in the power to communicate ideas just as there is inequality in economic bargaining power; to recognize the latter and deny the former is quixotic."[1] In this view, the marketplace of ideas is more metaphor than reality. New developments in technology combined with the emergence of great corporate entities such as Time-Warner or the Murdoch media holdings have created a potentially repressive marketplace of ideas, to which access controlled by the owners and operators of these great mass communication conglomerates. When a small number of owners controls the marketplace, it is argued, some rights to present ideas through the media must be guaranteed. These rights include access rights or rights of reply.

People holding these views are sometimes called advocates of "market failure." They contend that the marketplace of ideas does not work and that the legal system must take some corrective steps to make it work by providing rights of access and reply. Others, however, believe that the remedy proposed by those who advocate access for ideas is worse than the disease. Access advocates want government to make up for the shortcomings of the media.

Professor Edwin Baker warns them: "For the government to determine what access is adequate involves the government implicitly judging what is the correct resolution of the marketplace debates—or, more bluntly, allows the government to define truth."[2]

In this country, rights of access have fared very differently in the print media and in the electronic media. We will examine the nature of these distinctions. But first we shall discuss access and reply in the electronic media.

ACCESS AND REPLY IN THE ELECTRONIC MEDIA

- **Right of reply**

  No general right of reply exists in either the electronic media or the print media, but rights of reply are available in specialized contexts in the electronic media. A right of reply would provide space equivalent to the original attack in the print media and equivalent time in the electronic media. Persons attacked would respond in their own words.

- **Right of access**

  There is no general right of access to the media, but limited rights of access do exist in the electronic media. A right of access enables individuals and groups to present ideas through the media. The right would not be dependent on the media first attacking those seeking access.

- **Federal Communications Commission (FCC)**

  An administrative agency based in Washington, D.C., that is run by five commissioners. The FCC enforces the Federal Communications Act of 1934, which generally governs the U.S. electronic media.

The story of the legal fortunes of the **rights of reply** and **access** to the media in the United States begins with the *Red Lion* case, which was decided by a unanimous Supreme Court in 1969.[3] That case upheld the validity of **Federal Communications Commission (FCC)** principles such as the fairness doctrine, the personal attack rules, and the political editorializing rules.

The **fairness doctrine** required broadcasters to provide balanced coverage of controversial ideas of public importance to respond. The personal attack rules permit a person whose honesty, character, or integrity is attacked by a broadcast licensee while in the course of discussing a controversial issue of public importance. The political editorializing rules provide that when a broadcast licensee opposes or endorses a candidate in an editorial, that candidate or a spokesperson for the candidate must have a chance to respond. (For further discussion, see Chapter 12.) These rules, which were designed to promote debate in the electronic media, were attacked by broadcasters on First Amendment grounds. The broadcasters contended that the rules were wrong because they treated broadcasters differently from newspapers and other print media, which were free to be unfair and to editorialize at will. Some personal attacks in the print media, of course, would be vulnerable under libel law.

In *Red Lion,* the Supreme Court rejected the First Amendment assault on these regulations and policies. Given the "unique" characteristics of broadcasting, the Court decided these rules were entirely consistent with the First Amendment: "There is nothing in the First Amendment which prevents the government from requiring a licensee to share his frequency with others and to conduct himself as a proxy or fiduciary with obligations to present those views and voices which are representative of his community and which would otherwise, by necessity, be barred from the airwaves."[4] In reaching this conclusion, the Court relied on the public ownership of the airwaves and the **scarcity rationale** for broadcasting regulation (see Chapter 12).

Another important theme in *Red Lion* was the importance of public access to ideas, again especially in broadcasting: "It is the right of the public to receive suitable access to social, political, esthetic, moral, and other ideas and experiences which is crucial here. That right may not constitutionally be abridged either by Congress or the FCC."[5] What was the meaning of this "right of the public to receive suitable access" to ideas? Does the First Amendment itself give the public a right to receive access to the hurly-burly of debate? In the years following *Red Lion,* a great many cases came to the FCC seeking individual and group access to television.

If the Court recognized a right of the public to receive ideas in *Red Lion,* would it extend that theory and recognize that somebody without a broadcast station has a First Amendment right to compel a licensee to transmit that person's ideas to the public? Given the general ferment in the country over the Vietnam War and the pressure by anti-war activists for broadcast time to present their views, it was hardly surprising that a case raising this precise question came to the Supreme Court in 1973.

A First Amendment Right of Access to the Electronic Media

Two organizations complained to the FCC that WTOP, a CBS-owned radio station in Washington, D.C., refused to sell them time for editorial advertisements. One of the organizations was Business Executives' Move for Vietnam Peace (BEM), a group of business people opposed to the Vietnam War. BEM asked WTOP to sell time to it to broadcast some one-minute spot announcements expressing the organization's anti–Vietnam War views. WTOP responded that it presented full and fair coverage of controversial issues including the Vietnam War and, therefore, was not bound to accept a particular editorial advertisement.

Sometime after the BEM request, another organization, the Democratic National Committee (DNC), planned to buy time from CBS to present its views and to solicit funds. The DNC complained to the FCC, however, when CBS refused to sell time to broadcast the committee's editorial positions. The DNC wanted the FCC to rule that under the First Amendment and the Federal Communications Act, broadcasters could not flatly refuse to sell time to responsible organizations for the solicitation of funds and for comment on public issues.

The FCC ruled that a broadcaster could not be forced to sell advertising for comment on public issues, but it upheld the DNC's position that political parties had a right to buy broadcast time to solicit funds. A federal court of appeals disagreed with part of the FCC ruling and said that a flat ban on paid public announcements or on editorial advertisements violated the First Amendment.

The Supreme Court sided with the FCC on the editorial ad issue. The First Amendment did not prevent networks or stations from banning editorial advertisements. In short, the Supreme Court in *CBS v. DNC* refused to read the First Amendment as creating an enforceable right of access to the electronic media.[6] Chief Justice Warren Burger for a plurality of the Court ruled that the access requests of the DNC would involve the FCC too closely in the day-to-day editorial decisions of broadcasters.

Chief Justice Burger emphasized that, unlike the situation in *Red Lion,* no law or FCC policy was at stake here. Here the contention was that the First Amendment itself commanded the FCC to issue a ban against broadcaster blanket policies of refusing to accept editorial advertisements. But broadcasters

---

● **Fairness doctrine**
A policy, no longer in force, promulgated by the FCC that required broadcasters over the license period to cover controversial issues and provide a balanced presentation of those issues when they did so.

● **Scarcity rationale**
Refers to the fact that the electromagnetic spectrum is finite. Since it is not possible for all who might wish to use the spectrum to broadcast to do so, government is justified in regulating broadcasting in the public interest.

● **No First Amendment right of access to the electronic media**
There is no enforceable First Amendment–based right of access to the broadcast media. Recognition of such a right would involve the FCC too closely in the day-to-day editorial decisions of broadcast journalists.

were private parties, and the First Amendment did not apply to the actions of private parties. Ruling against blanket network editorial policies in the name of the First Amendment would trespass too deeply on editorial freedom and autonomy. "Journalistic discretion would in many ways be lost to the rigid limitations that the First Amendment imposes on government."[7] The access requests were basically complaints about editorial decisions. In such a situation, the First Amendment scales weighed in favor of supporting the editorial discretion of broadcasters: "For better or worse, editing is what editors are for; and editing is selection and choice of material."[8]

Justice William Brennan, joined by Justice Thurgood Marshall, dissented. They contended that government involvement in broadcasting was so extensive that broadcaster decisions refusing to sell time to groups or individuals wishing to speak on controversial issues should be subjected to the demands of the First Amendment: "[A]ny policy that *absolutely* denies citizens access to the airwaves necessarily renders even the concept of 'full and fair discussion' practically meaningless."[9] Justice Brennan concluded:

> The First Amendment values of individual self-fulfillment through expression and individual participation in public debate are central to our concept of liberty. If these values are to survive in the age of technology, it is essential that individuals be permitted at least *some* opportunity to express their views on public issues over the electronic media.[10]

An interesting aspect of the *CBS v. DNC* decision is that the Court justified its rejection of access to the media by citing the then-active FCC fairness doctrine. Since that doctrine required broadcasters to air ideas, the Court reasoned there was little need to protect any right of individuals to have access to stations. Now, however, the fairness doctrine has been abolished (see Chapter 12). Does that undermine the arguments against access to broadcasting in *CBS v. DNC?*

CBS v. DNC did not decide whether Congress or the FCC could originate and mandate a policy guaranteeing private access to broadcasting. It simply said that the Court would not interpret the First Amendment as requiring such a policy. What would the Court decide if a case involving access required by Congress or the FCC were presented to them?

"Reasonable Access" for Federal Political Candidates

- **Reasonable access**
The Federal Communications Act of 1934 provides in § 312 (a) (7) that the FCC can revoke a broadcaster's license for willful or repeated failure to provide reasonable access for federal political candidates.

In 1981, the Supreme Court finally decided a case, *CBS v FCC*, challenging an access law enacted by Congress. The case involved the "reasonable access" provision of the Federal Communications Act of 1934.[11] This part of the act provides that the FCC can revoke a broadcaster's license for willful or repeated failure to provide reasonable access to federal political candidates.

Lying in the background of the reasonable access case is another important U.S. Supreme Court decision, *Miami Herald Publishing Co. v. Tornillo.*[12] Decided a year after *CBS v. DNC*, *Tornillo* struck down a Florida law providing a right of reply to political candidates attacked by newspapers. The case is discussed later in the print media section of this chapter.

Just as the *DNC* case gave primacy to the editorial judgment of broadcast editors, so the *Tornillo* case gave primacy to the First Amendment rights of print media editors over political candidates seeking to reply to print media editorials. Even though the Court in *Red Lion* had declared that the access claims of the public were paramount, it rejected such claims in *Tornillo*. Thus, the problem of reconciling the free expression claims of editors and the public they serve is a difficult, troubling, and enduring one. *CBS v. FCC* was decided in this context of conflicting opinions. *Red Lion* said the public had the right to receive information from unwilling broadcast stations, but *CBS v. DNC* had rejected the idea that this also meant outsiders had a First Amendment right to buy broadcast time to present their views. *Tornillo* held that the public's right to receive information, in theory, did not include print media. Would the Court uphold or overturn an act of Congress guaranteeing federal candidates access to broadcast media? In *CBS v. FCC*, the Court decided that at least this form of "reasonable access" to broadcasting did not violate the First Amendment.[13]

The Carter-Mondale campaign had requested time on the three major television networks—ABC, NBC, and CBS—for a 30-minute program in early December 1979 to present a documentary outlining the achievements of the Carter administration and opening President Carter's reelection campaign. The networks refused to provide the time, and the Carter-Mondale Presidential Committee complained to the FCC that the "reasonable access" provision had been violated. The FCC, the federal court of appeals, and the Supreme Court all validated this complaint. In addition, the Supreme Court rejected the networks' contention that the reasonable access provision violated the First Amendment.

Falling back on *Red Lion*, the Supreme Court concluded the provision enhanced "the ability of candidates to present, and the public to receive, information necessary for the effective operation of the democratic process."[14] The networks relied on *CBS v. DNC* and *Tornillo* for the proposition that there was no right of access to the media. But Chief Justice Burger responded that although there was no "*general* right of access to the media," the reasonable access provision of the Federal Communications Act created a constitutional, limited, right of access to the media that could be invoked only by legally qualified federal political candidates.[15] Therefore, the *CBS v. DNC* and *Tornillo* decisions were not applicable. The Court concluded that the reasonable access provision properly balanced "the First Amendment rights of federal candidates, the public and broadcasters."[16]

In *Tornillo*, the newspaper right of reply case, and *CBS v. DNC*, the electronic right of access case, the Supreme Court came down squarely on the side of editorial autonomy and against the access claims of the public. In *Red Lion*, the fairness doctrine case, and *CBS v. FCC*, the reasonable access case, the Court came down squarely on the side of the free speech and access claims of the public and subordinated the editorial freedom claims of broadcast journalists. The reasonable access case illustrates once again the schizophrenic pattern of the Supreme Court in responding to the difficult task of reconciling the First Amendment interests of the media and the public.

● **Limited rights of access to the broadcast media** Although there is no general right of access to the media, limited rights of access to the broadcast media such as the reasonable access provision for federal political candidates properly balance the First Amendment rights of federal candidates, the public, and broadcasters.

Access for What?

Access claims present difficult problems, so the Court's ambivalence is understandable. For example, does access mean that anything the access claimant wants to say goes? If, as in a recent reasonable access case, a federal political candidate is eligible for access, must anything the candidate wishes to broadcast be aired?

Dan Becker, a vigorously anti-abortion congressional candidate in Georgia, submitted a videotape of a thirty-minute paid political ad to a television station in Atlanta for presentation between 4 and 5 P.M. on Sunday, November 1, 1992. Becker wanted his videotape to be shown immediately after the broadcast of a National Football League game between the Atlanta Falcons and the Los Angeles Rams. The videotape depicted the surgical procedure for abortion and also contained "graphic depictions and descriptions of female genitalia, the uterus, excreted uterine fluid, dismembered fetal body parts, and aborted fetuses."[17]

The broadcaster refused to air the program at the time the candidate requested. Arguing that the content was "indecent," the broadcaster asked the court to allow "channeling" of the videotape to the hours between midnight and 6 A.M. when children were less likely to be in the audience.

A major argument, of course, against allowing access to television is that broadcasters will be forced to air material that they would not voluntarily choose to broadcast. The "equal opportunities" or **"equal time"** provision of the Federal Communications Act specifically provides that broadcasters cannot censor material broadcast under it.[18] The reasonable access provision does not contain such a no-censorship provision. Nevertheless, the court held that the federal law that prohibits the broadcast of indecent material[19] constitutes an exception to the Federal Communications Act requirements of reasonable access, equal opportunities, and no censorship. Moreover, the videotape that Dan Becker wanted broadcast in the late afternoon qualified as indecent programming, and the station was authorized to schedule it for postmidnight viewing.[20] (For a discussion of what constitutes indecent programming, see Chapter 12.)

The Georgia federal court believed it had reached a Solomon-like judgment. Federal law allowed regulation of indecent programming and mandated "reasonable access" for political advertising. Accordingly, congressional candidate Becker got to air his political advertisement on WAGA-TV, but "decidedly indecent" material was exiled to a time slot that substantially diminished the likelihood of injury to the psychological well-being of children in the audience.[21]

One can view the Georgia case as a censorship decision. At the same time, one can view it as a decision that will encourage access. Arguably, if some limitations are placed on what can be aired, broadcasters, the FCC, and the courts will be more sympathetic to calls for "reasonable access."

Contemporary Status of Rights of Access and Reply to Broadcasting

What is the status of rights of access and reply to broadcasting today? To start with, political candidates have more access and reply rights in the electronic

● **"Equal time"**
Section 315 of the Federal Communications Act obliges broadcasters to give equal opportunities to political candidates. If a broadcaster sells time to a candidate, the station must sell time to the opponent.

media than ordinary citizens enjoy. Political candidates may invoke the equal time law and secure opportunities equal to those given by broadcasters to their opponents. (See the discussion of Section 315 of the Federal Communications Act in Chapter 12.) As we have seen, however, the reasonable access provision of the Federal Communications Act applies only to *federal* political candidates.

For many years, the fairness doctrine was also in effect. Theoretically available to the public at large, the doctrine required broadcasters to affirmatively seek to cover controversial issues and to provide a balanced presentation of controversial issues of public importance in their programming. The fairness doctrine was upheld against a First Amendment challenge in the *Red Lion* case in 1969, but it was abolished by the FCC in 1987 out of First Amendment concerns and as part of the Reagan administration's deregulation program. The **abolition of the fairness doctrine** was then affirmed by a federal appeals court (see Chapter 12).[22]

Broadcasters are still bound by the personal attack rules—a spin-off of the fairness doctrine. The **personal attack rules** permit individuals who are attacked during broadcasts to have equivalent time to respond without cost. The FCC did not abolish the personal attack rules and still considers complaints brought under the rules, albeit not very sympathetically.

An illustrative personal attack case was a 1991 complaint by Professor David Berkman. A talk show host on radio station WISN had said that Berkman would not "be happy until we see Iraqi soldiers jumping for joy." The professor felt this amounted to calling him a traitor and, therefore, constituted an attack on his integrity entitling him to a reply. The FCC ruled that the radio station's comments about Berkman's views on American involvement in the Gulf War were not a personal attack upon his "honesty, character, integrity, or like personal qualities" within the meaning of the personal attack rules. In short, since the comments were not personal, no response was warranted.[23]

Thus, the reasonable access rule still has vitality as does the equal time rule. The fairness doctrine, at least for the moment, is dead. The personal attack rules, though alive, are barely enforced. A structure for reply and access in the broadcast media still exists, but if it is to be meaningful, it will require sympathetic and effective enforcement. Whether the current administration will be as dedicated to deregulation in this field as were the Reagan and Bush administrations is hard to say.

The 1992 Presidential campaign may provide a preview of the future of access and reply to the broadcast media. The 1992 campaign saw the coming of age of broadcast "talk shows." Following in the footsteps of the pacesetter, Ross Perot, who announced his presidential candidacy on *Larry King Live,* candidates sought out talk shows on both radio and television. Both George Bush and Bill Clinton appeared on radio and television talk shows—sometimes eagerly. The format of the 1992 presidential debates where journalists served as moderators for direct questions to the candidates from the public, is also likely to recur in future campaigns.

The popularity of call-in radio and television talk shows demonstrates an intense public interest in playing an active rather than a passive role in the opinion process. Both radio and television are transforming themselves into

● **Fairness doctrine abolition**
The fairness doctrine was abolished by the FCC in 1987 as part of President Reagan's deregulation program and out of First Amendment concerns.

● **Personal attack rules**
Permit a person whose honesty, character, or integrity is attacked on broadcasting during the discussion of a controversial issue of public importance to respond without cost through the provision of equivalent time.

participatory media of their own volition without being prodded by law. In an effort to stay alive, AM radio—beleaguered by FM radio, "over the air" television, and cable television—sought out its audience and invited it in. In its hunger to speak, the public responded. Whether such developments will make legal requirements for access and reply obsolete or will stimulate further efforts to use the law to provide for public entry into the electronic media remains to be seen.

ACCESS TO CABLE TELEVISION

One area with a long history of mandatory public access to the media has been cable television. Franchise agreements between cable systems and cities often feature an obligation to dedicate one or more channels to public access, although such requirements have been resisted by many cable companies.

Lower courts are deeply divided on whether imposing mandatory public access obligations on cable systems violates the First Amendment. As we shall see, some courts say that such obligations are intolerable limitations on editorial freedom. Other courts say that imposing access obligations on cable systems simply implements the First Amendment interest in bringing the full spectrum of ideas to the community. So far the U.S. Supreme Court has not grappled with this specific issue.

One of the first cases to ask whether mandatory public access channels on cable are a violation of the First Amendment was *Berkshire Cablevision of Rhode Island v. Burke.*[24] This case arose before either the Cable Communications Policy Act of 1984 or the Cable Television Consumer Protection and Competition Act of 1992 was enacted. A Rhode Island state agency required cable operators to reserve seven of fifty or more channels for public access as well as one channel for use without charge by the general public on a first-come, first-served nondiscriminatory basis. Among other things, the mandated public access channels broadcast programming that originated from public institutions, religious institutions, and parochial schools. A federal district court upheld these mandatory public access requirements.

Seeking protection under the *Tornillo* decision, the cable operators argued that the First Amendment protected them no less than daily newspapers against compulsory access. They made a now-familiar argument in cable access litigation: cable is more like the newspaper press than the broadcast press and should, therefore, be given the greater First Amendment protection accorded the newspaper press. With their multichannel capacity, cable systems are a medium of abundance and resemble newspapers in the sense that they are not technologically finite—at least in the way VHF television is. The federal district judge in Rhode Island did not agree. "Newspapers and cable television cannot be equated," he held.[25] The print media have traditionally been free of government control. In contrast, government franchising of the cable industry is almost indispensable. For the Rhode Island federal court, the decisive precedent on whether mandatory public access channels on cable violated the First Amendment was the *Red Lion* case.

Red Lion, governing the electronic media, had validated regulation; *Tornillo,* governing the print media, invalidated regulation. Which model was more suitable for cable television? Even though broadcasting was a medium of scarcity and cable, a medium of abundance, the mandatory access rules should be upheld. According to the Rhode Island federal court, the goal of both the mandatory public access channels on cable, and the broadcast policies in *Red Lion,* was "to *promote* the First Amendment by making a powerful communications medium available to as many of our citizens as is reasonably possible."[26] This view, however, was hardly the last word on the matter.

In 1987, a federal court in Pennsylvania sustained a city's requirement that a cable operator reserve thirteen of eighty-four channels for public access purposes.[27] The cable operator argued that the city ordinance violated the First Amendment. The court disagreed and said the First Amendment was implemented by the access requirements: they secured "the foundation upon which the First Amendment is grounded—promotion of a marketplace of ideas."[28] Are public access requirements an impermissible intrusion on the editorial freedom of the cable operator? Relying on the rich multichannel capacity of cable, the court said that the mandatory access requirements only minimally intruded on the cable operator's First Amendment rights. The great majority of the eighty-four channels controlled by the cable operator were under its editorial control.

Not all First Amendment challenges to mandatory public access channels have failed. Illustrative was the fate of a proposal by the city of Santa Cruz, California, requiring a cable operator to dedicate separate access channels for public, governmental, and institutional use. Santa Cruz planned to create a city agency that would adopt rules to govern the time, scheduling, and use of these channels. The city agency would be funded by the cable operator. A California federal court declared: "If applied to the press, these requirements would surely violate the First Amendment."[29] The court pointed out that, unlike the Pennsylvania situation, the city of Santa Cruz reserved to itself the power to designate when and for how long speakers could use the cable operator's system. In these circumstances, Santa Cruz had failed to show that cable operators were less entitled to First Amendment protection than newspapers.[30]

In a case involving the city of Palo Alto, California, a federal court held that municipal requirements that cable operators must provide three public access educational channels and two governmental channels violated the First Amendment. Mandatory public access created a risk that a cable operator's expression would be "chilled." A cable system might not disseminate something on channels it controlled for fear that it would be attacked on the public access channels. Forcing access channels on a cable operator who did not want them unconstitutionally intruded into the cable operator's "editorial judgment of what to cablecast and not to cablecast."[31]

Mandated access was provided for when Congress adopted the Cable Communications Policy Act of 1984, which specifically required cable systems with thirty-six or more channels to reserve 10 percent of their **channel capacity for leased commercial use** by those who were not affiliated with the cable operator. Cable systems with a capacity of fifty-five or more channels were

---

● **Red Lion standard**
Red Lion Broadcasting Co. v. FCC (1969) upheld the fairness doctrine as reasonable regulation of the broadcast media that served the public interest, implemented the First Amendment, and was justified by the scarcity rationale. The Red Lion standard is shorthand for a First Amendment approach that permits reasonable regulation of the media.

● **Tornillo standard**
Miami Herald Publishing Co. v. Tornillo (1969) invalidated a state law requiring a right of reply for political candidates in newspapers attacking them as an impermissible intrusion on editorial autonomy. The *Tornillo* standard is shorthand for a First Amendment approach that is hostile to government regulation of the media.

● **Leased access channels**
The Cable Communications Policy Act of 1984 required that cable systems with a specified channel capacity reserve some channels for leased commercial use by entities not affiliated with the cable system. This requirement was designed to prevent a cable operator from dominating programming.

required to reserve 15 percent of their channel capacity for leased use.[32] The Cable Act of 1984 also permits, but does not require, cable operators to reserve channels for public, governmental, and educational use. Such congressional endorsement of cable access may affect how courts decide future access cases.

In a recent case, where a cable operator challenged the First Amendment validity of some mandatory public access regulations issued by a Florida town, the court upheld the regulations by specifically relying on the authority given to cities by the 1984 Cable Act.[33] The regulations required cable operators to provide service to schools and public hearings. In addition, one channel had to be dedicated to the city for public, educational, and governmental access requirements. The court noted: "Congress specifically granted franchising authorities the right to require public access channels through the Cable Act. Congress considered the First Amendment implications of this requirement in enacting the Cable Act."[34] Only one channel out of fifty was to be devoted to public access so the access requirements had "little impact on the cable operator's programming choices."[35] The court explained Congress's reasons for allowing municipalities to require public access channels on cable systems:

> Public access channels are often the video equivalent of the speaker's soap box or the electronic parallel to the printed leaflet. They provide groups and individuals who generally have not had access to the electronic marketplace of ideas with the opportunity to become sources of information in the electronic marketplace of ideas.[36]

Clearly, there is a congressional policy behind the leased access and mandatory public access channel provisions of the Cable Communications Policy Act of 1984. Usually, only one cable system operates in a given area. Therefore, it is important that admission into the conduit is not entirely controlled by a single cable operator. The 1984 Cable Act authorized franchising authorities to require cable operators to dedicate some of their channel capacity for **public, educational, and governmental programming (PEG)** as well as leased access channels. These PEG and leased access channels are not subject to the editorial control of the cable system operator. The Cable Television Consumer Protection and Competition Act of 1992[37] gave the FCC authority to regulate the prices, terms and conditions for leased access.

The cable industry has not taken kindly to being required to dedicate a portion of its channel capacity for uses it might not elect on its own. In 1993, in *Daniels Cablevision v. United States,*[38] some cable operators and programmers attacked the PEG and leased access provisions of the 1984 and 1992 cable laws on First Amendment grounds. The cable operators contended that these provisions mandated them "to engage in 'speech' they might not otherwise undertake."[39] The cable operators contended they had a First Amendment right to dedicate their channels for the speech they favored, not the speech favored by others.

Relying on the mid-level standard of scrutiny set forth in *United States v. O'Brien,*[40] the court in *Daniels* held that the challenged provisions were content-neutral and met the mid-level standard of review:

● **Mandatory PEG channels**

The Cable Communications Policy Act of 1984 authorized municipalities to require the dedication of some of their channels for public, educational, and governmental programming.

> The PEG and leased access provisions were enacted to serve a significant regulatory interest, *viz.*, affording speakers with lesser market appeal access to the nation's most pervasive video distribution technology. Enabling a broad range of speakers to reach a television audience that otherwise would never hear them is an appropriate goal and a legitimate exercise of federal legislative power.[41]

The court also held that the leased access provisions were valid under the First Amendment. The provisions did not impose too heavy a burden on cable operators, who still had complete control over most of their channel capacity:

> Nor do the PEG and leased access provisions overreach. PEG use is negotiable, and leased access provisions are directly proportional to the number of channels a cable operator has available, never exceeding 15 percent of total capacity. Operators retain discretion over the remainder, and may of course utilize them as they wish for their own programming or that of affiliated programmers.[42]

Although the *Daniels* case upheld the First Amendment validity of public access requirements on cable systems, the battle over whether cable operators may be required by government to dedicate some of their channel capacity for public purposes is hardly over. The results will ultimately depend on which standard of review is applied to cable systems. Under strict scrutiny, the standard the courts use in reviewing laws regulating the newspaper press, the imposition of public access requirements on cable systems would clearly be unconstitutional. If the courts were to treat cable systems like newspapers, public access requirements would probably be violative of the First Amendment for the same reasons that access requirements were held invalid in *Tornillo*—they impose too heavy a burden on editorial freedom. Under the more lenient rational basis standard of review, which is generally used in broadcast regulation, public access requirements on cable system would be valid. If the mid-level standard used in *Daniels* becomes the dominant standard of review for evaluating regulation, the results will be less predictable. The Supreme Court may disagree and conclude that conscripting part of a cable system's channel capacity serves no substantial government interest and is an impermissible burden on the First Amendment rights of cable operators.

In 1994, in *Turner Broadcasting System, Inc. v. FCC*,[43] the Supreme Court considered a First Amendment challenge to the **must-carry provisions** of the 1992 Cable Act.[44] These provisions required cable systems to carry local over-the-air broadcast signals. Using arguments similar to those used in the First Amendment challenges to mandatory public access channels, cable operators contended that the must-carry provisions violated the First Amendment. Government requirements that cable operators dedicate any part of their channel capacity for purposes that the cable operators had not selected violated their editorial freedom and, therefore, their First Amendment rights.

Ignoring the cable operators' insistence that their abundant channel capacity put them in the position of newspapers, Justice Anthony Kennedy, writing for a divided Court in *Turner*, declined to give the cable operators the full

● **Must-carry provisions**
To preserve over-the-air free broadcasting, the Cable Television Consumer Protection and Competition Act of 1992 required cable operators to carry local over-the-air broadcast signals.

First Amendment protection conferred on newspapers in *Tornillo*. At the same time, the Court declined to treat cable for First Amendment purposes with the more relaxed *Red Lion* standard of review used for broadcast regulation. Cable's multichannel capacity made the scarcity argument that had justified broadcast regulation in *Red Lion* inapplicable.

● **Standard of review for must-carry rules**
In *Turner Broadcasting System, Inc. v. FCC* (1994), the Court deemed the must-carry rules to be content-neutral and reviewed them under the mid-level standard of review set forth in *United States v. O'Brien* (1968). The *O'Brien* standard is not as hostile to government regulation as the *Tornillo* standard nor as lenient to government regulation as the *Red Lion* standard.

The *Turner* Court reviewed the must-carry rules under the mid-level standard set forth in *United States v. O'Brien;* this standard is used for content-neutral regulation. Justice Kennedy explained why the regulations were deemed to be content-neutral:

> Congress' overriding objective in enacting must-carry was not to favor programming of a particular subject matter, viewpoint, or format, but rather to preserve access to free television programming to the 40 percent of Americans without cable.[45]

The standard used in *O'Brien* is not as hostile to government regulation as the standard used for print media regulation nor as lenient as the standard used for broadcast regulation. Nevertheless, the *Turner* Court declined to hold that the must-carry rules were invalid under the *O'Brien* standard and instead remanded the case to the lower courts for further fact finding. The Court declared that the government had failed to show that the economic health, stability, and future of local over-the-air broadcasting was dependent on the must-carry rules.

Justice Kennedy said in *Turner* that the must-carry rules were content-neutral. If the Court were to hold that the public access requirements in federal cable legislation were content-based, then a more exacting standard of review would be used. In short, the question of the First Amendment validity of mandatory public access requirements in cable regulation depends on whether they are characterized as content-based or content-neutral. It is hard to predict which characterization the Supreme Court would choose.

ACCESS TO THE PRINT MEDIA

As already noted, in 1973 the Supreme Court in *CBS v. DNC* said that the First Amendment protected the editorial freedom of broadcasters. Editorial autonomy was deemed more important and fundamental than public rights of access to broadcasting under the First Amendment. Such competing claims of access and editorial freedom illustrate First Amendment rights in conflict regardless of medium. How would access claims fare in the context of the print media? The worlds of law and journalism did not have long to wait. The answer came a year later.

The landmark decision on whether those attacked by newspapers should have a right of reply or access to newspapers came in the case of *Miami Herald Publishing Co. v. Tornillo*.[46] Pat Tornillo, head of the teachers union in Miami, ran for the state legislature. Tornillo had recently led the public school teachers on strike at a time when strikes by public school teachers were illegal under state law. When Tornillo announced his candidacy, the *Miami Herald*, a nonunion newspaper, attacked him in two editorials. One editorial charged that "lawbreakers" now wished to be "lawmakers." Tornillo, in turn, furnished replies to the editorials, but the *Herald* refused to publish them. In most places in the United States, Tornillo would have had no chance of having his reply published if the paper did not choose to do so. But Florida at that time was a special situation. In 1913, **Florida** had enacted a **right of reply law** that specifically authorized political candidates to respond to attacks by newspapers during a political campaign. The law provided that if a newspaper attacked the personal character of a political candidate or charged that person with wrongdoing in office during a political campaign, then upon the request of the candidate, the newspaper had to publish free of charge any reply the candidate chose to submit. The only limitation was that the reply could take no more space than the original attack.

The *Miami Herald* refused to comply with the right of reply law, contending that the law violated the First Amendment. The Florida Supreme Court held that the statute was not in conflict with the First Amendment but instead constituted an implementation of the First Amendment.[47] But the U.S. Supreme Court disagreed and unanimously ruled that the Florida right of reply law violated the First Amendment.[48] Writing for the Court, Chief Justice Burger set forth the arguments of the access advocates:

> Chains of newspapers, national newspapers, national wire and news services, and one-newspaper towns, are the dominant features of a press that has become noncompetitive and enormously powerful and influential in its capacity to manipulate popular opinion and change the course of events.[49]

In addition, Chief Justice Burger observed: "The result of these vast changes has been to place in a few hands the power to inform the American people and shape public opinion."[50]

In *Tornillo*, the Supreme Court had two major reasons for invalidating the Florida right of reply law under the First Amendment. First, to compel newspapers to publish something they would otherwise choose not to publish was seen as a penalty. The Florida right of reply law penalized freedom of expression, a penalty that newspapers would have to bear based on the content of what they had published. This penalty chilled speech by newspapers. The end result, the Court feared, might be less rather than more speech. If a newspaper knew that by publishing *x* it would have to publish *anti-x*, it might choose to publish nothing on the subject at all.

Second, imposing an obligation on a newspaper to publish a reply was seen as an invalid interference with editorial freedom. Chief Justice Burger made a strong statement on the primacy of editorial freedom:

> A newspaper is more than a passive receptacle of or conduit for news, comment, and advertising. The choice of material to go into a newspaper, and the decisions made as to limitations on the size of the paper, and content, and treatment of public officials—whether fair or unfair—constitute the exercise of editorial control and judgment.[51]

● **Florida right of reply law**
Enacted in 1913, the law, struck down in *Miami Herald Publishing Co. v. Tornillo* (1974), required a newspaper to publish without cost a reply by a political candidate attacked by the newspaper during a political campaign.

A significant omission in the *Tornillo* case was that the Court made no mention of the *Red Lion* decision. Yet the cases were quite similar. Both involved rights of reply. In *Red Lion,* of course, a right of reply in an electronic media context was held to be consistent with the First Amendment. In *Tornillo,* a right of reply in a print media context was held not to be consistent with the First Amendment. Possibly, the Court by its silence on the relevance of *Red Lion* to *Tornillo* was signaling an intention to use quite different First Amendment approaches for the print media and for the broadcast media.

The *Tornillo* decision had significant consequences. Many in journalism thought the case was unfortunate in the sense that as a matter of ethics or fairness, the *Herald* should voluntarily have given Tornillo an opportunity to respond to the attacks against him. The development of op-ed pages and the appointment of press *ombudsmen* are to some extent **voluntary responses by the newspaper press to the problem of access.**

Compulsory Retraction Statutes

The *Tornillo* decision answered some questions and raised others. A feature of libel law in many states is that the defendant can mitigate damages by publishing a retraction. Since damages are coercive—in *Tornillo* terms, a penalty—this raised a question. If a newspaper printed a retraction to diminish its libel damages, wasn't this a form of the compulsory publication forbidden by *Tornillo?* Interestingly, Justice William Brennan, joined by Justice William Rehnquist, anticipated the problem in a short concurring opinion in *Tornillo.* They pointed out that the Court's opinion dealt only with "right of reply statutes" and observed that the Court had taken no position on the validity of libel-related retraction statutes." Today, retraction statutes in a libel setting appear to have survived the *Tornillo* case.[52]

One remedy that is still unclear after the *Tornillo* case is the validity of right of reply statutes limited only to defamation cases. The statute in the *Tornillo* case applied to political candidates who were attacked by a newspaper during an election. The statute was not limited to defamatory attacks. Would a statute that provided a right of reply as an option—an alternative to damages—be valid? The threat of heavy damages in libel cases and the cost of defending libel suits are increasingly worrisome costs of doing business for the media and for journalists. Would a right of reply be preferable? Although such proposals have received considerable discussion in the literature, the states have yet to enact such statutes.[53]

Reply and Retraction Compared

From an access point of view, even a right of reply remedy limited to libel is preferable to a retraction because the defamed party gets to respond in her or his own words. From the point of view of those for whom editorial freedom is the primary value, however, the fact that the editor loses control over the subject matter of the reply is the principal defect of right of reply legislation. It allows someone to be published whom the editor would not otherwise publish.

• **Voluntary access to the press mechanisms**

Although the *Tornillo* case held that the press was not required to provide access, voluntary responses to the problem of access include the op-ed page and the establishment of a press ombudsman.

• **Retraction statutes**

Typically provide that a defendant can mitigate damages in a libel suit by publishing a retraction. One difference between retraction and a right of reply is that the newspaper prepares the retraction whereas the person attacked writes the reply.

At least the retraction is prepared by the newspaper staff. If a newspaper is willing to take the consequences, a retraction does not have to be published.

Access for Advertising to the Private Press

The *Tornillo* case, unlike *CBS v. DNC*, involved an editorial attack against a political candidate. What about a newspaper's advertising columns? Does editorial control have the same importance in that context? Unlike the news and editorial columns of a newspaper, the advertising columns are the traditionally "open" part of the paper. Several cases in state and federal courts have dealt with the question of whether the First Amendment provides a right of access on a nondiscriminatory basis to the advertising pages of a daily newspaper if the advertiser is willing to pay the going rate. The response of the courts has been, "No, it doesn't." In a recent West Virginia decision, the court declined to see any reason to differentiate rights of access claims for advertising from claims to news column or editorial space: "In short, government can never compel a private newspaper to print anything without violating the First Amendment's guarantee of a free press."[54]

Does it matter that the dominant newspaper in an area denies access to its ad columns? The answer, again, is "no." In a 1991 case, a union had been trying to organize the employees of a company store in Danbury, Connecticut. The union sought to purchase an ad in the Danbury *News-Times*, the newspaper with the largest circulation in the area, to present the advantages of union representation. The newspaper refused to publish for fear of offending the store, which was a large advertiser. The union asserted that the newspaper's refusal to publish the ad violated the First Amendment by silencing the union's right to free speech. The court flatly rejected this contention by saying there was no place "for a governmental check on a privately owned newspaper."[55]

In short, the courts have refused to construe the First Amendment as a source of rights to obtain access to the advertising columns of newspapers. Nevertheless, the control newspapers may exert over advertising is subject to some legal restrictions. Newspapers' decisions as to what advertising they will print must be made in a manner that is consistent with antitrust laws.[56] When a newspaper refused to accept classified advertising from an apartment rental service that charged a fee, the refusal was held to constitute a violation of the antitrust laws. The newspaper could not use its monopoly power to protect its classified rental advertising.[57]

Access for Advertising to the Public Press

What about publicly, rather than privately, owned media? Around the time of the Vietnam War, student groups opposed to the war were successful in persuading the courts to force **"public" print media**—state university student newspapers in these cases—to run the students ads expressing their views. In a case involving the campus newspaper, the *Royal Purple,* at Wisconsin State University—Whitewater (now the University of Wisconsin at Whitewater), the paper turned down an ad protesting the Vietnam War. The legal question was

● **Right of access to advertising**
Although there is no First Amendment right of access to advertise in a daily newspaper, a newspaper's refusal to accept advertising may in some circumstances violate the antitrust laws.

● **Public press**
The press that is funded by the state, such as college newspapers at state-supported colleges. In some circumstances, the access obligations of the public press may be greater than is the case with the private press.

whether, having published other kinds of advertising, the paper could refuse to publish an ad because the paper disapproved of its editorial character. A federal court of appeals said that a state university newspaper like the *Royal Purple* was in a different position than a privately owned newspaper. In *Lee v. Board of Regents,* the court held that a state facility that had opened the campus newspaper to some kinds of editorial advertising lost the option to reject other kinds of editorial advertising.[58]

One of the reasons suits to compel publication of editorial advertising succeed when brought against the state university student press is that the First Amendment is directed to government and not to private individuals. When a private newspaper refuses advertising, this is a private exercise of editorial discretion. But when a government-supported newspaper refuses some kinds of editorial advertising, it appears that government is taking sides. Government, however, is obliged to provide equal protection to all its citizens. Government can not make the kinds of ideological distinctions and discriminations that private newspapers routinely make.

The *Royal Purple* case was decided before *Tornillo.* An interesting question is whether the access cases involving the state university campus press have survived the *Tornillo* decision with its emphasis on the importance of editorial autonomy. Did *Tornillo* restore editorial freedom to state college newspaper editors? A federal court of appeals confronted this issue in a case involving the *Reflector,* the campus newspaper at Mississippi State University. The chairwoman of the Mississippi Gay Alliance submitted an ad to the student newspaper that stated:

> Gay Center—open 6:00 P.M. to 9:00 P.M. Monday, Wednesday and Friday nights.
> We offer—counseling, *Legal aid,* and a library of homosexual literature.
> Write to—The Mississippi Gay Alliance, P.O. Box 1328., Mississippi State University, Ms. 39762.

The student newspaper refused to run the ad, and the organization brought a suit against the paper to compel publication.

The Gay Alliance was not successful. The federal court of appeals pointed out that a student editor rather than university officials had made the decision not to publish. Although the university involved was funded by the state, no official of the university had been involved in the decision. Therefore, the case really involved the exercise of discretion by an editor selected by the student body. In such circumstances, the First Amendment prevented judicial interference with the editorial decision. Additionally, the federal appeals court noted, sodomy was a crime in Mississippi and, therefore, there were "special reasons for holding that there was no abuse of discretion by the editor of *The Reflector.*"[59]

A dissenting judge urged that the right to edit of a student editor even in a state-supported newspaper should be recognized insofar as the editorial and news columns were concerned. With respect to the advertising columns, however, the dissent urged that a principle of equal access for editorial advertisements in state-supported student publications be recognized. In view of the special circumstances of the *Mississippi Gay Alliance* case, it is hard to tell whether the principle of equal access for advertising in the state-supported college press has survived the *Tornillo*.

ACCESS TO THE TELCOS

When Judge Harold Greene of Washington, D.C., ordered the breakup of AT&T,[60] he also created the seven Regional Bell Operating Companies (RBOCs). His subsequent monitoring of that order made him the virtual czar of the telecommunications industry. On July 25, 1991, Judge Greene removed the restrictions on the provision of information services by the telephone companies (telcos).[61] Although other legal barriers to the **dissemination and origination of** information and **video services by the telcos** remain, his decision removed one major barrier.

Another major barrier was removed when a federal district court held in *Chesapeake and Potomac Telephone Co. v. United States*,[62] that the provision of the Cable Communications Policy Act of 1984 that prohibited telephone companies and their affiliates from providing video services to subscribers within their service areas violated the First Amendment.[63] Reasoning that the prohibition in the 1984 Cable Act preventing telcos from disseminating their own video programming was content-neutral, the court concluded that the mid-level *O'Brien* standard of review was applicable. Even though it used the *O'Brien* standard, the court nevertheless found that the prohibition violated the First Amendment. The interests asserted by the government were not deemed sufficiently substantial.

The government had argued that telcos should be kept out of the video programming business for two reasons. The first reason was that the prohibition promoted competition in the video programming market. The court said, however, that by limiting video programmers to the cable industry, the prohibition actually limited the "number of outlets through which [video] programming can be distributed."[64] The second reason for the prohibition, the government contended, was to protect diversity of ownership of communications outlets. The court took this argument more seriously and described the government's argument forcefully:

> In essence, the government contends that the telephone companies would be *too* successful if they were allowed to compete in the cable television market. [T]he resulting situation would be worse for consumers than the *status quo* because rather than having two monopolists—one providing cable television and related services and one providing local telephone exchange service and related services—consumers would be faced with a single monopolist, the telephone company, providing all of their telecommunications services.[65]

The government feared that entry of the cash-rich telcos into the cable television market would drive the cable operators out of business and lead "to a

● **Telco entry into video programming** There is a controversy about whether the regional Bell telephone companies (telcos) should be allowed to originate and disseminate video programming. The newspaper and the cable industry have in the main opposed such entry, but existing legal barriers are increasingly being successfully challenged on First Amendment grounds.

single entity in control of *all* electronic communications sources entering an individual's home."[66] In short, the government feared what might be called the ultimate access problem. Entry into the video programming market would be in the control of a singe entity in each service area.

The court said that in responding to this concern, Congress had chosen the most "draconian approach"[67]—a complete bar to telco entry into the cable television industry. Less drastic alternatives were available. For example, the FCC had recommended to Congress that the prohibition on telco entry into video programming should be repealed. But the FCC also suggested that the telcos should be limited in the "direct provision of video programming to a specified percentage of the channel capacity" available to the telco. The FCC suggested further that "the balance of the channel capacity would be required to be leased on a common carrier basis, and the system would be required to have the capability to accommodate multiple video programmers."[68] Since Congress could have chosen other alternatives less burdensome to the First Amendment rights of the telcos, the court concluded that the provision in the 1984 Cable Act prohibiting telco entry into video programming was invalid.[69] In 1994, a federal court of appeals upheld the lower court's ruling that the prohibition against the direct provision of video programming by the telcos violated the First Amendment. The prohibition was not narrowly tailored to achieve the government interest in diversity of ownership of the means of communication. In fact, it was a *total* ban directed against the telcos. Furthermore, the prohibition did not leave open alternative means of communication in the dissemination of video programming to the telcos.[70]

Eventually, the telcos will be able to provide **electronic yellow pages**, news services, sports results, financial market results, and entertainment programming—all by way of the video screen. These developments will have a tremendous impact on existing media. Newspapers will have to fight the telcos for diminishing advertising revenues. Telcos will be able to develop their own video services. Given the technological capacity and economic strength of the telcos, their ability to originate and disseminate their own video programming services may ultimately overwhelm the existing cable and broadcast industries.

These developments will raise an intriguing question in the future. What **First Amendment standard** will be used to govern the telcos once they are engaged in disseminating and originating information and programming services in a major way?[71] Will they be governed by a common carrier standard?[72] A **common carrier standard** means that the conduit is open to all comers with no editorial control by the carrier whatever. Such a standard is almost the paradigm of mandatory access since it means that use of the conduit cannot be denied on the basis of content.[73]

Another approach that could be applied to the telcos as they enter the information age would be to use the *Red Lion* standard. This standard permits a large measure of government regulation as well as substantial editorial control. Another option would be to apply the *Tornillo* standard when telcos act as originators or disseminators of video programming. Under this standard, they would be treated as publishers or editors rather than as common carriers.[74] Still another alternative would be to adopt the approach of the *Turner* court with

- **Electronic yellow pages**
  The video services offered by telephone companies (telcos) such as sports results, news services, financial market quotations, and entertainment advertising.

- **First Amendment standard for telcos**
  The question of whether telcos offering video programming should be held to a common carrier standard or have the editorial autonomy enjoyed by newspapers.

- **Common carrier standard**
  The legal approach used to describe the obligation of public utilities such as phone companies to their subscribers. As a common carrier, the phone company must transmit the messages of all subscribers without regard to the message.

respect to cable. If the regulation is content-neutral, the *O'Brien* standard applies. If the regulation is content-based, then the strict scrutiny standard applies.

The problem with applying the *Tornillo* or print media standard to the telcos is that complete control over entry to the conduit, as well as control over the content of the conduit, would then belong to the telcos. Because only one telco operates in a geographic area, the telco, given its economic strength, might be in a position to dominate the opinion process in that area.

So far the courts have not had to face these questions in any overall or ultimate sense. When courts have faced these issues in specialized situations, such as the "dial-a-porn" cases, they have tended to abandon the common carrier standard and treat the telcos as editors.[75] In such circumstances, the telco is empowered to become the ultimate censor. How much access for the public and for service providers can be afforded once the telcos enter into the origination and dissemination of information and programming in a substantial way? This is one of the most important unresolved issues that will confront the communications law of the future.

SUMMARY

The approach to the responsibilities imposed by law on the electronic media and the print media in this country can be described as divided—perhaps even schizophrenic. The public enjoy greater rights of access and reply to the electronic media than they do with respect to the print media. In the case of the electronic media, the law in certain circumstances confers some rights of access or reply on political candidates and members of the public. Section 315(a) of the Federal Communications Act gives political candidates equal opportunities to use a broadcast station. Section 312(a)(7) of the Communications Act provides federal political candidates with the right of "reasonable access" to broadcast time to promote their candidacy. If a person is attacked on broadcasting, the personal attack rules give him or her the right to respond in some circumstances. Despite the existence of these laws, the extent to which rights of access and reply obtain even in broadcasting should not be overstated. The fairness doctrine was abolished in 1987. Although the personal attack rules are still alive, they are rarely enforced.

The status of a public right of access to the print media is much easier to summarize. There is no such right. In *Miami Herald Publishing Co. v Tornillo*, the Supreme Court invalidated a Florida law giving a political candidate a right of reply to newspaper criticism of the candidate because such a right could chill free speech and was an invalid interference with editorial freedom.

Although the rights of access and reply are greater with respect to the broadcast media than to the print media, the Supreme Court has not charted a straight course even in this area. Indeed, the Supreme Court seems to give the public a right of access to the electronic media in one case only to restrict that right in the next. For example, in *Red Lion* in 1969, the Supreme Court

● Political editorializing rules

Rules issued by the FCC that provide that when a broadcaster editorializes against a political candidate, the candidate or a spokesperson must be afforded an opportunity to respond.

considered a First Amendment challenge to FCC policies, such as the fairness doctrine, the personal attack rules, and the **political editorializing rules,** that provided certain rights of access to the public. Relying in large part upon the "unique" nature of the broadcast medium and the scarcity rationale, the Court held that these policies were valid under the First Amendment.

But in *CBS v. DNC* in 1973, the Supreme Court held that the First Amendment itself could not be relied upon to force broadcasters to grant rights of access to the public. In *CBS v. FCC* in 1981, the Court, moving this time to the pro-access side of the pendulum, held that a law providing that federal political candidates may have "reasonable access" to broadcast time was valid under the First Amendment. Thus, Congress can grant limited rights of access to the broadcast media, but the First Amendment itself is not a source of rights of access to the electronic media.

Public access has probably enjoyed its most significant success in cable television rather than in over-the-air broadcasting. Cable television is the medium where public rights of access are currently most visible. The multi-channel capacity of cable has encouraged Congress in both 1984 and 1992 to specifically authorize cable systems to dedicate some of their channels for public access purposes. Finally, the desire of the regional Bells to enter into the dissemination and origination of information and video programming presents many novel, difficult, and unresolved issues. It is uncertain whether the telcos will be treated like broadcasters and cable and subjected to certain access responsibilities. Alternatively, telcos may be treated like the print media. In that case, telco decisions on what video programming to disseminate will be treated as editorial decisions rather than as acts of censorship.

In sum, if we compare the print media with the electronic media, we find that the rights of the communicator are paramount in the former while the rights of the communicator and the public are constantly being balanced against each other in the latter. Journalists, lawyers, and the citizenry at large must decide which system serves society best.

KEY TERMS

Right of reply
Right of access
Federal Communications Commission
Fairness doctrine
Scarcity rationale
First Amendment right of access to the electronic media
Reasonable access
Limited rights of access to the broadcast media
"Equal time"
Fairness doctrine abolition
Personal attack rules
Participatory media
Public access channels
Red Lion Standard

Tornillo Standard
Leased access channels
Mandatory PEG channels
Must-carry provisions
Standard of review for must-carry rules
Florida right of reply law
Voluntary access to the press mechanisms
Retraction statutes
Right of access to advertising
Public press
Telco entry into video programming
Electronic yellow pages
First Amendment standard for telcos
Common carrier standard
Political editorializing rules

CASE PROBLEMS

1. A "political" group called 21st Century has recently been formed in Chicago. Police officials and others charge that a criminal street gang called the Gangster Disciples, with approximately 30,000 members, is behind 21st Century. They further charge that the group wants political power to further the criminal activity of the Gangster Disciples. Suppose that 21st Century decides to dispute these charges, which have been repeated in both the local and the national broadcast media? 21st Century decides it wants to buy ten minutes of airtime on a Chicago television station. Does 21st Century have a right of access to airtime on the station? 21st Century's leaders want to explain the true nature of the organization, which they claim provides funds to help troubled youth acquire an education. Does your answer change if a candidate for office under the sponsorship of 21st Century seeks to buy ten minutes of airtime?

2. Suppose that popular radio talk show host Howard Stern has a retired U.S. military officer on his show. This officer says, among other things, that the Activist Faculty (a fictional group) has an agenda in regard to Haiti that differs markedly from that of the rest of the nation. He then goes on to say, in reference to a particular member of the group, "Bob wants us to go in for one reason—he expects to make a lot of money writing a book about what happened to all the dead American boys over there." "Bob" (Robert Smith) asks the radio station to allow him to make a reply. If the station refuses, is the FCC likely to rule that a personal attack entitled to a reply has taken place?

3. Jane Jones is running for reelection to the U.S. Senate. She strongly believes that it is time to take action in Bosnia to stop what she feels is genocide. She has asked a local television station network affiliate for fifteen minutes after the popular television show *Seinfeld*. Her proposed presentation includes scenes of a violent and gruesome nature, depicting acts of violence including murder, rape and numerous dead bodies. Can the station refuse to run the programming?

4. Gotham Cable Co. has applied for a cable franchise in Gotham City. The city says that it will enter into a franchise agreement with Gotham Cable if the cable operator agrees to dedicate one of its channels to public access. Gotham Cable would rather not have a public access channel. Can the city refuse to give a franchise to Gotham Cable unless it agrees to dedicate one of its channels to public access purposes?

5. The Revisionists, a group that challenges the occurrence of the Holocaust, want to take a half-page ad in a state university newspaper, the *Ivory Tower*. They are willing to pay as much as other groups have paid for similar space. Steve Summers, the editor of the *Ivory Tower*, while disagreeing with the Revisionists' views, thinks that the paper should run the ad. University administrators feel differently and exert pressure on Summers not to run the ad. The Ivory Tower ends up not running the ad. The Revisionists go to court to require the paper to run the ad. What should the result be? Does it matter whether Summers or university officials made the final decision not to run the ad?

ENDNOTES

1. Jerome A. Barron, "Access to the Press—A New First Amendment Right," *Harvard Law Review* 80:1641 (1967).

2. Edwin Baker, "Scope of the First Amendment Freedom of Speech," *U.C.L.A. Law Review* 25:964, 986–987 (1978).

3. *Red Lion Broadcasting v. FCC*, 395 U.S. 367, 89 S.Ct. 1794 (1969).

4. *Id.* at 389, 89 S.Ct. at 1806.

5. *Id.* at 390.

6. *CBS v. Democratic National Committee*, 412 U.S. 94, 93 S.Ct. 2080 (1973).

7. *Id.* at 121, 93 S.Ct. at 2095.

8. *Id.* at 124, 93 S.Ct. at 2097.

9. *Id.* at 196, 93 S.Ct. at 2133.

10. *Id.* at 201, 93 S.Ct. at 2136.

11. Section 312(a)(7).

12. 418 U.S. 241, 94 S.Ct. 2831 (1974).

13. *CBS, Inc. v. FCC,* 453 U.S. 367, 101 S.Ct. 2813 (1981).

14. *Id.* at 396, 101 S.Ct. at 2829.

15. *Id.*

16. *Id.* at 397, 101 S.Ct. at 2830.

17. *Gillett Communications of Atlanta, Inc. v. Becker,* 807 F.Supp. 757, 20 Med.L.Rptr. 1947, 1951 (1992).

18. 47 U.S.C.A. § 315.

19. 18 U.S.C.A. § 1464 provides: "Whoever utters any obscene, indecent or profane language by means of radio communications shall be fined not more than $10,000 or imprisoned not more than two years, or both.

20. See *Gillett Communications of Atlanta, Inc. v. Becker,* 807 F.Supp., 757, 20 Med.L.Rptr. 1947 (1992).

21. *Id.*

22. *Syracuse Peace Council v. Television Station WTVH,* 2 F.C.C.R. 5043, 5057 (1987), *affirmed after remand, Syracuse Peace Council v. FCC,* 867 F.2d 654 (D.C.Cir. 1989), *cert. denied Syracuse Peace Council v. FCC,* 493 U.S. 1019, 110 S.Ct. 717 (1990).

23. *Letter to Professor David Berkman,* 6 F.C.C.R. 6640 (1991). See also *Letter to John Price, Esq.,* 6 F.C.C.R. 7122 (1991) where the FCC refused to order a reply since the radio station involved had offered the complainant reply time on two previous occasions.
    Much of the discussion in this section of the chapter is based on Jerome A. Barron, "The Right of Reply to the Media in the United States— Resistance and Resurgence," *Hastings Communication and Entertainment Law Journal* 15:1 (1992).

24. 571 F.Supp. 976 (D.C.R.I. 1983), vacated as moot 773 F.2d 382 (1st Cir. 1985).

25. *Id.* at 985.

26. *Id.* at 986.

27. *Erie Telecommunications, Inc, v. City of Erie,* 659 F.Supp. 580 (W.D.Pa. 1987).

28. *Id.* at 599.

29. *Group W Cable, Inc. v. Santa Cruz,* 669 F.Supp. 954, 968 (N.D.Cal. 1987).

30. *Id.*

31. *Century Federal, Inc. v. City of Palo Alto,* 710 F.Supp. 1552 (N.D.Cal. 1987).

32. 47 U.S.C.A. § 532(a) (Supp. III 1985).

33. *Telesat Cablevision, Inc. v. City of Riviera Beach,* 773 F.Supp. 383 (S.D.Fla. 1991).

34. *Id.* at 411.

35. *Id.* at 412.

36. See H.R. Rep. No. 934, 98th Cong. 2d Sess. 30, *reprinted in* 1984 U.S. Code Cong. & Admin. News at 4667, cited in *Telesat Cablevision, Inc. v. City of Riviera Beach,* 773 F.Supp. 383 (S.D.Fla. 1991).

37. P.L. No. 102–385, 106 Stat. 1460 (1992).

38. 835 F.Supp. 1 (D.D.C. 1993).

39. *Id.* at 6.

40. 391 U.S. 367, 88 S.Ct. 1673 (1968). See the discussion of the *O'Brien* standard in Chapter 1.

41. *Daniels Cablevision, Inc. v. United States,* 835 F.Supp. 1, 6 (D.D.C. 1993).

42. *Id.* at 7.

43. ____ U.S. ____, 114 S.Ct. 2445 (1994).

44. See §§ 4 and 5 of the Cable Television Consumer Protection and Competition Act of 1992, P.L. 102–385, 106 Stat. 1460.

45. *Turner* at ____, 114 S.Ct. at 2461.

46. 418 U.S. 241, 94 S.Ct. 2831 (1974).

47. *Tornillo v. Miami Herald,* 287 So.2d 78 (Fla. 1973).

48. *Miami Herald Publishing Co. v. Tornillo,* 418 U.S. 241, 94 S.Ct. 2831 (1974).

49. *Id.* at 249, 94 S.Ct. at 2835.

50. *Id.* at 250, 94 S.Ct. at 2836.

51. *Id.* at 258, 94 S.Ct. at 2839.

52. An Ohio trial court case in 1980 is an exception to this generalization. But the Ohio retraction statute was unusual; it permitted the retraction to be

written by the defamed party. The Ohio trial court declared: "Ohio's retraction statutes clearly result in the coerced publication of particular views and thus violate the First Amendment." See *Beacon Journal v. Landsdowne,* 11 Med.L.Rptr. 1094 (1984).

53. See generally Jerome A. Barron, "The Search for Media Accountability," *Suffolk University Law Review* 19:789 (1985). [A right of reply would be a remedy in lieu of damages in a libel action if the media defendant consented.] John G. Fleming, "Retraction and Reply: Alternative Remedies for Defamation," *University of British Columbia Law Review* 12:15 (1978); George E. Frasier, "Note: An Alternative to the General-Damage Award for Defamation," *Stanford Law Review* 20:504 (1968). [Plaintiff can choose reply or retraction in lieu of damages in a libel action whether the plaintiff agrees to that choice or not.]

54. A local political action committee (PAC) failed in its attempt to require a newspaper to publish a paid political advertisement submitted to the newspaper by the PAC. *Citizen Awareness v. Calhoun County Publishing Co., Inc.,* 185 W.Va. 168, 406 S.E.2d 65 (1991).

55. *Union Food and Commercial Workers v. Ottaway Newspapers, Inc.,* 19 Med.L.Rptr. 1792 (D. Conn. 1991).

56. *Lorain Journal Co. v. United States,* 342 U.S. 143, 72 S.Ct. 181 (1951).

57. *Home Placement Service v. Providence Journal,* 682 F.2d 274, 8 Med.L.Rptr. 1881, (lst Cir. 1982).

58. *Lee v. Board of Regents,* 441 F.2d 1257, 1 Med.L.Rptr. 1947 (7th Cir. 1971).

59. *Mississippi Gay Alliance v. Goudelock,* 536 F.2d 1073 (5th Cir. 1976).

60. *United States v. Western Electric Co.,* 552 F.Supp. 131 (D.D.C. 1982), *affirmed sub nom., Maryland v. United States,* 460 U.S. 1001, 103 S.Ct. 1240 (1983).

61. *United States v. Western Electric Co.,* 767 F.Supp. 308 (D.D.C. 1991).

62. 830 F.Supp. 909 (E.D.Va. 1993), *app. pending.*

63. See 47 U.S.C.A. § 533(b).

64. 830 F.Supp. at 927.

65. *Id.*

66. *Id.*

67. *Id.* at 928.

68. *Id.* at 931.

69. *Id.* at 931–932.

70. *Chesapeake & Potomac Tel. Co. v. United States,* 42 F.3d 181 (4th Cir. 1994).

71. Much of the discussion in this section is based on Jerome A. Barron, "The Telco, the Common Carrier Model and the First Amendment—The 'Dial-A-Porn' Precedent," *Rutgers Computer & Technology Law Journal* 19:101 (1993).

72. The late Ithiel de Sola Pool argued that the common carrier tradition was entirely consistent with the First Amendment. He emphasized the participatory and inclusive character of the common carrier tradition:

"The traditional law of a free press rests on the assumption that paper, ink, and presses are in sufficient abundance that, if government simply keeps hands off, people will be able to express themselves freely. The law of common carriage rests on the opposite assumption that, in the absence of regulation, the carrier will have enough monopoly power to deny citizens the right to communicate. *The rules against discrimination are designed to ensure access to the means of communication in situations where these means, unlike the printing press, consist of a single monopolistic network.*" (Emphasis supplied.)

Ithiel De Sola Pool, *Technologies of Freedom* (Cambridge: Harvard University Press, 1983), p. 106.

73. For the view that when telcos disseminate and originate information, they necessarily have to make choices and, therefore, should be treated as editors rather than as common carriers, see Daniel Brenner, "Telephone Company Entry into Video Services: A First Amendment Analysis," Notre Dame Law Review 67:97, 138–140 (1991).

74. For a discussion of the range of First Amendment approaches that might be relevant when the telco operates as an information and video service provider, see Angela J. Campbell, "Publish or Carriage: Approaches to Analyzing the First Amendment Rights of Telephone Companies," *North Carolina Law Review* 70:1071, 1078–1079 (1992).

75. See *Carlin Communications, Inc. v. Mountain States Telephone & Telegraph,* 827 F.2d 1291 (9th Cir. 1987), *cert. denied* 485 U.S. 1029, 108 S.Ct. 1586 (1988). See also *Carlin Communications, Inc. v. Southern Bell Telephone & Telegraph Co.,* 802 F.2d 1352 (11th Cir. 1986). In both of these cases, telcos were permitted by courts to refuse to carry "dial-a-porn" messages even though under conventional common carrier law theory, they would have had to transmit these messages.

Advertising: Law and Regulation

COMMERCIAL SPEECH

Advertising is part of a larger content area labeled "commercial speech" by bar, bench, and legal commentators. Historically, it has been held by the courts to be less deserving of full First Amendment protection than forms of speech that deal with political or public affairs. The U.S. Supreme Court expressed this distinction clearly in a 1978 case:

> Commercial speech enjoys a limited measure of protection commensurate with its subordinate position in the scale of First Amendment values [and is subject to] modes of regulation that might be impermissible in the realm of noncommercial expression.[1]

One might expect that in a market economy advertising would be considered very much a public affair, but not necessarily. The debate in legal circles and on the Supreme Court goes something like this: Justice John Paul Stevens emphasizes the value of commercial speech to economic decision making, which is part of almost everyone's daily routine; Justice Sandra Day O'Connor, on the other hand, sees a need for the regulation of commercial speech where self-regulation fails and there is no standardization in the quality of a product or service, placing the buyer at the mercy of the seller.[2]

Both courts and scholars argue that to protect advertising in all its forms as zealously as one would protect speech about political affairs would be to trivialize the core values that the First Amendment is designed to nurture. And it would make the citizenry cynical about the importance of free speech. Moreover, the Supreme Court in a famous footnote observed that commercial speech may be more "durable" than other forms of speech and that "since advertising is the *sine qua non* of commercial profits, there is little likelihood of its being chilled by proper regulation and foregone entirely.[3]

● *Sine qua non*
A thing or condition that is indispensable.

The *Central Hudson* Test

The conditions attached to the constitutional defense of advertising, then, which are unthinkable in the political realm and irrelevant if a commercial message has a political or public interest tilt to it, are best represented by the four-part test for the defense of commercial speech that the Supreme Court set out in the 1980 case *Central Hudson Gas & Electric Corp. v. Public Service Commission.*[4] In that case the Court invalidated a state regulation prohibiting advertising that promoted the use of electricity. But to earn First Amendment protection, said the Court:

- **Central Hudson Gas & Electric Corp. v. Public Service Commission**
The 1980 case that set down the four-part test for the First Amendment protection of commercial speech.

1. Commercial speech must concern a lawful activity and *not* be misleading;

2. The state must prove the existence of a substantial state interest to be served by regulation;

3. The regulation must advance that interest; and

4. It must be no more extensive than necessary to serve that interest.

On the last point—a kind of "least restrictive means test"—the Court has spoken of the necessity of a "fit" between the legislature's goals and the means chosen to reach those goals.[5] It contemplates a narrowly drawn statute. An example of a "fit" was a university rule that prohibited private enterprises from doing business in university facilities. Campus police interrupted a "Tupperware party" in a dormitory at the State University of New York. Some students claimed a violation of their First Amendment rights. SUNY argued that its rule promoted educational rather than commercial activities that could exploit students. The Supreme Court agreed. "What our decisions require," wrote Justice Antonin Scalia for the Court, "is a 'fit' between the legislature's ends and the means chosen to accomplish those ends."[6] Any "substantial" state interest would take the place of the "least restrictive means" test. This weakens the fourth part of the original *Central Hudson* test.

Conversely, a postal law prohibiting the mailing of "(a)ny unsolicited advertisement of matter which is designed, adapted, or intended for preventing conception" was struck down by a unanimous Supreme Court. None of *Central Hudson's* conditions applied.[7] But the material still qualified as commercial speech because a commercial transaction was envisioned; the Court did not want false and misleading advertising in other cases to ride on the back of political content such as the discussion in this case of how venereal disease might be prevented by the use of condoms.

Nevertheless, much of the debate about what constitutional protection advertising deserves has revolved around the *Central Hudson* test. So far, the Supreme Court has wavered on and tinkered with the four-part test but has not abandoned it, reinforcing the conclusions that advertising can be regulated but not banned outright, and that its protection, although waxing and waning, has increased incrementally over the years.

One perplexing example of tinkering with broad implications was the Court's upholding of a Puerto Rican law that prohibited the advertising of casino gambling within the commonwealth, but encouraged such advertising to tourists. In *Posadas de Puerto Rico Associates v. Tourism Co.*, the Court held that Puerto Rico's interest in protecting its own citizens from gambling was "substantial" enough because casino gambling attracted prostitutes and drug dealers. It apparently felt no similar obligation to other Americans who visit Puerto Rico.[8]

Similarly, late in its October 1992 term, the Court, reversing lower federal courts, held in *United States v. Edge Broadcasting Co.*[9] that a federal regulation prohibiting the broadcasting of lottery ads, not only within a state that forbids lotteries, but also in adjoining states that have legalized them, met the requirements of the *Central Hudson* test. The Court found a substantial federal governmental interest in balancing the lottery policies of different states. The restrictions would reasonably accomplish this; in other words, they "fit."

Although the speech involved in both cases was neither false nor deceptive, the Court's action appears to be premised on the view that gambling is a "vice" that Congress or a state legislature could or might wish to curtail. It is apparently of no significance that enforcement may be impossible and that a large proportion of society's lawmakers elsewhere have made gambling of various kinds not only legal but "respectable."

A long-standing federal law also prohibits the mailing of any publication containing an advertisment of a **lottery.** New federal laws, however, have eased the situation considerably. Occasional lotteries operated by nonprofit organizations and legal in their own communities and lotteries conducted by Indian tribes are exempt from the law. So are lists of prizes and prize winners appearing in news stories and editorial copy.

In a different dimension of the issue, when a statute forbidding certified public accountants from advertising did not in any way advance a state's interest in protecting people from fraud or invasions of privacy or in maintaining the independence of CPAs, the Supreme Court said it violated the First Amendment.[10] In other words, the law didn't "fit" the intended legislative purpose.

The Right to Refuse Advertising

While the government and its agencies must carefully weigh the degree to which their laws and regulations may interfere with commercial speech, publishers and broadcasters are under no such strictures. Their **right to refuse** advertising, for example, is near absolute. Business enterprises, labor unions, and political action groups continue to test this hypothesis but are thwarted by First Amendment defenses: "(A)ny . . . compulsion to publish that which 'reason' tells [a newspaper] should not be published" is unconstitutional, said a federal district court in *Person v. New York Post.*[11]

Among the few exceptions are antitrust violations, notably where the advertiser is a competitor of the media company,[12] or where a breach of contract has occurred.[13] In the former case, a monopoly newspaper refused to accept an ad from a direct competitor for real estate advertising. At the same time, a publisher can be penalized for an ad that does direct and grievous harm to an

● **Lottery**
A scheme involving the three elements of prize, chance, and consideration, the third element requiring a player or participant to give up something of value such as time or money.

● **Right to refuse**
Advertising media have an absolute right to refuse any ad submitted to them, except in some antitrust situations or where there has been a breach of contract.

individual. For example, a "gun-for-hire" ad led to murder. The person placing the ad had offered to consider "any job" and promised confidentiality. The publisher of the ad, whom the court called "imprudent," was held liable to the victim's sons.[14]

Media managers are not responsible, however, for false or deceptive, advertising or for injuries resulting from defective products unless the newspaper, magazine, or broadcaster is a party to the creation of the ad. Nor do they have a duty to investigate each and every advertiser and message. **Indemnification clauses** are common in media rate cards and in advertising contracts as a further protection. Typical language might be the following:

> The advertiser and/or advertising agency agrees to defend and indemnify the publisher against any and all liability, loss, or expenses arising from claims of libel, unfair competition, unfair trade practices, infringement of trademarks, copyrights, trade names, patents or proprietary rights, or violation of rights of privacy resulting from the publication of advertiser's advertisement.

Although it happens frequently, advertisers may not legally conspire to withdraw advertising from a newspaper for economic reasons; in other words, they may not attempt to put a publication out of business. Political boycotts, on the other hand, are permitted.[15] It is not clear how the courts are to distinguish between "economic" and "political" motivation, a distinction that is no less difficult to make than that between commercial and noncommercial speech.

Government entities face even greater strictures in this respect. A federal appeals court said a city could not withdraw its advertising to punish critical commentary,[16] and publications that are state owned or sponsored may not prohibit the running of ads on particular controversial issues. A state college newspaper, for example, could not single out abortion ads for rejection, said an Oregon court.[17] Similarly, a school board was taken to task by a federal appeals court for refusing to allow publication of an antidraft ad in a high school newspaper when almost everyone and everything else had access.[18] Since *Hazelwood*, a 1988 Supreme Court ruling,[19] however, school districts have been given broad discretion in deciding what goes into secondary school newspapers. In *Planned Parenthood of S. Nevada, Inc. v. Clark County School District*,[20] for example, a divided federal appeals court held that high school newspapers that are part of the curriculum are **nonpublic forums**. Therefore, reasonable judgments could be made as to what content may be excluded.

FALSEHOOD, DECEPTION, AND UNFAIRNESS

The regulation of advertising grew out of a general assault on the excesses of *laissez-faire* capitalism at the turn of the century and the cynical doctrine of *caveat emptor* (let the buyer beware). Stimulated by the writing of the muckrakers, notably Samuel Hopkins Adams's 1906 *Colliers* series on patent medicines, "The Great American Fraud," the

---

● Indemnification clause
A statement, usually in a contract for the purchase of time or space, in which the seller indicates that he or she is not responsible for any damage or injury or lawsuits resulting from the use of the advertised product or service.

● Nonpublic forum
A place traditionally not thought to be suitable for speech activities, unless by invitation, e.g., a private home.

● *Laissez faire*
Letting people do what they choose to do, especially in the world of business and economics.

● *Caveat emptor*
Let the buyer beware, the state of being victimized by a seller.

regulatory movement took root in passage of the Pure Food and Drug Act in 1906 and the creation of the Federal Trade Commission (FTC) in 1914.

Other forces were also at work in this period. The advertising business itself had called for "truth in advertising" as early as 1911. A year later the **Better Business Bureau** took shape. States began adopting a code that *Printers' Ink*, a trade magazine, had fashioned.

At first, the FTC was primarily concerned with reinforcing the antitrust provisions of the Sherman and Clayton Acts. The **FTC Act** declared unfair methods of competition in commerce to be unlawful. Its purpose was to promote the "preservation of an environment which would foster the liberty to compete." In its early years, the act was used by the courts to protect competitors against each other's false and deceptive advertising: the protection of consumers was incidental.

Today the FTC through its Bureau of Consumer Protection monitors the advertising business—although it sometimes seems like a gnat corralling an elephant. Theoretically, substantiation is required for all factual claims made in ads. Implied falsehoods are scrutinized. Since 1914, the five-member commission has had a broad congressional mandate to monitor false, deceptive, and unfair advertising. Since the 1938 Wheeler-Lea Amendments to the FTC Act, consumers have been protected. This authorization is contained in Sections 5, 12, and 15a of the 1914 Federal Trade Commission Act and in Section 43(a) of the 1946 Lanham Trademark Act. The latter is a separate law intended primarily to protect business competitors from one another by enabling them to obtain injunctions against deceptive advertising as an unfair trade practice. In 1989, the **Lanham Trademark Law Revision Act** of 1988 became law. It provides broad remedies to those hurt by false advertising or by the disparagement of another's goods, services, or commercial activities by misrepresentation, deception as to affiliation, sponsorship, or origin—as long as the offending words have a strictly commercial purpose. For First Amendment reasons, careful judicial review is required of any FTC order regulating advertising to ensure that it does not to infringe upon more highly protected forms of speech. Federal courts disagree on whether individual consumers have standing to sue under the revised Lanham Act. The commission may also challenge unfair or anticompetitive practices that violate the Sherman and Clayton antitrust laws.

A deregulatory mood in Washington beginning in 1980 left uncertain whether the jurisdiction of the FTC still extended to advertising deemed "unfair." In 1981, Congress temporarily withdrew from the commission authority to base trade regulation rules on *unfair* as opposed to false and deceptive advertising. Immediately, the D.C. Circuit Court of Appeals found Congress's attempt to run the agency by legislation an unconstitutional violation of the separation of powers doctrine.[21]

The FTC's difficulties and the ultimate demise of the unfairness standard were partly due to the earlier **"Kid-Vid"** rule-making proceedings. Under the promise of a trade regulation rule, the commission had examined the effects on presumably vulnerable children of television advertising, notably the advertising of sugared cereals and toys.[22] After congressional intervention, a docile commission said lack of resources had forced it to conclude its search for legal

---

● **Better Business Bureau**
An organization founded in 1912 to keep on file complaints brought against businesses by those who have used their products or services.

● **FTC Act**
The 1911 federal law that established the Federal Trade Commission and made unfair methods of competition in commerce unlawful.

● **Lanham Trademark Law Revision Act**
A 1989 federal law that provides remedies for those hurt by false advertising, as well as protecting competitors from one another.

● **Kid-Vid**
The name given to hearings before the Federal Trade Commission intended to explore how to protect children from the advertising of certain products such as toys and sugared cereals.

Trade Regulation Rules

Rules developed by the Federal Trade Commission to protect consumers against false and deceptive advertising and marketing practices by defining the outer boundaries of behavior for specific goods and services.

Reasonable person

A standard of culpability that is just, proper, ordinary, usual, or reasonable, or based on the views of a person with those characteristics.

Puffery

In advertising, exaggeration for effect, sensationalizing, phantasizing.

Testimonial

Celebrity endorsement of a product or service.

Demonstration

Showing in an advertisement how to use a product or what that product can do.

and policy solutions to the problems of children's advertising. Shortly thereafter and in the same political environment, the Federal Communications Commission (FCC) suspended the fairness doctrine in broadcasting.

The FTC also attempts to enforce an array of specific consumer protection laws. *Industry Guides* and **Trade Regulation Rules** developed by the FTC, the latter having the force of law, are unusually detailed. They are also subject to congressional scrutiny. These rules define with specificity the outer boundaries of product or service advertising or marketing practices that could constitute false or deceptive trade practices (bait and switch, for example, promising one kind of product or service as a premium or come-on and substituting something else once the consumer has responded).

A **"reasonable person"** standard is applied somewhat subjectively by the FTC to advertising claims. However, the line between **puffery** and factual misrepresentation or serious omission is often hard to draw. Terms such as "environmentally friendly," "stupendous," "lite," "fresh," and "nutritious," the daily stuff of television commercials, may get special scrutiny from the FTC. But the commission first draws the line, and courts defer to its expertise and experience in defining the words "false and deceptive." Higher standards may be required where child consumers are concerned and where the health and safety of the public may be at stake.

Generally, the commission and courts have been especially sensitive to misleading demonstrations, testimonials, and endorsements. The classic case involving a demonstration began in 1959 when Colgate-Palmolive and its advertising agency ran television ads suggesting, by means of a Plexiglas mockup, that a shaving cream product could shave sandpaper. The FTC stuck to its claim that viewers would be misled into thinking they were seeing an actual experiment all the way to the Supreme Court. The Court upheld the commission.[23] In 1978, the FTC for the first time was able to get a product endorser to be personally accountable for advertising claims. Using its injunctive, complaint, and consent powers to challenge the alleged deceptive marketing practices of an acne treatment, the commission got celebrity Pat Boone to agree to pay part of any restitution to consumers that would be ordered in the case and to make a reasonable inquiry before endorsing products in the future.[24]

Human Safety and Cigarette Advertising

Substantial test data are required to support claims that involve matters of human safety that consumers cannot possibly verify for themselves. Advertisers, therefore, are expected to substantiate claims made for these kinds of products and services.

The difficulties involved in carrying out this mandate are well illustrated by the seemingly endless debate on cigarette advertising. As early as 1964 in its "Statement of Basis and Purpose of Trade Regulation Rule 408, Unfair or Deceptive Advertising and Labeling of Cigarettes in Relation to the Health Hazards of Smoking,"[25] the FTC spoke of practices that "offend public policy," because they are "immoral, unethical, oppressive or unscrupulous" and cause "substantial injury to consumers or competitors or other businessmen." That was the same year the Surgeon General issued his first report linking smoking to cancer and other deadly diseases. Warning labels on cigarette packaging and cigarette advertising followed, a form of compelled speech that would not be condoned in the political realm. In 1969, after a short-lived period of **counter-advertising** under the fairness doctrine (one anti-smoking ad on radio and TV for every six commercials), Congress banned tobacco advertising on the electronic media altogether. The FTC, FCC, and the National Association of Broadcasters agreed with this move. A federal district court upheld the congressional ban.[26] The tobacco industry switched to advertising in print media, expending billions with no threat of counteradvertising.

> ● **Counteradvertising**
> Advertising that directly rebuts a message already presented.

On a broader First Amendment scale, the debate continues on whether the advertising of documentably harmful products can be banned when it is legal to manufacture and sell those products. Tobacco and liquor are the two best examples. Outlawing such products, as Prohibition attempted to do with liquor, is unlikely since that experiment turned out to be a social disaster. In 1985, a federal appeals court did find a cigarette manufacturer's use of FTC test results in its advertising to be false and misleading.[27] A year later, the FTC got another tobacco company to enter into a consent decree, admitting no violations but agreeing not to misrepresent scientific studies in future ads.[28] At this point, of course, one must ask whether **editorial ads** discussing the pros and cons of smoking or the validity and reliability of scientific studies constitute commercial or noncommercial speech. If the latter, they are not subject to FTC regulation. If the former, they have at least partial First Amendment protection. Not without difficulty, the FTC and the courts found that the speech in the "scientific studies" case was indeed commercial speech. The ads referred to a specific product, talked about its attributes, and had an economic motivation. As an aside, one might ask whether it demeans the civil rights movement to analogize the *New York Times v. Sullivan* advertorial to the tobacco industry's ads disputing scientific research into smoking and health?

> ● **Editorial advertising**
> Advertising in which the primary purpose is to promote a social, political, or cultural idea.

Numerous bills have been introduced in Congress to put pressure on tobacco company advertising. The *Posadas* ruling by the Supreme Court may allow bans on the advertising of legal but harmful products and services. In the meantime, local ordinances have banned tobacco advertising in certain places such as New York buses, subways, and platforms. Counteradvertising, but on a much larger scale than its initial use against smoking, may ultimately prove to be the best solution.

THE REGULATORY PROCESS

Though the regulatory process is complex and time-consuming, it is designed to secure maximum input from all interested parties. For example, an initial notice of proposed rule making by the FTC, leading to *Trade Regulation Rules*, includes (1) the terms or substance of the proposal or a description of the subjects and issues involved, (2) the legal authority under which the rule is proposed, (3) particular reasons for the rule, and (4) an invitation to all interested persons to raise questions within the framework of the proposal. The commission invites written comments from manufacturers, advertisers, and the public and holds hearings on the proposal. Petitions are entertained for later modifications in or challenges to the issues before the commission. Finally, a staff report and a report from the presiding officer, who may be an administrative law judge, go to the commission. The commission may hold open meetings before any new rules are laid down.

Once rules are made, violations of the rules are uncovered either through public or competitor complaints or through commission investigations. An FTC advisory committee will recommend which complaints seem to have merit. At an early point, the FTC may waive a right to bring court action in return for an advertiser's or advertising agency's agreement to provide consumer or competitor relief through a **letter of compliance** or, in a more serious vein, a **consent agreement.** While such agreements do not constitute an admission of guilt, they do carry the force of law with respect to future actions and have the same effect as an FTC adjudication. In addition, they allow an advertiser to avoid both negative publicity and expensive litigation. Further violations of these orders may result in a **cease-and-desist order** after a hearing before an administrative law judge and a ruling by the full commission. These actions may lead to heavy civil penalties of up to $10,000 per day per violation. Some advertisers have found it more profitable, however, to pay the fines than to interrupt lucrative advertising schemes. Most cases, however, end before any penalties need be imposed.

The Magnuson-Moss Warranty–FTC Improvement Act of 1975 greatly expedited consumer relief. Consumer protection rules are now directly enforceable in a U.S. district court with civil penalties available for noncompliance. Industry-wide *Trade Regulation Rules* covering similar but competitive products or services may be enforced in the same manner. Dishonest or fraudulent trade practices—more serious than practices that are deceptive but less serious than those amounting to criminal fraud—still require administrative proceedings before an administrative law judge. These may lead to dismissal of the complaint or to a final cease-and-desist order. The full commission will review the results before any court actions are taken.

Violations of cease-and-desist orders or other final orders of the commission justify the grant of **temporary restraining orders** (temporary injunctions) in U.S. district courts, especially where public health and safety are involved. Permanent injunctions are possible but uncommon. Advertisers may appeal either type of order to a federal court of appeal. Violators ultimately may have to pay damages to injured consumers as well as civil penalties.

A much more informal avenue is also open to advertisers. They make seek staff opinion letters or advisory opinions from the commission as to the legality of a proposed advertising campaign or series of ads. *Industry Guides* developed by the FTC are also available. They are standards of advertising interpreting federal laws that apply across an industry, for example, hearing devices, insurance, funeral services, chiropractors. Continued inattention to these guides can lead to formal FTC action, although Industry Guides are not taken as seriously as Trade Regulation Rules.

● Letter of compliance
An advertiser's agreement with the FTC not to repeat advertising that has resulted in complaints from consumers or competitors.

● Consent decree agreement
An agency agreement with an advertiser not to run certain ads in the future, but with no admission of fault on the part of the advertiser.

● Cease-and-desist order
An order from an administrative agency such as the FTC, similar to a court injunction.

● Temporary restraining order (TRO)
A judge's order prohibiting certain action prior to a hearing on the matter.

● *Industry Guides*
Guidelines as to standards of advertising across an industry based on the FTC's interpretation of federal laws.

Advertising may also be regulated by about twenty additional federal agencies including the Securities and Exchange Commission, the Alcohol and Tobacco Tax Division of the Internal Revenue Service, the Civil Aeronautics Board, the Interstate Commerce Commission, and the Federal Power Commission.

Most states have parallel statutes and regulatory agencies that tend to follow federal guidelines. And there are scores of state and local regulations governing, for example, the size and placement of billboards, as well as laws governing the advertising of myriad goods and services. In recent years, some state attorneys general have pursued cases of consumer fraud and deception more vigorously than in the past.

Corrective Advertising

If the FTC cannot persuade an advertiser to make an **affirmative disclosure** to overcome deception in an ad, a corrective ad may be ordered, although this happens infrequently. Corrective advertising has had its ups and downs in the past twenty years. The movement reached its zenith in 1975 when the full commission upheld an administrative law judge's order forbidding Warner-Lambert, maker of Listerine, from advertising unless every ad it ran included the following language:

> Contrary to prior advertising, Listerine will not help prevent colds or sore throats or lessen their severity.

The corrective advertising was to continue until the company had spent $10 million on Listerine advertising, an amount roughly equal to the annual Listerine ad budget for the years 1962 to 1974. The D.C. Circuit Court of Appeals affirmed the commission's ruling but with the words "contrary to prior advertising" deleted.[29] At the time this was considered a victory for advertisers because the correction had lost its retrospective clout.

Corrective ads are rare. With references to past advertising deleted, they have little more effect than the affirmative disclosures sometimes ordered by the FTC.

Comparative advertising, if truthful, can be more successful, at least until it becomes what in a brief but failed experiment was called *counteradvertising,* a more confrontational and cacophonous disagreement among competing advertisers. Ideally, a fair and truthful comparison of goods and services is what the First Amendment contemplates. Some courts and the FTC have therefore endorsed comparative advertising. Too often, and in spite of FTC and congressional directives prohibiting misrepresentations or omissions of fact, comparative advertising turns into disparagement or unfair competition and provides little useful information to the consumer. The result is often consumer confusion such as that created by the manufacturers of pain relievers like Anacin, Tylenol, and others, who have been suing one another for decades. If advertisers are not suing one another, they are using an industry complaints process, discussed below.

● **Affirmative disclosure**
A request from the FTC that an advertiser admit to a deception or a falsehood before ordering a corrective ad.

● **Comparative advertising**
Advertising messages that attempt to compare, usually negatively, or distinguish similar products from one another.

Self-Regulation

● **National Advertising Review Board (NARB)** Part of a self-regulatory system in advertising that acts upon complaints from industry about truth and accuracy in national advertising.

Spearheading self-regulation in advertising is the **National Advertising Review Board (NARB)**, which acts upon industry, but not consumer, complaints about truth and accuracy in national advertising. The board's membership comprises national advertisers, advertising agencies, and representatives of the public. It is sponsored by the American Advertising Federation, the American Association of Advertising Agencies, the Association of National Advertisers, and the Council of Better Business Bureaus. Direct mail and telemarketing associations have similar review boards.

● **National Advertising Division (NAD)** Staff of the Council of Better Business Bureaus screen complaints before they move on to the NARB. A query from NAD can lead to modification of an unsubstantiated advertising claim.

Complaints are handled initially by the staff of the Council of Better Business Bureaus. They are called the **National Advertising Division (NAD)**. A query from NAD can lead major national advertisers to modify or discontinue unsubstantiated advertising claims. NAD fields about 150 complaints annually, and advertisers are found to be at fault in at least half of them. Compliance is nearly perfect. NAD monitors and advises and, in unresolved cases, carries appeals to the National Advertising Review Board. If an advertiser remains unrepentant after the NARB reaches an adverse decision, the board will notify the appropriate governmental agency. There is seldom any need for such draconian action.

Individual newspapers, magazines, broadcast stations, networks, and other media have their own advertising acceptability or broadcast standards departments. There is disagreement as to how successful or sincere these self-regulatory bodies have been. Self-regulation grew in part as a defense against government regulation prior to First Amendment protection being extended to commercial speech.

LEGAL OR PUBLIC NOTICE ADVERTISING

● **Legal advertising** The means by which government communicates formally with the citizenry. Also called public notice advertising.

Legal or public notice **advertising** is a means by which government communicates with the citizenry. It began with the publication of the *Oxford Gazette* (later the *London Gazette*) in 1665 to convey the thoughts of the king and to answer such questions as: What are the laws? When will one's rights or property be affected by the action of local government? How is government being conducted? How is tax money being used? Those questions are still relevant.

In every state, laws define the classifications of information that are to be published and how they are to be presented. Examples of typical publications include statutes and ordinances, articles of incorporation, registration of titles, probate notices, bankruptcies, delinquent taxes, notices of elections, taxes, bids for public works, and appropriation of public funds. In many states, the proceedings of county boards, town councils, and school boards, for example, may be published in summary form.

State laws also define the qualifications that newspapers must possess to qualify for legal advertising and how they are to be chosen for the task. These requirements will depend upon some combination of the following factors: location where published or printed; paid subscription; required frequency; years published; circulation; second-class permit; and format and type (title, size, pages, and other technical elements).

In some states, the maximum rate charged for publication of a public notice may not exceed the lowest or the highest classified rate paid by commercial advertisers for comparable space. Some state laws further require that cash discounts, multiple insertion discounts, and similar benefits extended to the newspaper's regular customers be available to governmental entities. Sometimes a higher rate is set for material in tabular form.

Other states calculate their charge for legal advertising by column inch, column line, column, line, word number, display rate, or national rate. Rates may be determined by the newspaper's established rates (16 states), the market rate (12 states) or a statute that sets a market rate (2 states), population (3 states), or newspaper circulation (4 states). In 13 states the rate is tied to a standard charge (maximum, minimum, or fixed) per insertion. Some states have mechanisms for rate increases.

Legal or public notice advertising is an integral part of the democratic process. Surveys indicate that readers overwhelmingly agree and that public notices are read by a substantial segment of the newspaper audience.

SUMMARY

The tension between the First Amendment and the regulation of commercial speech and advertising has led to a substantial volume of case law covering everything from fair housing and fair employment to political and professional advertising, with, for example, eyeglasses, tobacco, gasoline, automobiles, and funeral services ads in between. The law and regulation of advertising remain a complex and fluid matter. Federal courts have often noted that all prior restraints on publication are suspect and that remedies, even for false and deceptive advertising, must go no further than necessary. Certainly, commercial speech has more First Amendment protection now than it has had in the past.

KEY TERMS

Sine qua non
Central Hudson Gas & Electric Corp. v. Public Service Commission
Lottery
Right to refuse
Indemnification clause
Nonpublic forum
Laissez faire
Caveat emptor
Better Business Bureau
FTC Act

Lanham Trademark Law Revision Act
Kid-Vid
Trade Regulation Rules
Reasonable person
Puffery
Testimonial
Demonstration
Counteradvertising
Editorial advertising
Letter of compliance
Consent agreement

Cease-and-desist order
Temporary restraining order
Industry Guides
Affirmative disclosure

Comparative advertising
National Advertising Review Board (NARB)
National Advertising Division (NAD)
Legal advertising

CASE PROBLEMS

1. What case contains the formula or rule for mounting a First Amendment defense of commercial speech, notably advertising, or for permitting its regulation? What is the rule? Find and brief a case in which the requirements of the rule were not met and a regulation was struck down by the courts.

2. *Posadas de Puerto Rico Associates v. Tourism Co.* is considered an aberration by some legal commen-

tators. Read all of the opinions in the case and debate the validity of some of the major arguments you find on both sides of the Supreme Court.

3. Compare the self-regulatory system in advertising with the self-regulatory system in news.

ENDNOTES

1. *Ohralik v. Ohio State Bar Ass'n*, 436 U.S. 447, 98 S.Ct. 1912 (1978).

2. *Peel v. Attorney Registration and Disciplinary Comm. of Illinois*, 496 U.S. 91, 110 S.Ct. 2281 (1990).

3. *Virginia State Board of Pharmacy v. Virginia Citizens Consumer Council, Inc.* 425 U.S. 748, fn. 24, 96 S.Ct. 1817, fn. 24 (1976).

4. 447 U.S. 557, 100 S.Ct. 2343, 6 Med.L.Rptr. 1497 (1980).

5. *Board of Trustees of the State University of New York v. Fox*, 492 U.S. 469, 109 S.Ct. 3028 (1989).

6. *Board of Trustees of the State University of New York v. Fox*, 492 U.S. 469, 109 S.Ct. 3028 (1989).

7. *Bolger v. Youngs Drug Products Corp.*, 463 U.S. 60, 103 S.Ct. 2875 (1983).

8. *Posadas de Puerto Rico Associates v. Tourism Co.*, 478 U.S. 328, 106 S.Ct. 2968, 13 Med.L.Rptr. 1033 (1986).

9. ____ U.S. ____, 113 S.Ct. 2696 (1993).

10. *Edenfield v. Fane*, ____ U.S. ____, 113 S.Ct. 1792, 21 Med.L.Rptr. 1321 (1993).

11. 427 F.Supp. 1297, 2 Med.L.Rptr. 1666 (E.D.N.Y. 1977), affirmed without opinion 573 F.2d 1294, 3 Med.L.Rptr. 1784 (2d Cir. 1977). See also *United Food and Commercial Works Local 919 v.*

Ottaway Newspapers, Inc. 19 Med.L.Rptr. 1792 (D.Conn. 1991); *Citizen Awareness Regarding Education v. Calhoun County Publishing, Inc.*, 406 SE 2d 65, 19 Med.L.Rptr. 1061 (W. Va. 1991).

12. *Home Placement Service, Inc. v. Providence Journal Co.*, 682 F.2d 274, 8 Med.L.Rptr. 1881 (1st Cir. 1982).

13. *Herald-Telephone v. Fatouros*, 431 N.E.2d 171, 8 Med.L.Rptr. 1230, (Ind. 1982). See also *Soap Opera Now, Inc. v. Network Publishing Corp.*, 867 F.2d 1424, 16 Med.L.Rptr. 1415 (2d Cir. 1988).

14. *Braun v. Soldier of Fortune Magazine, Inc.*, 968 F.2d 1110, 20 Med.L.Rptr. 1777 (11th Cir. 1992).

15. *Environmental Planning and Information Council v. Superior Court*, 36 Cal.3d 188, 203 Cal.Rptr. 127, 680 P.2d 1086, 10 Med.L.Rptr. 2055 (Cal. 1984).

16. *North Mississippi Communications, Inc. v. Jones*, 951 F.2d 652, 19 Med.L.Rptr. 1897 (5th Cir. 1992).

17. *Portland Womens's Health Center v. Portland Community College*, No. 80–558 (D.Or. 1981).

18. *San Diego Committee against the Draft v. The Governing Board of Grossmont Union High School District*, 790 F.2d 1471, 12 Med.L.Rptr. 2329 (9th Cir. 1986).

19. 484 U.S. 260, 108 S.Ct. 562 (1988).

20. 887 F.2d 935, 17 Med.L.Rptr. 1065 (9th Cir. 1989), *affirmed en banc* 941 F.2d 817 (9th Cir. 1991).

21. *Consumers Union, Inc. v. FTC,* 691 F.2d 575 (D.C.Cir. 1982).

22. *Summary and recommendation: Federal Trade Commission Staff Report on Advertising to Children,* summarized in *Advertising Age,* February 27, 1978.

23. *FTC v. Colgate-Palmolive Co.,* 380 U.S. 374, 85 S.Ct. 1035 (1965).

24. FTC News Summary, No. 20, May 19, 1978.

25. 29 Fed. Reg. 8355 (1964).

26. *Capital Broadcasting Company v. Mitchell,* 333 F.Supp. 582 (D.D.C. 1971).

27. *FTC v. Brown & Williamson Tobacco Corp.,* 778 F.2d 35 (D.C.Cir. 1985).

28. FTC Dkt. No. 9206, 54 Fed.Reg. 41342.

29. *Warner Lambert Co. v. Federal Trade Commission,* 562 F.2d 749, 2 Med.L.Rptr. 2303 (D.C.Cir. 1977), *cert. denied* 435 U.S. 950, 98 S.Ct. 1575 (1978).

Monopoly, Diversity, and Antitrust Law

ORIGINS

In the last decade of the nineteenth century, Congress decided that a market economy would not work well or fairly if monopolies were permitted to form; accordingly, in 1890 it passed the Sherman Act. The act prohibits contracts, combinations, trusts, and conspiracies that restrain trade or encourage monopoly.

In 1914, Congress passed the Clayton Act to discourage specific anticompetitive practices such as corporate mergers, interlocking directorates, discriminatory or predatory pricing (pricing so low that a competitor is destroyed), and tying (conditioning the sale of one product or service on the purchase of a second). The Clayton Act has been amended many times since 1914 in order to sharpen its teeth against all forms of anticompetitive behavior. The underlying assumption is that fair competition among entrepreneurs ultimately benefits the consumer by providing both choice and quality and thereby contributes to the general welfare.

In the media world, two trends are occurring simultaneously. New technologies are providing new and diverse media of communication such as the expansion in specialized cable channels with some soon to be interactive (that is, you will be able to talk to your TV set), VCRs, digital systems, direct broadcast satellite (DBS), and fiber optics with its greatly increased capacity for carrying messages. At the same time, fewer and fewer owners are controlling more and more of the system.

Nearly 80 percent of daily newspapers now belong to chains, and bigger chains are buying smaller chains. These are called **horizontal mergers.** One-on-one newspaper competition is almost a thing of the past. Consolidation, merger, and conglomeration (the coming together of unrelated businesses) were rife in the 1980s and continue into the 1990s. Magazines, record and film

● **Sherman Act**
An 1890 act of Congress that prohibits contracts, combinations, trusts, and conspiracies that restrain trade or encourage monopoly.

● **Clayton Act**
A 1914 federal law that prohibits anticompetitive practices such as corporate mergers and predatory pricing.

● **Horizontal merger**
The addition of similar outlets to a corporation, such as newspaper chains.

companies, movie theaters, book publishers, broadcast and cable companies, and even newspaper marketing and trade organizations have all been affected.

The much maligned union of Warner Communication and Time, Inc. in 1989 is an example of a merger. General Electric's acquisition of RCA and its NBC network three years earlier illustrates **conglomeration**. In the fall of 1994, Time-Warner was eyeing NBC, and it was rumored that Disney and Turner Broadcasting were both in pursuit of CBS. These developments toward even greater vertical integration have serious implications for the public interest in that they could lead to a lack of access for diverse programming and a lessening of journalistic competition. Rupert Murdoch, an Australian magnate who became an American citizen, bought UHF television stations in many of the nation's largest markets and with them Fox studios to form a fourth network. Three of the original networks, NBC, ABC, and CBS, have traditionally been prohibited by the antitrust laws from this very kind of **vertical monopoly** of both production and distribution systems.

At the same time, intermedia competition is now greater than it has ever been; local radio stations compete with the local newspaper for a larger share of the advertising dollar, and national newspapers such as *USA Today* compete with CNN (Cable News Network) for national advertising. Consequently, there is always a temptation to resort to unlawful methods of competition. This is where the Antitrust Division of the Department of Justice, the **Federal Trade Commission (FTC),** and the Federal Communications Commission (FCC) become involved in enforcing the Sherman and Clayton Acts, as do their counterpart state agencies in enforcing parallel state antitrust laws. Penalties for violation of either state or federal laws can be severe. In addition to facing fines and imprisonment, convicted antitrust violators may be prohibited from holding federal licenses or privileges, a substantial concern to broadcasters, for example, where licenses are required and profits are high. To avoid going to trial, many violators will accept consent agreements that require them to discontinue certain activities or sell off certain assets.

Antitrust law affects media in complex ways. Understanding it requires a knowledge of how the courts define such terms as markets, products, services, and monopoly, for starters. Courts have hesitated to view communication markets as **multimedia markets:** markets within which all media compete for advertisers and audience. This makes the single daily newspaper in town seem more of a monopolist than it really is.

Monopolization of a product or a geographic market is not necessarily bad or illegal. It can happen unintentionally, as when your only competitor leaves the market through no fault of yours or because of its inability to match your skillful merchandising. There is also such a thing as a natural monopoly. For example, most communities cannot economically support more than a single daily newspaper or a single cable television company. What is illegal is the *abuse* of **monopoly power,** the exercise of market power to control prices or exclude competitors. A newspaper runs the risk of abusing its monopoly power if, for example, it prices its advertising space so low as to put a competing shopper or a weekly out of business, or if it requires those who buy newspaper space to buy time on the radio station it owns to the detriment of a competing radio station.

- **Conglomerate merger**
  The joining together of different kinds of businesses, for example, a defense contractor and a television network.

- **Vertical merger**
  The merging of program production and distribution systems.

- **Federal Trade Commission (FTC)**
  The federal agency largely responsible for the regulation of advertising.

- **Multimedia market**
  A market in which all media compete for advertisers and audience.

- **Monopoly power**
  The exercise of market power to control prices or exclude competitors.

CONSTITUTIONAL CHALLENGES

I
t should not be surprising that antitrust laws directed at the print and broadcast media have been challenged as unconstitutional. The first great challenge came in 1943 when the regulatory system governing broadcasting—the Federal Communications Act of 1934—was attacked by NBC and CBS as an unconstitutional infringement of their First Amendment rights. In *National Broadcasting Company v. United States,* the U.S. Supreme Court upheld the constitutionality of the act in a decision that dealt in part with antitrust questions.

A 1938 study by the FCC revealed that more than half the radio stations then in operation were affiliated with one of the two networks, and they were the powerful stations. Of these stations, the most powerful were the eighteen owned by CBS and NBC. Stations affiliated with the national networks (including the Mutual Broadcasting System) utilized more than 97 percent of the total nighttime broadcasting power of all the stations in the country. NBC and CBS together controlled more than 85 percent of the total nighttime wattage, and the broadcast business of the three national network companies amounted to almost half of the total business of all stations in the United States. Network control over programming and advertising rates, the government argued, subverted the authority of local broadcasters and was anticompetitive. New networks were being kept from developing. This situation had led the FCC to adopt the "chain broadcasting regulations," and their constitutionality as well as the constitutionality of the entire regulatory system was being challenged.

"If a licensee enters into a contract with a network organization which limits his ability to make the best use of the radio facility assigned him," said the Supreme Court in upholding the constitutionality of the FCC regulations, "he is not serving the public interest. . . . The net effect . . . has been that broadcasting service has been maintained at a level below that possible under a system of free competition."[1]

The next challenge to the constitutionality of antitrust laws came two years later from the Associated Press. Cooperatively owned by its newspaper members, the AP had denied membership to Marshall Field's *Chicago Sun,* a new paper founded to compete with the *Chicago Tribune.* The AP wire service, it would be argued, was necessary for survival.

In a landmark opinion for the U.S. Supreme Court in *Associated Press v. United States,* Justice Hugo Black wrote that the AP bylaws used to exclude the *Sun* violated the Sherman Act. To the argument that applying antitrust law in this way to an association of publishers constituted an abridgment of freedom of the press guaranteed by the First Amendment, Justice Black replied in language that is both puzzling and inspirational:

> The First Amendment, far from providing an argument against application of the Sherman Act, here provides powerful reasons to the contrary. . . . Surely a command that the government itself shall not impede the free flow of ideas does not afford nongovernmental combinations a refuge if they impose restraints upon that constitutionally guaranteed freedom.

● *National Broadcasting Company v. United States*
The 1943 Supreme Court ruling that upheld the constitutionality of the broadcast regulatory system.

● *Associated Press v. United States*
The 1945 Supreme Court holding that the antitrust law did apply to newspapers and that they were not immune under the First Amendment.

Freedom to publish means freedom for all and not for some. Freedom to publish is guaranteed by the Constitution, but freedom to combine to keep others from publishing is not. Freedom of the press from governmental interference under the First Amendment does not sanction repression of that freedom by private interests."[2]

Black's declaration is puzzling in that it suggests that private power as well as state action, i.e., governmental interference, may invoke the First Amendment. Generally, the First Amendment has been interpreted to mean that only Congress or other branches or agencies of government are precluded from abridging First Amendment rights.

Together these two cases leave little doubt that antitrust laws do apply to the media.

ANTITRUST VIOLATIONS

Most antitrust claims are made as a result of anticompetitive practices violating the Sherman Act, the Clayton Act, or both, such as:

1. *Predatory pricing.* Setting advertising rates below cost to harm a competitor.

2. *Forced combination rates and refusals to deal.* Unit advertising rates compelling advertisers to use, for example, both a monopoly newspaper and an affliated broadcast station, and the policy of rejecting ads if the advertiser used competing media. An agreement between a newspaper and an advertiser not to sell space to that advertiser's competitor, if provable, would be illegal; but a newspaper, whether a monopoly or not, may refuse ads that do not comply with the company's stated rules for accepting advertising.

3. *Tying.* Like combination rates, this practice is legal if, for example, morning and afternoon editions of a newspaper are separately available to an advertiser on a basis as favorable as the proposed tie-in. Tie-ins offering substantial discounts are legal if advertisers are free to accept or reject them.

4. *Conscious parallelism.* Conspiring across media to set advertising rates.

5. *Zoned editions.* Illegal if they are based on secret payments to advertisers, or if their advertising space is sold regularly below cost, or if a monopoly daily establishes a shopper to draw advertisers away from a competing suburban newspaper.

6. *Blanketing.* Giving free copies to every residence in a specific circulation area should not last too long and should not be designed to drive a weaker competitor out of that market.

Know These?

7. *Vertical price fixing.* Illegal when done by a newspaper in an attempt to coerce independent distributors (those who buy the newspapers outright) into keeping their prices as low as possible.

8. *Feature syndicates.* Newspapers should not sign contracts that unreasonably handicap competitors by denying them features where, for example, the newspaper has a penetration rate of less than 20 percent and a circulation of less than 5,000.

Many antitrust violations are more structural than behavioral and therefore more potentially permanent and difficult to deal with—for example, mergers and acquisitions. These may be vertical as when a newspaper buys a paper mill or a distribution company; or they may be horizontal as when one newspaper buys another newspaper in the same geographic market, or when a chain or group adds another newspaper to its national or international stable.

When faced with a merger, the Antitrust Division follows a three-step procedure. It defines the product and its geographical market; calculates the percentage of the market that would be controlled by the new, merged firm; and decides whether that figure is sufficient to create a "reasonable probability" of lessened competition through "the willful acquisition or maintenance of that power as distinguished from growth or development as a consequence of a superior product, business acumen, or historical accident," to use the language of the Sherman Act.

These principles of the Sherman and Clayton Acts were applied in 1967 when the *Los Angeles Times* tried to buy the *San Bernardino Sun and Telegram.* The *Times*, a newspaper of national importance, had the largest daily circulation in California, whereas the *Sun* dominated the newspaper market in San Bernardino County and was the largest independent publishing company in southern California. These newspapers, while existing in different categories, nevertheless engaged in what the court called "interlayer" competition, and the merger was disallowed. Direct competition was much less important than whether the overall effects of the merger were anticompetitive, and they were held to be. Had the merger been allowed, total morning circulation for the merged firm would have increased from 24 percent to 99 percent. "The acquisition of the *Sun* by the *Times*," said the court, "was particularly anticompetitive because it eliminated one of the few independent papers that had been able to operate successfully in the morning and Sunday fields. . . ."[3]

Economic pressures toward group ownership are overwhelming. Tax laws and inheritance taxes favor expanding groups. Groups enjoy the advantages of central planning and management. Perhaps groups now compete with one another for new acquisitions and ought to be considered a line of commerce for Clayton Act purposes.

Cross-media competition may be the competition of the future. In this dramatic form of interlayer competition, forms of competition that are already well established will become increasingly complex: newspapers will compete with television, television with cable, and magazines with books.

NEWSPAPER IMMUNITY

- **Newspaper Preservation Act**
  A 1970 federal law that permits the business merger of competing daily newspapers, if one is failing; editorial departments remain separate. Such mergers are called joint operating agreements (JOAs) and, in effect, give newspapers in these situations immunity from such antitrust violations as profit pooling and price fixing.

P owerful lobbying by the American Newspaper Publishers Association (ANPA), now known as the Newspaper Association of America (NAA) as a result of trade organization mergers, led to passage of the Newspaper Preservation Act in 1970. Under certain conditions, the act immunizes newspapers from some structural purposes of the antitrust laws.

If there is no obvious intent to monopolize and a geographic market is deemed unable to support competing daily newspapers, the act permits a merger of some or all of the business departments of two papers where one paper is failing. Their editorial departments must remain separate, preserving two newspaper voices, and presumably editorial diversity, in the community. It is argued that the act serves the First Amendment by saving editorial competition in a situation where it is in imminent danger of disappearing.

Since 1930, mergers in all businesses have been protected where there is clear evidence that a competing company is failing.[4] Hence there must be a "failing newspaper" before the act permits a merger. The act was an attempt in part to undo the work of the U.S. Supreme Court in *Citizen Publishing Co. v. United States*,[5] a case that began in Tucson, Arizona. In disallowing the merger, the Court stipulated that the acquired company, there a faltering evening newspaper, had to be so close to failing that no reorganization could save it. In addition, the proposed merger had to be the only way to save the failing firm, there being no prospective purchaser. That energized the ANPA to lobby the Congress for what was first called the Failing Newspaper Act and would become the Newspaper Preservation Act, a more tuneful title.

Before passage of the act, competing newspapers in twenty-three cities had already merged in what are now called joint operating agreements (JOAs); they were "grandfathered" by the act. In the past two decades, some have disappeared and new JOAs have been formed under the act's more precise and restrictive rules. As of this writing, there are twenty-one JOAs.

- **Downward spiral**
  A newspaper in economic stress. Circulation falls, advertising linage follows, first-issue costs increase under what is called the economies of scale, profitability falls, and the only remedy is to raise prices or cut costs, and thereby quality, further reducing circulation. So the spiral continues downward.

Again, under the "failing company" doctrine, newspapers have to show that the resources of one of the newspapers are about to be depleted. In other words, the weaker newspaper must be in what media economists call a **downward spiral.** In addition, the failing newspaper has to demonstrate that every effort toward rehabilitation or reorganization of the company has been made and that no potential buyer has come forward.

Subscriber and advertiser demands are interdependent. When circulation drops, advertising sales drop. The **economies of scale** (another economics term) dictate that fixed first-issue costs (paper, ink, labor, capital equipment, taxes, administration) diminish as circulation increases. When circulation decreases, fixed first-issue costs rise as a percentage of total costs. This leads to lower profitability, which can only be remedied by raising advertising and subscription rates or by cutting costs and thereby quality. Either course accelerates the downward spiral. The weaker newspaper appears to be doomed.

- **Economies of scale**
  In the case of a newspaper, a large part of production costs for labor, paper, and ink are spent in producing the first copy. Thereafter cost per unit decreases as circulation increases.

Newspaper employees, advertisers, and the publishers of suburban newspapers often oppose JOAs for obvious reasons—loss of jobs, higher advertising rates, and unfair competition. They have also opposed JOAs as a special privilege to powerful publishers who no longer wish to compete for advertisers and subscribers. Strong opposition to mergers developed in Seattle and Detroit in recent years.

In Seattle, the U.S. attorney general, who must approve all such mergers, said the financial health of a newspaper could be considered apart from the financial condition of the chain to which it belonged. The "failing" *Post-Intelligencer* belonged to the financially sound Hearst organization. Nor was it necessary, said the attorney general, to prove the absence of a qualified buyer. A federal district judge disagreed with this interpretation of the act, but was reversed by the Ninth Circuit Court of Appeals. The *P-I*, it held, was clearly in a "downward spiral."[6]

A battle of behemoths took place in Detroit between the two largest newspaper groups in the country, Gannett and Knight-Ridder. The latter claimed losses of $35 million over a five-year period for its *Free Press*, the second newspaper in Detroit and eighth largest in the country. Gannett claimed losses of $20 million for its *News*, the seventh largest U.S. daily.

Opponents charged that the two newspapers were engaging in what lawyers call **self-predation:** they were orchestrating their own failure by selling subscriptions and advertising space far below costs in order to be granted the privileges of a JOA. Knight-Ridder threatened to close the *Free Press* unless the merger were allowed. Opponents argued that jobs would be lost and advertising and subscription rates would certainly go up if the JOA went through. It did. And advertising and subscription rates went up.

Again the U.S. attorney general approved the merger, this time against the better judgment of an assistant and an administrative law judge. In spite of opposition from a committee of advertisers, readers, and employees, a federal district court approved the merger, defining the *Free Press* as a "failing newspaper." In 1989, a divided panel of the D.C. Circuit Court of Appeals upheld that decision, finding the attorney general's interpretation of both the law and the precarious position of the *Free Press* "reasonable."

Judge Ruth Bader Ginsburg, now a Supreme Court justice, dissented. She did not see the *Free Press* in a downward spiral. Both papers were maintained by "deep-pocket" parent companies, and the competition was close. A JOA had been talked about when Gannett acquired the *News* some years before. "No 'failing' paper in Newspaper Preservation Act history," she wrote, "has emerged so advantageously under an approved JOA." She also noted Congress's desire to prevent newspapers from engaging in destructive competition in the hope of gaining long-term financial rewards through a JOA—profit pooling, price fixing, and market allocation.[7]

The U.S. Supreme Court affirmed the circuit court decision in a tie vote, and the highly profitable merger went forward. The combined circulation of the two newspapers reached 1.2 million and then began to tumble, especially that of the *News*. The success of the merger is by no means assured.

Even though the *Las Vegas Sun* was not in a downward spiral, the attorney general ruled in 1990 that it was "failing" within the meaning of the Newspaper Preservation Act because of irreversible losses. These kinds of appeals are not uncommon.

● **Self-predation**
Where a newspaper sells advertising and subscriptions below costs in order to be seen as failing and therefore eligible for a JOA.

In fact, in 1991 the Antitrust Division approved a proposed JOA between the weekly Manteca (Calif.) *News* and the daily Manteca *Bulletin,* the first merger of its kind, even though antitrust lawyers at first suspected that the weekly's financial difficulties were due primarily to bad management. The weekly died, however, before the marriage could be consummated.

ANTITRUST IN OTHER MEDIA

Broadcasting

The FCC may consider antitrust behavior when measuring a licensee's performance against the **"public interest, convenience, and necessity"** standard applied in the renewal process.

Although the FCC twice approved the proposed acquisition of ABC by International Telephone and Telegraph (ITT) in the late 1960s, continuing Antitrust Division objections led to the canceling of the sale in 1968. In the 1980s, however, the same government agency raised no significant objections to the sale of the same network to Capital Cities Broadcasting, admittedly a more compatible takeover, nor did it object to the acquisition of NBC by General Electric.

In the 1970s, the Department of Justice limited network control over prime-time programming by severely restricting network control over production, syndication, and talent. These restrictions seem less necessary now in light of the rapid growth of cable competition.

The authority of the National Association of Broadcasters (NAB) over programming was also limited by antitrust forces. The Writers Guild of America argued that the NAB code exhorting broadcasters to implement socially responsible practices in both advertising and programming was *government* regulation in disguise. In particular, "family viewing" rules—setting aside early evening hours for programming that would insulate children from sex and violence—were seen as an infringement of writers' First Amendment freedoms.

A federal district court judge agreed. Although his ruling was later vacated by an appeals court,[8] for the three years the rules were in effect, the NAB, a trade association, lived the public relations nightmare of being charged with violating the First Amendment rights of its own members.

At about the same time, the Department of Justice claimed that three provisions in the NAB television code limiting commercial time were a conspiracy to drive up the price of commercials and therefore violated the Sherman Act. A federal district court judge agreed in part.[9] A later settlement between the Department of Justice and the NAB closed the matter, but not before the NAB dropped its radio and television codes altogether. However, the federal Children's Television Act of 1990 does limit commercial advertising time to 10.5 minutes per hour on weekends and 12 minutes per hour on weekdays for children under twelve.

One broadcast antitrust suit that did not end in a **consent agreement** or a settlement involved the question of whether the television contracts negotiated

---

● **Public interest, convenience, and necessity**
Vague language in the Federal Communications Act that sets the standard for the granting and renewal of broadcast licenses.

● **Consent agreement**
A voluntary yielding to the will of another; the act or result of coming into harmony or accord.

by the National Collegiate Athletic Association (NCAA) violated the Sherman Act. The Supreme Court ruled in 1984 that the association had monopolized the market for college football television and thereby violated the act.[10] As a result of the ruling, the amount of college football on both broadcast and cable television expanded dramatically, as colleges signed contracts of their own or banded together in smaller regional or national associations.

Broadcasters owning or controlling a station in a particular area may not own other stations, daily newspapers, or cable TV systems in the same area. Under 1992 rule changes, nationwide ownership is limited to 18 AM and 18 FM stations, and up to 12 TV stations, if together they do not account for more than 25 percent of the national audience. A UHF television station, because of signal limitations, counts as only half a station in this calculation. An owner may go up to 21 AM and FM stations and up to 14 TV stations if the additional stations are minority owned.

Cable Television

The Cable Communications Policy Act of 1984 and the Local Government Antitrust Act passed by Congress a year later relieved municipalities that license cable companies (usually one to a community) of having to worry about antitrust violations.

Cable may also be a **natural monopoly.** Local government franchisers generally recognize this in choosing a single company to wire their communities. Technological improvements, however, have led to cable competition in some larger cities. Municipal cable regulators are immune to antitrust laws if what they do is based on "clearly articulated and affirmatively expressed state policy."[11]

An unsuccessful cable applicant was awarded $6 million after proving that Houston business leaders, the mayor, and the applicant who won the franchise conspired to violate the Sherman Act in order to block him from the area. TCI, one of the country's largest cable system operators, got into the same kind of trouble when it was proved that the company had conspired with the mayor and other city officials to retain its franchise in Jefferson City, Missouri. The penalty there was $35 million.

Cable has continued to consolidate both horizontally and vertically. **Multiple system operators (MSOs)** have bought more and more systems, and major MSOs have bought into many of their sources of programming. Cable's problems with antitrust laws are by no means over. In the 1990s, Congress was struggling with such questions as how to make cable more competitive, what power local authorities should have over cable rates and services where there is no local competition, and whether network television should be permitted to own cable systems, especially in large and competitive markets. Congress did pass a complex Cable Act in 1992.[12] A national debate immediately erupted over whether the act's "must-carry" provisions (requiring cable companies to carry all local commercial and noncommercial broadcasts) on top of the cable operator's obligation to provide public access, educational, and governmental channels violated cable's First Amendment rights. In 1994, the U.S. Supreme

● **Natural monopoly**
A situation in which economics dictate a single newspaper or cable company in a particular community. Competitors could not survive.

● **Multiple system operator (MSO)**
A company that owns more than one cable system.

Court declared that the "must-carry" rules would be constitutional so long as they were content-neutral restrictions on speech that furthered a substantial governmental interest and were no more restrictive than neccessary to serve that interest. The case was remanded to a federal district court to consider the question.[13]

Telephone

On January 8, 1982, the Department of Justice and AT&T reached a settlement in a protracted antitrust suit against AT&T, Western Electric, and Bell Labs, Inc. Finally, AT&T agreed to give up control of local telephone service, but retain its long-distance operations in competition with new companies such as MCI and U.S. Sprint. It could also enter into new, unregulated businesses. A major consequence of this settlement was the spin-off of seven regional Bell companies or Regional Bell Operating Companies (RBOCs). The breakup went into effect in 1984.

From the beginning, the newspaper industry feared the entry of AT&T and the regional Bells into the electronic information services market, notably videotex or electronic yellow pages. Ultimately, the newspapers convinced the presiding federal district court judge, Harold Greene, of the rightness of their position. The newspapers' main argument was that the telephone companies would have an unfair advantage because they controlled the equipment needed to deliver such services. Under Judge Greene's order, AT&T was constrained for seven years—until 1989—and the regional Bells indefinitely.

In mid-1991, under intense lobbying pressure, Judge Greene reluctantly removed the provision prohibiting the regional Bells from providing information services but stayed his order until it could be reviewed by a higher court. In the meantime, the Senate passed a bill allowing the seven Bell companies to participate in research, design, and manufacture of communication equipment.

Counterlegislation was immediately forthcoming. A bill introduced by Representative Jim Cooper of Tennessee, supported by the newspaper lobby, would bar the Bells from offering information services as long as they had a monopoly on local telephone services. The newspaper industry and twenty-three other media and consumer groups, joined by AT&T and other long-distance companies, urged reimposition of Judge Greene's stay delaying entry of the regional Bells into the information services business. The U.S. Supreme Court refused to allow this until the appellate court had considered the case.

"Fair competition cannot exist," the American Newspaper Publishers Association argued, "where you are forced to rely on a competitor for delivery of your product." Opponents retorted that restrictions on the Bell companies were unconstitutional because they denied the companies "the right to use their natural advantages to communicate with their intended audiences."

Congress continues to sort out these arguments as new technologies in personal communications, fiber optics, and video dial tone rapidly emerge. The outcome will have significant implications for the future of telecommunication services.

SUMMARY

Antitrust laws reflect a longtime commitment to the protection and encouragement of competition in business affairs. The underlying purpose is to ensure diversity and choice in products, services, and ideas.

Though society is enjoying a profusion of new communication technologies, both the accelerating concentration of ownership in some of the major systems and the possibility of monopolies in ideas cast a shadow over the future. Antitrust oversight is the responsibility primarily of the Antitrust Division of the Department of Justice, but the Federal Trade Commission and the FCC also participate.

Antitrust laws take pains to define products and markets. In the sphere of communications, these definitions have too often worked to the benefit of media magnates. However, some media, notably small or medium-sized daily newspapers or cable companies, may be seen as natural monopolies.

Still, media power, whatever its dimensions, must not be abused by predatory pricing, price fixing, tying, or forced combinations. Juries tend to be unsympathetic toward media violators, and where intent is paramount, as it is in antitrust suits, managers should be careful not to put anything on paper that suggests an intent to monopolize. Antitrust compliance rules should be posted in every media business office.

First Amendment challenges to antitrust laws have not been successful, but legislation giving immunity to the newspaper industry in certain circumstances has been, to the consternation of media employees, advertisers, and competing weekly and suburban newspapers.

Antitrust laws, of course, apply to broadcasting, cable, and telephone. Certain network practices and some NAB code requirements have been restricted by antitrust actions. Cable companies have been severely penalized for conspiring with public officials either to gain or to retain cable franchises.

After the breakup of AT&T as the result of an antitrust suit, the question became whether the resulting independent regional Bell companies should be allowed to enter the electronic information market. The newspapers thought not because the Bells would have the unfair advantage of controlling the equipment needed to deliver such services. That debate continues in Congress.

KEY TERMS

Sherman Act
Clayton Act
Horizontal merger
Conglomerate merger
Vertical merger
Federal Trade Commission (FTC)
Multimedia market
Monopoly power
National Broadcasting Company v. United States

Associated Press v. United States
Newspaper Preservation Act
Downward spiral
Economies of scale
Self-predation
Public interest, convenience, and necessity
Consent agreement
Natural monopoly
Multiple system operator (MSO)

CASE PROBLEMS

1. Why have the antitrust laws generally survived tests of unconstitutionality when applied to the media? What case set the stage for use of the antitrust laws against the media?

2. What premise provides the foundation for the regulation of broadcasting? Is this premise defensible in the late twentieth and early twenty-first centuries? What premise have the courts suggested may be substitutable for the earlier premise? Would you substitute it?

3. The Newspaper Preservation Act relieves newspaper mergers from antitrust compliance. Make arguments for and against this special treatment of newspapers.

4. *Turner Broadcasting* is a good case to use to debate the question of whether electronic media should continue to be treated differently from print media for First Amendment purposes. Examine the various opinions in the case for arguments on both sides of the question.

ENDNOTES

1. *NBC v. United States*, 319 U.S. 190, 63 S.Ct. 997 (1943).

2. *Associated Press v. United States*, 326 U.S. 1, 65 S.Ct. 1416 (1945).

3. *United States v. Times Mirror Co.*, 274 F.Supp. 606 (C.D.Cal. 1967), *affirmed per curiam* 390 U.S. 712, 88 S.Ct. 1411 (1968)

4. *International Shoe Company v. FTC*, 280 U.S. 291, 50 S.Ct. 89 (1930).

5. 394 U.S. 131, 89 S.Ct. 927 (1969).

6. *Committee for an Independent P-I v. Hearst Corp.*, 704 F.2d 467 (9th Cir. 1983).

7. *Michigan Citizens for an Independent Press, et al. v. Richard Thornburgh, United States Attorney General, et al.*, 868 F.2d 1285 (D.C.Cir. 1989).

8. *Writers Guild of America v. American Broadcasting Co.*, 609 F.2d 355 (9th Cir. 1979).

9. *United States v. National Association of Broadcasters*, 536 F.Supp. 149 (D.D.C. 1982) and 553 F.Supp. 621 (1982).

10. *NCAA v. Board of Regents of the University of Oklahoma*, 468 U.S. 85, 104 S.Ct. 2948 (1984).

11. *Community Communications Co. v. City of Boulder*, 455 U.S. 40, 102 S.Ct. 835 (1982).

12. Cable Television Consumer and Competition Act, 47 U.S.C.A. §§ 534 and 535.

13. *Turner Broadcasting System v. FCC*, ____ U.S. ____, 114 S.Ct. 2445, 22 Med.L.Rptr. 1865 (1994).

Student Press Rights

TINKER AND *HAZELWOOD:* LIBERALS VERSUS CONSERVATIVES

In 1969, a liberal Supreme Court held that certain First Amendment rights of students could not be abridged unless school authorities could convince the courts that the expression involved would "materially and substantially interfere with the requirements of appropriate discipline in the operation of the school." The case was *Tinker v. Des Moines Independent School District;*[1] it involved symbolic speech—black armbands worn by schoolchildren to symbolize the opposition of their parents to the Vietnam War.

"It can hardly be argued," the Court declared, "that either students or teachers shed their constitutional rights to freedom of speech or expression at the schoolhouse gate." Citing a landmark case in which the Court had rejected compulsory flag salutes in the public schools of West Virginia in World War II, the Court added:

> That they are educating the young for citizenship is reason for scrupulous protection of Constitutional freedoms of the individual, if we are not to strangle the free mind at its source and teach youth to discount important principles of our government as mere platitudes."[2]

That foundational principle may have become a minority view nineteen years later when a conservative Court held that a high school principal had the authority to remove two pages from the school newspaper without consulting the student staff. The principal was concerned about the effects two stories about pregnancy and abortion would have on students and the effects stories about divorce would have on the privacy of parents.

While not overturning *Tinker,* the case, *Hazelwood School District v. Kuhlmeier,*[3] now seems to govern high school press law. "A school," wrote Justice Byron White for the Court, "need not tolerate speech that is inconsistent with its basic educational mission, even though the government could not censor similar speech outside the school." The Court chose not to direct its rule to college papers, but in a footnote suggested that such an application could be considered in the future; and *Hazelwood* may not apply to high school newspapers that are independent of the school curriculum, although that distinction may be spongy. The Hazelwood high school newspaper was part of a journalism class.

Between the symbolic speech of an armband and the press rights of a scholastic newspaper, a third case defining the boundaries of pure speech in high schools was decided by the Court two years before *Hazelwood*. It was a tougher case and one that may bridge the liberal/conservative chasm. In *Bethel School District No. 403 v. Fraser*[4] the Court permitted restrictions on language it characterized as vulgar, lewd, and plainly offensive. A student endorsing a candidate for student government at a school assembly used sexual double entendres to further his cause. Aside from the language being tasteless, fourteen-year-olds were required to be in the audience. Sooner or later, the Court noted, they would be getting graphic interpretations of the speaker's allusions from older or more mature classmates. Primary to the mission of the school, said the Court, is the inculcation of fundamental values, and the "First Amendment does not prevent . . . school officials from determining that to permit a vulgar and lewd speech . . . would undermine the school's basic mission."

So, when the contested school-sponsored expression takes place in a school setting, which is largely a nonpublic forum, a principal, a superintendent, or a school board, acting on behalf of the public, may suppress speech or press in the interests of education. This could be called a majoritarian position—the public or representatives of the public know best. *Tinker*'s liberalism, representing a constitutionalist doctrine more respectful of civil liberties, considered the public school to be at least a limited public forum where viewpoints, whether school sponsored or not, should not be suppressed unless they demonstrably disrupt the educational process. Both positions are defensible. In a psychological sense at least, Fraser's speech in the Bethel school may have been disruptive.

The liberal view, however embattled it may now be in the federal judiciary, and very likely the dominant conservative view as well, still insist that school officials give adequate warning to students as to what forms and topics of expression may be subject to prior restraints; what constitutes disruption, defamation, obscenity, or an invasion of privacy; and what steps are available for a prompt hearing and appeal when an administrative interference with publication or distribution takes place. Few if any of these elements of due process were available to students in *Hazelwood*. And the authority of the case is being felt elsewhere. *Hazelwood* has been used to remove educational material from school curricula.[5] Some assert that the case has wiped out twenty years of student press law, most of it forged in the federal appeals courts, and that students may now have to look to state constitutions for protection. By early 1994, five states—California, Colorado, Iowa, Kansas, and Massachusetts—had passed anti-censorship laws to protect the scholastic press, and other states were considering such legislation.

The Student Press Law Center (SPLC) in Washington, D.C.,[6] assists students who have serious problems with censorship, access to information, libel, privacy, or the litigation process.

BEFORE AND AFTER *HAZELWOOD*

Before *Hazelwood*, the Supreme Court held that books could not be removed from high school libraries simply because school authorities objected to their philosophical themes.[7] The First Amendment rights of students were violated, said a federal district court, when a school board removed all issues of *Ms.* magazine from a high school library without any showing of a countervailing governmental interest, beyond the personal views of individual board members.[8]

In *Pratt v. Independent School District, No. 831,*[9] the Eighth Circuit Court of Appeals held that a "school board cannot constitutionally ban ... films because a majority of its members object to the films' religious and ideological content and wish to prevent the ideas contained in the material from being expressed in the school." A California school board that permitted military service ads to be placed in the school paper but prohibited ads promoting alternatives to military service was said to have violated the First Amendment rights of the anti-war sponsors.[10]

For years, only serious disruptions of the educational process had justified restrictions on student expression. Fraudulent notices announcing the closing of a university met the test, as did leaflets calling for a boycott of registration, and the breaking up of campus meetings.[11] The majority of these cases, however, had gone the other way.

For instance, a unanimous Supreme Court held in *Healy v. James*[12] that fear of or a prediction of disruption was an inadequate reason for a college president to deny recognition to an SDS (Students for a Democratic Society) chapter on campus. Nor was the distinct possibility of public disapproval sufficient to keep a gay organization off a campus.[13]

The First Amendment would also prohibit school administrators from taking away a publication's funding or suspending its editor because of objections to editorial points of view. "We are well beyond the belief," said a federal district court in *Antonelli v. Hammond,*[14] "that any manner of state regulation is permissible simply because it involves an activity which is part of the university structure and is financed with funds controlled by the administration." The Fourth Circuit Court of Appeals put it even more bluntly:

> It may well be that a college need not establish a campus newspaper, or, if a paper has been established, the college may permanently discontinue publication for reasons wholly unrelated to the First Amendment. But if a college has a student newspaper, its publication cannot be suppressed because college officials dislike its editorial comment.... Censorship of constitutionally protected expression cannot be imposed by ... withdrawing financial support, or asserting any other form of censorial oversight based on the institution's power of the purse."[15]

Nor could a fee system be modified because of legal but distasteful editorial content.[16]

But the courts have changed, and perhaps what has been referred to as majoritarianism (the majority rules) is gradually replacing constitutionalism (the First Amendment protects individual dissenters and rabble-rousers from the wrath of the majority) in our body politic. More and more voices are calling for students to be protected from offensive or hateful speech through criminal or administrative sanctions. The campus is no longer a haven for conflicting views because, it is felt, speakers representing society's majority have an unfair advantage: their voices are louder. Here the constitutional model is turned upside down: minorities are being protected from majorities, but the minority persons in these cases are not speakers but harassed individuals or members of a victimized audience.

It is hazardous to predict the future course of these cases or the public mood that may govern them. Shortly after *Hazelwood*, the Ninth Circuit Court of Appeals took the Supreme Court at its word by holding that a high school policy violated the First Amendment rights of students because it required that all student-written material not sponsored by the school be reviewed by school authorities before distribution. An off-campus newspaper had been brought to an on-campus barbecue. The court seemed to be applying a *Tinker* standard. School sponsorship may now be the key question in school cases.[17]

STUDENT BROADCASTERS

The Federal Communications Commission (FCC) has had no trouble deciding who's "in charge" where campus broadcast stations are concerned. Though radio stations are rare on high school campuses, they are common on college campuses, and so it is college students who are apt to find themselves in hot water on occasion. In 1978, the FCC voted to deny license renewal to a noncommercial, educational FM station at the University of Pennsylvania. There had been complaints about obscenity in programming, and the FCC felt that the licensee, the trustees of the university, had lost control over the operation of the station.[18]

Tracing control of the station through a bewildering campus bureaucracy, the commission concluded: "In sum, the daily operation of WXPN-FM was in the hands of student-run organizations and was considered by the licensee to be just one of many 'student' activities supervised by the Student Activities Council." This was not good enough. The station was licensed to the trustees, yet they exercised no control over what was broadcast. Under the law, the licensee is responsible for everything that goes out over the air.

There was no wish to discourage student-run stations, but ultimate responsibility for content, said the commission, rested with the licensee, and total abdication of this role was unacceptable. Penn lost its license, but a year later, the FCC broke its own rule on how long one must wait to reapply and entertained a hasty reapplication from the trustees. A new license was granted but with the understanding that the station would be controlled by a professional manager and staff and that the president of the university and a Board of Governors would assume ultimate responsibility for programming.

Cases such as *Hazelwood* and *Trustees of the University of Pennsylvania* may seem troublesome. If in any sense schools are breeding places for democratic citizenship, these cases could be said to breed cynicism, although many would disagree. In any case, sooner or later scholastic journalists and broadcasters must learn to be responsible for their own mistakes and misjudgments. While student groups may have difficulty getting broadcast licenses, their newspapers ought at least to consider the advantages of being free of credits, grades, and coursework. Although some excellent publication are woven into curricula, those independent of curricula seem to have many fewer problems with administrative censorship.

By serving on boards of publication that include faculty and administrative representatives and playing the role of publisher, students can learn how to judge fellow students. This is how society functions. Libelous, obscene, or potentially disruptive content ought to be examined by faculty advisers and campus or publication lawyers. This is how the commercial press does it. Responsible citizenship cannot be learned in an oligarchy.

Private school students will find the Constitution less accessible to them because censorship of their publications does not constitute state action. Nevertheless, they may still look to state constitutions, statutes, and legal precedents when they run afoul of the censor. And their institutions may have traditions or written guarantees reflecting a respect for constitutional rights.

Although few student cases can command the funds and the time necessary to take cases up the judicial appeals ladder, any issue of *Report*, the official publication of the Student Press Law Center, reflects the turmoil over free speech and press on high school and college campuses. The Center received 1,473 requests for legal assistance in 1993. In the past six years, calls to the Center have increased almost 170 percent. Almost 30 percent of the calls are related to censorship by administrators. Nearly half of the calls come from public colleges, a quarter from public high schools. The Center believes *Hazelwood* is in large part responsible for this increase.[19]

Political correctness (PC), as interpreted by radicals of both left and right, is also taking its toll on traditional campus values of free expression. Although much of this conflict revolves around the appropriateness of library books, campus publications have not been immune. When "objectionable" material is printed in a school newspaper, a frequent response has been to steal and confiscate copies of the offending publication. The SPLC reported thirty-one incidents of newspaper theft in the 1993–1994 school year, including those at the University of Maryland, Duke University, and Tufts.[20]

SUMMARY

Censorship on high school and college campuses continues to burden the scholastic press. It is not the only problem confronting student journalists, however. Access to information is another. A whopping 19 percent of all calls to the SPLC were about access to information. Seemingly endless arguments take place between college editors and administrators over how a state's open records and open meetings laws apply to public educational institutions. Frequently, the federal Family Educational Rights and Privacy Act (the Buckley Amendment)—discussed in Chapter 7—is cited as a justification for keeping records closed. The U.S. Department of Education in 1994 was asking for public comment on rule changes in the Buckley Amendment that would privatize student judicial records. Campus journalists were generally against the changes, administrators in favor of them. Students argued the importance of fair and open trials and useful information about campus crime; administrators argued the need for privacy and the education rather than the punishment of students. Administrators are not the only adversaries college and high school journalists find themselves confronting. Radical liberals and radical conservatives increasingly insist that certain words must not be written and certain topics must not be discussed. To ignore such threats can lead to the theft and destruction of student newspapers.

CASE PROBLEMS

1. What two principles connecting speech and education run through the student press rights cases?

2. Have the class read the Court's opinions in *Bethel School District No. 403 v. Fraser* and debate the following question: Did the student's speech to a school assembly undermine or disrupt the school's basic educational mission, as the Court held, or should more latitude have been given the failed and vulgar humor of what after all was a political speech in a school setting?

3. If administrators and trustees cannot suppress or control a college newspaper because they don't like its editorial content, what can they do about a radio station whose broadcasts lead to complaints about obscenity?

ENDNOTES

1. 393 U.S. 503, 89 S.Ct. 733 (1969).

2. *West Virginia State Board of Education v. Barnette*, 319 U.S. 624, 637, 63 S.Ct. 1178, 1184 (1943).

3. 484 U.S. 260, 108 S.Ct. 562 (1988).

4. 478 U.S. 675, 106 S.Ct. 3159 (1986).

5. *Virgil v. School Board*, 862 F.2d 1517 (11th Cir. 1989).

6. Suite 504, 1735 Eye Street, N.W., Washington, D.C., 20006; (202) 466–5242. See also the 1994 edition of SPLC's *Law of the Student Press*.

7. *Board of Education Island Trees Union Free School District No. 26 v. Pico*, 457 U.S. 853, 102 S.Ct. 2799 (1982).

8. *Salvail v. Nashua Board of Education*, 469 F.Supp. 1269 (D.N.H. 1979).

9. 670 F.2d 771 (8th Cir. 1982).

10. *San Diego Committee v. Grossmont Union High School*, 790 F.2d 1471 (9th Cir. 1986).

11. *Speake v. Grantham*, 317 F.Supp. 1253 (S.D. Miss. 1970); *Jones v. State Board of Education*, 407 F.2d 834 (6th Cir. 1969).

12. 408 U.S. 169, 92 S.Ct. 2338 (1972).

13. *Gay Students of University of New Hampshire v. Bonner*, 509 F.2d 652 (1st Cir. 1974).

14. 308 F.Supp. 1329 (D. Mass. 1970).

15. *Joyner v. Whiting*, 477 F.2d 456 (4th Cir. 1973).

16. *Stanley v. Magrath*, 719 F.2d 279 (8th Cir. 1983).

17. *Burch v. Barker*, 861 F.2d 1149 (9th Cir. 1988).

18. *Trustees of the University of Pennsylvania*, 69 F.C.C.2d 1384 (1978). See also 45 RR2d 565 (1979).

19. Student Press Law Center *Report*, Spring 1994, pp. 3, 4.

20. Ibid., p. 31ff.

Electronic Media Law

CHAPTER OUTLINE

U ntil now, this book has rarely dealt with what could be called media-specific communications law. Most topics have been presented as if it didn't matter whether messages were delivered by a newspaper carrier, handed out on a street corner, shouted from a public park, or delivered electronically. Now, however, we must focus on laws uniquely applicable to electronic media. Courts, Congress, presidents, local government, and media consumers have long perceived that the nature of and unique characteristics of different communications media, especially electronic ones, call out for special forms of communications law. To paraphrase a popular advertising campaign, things are different in electronic media law.

These differences begin at a very basic level. Electronic media, unlike print media, require government licenses or franchises. Various justifications for this have been offered, but most turn on either the use of a public resource (the electromagnetic spectrum or **public rights of ways** that can be used to string wires and cables), some perceived unique **intrusiveness** or **pervasiveness,** or the belief that a particular electronic medium has gained monopolistic "bottleneck" control over a form of electronic communications in a community.

- **Public rights of way**
Physical spaces (roads, sidewalks, areas where power poles are located) that are owned by the public and dedicated to providing services that all citizens enjoy.

- **Intrusiveness**
In broadcast law, the idea that radio and television signals come uninvited into the homes, cars, and offices of listeners and viewers and, as a result, can be regulated by the federal government.

Pervasiveness
Similar to intrusiveness in indecency law. Electronic media are presumed to be different than print media because they are thought to influence everyone's life.

Public offices
Governmental offices where public elections—rather than appointment—determine who serves.

Fairness doctrine
An abandoned FCC policy that required broadcasters to (1) present some programming about controversial issues of public importance and (2) reasonably present opposing viewpoints on those issues.

Obscenity
Sexual content that may be banned by the government. Specifically defined by the U.S. Supreme Court. If content meets the definition, it is not protected under the First Amendment to the U.S. Constitution.

Indecency
Different from obscenity. Regulated in broadcasting but, so far, not in other media. Indecent broadcasts involve patently offensive depictions of sexual or excretory activities or organs broadcast when children are likely to be in the audience.

The very fact that electronic media are licensed media has compelled courts to develop First Amendment theories that can justify such government control. Theories have also been formulated to justify the regulations government imposes on these licensed media. Our current theories for electronic media regulation—and for squaring that regulation with First Amendment promises of freedom of speech and press—were developed independently for various forms of electronic communication. As all of these forms converge, however, our older media-specific notions are being strained.

Electronic media law can come from the executive, legislative, and judicial branches of federal and state government. Much of it, however, is also created by allegedly "independent" regulatory agencies. At the federal level, the relevant agency is the Federal Communications Commission (FCC). State public utility commissions regulate some aspects of telephony. Municipal agencies play a major role in the lives of cable systems.

Ultimately, these government agencies must grant and renew licenses and franchises. Sometimes renewal is denied, and occasionally licenses are revoked before they expire. Standards and procedures for accomplishing all this must be developed and require periodic revision. Although some attention is paid to content in making licensing decisions, these are, today, largely content-neutral matters. Government regulates some business aspects of electronic media, such as ownership patterns, in order to maximize service to the public, and sometimes to minimize costs and promote diversity.

Although content rarely determines licensing matters, some aspects of electronic media content remain regulated in ways not applicable to print media. Whether they want to or not, broadcasters must provide some access to their stations by candidates for federal elective office. They, along with cablecasters, must treat opposing candidates for all **public offices** equally. Many uses of broadcasting and cable by candidates cannot be censored by media owners or employees, and the rates electronic media can charge candidates are subject to federal regulation. Television broadcasters are compelled to offer at least some programming that assists in the development of children while cable operators must retransmit the signals of all local television stations to their cable customers.

With the abandonment of the FCC's **fairness doctrine**, broadcasters can be as unfair as their ethics and morals allow. But on other moral issues, government opinion can prevail. All electronic media face laws preventing them from carrying obscene content, but **obscenity** laws originally designed for print and movies are hard to apply to electronic forms of communication. In addition, only electronic media are compelled to keep a different kind of content, **indecency**, away from ready access by children. Broadcast promotion of lotteries and other gambling activities is regulated, and the broadcast of song lyrics glorifying drug use and other content that may promote antisocial behaviors can be sanctioned. Broadcasters whose programming panics or deceives a community can also be disciplined by law.

Some alternatives to traditional commercial broadcasting and cable exist, notably noncommercial broadcasting. Noncommercial licenses can be held by religious organizations, but that can create tension between freedom of religion and media law. Nonreligious public broadcasters have received government funds and are sometimes government agencies themselves. This government connection has raised hard-to-solve problems about how public broadcasting can be kept both free of control from the government hand that feeds it and accountable to the public. This balancing act becomes especially tricky, in First Amendment terms, when the government owns and runs the medium.

Continued electronic media **convergence**—our ongoing transformation into an information society—is putting new faces on some old electronic media law problems and creating new problems that are unprecedented. Nevertheless, knowledge of past and present electronic media law is crucial to citizens and electronic communicators, now and in the future.

● **Convergence**
The merging or melding of previously distinct communications media, making business, technical and legal distinctions among forms of electronic media less meaningful.

WHY HAVE THINGS BEEN DIFFERENT?

Print media obviously existed long before electronic media came along. Gutenberg preceded electronic media figures such as Marconi, de Forrest, Armstrong, Zworkin, Paley, Cronkite, and Koppel by several centuries. Not surprisingly, we developed traditions of print media law long before we began to think about how media law should apply to nonprint media. Those traditions stressed freedom from government control and left responsibility largely in the hands of media owners and employees with very minimal governmental guidance. So far, this print tradition has dominated this book. The United States has no Federal Print Media Commission deciding whether one can publish a newspaper or magazine or, if one does, whether that newspaper must provide equal space to candidates for public office. If you have the money, you can start a newspaper or magazine whenever you like. You simply raise the money, offer a product to the public, and sink or swim based on the willingness of readers and advertisers to pay for your publication.

Things have always been different for electronic media. In the 1910s and 1920s, when electronic media first emerged, two ideas drove the notion that electronic media were different than print. First, unlike newspapers, early wireless services used the electromagnetic spectrum rather than paper to transmit information. Lawmakers viewed that spectrum as a public resource different from the roads, for example, used to deliver newspapers. Second, the electromagnetic spectrum was considered a type of scarce or limited public resource. When radio began, partly because of primitive transmission and reception technology, it quickly became clear that everyone who wanted to operate a broadcast station would not be able to do so. If no control was exercised over who ran stations and how they did it, service to the public would decline as different transmitters placed signals on top of each other causing interference.

Early U.S. efforts at regulating spectrum use tried to address these problems by limiting the number of stations and adopting technical standards to reduce interference. After adopting two early statutes—the Radio Act of 1910 and the Wireless Ship Act of 1912—that regulated the radio spectrum only to control wireless equivalents of telegraphs and telephones, Congress enacted the

- **Radio Act of 1927**
Federal statute regulating users of the spectrum from 1927 until 1934 when the Communications Act of 1934 was adopted. Broadcast portions of the 1927 act were nearly identical to those of the 1934 act.

- **Public interest, convenience, and necessity**
The standard by which all actions of the FCC must be justified. If challenged, the FCC must be able to prove that what it has done advances the public interest, convenience, and (sometimes or) necessity.

- **Federal Radio Commission (FRC)**
Predecessor to the Federal Communications Commission. Governed interstate uses of radio (but not wired services like telephones and telegraphs) from 1927 until the FCC was created in 1934.

- **Communications Act of 1934**
The major federal statute that still governs wired and wireless interstate electronic media. Has been amended many times since 1934.

Radio Act of 1927 as the first federal law intended to regulate the new and booming industry of wireless broadcasting.[1]

The Radio Act of 1927 accomplished several purposes. It established that federal law would govern uses of the spectrum, including broadcast uses. Radio, with signals that crossed readily from state to state, should be uniformly regulated by national law. Federal regulation of broadcast media persists. Even today, local communities do not have much say in who owns local television and radio stations or how they work.

Congress also said in 1927 that federally licensed broadcast stations should serve the **public interest, convenience, and necessity**. While Congress, at the time, almost certainly had no clear idea of what this meant in fine detail, it believed broadcasters were lucky to be given spectrum space and should use it for the public good.

Since all the details needed to cope with a rapidly changing industry could not be included in legislation, Congress established a regulatory body—the **Federal Radio Commission (FRC)**—to work out the fine points of broadcast law by adopting rules and regulations having the force of law. Like broadcasters, the FRC was supposed to promote the public interest. Its rules and regulations had to meet that standard. As things turned out, while some of these rules and regulations covered technical aspects of broadcasting as everyone expected they would in 1927, the FRC also adopted rules and policies pertaining to content. It prohibited broadcasters, for example, from using their stations to mislead the public or to promote their own views or business interests. Like federal control over broadcasting, the public interest standard persists today although what it means in practice has been subject to constant change.

Technically, the Radio Act of 1927 had a short life. Seven years after its adoption, Congress replaced it with the statute that, with modifications, continues to guide broadcasting and other electronic media today—the **Communications Act of 1934**.[2] The 1934 act replaced the FRC with the Federal Communications Commission and made that body more permanent than the FRC had been intended to be. The new FCC, like the FRC, was in charge of wireless services such as broadcasting and radiotelephony, but it also assumed regulatory authority over interstate wired services such as telephones and telegraphs that had previously been regulated by the Interstate Commerce Commission. Since the broadcast parts of the 1927 act were incorporated with few changes into the Communications Act, our statutory framework for broadcast law dates from the earlier statute.

Justifications for Broadcast Regulation

Congress gained power to regulate broadcasting because it was a form of interstate commerce. So are newspapers, but we have never licensed newspapers as we license broadcast stations. The key justification for treating broadcasting differently in 1927 and 1934 was the concept of spectrum scarcity. As a scarce resource, the spectrum seemed to need a technological traffic cop regulator. Ever since 1927, however, the theory has also resulted in at least some content regulation. The 1927 act, for example, required broadcasters to provide opposing candidates for public office with equal opportunities to use their stations. In general ways, both the FRC and the FCC have adopted rules and policy statements attempting to describe what kind of content is in the public interest and what is not, although such policies are not in vogue today. Like technical regulations, these rules were often justified in the name of scarcity; since we could have only a few governmentally selected broadcasters, they had to function, even in programming terms, as trustees of a public resource. This meant, at least until fairly recently, that the FRC and FCC promulgated broad guidelines about public interest programming expected of broadcasters. These guidelines were usually quite general because the First Amendment and the 1927 and 1934 acts all recognized that broadcasters enjoyed rights of free speech and press that might be violated if government got too specific about content. The issue then, as now, was how far the government could go in influencing content when the speakers were trustees of a scarce public resource who were supposed to operate in the public interest.

In 1943, the U.S. Supreme Court accepted the **scarcity theory** as a basis for imposing regulations on broadcasters that probably could not be imposed on print media. *National Broadcasting Company v. United States* involved FCC regulations of the contracts that could exist between radio networks and affiliated stations.[3] The regulations were designed to protect the programming decision making of local stations by prohibiting such things as contractual restrictions on when stations could choose not to run network shows or limits on the ability of stations to run programs from sources other than their networks. NBC and CBS attacked the rules, in part, by arguing that they violated the First Amendment. Relying on the scarcity principle, Justice Felix Frankfurter responded that they did not:

● **Scarcity theory**
The idea that broadcast media must be regulated by the government because only a limited number of broadcasters can use the spectrum at the same time.

> The regulations, even if valid in all other respects, must fall because they abridge, say the [broadcasters], their right of free speech. If that be so, it would follow that every person whose application for a license to operate a station is denied by the commission is thereby denied . . . constitutional right of free speech. Freedom of utterance [however] is abridged to many who wish to use the limited facilities of radio. Unlike other modes of expression, radio inherently is not available to all. That is its unique characteristic, and that is why, unlike other modes of expression, it is subject to governmental regulation. Because it cannot be used by all, some who wish to use it must be denied. . . . The question here is simply whether the commission, by announcing that it will refuse licenses to persons who engage in specified network practices . . . is thereby denying such persons the constitutional right of free speech. The right of free speech does not include, however, the right to use the facilities of radio without a license. The licensing system established by Congress in the Communications Act of 1934 was a proper exercise of its power over commerce. The standard it provided for licensing of stations was the "public interest, convenience, or necessity." Denial of a license on that ground, if valid under the Act, is not a denial of free speech.

Belief in spectrum scarcity later added another important idea to First Amendment theory for broadcasting—that broadcasting was a medium in which the First Amendment rights of broadcasters to decide what to transmit might conflict with First Amendment rights (or at least interests) of listeners and viewers to receive diverse information. This balance of First Amendment rights was directly addressed by the Supreme Court in *Red Lion Broadcasting v. FCC* (1969).[4]

A fundamentalist minister, Rev. Billy James Hargis, bought time on religious format radio station WGCB in Red Lion, Pennsylvania, to run a program that, among other things, vigorously criticized a book written by Fred Cook about Hargis's favorite 1964 Republican presidential nominee, Barry Goldwater. The FCC, under the fairness doctrine (a policy discussed later in this text), ordered WGCB to let Cook respond to the attack for free. WGCB appealed all the way to the Supreme Court.

Writing for the Court, Justice Byron White juxtaposed the First Amendment claims raised in the case—WGCB's claim that the FCC order violated its First Amendment rights and the FCC's position that its order furthered the First Amendment rights of listeners and viewers. White supported Cook and the FCC based on a continuing belief in spectrum scarcity:

> Because of the scarcity of radio frequencies, the government is permitted to put restraints on licensees in favor of others whose views should be expressed in this unique medium. But the people as a whole retain their interest in free speech by radio and their collective right to have the medium function consistently with the ends and purposes of the First Amendment. It is the right of the viewers and listeners, not the right of the broadcasters, which is paramount. . . . It is the purpose of the First Amendment to preserve an uninhibited marketplace of ideas in which truth will ultimately prevail, rather than to countenance monopolization of that market, whether it be by the government itself or a private licensee. . . . It is the right of the public to receive suitable access to social, political, esthetic, moral, and other ideas and experiences which is crucial here.

Although the FCC has since abandoned the fairness doctrine, the Supreme Court still believes that spectrum scarcity justifies unique treatment of broadcasting under the First Amendment.[5] Others, however, argue that the theory is outmoded and should be abandoned.

Even if spectrum scarcity no longer justifies regulation, however, other justifications for treating broadcasting uniquely have been advanced and would remain. The most significant of these was developed by the Supreme Court in a 1978 decision involving a broadcast of a comedy routine by George Carlin.

WBAI, a noncommercial radio station in New York City, broadcast a twelve-minute recording of Carlin's "Filthy Words" monologue at about 2 o'-clock in the afternoon. Complaints were filed with the FCC that the broadcast was indecent and thus violated parts of the U.S. Criminal Code prohibiting "obscene, indecent, or profane language by means of radio communications."[6] The contributions of the eventual U.S. Supreme Court decision in *FCC v. Pacifica Foundation* to obscenity and indecency law are treated later. Of equal importance, however, was the articulation by the Court of additional, non-

• **Red Lion Broadcasting v. FCC**
The U.S. Supreme Court decision upholding the FCC's fairness doctrine because it advanced the First Amendment rights of listeners and viewers to receive information even though doing so required some government supervision of content.

• **FCC v. Pacifica Foundation**
The U.S. Supreme Court decision upholding FCC regulation of broadcast indecency.

scarcity-based justifications for broadcast regulation. According to Justice John Paul Stevens's majority opinion:

> We have long recognized that each medium of expression presents special First Amendment problems . . . . And of all forms of communication, it is broadcasting that has received the most limited First Amendment protection. . . .
>
> The reasons for these distinctions are complex, but two have relevance to the present case. First, the broadcast media have established a uniquely pervasive presence in the lives of all Americans. Patently offensive, indecent material presented over the airwaves confronts the citizen, not only in public, but also in the privacy of the home where the individual's right to be let alone plainly outweighs the First Amendment rights of an intruder. . . . To say that one may avoid further offense by turning off the radio when he hears indecent language is like saying that the remedy for an assault is to run away after the first blow. . . .
>
> Second, broadcasting is uniquely accessible to children, even those too young to read . . . . Other forms of offensive expression may be withheld from the young without restricting the expression at its source. . . . The ease with which children may obtain access to broadcast material [however] . . . amply justify special treatment of indecent broadcasting.

While the *Pacifica* rationale of unique pervasiveness or intrusiveness may be limited to narrow circumstances involving children, the decision did demonstrate that broadcasting was different than print for reasons beyond scarcity. On occasion, arguments about intrusiveness or pervasiveness have been made to justify regulation of nonbroadcast media, such as cable television or even persistent telephone solicitation. When these arguments have failed—as they most commonly have in court cases to date—the result tends to reaffirm *Pacifica*'s holding: other electronic media are not uniquely intrusive or pervasive, but broadcasting still is. That's the case, at least, until the Supreme Court changes its mind.[7]

Justifications for Cable Television Regulation

Different arguments support regulation of cable television, not all of them universally accepted. There are many kinds of cable television systems. What they all share, however, is their reliance on physical interconnection by coaxial or fiber optic cable of a central headend with television receivers in a community. Cable, in other words, must establish a physical pathway to viewers that, in broadcasting, is accomplished through wireless, nonphysical means.

If cable's physical pathways are constructed entirely on private property, for example, within a large multi-unit apartment complex, then the arguments for government control of the system are weak. Large cable systems, however, must inevitably string wires over or under public property. This use of public rights of way to build cable systems is one of the major justifications for cable regulation, both by the federal government and by the states. Municipalities have traditionally regulated at least some aspects of public utilities, like telephone, electric, and gas companies, that use public rights of ways. They argue that cable is little different. Disputes arise, however—much as in broadcasting—over the scope or limit of appropriate regulation. Government regulates more than the physical or technical aspects of broadcasting. Cable law has varied, over its short history, in how far it will go in allowing government to regulate the nonphysical or nontechnical aspects of cable.

Increasingly, the argument is also being made that local cable systems are monopolies and that most cable subscribers have no available alternatives for similar high-capacity video and audio service. Cable regulation proponents urge that this local monopoly status of cable also justifies regulation, at least until cable systems receive direct competition from other cable providers, from multichannel wireless services such as direct satellite broadcasting (DBS), or conceivably from telephone companies.

Despite the variety of arguments advanced for broadcast and cable regulation, the result is the same. Government approval is needed to enter these businesses, and some level of government supervision of what they do is ongoing. In these ways, our electronic media have always been, and remain today, quite different from print media. Today they often chafe at these differences. Broadcast, cable, and even telephone industry leaders argue that their media businesses are forced to play on "uneven playing fields" when the laws that govern them are different than the laws that govern print and even some of their electronic competitors. They question whether the justifications for cable and broadcast regulation developed in the past remain valid today in light of changes in the media and media marketplaces.

MODERN CONDITIONS AND OLD ARGUMENTS

The last twenty years or so have been hectic for the electronic media industries and turbulent for electronic media law. We have gone from a broadcast industry dominated by three major national networks to a much more fragmented electronic media industry in which cable television is a major player and in which broadcast stations have become just one of many sources of content. Broadcast regulation largely developed in a less diverse and less competitive world. Much cable regulation resulted from comparisons of cable with old-fashioned broadcasting. Some argue that times have changed. The old justifications should be rejected and laws, rules, and regulations modified or deleted. It is time, some say, for deregulation and equality among the rules governing electronic media.

To some extent, calls for deregulation have been characteristic of recent American business law in general. Some argue that traditions of governmental regulation of business, largely established during Franklin Roosevelt's New Deal era, are out of date. They argue that as was the case before the New Deal's reaction to the Great Depression, we should rely primarily on competitive marketplace forces rather than government dictates to keep businesses in line. The United States has substantially deregulated industries such as airlines and trucking. We have also, at least to a degree, deregulated broadcasting and cable and, in this climate, have been reluctant to impose new regulations on newer competitors.

The scarcity rationale for unique treatment is perhaps the hardest to sustain today. Broadcasters still use the spectrum, but it is hard to argue broadcasters are scarce. Communities almost always have many more local electronic media outlets than they have local print outlets. New networks come along regularly—Fox, Paramount, and Warner Brothers have joined the much older ABC, CBS, and NBC networks in broadcasting, while ESPN, CNN, and others offer options to viewers through cable. If scarcity really does justify government regulation of media, some would say, then we should regulate scarce newspapers rather than not-so-scarce radio and TV broadcasters. Deregulation proponents argue that the real scarcity today is money, that anybody with enough money can buy their way into radio or TV by purchasing stations just as they can buy their way into print media, and that—in this sense—all media are equally scarce and ought to be treated alike under the law.

Predictions for media in the twenty-first century are staggering. Cable television companies, combining fiber optic transmission systems with digital signal processing, are actively making plans to offer up to 500 channels to American homes by the turn of the century. There may be something to the broadcasters' argument that scarcity is a thing of the past and that unique rules for broadcasting are now unjustifiable and should be dropped.

Convergence of Modes

The mention of cable as a competitor to broadcasting highlights another trend that is both undermining and reviving the old justifications for unique treatment. Scholars have called this trend "convergence of modes,"[8] which is a fancy term for a fairly simple idea. For much of our media history, people primarily used radio and TV for different purposes than they used print. They turned to newspapers, primarily, to be informed through reading. Broadcasting, although often informative, was primarily used for entertainment. If people wanted to converse electronically with a friend or a business, they did so through yet another mode of communication, telephony. In recent years, however, those distinctions—which underlie much existing electronic media law—are blurring. Although they haven't been rousing economic successes, broadcasters and cable operators have offered teletext services that let people read from their TV monitors. Computer networks, often using telephone lines, permit individuals to access information in text, audio, and video form from far-flung locations. Newspapers are increasingly forming partnerships with cable TV systems to transmit mini-local newscasts from their newsrooms, which, of course, compete with local broadcasters. In other words, convergence has resulted in people using media to meet their needs with less concern about the mode of information transmission the medium uses. In a business sense, convergence characterizes most media companies, which are no longer solely print or broadcasting or cable companies but, instead, have divisions involved in all of these industries. Time-Warner Communications, for example, publishes magazines (*Time,*

People, *Sports Illustrated*), owns cable television systems and cable networks (HBO), and produces motion pictures and TV shows (Warner Brothers). It is actively exploring most other forms of modern communications. Yet it confronts media law that often remains media-specific.

The ultimate in convergence—perhaps not too far away—seems likely to involve a mode of electronic communications that, until very recently, we did not even think of as a mass medium although almost every citizen used it. This is telephony. For years, all the telephone system did for most people was automate interpersonal communications. It provided one-to-one rather than one-to-many communications services such as those provided by traditional mass media. Today, however, many uses of the telephone network, and related computer networks, are taking on decidedly mass-media-like characteristics. People use the telephone as a means of getting information—from dial-a-porn sexual services to stock reports and sports scores. In today's information age, laws rooted in the old ways radio, television, cable, and even telephony operated look to some to be increasingly outdated.

These developments suggest that the inevitable result will be continued deregulation and that future editions of this book will have no need for separate electronic media chapters. That much convergence of media and media law, however, seems unlikely. Cable TV, for example, has recently bucked the deregulation/convergence trend. Rate increases associated with a largely deregulatory statute adopted by Congress in 1984[9] led to adoption of the **Cable Television Consumer Protection and Competition Act of 1992**, which reregulated some aspects of cable.[10] In this case, for at least a while, policymakers believed cable had had a little too much deregulation and consumers had suffered. By 1995, however, a newly Republican Congress actively considered modifying or repealing the rate control sections of the 1992 act.

The remainder of this century is likely to see intensive debate over communications policy making. Under the Clinton administration, many government agencies have studied what policies, if any, must be modified, repealed, or adopted in order to build a modern "National Information Infrastructure"—the so-called Information Superhighway. The improved infrastructure would meld together wired and wireless means of high-capacity information exchange. It would mingle what broadcasting, cable TV, telephony, and related industries do today. Theoretically, the superhighway would give citizens and business vast abilities to retrieve and exchange information and to tailor that information to unique personal and corporate needs. Few seem to doubt, however, that the superhighway will require at least some special rules, so electronic media regulation seems likely to persist. Development of the superhighway may even result in yet another justification for electronic media regulation—the uniquely central role of information in modern corporate and individual affairs.

At least the following fundamental issues endure. Entry into most electronic media requires government permission. How is that obtained? How is it renewed or preserved? Special laws still affect electronic media content. What are they? How do they affect the practice of electronic journalism? How can they be reconciled with freedom of speech and press? These are the topics for the remainder of this chapter. Understanding them, however, requires knowing

● **Cable Television Consumer Protection and Competition Act of 1992**

Legislation adopted by the U.S. Congress that, in part, increased federal, state, and local regulation of cable television especially of rates cable systems could charge subscribers.

a bit more about the government agencies responsible for electronic media law and policy.

FEDERAL AND STATE REGULATORS OF ELECTRONIC MEDIA

Much electronic media law is what lawyers call administrative law. Such law is adopted and enforced a bit differently than the statutes adopted by legislatures and interpreted by courts that have so far been the focus of this book. Administrative law is created by what some have called the fourth branch of government—administrative agencies. These agencies can exist at both the federal and state levels of government. Agencies such as these began in the early twentieth century and grew dramatically from the 1930s to the 1960s as legislative bodies realized that specialized areas of the law were so complex, technical, or fast-changing that their details could not be routinely handled by often slow-moving and in-expert legislatures.

To address this problem, legislatures adopted broad statutes granting some of their regulatory powers to specialized agencies. These agencies often focused on specific industries such as airlines, banking, or communications. Once given general mandates and powers by statute, the agencies had the power to adopt additional laws, generally called rules or regulations, that fleshed out the details and, at least theoretically, were consistent with the goals of the legislature. Agencies could change or delete these rules and regulations as conditions warranted. If the agency did something the legislature really objected to, of course, that legislature could intervene by adopting additional statutes undoing what the regulatory agency had done, but such intervention has historically been rare.

The Federal Communications Commission is a classic example of an administrative agency. Its basic job is to implement the Communications Act of 1934. Legislation did not come to a complete stop in 1934, however. For more than sixty years, Congress has modified the statute in two important ways. First, it has adopted hundreds of minor changes and adjustments, either in response to changes in the electronic media or in reaction to FCC or judicial decisions. Second, it has added large sections to the act to deal with matters that were not problems in 1934, such as satellite communications (1962),[11] public broadcasting (1967),[12] and cable television (1984 and 1992).[13] These changes have attempted to keep the act up-to-date.

In less sweeping, but very significant, ways, the act is also kept up-to-date by the commission. The statute is often very nonspecific, so many things are governed by rules and regulations written by the FCC. Licensing of broadcast stations is an example. Except for setting the length of licenses, stipulating that they cannot be granted to foreigners, mandating that the character of licensees be scrutinized, prescribing some ownership restrictions, and a few other matters, Congress has left many of the most important elements of licensing unaddressed. The FCC adopts rules and regulations deciding these matters—in that sense, it is quasi-legislative—and then applies and enforces its own policies, which makes it quasi-judicial.

The FCC Described

The FCC is a bureaucracy. Situated in Washington, D.C., it has about 2,200 full-time employees; most are in the nation's capital, but a few are in field offices around the country. Atop the bureaucracy are five commissioners nominated by the president and, like many other federal officeholders including judges, confirmed for office by the U.S. Senate. Commissioners serve five-year terms and can be reappointed, although they rarely are. The president can, at any time, name one of them FCC chair without Senate approval.

Beneath the commissioners is a staff structure that does most of the FCC's work (see Figure 1). Various bureaus (for example, the Mass Media Bureau and the Common Carrier Bureau) handle the details of drafting, monitoring, and enforcing rules and regulations affecting their parts of the FCC's responsibilities. In most cases, the bureaus also have the power to grant licenses in the ser-

FIGURE I
THE FEDERAL COMMUNICATIONS COMMISSION

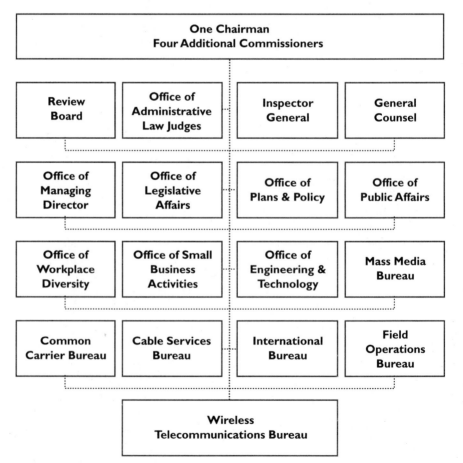

vices they regulate unless a great dispute arises over who should hold the license. The offices (for example, the Office of Engineering and Technology and the Office of the General Counsel) broadly advise the FCC on professional matters cutting across the industries the FCC regulates (here, engineering or legal issues). Other quasi-independent parts of the FCC (the Office of Administrative Law Judges and the Review Board) function much like courts, hearing disputes among parties, sometimes pitting outside parties against the commission, and making at least initial decisions almost as if they were judges. Decisions of almost all parts of the FCC, however, can be reviewed by the five commissioners who have ultimate responsibility for the agency's actions. They vote as a collegial body—the chair has no more power than any of the other members.

Although the FCC is sometimes called an independent agency because it is not a part of the executive, legislative, or judicial branches of government, this term can be quite misleading. Actually, the FCC is subject to influence from all of these other branches of government. An agency finds it hard to be independent when its members must seek presidential approval to be appointed and Senate confirmation to take office. Like all parts of the federal government, the FCC must go to Congress annually as part of the budgeting process and can, through that process, be not-so-gently guided by senators and representatives. The very statute leading to the commission's existence and defining its powers and responsibilities can be amended by Congress. Nearly all of the FCC's decisions can be appealed in federal courts, so it is hardly independent of the judiciary either. Actually, like all parts of government, administrative agencies are political bodies subject to multiple influences.

In addition to the responsibilities it has had over broadcasting, telephony, and telegraphy since 1934, since 1984 the FCC has some authority over cable TV. It shares that authority, however, with state and local governments, which are much more involved in the regulation of cable than in broadcast regulation. Although Congress increased the FCC's authority substantially in 1992, much of the action in cable TV law still comes from state and local governmental agencies. As has already been mentioned, cable TV systems (unlike broadcasters) do not need licenses from the FCC. What they do need is a **franchise**. In most instances, they get that from local government.

● **Franchise**
Authorization from one party to another authorizing the second party to engage in a specific activity. Cable operators usually obtain franchises from local government.

Cable Franchising

The cable franchising process begins when a local government legislature, such as a city council, adopts an ordinance establishing a legal framework for cable television in a community. The ordinance states the basic expectations of the community for cable service and the conditions under which it will grant franchises. What cities can ask for or regulate, however, is limited by federal law. The ordinance establishes some system under which companies interested in providing service under those conditions can apply for franchises and sets up a mechanism for making the decision about who receives them. At least sometimes, the ordinance puts some part of city government in charge of the franchising process and/or monitoring the behavior of successful applicants once a franchise is granted.

The specifics of local government regulation of cable TV vary. In some communities, responsibility is vested in city administrators who have many other responsibilities as well. It might be given to the city manager or a generic board of public works or public utilities. In other communities, however, specific cable or telecommunications councils are established. Their operation is often paid for out of the franchise fee most cities collect from cable TV operators. The structure, behavior, duties, and levels of sophistication of these bodies vary widely, but the local cable system operator must learn to deal with them. As a result, cable regulation is much more diverse than broadcast regulation. Broadcasters primarily worry about only one federal agency—the FCC. A cable television **multiple system operator** (MSO) is likely to run hundreds of cable systems in communities across the country. Things will be handled a little differently in each of those communities, although federal law imposes some uniformity. In addition to these local ordinances, all cable systems must comply with FCC rules and regulations that govern cable nationally. As in broadcasting, there are usually ways to get courts to review actions of both federal and local cable regulators.

● **Multiple system operators (MSOs)**
Cable companies that operate many cable systems throughout the country.

GETTING AND KEEPING A LICENSE OR FRANCHISE: HOW THE PROCESS WORKS

As you can sense from this brief discussion of cable franchising, getting government approval to enter electronic mass media is often complex. Textbooks specifically oriented toward electronic media law contain a much fuller description of the franchising and broadcast licensing process than is included here. Our account focuses on aspects of licensing and franchising that are of particular importance to those who practice electronic communications. We include the basics that are relevant to employees of media companies and leave out some issues that are primarily of importance to owners.

Although we have said that government determines entry into electronic media, that is, perhaps, more true in theory than in practice. In theory, government's strongest opportunity to shape the electronic media could be at the point where franchises and licenses are first granted. Government might carefully scrutinize applicants and do all that it could to pick the very best among them. Indeed, a whole set of laws and policies govern the initial selection of totally new broadcasters and cable system operators, and making predictions about who will do best is part of that process.

In fact, however, government today rarely has this kind of opportunity. Almost all desirable—meaning profitable—broadcast licenses and cable franchises were awarded by government long ago. In a practical sense today, one does not often enter broadcasting or cable system operation by asking the government for a new license or franchise. Instead, entry occurs by locating a broadcast station or cable system owner willing to sell, negotiating a price, and then seeking government's approval to acquire the license or franchise. Government is still involved, but its role is more one of approval than selection.

Thus, our focus will be on how law affects the sale and transfer of broadcast licenses and cable franchises.

We will also describe license and franchise renewal. Unlike some other areas of business, these grants of the right to engage in a business are not indefinite. Currently, radio station licenses run for seven years and television licenses for five. In mid-1995, there was the possibility that could change since Congress considered extending the length of both radio and TV license terms to ten years. The length of cable franchises may vary through negotiation between the **franchisor** and **franchisee** but may not currently exceed fifteen years. When these licenses and franchises end, owners nearly always expect them to be renewed. Government decides when renewal is justified.

The Broadcast Licensing Process

To hold any broadcast station license, a party must meet standards created by Congress through the Communications Act of 1934 and by the FCC through its rules and regulations. The act currently prevents foreigners from holding licenses (although Congress may change this), stipulates that the FCC consider legal, financial, technical, character, and public interest qualifications, and specifically governs a few matters such as some forms of ownership. While statutory requirements are often general and nonspecific, the FCC must establish clear licensing requirements that people can understand sufficiently well to know what they must do to qualify to receive an initial license or, much more often, acquire the license to a broadcast facility they are purchasing.

These requirements can be grouped into several categories. It is relatively easy to prove one satisfies the financial qualifications to hold a license. Applicants must show that they have the resources available to build or acquire the station and run it for three months without counting on revenues. While there are many technical requirements, concerning such things as acceptable power, hours of operation, transmitter locations, and types of equipment, a good engineer usually works those out and produces an acceptable application. In the case of a transfer application, an existing facility is being purchased. Showing that it meets the FCC technical standards is rarely a problem. Citizenship is a go or no-go proposition and therefore fairly easy for applicants to demonstrate. Beyond these financial, technical, and citizenship showings, however, are slightly more complex matters related to legal qualifications and, sometimes, character.

Many of the most important legal qualifications relate to ownership patterns and limits. For many years, all ownership rules were creations of the FCC. More recently, Congress has added some ownership limits to the Communications Act but also considered deleting others. Collectively, Congress and the FCC regulate many aspects of electronic media ownership.

The FCC long prohibited what it called local **duopolies**. This meant that nobody could own two AM stations or two FM stations or two TV stations serving the same communities. Responding to changes in radio economics, however, the FCC has changed its rules, and radio duopolies are now possible. The conditions are very complex. In communities with fourteen or fewer commercial radio stations, an owner may own up to three radio stations (but no

● **Franchisor**
The party that grants a franchise (in cable television, usually cities or counties).

● **Franchisee**
The party that holds a franchise.

● **Duopolies**
Common ownership of two electronic media of the same type in the same community—for example, owning two TV stations in the same town.

more than two of them in a single service, AM or FM) provided that the stations commonly owned do not equal more than 50 percent of all stations in the market. In communities with fifteen or more commercial radio stations, a single owner is allowed up to four radio properties (no more than two in each radio service) provided that the audience share in the market reached by those stations is not more than 25 percent of all listening in the market![14]

Consider the following example. There are four radio stations in a small market. Three of these are AM stations while one is FM. The owner of the FM station could acquire only one of the AMs because that would result in common ownership of two of the four stations in the market. The remaining AM stations, however, could not merge because the resulting company would own two stations in the same service in the market.

Now imagine a larger market with twenty-four radio stations. There are both AM and FM stations for sale here. The owner of one of the FM stations decides to purchase other properties. That owner might be able to buy up to two AM stations, but only one more FM. Such a purchase would result in the maximum number of co-owned stations (four) with only two stations in each service. Whether this purchase could actually be made, however, also depends on the ratings of the stations acquired. To decide what stations to buy, the purchaser must add the audience share of the currently owned FM station (say, 6 percent of the total audience) to the shares of the stations being purchased (say, in this case, 6, 4, and 2 percent). Since the total here is 18 percent, which is less than the 25 percent combined share allowed under the rules, these purchases would be acceptable. Purchases of more successful stations might push the combination over the audience share limit.

The rules for television are easier to understand, at least as of mid 1995. Local duopolies (meaning UHF-UHF, VHF-VHF, and UHF-VHF combinations) are simply prohibited. Under current policies, commonly owned TV stations must usually be at least fifty to seventy miles apart. In late 1994, however, the FCC proposed to liberalize these standards and narrow the required distance between commonly owned stations to around forty miles.[15] By 1995, Congress was considering deleting all rules prohibiting local radio or television duopolies.

Common ownership of radio and TV stations in the same market is also subject to FCC review. In general, owners of TV stations cannot buy radio stations in their markets and vice versa. Some exceptions, however, allow combinations of economically weak UHF stations with radio or economically weak AM stations with TV. Such combinations are usually permitted if the market is one of the nation's twenty-five largest and if, after the acquisition, at least thirty separately owned radio and TV stations would remain. This rule, too, was under FCC and Congressional review as of mid-1995.[16]

The FCC has capped the number of stations a single owner can own since the 1940s. As of mid-1995, a single owner could own up to 20 AM stations, 20 FM stations, and 12 TV stations (either UHF or VHF) throughout the country. In addition, a single owner's TV stations could not serve markets containing more than 25 percent of the nation's TV households. More stations (up to 3 AMs, 3 FMs and 2 more TVs) can be combined with other properties if the stations are controlled. If this happens, the share of TV households can rise to 30%. UHF-

TV stations count for only half of the homes in a market in computing the 25 or 30 percent cap, so a UHF station in a market with 6 percent of all TV house-holds in the nation would count as if it were in a market with only 3 percent of households. Congress, as of mid-1995, was considering lifting all radio owner-ship limits and permitting TV owners to own an unlimited number of stations so long as they did not exceed an audience cap of between 35 and 50 percent.

Suppose that a single party already owns 18 AM stations, 19 FM stations, and 11 TV stations. Looking at possible purchases in a market where the com-pany does not currently own any properties, the owner finds 4 AM stations, 3 FM stations, and 3 TV stations for sale. Under the national cap, this owner might acquire 2 AMs and 1 FM, which would top out the company's radio own-ership at 20 stations in each service. This market has at least seven radio sta-tions—the ones that are for sale—and probably more. In any event, after this ac-quisition, our owner would own three radio stations in a market that has at least seven. That is not more than half of the stations in the market. After the pur-chase, the owner would still not hold licenses for more than two stations in the same service (two AM and one FM). Under the combination of the radio duop-oly rules and the national radio station cap, such a purchase is permissible.

Any decision about purchasing a television station may be more complex. In terms of the number of stations, one more can be acquired since it would bring the combination to the maximum—twelve. However, the owner would have to compute the percentage of all TV households represented by the mar-kets in which stations are already owned and add this to the percentage of TV households in the market where the purchase is contemplated. The combined total of TV households must not exceed 25 percent. In addition, the purchase of the radio stations might, or might not, preclude acquisition of a TV station in the same market. This would depend on the size of the market—for the ac-quisition to be allowable at all, the market would have to rank within the top twenty-five TV markets—and the number of separately owned radio and TV stations that would remain in the market after the acquisitions (which would have to be at least thirty). To further complicate things, the proposed purchaser will probably be aware that, in late 1994, the FCC began considering modify-ing the caps on TV station ownership too.[17]

Finally, there are **crossmedia ownership** limits. The FCC restricts com-mon ownership of local broadcast stations by local daily newspapers. Under current rules, if only one daily newspaper is serving an area and only one broadcast licensee is serving the same area, then those two properties cannot be commonly owned. This situation obviously occurs rarely and is likely to happen only in very small communities. Combining local cable TV systems with local TV stations or local telephone companies is also generally prohib-ited although some courts have ruled the prohibition on cable/telephone crossownership is invalid. In 1995 Congress was considering deleting all crossownership limits or allowing combinations of some media in a market so long as others remained independent.[18]

The other major legal limit falls under the heading of character. Since Congress required by statute that the FCC consider character but did not spec-ify what it meant, the FCC has discretion and, for years, considered a wide

● **Crossmedia owner-ship**
Ownership of different me-dia by the same party—for example, combined own-ership of broadcast stations and daily newspapers.

range of factors in deciding whether licensees had the appropriate character. Some of the things considered were fairly inconsequential, such as past bad checks, marital matters, and the like. Today, licensees do not have to prove good character, but certain types of past misbehavior can demonstrate bad character and be disqualifying. Bad character includes fraud or misrepresentation in dealing with the FCC or any other government agency; prior violations of the Communications Act or FCC rules; criminal convictions if they involve fraud, deceit, dishonesty, or lying; convictions for violating antitrust laws; and felony convictions especially any related to illegal drugs. The FCC's goal is to make sure that at least licensees can be trusted to deal with it, with the public, and with the business community fairly.[19]

If applicants can prove that they meet all these legal, financial, and technical standards, then they qualify for a license assuming one is available. Most commonly, a license becomes available because an existing broadcaster is willing to sell a station. When such transfers are proposed, the FCC is prohibited from seeking out a "better" applicant than the one presented to it by the seller. If the buyer is minimally qualified, then that buyer obtains the license.

Broadcast License Renewal

When licenses expire, the FCC's permission is needed to continue in business. In most respects, the standards for renewal are the same as those for obtaining a license in the first place. The process, though not simple, is usually routine. Technical matters are presumably not a problem—the station is in current compliance with all the FCC's technical rules. Financial matters are not reviewed. Questions are asked about character, but presumably, licensees have been careful not to commit any of the prohibited misdeeds. Ownership matters should also not be a problem since all acquisitions made since the last license was granted have, one hopes, been made in line with the FCC's rules.

One thing, however, makes the renewal applicant quite different from a new applicant or even a purchaser. Unlike the new applicant or new owner of a station, incumbents have track records running the facilities for which they seek license renewal. That record is not ignored when the FCC makes a renewal decision, but it is also not examined in quite the way one might imagine.

There are at least two ways the track record could be reviewed. One way would be to analyze the incumbent's performance as a business and as an employer. That is the way the FCC primarily evaluates incumbents at renewal time today. If the radio or TV business has seriously misbehaved—by violating FCC rules, lying to government agencies, or engaging in employment discrimination—it can conceivably encounter trouble at renewal time.

Since the 1960s, the FCC has been a fairly vigorous enforcer of **equal employment opportunity (EEO)** policies. Broadcasters report annually on employment and hiring at their stations, paying special attention to the hiring of women and minority group members. At renewal time, the FCC reviews the station's achievements with primary emphasis on how closely the workforce at the station mirrors the availability of minority and female workers in the community workforce at large. It also evaluates **affirmative action** plans that larger

● **Equal employment opportunity (EEO)**
Laws and policies that require employers to select employees without regard to gender or ethnic background except where those characteristics can be shown to be truly relevant to the performance of a job.

● **Affirmative action**
Federal and state laws and policies that require organizations, usually employers, to take steps to make sure that opportunities are known by and available to "protected groups" such as women and members of ethnic minorities.

stations create and implement to locate and promote qualified minority and female employees.[20] Serious EEO problems here may result in a short-term renewal (less than five or seven years), but only the most blatantly racist or sexist employers have ever lost licenses for EEO violations. By 1995, however, Congress and the president were reviewing whether the vigor of more than thirty years of civil rights law should be reduced and a U.S. Supreme Court decision implied that at least some FCC EEO and minority ownership policies may be unconstitutional. Unless a licensee has engaged in misrepresentation (lying) to the FCC, the commission is usually tolerant of other violations of its rules and regulations that may have been investigated and resolved prior to license expiration.

Another way to consider an incumbent's track record would be to focus on the programming the licensee has offered its community in the recent past. Evaluation of past programming at renewal time, however, has varied much in specificity through the years. Currently, the FCC's review of programming in making licensing decisions is minimal.

From the 1920s through the 1970s, programming promises and performance were among the most extensive parts of license applications. Applicants for new or renewed licenses had to make promises about how much news, public affairs, and other noncommercial, nonentertainment programming they would offer. At renewal time, their performance on these promises was checked. A significant promise-versus-performance shortfall raised questions about renewability but almost never resulted in denial of renewal. Beginning in the 1960s, applicants were also required to conduct three-part ascertainments of community needs. This entailed asking a sample of the public and community leaders what they thought were the "problems, needs and interests" of the community. The results of these ascertainments, plus information about programming related to past ascertainments and plans for future programming, were considered at license renewal time. To some extent, this system permitted the FCC to avoid examining programming directly while, at least in theory, considering the more content-neutral issue of how broadcasters made decisions about how much informational programming to offer and what topics to address.

By the mid-1980s, the FCC had eliminated nearly all of these programming-related aspects of licensing.[21] The FCC had always been cautious about examining programming too closely because of the First Amendment, and this reluctance limited the rigor of its program review. Broadcasters and their attorneys, moreover, had converted the ascertainment process into a ritual, and there was some doubt that it really had much effect on programs actually aired. Enforcement of these policies had never been too vigorous—it didn't have to be. Broadcasters knew the minimum amounts of informational programming the FCC staff expected and the maximum amounts of commercial time it would allow. As a result, nearly every applicant promised the expected minimum and maximum amounts of each. Under the Carter and, especially, Reagan administrations, advocates of marketplace-based regulation convinced the FCC that it should eliminate quantitative programming and advertising review, ascertainment, and the required keeping of logs by stations as records of their programming and advertising. The commission decreed that if a specific type of programming was profitable, economic forces would lead stations to offer it. If it was not profitable, then probably the public did not need it, and the FCC should not require it. If unprofitable programming was mandated, the FCC reasoned, broadcasters would meet any such obligation only halfheartedly.

Today, broadcast license applicants do not promise much about program service, and their programming is not much reviewed at renewal time. Applications still must describe how broadcasters plan to meet the programming needs of their communities, but the FCC accepts very general descriptions here. Broadcasters must air some "issue responsive" programming and put quarterly records describing what they have done in public files at their stations. The commission, however, does not specify how much such programming must be run or when it should be scheduled. Nor does the FCC typically review these matters unless there is an outside objection to a license application. The issues/programs lists come up in renewal cases only if they are submitted to the FCC by some outside party questioning an incumbent's application. So far, the FCC has shown little inclination to pay much heed to challenges based on programming grounds.

Congress has created one exception to this lack of concern about programming at license renewal time. This exception, applicable only to television broadcasters and not radio applicants, requires the FCC to consider both programming for children and advertising practices in children's programming at renewal time. Congress added these requirements to the Communications Act in 1990 after the FCC, choosing to rely on the marketplace to provide children's shows, eliminated most prior policies that had prodded TV broadcasters to present informational or educational shows for children.[22] The act requires each TV station to provide at least some programming designed to serve the "educational and informational needs of children." The FCC has defined this as applying to children sixteen years old and under; at least initially, the commission indicated it would count "programming that furthers the positive development of the child's intellectual/cognitive or social/emotional needs" in any way. The FCC has no standards about the amounts, lengths, or scheduling of such programming. Indeed, broadcasters can offset their obligation to serve children through their own programming if they engage in "nonbroadcast efforts which enhance the value of children's educational and informational television programming." This can include such things as sponsoring and promoting "learn to read" programs at local libraries, provided that the activity is arguably broadcast related. Commercial broadcasters can offset their programming obligations by demonstrating that they help support educational and informational programming by other TV stations, including noncommercial stations, in their market.[23]

Congress also limited the amount of permissible advertising in children's shows to 10½ minutes per hour on the weekend and 12 minutes per hour on weekdays. This limit, however, has not halted what some children's TV advocates describe as program-length commercials for kids. Activists argue that programs featuring characters who are sold to kids in other contexts should count, in their entirety, as ads and thus automatically exceed the commercial time limits. Under such a standard, programs like *The Smurfs* would be unlawful because they would be viewed as entirely commercial. The commission's initial implementation of the statute, however, was narrower. Under current FCC policies, *The Smurfs* and programs like it, count as commercial matter only if the programs include ads for character-related paraphernalia.[24]

The act was initially implemented by a Republican-dominated FCC that had urged Congress not to adopt it. The FCC's "permissive" implementation of its programming and advertising requirements incensed many who had pushed Congress for its adoption. Some broadcasters, in initial filings with the FCC, listed programs like *Leave it to Beaver* and *G.I. Joe* as furthering the social development of children. Many stations appeared to be exceeding some of the commercial time limits. As the Clinton administration began to have an impact on the FCC in early 1993, the new commission began an inquiry into whether broadcasters were complying with the spirit of the law and asked if the FCC rules implementing it under President Bush needed to be modified. In April, 1995, they proposed a tighter "clarification" of its definition of "educational and informational programming" that would exclude many of the questionable children's shows some broadcasters had listed. Republicans in Congress, however, discussed repealing the 1990 Act.[25]

In sum, all applicants for licenses—through purchase, renewal, or even initial application—must prove they meet basic legal, financial, and technical qualifications established by Congress and the FCC. Renewal applicants must also show that they have been good, dependable licensees in the past, retained their character, still comply with ownership rules, have adequate EEO records, have offered some "issue responsive" programming, and, in the case of TV, have done something for the child audience. For the overwhelming majority of applicants, renewals or grants of transfers are routine. Indeed, the FCC has come to recognize that good broadcasters enjoy a renewal expectancy that is close to a property right.[26]

Not every license application is so routine, however. Applications can be challenged, occasionally successfully. Applicants for new licenses or for renewal can find their applications opposed by others who are filing what is known as a competing application. Competing applicants almost never prevail, although at first glance it may look as though they should. The FCC has long said that if it is confronted by multiple applicants for new licenses, it will pick the applicant who is most likely to diversify media ownership and/or is predicted to be able to provide the best practicable service.[27] All other things being equal, the FCC has preferred to give new licenses to individuals and groups who do not already own media properties rather than to applicants who do. This promotes diversified ownership of mass media. All other things being equal, the FCC has also preferred to grant licenses to applicants who will be deeply involved with station management rather than to applicants who will hire others to manage stations for them. Until recently, these factors guided comparative contests for new full-power AM, FM, and TV licenses in the rare instances where such contests occurred.

In late 1993, however, a federal appeals court decided that the FCC could not prove that its preference for owners who would also be managers necessarily resulted in picking the best applicant.[28] The same complaint could readily be raised about all the other comparative criteria. In early 1994, the FCC froze its review of all competing applications for new facilities. Although it said it might revive a 1992 rulemaking proceeding aimed at clarifying comparative criteria, it urged applicants then stuck in comparative battles to try and settle with each other.[29] Until this matter is resolved, the commission appears to have no mechanism for resolving comparative contests over new full-power broadcast licenses.

The situation also becomes complicated when comparative battles develop between incumbent broadcasters seeking license renewal and challengers who seek to displace them. Rigid application of the standard comparative criteria to contested renewal applications seems unfair to incumbents. An ideal competing applicant would probably be a minority female who owns no other media properties and promises to become the full-time general manager of the station. Such an applicant could, under standard comparative criteria alone, credibly challenge renewal applications of most radio and TV stations, which are owned by companies or individuals who own other media. Many stations, especially those owned by large public corporations, do not have owners intimately involved in day-to-day station management. It would be easy to design an ideal competitor who could pick off the licenses of such stations for the costs of lawyer's fees and the construction of new facilities.

Not wanting incumbents to be so vulnerable, the FCC has long struggled to include the past broadcast record of incumbents in comparative renewal cases. This effort has a tortured history.[30] It is difficult to do because a past record with a station is obviously something the incumbent has but the challenger lacks. Consequently, their records can hardly be compared. Under current policies, an incumbent earns a renewal expectancy if it can show it has provided "substantial past service not characterized by serious deficiencies." Such past service can include offering more-than-average amounts of informational programming or having a good reputation for community service among civic leaders.[31] In theory, applicants who earn this renewal expectancy are not guaranteed renewal against a competing application. The FCC claims to consider all of the traditional comparative factors as well. In practice, however, no incumbents faced with challenges have failed to earn a renewal expectancy in recent years, and no challenger, no matter how good on other criteria, has displaced an incumbent through the comparative hearing process.

● **Petitions to deny**
Paperwork filed with the FCC asking the commission not to grant a license sought by a broadcaster.

Petitions to deny are slightly more likely to cause licensing difficulties for applicants. Such a petition is filed with the FCC by someone who does not want the license themselves but believes a license application filed by somebody else should be denied. To force the FCC to hold a hearing on the petition with denial of the license application a possible outcome, petitioners must prove there are "substantial" (meaning significant or important) and "material" (meaning relevant) matters in dispute that the FCC must clear up before it can grant an application.[32] This is hard for petitioners to do, and most times they fail. In that event, the FCC denies the petition to deny, and the license application proceeds routinely.

While a petition to deny is pending at the FCC, however, license applications are in limbo, legal bills run up, and sometimes negotiations take place between the applicant and the petitioner to resolve their differences. In recent years, most petitions to deny have focused on stations' hiring practices for minorities and women. Without admitting they are doing a bad job, applicants often promise to change their hiring and promotion systems in ways likely to improve opportunities for minorities or women. If that occurs, petitioners may withdraw their petitions, and the application progresses normally at the FCC. The fact remains, however, that applications for renewals and transfers of licenses nearly always sail through the FCC without difficulty.

Cable Franchising and Franchise Renewals

Parts of the cable franchising system were described earlier to demonstrate the role state and local governments play in cable regulation. As was mentioned there, what franchisors (those who grant franchises) can ask of or do to cable systems is limited by federal law. Franchisors cannot make very specific demands about the kinds of cable programming they would like to see on the system, although they can negotiate over broad categories of program service. They can negotiate for "public, educational and public access channels" (**PEG access**) that can be used by schools and to transmit coverage of public meetings. They can seek a franchise fee that may not exceed more than 5 percent of a system's annual gross revenues and regulate rates for basic cable service (retransmission of over-the-air TV stations and access channels) only if the cable system does not face effective competition and subject to FCC procedures and standards. They can also regulate some technical and customer aspects of cable operation, but here too FCC rules check what they can demand. Although the 1992 Cable Act specifies that franchises cannot be exclusive—a city cannot grant the right to offer cable service in an area to only one company—competing applications for new cable franchises are rare. If one of the "600-pound gorilla" multiple system operators applies, others usually do not. If a franchisor does find itself confronted with multiple applicants, it can take the option—not available to the FCC in distributing broadcast licenses—of accepting all the applicants it finds basically qualified. The economics of the industry, however, generally result in only one system being built.

> ● **PEG access**
> Channels on cable television systems reserved for use by public, educational, or governmental cablecasters.

The real action is, or at least shortly will be, focused on franchise renewal. Under the Cable Communications Policy Act of 1984, many new franchises were granted for the fifteen-year terms. Accordingly, many franchises will not expire until 1999. Renewal is thus a bit more of a theoretical than a practical matter at present. The cable industry, however, worried about it in 1984 and successfully lobbied for renewal systems and standards to protect its interests.

In broadcasting, there is no legal guarantee that an incumbent seeking renewal will prevail over a challenger. The FCC's practice of almost inevitably granting a renewal expectancy to incumbents, however, nearly always eventually protects them. Despite this practice, broadcasters have long urged Congress to change the Communications Act and create a two-step renewal system. Under such a system, the FCC would first decide whether an incumbent deserved renewal. Competing applications would be received only if the incumbent's renewal application was denied.

Cable industry advocates successfully sought to avoid these uncertainties when they lobbied Congress in the 1980s. Under current law, either the cable operator or the franchisor can open public renewal proceedings as early as three years before a franchise ends. The public is encouraged to comment on a cable operator's service. After the hearings, the incumbent submits a renewal application. If the franchising authority initially decides to deny renewal, there will likely then be a more formal administrative proceeding. In that proceeding, only four issues are relevant. First, has the applicant substantially complied with the law and the existing franchise? Second, considering everything except programming offered, has the operator's service been reasonable in light of the community's need for cable television? Third, can the operator provide the facilities and services described in the renewal application? Finally, does the proposal meet the future "cable-related" needs of the community?[33] Franchisors can deny renewal only on these grounds. Unsuccessful renewal applicants can appeal in court.

This process is so new that we have little idea what it means in practice. It appears, however, to favor renewal applicants. Unless an incumbent has seriously misbehaved, it seems likely to be able to gain renewal, and challengers will not be offered the chance to start a new system unless an incumbent has been evicted. Others can always apply for their own nonexclusive franchises to "overbuild" existing systems, but given the cost of building systems and the likely competitive strategies an incumbent would use, such overbuilds are most unlikely. While events could prove otherwise, it seems reasonable to expect that cable franchise renewal will become as routine as broadcast station license renewal.

Franchisors may have slightly more influence over cable television system sales and transfers. The Cable Communications Policy Act of 1984 dissatisfied many municipalities by seeming to leave them out of the transfer process almost completely. Cable companies would announce, often without warning, that the system had been sold without the cities having any say at all. As a result of municipal lobbying, Congress changed these laws in 1992.[34] Newly built or newly purchased systems cannot normally be sold for three years. When sales are contemplated, and existing franchises require franchising authority approval of any sale, franchisors must be notified in advance and have 120 days to approve or deny the proposed sale. They may certainly consider any provisions of the franchise that govern proposed sales. What else they may consider will only become clear when cases are decided by franchising bodies and, ultimately, by courts.

The 1992 Cable Act and the FCC rules implementing it have begun to impose EEO obligations on cable system operators similar to those that have been applied to broadcasters for years.[35] Cable operators file annual reports with the FCC for each location where they have five or more full-time employees. If the report indicates compliance with the FCC's policies, the commission issues a Certificate of Compliance to the operator. Systems are thoroughly reviewed on five-year cycles. When the five-year review is done, additional information on EEO and affirmative action must be submitted. The potential penalty here, however, cannot be denial of a franchise because that is not under the control of the FCC. Instead, the commission may assess fines against cable systems that flagrantly disregard its EEO standards.

Ownership patterns in cable are also subject to some regulation. Unlike broadcast ownership policies, which are often embodied in FCC rules, cable crossownership standards are included in the Communications Act.[36] Just as national ownership of broadcast stations is limited, since 1992, the number of cable households a single multiple system cable operator can serve has been limited. No single owner can own cable systems reaching more than 30 percent of all cable households in the United States. If the system includes significant minority ownership, that limit can rise to 35 percent. These levels did not force any existing multiple system operator to sell systems owned at the time the rules were adopted. The rules will, however, prevent some of the largest MSOs from getting much larger. Local TV stations, telephone companies, and multichannel, multipoint distribution services cannot, except in special circumstances, own cable systems in their communities. Two U.S. district courts, however, one in Virginia and another in Washington State, have declared that the federal law prohibiting cable companies from offering video services in their telephone service areas violates the First Amendment rights of telephone companies.[37] Other cases are pending as are appeals of these decisions, and it seems likely that, partly in response to these court decisions, Congress may repeal the cable/telco crossownership laws and actually encourage telephone companies to offer cable service in order to provide competition to existing cable companies.

For many years, vertical integration broadcasting was limited by FCC financial interest and syndication rules (Fin/Syn). These rules restricted the ability of the major broadcast networks to own the programs they air. In theory, the rules prevented the networks from dominating the program production market. In 1993, however, the FCC so weakened and modified the rules that, in practice, they could be considered abolished.[38] As of early 1995, the courts were still dealing with appeals of this FCC action by parties who wanted the rules retained.

Somewhat similar policies have been developed for cable TV, where almost all the major cable program services (e.g., CNN, TBS, HBO, ESPN) are, wholly or partially owned by the major national cable multiple system operators such as TCI and Time-Warner. Only 40 percent of the channels on a cable system can be used for programming from sources in which that cable system has a significant degree of ownership. If the programming sources are minority controlled, however, up to 45 percent of a co-owned cable system can be occupied by such programming.[39] In addition, cable program suppliers are required to make their program services available to cable competitors such as MMDS, direct broadcast satellite services, and others on the same terms they offer to cable systems.[40]

REGULATION OF ELECTRONIC MEDIA CONTENT

 s we have seen, content and programming play a minimal role in determining who is authorized to enter or remain in regulated electronic media. This does not mean, however, that government exercises no control over electronic media content at all. Despite

First Amendment theories that recognize rights of electronic communicators and media and substantial federal and state deregulation since the 1980s, a number of laws and policies that regulate electronic media content still linger on. Many, but not all, of these laws directly affect electronic journalism in ways quite unlike the laws affecting print communicators. In theory, willful or repeated violation of a few of these laws could jeopardize licenses or even franchises. Nearly always, however, penalties for violating these policies take the form of monetary fines from regulatory agencies, orders from courts or regulatory agencies to obey the rules, or little more than a raised eyebrow from regulators suggesting that a violator had better not get caught again.

Self-Regulation

It is important to remember that government imposes few content regulations. By and large, electronic communicators, like their print colleagues, are free to transmit what they choose subject to postpublication accountability through laws that apply to all media, such as libel and privacy law. In practice, this means that much depends on the conscience and self-imposed standards of electronic communications.

These media-derived standards have sometimes been reduced to written codes. From 1929 until 1988, for example, the National Association of Broadcasters (NAB), the major trade association for commercial broadcasters, promulgated Radio and Television Codes for its members. The codes guided both advertising and nonadvertising content. They were usually cast more in the form of advice than mandates—"broadcasters should not" rather than "broadcasters cannot"—and, being enforced by self-interested industry members, were often interpreted in ways favorable to broadcaster-members of the NAB. Some of the advice related to noncommercial content, such as appropriate things to do and not do in news and entertainment programming. Much of the codes, however, addressed advertising practices. The codes, for example, long kept advertising showing models in undergarments off TV and hard liquor advertising off both radio and television. Perhaps most significantly, it was really the NAB codes and not the FCC rules that, for many years, established the amount, frequency, and duration of radio and TV ads. These advertising limits, however, eventually brought down the NAB codes. The U.S. Department of Justice successfully argued in court that these restrictions violated antitrust laws by artificially limiting the amount of TV advertising available and driving up prices. Faced with legal expenses if it attempted to overturn this decision and the possibility of having to pay damages to advertisers allegedly harmed, the NAB dropped its codes in 1988 and ceased trying to guide broadcasters into self-regulation.

Nevertheless, self-regulation persists at many other levels of the electronic media. Major networks, both broadcast and cable, have internal guidelines about what they will and will not do. Groups of stations and cable MSOs often develop similar policies. Individual stations sometimes formulate codes for themselves. Because codes like these are not industry-wide or imposed by a national trade association, they are less vulnerable to an antitrust law attack. Such

● **Self regulation**
Systems and standards that individuals and groups develop for themselves to guide their conduct. Often created to head off regulation by government.

codes continue to cover many aspects of electronic media programming that cannot be, or at least should not be, governed by formal law.

Some evidence suggests that we may see a revival of limited industry-wide codes focused on reducing the exposure of children to violent content. Such a move would at least in part receive Congress's blessing. Although the impact of violent content, especially upon children, has been a matter of concern for years, there is little formal law on this subject. Courts have generally protected broadcasters from having to pay damage awards when a viewer or listener mimics some violent act seen on TV or heard on radio. Broadcasters are liable only if they intended that the viewer or listener commit the violent act. They are not held accountable if that was not their intent and, of course, it rarely is.

In 1990, however, Congress created an exception to the antitrust laws to permit broadcasters, cable companies, and the producers of programming to cooperate to develop codes that might limit violence in electronic media.[41] Public and industry interest in the topic has waxed and waned greatly since then, but the perception persists among congressional leaders and public activists that American media are unreasonably violent. Television networks agreed to air warnings before programs whose content might require parental discretion and promised additional studies and action on the problem.[42] The cable industry, through the National Cable Television Association, announced in 1994 that major cable networks would also adopt warnings about violent content, attempt to schedule such programs at times when few children are watching, make sure that promotional announcements for such programs are appropriate, adopt and publicize a violence ratings system, and even attempt to run an educational campaign for children aimed at deglamorizing violence.[43]

Cable Content Regulations

Unlike broadcasting, where the FCC historically had overall broadcast content policies, the content of cable television has never been subjected to national content expectations by law. Until 1984, when Congress adopted the Cable Communications Policy Act, what content control there was came from a mixture of FCC rules and regulations, often of debatable validity, with policies enforced by state and local cable franchisors. Franchisors often attempted to influence the mix of cable services an operator offered. They accomplished this through their regulation of cable television rates. Until 1984, cable systems had to get the franchisor's permission to raise rates. When those requests were made, franchisors in turn often demanded new or modified channels or services. They might ask for the addition of a specific channel (say, ESPN) or that the system drop a channel (perhaps Playboy). Franchisors also often required franchisees to set aside some channels on the system for public access. Government and community groups used these channels to transmit programming ranging from cooking shows to government meetings to education to soft-core pornography.

Under FCC rules, cable operators were required to retransmit most local broadcast signals but also provide some protection to local stations against duplication of programs for which they held local broadcast rights; the problem

● **Syndicated exclusivity rules**

FCC rules that require cable systems to "block out" syndicated programming coming from a nonlocal TV station if a local TV station has the right to broadcast that program in a community.

● **Network nonduplication rules**

Laws requiring cable systems to block out network signals from distant TV stations if the same programs are being aired by local network affiliates. Protects the local network affiliates from losing viewers to nonlocal stations.

here was that, in some cases, non-local stations whose signals were imported into the market by cable were broadcasting the same syndicated programs as the local stations. These rules were known as the **syndicated exclusivity rules.** Local network affiliates were also protected against duplication of their network programming by an imported station under **network nonduplication rules.** The problem with these FCC rules and policies was that it was unclear that the FCC had the authority to adopt them. Prior to 1984, cable television was not mentioned in the Communications Act. Courts had ruled that the FCC could regulate cable if what it did was "reasonably ancillary" to the FCC's regulation of broadcasting.[44] What this included was always debatable.

The Cable Communications Policy Act of 1984 was intended to clarify this situation and significantly deregulate cable.[45] It sorted out responsibilities among the federal government, mostly the FCC, and state and local bodies. Facing taxpayers demanding "no new taxes," municipalities had become pressed for revenue and, more than anything else, wanted to protect and perhaps increase their revenues from the franchise fees they charged cable systems. In exchange for clear congressional authorization to charge franchise fees based on a percentage of all the revenue taken in by a cable system (rather than just on the lowest tier of cable service a company offered), some ability to regulate the customer service aspects of the cable industry (cities were tired of hearing horror stories about poor service, sloppy installations, and perpetually busy telephone lines at cable companies), and a clear ability to seek public, educational, and governmental access channels from cable operators during the franchising process, municipalities eventually supported the 1984 act's deregulation of local control over both subscriber fees and channels or services cable systems carried. As a result, the setting of customer rates and decisions on what channels and services to offer were left to cable system operators who, presumably, would respond to economic marketplace forces. The cable industry also got the improvements, from its perspective, in the franchise renewal system that have already been described. The results for cable were a few remaining content regulations from Congress but much less intervention in content and rate setting at the local level. Multiple system operators who ran many systems across the country could count on somewhat greater regulatory uniformity among their systems.

By 1992, however, Congress decided this had not been a very good legislative compromise. Cable industry, congressional, and municipal figures varied, but the evidence was clear that cable rates had gone up dramatically under deregulation. The cable industry argued that service had improved too and that the public was getting more services for slightly more money. It also argued that the price rises were simply a natural response to prices that had been kept artificially low for so long by local regulators. Lawmakers, both federal and state, heard more from angry constituents about gouging cable rates, however, and Congress decided to roll back some of the 1984 act. The most important rollback reregulated cable rates. Following FCC guidelines, municipalities that want to do so can regulate rates for basic cable service (retransmitted over-the-air TV signals plus access channels), except where systems receive "effective competition." If requested to do so, the FCC can regulate the rates systems charge for premium channels, such as HBO. In 1995, however, Congress considered modifying or repealing this system for rate regulation.

Taken together, some portions of the 1984 and 1992 acts continue to allow some forms of government regulation of cable content. Cable franchisors are permitted to negotiate with cable companies over "broad categories of video programming." In other words, a franchisor could seek to require, through the franchise, that an operator carry a sports channel. If the operator agreed to do this, the franchisor could not order the operator to select, for example, ESPN over a regional sports service.[46]

Cable systems offer a basic tier of service that includes, at minimum, all the broadcast TV signals a system carries plus any access channels that are mandated by the franchise.[47] This basic tier must include local commercial TV stations, most local noncommercial educational TV stations, and on rare occasions local low-power TV stations. Very small systems with twelve or fewer channels cannot be compelled to carry more than three commercial and one noncommercial station. Systems with more than thirty-seven active channels cannot be compelled to devote more than one-third of their channels to commercial TV stations, but they must carry all noncommercial TV stations that request carriage unless programming is duplicated among multiple noncommercial TV stations. Cable systems are required to run the must-carry stations under the same channel numbers they use over the air if the station so requests. Under these **must-carry rules,** operators have to carry all the programs a must-carry station offers throughout the day, but must delete imported syndicated and network programming that is duplicated on local stations.[48]

For obvious reasons, the cable industry did not welcome reregulation. Many court challenges, quite a few of which are still pending, were filed seeking to overturn most significant parts of the 1992 act. The most significant of these challenges to reach the U.S. Supreme Court as of early 1995 focused on the constitutionality of the must-carry requirements.

Turner Broadcasting System and numerous other cable industry organizations argued that these rules violated cable's free press rights. In *Turner Broadcasting v. FCC* (1994), the Supreme Court agreed that the rules might do that but refused to strike them down without further review by lower courts. At least eight members of the Court implied that cable stood somewhere between print and broadcasting on a First Amendment rights continuum. Broadcasters who used the spectrum were limited-capacity systems that could technically interfere with each other. Cable systems, on the other hand, were high-capacity systems that could accommodate many speakers. Cable operators, however, were not quite newspaper publishers. A local newspaper publisher, Justice Anthony Kennedy noted, could not prevent other newspapers from entering a circulation area. Cable system operators, however, could prevent cable subscribers from receiving video services that others might wish to offer. The decision actually did little to clarify the First Amendment status of cable operators. At most, it tentatively decided that they are not broadcasters, but neither are they print publishers.

Having agreed that cable enjoys some First Amendment rights, the Court analyzed the must-carry rules. It concluded that the rules could restrict cable speech. The government command to carry some broadcast signals that an operator might not wish to retransmit limited the editorial discretion of cable operators. Channels that had to be dedicated to must-carry channels were not

● **Must-carry rules**
Laws requiring cable television systems to retransmit the signals of broadcast stations.

● *Turner Broadcasting v. FCC*
Decision of the U.S. Supreme Court upholding federal statutes requiring cable systems to carry local broadcast TV stations ("must-carry" rules).

available for other nonbroadcast program services an operator might prefer to run.

The greatest split within the Court occurred when it sought to apply a standard to decide whether or not these restrictions on editorial discretion violated the First Amendment. The options were to regard the restrictions as content-based rules or as content-neutral policies having an incidental effect on content; if they were classed as content-based rules, they would be subject to a "strict scrutiny" review and probably would not survive. By a 5–4 vote, the Court settled on a content-neutral analysis and applied the test, described previously, that was first announced in *United States v. O'Brien.*[49]

The must-carry rules, said Justices William Rehnquist, Anthony Kennedy, Harry Blackmun, John Paul Stevens, and David Souter, focused on the means of transmission rather than the content of cable or broadcasting. They did not command operators to carry specific views or programs. The Court accepted the government's argument that the objective of preserving local broadcast stations from economic harm through not being carried by cable was a legitimate and substantial governmental interest. Four of the five justices who adopted the *O'Brien* test—all but Justice Stevens—decided, however, that there was inadequate economic information in the record to complete the *O'Brien* analysis. Thus, the case was remanded to the court of appeals for further review.

Dissenting Justices Sandra Day O'Connor, Antonin Scalia, Clarence Thomas, and Ruth Bader Ginsburg believed the must-carry law was a content regulation that unconstitutionally put the First Amendment rights of broadcasters ahead of the First Amendment rights of cable system operators. Justice O'Connor's opinion argued that Congress had intended to favor the kind of content broadcast stations offered, for example, noncommercial educational programming and local news and public affairs. Applying a strict scrutiny test, O'Connor concluded that the government's interest in educational or local content lacked the requisite "compelling state interest." Admitting that the goal might be praiseworthy, O'Connor still concluded that government mandates to cable operators to carry broadcast content constituted a threat to freedom of expression and violated the First Amendment.[50]

Much remains to be decided about the limits of government content control in cable. The First Amendment status of cable is just emerging. The must-carry case is likely to return to the U.S. Supreme Court, which will also likely see challenges to provisions of the Cable Act dealing with obscenity, indecency, and other program matters.

Political Broadcasting and Cablecasting

Section 315 and "Equal Time" • As early as the 1920s, politicians realized that how they were treated by radio could affect their political careers. In response to their concerns, Congress decided that since radio could affect politics, it was best to try to regulate radio broadcasts in ways that would assure equal treatment to all candidates. Being both political and realistic, Congress in 1927 adopted radio laws that appeared favorable to all but, in fact, favored incumbent candidates for public office and have done little, over the years, for fringe or non-major-party office seekers.

The Radio Act of 1927 was the first federal law to require broadcasters to provide equal opportunities to use their stations to all legally qualified opposing candidates for office. This requirement was continued by Congress in the Communications Act of 1934 and slightly modified in 1959. Today, the requirement applies in limited ways to cable as well as to broadcasting.

Under what is now **Section 315** of the Communications Act, broadcasters who have permitted initial **use** of their station by one candidate for political office must allow the candidate's legally qualified opponents an equal opportunity to use the station. Assume, for example, that three persons are seeking the same office. If a broadcaster lets Candidate A use the station, then both candidates B and C must be provided an equal opportunity to use it too. This requirement is popularly, if inaccurately, known as the equal time standard.

Section 315 does not require the station to let Candidate A on the air in the first place. Instead, it places a contingent responsibility on broadcasters and comes into play only if they have opened their stations to use by at least one candidate initially. Other laws, to be covered shortly, occasionally force stations to allow initial uses by candidates for federal office. In general, however, broadcasters can decide whether to permit an initial use of a station by a candidate and may legally ignore some races for public office altogether.

Uses of stations by **legally qualified candidates** for public office set the law in motion. What, however, is a "public office"? Who is a "legally qualified candidate"? What is a "use"? Public office is straightforward. It is any government position where officeholders are elected by popular vote. Thus, it includes the president, vice president, mayor, school board member, and even dogcatcher provided there is a public election. It applies to elected judges. Appointed public officials, such as most city managers, are excluded even if government bodies vote to hire them.

Determining who is a legally qualified candidate can be harder. The FCC has issued a few guidelines. Persons are not legally qualified candidates until they declare that they are. Neither broadcasters nor the FCC must guess. Even if candidates declare years before an election, they are, at that point, probably legally qualified candidates. "Probably" is necessary here because, if there are specific legal qualifications to hold an office, such as residency or age, persons are not candidates for public office unless they meet those standards. A candidate's name does not necessarily have to be on a ballot in order to be legally qualified under Section 315. If a state allows write-in candidates, then a declared candidate who does the things candidates usually do such as forming committees, raising funds, giving speeches, and the like benefits from Section 315. Persons approved to be placed on ballots are, almost inevitably, legally qualified and declared, so they obviously have Section 315 rights. A legally qualified candidate for a public office, then, is somebody who has declared that she or he is seeking a public office and, if elected, would meet the legal qualifications for holding it and could assume it if elected. The popularity of a candidate, the depth of his or her support, the oddity of campaign planks, and the likelihood of winning are all irrelevant.

The hardest part of Section 315 to understand is the concept of use. Prior to 1959, this was extraordinarily easy. Although some broadcasters did not

---

● **Section 315**
Provision of the Communications Act of 1934 that requires broadcasters to treat opposing candidates for the same public office "equally" except in many news-related contexts.

● **Use**
In broadcast law, occurs when one legally qualified candidate for a public office appears on a radio or TV station during a campaign (with certain exceptions). Broadcasters must allow opposing candidates equal opportunities to use the station.

● **Legally qualified candidate**
A candidate for a public elected office who, if elected, could hold the office. Qualifications typically include age and residence.

realize it, the FCC's policy was that absolutely any identifiable appearance, either by voice or picture, of a legally qualified candidate for public office on a station was a Section 315 use and would result in the station owing equal opportunities to all qualified opponents. Broadcasters were appalled in 1959 when the FCC ruled that uses could occur in news programs. A very fringe candidate for mayor of Chicago asked the FCC for equal opportunity after Chicago stations ran newscasts picturing the incumbent mayor. The FCC, calling all appearances Section 315 uses, ruled in the minor candidate's favor.[51] Broadcasters turned almost immediately to Congress for relief.

Uses That Do Not Count • Congress changed Section 315 within weeks. It specified four types of candidate appearances that would no longer count as uses requiring equal response opportunities:

1. Appearances in *bona fide* newscasts.

2. Appearances in *bona fide* news interviews.

3. Appearances in *bona fide* news documentaries (but only under somewhat specialized circumstances).

4. Appearances in on-the-spot coverage of *bona fide* news events.

Congress, however, did not intend to exempt candidate appearances in anything and everything a broadcaster might call news. The term *bona fide* is used in each of these exemptions. It means real, true, or genuine. If a broadcaster, for example, trumped up something called "The Frank Smith Report" while Frank Smith—perhaps the broadcaster's brother-in-law—was running for public office, the FCC could rule the appearance nonexempt and order that equal opportunities be granted Smith's opponents.

Over the years, these exemptions have allowed broadcasters to readily cover news without worrying too much about equal opportunities for minor, fringe candidates. The regularly scheduled newscasts of stations are exempt as, in general, are on-the-spot field reports. Most news interview programs are exempt, although occasionally the FCC ruled that a show was not consistently newsy enough to fit the definition—an approach the commission abandoned in the 1980s. Special conditions attached to the documentary exemption can be troublesome because uses are exempt only if candidate appearances are incidental to the main subject of the documentary. A documentary about labor history including film clips of former union leader Ronald Reagan would be exempt even if Reagan was running for public office. A documentary about the campaign that included Reagan clips, however, would not be exempt. By the 1970s this distinction had little significance because broadcasters had largely abandoned documentaries anyway.

The most controversial and problematic of the exemptions was the one exempting "on-the-spot coverage of *bona fide* news events." When it created the exemptions in 1959, Congress made it clear that some things were definitely covered by this language. It specifically mentioned coverage of political conventions. The problem was figuring out what else Congress had in mind.

Attention focused almost immediately on broadcast coverage of candidate debates and press conferences. Early FCC rulings suggested so strongly that debates were not *bona fide* events that, in 1960, Congress passed a special, "this election only," modification to Section 315 that permitted debates between Vice President Richard M. Nixon and Senator John F. Kennedy that excluded minor candidates to be broadcast.[52] This 1960 law reinforced the belief that broadcast coverage of candidate debates was not exempt and could create problems for broadcasters if minor candidates were not included. The same idea generally applied to candidate press conferences. In the 1960s, these were considered pseudo-events rather than real ones, and broadcasters generally believed that if they covered a press conference by one candidate, they would have to provide equal opportunities for all of that candidate's opponents. As a result, broadcasters almost never aired candidate debates or press conferences.

Things changed in time for the 1976 presidential campaign pitting Georgia Governor Jimmy Carter against unelected President Gerald Ford. Reinterpreting legislative history, the FCC concluded that its 1960s policies were wrong and that candidate debates could be *bona fide* news events if the debates were conducted by parties other than broadcasters or the candidates themselves.[53] The League of Women Voters stepped in and ran debates between Ford and Carter, and broadcasters covered them without including a significant independent presidential candidate, former Senator Eugene McCarthy. Debates in 1980 between President Carter and his major opponent, California governor Ronald Reagan, excluded Illinois Congressman John Anderson. The debates had to be covered live, or with a short delay, because the law required on-the-spot broadcasting and had to be broadcast in their entirety, but at last, after about fifteen years, broadcasters were relieved of significant legal impediments to broadcasting candidate debates. Somewhat similar policies were adopted regarding coverage of press conferences.

In subsequent years, the FCC liberalized even these interpretations. Broadcasters wanted to present debates themselves in their studios, where they would have more control and lower costs. The FCC eventually agreed. If a broadcaster were to set up a debate in a patently unfair fashion, for example, including only one major party candidate and some minor candidates while leaving out another major party office seeker, the FCC can still rule the debate is not *bona fide*. Assuming that major candidates are included, however, and that the format provides a decent opportunity for all candidates to present their views, then the debate is probably exempt and does not create equal opportunity obligations.

Thus, most, but not all, news-related appearances do not trigger Section 315 obligations. The two primary elements of broadcast service that still do are political advertising and, occasionally, entertainment programming. For many years, the FCC followed its pre-1959 approach when dealing with this kind of content. If a legally qualified candidate for a public office appeared in any ad, either a political ad or a commercial for a good or service, in anything but the most fleeting way, the appearance was a use and Section 315 applied. If a candidate appeared in an entertainment show, that, too, was a use. When Ronald Reagan campaigned for public office, for example, television stations generally stopped running his movies and old TV shows. Reagan's movie and TV career had ended years before he became a politician, and the movies and shows had clearly not been designed for political purposes. The FCC, however, believed it would be unwise for a government agency to decide, based on content, which uses counted and which did not. It was better, the FCC reasoned, to simply say that any appearance would count if it occurred in anything except the four kinds of programming Congress exempted.

The FCC deviated from this standard slightly between 1991 and 1994. The commission decided that candidate appearances counted as uses only when they were approved, controlled, or sponsored by the candidate or the candidate's campaign committee.[54] This meant that old movies including people who became candidates and negative campaign ads featuring unflattering images that a candidate would never have approved no longer resulted in free time for opponents of the candidate depicted in the movie or ad.

Partly because of the difficulties stations faced in deciding when candidate approval was present, but largely because of changes in the FCC after the election of President Clinton, the FCC in 1994 switched back to its pre-1991 definition of use with one slight modification. The commission ruled that any identifiable voice or image appearance of a candidate in anything other than a statutorily exempt program created equal opportunities for that candidate's opponent. The slight modification was to stipulate that the appearance had to be "positive." Otherwise, unflattering depictions of candidates by their opponents would result in rights to equal opportunities for those opponents themselves.[55]

Wise candidates and their managers carefully manipulate political advertising. Campaign spots that do not include candidates in an identifiable way— for example, a series of interviews with voters praising the candidate or patriotic scenes of amber waves of grain—result in no equal opportunity rights for opposing candidates. Rates broadcasters can charge candidates for ads depend on whether the ad is a use. A candidate seeking to hold down costs might run mostly spots that were uses. An unphotogenic candidate might include a very small picture at the end of the ad and still qualify for a low rate.

What Is an "Equal Opportunity"? • Once any nonexempt use occurs, broadcasters must provide all legally qualified opposing candidates with equal opportunities to use their station. The person claiming an equal opportunity must be a direct opponent of the candidate who has made the initial use. Thus, during primary campaigns, a candidate for the Democratic nomination for an office cannot claim an equal opportunity right in response to a nonexempt appearance by a candidate for the Republican nomination for the same office. During primaries, Democrats oppose other Democrats, and Republicans oppose other Republicans. Once the primaries are over and the general election campaigning begins, however, the Republican nominee will be an opponent of the Democratic nominee and can claim equal opportunity rights in response to any nonexempt appearances of the Democrat.

Equal opportunity requires four things of broadcasters. First, stations must provide an equal amount of time to opposing candidates. In part, this requires figuring out how much time Candidate A has had in order to determine the amount Candidate B is due. As noted, "fleeting" uses do not count at all.[56] Candidate appearances in political spots, even if only for a small part of the total ad, usually entitle an opponent to the same amount of time as the entire ad. When candidates appear in nonexempt talk or variety shows, opponents are only entitled to an amount of time equal to the time the first candidate was identifiable. Movies and entertainment shows remain somewhat less precise. If the candidate's appearance is substantial and integral to the plot of the show—in other words, if the candidate is a major player—then the FCC may rule that an opponent is entitled to an amount of time equal to the entire movie or show. It might be risky, for example, to run *Die Hard II* on television at a time when one of its stars, Fred Thompson who is now a senator from Tennessee, was campaigning for reelection. Less integral appearances would qualify opponents only for the amount of time a candidate was identifiable.

Second, opposing candidates must be provided generally comparable time in terms of audience potential. Radio and TV audiences are never equal on different days so the FCC knows a broadcaster cannot possibly deliver to one candidate an audience exactly like the one an opponent reached. The licensee must come close, however. It would not be lawful to offer one candidate time in a low-rated show if the opponent's nonexempt uses occurred in very highly rated programs.

Third, opposing candidates must be provided comparable numbers of uses. If a licensee, for example, sold sixty thirty-second spots to one candidate, a total time of thirty minutes, that broadcaster could not comply with Section 315 by offering an opponent a thirty-minute block of time elsewhere in the broadcaster's schedule. Similarly, a candidate seeking time to respond to a thirty-minute political program would be entitled to a single thirty-minute block of time and could not request an equal amount of time divided into campaign spots.

Finally, opposing candidates must be offered time on equal commercial terms. If Candidate A has paid $100 for his or her use, then Candidate B can be required to pay the same, but no more. If Candidate B does not want to pay, or cannot afford to pay, the candidate is out of luck. Equal opportunity does not mean providing free time to respond to paid time. However, positive appearances by one candidate in a nonexempt nonpaid program entitle opposing candidates to free time. Opponents of Fred Thompson, for example, would get free time in response to *Die Hard II* because Thompson is depicted positively and most likely would not have paid broadcasters to air it.

Federal Candidates and "Reasonable Access" • Since Section 315 does not require broadcasters to allow any candidates to use their stations initially, broadcasters can safely decide not to sell advertising time to candidates for most minor races in their communities. An exception to this rule, however, has been created by Congress through **Section 312(a)(7)** of the Communications Act.[57]

Under this part of the act, all broadcasters—radio and TV, commercial and noncommercial—must provide **reasonable access** to their stations to legally qualified candidates for federal office. Thus, candidates for president, vice president, and Congress have rights that candidates for state offices, such as governors, and local offices, such as mayors, lack.

- **Section 312(a)(7)**
Provision of the Communications Act of 1934 that requires broadcasters to provide "reasonable access" to their stations to federal candidates for campaigning.

- **Reasonable access**
Broadcast stations must allow candidates for federal public office to purchase reasonable amounts of time during campaigns or other reasonable amounts of free time.

Congress added this provision in 1972.[58] At the time Congress was concerned about the cost of campaigning and wanted to lower the rates charged for political ads. Some members realized, however, that if rates were driven down, some broadcasters might choose not to sell time for political ads at all. Panicked by this thought, Congress added Section 312(a)(7) to the act.

What is "reasonable access"? An affirmative answer is hard to provide because what is reasonable can vary from market to market, office to office, and campaign to campaign. Things are not as clear-cut as determining equality under Section 315. Negative answers are easier. The FCC has more often declared certain actions by broadcasters unreasonable than it has been able to specify exactly what is reasonable.

- **Federal candidates**
Candidates for offices of the federal government: president, vice president, senator, and representative.

To start with, **federal candidates** cannot be completely ignored. If even the most obscure federal candidate seeks access on a radio or TV station, that station must have some plans for providing reasonable access. The FCC has ruled, however, that it is reasonable to require all federal candidates to pay. A broadcaster can turn to a candidate and state reasonable rates for advertising; then, if the candidate chooses not to pay, the broadcaster need do no more. Clearly, underfunded candidates do not benefit much from Section 312.

The FCC has also declared it unreasonable to have policies that flatly ban candidates from specific types of access they might seek. "Top 40" music stations, for example, might want to bar candidates from buying long, program-length ads. A TV station might, out of conscience, seek to prohibit candidates from buying ten-second ads. Both policies, if uniformly and consistently applied to all federal candidates, would probably violate Section 312(a)(7) because they put the needs of broadcasters ahead of the needs of candidates. To the extent possible, broadcasters must try to meet the needs of candidates even if those needs conflict with some of the station's programming objectives. If they choose to deny a candidate's request, broadcasters need a specific, reasonable, not totally self-serving explanation that shows that the needs of candidates have been fairly considered.

Stations need not handle every race in the same way or apply the same policies to races across election years. In a presidential campaign year, for example, a station might well have different policies for presidential candidates than for congressional candidates. A station expecting many candidates in one race but few in others could have different policies for each office. Stations in large urban areas, with many candidates vying for many federal offices, can have different policies than broadcasters in rural areas who must meet the needs of fewer federal candidates. Policies can change from year to year so long as the policy is reasonable when applied. Although the FCC is ultimately the judge of what is reasonable, it usually defers to the judgment of broadcasters so long as the broadcaster has not done something previously determined to be unreasonable or clearly outrageous.

In 1981, the U.S. Supreme Court decided that Section 312(a)(7) did not violate the First Amendment rights of broadcasters, even though it compelled them to provide some access to their stations to candidates. Early in the 1979–1980 presidential campaign, the reelection committee for President Carter asked all three major TV networks to sell it time for a thirty-minute campaign documentary to kick off Carter's reelection bid. All three refused to sell the time the committee requested. CBS offered to sell five minutes of prime time; NBC and ABC said they were not yet selling any time for the 1980 elections.

The Carter-Mondale committee appealed these network decisions to the FCC, which ruled them unreasonable. The U.S. Court of Appeals for the D.C. Circuit upheld this decision. So did the U.S. Supreme Court in *CBS v. FCC* (1981).[59]

The networks attacked Section 312 on First Amendment grounds. After all, it affected their programming decisions. Chief Justice Warren Burger, writing for himself and six other members of the Court, admitted that was so, but reasoned that the statute did not severely impair the ability of broadcasters to present their views or to carry other kinds of programs. Looking back to the *Red Lion* decision, in which the Court had affirmed a paramount First Amendment right of listeners and viewers to receive information, Burger concluded that at least in the broadcast media, access requirements such as Section 312 were constitutional. The First Amendment rights of candidates to reach the electorate and voters to receive political information outweighed the First Amendment interests of broadcasters.

The networks also claimed that the requests for time in 1979 were premature because the election was almost a year away. Noting that Congress had adopted Section 312(a)(7) at the same time as another part of the law affecting what broadcasters could charge during thirty- and sixty-day periods before elections, the broadcasters argued that reasonable access only applied when these related restrictions on rates were in effect. Both the FCC and the Supreme Court rejected these arguments. Candidates, not broadcasters, determine when campaigns are on, and once there are clear indications campaigns have begun, broadcasters must have some system for providing reasonable access to candidates, no matter how far away the election is. Reasonable access years in advance of an election, however, might be quite different than reasonable access as the election draws near.

Regulating Rates for Political Broadcasting • As the argument about reasonable access indicates, regulations exist today—and have existed for years—governing what broadcasters can charge candidates for advertising time. Rates are regulated in three ways.

Ever since 1927, rates charged a candidate who gets a right to use a station because of the appearance of an opponent must be equal to what the first candidate paid. In 1959, Congress changed the law to stipulate that candidates could never be charged more for political advertising time than other advertisers paid for comparable uses. This rule prevents broadcasters from either discouraging candidates from advertising or gouging them through artificially high political rates.

A far more complicated regulation of candidate advertising rates is the one Congress adopted along with reasonable access in 1972.[60] During the forty-five days before a primary election or the sixty days before a general election, a broadcaster may not charge any candidate, federal or nonfederal, more than the "lowest unit charge" paid by other advertisers for the same type and amount of advertising on the station.[61] With this rule, Congress tried to go beyond what it had done in 1959. The 1959 legislation prevented broadcasters from charging candidates rates higher than those charged other advertisers. Since 1972, broadcasters must give candidates the lowest rate they offer for various kinds of radio and TV ads.

Although this rule sounds simple, it has proven difficult to implement in practice because of the incredible variety of ways radio and TV advertising is packaged and sold. It is impossible to cover this topic in detail here, but some basic principles can be noted. If package or volume rates are available to commercial advertisers, candidates must get the same price breaks even when they do not buy enough advertising to qualify for the special rate. Suppose a broadcaster sells thirty-second spots for $20, but would sell six such spots for $100. When the lowest unit charge rule is in effect, a candidate could be charged no more than $16.67 for even a single spot. After a 1990 audit of thirty radio and TV stations for compliance with the lowest unit charge requirements, the FCC stressed that broadcasters must deal with candidates exactly as they deal with all other advertisers. If the broadcaster's system for selling time emphasizes flexibility and negotiation over rates and discounts, candidates must have the same flexibility other advertisers are granted. Policies for bumping, rescheduling, and selling nonpreemptable spots must be the same and must be clearly explained to candidates and their representatives. Stations can adjust and raise rates as campaigns progress but must do so as a result of variations in ratings or seasonal program adjustments. When rates are adjusted, candidates must be subject to terms identical to those applying to other advertisers.[62] A few stations that have violated the lowest unit charge requirements have been assessed hefty fines, and some candidates, claiming to have been overcharged, have attempted to recover damages in state courts.[63]

Censorship and Cable Political Advertising • Two more points must be made about both Section 315 and Section 312(a)(7). Candidate uses resulting from either of these sections of the Communications Act cannot be censored by broadcasters. In turn, however, only the candidate, and not the broadcaster, is liable for any consequences that may result from the candidate's use. In 1959, the U.S. Supreme Court decided that WDAY-TV in Fargo, North Dakota, could not be held responsible for damages when a candidate libeled the North Dakota Farmers Union by calling it communistic. The no-censorship provisions in Section 315, said the Court, preempted states from holding broadcasters accountable for libels they could not avoid. The candidate could be liable, but in this case, that was of no significance to the Farmers Union since the candidate had no assets.[64]

> **No-censorship requirement**
> Part of Section 315 of the Communications Act of 1934 that prohibits broadcasters from editing the uses candidates for public office make of broadcast stations under that law.

Since 1959, this **no-censorship requirement** has affected other controversial issues. J. B. Stoner, a candidate in a U.S. Senate race in 1972, ran radio spots claiming to be the only candidate "for the white people." He ranted that civil rights laws took "jobs from whites and [gave] those jobs to the niggers." "[V]ote your convictions by voting white racist J. B. Stoner into the runoff election for U.S. Senator," his radio ads proclaimed. The FCC rejected requests by broadcasters and civil rights groups that Stoner's uses be censored.[65]

During the 1992 and 1994 federal campaigns, several candidates sought to run ads explaining their anti-abortion positions by including photos of aborted fetuses, placentas, dismembered fetal body parts, and female sexual organs. The FCC refused to rule that such spots were indecent, and presumably could be banned by broadcasters. Instead, the commission said that TV stations could, at their own expense, precede the ads with disclaimers warning that the ads might disturb children.[66] If political ads are, indeed, obscene or indecent, broadcasters may be able to refuse to run them. That, at least, was the position of the FCC in 1983 when *Hustler* publisher Larry Flynt threatened to run for president and include sexually explicit images in his TV ads.[67] To the great relief of the FCC and broadcasters, however, Flynt decided not to run, and the question of what to do about ads he might have aired remained theoretical.

The final point about political broadcasting law is that much of it applies to cable television in special ways. Broadcast stations, not cable systems, are responsible for complying with Sections 312 and 315 in their on-air service. If that service is retransmitted by a cable system and a violation of the law occurs, the FCC may sanction the broadcaster but will not sanction the cable system.

When cable systems originate programming or sell political ads, however, Section 315 and all of the associated standards about equal opportunities and rate regulation apply to the cable system. Section 312 does not apply because it is embedded in a part of the Communications Act applying only to broadcast stations and their federal licenses. Few cable systems originate much political programming, but many have become campaign advertising vehicles for candidates who find cable advertising rates similar to radio rates and much less expensive than over-the-air TV rates. With regard to such ads, cable systems must do everything that political broadcasting law requires except provide reasonable access to federal candidates.

Fairness

Except for some talk and tabloid hosts, most electronic journalists would probably agree with the ethical proposition that their broadcasts should be fair. Most broadcast journalists, however, objected strongly to a policy pursued for thirty-eight years (1949–1987) that converted that ethical principle into law.

The policy, known as the fairness doctrine, began in the 1920s when the FRC lifted licenses from one-sided "propaganda" broadcasters on the ground that the public interest required that all sides of a controversy be presented.[68] Its most cogent articulation, however, came in 1949 when the FCC released a policy statement on editorializing by broadcasters.[69] The FCC had banned editorializing by licensees in 1941, arguing that if broadcasters aired editorials, listeners would not get balanced information about controversies. In 1949, however, the commission decided that broadcasters could and, in fact, should editorialize and present programming about controversial issues of public importance, as long as they provided a "reasonable opportunity" for opposing views on those issues to be heard.

These two things—presenting a reasonable amount of controversial issue programming and providing reasonable opportunities for opposing views to be aired—were all that the fairness doctrine ever required. Both broadcasters and the public, however, often confused the doctrine with Section 315's equal opportunity requirements. Yet the fairness doctrine never required equal time for opposing views and never compelled broadcasters to put advocates of views on their stations. Broadcasters could present opposing views themselves, and balance among views only had to be reasonable. Individual programs did not have to be balanced; opposing views could be aired in other programs at other times. The FCC only once enforced the "first prong" of the doctrine—the requirement to devote time to controversial issue programming. This came in an extraordinary case where a West Virginia broadcaster admitted to the FCC that it had devoted no attention at all to controversies surrounding proposed federal regulation of strip mining. The issue was shown to be perhaps the most important controversy facing the community at that time. Failure to discuss the issue, the FCC concluded, was not reasonable. The station was told to run at least some programming about it.[70]

Even the "second prong"—the obligation to provide a reasonable opportunity for the presentation of opposing views—was not enforced rigorously or very often by the FCC. Broadcasters were given great latitude about frequency, scheduling, and amount of time dedicated to opposing viewpoints so long as they acted reasonably and in good faith. Presenting only one side or offering opposing viewpoints in a blatantly imbalanced way was sometimes sanctioned, but in general, the FCC supported what broadcasters had done when complaints of violations of the doctrine were filed with it. As actually applied, the doctrine probably did no more than codify the typical news ethics of the time. Nevertheless, the doctrine was much resented because it regulated content, and broadcast journalists thought that was none of the FCC's business.

The Red Lion Case: Fairness and the First Amendment • In 1969, in *Red Lion Broadcasting v. FCC,*[71] the U.S. Supreme Court decided that the doctrine was basically constitutional. Before the Court, the FCC argued that the doctrine was necessary to assure that the public was fully informed about important public issues. The Court accepted the FCC's position, balanced the First Amendment rights of the public to be informed against the lesser First Amendment rights of broadcasters to have absolute control over all broadcast content, and upheld the commission's decision that the broadcaster had violated the law. The Court affirmed this position a few years later when it rejected arguments that nonbroadcasters should have a right to buy radio and TV time to present their opinions on controversies. In *CBS v. Democratic National Committee* (1973), the Court concluded that access rights such as these were unnecessary because the fairness doctrine protected the public's right to be informed.[72]

Demise of the Fairness Doctrine • Under Mark Fowler, who was appointed FCC chairman by President Reagan, the groundwork was laid that, by 1987, had resulted in the FCC's repeal of the doctrine. Fowler, who was something of a First Amendment absolutist, made no attempt to hide his dislike for governmentally mandated fairness. One impediment to eliminating the doctrine disappeared in 1986 when the U.S. Court of Appeals for the D.C. Circuit ruled that Congress had not made the doctrine statutory when it amended Section 315 in 1959.[73] If Fowler and his colleagues wanted to eliminate the doctrine, they could—provided that they could do so in some way consistent with *Red Lion*, which the Supreme Court had not abandoned.

A complex series of events occurred. An FCC that normally found almost any broadcast response adequate to satisfy the doctrine concluded that a Syracuse television station had violated the second prong of the doctrine in its treatment of a controversy surrounding a nuclear power plant. As the FCC almost certainly expected, the broadcaster, Meredith Corporation, appealed to the U.S. Court of Appeals for the D.C. Circuit. The case bounced back and forth between the court and the FCC until 1987. Then the commission decided that the fairness doctrine, although upheld in *Red Lion*, actually violated the logic underlying that case and should be abandoned because it was ineffective at informing the public and, more likely than not, resulted in broadcasters airing less programming about controversial issues rather than more. As the FCC put it:

> . . . the fairness doctrine in operation disserves both the public's right to diverse sources of information and the broadcaster's interest in free expression. Its chilling effect thwarts its intended purpose, and it results in excessive and unnecessary government intervention into the editorial processes of broadcast journalists. . . . [U]nder the constitutional standard established by *Red Lion* and its progeny, the fairness doctrine contravenes the First Amendment and its enforcement is no longer in the public interest.[74]

Two years later, the U.S. Court of Appeals for the D.C. Circuit upheld the commission, and the U.S. Supreme Court subsequently decided not to review the matter.[75]

Congress tried to thwart the commission's elimination of the doctrine by explicitly writing the doctrine into the Communications Act in 1987. President Reagan, however, vetoed that legislation and threatened to veto similar legislation proposed a few years later. President Bush implied that he would veto fairness legislation, but never was tested because Congress did not adopt any during his presidency. Although a few die-hard fairness doctrine advocates hoped Congress might reinstate it during the Clinton administration, the doctrine failed to get serious attention from Congress prior to the 1994 elections. Opposition fomented by talk show hosts and religious broadcasters who argued that the doctrine would destroy opinionated programming helped keep the doctrine off the agenda. Domination of the Congress beginning in 1995 by conservatives who do not favor additional regulation of business—and are often fans of Rush Limbaugh—makes it most unlikely that the doctrine will return anytime soon or, probably, ever. Arguments against it—that it violates the First Amendment and that in an age of diverse media the public has many sources of opinion available—seem to have prevailed.

Personal Attacks and Political Editorials • A few legacies of the fairness doctrine persist. Their future is in doubt because many of the arguments mounted against the doctrine could be mounted against them by the FCC or through the courts by fairness doctrine opponents. As of mid 1995, however, broadcasters must follow special policies when they editorially endorse or oppose candidates for public office or when they run a "personal attack" on an identified individual or group while discussing controversial issues of public importance.

● **Personal attack rules**
FCC rules that sometimes require broadcasters to let persons they attack use their station to respond.

Under the **personal attack rules**, a station that broadcasts strident criticism of an individual or group's "honesty, character or integrity" while discussing a "controversial issue of public importance" must contact the attacked party within a week, provide a copy or a summary of the attack, and offer a reasonable opportunity for that party to respond via the station.[76] The FCC applies these standards very conservatively. Strident criticism is permissible so long as it focuses on ability or knowledge. A business person, for example, can be criticized as an incompetent manager. Calling that person "unethical" or "a cheat," however, is an attack on "honesty, character or integrity" and might set the personal attack rules in motion. The commission sometimes avoids personal attack cases by ruling that, although attacks may have occurred, they did not take place while discussing a controversial issue of public importance. The rules exempt attacks on foreign individuals and groups and on public figures. They also do not apply to attacks occurring in newscasts, news interviews, and on-the-spot coverage of news events exempt under Section 315 of the Communications Act. Given all these limitations, personal attack complaints rarely reach the FCC, and it is rarer, still, for the commission to conclude the rules have been violated.

● **Political editorializing rules**
FCC rules that sometimes require broadcasters to offer time to candidates they have editorialized against or opponents of candidates they have editorially supported.

Since broadcasters can either editorially support or oppose candidates for public office, it is understandable that the FCC's **political editorializing rules** require them to do slightly different things when they run different kinds of candidate-related editorials. Endorsement of one candidate for a public office requires the station to notify opposing candidates of that endorsement and provide them with a reasonable opportunity to respond. If, on the other hand, a station decides to oppose one candidate, it need only notify that candidate of its stance and offer a reasonable response opportunity.[77]

As a result, in the rare cases where stations do editorialize about candidates, they tend to run opposing rather than endorsing editorials, especially when there are many contenders for the same office. Like the personal attack rules, however, the political editorializing rules have limited application. Under the rules, response opportunities only arise if editorials clearly represent the opinions of station management or ownership. If a station has an independent editorialist whose views are not those of management or ownership, comments by that editorialist do not come under the political editorializing rules.

Morality and the Electronic Media

Obscenity and Indecency • As much as Americans value their personal free speech, they have long displayed a tendency to censor at least some speech by others. This is especially true when sexual speech is involved. The general history of obscenity law has been treated earlier in this book. Obscenity law, of course, applies to broadcasting and cable just as it applies to print media, movies, and audio recordings. Because of the nature of broadcast and cable speech, however, there are some twists and turns to how obscenity law is applied. In addition, almost exclusively to broadcasting, Congress, the FCC, and the courts have developed a parallel line of law that permits the FCC to regulate "indecent" although not obscene radio and television content.

Federal concern about broadcast obscenity and indecency goes back to the Radio Act of 1927. Portions of that act prohibited "obscene, indecent or profane utterances" by means of radio communication. The restrictions were carried over to the Communications Act of 1934. In 1948, they were moved from the Communications Act to the U.S. Criminal Code.[78] Today, it is a federal crime, conceivably punishable by fines and prison time, to use radio, television, or cable for the transmission of obscenity or indecency.

Prosecution of such crimes would have to be begun by a U.S. District Attorney. While criminal obscenity prosecutions are fairly common in nonbroadcast media, they have been infrequent in broadcasting. This is probably because the FCC's rules and regulations allow it to punish stations as well as cable systems and even telephone information service providers for producing or transmitting some types of sexually explicit content.

In electronic media obscenity cases, the FCC says it applies the definition of obscenity from *Miller v. California* described earlier in this book.[79] Critics have long argued, however, that this is not what the FCC actually does. *Miller* requires that obscenity judgments be based on consideration of works "as a whole." The FCC, however, claims that because listeners and viewers can wander in and out, broadcasting lacks the "wholeness" of print media or even films.

Miller also says that obscenity is judged by "contemporary community standards." In criminal prosecutions for obscenity, there is usually a jury, drawn from a community, that is presumed to know and be able to apply that community's standards toward sexual expression. The FCC, however, does not use juries. Obscenity and indecency complaints are decided by FCC staff members and commissioners who may have little or no knowledge of community standards in the area served by the allegedly offending broadcaster. Fortunately perhaps, the FCC rarely handles obscenity cases.

Indecency and the Pacifica Case • Indecency, however, is another matter. Although indecent broadcasts have been prohibited since 1927, and efforts to prevent them in cable and telephony have been made more recently, the most significant indecency case began in 1973 when a noncommercial New York City radio station, WBAI, broadcast a twelve-minute monologue called "Filthy Words" by comedian George Carlin. Carlin's monologue repeatedly used seven common, but some would say vulgar, sexually explicit words the first being shit. On occasion, these words were used in a sexual context. At other times, however, they were not. This routine, like so many of Carlin's, achieved its humor by forcing listeners to consider odd justapositions of words.

The 2:00 P.M. broadcast upset a man driving in his car with his teenage son. He complained to the FCC, which was then under pressure from Congress to do something about broadcast sex and violence. Although indecency cases had been decided earlier, the FCC pursued this one with vigor. Earlier cases had been decided while the *Roth-Memoirs* standard defined obscenity. The FCC had fashioned its definition of broadcast indecency by drawing from *Roth-Memoirs*. The switch to *Miller* meant that if the FCC was going to continue to regulate indecency, it needed a new definition.

The FCC decided WBAI's broadcast was indecent both because of the content it contained and the time of day it aired. According to the FCC, the content "depicted sexual and excretory activities and organs in a patently offensive manner"—at least given the public's expectations of broadcasting. In addition, however, WBAI had broadcast the monologue "at a time of day when there was a reasonable risk" that children were in the audience.

The commission likened broadcast indecency to a nuisance. A given behavior or item often becomes a nuisance not so much because of what it is but because of when and where it occurs. Rather than banning indecency altogether, the FCC sought to define it and then channel it away from children. As in obscenity cases, the commission rejected arguments that it make this decision by considering the entire program about contemporary language within which WBAI had aired the monologue. Instead, the FCC focused on Carlin's repeated use of specific dirty words. It also held that even if indecent language had the serious literary, artistic, political, or scientific value that would prevent it from being classified as obscene, it should still be channeled away from children.[80]

Although the FCC's ruling was overturned by the U.S. Court of Appeals for the D.C. Circuit, it was reinstated in 1975 when the U.S. Supreme Court decided *FCC v. Pacifica Foundation*.[81] All members of the Court agreed that Carlin's monologue was protected speech under the First Amendment. A group of four dissenters led by Justice Potter Stewart believed that only obscenity could be sanctioned, that the monologue was not obscene, and that, accordingly, the broadcast could neither be banned nor channeled by the commission.

Justice Stevens, writing for a sometimes divided five-member Court majority, maintained that indecency was different from obscenity, that broadcasting was uniquely pervasive, intrusive, and accessible to children, and that the commission could channel indecent broadcasts featuring repetitive uses of vulgar sexual words exceeding "normal standards of morality" to times when children were unlikely to be listening. The FCC appeared to have gained quite substantial powers to regulate broadcast content when it pertained to sex.

For almost twelve years, however, the FCC exercised its powers cautiously. The commission indicated it would only punish repetitious broadcasts of the seven words Carlin used. Knowing that, broadcasters avoided their repetition. Even under the chairmanship of Mark Fowler, when some expected that the FCC might enforce anti-indecency policies more rigorously, Fowler's near-absolute approach to the First Amendment resulted in the commission rejecting indecency complaints.

This situation changed in 1987, when Fowler's term as FCC chairman ended. His replacement, Dennis Patrick, had been pressured by conservatives during his Senate confirmation hearings into suggesting that the commission would be more watchful about indecent programming under his leadership.

With more and more stations on the air, plus the alternatives available through cable TV and video rental, broadcasters found their audiences fragmenting. Cable offered uncut R-rated theatrical movies including scenes that broadcasters typically never aired. In large urban areas, radio stations competed fiercely for small shares of the audience. Television and radio both dared to be bolder in an effort to hold onto smaller shares of the audience in a market.

In a 1987 case involving Pacifica broadcasting, the FCC repeated its indecency definition of years earlier but indicated it would enforce the law more vigorously. Any repetition of patently offensive depictions of sexual or excretory activities or organs—not just repeated uses of Carlin's words—when children were in the audience and in ways emphasizing their vulgarity or "shock value", the FCC warned, would be sanctionable.[82] The U.S. Court of Appeals upheld this policy one year later.[83] In mid-1995, the same court said "indecent broadcasts" were okay only within a 10 p.m. and 6 a.m. "safe harbor" when few children watched or listened.

Since 1989, the FCC has fined several broadcasters for allegedly indecent programs. Many of these cases result from shows hosted by radio "shock jocks." Like their most notorious leader, Howard Stern, shock jocks use raunchy language—Carlin's words and many more—to describe sex and attract audiences. For Stern and his syndicator, Infinity Broadcasting, the format works. Stern's program is usually highly rated in markets where it airs. As has already been noted, however, the commission has issued nearly $2 million worth of fines to broadcasters associated with the Stern program. Infinity and others are appealing all these decisions. No immediate resolution is in sight.

In its 1987 decision, the commission stressed that context mattered. When words are used to shock, titillate, or pander, they may be indecent. In different contexts, the same words may be permissible. This is especially true in news. A National Public Radio broadcast of a taped conversation between alleged mobster John Gotti and a colleague included repeated use of the words fuck and fucking. Citing the news context of the broadcast, the FCC rejected a listener's complaint. The Court of Appeals refused to consider the listener's appeal of the FCC's decision.[84]

Obscenity and Indecency Beyond Broadcasting • Since 1984, it has been a crime, punishable by up to two years in prison and a $10,000 fine, to transmit obscene materials by cable.[85] The 1992 cable act authorized the FCC to adopt rules regulating cable indecency.[86] Under the act, the commission has adopted rules attempting to reduce exposure of children to indecent materials on cable leased access channels. The rules require cable operators to block access to leased channels carrying indecent programs unless individual subscribers make written requests for the programming. The channels, however, can only be blocked when indecent programs are on. This could be a problem for cable system operators since it implies that they must have advance knowledge of leased access channel content. Cable operators, however, can obtain and rely upon certification from program suppliers that programming is not obscene or indecent. This may transfer liability away from the cable operator.[87] Although a panel of the U.S. Court of Appeals for the D.C. Circuit found the FCC's access channel indecency restrictions unconstitutional in 1993, that decision was suspended in 1994 when the full Court of Appeals decided to rehear the case *en banc*.[88] Efforts by some states to adopt cable indecency statutes building upon *Pacifica* fared poorly in the courts prior to 1992.[89] Noting that cable entered households only if subscribers paid for it and was not a spectrum-using service, these courts declined to extend broadcast-based principles to cable. After 1992, courts probably would hold that federal efforts to regulate cable indecency preempt states from trying to do so on their own.

Perhaps the most interesting developments in electronic media obscenity and indecency are occurring as a result of the telephone systems evolution into a mass medium. Recognizing that information services, including dial-a-porn, were becoming an increasingly important part of telephone service, Congress in 1988 attempted to ban the commercial offering of obscene or indecent telephonic information. Sable Communications, a provider of dial-a-porn services, asked the Supreme Court to consider the constitutionality of the 24-hour-a-day ban.

In 1989, the Court upheld the ban on obscenity but invalidated the ban on indecency.[90] Noting that *Pacifica* held that indecent speech was protected under the First Amendment, Justice White—writing for a 6–3 majority—said that banning it to protect children unconstitutionally denied adults access to dial-a-porn services. Congress responded almost immediately by enacting another statute. Under this one, dial-a-porn service providers must limit their services to consenting adults over the age of eighteen. Telephone companies must block the services to subscribers who have not previously subscribed in writing. In response to this legislation, the FCC adopted rules requiring services to force customers to use credit or access codes; alternatively, the services can employ electronic scrambling. These laws have fared somewhat better in the courts, although Supreme Court review of them remains possible.[91] Law in this area and in the related area of obscene or indecent content delivered via computer networks is likely to remain unsettled for years. Neither Congress, the FCC, nor the courts have had anything like the last word yet.

Gambling • America seems just about as schizophrenic about gambling as it is about sex. On the one hand, we have a gambling streak as witnessed by everything from Saturday night poker games and church bingo to Las Vegas and Atlantic City to state-run lotteries. At times, however, we have adopted laws intended to discourage such "immoral" activities. Prohibitions on using radio to promote lotteries and gambling first appeared along with prohibitions on broadcast obscenity and indecency in the Radio Act of 1927 and the Communications Act of 1934. They persist today, but in much modified form.[92]

Broadcast restrictions today focus primarily on lotteries and lottery advertising. The details of what lotteries are can be found elsewhere in this book.[93] Basically, however, lotteries are a form of gambling. They occur, in law at least, whenever a prize (something of value) is awarded to contestants who have themselves given up something of value (consideration) to participate in a contest, the outcome of which is determined by chance rather than by knowledge or skill.

Lotteries can be run by many individuals and organizations. Organized crime has run numbers rackets for years. All but two states now operate some form of public lottery. Churches and other charities often hold lotteries or drawings as fund-raisers. Businesses may conduct giveaways or contests to attract customers. From 1927 until 1988, broadcasters were prohibited from advertising or promoting all private lotteries or, for that matter, running contests or promotions amounting to lotteries themselves. This ban was relaxed somewhat in the 1970s when Congress amended the law to allow broadcasters licensed to states that hold lotteries to advertise those lotteries and the state-run lotteries, if any, in adjacent states.

Since the Charity Games Advertising Clarification Act of 1988 was enacted, some broadcasters can advertise and promote both governmental and private lotteries under very precise conditions.[94] State law regarding lotteries and gambling is now more crucial than before. If a state law prohibits lotteries, gambling, or advertising for lotteries or gambling, broadcasters licensed to those states are not exempt from the laws. If a state chooses to run its own lottery, however, that lottery can be advertised or promoted by broadcasters in that state or in any other state with a state-run lottery. Lottery drawings are often televised live. Broadcasters licensed to states without state-run lotteries, however, may not advertise or promote state-run lotteries even if most of their listeners or viewers are in states with such lotteries. Treating lottery advertising as a form of commercial speech, the U.S. Supreme Court upheld this distinction in 1993.[95]

Broadcasters can advertise or promote lotteries run by not-for-profit organizations in their state if state law permits such gambling. Many states allow churches and fraternal organizations to run lotteries and games of chance, but require these organizations to register with or get permission from the state before they do so.

The most difficult area of lottery law for broadcasters to comply with concerns lotteries run by commercial organizations, which can include not only businesses that advertise on the station but the station itself if it runs lotteries to increase audience interest. Federal law allows broadcasters to promote lotteries run by commercial entities only if the lotteries are "occasional" and "incidental to" the primary activity of the business. Under this law, a radio station might be able to hold or promote its own lottery occasionally because its primary business is broadcasting. It might also be able to promote a lottery for a car dealer whose primary business is selling cars. It would not be able to accept an ad from the local numbers runner whose only business is gambling.

The numbers runner raises another point about this law. In addition to being incidental or occasional activities, private lotteries can be promoted only if they are lawful under state and federal law. Many states have never changed their very old, very broad statutes and constitutional provisions that were originally enacted to stamp out private gambling. Thus, probably more often than broadcasters and their advertisers realize, private lotteries, whether run by broadcasters or car dealers, are illegal as is promotion of them by broadcasters.

Finally, broadcasters are allowed to promote lawful gambling activities conducted on Indian reservations. Since Congress adopted the Indian Gaming Regulatory Act in 1988, **Indian gaming** has brought games of chance to many states that forbid other forms of gambling.[96] Acting under the sovereignty most tribes enjoy under treaties with the U.S. government, Indian tribes have developed gambling into a major source of revenue. Non-Indians are good customers and frequent gamblers. The business has become highly profitable for Indian tribes, and advertising it has become good business for broadcasters.

Broadcasters can promote Indian gaming provided that (1) the gaming is run on Indian lands; (2) it is owned and operated by a recognized Indian tribe; (3) it is permitted by law in the state where it is held; and (4) it complies with a state–Indian tribe compact if it includes forms of gaming where participants play against the house (for example, 21 or slot machines) rather than against each other (as in poker). Congress has begun to question the scope of Indian gaming and may amend the law to block interstate Indian lotteries using, in part, the Internet.

A few other policies apply when broadcasters run contests or lotteries themselves. The FCC requires that broadcasters fully disclose how the contest is to run and then run it according to those terms. They have to disclose what prizes do and do not include. If a prize described as "a trip to Florida" includes Florida lodging but not airfare, then that limit must be clearly announced. The contest and the advertising for it cannot be false, misleading, or deceptive. Broadcasters must actually have and award the prizes they announce. Failure to follow these rules can result in FCC fines and, conceivably, loss of license.[97]

Lyrics • In the 1970s, the FCC issued a public notice requiring licensees to be aware of the meaning of songs that might contain drug-oriented lyrics. Repeatedly airing songs that promoted drug use, the FCC warned, might jeopardize a broadcaster's license.[98] The general policy was upheld by a U.S. Court of Appeals in 1973. The court interpreted the policy as an FCC reminder that broadcasters should not air programming not in the public interest rather than as a policy directly targeted at specific songs with specific lyrics.[99] The policy remains in force although it has rarely been applied. Today, however, broadcasters might profitably consider the implications of the policy outside the drug lyric context that gave it birth. Artists, especially rap artists, are sometimes accused of glorifying violence, often against police or women, and other antisocial behaviors. The recording industry has adopted self-regulatory codes that label recordings with adult content. Given the court's interpretation of the 1971 FCC policy, broadcasters should at least consider it when they air these kinds of recordings. These lyrics, too, may be contrary to the public interest. As in so many other areas, however, broadcasters complain they are subjected to unfair treatment since this policy statement does not apply to cable services like MTV.

Disturbing, Misleading, or Deceiving the Community • Exuberant radio personalities sometimes get carried away and conduct hoaxes that can mislead and

● **Indian gaming**
Gaming and gambling activities lawfully conducted by Native American tribes, usually on reservations. An increasing source of income for many tribes.

disrupt communities. Under rules adopted by the FCC in 1992, licensees can be fined for "knowingly broadcasting false information concerning a crime or a catastrophe" whenever they ought to anticipate public harm that, in fact, occurs. Public harm can include harm to public health or safety, damage to property, or the diversion of law enforcement or health officials from their responsibilities. Fictitious programming is acceptable if it is accompanied by disclaimers run before, during, and after the programming.[100]

Examples, unfortunately, are all too common. When radio station WALE-FM in Providence, Rhode Island, broadcast a report that a talk show host had been shot outside the station, police rushed to investigate and the FCC admonished the station.[101] When a "Confess your Crime" segment ran on KROQ-FM in Pasadena, California, Doug Roberts, a disc jockey on an Arizona station, called in to falsely report killing his girlfriend. Police investigated, and NBC's *Unsolved Mysteries* ran a segment about the unsolved murder. In this case, too, the FCC only admonished the station.[102] The FCC was less understanding, however, when KSHE-FM in St. Louis, Missouri, broadcast a false warning of a nuclear attack with exploding bomb sound effects. For this incident, the FCC assessed the maximum fine allowed under its rules—$25,000![103]

The commission also has rarely enforced policies prohibiting news staging, rigging, or distortion. In 1967, the FCC told a Chicago TV station that arranged a pot party so that a news crew could film it that the station should have explained to its viewers that the event was staged.[104] Instructing a news department to slant the news was part of the reason Indiana broadcaster Don Burden lost licenses for five radio stations in 1975.[105] More recently, the FCC investigated *60 Minutes* after a California doctor obtained access to video outtakes and complained that an interview with an employee of his clinic admitting fraud had been staged. The FCC concluded that the staging and distortion were not significant—there was plenty of other evidence that fraud had been committed—and dismissed the doctor's complaint. Courts upheld the FCC.[106]

One ethically questionable, but commonly employed, news-gathering tactic is also prohibited by FCC rules. In an effort to protect personal privacy, the FCC prohibits the broadcast of live or recorded telephone conversations unless the person on the other end of the line has given advance permission to the broadcast. The only exceptions are when the phone call is between the station and station personnel or when it is absolutely certain that the nonstation participant knows the call is being broadcast.[107] These rules have never been applied in a news context, but some broadcasters have been fined or admonished for violating them during station contests or promotions. The use of hidden cameras and microphones to gather news for later broadcast is not forbidden by FCC rules, but may violate state law.

Special Types of Broadcasting—Religious and Public Broadcasting

Two special kinds of programming have posed problems for the FCC over the years—religious broadcasting and public broadcasting. They may seem an odd pair, but the two services have much in common. Both offer alternatives to regular commercial fare. Religious organizations can qualify for the kinds of licenses held by public broadcasters. Both often employ nontraditional means of raising revenue.

When the FCC had overall programming expectations, religious programming was one of the types of programming it typically expected. The commission, however, never really questioned failure to offer such programming. When the fairness doctrine was in effect, religious broadcasters were required to adhere to it and got in trouble with the FCC when they did not.[108] The commission has rejected arguments that freedom of religion exempts religious licensees from general broadcast law. When a TV evangelist misled his contributors about what he was doing with their money and then cited religious freedom as a reason for not telling the FCC who the contributors were, the FCC refused to renew the preacher's license.[109] If it had been more tenacious, the FCC might have revealed Rev. Jim Bakker's misdeeds long before they became public. The FCC spent years investigating the affairs of Bakker's Heritage Village Church and Missionary Fellowship in Charlotte, North Carolina. When it discovered some questionable practices, it dropped its investigation and passed the matter off to the U.S. Department of Justice, which, unfortunately for Bakker's supporters and contributors, did not follow up immediately on what the FCC had discovered.[110]

The FCC grants noncommercial, educational radio and television licenses to applicants who can prove their "primary thrust" will be "educational." Recognizing some inevitable overlap between religious and secular education, the FCC nevertheless tries to determine which purpose is primary and which is incidental.[111] It typically expects religious organizations seeking noncommercial licenses to operate schools in the communities for which they seek licenses. That is taken as a sure sign of the educational thrust of the licensee. Deregulation has probably advantaged some religious broadcasters. Freed from the fairness doctrine, some have become more bold about advancing their views on controversial issues such as abortion.

Congress and the FCC have long believed that commercial market forces and commercial radio, television, and cable may not necessarily provide every type of service the public needs. Thus, the United States—like most other nations—has promoted an alternative system of noncommercial telecommunications. In the United States, this system has focused on public television (PBS) and public radio (NPR). The effort has not been without problems and controversy.

One major set of problems has focused on how to publicly finance the system while preventing it from becoming a government propaganda operation. Can public broadcasting be simultaneously dependent on government for money and a source of criticism of the hand that feeds it? Congress finally began to address this problem when it adopted the Public Broadcasting Act of 1967, which created the basic framework for public radio and television in the United States.[112] What eventually emerged is a system where funds for public television programming are funneled through a quasi-governmental nonprofit corporation, the Corporation for Public Broadcasting (CPB). The CPB, in turn, makes programming grants to producing stations and individuals. Money for construction of public telecommunications facilities is administered by the National Telecommunications and Information Administration, a part of the Department of Commerce.

Levels of federal government funding have not risen much over the years, but the funding stations receive is keyed to requirements that public broadcasters raise matching funds locally to qualify for federal dollars. Congress also put public broadcasting into a unique funding system. Unlike all other parts of government, which are funded just year-to-year, public broadcasting is guaranteed its money three years in advance. In theory, this means that public broadcasting can criticize government without fearing immediate financial reprisals.

Under Republican leadership, Congress in 1995 considered major changes in funding for public broadcasting. Options discussed ranged from a cutback of already approved funds for fiscal year 1995 to an immediate cutoff of all federal funding to continued funding without inflation increases. By mid–1995, Congress seemed likely to adopt changes including a two-to-four-year phaseout of federal support which, by 1995, amounted to about 14 percent of public broadcasting's budget.

Public broadcasters have always subsisted, however, on a diet of mixed federal, state, and locally raised funds. Many of the nongovernment dollars come from companies that would otherwise advertise on commercial media. These companies provide grants to support specific programs. While unquestionably motivated to do good in many instances, these supporters have also always expected some acknowledgment of their support for public broadcasting programs. In effect, they want at least some of the benefits of a commercial in what is theoretically a noncommercial medium. Station desires to be more successful—to attract larger audiences than underwriters will support—have focused attention on two main issues for public broadcasting. First, what should be the nature of the service public broadcasters provide? How alternative must it be? Second, how commercial can they become in acknowledging support received from underwriters?

Public broadcasting has always been perceived as some kind of alternative to commercial broadcasting. The need for the alternative is reflected in FCC policies since the 1940s that reserve spectrum space exclusively for educational, noncommercial television and radio. As the phrase *educational, noncommercial* indicates, the early focus was on fairly formal education. Many pioneer public licensees were educational institutions—school districts, colleges and universities, and others. These licensees often devoted most of their programming to clearly educational programming such as "sunrise semesters." Many public broadcasters still do some of that.

Over the years, however, public broadcasting evolved into a broader service. Governmental bodies, such as the FCC, did not object to the evolution. Today, many public stations offer a mix of program services, occasionally overtly educational but more often just targeted to audiences ignored by commercial broadcasting and, sometimes, no more than alternative forms of popular entertainment.

In recent years, the FCC has not subjected the general programming services offered by public broadcasters to an in-depth examination, and its general deregulation of broadcast programming has benefited public as well as commercial licensees.

At least occasionally, however, both commercial broadcasters and the FCC use public broadcasting as a justification for not expecting commercial broadcasters to provide less than maximally profitable programming. Beginning with *Sesame Street*, public television has taken a high-profile lead in serving children. On the radio side, public stations are the home of classical, jazz, and new age music that is rarely attractive to commercial broadcasters. Nearly all the serious news and public affairs programming done in radio comes from National Public Radio. PBS runs television news documentaries, which have all but disappeared from commercial TV. To some extent, deregulation of commercial radio and TV in the 1980s was justified because public broadcasters had stepped in and filled programming niches the FCC, under regulation, had compelled commercial broadcasters to grudgingly fill.

Some question, however, whether public radio and TV can continue in their current mode and role. Funding is one problem. Conservative federal politicians often characterize public broadcasting as liberal and argue that tax dollars should not support it. Cable television threatens public broadcasting because some of its channels profitably offer programs similar to those traditionally shown on public television, for example, Nickelodeon and Disney (children's services), Discovery Channel (science), and A&E (high-culture BBC imports). If these services can be commercially viable, some argue, why should they be supported by government?

The constant quest for more nongovernment funds has brought changes in permissible underwriting announcements. From the late 1960s through the early 1980s, acknowledgment of support for programs was fairly nonobtrusive. There might be a brief audio mention of program underwriters—"brought to you by a grant from. . ."—accompanied on TV by a slide presenting the full name of the underwriter in block letters. Corporate logos were prohibited, and underwriting acknowledgments had little of the character of traditional commercials.

That changed in 1981. Faced with congressional reluctance to increase federal support or even keep funding level with inflation, Congress and the FCC relaxed the law about acknowledgment of private program support.[113] Today, corporate logos and slogans can be incorporated into underwriting acknowledgements. Objective statements about the goods or services an underwriter offers can be broadcast. For example, a TV underwriting announcement could include the XYZ Corporations's corporate logo and say "brought to you by a grant from XYZ Corporation, manufacturer of widgets and other home accessories." Sales pitches or claims are still prohibited. Underwriters still cannot say that they offer the best of some product or service. The distinction is a fine one, but does persist as one of the ways in which noncommercial broadcasting differs from commercial radio and TV. If federal funding is eliminated, it appears likely that commercialization will become even more overt.

Disputes have arisen about whether any special programming standards should apply to public broadcasting. The Public Broadcasting Act advised CPB to use its money to fund programs with "strict adherence to objectivity and balance in all programs . . . of a controversial nature." If enforced, this would be a stronger mandate than even the fairness doctrine, which did not apply to individual shows. When a conservative media watchdog group, Accuracy in Media (AIM), tried to force the FCC to enforce this standard, the U.S. Court of Appeals ruled that the language was not enforceable by the commission and was, instead, only congressional advice to CPB.[114] At this time, however, the FCC still enforced the fairness doctrine and applied it to noncommercial as well as commercial broadcasters.

Abolition of the doctrine and continued concern among conservatives about a perceived leftward tilt led Congress to incorporate special provisions in CPB's 1992 appropriations. CPB was admonished to step up its pursuit of "objectivity and balance in all programs." It must review programming for "quality, diversity, creativity, excellence, innovation, objectivity and balance" and, if found lacking, redress deficiencies. Mechanisms must be created for CPB to receive public comment on programming.[115] These conditions seemed to be largely a response to *POV* (Point of View), a public TV series that, among other things, had broadcast a provocative program by a homosexual producer graphically presenting many elements of homosexual speech and lifestyle.

Public broadcasting remains something of an enigma. It is the mass medium most subsidized by public funds in contemporary America. Although federal funding is relatively stagnant and may be eliminated, state and local funding remains quite substantial and may increase. Many public stations are licensed to public school systems and state colleges and universities. Not only is government more deeply involved in public broadcasting than in any other mass media, but there is no print analogy to such a heavily governmentally supported mass medium.

This relationship has raised significant First Amendment questions. Actions of commercial broadcasters normally are not viewed as actions of government. Although they take place under an FCC license, they are still considered to be the actions of private, nongovernmental communicators, and programming decisions by commercial broadcasters cannot violate the First Amendment because they are not considered government actions.[116] When the government of Saudi Arabia objected to PBS's airing of "Death of a Princess," a dramatization of the execution of a Saudi Arabian princess for adultery, some public broadcasting stations decided not to carry the program. Viewers who wanted to see it went to court and argued that the decision of such public broadcasters who were also part of state government violated the First Amendment rights of viewers to receive information. Courts eventually decided that, at least in this case, stations run by the University of Houston and the Alabama Educational Television Commission were not public forums, that their editorial discretion had to be respected, and that their programming decisions did not violate the First Amendment rights of viewers.[117]

In 1994, however, a minor party candidate for the U.S. House of Representatives, who had been excluded from a debate sponsored by the Arkansas Educational Television Network (AETN), asked the U.S. Court of Appeals for the Eighth Circuit to rule that AETN's editorial decision violated both the public's and the candidate's First Amendment rights. Sitting *en banc*, a 6–5 majority distinguished this case from "Death of a Princess." Here, said the court, the issue was different. The earlier case simply involved decisions about what shows to air. In the 1994 case, the government (AETN) was expressing a preference for some candidates over others. The court ruled that in choosing to run debates, AETN might have created a limited public forum and dedicated some of its facilities and resources to political discourse. It remanded the case to a federal district court, directing that court to examine the public forum issue more closely. Thus, the debate is still alive: at least in some instances, public broadcasters are the government, and although they enjoy First Amendment protections, they must also respect the First Amendment rights of viewers, listeners, and those who might wish to use their stations in ways distinct from those available in commercial broadcasting.

The dispute has wide-ranging implications. As the United States moves toward an information superhighway of interconnected computer networks, many are likely to argue that such a network is also some kind of public forum. Much of today's network has been built and is operated by the federal government, notably the Department of Defense; in addition, as in the case of public broadcasting, public universities and colleges are much involved in providing computing and transmission capability.

Congress and the courts are just beginning to tackle disputes about when those government bodies can censor computer communications and who, if anyone, is responsible for harmful content, libel, or obscenity distributed over computer networks. As these technologies progress, they will profoundly change all forms of communication—print, broadcast, cable, and telephonic. They will change the nature of communication and the substance of communications law. They are likely to force us to reconsider fundamental ideas about how the First Amendment applies to electronic communications and whether there are any relevant differences among electronic media. Media law to date has largely governed one-way, noninteractive communications that are much different than what is predicted for the future. Editing used to be what editors did. In an information-on-demand society, editing may mostly be done by readers, viewers, and listeners. In a global communications village, which the computer age has already begun to create, the question may not be just how freedom of speech and press and the First Amendment apply to new forms of communication in this country. It is likely that our traditions of free expression will be much more directly challenged by the traditions of other political systems whose beliefs are different than ours. John Milton believed that truth would prevail when it grappled with falsity in a free and open encounter. It is quite unlikely that old First Amendment theories and practices will prevail unchanged in a global grapple over communications technology and appropriate communications laws and policies.[118]

SUMMARY

For nearly seventy years, electronic mass media in the United States have been subject to laws and regulations treating them differently than print media. These differences began with decisions that broadcasting had to be regulated because of its use of the spectrum. By 1934, the Federal Communications Commission was not only licensing and regulating broadcasting but also regulating interstate aspects of wired services like telephones and telegraphs. Much later, it acquired responsibilities for regulating cable television although states and local governments regulated that industry as well.

Such extensive regulation of broadcasting, cable, and telephony inevitably led to the development of First Amendment law pertaining to these media. Focusing on technical differences among means of electronic communications, the U.S. Supreme Court eventually gave broadcasting less First Amendment protection than print media. In addition, courts ruled that in broadcasting, First Amendment rights and interests of listeners and viewers often were more significant than First Amendment rights of broadcast employees and owners. First Amendment theory for cable television is not extensively developed, but at the moment the Supreme Court says the medium is not broadcasting but also is not identical to print. Cable seems to be finding a First Amendment status somewhere between these traditions. First Amendment theory for telephony and computer communications is in its infancy because these communication modes have only begun to work like mass media in recent years. In the long run, broadcasting, cable, telephony, and even print (if one thinks of it as text) are converging. This process may not be compatible with our past history of media-specific First Amendment law.

While fundamental electronic media law is statutory, these industries have been regarded as so rapidly changing and specialized as to require ongoing attention from specialized regulators. Federal and state administrative agencies are responsible for many of the regulations affecting the electronic media. Rules from such agencies can be readily changed as media and the conditions under which they operate evolve.

One problem these agencies face is deciding how to grant, renew, deny, and revoke licenses. Today, licensing and franchising decisions are very content-neutral, although they were not always that way in the past. Legal, financial, and technical requirements have been developed that determine basic fitness to hold licenses and franchises. In most cases, entry is gained by purchasing an existing electronic media system from its owner and then getting the government's permission to hold the license or franchise required to operate it. Criteria such as ownership of other media, financial qualifications, character, and citizenship primarily determine licensee and franchisee fitness.

Content regulation of the electronic mass media persists in a few specific areas. In broadcasting, much law governs the treatment of candidates for public office by licensees. Equal treatment is required of all candidates; federal candidates have special rights of access to broadcast time. Under some circumstances, candidate uses of stations cannot be censored by station personnel. Political advertising rates on electronic media are subject to government regulation. These regulations of political content have survived First Amendment attack when courts have reasoned that they promote the First Amendment rights of listeners and viewers to receive political speech.

Additional law requires special TV programming for children and governs such things as the advertising and promotion of lotteries, news distortion and staging, hoaxes that harm the public, and religious programming. Deregulation has lifted many content constraints in recent years out of a belief that economic factors—competition—can regulate electronic media better than the government can. Another consideration is that as the media environment grows richer and more varied, it may no longer be necessary to require one medium or one outlet to do everything since other fungible media and outlets are available to fulfill the public's needs.

The convergence of electronic media is likely to continue, and as it does, the distinctions among electronic media will become more transparent in the eyes of both consumers and media personnel themselves. The national information infrastructure of the future is likely to meld our existing modes of electronic communication into a hybrid system in which visual, aural, and text information, reduced to digital form, moves seamlessly through many wired and wireless channels. Information will be more consciously and interactively chosen by consumers. The traditional role of electronic media and their employees as gatekeepers between information sources and information users will change. The nearly inevitable result will be substantial change in our existing system of electronic media law, which was built on assumptions of a simpler, less-diverse, less–consumer-oriented, and less–interactive media world.

KEY TERMS

Public rights of way
Intrusiveness
Pervasiveness
Public offices
Fairness doctrine
Obscenity
Indecency
Convergence
Radio Act of 1927
Public interest, convenience, and necessity
Federal Radio Commission (FRC)
Communications Act of 1934
Scarcity theory
Red Lion Broadcasting v. FCC
FCC v. Pacifica Foundation
Cable Television Consumer Protection and
  Competition Act of 1992
Franchise
Multiple system operator (MSO)
Franchisor
Franchisee

Duopolies
Crossmedia ownership
Equal employment opportunity (EEO)
Affirmative action
Petitions to deny
PEG access
Self-regulation
Syndicated exclusivity rules
Network nonduplication rules
Turner Broadcasting v. FCC
Must-carry rules
Section 315
Use
Legally qualified candidates
Section 312(a)(7)
Reasonable access
Federal candidates
No-censorship requirement
Personal attack rules
Political editorializing rules
Indian gaming

CASE PROBLEMS

1. Little Mary Sunshine, whose name will appear on the primary election ballot in twenty-five days as a candidate for the Republican nomination for mayor, strolls into the office of WARM-TV. Last night Sunshine saw a commercial on WARM for Dan Divine, one of four candidates for the Democratic mayoral nomination. Sunshine confronts WARM's general manager and demands "equal time" to respond to Divine's ad the previous evening. Can the manager respond to Sunshine's demand based on just this information? If so, what is the response and why? If not, what other information does the manager need?

Five days later, Sunshine returns. This time her request is for "reasonable access" to the station. Again, can the manager respond to her request? If so, how? If not, what further information is required?

Assume that, for whatever reasons, the manager agrees to sell political advertising time to Sunshine. Can the manager simply charge Sunshine whatever she is willing and able to pay? What constraints does the law place on what Sunshine can be charged for political advertising at this time? Why do these constraints, and not others that may apply at other times, apply here?

2. You are the president of your town's Telecommunications Council. Under a recently enacted ordinance, your council is in charge of overseeing cable television. The town has a population of about 100,000 people. A single cable operator, TCPPT, Inc. (Telecommunications, Paramount, Pacific Telesis, Inc.), runs your cable system. No other multichannel video services are available to your citizens. Name three major things about TCPPT's operation that your council can lawfully regulate or influence. Name three other things that are likely to be of great importance to your citizens but, unfortunately, are beyond your regulatory authority over cable TV.

3. As general sales manager of KLDS-AM, a high-powered AM station licensed to Salt Lake City, Utah, you are contacted by officials of the Colorado State Lottery. Colorado officials know that Utah, a strict Mormon state, has no state-run lottery and prohibits all forms of private wagering. The Colorado officials hope to urge lottery-hungry citizens of northern Utah to drive east to Colorado and buy Colorado lottery tickets. Can you sell advertising time to the Colorado State Lottery on your Salt Lake City radio station? Why or why not? Can you think of (other) lawful ways Colorado State Lottery officials could get electronic ads for their lottery into Salt Lake City? If so, what would they be?

4. You are the chief executive officer for MegaMedia, Inc. Your company already owns four VHF-TV stations and five UHF-TV stations in nine different communities in the U.S. Collectively, these nine markets equal 17 percent of all TV households in the country. You also own 13 FM stations and 15 AM stations around the country. Three of these radio stations are in towns where you also own TV stations. These jointly owned radio-tv combos were created before the FCC began prohibiting such combinations. MegaMedia owns newspapers too, but right now they are not in communities where you own broadcast properties. Your company wants to expand. What limits does the Communications Act and the FCC's rules currently place on buying more radio or TV stations? What about buying cable television systems? Could you buy broadcast stations or cable systems in the communities where you run newspapers? Could a telephone company or a motion picture studio buy up MegaMedia, Inc? Could you buy broadcast properties abroad? Finally, would the Communications Act let a foreign corporation buy you out?

5. The FCC relied on *Red Lion Broadcasting v. FCC*, which sustained an FCC action under the fairness doctrine, to eventually overturn the doctrine. The FCC had to accept *Red Lion* because the U.S. Supreme Court still considers the case good law. Suppose that, in the late 1990s, Congress rewrites the fairness doctrine into the Communications Act of 1934 and a Supreme Court case results in which the Court can either continue to follow *Red Lion* or vote to overturn it and do something else. What do you think the Court should do? Are the justifications behind *Red Lion* still valid today? Why or why not? Could other justifications be advanced to support a modern fairness doctrine against First Amendment attack? If they *could* be developed, do you believe they *should* be developed? Why?

6. Sam Bonehead, manager of WASP-TV, knows he has a problem. For each of the first four years of his current license, he has reported to the FCC that minority employment at his station is much lower, as a percentage of the workforce, than minority employment in his community. Assuming the situation

is no better when he applies for renewal, and also that there is no evidence of overt discrimination against minorities at the station, is it likely that the FCC will strip Sam of his license because of the statistical shortfall alone? Why or why not? Given this information, what is the FCC most likely to do to WASP-TV? Why? Suppose Sam decides that he will simply fabricate higher minority employment figures on his fifth annual EEO report. Is this a good idea? If the FCC finds out about this fabrication, how will it affect Sam's chances for renewal? Why? Assuming Sam decides to complete his form truthfully, what if anything can he do during the final year before his renewal to increase his chances of gaining renewal without dispute?

7. A local chapter of HSA (Home Shoppers Anonymous) files a petition to deny with the Federal Communications Commission when KSEL-TV, a "home shopping" TV station applies for renewal. HSA has conducted a careful social scientific analysis of KSEL's programming during its last year of operation. The study clearly supports the conclusion that KSEL has offered absolutely nothing except nationally syndicated home shopping programs. It is, in other words, 100 percent commercial. If HSA formulates the most compelling petition to deny it can, on what grounds will it urge the FCC to deny the renewal? Assuming that HSA files this best possible petition to deny, what can KSEL argue in exchange? Suppose that instead of filing a petition to deny, HSA files a competing application for KSEL's license. Do you think that KSEL can claim a "renewal expectancy" for the record described here? Why or why not?

ENDNOTES

1. Radio Act of 1927, P.L. 69-632, 44 Stat. 1162 (1927).

2. Communications Act of 1934, 48 Stat. 1064 (1934). All federal statutes governing telecommunications today, including the Communications Act and its amendments, are codified in Title 47 of the United States Code.

3. 319 U.S. 190, 63 S.Ct. 997 (1943).

4. 395 U.S. 367, 89 S.Ct. 1794 (1969).

5. *Metro Broadcasting, Inc. v. FCC,* 497 U.S. 547, 110 S.Ct. 2997 (1990).

6. 18 U.S.C.A. § 1464 (Supp. 1995).

7. For a solid argument that the Supreme Court should change its emphasis on media–specific First Amendment theory, see Patrick M. Garry, *Scrambling for Protection: The New Media and the First Amendment* (Pittsburgh: University of Pittsburgh Press, 1994).

8. Ithiel de Sola Pool, *Technologies of Freedom* (Cambridge, Mass.: Belknap Press, 1983).

9. Cable Communications Policy Act of 1994, P.L. 98–549, 90 Stat. 2779 (1984).

10. Cable Television Consumer Protection and Competition Act of 1992, P. L. 102–385, 106 Stat. 1460 (1992).

11. Communications Satellite Act of 1962, P.L. 87–624, 76 Stat. 419.

12. Public Broadcasting Act of 1967, P.L. 90–129, 81 Stat. 889.

13. Cable Communications Policy Act of 1984, P.L. 98–549, 98 Stat. 2780; Cable Television Consumer Protection and Competition Act of 1992, P.L. 102–385, 106 Stat. 1460 (1992).

14. 47 C.F.R. § 73.3555.

15. The FCC is considering prohibiting only duopolies whose "Grade A" signals overlap. Under current rules, "Grade B" overlap is prohibited. "Economic Analysis Sought; FCC Starts Rulemaking on TV Station Ownership," 14 Communications Daily No. 242, December 16, 1994, p. 2. By mid–1995 Congress was also considering changes here.

16. 47 C.F.R. § 73.3555(c) (1992). The commission may decide to eliminate all prohibitions on common ownership of radio and TV stations within markets. "Economic Analysis Sought; FCC Starts Rulemaking on TV Station Ownership," 14 Communications Daily No. 242, December 16, 1994, p. 2. Congress, by 1995, was also reviewing these policies.

17. 47 C.F.R. § 73.3555(c) (1992). Under the proposed changes, the audience cap might rise by

5 percent every three years up to a maximum of 50 percent of national TV households. Commission staff members indicated that the proceeding might also result in changes in the number of TV stations a single entity could own. "Economic Analysis Sought; FCC Starts Rulemaking on TV Station Ownership," 14 Communications Daily No. 242, December 16, 1994, p. 2. This too was under Congressional review in 1995.

18. 47 C.F.R. § 73.355(d) (1992).

19. Policy Regarding Character Qualifications in Broadcast Licensing, 102 FCC 2d 1179 (1986). Policy Regarding Character Qualifications in Broadcast Licensing, 5 FCC Rcd. 3252 (1990).

20. 47 C.F.R. § 73.2080 (1992). By mid–1995 the possibility existed that Congress would prohibit the FCC from enforcing equal employment opportunity rules. The U.S. Equal Employment Opportunity Commission (USEEOC) would still enforce EEO law. However, the U.S. Supreme Court's June, 1995 decision in *Adarand Constructors Inc. v. Peña,* 1995 WL 347345 could sharply reduce the vigor of EEO enforcement.

21. Deregulation of Radio, 84 FCC 2d 968 (1981), generally affirmed *Office of Communications of the United Church of Christ v. FCC,* 707 F.2d 1413 (D.C.Cir. 1983), Revision of Programming and Commercialization Policies, Ascertainment Requirements, and Program Log Requirements for Commercial Television Stations, 98 FCC 2d 1076 (1984).

22. Children's Television Act of 1990, P.L. 101–437, 101 Stat. 996 (1990).

23. Policies and Rules Concerning Children's Television Programming, 6 FCC Rcd. 2111 (1991), *reconsidered* 6 FCC Rcd. 5093 (1991).

24. Policies and Rules Concerning Children's Television Programming, 6 FCC Rcd. 2111 (1991), *reconsidered* 6 FCC Rcd. 5093 (1991).

25. Policies and Rules Concerning Children's Television Programming Policies, Revision of Programming for Television Broadcast Stations, 8 FCC Rcd. 1841 (1993), Broadcast Services; Childrens Television, 60 Fed. Reg. 20586 (April 26, 1995).

26. *Cowles Broadcasting, Inc.,* 86 FCC 2d 993 (1981). *Affirmed Central Florida Enterprises, Inc. v. FCC,* 683 F.2d 503 (D.C.Cir. 1982). Cert

denied 460 U.S. 1084, 76 L. Ed. 2d. 346, 103 S. Ct. 1774 (1983).

27. Policy Statement on Comparative Broadcast Hearings, 1 FCC 2d 393 (1965).

28. *Bechtel v. FCC,* 10 F.3d 875 (D.C.Cir. 1993).

29. FCC Freezes Comparative Hearings, 9 FCC Rcd. 1055 (1994).

30. For a summary of the history, see *Central Florida Enterprises, Inc. v. FCC,* 683 F.2d 503 (D.C.Cir. 1982), *cert. denied* 460 U.S. 1084, 103 S.Ct. 1774 (1983). Here, too, Congress was by mid–1995 considering changes in the Communications Act that would eliminate comparative renewal battles.

31. *Central Florida Enterprises, Inc. v. FCC,* 683 F.2d 503 (D.C.Cir. 1982), *cert. denied* 460 U.S. 1084, 103 S.Ct. 1774 (1983).

32. 47 U.S.C.A. § 309(d) (1991).

33. 47 U.S.C.A. § 546 *et. seq.* (1991 & Supp. 1995).

34. 47 U.S.C.A. § 537 (Supp. 1995).

35. 47 U.S.C.A. § 554 (1991 & Supp. 1995).

36. 47 U.S.C.A. § 533 (1991 & Supp. 1995).

37. *U.S. West v. United States,* 855 F. Supp. 1184 (W.D.Wash. 1994), *Chesapeake & Potomac Telephone Company v. United States,* 830 F.Supp. 909 (E.D.Va. 1993). Affirmed, 42 F. 3d. 181 (4th Cir. 1994).

38. Evaluation of the Syndication and Financial Interest Rules, 8 FCC Rcd. 3282 (1993).

39. Implementation of The Cable Television Consumer Protection and Competition Act of 1992, MM Docket, No. 92-265, 9 FCC Rcd 4415 (1994).

40. 47 U.S.C.A. § 548 (Supp. 1995).

41. Television Program Improvement Act of 1990, P.L. 101–650, Title V, 104 Stat. 5127 (1990).

42. "Washington Watch," *Broadcasting & Cable,* July 4, 1994, p. 36, "TV Industry to Senate: Self-Regulation, Not Legislation, the Answer to Violence," *Broadcasting,* May 24, 1993, p. 14.

43. "Voices against Violence; A Cable Television Industry Initiative," Satellite Network Committee, National Cable Television Assn., Washington, D.C., January 1994.

44. *United States v. Southwestern Cable Co.*, 392 U.S. 157, 88 S. Ct. 1994 (1968).

45. For a basic legislative history of the Cable Communications Policy Act of 1984, see 1984 *U.S.C.C.A.N.* 4655.

46. 47 U.S.C.A. § 544(b)(2)(B) (1991 & Supp. 1995). One court held that a Wisconsin franchisor could enforce franchise provisions calling for the general category of "east coast programming." *Jones Intercable, Inc. v. City of Stevens Point*, 729 F.Supp. 642 (W.D.Wis. 1990).

47. 47 U.S.C.A. § 543(b)(7) (Supp. 1995).

48. See 47 U.S.C.A. §§ 534 and 535 (Supp. 1995).

49. See Chapter 1, page 14 of this book.

50. *Turner Broadcasting System, Inc. v. FCC* ___U.S.___, 114 S.Ct. 2445 (1994).

51. Lar Daly, 22 FCC 2d 16, 18 RR 2d 701 (1959).

52. P.L. 86–274, § 1, 73 Stat. 557 (1959). For analysis of those debates, see Sidney Kraus, ed., *The Great Debates* (Bloomington: Indiana University Press, 1962).

53. *In re Aspen Institute and CBS, Inc.*, 55 FCC 2d 697 (1975), *affirmed, Chisholm v. FCC*, 538 F.2d 349 (D.C.Cir. 1976). Cert den. Democratic National Committee v. FCC, 429 U.S. 890, 97 S. Ct. 247 (1976).

54. Codification of the Commission's Political Programming Policies, 7 FCC Rcd. 678 (1991).

55. Codification of the Commission's Political Programming Policies, 9 FCC Rcd. 651 (1994).

56. National Urban Coalition, 23 FCC 2d 123 (1970).

57. 47 U.S.C.A. § 312(a)(7) (1991).

58. Federal Election Campaign Act of 1971, P.L. 92–225, Title 1, § 103(a)(2)(A), 86 Stat. 3 (1972).

59. 453 U.S. 367, 101 S. Ct. 2813 (1981).

60. Federal Election Campaign Act of 1971, P.L. 92-225, Title 1, §§ 103(a)(1)(2)(B), 104(c), 86 Stat. 3, 7 (1972).

61. 47 U.S.C.A. § 315(b)(1) (1991).

62. Codification of the Commission's Political Programming Policies, 7 FCC Rcd. 678 (1991)

63. Chronicle Publishing Co., 6 FCC Rcd. 7497 (1990). Broadcasters have argued in state courts, however, that federal regulation of broadcast advertising rates blocks recovery at the state level.

64. *Farmers Educational and Cooperative Union v. WDAY*, 360 U.S. 525, 79 S. Ct. 1302 (1959).

65. Atlanta NAACP, 36 FCC 2d 636 (1972).

66. Vincent Pepper, 7 FCC Rcd. 5599 (1992).

67. The Law of Political Broadcasting and Cablecasting: A Political Primer, 100 FCC 2d 1476, 1513 (1984).

68. *Trinity Methodist Church, South v. FRC*, 62 F.2d 850 (App. D.C. 1932), *cert. denied*, 284 U.S. 685, 53 S. Ct. 317 (1932).

69. In the Matter of Editorializing by Broadcast Licensees, 13 FCC 1246 (1949).

70. Representative Patsy Mink, 59 FCC 2d 987 (1976).

71. 395 U.S. 367, 89 S. Ct. 1794 (1969).

72. 412 U.S. 94, 93 S.Ct. 2080 (1973).

73. *Telecommunications Research and Action Center v. FCC*, 801 F.2d 501 (D.C. Cir. 1986), *cert. denied*, 482 U.S. 919, 107 S.Ct. 3196 (1987).

74. Syracuse Peace Council, 2 FCC Rcd. 5043, 5052 (1987).

75. *Syracuse Peace Council v. FCC*, 867 F.2d 654 (D.C.Cir. 1989), *cert. denied* 493 U.S. 1019, 110 S. Ct. 717 (1990).

76. 47 C.F.R. § 73.1920 (1992).

77. 47 C.F.R. § 73.1930 (1992).

78. 18 U.S.C.A. § 1464 (Supp. 1995).

79. See Chapter 5, page 144 of this text.

80. Pacifica Foundation Station WBAI(FM), 56 FCC 2d 94 (1975).

81. 438 U.S. 726, 98 S.Ct. 3026.

82. Pacifica Foundation, Inc., 2 FCC Rcd. 2698 (1987).

83. *Action for Children's Television v. FCC*, 852 F.2d 1332 (D.C.Cir. 1988). Vacated and remanded, 932 F 2d 1504 D.C. Cir. (1991), *cert. denied* ___ U.S.___ 112 S. Ct. 1281 (1992).

84. Peter Branton, 1991 WC 639759, 6 F.C.C.R 610 (January 25, 1991). *Branton v. FCC*, 993 F.2d 906 (D.C.Cir. 1993), *cert. denied* ___U.S.___ , 114 S.Ct. 1610 (1994).

85. 47 U.S.C.A. § 559 (1991).

86. 47 U.S.C.A. § 532(h) (Supp. 1995).

87. Implementation of Sec. 10 of the Cable Consumer Protection and Competition Act of 1992: Indecent Programming and Other Types of Materials on Cable Access Channels, 58 Fed.Reg. 79990 (1993).

88. *Alliance for Community Media v. FCC*, 10 F.3d 812 (D.C.Cir. 1993), *vacated* 15 F.3d 186 (D.C.Cir. 1994).

89. *Community Television of Utah v. Wilkinson*, 611 F.Supp.1099 (D. Utah 1985), *affirmed* 800 F.2d 989 (10th Cir. 1986), *affirmed* 480 U.S. 926, 107 S.Ct. 1559 (1987), and *Cruz v. Ferre*, 755 F.2d 1415 (11th Cir. 1985).

90. *Sable Communications v. FCC*, 492 U.S. 115, 109 S.Ct. 2829.

91. Regulations Concerning Indecent Communications by Telephone, 5 FCC Rcd. 4926 (1990), *Dial Information Services Corp. v. Thornburgh*, 938 F.2d 1535 (2d Cir. 1991), *cert. denied* 502 U.S. 1072, 112 S.Ct. 966 (1992), *Information Providers' Coalition for Defense of the First Amendment v. FCC*, 928 F.2d 866 (9th Cir. 1991).

92. 47 U.S.C.A. §§ 1304 and 1307 (1984 & Supp. 1995).

93. See Chapter 13 of this book, pages 357–359.

94. 18 U.S.C.A. § 1307 (1984 & Supp. 1995).

95. *United States v. Edge Broadcasting Co.*, ___ U.S. ___, 113 S. Ct. 2696 (1993).

96. Indian Gaming Regulatory Act, P.L. 100–497, 102 Stat. 2467, 25 U.S.C.A.§§2701–2721 (Supp. 1984–1994).

97. 47 C.F.R. § 73.1216 (1992).

98. Licensee Responsibility to Review Records Before their Broadcast, 28 FCC 2d 409 (1971), *clarified* 31 FCC 2d 377 (1971).

99. *Yale Broadcasting v. FCC*, 478 F.2d 594 (D.C.Cir. 1973), *cert. denied* 414 U.S. 914, 94 S.Ct. 211 (1974).

100. Amendment of Part 73 Regarding Broadcast Hoaxes, 7 FCC Rcd. 4106 (1992).

101. WALE-FM, 7 FCC Rcd. 2345 (1992).

102. KROQ-FM, 6 FCC 2d 7262 (1991).

103. KSHE-FM, 6 FCC 2d 2289 (1991).

104. WBBM-TV, 18 FCC 2d 132 (1969).

105. Star Stations of Indiana, 51 FCC 2d 95 (1975).

106. *Galloway v. FCC*, 778 F.2d 16 (D.C.Cir. 1985).

107. 73 C.F.R. § 1206 (1992).

108. Brandywine-Main Line Radio, Inc. v. FCC, 473 F.2d 16 (D.C. Cir. 1972).

109. Scott v. Rosenberg, 702 F.2d 1263 (9th Cir. 1983).

110. PTL of Heritage Village Church, 71 FCC 2d 324 (1979).

111. Bible Moravian Church, Inc., 28 FCC 2d 1 (1971).

112. Public Broadcasting Act of 1967, P.L. 90-129, 81 Stat. 365 (1967).

113. 47 U.S.C.A. §§399(a) and 399(b) (1991).

114. Accuracy in Media, Inc. v. FCC, 521 F.2d 288 (D.C. Cir. 1975), *cert. denied* 425 U.S. 934, 96 S.Ct. 1664 (1976).

115. Public Telecommunications Act of 1992, P.L. 102-356, 106 Stat. 949 (1992).

116. CBS v. Democratic National Committee, 412 U.S. 94, 93 S.Ct. 2080 (1973).

117. Muir v. Alabama Educational Television Commission, 688 F.2d 1033 (5th Cir. 1982) *en banc*.

118. Bartlett, David, "The Soul of a News Machine: Electronic Journalism in the Twenty-First Century," 47 Fed. Comm. L.J. 1 (1994), Terry, Herbert A., "Changes that Challenge the Soul," 47 Fed. Comm. L.J. 25 (1994).

CHAPTER 13

Intellectual Property and Media Business Issues

C reators of original news stories, novels, poems, photographs, television shows, and similar forms of communication naturally take pride in their work. Morally, they may feel hurt if others use it without permission or acknowledgment. Economically, unauthorized use threatens the creators' livelihood. **Intellectual property** law gives them legal recourse when unauthorized uses are made of their creations.

Copyright is the most significant part of intellectual property law for those whose life is information. Once communicators create something, they have a copyright in it that gives them exclusive control over its uses for fixed periods of time. When they want to use someone else's copyrighted work, they must find a way to do so without violating the copyrights that person has in their creations.

Works are copyrighted when ideas are set down in some fixed form. Ideas and events themselves cannot be copyrighted. Only fixed versions of them can be. Once the form is fixed, the creator of the work controls an enumerated set of rights affecting uses of the work made by others. Normally, lawful use of a copyrighted work requires negotiation and payment, but limited uses without permission are possible for certain purposes under the fair use doctrine. In fair use cases, the court must simultaneously consider four concepts. Outcomes are often hard to predict because of the interplay among the elements of fair use. Uses without permission can result in payment of damages.

- **Intellectual property**
  Intellectual property is the product of creativity or invention, and intellectual property law regarding copyrights, trademarks and patents is designed to encourage its creation.

- **Copyright**
  An intangible property interest in literary or artistic creations. The Copyright Act gives creators or owners specific exclusive rights to control sales and uses of their creations.

● **Fair use.**
A doctrine that allows others to use copyrighted materials without the consent of the copyright owner, but only for news, criticism, education, or similar purposes.

● **Unfair competition**
Occurs when a competing business attempts to "pass off" its product or service as if it were the product or service of a competitor.

● **Trademark**
A symbol, name, logo, or other device that is used to identify the source of a product for consumers. The best trademarks are immediately recognizable.

● **Service mark**
Similar to a trademark but used to identify a service rather than a product.

The law also punishes **unfair competition** through the use of another's intellectual work. **Trademark** law protects a business's interest in a clearly identifiable sign, word, or symbol that it has worked to link positively with its product. Unauthorized use of a trade or **service mark** is unfair and punishable. So is appropriating even the uncopyrighted creations of an individual or company for commercial gain.

COPYRIGHT LAW

Suppose someone designed and built a house, and as soon as it was completed, another person moved in without permission, perhaps remodeled it, used it for a while, sold it to somebody else, and kept all the money received. Appropriate cries of "foul" or "theft" would ensue from the builder. Somebody would have taken property without permission and made unauthorized use of it. American law prevents that when it comes to physical property.

The same thing is true when intellectual property is involved. Under copyright law when one person has an idea and converts that idea into a fixed tangible form such as a word-processed manuscript, a published book, a musical score, or an audio or video recording, the law treats that intellectual work as property.[1] The person who created it, or that person's employer if the work was created for hire, is regarded as the author of the work and owns it just as certainly as an architect/contractor/builder would own a house. Owners of intellectual property can control most of the uses others make of their works. They can make money through that control. If unauthorized uses are made, they can recover money from the unauthorized infringers of their copyrights.

Origins and Purpose of Copyright Law

The earliest copyright laws date from the fifteenth and sixteenth centuries when European governments, faced with emerging mass media such as printing presses, sought to control publishing in order to prevent heresy or sedition. Laws were adopted to prohibit publishing except through officially sanctioned printers' guilds, which were authorized to publish by the government. Those who published through the guilds had copyright protection. Those who didn't risked the dire punishments meted out for unauthorized publication.

Initially, then, the purpose of copyright law was to control the creation of intellectual property rather than to stimulate it. That changed in 1710 when the British Parliament adopted the **Statute of Anne**, the first modern copyright law.[2] The Statute of Anne contained two important ideas. First, it gave copyrights to the creators of works rather than to printers. Second, it let the creator/author control the work for a limited period of time. After that time, copyright control expired, and the work could be used, for free, by anyone. This law was intended to erect a system where the creators of works could profit from their intellectual labors and, because of that, be encouraged to create more.

● **Statute of Anne.**
The first copyright law enacted in England. It established the modern principle that a primary purpose of copyright protection is encouragement of writers and artists.

British copyright principles influenced the early development of copyright law in the United States. Between the end of the Revolutionary War and the adoption of the U.S. Constitution in 1789, the thirteen former colonies organized themselves loosely under the Articles of Confederation. Although there was no uniform federal law—there was not even a federal government—twelve of the thirteen colonies adopted copyright laws. When the U.S. Constitution was adopted in 1789, the Framers included the power to adopt intellectual property laws among the powers of the new Congress listed in Article I:

> . . . Congress shall have the Power . . . to promote the Progress of Science and useful Arts, by securing for limited Times to Authors and Inventors the exclusive Right to their respective Writings and Discoveries.[3]

This section of the Constitution reflected the spirit of the Statute of Anne. Creators, it was believed, would not create new things unless given exclusive control for limited times. Although giving creators control would make it difficult for others to use these creations during that time, this was, on balance, thought to be necessary in order to promote progress. The first Congress acted on this section of the Constitution in 1790 by adopting the nation's first comprehensive copyright statute.[4] Hundreds of minor revisions have since been made to the copyright statutes, which must be constantly revised as the means of creating and copying intellectual property change. Major copyright revisions occurred in 1831, 1870, 1909, and, most recently, in 1976.

What Can Be Copyrighted?

Under the current copyright statute, "original works of authorship fixed in any tangible medium of expression now known or later developed, from which they can be perceived, reproduced or otherwise communicated, either directly or with the aid of a machine or device" can be copyrighted.[5] This language has several consequences.

First, a work must have an author who will hold the copyright, and it must in some sense be the original work of that author. The author must be a human being. That author must have done something creative in order for his or her work to be regarded as original. When copyright cases arise, the courts are rigorous in insisting that the work must have been produced by a creative rather than a mechanical act by its author. When some broadcasters rebroadcast without permission George Halliday's amateur videos of the beating of Rodney King by Los Angeles police and other videos of the beating of Reginald Denny during the 1992 Los Angeles riots shot by a news service, the original-ity of those works became an issue. Since camcorders are easy to use—essentially point-and-shoot devices—organizations that were sued for copyright infringement over use of these tapes (and others like them) have argued that such tapes require little originality or creativity and are therefore uncopyrightable. Rightsholders, on the other hand, focus on creative decisions about length of shots, camera angles, and composition that any photographer, no matter how amateurish, makes.

● **Originality**
A requirement for a work to qualify for copyright protection. A work is original if it represents the actual creative effort, no matter how little, of its author.

Not everything in a work need be created solely by that author in order to qualify as original. Compilations of materials can sometimes qualify for copyright protection. In 1991, in *Feist Publication, Inc. v. Rural Telephone Service Company, Inc.*, the U.S. Supreme Court held that the publisher of a regional phone directory assembled in part by unauthorized use of listings from a copyrighted phone directory published by a telephone company did not violate the phone company's copyrights.[6] The directory was not a creative or original work but was simply a logical arrangement of facts.

Subsequently, courts were asked to decide if video clipping services operated within copyright law.[7] Video Monitoring Services of America (VMS) edited together news clips from broadcast and cable newscasts for clients who wanted to see how they were depicted on television. Ted Turner's Cable News Network (CNN) sought a temporary **injunction** to stop VMS. A three-judge federal court of appeals panel denied CNN's request. It concluded that such an injunction would apply to things not yet created, things CNN had released to the public domain, content CNN did not own, and things it could not copyright.[8] CNN immediately appealed to the full circuit *en banc,* which vacated the earlier panel decision without issuing a written opinion. This allowed the injunction against VMS to stand. The lack of a written opinion means there is still no clear law on the matter, but the issuance of the injunction certainly gives pause to operators of video and, perhaps print, clipping services.

A second requirement of qualifying for federal copyright law protection is that the work must be fixed in some tangible way. In other words, it must be somehow recorded or preserved. This can take a variety of forms. A photographer fixes an idea through production of a negative and positive photographic prints. Composers write musical scores. Writers fix their works in manuscripts and, eventually, published books and articles. The form of the fixation does not matter.

The concept of fixation is crucial to copyright law, however. Understanding it can dispel common misunderstandings about copyright law. Nobody can copyright an idea, a fact, or, for that matter, a news event. Suppose that were possible. What would happen if a person could just have an idea and then prevent others from using that idea even if they thought of it independently? Or, suppose the first person to gather facts about a news event could prevent others from reporting the event in their own way. Either of those strategies would retard rather than advance progress. Thus, copyright protection extends to works about facts, events, and ideas only after they take some fixed form. The idea or thought behind a play cannot be copyrighted by anyone. But once the thought becomes a script, the fixed idea becomes copyrightable. News events cannot be copyrighted, but original news stories describing the event, either printed or in the form of audio or video tapes, can be.

Copyright law covers almost any subject matter that can be fixed. The law lists examples of types of works: literary works, musical works (including accompanying lyrics), dramatic works (including any accompanying score), pantomimes and choreography, pictorial, graphic and sculptural works, motion pictures and other audiovisual works, sound recordings, and architectural works.[9] Storage of sound or images on capacitance discs, for example, was al-

● **Injunction**

An order from a court prohibiting someone from continuing certain behavior. In copyright, an injunction is used to stop additional distribution of infringing materials.

most unknown when the latest major copyright law was adopted in 1976. Compact discs, however, are clearly a modern form of fixation of ideas, and content fixed on a CD can be copyrighted.

Rights of the Copyright Holder

Copyrights are initially owned by the author or creator of the work.[10] In most instances, therefore, copyrights are first held by the persons who put their ideas in fixed form. If a work is a collaboration with joint authors, then the copyright is shared. Works made for hire pose some problems. If the author is a full-time employee of somebody else and has the job of creating the type of work in question, then the employer, not the employee, owns the work and its associated copyrights. Sometimes, however, the line between employees and non-employees is blurred.

The work-for-hire issue is of great importance to freelancers. In a 1989 case dealing with who owned the copyrights in a sculpture made by an artist under commission from an organization, the U.S. Supreme Court announced eleven criteria that, considered together, should be used to determine whether a hired person is an independent freelancer, or an employee whose creative works belong to the party who pays for services. According to *Community for Creative Non-Violence v. Reid,* courts should consider (1) how much skill is involved, (2) who provides the tools or supplies needed to do the work, (3) where the work is done, (4) how long the relationship has existed between the parties, (5) whether the person doing the work can be forced to complete other assignments for the hiring party, (6) the amount of control the hired party has over when to work and how long, (7) how payment is made, (8) whether the hired party selects and pays any assistants, (9) whether the work is the regular business of the hiring party, (10) whether that party is a business, and (11) who pays for employee benefits and taxes of the hired party. Considering these factors, the Court concluded that the artist was an independent contractor and owner of the copyright in the sculpture rather than an employee of the Community for Creative Non-Violence that commissioned the work.[11]

Copyrights, whether held by an individual, collaborative creator, or an employing company, can later be sold or transferred, in whole or in part, to others—just as an owner can sell a house.

Distinctions between owning the copyright in a work and owning a copy of the work are very important. Under the **first-sale doctrine**, purchasers of copies of copyrighted work own that copy. They do not own the work in an intellectual property sense, however.[12] Important community institutions and businesses are built on the first-sale doctrine. When a library buys a book, for example, it owns that copy but not the fixed forms of the ideas in it. Libraries can lend copies they own to others, but they cannot, absent special circumstances, copy the work. You may be reading a used copy of this book. The used book market exists because of the first-sale doctrine. The original purchaser of this copyrighted book (the copyrights in this book, by the way, belong to the publisher because the authors have agreed to that by contract) owned the copy he or she bought. That buyer had the right to sell it to somebody else, probably

First-sale doctrine Guarantees that the person who buys a copy of a copyrighted work is entitled to exercise complete ownership over that copy, including the right to resell or rent the copy.

a broker dealing in used books. The broker owns the physical copy of the book and can lawfully sell that copy to others. None of these owners, however, truly owned "the work." All that any of them ever owned was a lawful copy of the work. Another industry built on the first-sale doctrine is the videotape rental industry. Video stores buy copies of videotapes. Like a library, a store does not own works, just lawful copies of them. The store can lease its copy to others and make a profit, but it cannot either copy or alter the work without permission under copyright law even though it owns a copy of the work.[13]

Copyrights are valid for limited times or durations.[14] Except in the case of works for hire, current copyrights extend for the author's life plus fifty years. The author's heirs can profit from the work for fifty years after the author's death. In the case of works for hire, copyrights extend either seventy-five years from publication, meaning public release of the fixed work, or a hundred years from the first fixation of the idea, whichever comes first. Once copyright terms expire, the copyrighted work passes into the public domain and can be used in any way by anybody without violating copyright law.

Copyright law gives owners of copyrights five exclusive rights.[15] Rights holders can either do these things themselves or, through a license, can authorize others to do them. The most obvious exclusive right is the right to reproduce the work—to make more copies. Owners of rights in a copyrighted newspaper article, for example, can prohibit others from reprinting it without permission. A second exclusive right involves control over what copyright law calls derivative works—works based on existing works that are somehow changed or adapted. Those who own the copyrights in novels, for example, can control adaptation of those novels into plays, movies, or musicals. Another exclusive right includes the right to publicly distribute copies of copyrighted works. Thus, even if a lawful copy of a work is made, the original rightsholder controls public distribution of that work to others. Likewise, a fourth type of exclusive right covers the performance of a copyrighted work in public. Owners of copyrighted music, for example, control the ability of orchestras or, for that matter, radio stations to perform the work—either by playing it in a concert hall or playing a recording of it over radio, TV, or some other electronic means of distribution. The fifth exclusive right prohibits public display of pictorial, graphic, or sculptural works unless the copyright owner consents.

How to Obtain a Copyright

Under current copyright law, creators of works have the protection of copyright law the moment the work takes its fixed form. An author, for example, using a typewriter or a word processor would have copyright protection for her or his article or book the moment the text was printed on a page or, presumably, saved on a computer disc. A composer receives protection as soon as notes are written down as a score. While copyright protection attaches the moment a work is created, this is largely protection in theory unless a creator is able to prove he or she made the work.

Protection is strongest, though, when the copyright is registered with the Copyright Office of the Library of Congress.[16] Forms for registration can be obtained from that office. A copy of the work usually must be sent to the Library of Congress along with the completed form and a registration fee. Registering a copyright can make it easier to get damages for unauthorized uses by others. Registration is not required, however, and a work is copyrighted as soon as its author creates a fixed version of the underlying idea. Authors usually attach notices of copyright (e.g., Copyright, Mary Smith, 1994 or © Bob Smith, 1995) to the work. Failure to attach the notice does not fatally undermine the copyright, however.

How to Lawfully Use Copyrighted Works

Obviously, for many reasons, others may want to use a work copyrighted by others. In most instances, this use is accomplished through one of two means. Just as with physical property, it is possible to buy the copyrights and transfer them to a new owner. In that case, the transfer of ownership must be in writing and can be recorded with the Copyright Office. More commonly, however, users of copyrighted works neither want nor need control of all the exclusive rights in a work. What they need is the right to do something specific such as converting a book into a screenplay or a work of history into a documentary film. To do that, they can negotiate a license from the rightsholder. This is usually handled through a contract. The parties agree on what uses of the copyrighted work the owner of the copyright allows the other party to make. The owner of the copyright usually is paid for the authorized uses. The holder of a license to use a copyrighted work can do only what was agreed to—no more.

The system usually rewards creation of intellectual property and thus encourages the creation of more—the intent of intellectual property law. Carried to extremes, however, absolute control over copyrighted works could retard progress of knowledge. Recognizing this, courts created exceptions to the generally absolute control over copyrighted works held by copyright owners under older copyright laws. In its 1976 revision of copyright law, Congress wrote these exceptions into the statute.[17]

The exception to the general rule that copyrighted works can only be used with permission of the copyright owner is known as fair use. The limits of fair use are sometimes difficult to understand because courts consider each case separately on its own facts. Congress, however, did specify four factors long used by judges that must be simultaneously considered in evaluating fair use claims.[18]

First, courts should consider the **nature and purpose of the use.** Uses for criticism, news reporting, comment, teaching, and research have a good claim to being fair uses. The fact that a use has a commercial dimension or motivation does not automatically make the use unfair, although it can weaken the argument for fair use considerably. Most of the time, copying excerpts for use in news stories or for students to read is no problem unless the copier is using a work in its entirety and possibly costing the copyright owner some sales. Parody, a form of criticism, is a special case. To be a fair use, a parody must do more than merely copy. It must in some sense transform the original work. Thus, as the U.S. Supreme Court recognized in *Campbell v. Acuff-Rose Music,*

● **Nature and purpose of the use**
A factor to be considered in fair use claims. The statute specifies criticism, news reporting, comment, teaching, and research as uses that are likely to be thought fair.

even commercial parodies of copyrighted works may be fair uses if the objective is to criticize the underlying song.[19]

Luther Campbell, lead singer for the rap group 2 Live Crew, wrote and performed a crude parody of singer Roy Orbison's 1964 hit, "Oh Pretty Woman." Orbison's song stressed sentiment and romance while Campbell's emphasized sexuality through crude descriptions, including "Oh hairy woman / You better shave that stuff." Campbell claimed his intent was to satirize Orbison's song and the society that produced and loved it.

In a unanimous opinion written by Justice David Souter, the Court concluded that, while the parody was hardly of high rank, its purpose had been comment or criticism. To presume all commercial uses unfair, Souter noted, would be to deprive all for-profit critics—including newspapers and broadcast stations—of the ability to criticize copyrighted works. On this criterion, then, Campbell's parody seemed to be a fair use. The Court remanded the case to the U.S. Court of Appeals for the Sixth Circuit so that court could evaluate the other fair use criteria and make an overall judgment about whether, all things considered, Campbell's use was fair.

- **Nature of the work**
  A factor to be considered in fair use claims; refers to the type of work that has been copied. Unpublished works are especially protected.

Second, Congress said that the **nature of the copyrighted work** also matters. The nature of the work includes such things as how long the work is, how much effort has gone into creating it, and how readily it is available. Fair use will rarely be found if unpublished letters or manuscripts are used without permission. When Random House prepared a book including excerpts from private letters written by author J. D. Salinger, Salinger registered the letters for copyright and then sought an injunction to prevent Random House from publishing the book. Attention focused on the nature of the unpublished letters. Although Salinger had placed some in libraries, he still controlled the letters' content. The court ordered the publisher not to print the book as planned. By carefully using only the facts in the letters, Random House eventually published the work.[20]

Two years earlier, the Supreme Court said the *Nation* magazine could not successfully claim fair use after it published 300 to 400 words from the unpublished manuscript of former President Gerald Ford's memoirs in 1979. Harper and Row, publisher of Ford's book, had contracted for *Time* magazine to publish an advance excerpt from Ford's book. The excerpts used by the *Nation*, however, dealt with the most intriguing aspect of Ford's memoirs—his pardoning of former President Richard Nixon. Focusing on the fact that Ford's book had not been released for publication, and concluding that the nature of this work suggested its unauthorized use was unfair, Justice Sandra Day O'Connor wrote that the *Nation* had gone beyond fair use. In addition to rejecting the fair use defense, O'Connor dismissed the *Nation's* argument that it should have some First Amendment right to publish the excerpts because of their newsworthiness. Accepting that kind of argument, according to O'Connor, would fundamentally undercut the objectives of copyright law.[21]

- **Amount and substantiality**
  A factor to be considered in fair use claims. In general, small amounts of copying are more likely to be considered fair uses, while use of entire works or chapters will likely be considered unfair.

A third element of fair use is the **amount and substantiality** of what is used without permission. It is much less risky to use only a small part of a work without permission than to use or copy it all. The *Nation* did not use much of the *Time* manuscript—only about 17 percent—but it also failed this test because of the substantiality of what it took. The account of the Nixon pardon was the most important part of the work.

It is sometimes possible to copy all of a work and, given the other three factors, still have a fair use. For example, private individuals may use home VCRs to record copyrighted broadcast programs for eventual private, non-commercial, at-home "time-shift" viewing.

Sony Corporation of America v. Universal City Studios, Inc. arose when Universal and other studios sued Sony, the manufacturer of the early "Betamax" VCRs, stores that sold the machines, and a customer who used one. Universal said viewer recording of entire shows for later entertainment could not possibly be a fair use. Admitting that the amount and substantiality of the copying were extensive, Justice John Paul Stevens concluded that the entertainment/convenience motive behind the recording, the nature of the work—broadcast programs readily offered to the public for free—and the minimal effect on subsequent sale of the TV programs made VCR recording fair.[22] The decision clearly did not approve of recording programs for subsequent commercial use. That, it suggested, would probably make the recording unfair.

Finally, and in many instances most important, courts are told to consider the economic effect of the use on the potential market for the work or for works that might be derived from it. Here courts are to project whether the use has diminished the ability of the copyright owner to profit from the copyright. If so, then the use may not be a fair use. In some instances, however, uses may actually expand rather than limit the market for the work. Positive economic consequences suggest that the use may be fair. Economic effect was a key part of the *Nation* case, since both *Time* and Harper and Row lost the benefits they expected. In the "Oh Pretty Woman" case, by comparison, there was no evidence that 2 Live Crew's spoof version had cost or was likely to cost the copyright owner any sales, and Justice Souter emphasized the vastly different markets for the spoof and for the original.

Courts must consider these four factors simultaneously when fair use defenses are raised in copyright lawsuits. Often a use will look fair under some of these factors, but unfair under others. Courts balance the factors and arrive at an equitable decision. The kinds of uses students generally make when they quote copyrighted materials in class papers are usually covered by fair use, for example. Uses in more commercial contexts are riskier. Because the news media are often engaged in criticism, however, many—but certainly not all—of their uses of copyrighted works can be justified under this doctrine. When the media move in the direction of providing commercial entertainment, however, fair use principles do not apply as readily.

● **Effect of the use**
A factor to be considered in fair use claims; refers to the economic effects of copying. If the economic impact is great, a use is less likely to be considered fair.

What Happens to Infringers

Violation of copyright law is serious business but can be avoided by owning the copyright outright, by having a license for uses , or by making a fair use. If what has been done does not fall within any of these categories, infringement has occurred, and the rightsholder can recover damages.[23]

Actual damages
Damages actually suffered by a copyright owner as a result of an infringement.

Specific damages
Damages defined by statute and provided automatically when infringement is proven. The amounts vary depending on the behavior of the defendant and on the size of the copying and market.

Striking similarity
Must be shown to prove infringement. It is usually enough to show that the original work and the infringing work are substantially identical in whole or in part.

Access
To prove infringement, a copyright owner must show that the defendant had access to the original work. Proof that the original was widely available to the public will usually be sufficient.

Berne Convention
The most important international treaty on intellectual property. It calls for member nations to generally recognize the copyright protections from an owner's home country.

Several kinds of damages are possible. Rightsholders may recover **actual damages**, which consist of two things. First, assuming that the use hurt the author's market for the work, the rightsholder could recover lost profits—money that might have been made had the unauthorized use not taken place. Moving in another direction, if the unlawful use brought profit to the infringer, then the rightsholder can seek to recover that ill-gotten gain as well.

If the work was properly registered with the Copyright Office, then rightsholders have an alternative. They can ask the court to award **specific damages** spelled out in the statute. These can range from a nominal $200 up to $100,000. They are highest if it can be shown that the infringement was willful. If the work was registered, it is also possible for the copyright owner to recover the costs of the lawsuit, including attorney's fees.

A final relief available to copyright owners is to ask courts to issue an injunction barring continuing violation of the copyright. This, obviously, can sometimes be fatal to the plans of the infringer.

Copyright plaintiffs, however, face stiff burdens to prove that infringement, rather than independent creation of a similar work, occurred. They must prove both that the allegedly unauthorized copy bears a "**striking similarity**" to the copyrighted work and that the alleged infringer unarguably had **access** to the copyrighted work. It is fairly easy to prove access to widely available copyrighted works, but much harder if the work has had limited dissemination. An exact copy of a copyrighted work is obviously "strikingly similar," but less than exact similarity can make this element of proof problematic.

Warner Brothers learned this when it sued ABC over "The Greatest American Hero." Warner Brothers claimed that ABC's television series featuring a caped flying hero violated rights in its Superman movies. The court, however, was more impressed with the dissimilarities. Ralph Hinckley, ABC's hero, was slight, unpresupposing, crashed into buildings, and penetrated walls only with great difficulty. This was not a case of "striking similarity."[24]

Copyrights in Foreign Countries

In an international information society, it is important for copyright holders in one nation to know that their rights will be respected in other nations. This promotes the international sale of works and discourages the importation back into this country of unauthorized works made in other nations.

For many years, U.S. copyright law was in many respects "out of synch" with foreign copyright systems. For example, U.S. copyright terms were different, and the American government did less than other nations to protect rights of artists against editing or distortion of their works. The 1976 Copyright Act brought the United States closer to international standards, but still left the country an outcast from the major international copyright convention—the **Berne Convention** for the Protection of Literary and Artistic Works.

To better protect holders of U.S. copyrights, Congress amended copyright law in 1988 so that the United States could join the Berne Convention. As a result, it is now easier for U.S. rightsholders to enforce their rights in foreign countries.[25]

Some Special Mass Media Copyright Issues

A few specific twists of copyright law are the result of modern mass media, especially the electronic media. Radio stations perform much copyrighted music when they play records, tapes, and CDs over the air. Performances require the permission of copyright holders. Because it would be cumbersome to get these rights individually from all the composers who own them, composers typically assign some or all of their public performance rights to **performing rights societies**. There are three such societies in the United States: ASCAP (American Society of Composers, Authors and Publishers), BMI (Broadcast Music, Inc.), and SESAC (Society of European State Authors and Composers).

> ● **Performing rights societies** Clearinghouses created to pool royalties for authors of musical and other works that are played on radio or elsewhere.

These societies simplify copyright life for radio stations. Stations take out licenses to play music from the societies. In exchange for payment to the societies, the station gets the right to perform any recorded music the society represents. Functioning as a clearinghouse, the society pays rightsholders based on the amount of use their music receives. Under current U.S. law, performers of music such as singers are not viewed as doing anything creative. The money goes to the authors—composers—of the songs or to the people to whom they have sold their rights. Singers and musicians may of course copyright their recorded performances of songs separately, but any financial benefit comes from sales rather than from radio play. This country's lack of a performer's right galls performers—they think of themselves as creative people and would like to profit. So far, however, they have been unable to persuade Congress to create a performer's right, although some other nations recognize such rights.

The cable television industry displays some interesting variations on copyright law. Just as it would be cumbersome for radio stations to negotiate with all the rightsholders of copyrighted music, Congress has decided that cable systems should not have to negotiate with all the rightsholders involved in video programs carried on TV stations retransmitted by cable systems.[26]

As one solution to this problem, Congress gave the cable industry access to what is called a **compulsory license**. In exchange for an annual payment, a cable system obtained the automatic right to retransmit the copyrighted programming contained in over-the-air broadcast signals that the cable system could lawfully carry. The pooled money was distributed back to the rightsholders. Until December 1993, the collection and distribution were handled by a little known and even less loved agency known as the Copyright Royalty Tribunal. Concluding that the tribunal was both costly and useless, Congress abolished it. Currently, the librarian of Congress selects arbitration panels to hammer out agreements over compulsory license rates and the distribution of money collected.[27] Little money goes to broadcast stations because they are not the author of most of the programming they carry. Instead, most of the money goes to the Hollywood studios that produce programming. A large amount also goes to professional sports leagues such as Major League Baseball and the National Football League.

> ● **Compulsory license** Statutory permission to use a copyrighted work without consent of the owner. License fees are set by formula.

Neither Hollywood nor the professional sports leagues like the system. They would rather negotiate for payment because they believe cable pays too little. Congress has repeatedly been asked to drop the compulsory license system, but so far it has not done so. Without a license, cable systems retransmitting copyrighted programming of broadcast stations would be "performing" copyrighted video works of others and would have to get permission from each of the rightsholders in broadcast programming just as they get it now for non-broadcast cable services such as HBO, ESPN, the Discovery Channel, and the Family Channel. Congress did, however, include an option for broadcasters as part of the 1992 cable act. If they wish to do so, broadcasters that could be must-carry stations can decline that right and negotiate with cable systems for "retransmission consent." Many broadcasters sought cash compensation when this part of the law was new, but few cable operators paid. Most local broadcast stations that appear on cable systems get there by claiming a right to be carried as must-carry stations.[28]

New technologies always pose new copyright law problems. When Congress revised the copyright law in 1976, the prospect of home digital audio tape recording (DAT) was not foreseen. Since DAT machines can make perfect copies of CDs, and thereby conceivably reduce the sale of discs, recording industry interests pressured Congress to amend the copyright law to deal with this new technology. Under this legislation, it is unlawful to sell or import into the United States any DAT machine not equipped with special circuitry that prevents the machine from making a tape copy of a tape copy (yes, that is right) of a CD.[29]

Copyright Law in Summary

Copyright law provides individuals and companies strong protections for the intangible property rights in creations. Copyright protects ideas in fixed forms from unauthorized use by others. Normally, copyright holders have exclusive control over all uses of a copyrighted work. If others wish to use works, they must get explicit permission, which will normally require negotiation and payment.

The defense of fair use in copyright, however, permits some uses without permission when the use is made for uses specified in the statute, such as news, criticism, or scholarship; when the nature of the work invites such uses; when the amount used is not substantial; and when the use does not diminish the economic value of the copyrighted work. Absent a defense, however, infringing unauthorized uses can lead to substantial damage awards.

TRADEMARK INFRINGEMENT AND UNFAIR COMPETITION

Trademark

Protections for intellectual property extend beyond copyright. Patent law, trademark and service mark law, and unfair competition law all, like copyright, protect creative materials. In many states, the right of publicity (see Chapter 3) has been interpreted more as an intellectual property issue than as a privacy issue. In general, patents protect inventions. While patent law is a key area of intellectual property law, it is usually the concern of engineers and investors, not mass communication professionals.

Since trademarks are a form of communication, they are an important matter for the mass media. Marks are words, names, pictures, devices, or graphic symbols used by one business to distinguish its goods or services from those of other companies. If the mark belongs to a company that manufactures goods, it is a trademark. If the mark belongs to a company that provides services, it is a service mark. Coca Cola's "The Real Thing" and McDonald's golden arches may the most widely recognized trademarks in the world. Both companies aggressively police other businesses to assure that no one infringes. AT&T's "The Right Choice" is an example of a well-known service mark.

Businesses, their advertising and public relations agencies, and their lawyers may spend tens and even hundreds of thousands of dollars creating a mark for a new product or service. If the mark is successful, they may spend as much or more in maintaining and defending it. An extensive search for similar marks usually precedes the introduction of a new trademark. Since marks are protected both under the federal **Lanham Act**[30] and by statute and common law in the various states, searches are difficult. If a company is convinced that it has created a "distinctive" trademark, it may file for federal and, perhaps, state registration. The company's claim is then available for future searchers to find—considerably speeding the process. Under the federal statute, registration lasts only ten years, but infinite renewals are possible.

Trademarks, thus, have no time limit. They are protected so long as the mark continues to be distinctive and used in commerce. The courts consider many factors when a company claims trademark rights, but two factors are key to making a trademark distinctive. First, it should be visually or textually unique. For example, labeling one's new product "Pain Killer" would fail because the name is descriptive rather than suggestive.[31] It is much better to use a made-up name such as "Aleve." Second, the trademark must develop "secondary meaning." In other words, the mark must conjure up the company, its product or service, and its reputation for quality, in the minds of consumers or audience members who see the mark.[32] One of the strongest examples in history is the Metro-Goldwyn-Mayer lion that roars at the start of MGM films, a mark that has actually survived the studio that created it.

Trademark law is based on two principles. One is consumer protection. By giving companies exclusive rights to marks, consumers will be protected from others who try to market substitute or poorer-quality goods using similar words or symbols. Originally, trademarks applied to goods of the craft trades; a shoemaker or potter, for example, would have a mark. Today trademarks are seen as guarantees of quality—or at least uniformity or consistency. The second rationale is to protect the goodwill and investment of the company. Under this rationale, the company has "earned" protection by providing a product—with its accompanying trademark—that is good enough to earn consumer support. This business investment should be protected against competitors who might try to profit by using a similar mark.[33] When a company tries to market confusingly similar marks or packaging, it is in effect passing off its goods as if they were the products of another company.

● **Lanham Act**
The federal statute protecting trademarks used in interstate commerce. The act also prohibits types of unfair competition.

● **Secondary meaning**
In trademark law, refers to the ability of a mark to instantly invoke the source of a product or service in the mind of a consumer.

● **Exclusive rights**
In both copyright and trademark law, include the rights to use material, to license uses of material, and to allow derivative uses of materials.

● Distinctiveness

Exists when a trademark or service mark uses a fanciful or imaginary term or symbol to set it apart.

● Generic mark

A trademark that has lost both its secondary meaning and its distinctiveness. It has instead become the everyday word used to describe a product.

● Descriptive mark

A trademark that on its face tells consumers what the product is. It is difficult to make a descriptive mark distinctive.

● Likelihood of confusion

Exists when a competitor uses a close copy of another's trademark and consumers are either misled or will likely be misled into mistaking the copy for the original.

● Dilution

Can occur where a noncompetitor uses the mark for commentary or other purposes, such as parody. The trademark owner argues that the use will mislead consumers into thinking the use was approved, thereby diluting the mark.

Trademark protection can last forever, at least in theory, if the mark remains meaningful to consumers. Not surprisingly, companies try to prevent marks from losing their **distinctiveness.** A mark can lose its distinctiveness in several ways. The most dreaded is to have a mark declared **generic.** It is then considered **descriptive.** Everyday terms such as aspirin and shredded wheat were once trademarks. If a mark is declared generic, any business may use it. Companies often send letters to news organizations advising or warning them to not use a term such as "Xerox", as a generic term for photocopying, or "Kleenex" without quotation marks and/or the trademark ™ symbol; companies also object to the use of lowercase letters on their trademarks, which suggests the words are not proper nouns as trademarks must be. Letters seeking to preserve trademarks typically imply that legal action may follow unless the news organization complies.[34] Since trademark infringement actions may only be brought against competitors, however, and competitors rarely include the press, this is not a significant legal threat. Whether or not to use a mark generically is left to the editorial and ethical judgment of the journalists.

Two other ways of losing distinctiveness appear in the court cases with some regularity. One is abandonment. A trademark may be considered abandoned unless it is used regularly in trade,[35] although proof of an intent to abandon is normally required as well. Occasional or token use, aimed at keeping the mark alive, will likely fail. An abandoned mark is available for another to use. Another way of losing distinctiveness is by cross-market competition. Trademarks are not necessarily nationwide. They are protected only in the geographic and product markets where the company operates. As a result, two firms could operate in different states with the same trade name. Should one expand its market, the other could face a loss of distinctiveness. For recently introduced trademarks, the comprehensive federal registration system should prevent cross-market disputes.[36]

Most trademark infringement claims against competitors involve close imitations of protected marks. The shelves of chain drug stores are full of generic over-the-counter remedies packaged to look as much like the name brand originals as possible. If the imitation is so close that it is **likely to confuse consumers, then an infringement action should succeed.**[37] The general test is whether or not average consumers would think they were buying from either the same company or from a source affiliated with or authorized by the company.

The biggest problem for the news and entertainment media has not been infringement cases but rather lawsuits for trademark dilution. A good example is *Anheuser-Busch, Inc. v. Balducci Publications.*[38] In this case, the defendant published a spoof of Anheuser-Busch's well-known advertising campaign for Michelob, Michelob Dry, Michelob Light, and Michelob Classic Dark beers. In the original campaign, advertisements announced, "One Taste and You'll Drink It Dry." In the *Snicker* magazine satire, under the headline "MICHELOB OILY," an actual photo of a bottle of Michelob Dry was used, along with the phrase, "One Taste and You'll Drink It Oily." The beer maker sued for trademark dilution under federal law and also under Missouri's antidilution statute.

The court, swayed by an Anheuser-Busch–sponsored survey concluding that most people thought permission was needed to use the trademarks, held that dilution was proved because consumers were likely to be confused into thinking that the plaintiff endorsed the satire. The defendant claimed that including the trademarks in the spoof was protected under the First Amendment as a "fair use." Although the federal statute does not specifically provide a fair use defense for trademark use, many courts have applied one under the First Amendment.[39] Applying a fair use test essentially similar to the copyright test used in the "Oh, Pretty Woman" case, the court said that *Snicker* would probably have won on its fair use claim had it used a disclaimer, modified the trademarks at least slightly, or somehow alerted consumers so they would not be confused. The U.S. Supreme Court refused to review the decision,[40] despite a number of conflicting decisions among the federal circuit courts of appeal.

The *Balducci* decision means that using trademarks and service marks in parodies carries risks. Just as in copyright fair use, the parodist must "conjure up" enough of the mark for the parody to work, but not so much that consumers are confused into thinking the parody was authorized by the trademark owner. Two earlier cases illustrate the difficulties here. In *L. L. Bean, Inc. v. Drake Publishers, Inc.,*[41] a spoof named "L. L. Beam's Back-to-School-Sex-Catalog" was published in the raunchy magazine *High Society*. Using Bean-style layout and type, it included explicit photos of sex acts. The court applied a broad First Amendment trademark fair use in deciding for the magazine, noting, "Denying parodists the opportunity to poke fun at symbols and names which have become woven into the fabric of our daily life would constitute a serious curtailment of a protected form of expression."

The opposite result was reached in *Mutual of Omaha Insurance Co., Inc. v. Novak.*[42] Mutual sued Franklyn Novak for trademark infringement and disparagement, which is essentially similar to the dilution claims discussed earlier. Novak produced T-shirts using modified versions of Mutual's Indian head logo and typeface logo, reading "Mutant of Omaha." Also included was the phrase, "Nuclear Holocaust Insurance." Novak apparently designed his satire to capitalize on the airing of an ABC movie, *The Day After,* which depicted the aftermath of thermonuclear war. Novak later expanded into selling Mutant of Omaha mugs, buttons, and caps. The court relied on a survey introduced by Mutual that showed that forty of four hundred people from New York, Denver, Chicago, and San Francisco thought that the insurer approved of the T-shirts. The court was also persuaded that the defendant was competing with Mutual because the insurance company placed its logos on coffee mugs and shirts that are sold to agents in the field. Entrepreneur Novak was enjoined from selling his products. The court majority suggested that Novak's First Amendment rights were not violated because he could have used alternative methods to spread his opinions on nuclear war.

Another problem for the media is the merger of right of publicity and service mark claims. A famous person can make a claim on either basis and, in any given case, is likely to claim both.[43] In 1994, Elizabeth Taylor argued that a planned television miniseries about her violated both service mark rights under the Lanham Act and her right of publicity.[44] A trial court refused to grant an injunction barring the broadcast, indicating that it doubted that Taylor could ever prove a likelihood of confusion at a later trial.

The value—and the costs—of trademarks and service marks have increased greatly over the last forty years. They have become one of the primary national advertising and marketing tools of business. Those holding them have worked to expand both the kinds of protection and also the strength of the protection available for trademarks. More conflicts with the news and entertainment media can be anticipated.

Unfair Competition

At one level, unfair competition is the same as trademark infringement. Under common law in most states, competitors who use the trade names, symbols, or unique packaging of other businesses can be sued for passing off and confusing consumers just as in statutory trademark law. Unfair competition has two additional aspects that are important to mass communication, however.

First, Section 43(a) of the federal Lanham Act prohibits unfair competition by deceptive marketing,[45] phrasing broader than in most states' laws. The section has for decades been applicable to traditional likelihood-of-confusion situations, but as amended has recently been used to bring suits against competitors for inaccurate or misleading comparison advertising. The plaintiffs usually seek an injunction, but under the statute, they may also seek damages for lost business.[46]

- **Comparison advertising**

  Advertising that directly contrasts the characteristics and features of competing products or services.

- **Misappropriation**

  Occurs when one takes another's product or work and peddles it as one's own.

Another form of unfair competition is perhaps better known, and better described, as misappropriation. For the media, this action arises when one organization takes and uses the product, such as a column or news story, of another and passes it off as its own. The leading case in this area is *International News Service v. Associated Press.*[47] INS had developed the habit of buying newspapers with AP stories in the morning. INS then edited or rewrote the stories in a cursory fashion and sent the "rewrites" by wire to its subscribers. The Supreme Court said that the misappropriation was unfair competition and that INS was stealing AP's labor, skill, time, and money invested in its news accounts.

The principle of *INS* survives today, but seldom leads to lawsuits because the rule is so clear-cut. The major area of misappropriation activity today involves the "rip 'n' read" news practices of some radio stations. Lacking news staffs of their own, they clip the local daily newspaper's stories. The practice led to many lawsuits in the 1930s, but court cases are rare today. Newspapers, fighting to keep subscribers, are happy to have stations read stories if the newspaper is named as the source. Some newspapers have entered into exclusive contracts with radio and television stations to share news product.

It is not unusual for journalists to use a published story as a starting point for additional investigation. This practice is allowed because misappropriation applies to the story itself, not the facts in the story. It is customary, though, to credit another news organization when using previously reported material.

Trademark Law in Summary

Trademark and service mark law and the law of unfair competition protect companies or individuals from having their intellectual property or work product passed off as another's. Trademark law protects symbols and short texts that provide an instant, "shorthand" communication with consumers. Infringement actions are designed as much to protect consumers from buying the wrong product or service as they are to protect the economic interests of businesses.

The courts have recognized a fair use defense, grounded in the First Amendment, for unauthorized trademark users, but the defense appears much narrower than the fair use defense in copyright law. Absent a defense, an infringer may face a court order to stop using a trademark, hefty money damages for diverted revenues, or both.

REGULATING LOTTERY AND CONTEST ADVERTISING

The ability of the proprietors of lotteries and contests to advertise their ventures is limited under both federal and state law. The traditional justification for close regulation—and occasional outright banning—of **lottery** and contest advertising was the legislative decision that gambling was either immoral or amoral. Lotteries have at times been severely suppressed, but at other times law enforcement officials have looked the other way if the stakes were small or the cause noble. Today, state-run lottery games compete with Las Vegas, Atlantic City, and Native American casinos for consumer gambling dollars. The moral argument has lost most of its force. The concern for the media is that, while some promotions of lotteries or contests are allowed and even encouraged, others can create legal minefields for broadcasters at the Federal Communications Commission (FCC)[48] and for all media with postal authorities.[49]

For legal purposes, lotteries must have three elements: a **prize**, given by chance, for consideration. **Consideration** refers to the transfer of something of value from one party to another. When an individual buys a state lottery ticket, the price is the consideration. On occasion **contests** have been treated as regulable lotteries because "consideration" in the form of personal time and effort, or nominal cost, was present.[50] Some lottery laws apply only when the person or organization running the lottery benefits financially. Sweepstakes such as those promoted by Publishers Clearing House do not match the definition because the consumer invests nothing beyond minimal postage.

Chance can best be defined negatively. Chance is present if the likelihood of winning cannot be controlled through skill or knowledge. Having a lucky number drawn from a barrel involves chance.

A moral argument for regulation of lotteries or contests run by private companies rather than by state or local governments persists. Federal and state statutes and regulations have historically reflected a fear that private game operators will prey on the public with unrealistic promises of winning odds or by

- **Lottery**
  Exists when the consumer is required to pay for a random chance at winning a prize.

- **Prize**
  For lottery purposes, anything of value for which a ticket or chance must be bought.

- **Consideration**
  In a lottery, the price the consumer pays to seek the prize.

- **Contest**
  Usually refers to a game in which some sort of skill or ability is used to determine a winner.

- **Chance**
  Exists when the odds of winning are set randomly and the participant has no way of affecting the outcome.

bilking consumers into buying related products or services in order to qualify as a contestant. That concern remains valid today as "free" offers flood consumers' mailboxes. Regulation of promotions in contest form has been infrequent during the 1980s and 1990s. The Federal Trade Commission has acted in this area before, however,[51] but primarily regarding contests run by companies in specific industries.

In the past, federal law forbade broadcasters and publishers from promoting lotteries, whether the promotion was by advertising or by news coverage.[52] The flat ban was loosened in the mid-1970s, and recently Congress decided the federal government should abandon its policy altogether. The Charity Games Clarification Act of 1988 now allows media companies to broadcast or publish advertisements for state-run lotteries if the state in which they are licensed allows such lotteries.[53] Ads for games in other states with legal lotteries are also allowed. Even ads for privately run lotteries sponsored by both nonprofit and for-profit groups are sometimes permitted. For-profit groups are limited to advertising irregular lotteries or contests that are "ancillary" to their main business. The statute reflects the shift in the attitudes of most Americans toward legalized gambling. The statute bans broadcast ads if lotteries are illegal in the state where a station is licensed, though. That part of the statute was challenged as a First Amendment violation in *United States v. Edge Broadcasting Co.*[54] A radio station licensed in the nonlottery state of North Carolina but located near the border of Virginia, a lottery state, wanted to run advertisements aimed at its Virginia audience, who accounted for about four-fifths of the station's listeners. The U.S. Supreme Court determined that the 1988 federal provision was constitutional under the *Central Hudson* test applied to commercial speech. In doing so, the 7–2 majority seemed especially impressed with the long history of regulation and prohibition of gambling and advertising for gambling.

In an earlier case, publishers in Minnesota had challenged the federal ban on mailing both lottery ads and lists of lottery winners. In *Minnesota Newspaper Association v. Postmaster General of U.S.*,[55] a federal district judge upheld the ad limits as a permitted commercial speech regulation. The ban on carrying lists of prizes or prize winners limited editorial speech, however, and was declared unconstitutional. Both sides appealed. In the meantime, Congress passed the 1988 act, and the government agreed that the outright ban no longer would be valid. The Supreme Court dismissed the dispute as moot—no longer a real controversy.[56]

Justice John Paul Stevens's dissenting opinion in the *Edge* case in effect argues that the entire idea of barring lottery or gambling advertising should be moot:

> The fact that the vast majority of the States currently sponsor a lottery, and that soon virtually all of them will do so. . . . [U]ndermines the United States' contention that non-lottery states have a "substantial" interest in discouraging their citizens from traveling across state lines and participating in a neighboring State's lottery.

Perhaps Justice Stevens would endorse traditional regulation of unfair or deceptive gambling or contest advertising, but he is surely right that most

Americans are no longer concerned with preventing this kind of advertising altogether.

Two other types of gambling are less widespread. Many states now authorize casino gambling. Sometimes this takes place on land, but it is also becoming common on riverboats. These activities are usually licensed and closely regulated by the states. State regulators may also closely monitor the types of advertising that casinos may use. Under FCC rules , broadcasters in states with casino gambling are not allowed to directly promote the gambling. They may stress accommodations, meals, or entertainment, but they cannot show gaming in progress or even use the word *casino* unless it is part of the official name of the business.[57] In cities such as Las Vegas, the result is some very strange television—casino gambling can be seen everywhere except on TV.

Indian gaming, which is allowed under federal law, is essentially the same as casino gambling in most locations where it is offered. Since the federal law preempts conflicting state laws, the media are free to promote the lawful gaming run by Native American tribes.

Lotteries in Summary

Regulation of both advertising and news coverage of lotteries, contests, and gambling has posed great risks for the mass media in the past. While a small amount of federal and state regulation remains today—and it therefore remains important to check local and national rules—it appears to be only a matter of time before liberalized attitudes toward gambling erase or reduce the risk.

TAXATION AND LICENSING OF THE PRESS

As long as there have been newspapers in North America, members of the press, especially newspapers, have worried that government would use taxes and licensing rules to suppress information. The colonial press's experience with taxes on paper and licensing of publishers by the British government was a major reason for the adoption of the First Amendment.[58] Heavyhanded use of taxes on paper and ink, along with oppressive administrative licensing measures, remains one of the primary ways of shackling the press worldwide.[59] Outside the United States, newspaper and other publishers usually register with the government and prove financial stability—a form of bond or surety.

Today in the United States, it is universally agreed that a primary purpose of the First Amendment was to prevent government from using these indirect tools as a way of restraining news coverage. Determining when a tax or license provision violates the First Amendment has not always proved easy, however. Since there is no historical support for an absolute ban on press taxation or licensing, conflict is inevitable when government imposes costs on the media.

The Supreme Court has decided several major cases on news media taxation and two other major cases on issues involving licenses. As a result of these cases, some general rules have been developed for each type of dispute.

● **Indian gaming**
Refers to casinos, keno parlors, and other gambling businesses operated by Native Americans under federal law as a result of their independent nation status.

The law regarding taxation and licensing is much clearer now than in the early 1980s. Throughout that decade and into the 1990s, mass media organizations challenged tax laws, license laws, and newspaper vending regulations in dozens of reported court cases.[60]

Taxation

The principle that government should not use taxes to punish or favor specific news organizations or to punish any news organizations for particular news coverage has been translated into the general rule that any tax provision that makes distinctions among media organizations and that threatens to suppress particular ideas is unconstitutional.[61] A second rule recognizes that many business laws that apply evenhandedly to all organizations or businesses, such as environmental regulations or civil rights laws, do not violate the First Amendment when applied uniformly to the press.

The rules have developed from the Supreme Court's first newspaper taxation case, *Grosjean v. American Press Co.,*[62] a 1936 case about a Louisiana statute imposing a 2 percent gross receipts license tax—but only upon publications with circulations above 20,000. Only thirteen Louisiana newspapers were subject to the tax.

The Louisiana legislature passed the law, introduced by controversial Governor Huey Long, despite knowing that the measure had been contrived by the governor as a way to punish newspapers that had opposed his rise to near-absolute power in the state. When nine publishers sued, they claimed that the tax law violated the First Amendment as well as their **equal protection** rights under the Fourteenth Amendment.

The Court decided that the Louisiana law was an unconstitutional violation of the First Amendment on its face. Since the law was invalid on that ground, the Court did not address equal protection directly. The holding has since been interpreted as applying to deliberate attempts to bridle the press; in other words, a statute or regulation that is designed to punish the press will be unconstitutional, no matter how neutral it may appear on paper. Since the records of the Louisiana legislative debate made the intent to punish clear, it was a relatively easy decision for the Court majority. The discriminatory application was the key, though, indicating a theme for future equal protection arguments:

> The form in which the tax is imposed is in itself suspicious. It is not measured or limited by the volume of advertisements. It is measured alone by the extent of the circulation of the publication in which the advertisements are carried, with the plain purpose of penalizing the publishers and curtailing the circulation of a selected group of newspapers.[63]

The issues about equal protection were raised again almost fifty years later in the *Minneapolis Star* case, but the situation was quite different. Like most states, Minnesota did not apply its retail **sales tax** to consumer purchases of newspapers. The state legislature, looking for additional sources of revenue, passed a "use" tax that applied to purchases of ink and paper by newspapers.

● **Equal protection**
Under the Fourteenth Amendment of the U.S. Constitution, all similarly situated persons are entitled to nondiscriminatory treatment so far as the guarantees of the Bill of Rights are concerned.

● **Sales tax**
A tax applied to purchase transactions, usually as a percentage of the total value of the sale. Most state sales tax laws apply to all sales of tangible products.

As in the Louisiana tax, exceptions were included for small-circulation newspapers. Unlike the Louisiana statute, though, the Minnesota legislature's purpose was to protect small businesses that might be hard-pressed to pay the tax. Large newspapers, which would end up providing almost all of the revenue from the tax, sued.

The newspapers argued, as had been argued in 1936, that the statute violated the First Amendment on its face, and that it also violated equal protection. The Supreme Court declared the statute unconstitutional, but not on its face. Instead, the Court's 8–1 majority, in one of Justice Sandra Day O'Connor's first opinions, said that any statute that singles out the press for "differential treatment" is presumed unconstitutional and will be upheld only if the government can show a compelling interest underlying the statute.[64] Raising tax revenues was a substantial but not compelling interest. The law was invalid even though it cost newspapers less than application of the regular sales tax would have cost. Under the rule that laws of general application are constitutional when applied to the press, imposing the full sales tax would have been approved. In fact, many states now tax newspaper sales. O'Connor stressed that allowing a tax singling out the press—even for preferred treatment—posed the risk that government would use the same statute to punish the press later.

Justice Byron White's concurring opinion used equal protection arguments. He said that the discrimination in favor of small newspapers was enough to make the use tax unconstitutional. No intent to influence content was needed to invalidate the tax in his view.

Justice William Rehnquist was the sole dissenter. He adhered to the traditional tax law rule that only a rational basis is required to uphold a tax unless it is shown that the tax somehow interferes with constitutional rights. Since Minnesota's use tax cost newspapers less than the sales tax would have, he found no interference with First Amendment rights. He seemed surprised that newspapers would complain when the state was giving them a break not enjoyed by other businesses.

The *Minneapolis Star* case spawned dozens of challenges to state and local government taxes. These cases usually arose when governments attempted to tax different media in different ways. A frequently tried issue was the tax status of free-circulation newspapers. In a typical case of the time, *Maryland Pennysaver Group, Inc. v. Maryland Comptroller of the Treasury*,[65] a group of free-circulation shoppers challenged the state's exemption of paid-circulation newspapers from the sales tax, claiming they were similarly entitled to exemption. The court found no statutory, administrative, or constitutional basis for the challenge despite the obvious discrimination in favor of traditional newspapers.

A similar claim was rejected in *Sacramento Cable Television v. Sacramento*.[66] The cable company challenged the application to it of a city "utility user's tax" applied previously to gas, water, and electric companies. The California Court of Appeals specifically approved some degree of differentiation among media businesses. In doing so, the court noted:

> [P]erfection in a taxing scheme has never been a prerequisite to validity. Equal taxation of all is not the constitutional mandate but only equal

taxation of those "similarly situated." There need only be a rational basis for the classification used, even though more equitable classifications may exist. And because the record contains no evidence of intent to suppress ideas and no evidence such suppression will result from enforcement . . . we find no First Amendment violation.

The California court had relied upon a U.S. Supreme Court interpretation of *Minneapolis Star* in 1991. In *Leathers v. Medlock*,[67] the Court upheld application of the Arkansas sales tax to cable companies despite the presence of an exemption for print media. In another opinion by Justice O'Connor, the Court changed direction slightly. From now on, the majority said, discrimination aimed at a small group of media companies or direct intent to interfere with First Amendment activities would be the keys. Since the Arkansas sales tax applied to all cable companies, it was considered a generally applicable law.

The Court's decision in *Leathers* has freed the states to design tax laws in ways that recognize differences in the structure, revenues, manufacturing, and economics of various communication media. In all likelihood the courts will move toward a standard that allows differential taxation when differences among the media require it.[68] Evidence that the overall economic effect of taxes is about equal for various media will also likely result in state tax rules being upheld.

Direct, and impermissible, discrimination against the press has been found in a number of cases. In *Arkansas Writer's Project, Inc. v. Ragland*,[69] the Court considered Arkansas's sales tax, which taxed general interest magazines while exempting newspapers and various other types of magazines, including religious, sports, and trade magazines. The tax was held to be unconstitutional. The state was clearly preferring some types of content. Similarly, in *Texas Monthly v. Bullock*,[70] exempting religious publications but no others from sales tax was found unconstitutional.

It appears that a tax will be upheld under the *Leathers* decision so long as the tax is a legitimate revenue-raising measure, the legislature has a rational basis for any classifications of media, and there is neither intent to affect content nor an effect on content. Given the variety of ways in which media are distributed, financed, and sold, such flexibility is probably necessary to assure that the mass media pay their share of taxes.

Tax Exemption

Tax exemption is another way tax laws can have an effect on the press. Organizations that engage in charitable activities, including educational activities, may qualify for **tax-exempt status** under both federal and state tax laws. Under the federal Internal Revenue Code Section 501(c)(3), a qualifying organization does not pay tax. In addition, donors to 501(c)(3) groups are allowed to deduct donations from their personal income taxes. State laws have similar provisions. In practice, then, these groups are subsidized because they pay no taxes and others must pay more to make up the difference.

For a period of about five years, the Internal Revenue Service (IRS) attempted to regulate expression by nonprofit groups. The IRS argued that tax-

---

● **Rational basis**
In federal constitutional law, a test used to uphold government regulation when no constitutional rights, such as freedom of speech, are involved.

● **Tax-exempt status**
Qualifying organizations are not required to pay the taxes a business might, although they are required to file informational returns. Available for certain types of charities, trade associations, and other groups.

exempt status brought with it an obligation that organizations claiming to be educational must be balanced and fair when publishing materials. The argument could also have been applied to nonprofit broadcasters.

The IRS was rebuffed in *Big Mama Rag, Inc. v. United States.*[71] but prevailed in *National Alliance v. United States.*[72] In both cases a nonprofit organization published a periodical. In *Big Mama Rag*, the IRS revoked the tax-exempt status of a group that published a feminist magazine. The IRS argued that the magazine's coverage of issues, especially lesbian issues, was too "doctrinaire" and must be balanced with competing views. The U.S. Circuit Court of Appeals for the District of Columbia held that the rules the IRS created to decide what constituted balanced coverage were vague, allowing too much interpretation by government.

Three years later, the same court upheld revocation of tax-exempt status for a Nazi group's newsletter. The newsletter consisted mainly of unsupported racist opinion. Using something it called the "Methodology Test," the IRS argued that it had eliminated vagueness. The court neither approved nor disapproved of the test. Instead, it declined to decide the test's constitutionality, concluding instead that the newsletter "Attack" could not be considered educational by any definition and therefore was ineligible for special tax status.

Together the two cases seem to establish general rules for tax-exempt publishers and broadcasters. Exemption will be allowed for groups that provide some supporting evidence, however scant, for positions advocated, and the government will not be allowed to supervise accuracy or fairness. Pure opinion may not qualify for tax exemption. In all likelihood, however, only fanatical opinion such as that in *National Alliance* would ever be acted against.

Closely related to the tax exemption cases are cases involving direct government subsidies and the application of the Supreme Court's **"unconstitutional conditions"** principle. The Court has said that the government may not require that the recipients of government funds waive their constitutional rights as a condition for receiving the subsidy. In *FCC v. League of Women Voters of California*,[73] the Court declared that a ban on editorializing by nonprofit educational broadcasters who received federal funds imposed by the Public Broadcasting Act of 1967 violated the First Amendment. Most public broadcasting comes from tax-exempt organizations. The *League of Women Voters* case may help explain why the IRS and other government agencies have not pursued content regulation of those receiving direct and indirect subsidies.

Arts funding and abortion counseling have been the two major exceptions to this principle. After several controversial grants in the 1980s, Congress imposed requirements to keep the National Endowment for the Arts from subsidizing obscene or indecent messages. The courts have traditionally supported the First Amendment rights of speakers rather than the regulatory goals of Congress. In doing so, they have found the rules put forward in support of content regulations attached to subsidies to be both too broad and vague.[74] In *Rust v. Sullivan*,[75] however, the Supreme Court narrowly upheld government limits on abortion counseling by medical staffers at federally subsidized family planning clinics. Medical staffers claimed that providing abortion counseling was

● **Unconstitutional conditions**
A doctrine used to void rules that require that the recipient of a government benefit or subsidy give up a constitutional right to get the benefit.

protected by the First Amendment. The majority opinion appears to generally authorize government to restrain subsidized speakers, using a rational basis test, whenever government pays part of the bills. Lower courts have been reading *Rust* narrowly, and as a result, it has had little effect.

Licensing

Formal licensing of the print media does not exist in the United States. No advance permission or qualifications tests are used or allowed. Anyone may publish. Nevertheless, licensing-like issues arise regularly. Regulation of newspaper vending boxes has been a major source of dispute between the press and government. Regulation of home delivery of newspapers and advertising shoppers has also been an issue. Another area of dispute has focused on postal classifications.

As with tax laws, laws or regulations that apply generally will be upheld. If a city has a business license fee that applies to all businesses, it may impose it on media companies as well.[76]

Newsracks • Licensing newsracks is entirely different because the regulation is specific to print media. Opportunities for confrontation between local governments and newspapers have grown extensively in the last fifteen years as the circulation markets of national, regional, and state newspapers have expanded. Upstart local publications have also multiplied in most cities. As a result, busy street corners are often jammed with vending boxes for a variety of newspapers. Many communities have attempted to regulate newsracks to reduce the clutter and ensure safety.

Government attempts at regulation face fairly strict constitutional limits, however. The courts have repeatedly said that cities must pass a time, place, and manner test to regulate placement of newsracks. Vagueness will invalidate the regulations. Dozens of cases have arisen in the last decade. Local governments have argued that aesthetics and public safety are the major justifications for regulating newsracks. An additional supporting argument urges that newspapers should bear the costs of using public property.

Twice the Supreme Court has addressed the issue. In *City of Lakewood v. Plain Dealer Publishing Co.*,[77] the Court held that a city ordinance that gave local officials wide discretion to interpret qualifications for installing machines violated the First Amendment. Officials might use the vague provisions as a weapon to chill the press, the majority said. Implicitly recognizing a constitutional right to distribute the news, the majority likened a vague licensing plan to a prior restraint.

When Cincinnati attempted to impose tighter controls on distribution of advertising and promotional publications than on mainstream newspapers, the Court declared the attempt unconstitutional. In *Cincinnati v. Discovery Network, Inc.*,[78] the city had relied upon the Court's commercial speech cases as a justification for stricter regulation of commercial speakers. The Court said the city could not discriminate between publications unless it could show a "reasonable fit" between the regulation and the publications regulated. In this case, there was no solid evidence that shoppers or other commercial publications posed more risk to safety or aesthetics than other publications.

For a newsrack regulation to be valid, then, it must be:

- Content-neutral.
- Designed to achieve a "substantial" government interest.
- Precise and clear enough to require little interpretation.
- Speaker-neutral—that is, all publications must be treated similarly.
- Written to allow reasonable alternatives.

Any limits on newsracks must be supported by evidence provided by the regulating government entity. Typical limits address the number of boxes at a specific location and requirements for liability insurance. A first-come, first-served policy is probably the only one that will be considered content-neutral. Numerical limits may be challenged if the city's real purpose is to reduce the number of newsracks rather than assure safety.[79] Aesthetics alone is likely to be an insufficient ground for regulating the appearance and number of boxes. In only one case, *Chicago Observer, Inc. v. City of Chicago,*[80] was an aesthetic argument for newsrack regulation upheld. But in that case the boxes were almost twice the size of others, and the company also used the huge boxes as billboards to sell advertising to other companies.

The major remaining argument—that publications should bear the cost of using the public ways—has gotten a mixed reception from the courts. Most courts apparently have thought the costs of city cleanup and maintenance resulting from newspaper vending boxes too small to be substantial.[81] In one case, however, the court closely examined rental and janitorial fees and found them reasonably related to the costs of newsrack placement.[82]

Attempts to regulate the circulation of free newspapers and advertising shoppers have generally failed the time, place, and manner test. When Doylestown, Pennsylvania, tried to argue that only publications requested by home owners should be granted the right to distribute, a federal appeals court demanded strong proof that unretrieved copies on front porches and stoops posed a safety or crime hazard. The township had no such proof, and the ordinance was declared unconstitutional.[83] Similarly, when Laramie, Wyoming, tried to enforce its littering law against free-circulation publications, the city's proof that a weekly newspaper caused considerable littering was weak. More importantly, the court indicated that the publisher's First Amendment rights would probably prevail over the ordinance anyhow.[84]

Postal Regulations • Preferential postal rates for newspapers, magazines, and books have long been offered as a way of promoting greater public awareness of news and public affairs.[85] Whenever one category of mailer gets lower rates, of course, others have to make up the difference. Not surprisingly, deciding who qualifies for postal subsidy rates can be hotly contested.

For the mass media, the major subsidies come with second-class postal status. This classification requires that a publication have a list of paid subscribers, that it presort and bundle mail, and that total advertising space be limited to a percentage specified by the U.S. Postal Service.

Third-class status is reserved for mass mailers and for nonprofit organizations. Normally, a group that gets tax exemption will also get third-class rates. The major third-class groups, however, are the bulk advertising mailers. Mainstream publishers have contended that the postal service gives ad mailers an unfair advantage with cheap rates[86]—although the service argues that the mailers more than cover their own costs.

Since 1970, with the passage of the Postal Reorganization Act, which called for the mails to eventually cover their own costs, there has been constant pressure to limit subsidy costs. Second-class rates represent more of their true cost today than in the past, but they are still a bargain for anyone who can qualify.

The courts have upheld classification rules so long as they are content-neutral. The **paid subscriber** requirement for second-class permits was upheld against a constitutional challenge by a free-circulation newspaper. It wished to mail copies to everyone in its circulation area and would enjoy big savings with second-class rates. In *Enterprise, Inc. v. United States,*[87] the U.S. Court of Appeals for the Sixth Circuit said that the postal service's rule requiring paid subscribers was content-neutral. The court also said that since a free newspaper could qualify if it obtained enough names on a "requester list," a reasonable alternative had been provided. The decision nevertheless favors established newspapers sold in traditional ways.

The rule requiring that postal classification decisions be content-neutral has a long history. In the 1940s, the postmaster general decided that *Esquire* magazine's suggestive cartoons and drawings should not be considered "information of a **public character**" qualified for second-class treatment under the postal statutes.[88] The U.S. Supreme Court told the post office that its action amounted to censorship. Emphasizing that postal classification should not depend on what officials thought of a publication's content, the Court limited the "public character" interpretation. If a publication had subscribers, it had content of a public character.

Taxation and Licensing in Summary

Under current rules, the government may apply the same tax and administrative rules to the news media as are applied to any other kinds of businesses. First Amendment issues arise only when the federal, state, or local government is somehow trying to have an effect on the content of the media. If that happens, the traditional fear of government chilling free expression calls for application of a compelling interest test.

Licensing is a bit different. Qualifying for a postal subsidy or getting approval to install a newspaper vending machine is similar to getting a license to operate. Here too government must remain content-neutral, but the courts have used the time, place, and manner test with its substantial interest requirement rather than the tougher compelling interest test.

In general, the courts have been sympathetic to media plaintiffs who can show that a government action that limits media activity is discriminatory, vengeful, or arbitrary.

● Paid subscriber

In postal law, a rule that requires a publication to have a list of genuine subscribers amounting to at least half its circulation to qualify for the subsidized second-class postal rate.

● Public character

Periodicals of a public character are given second-class mailing permits. The courts have concluded that having subscribers is sufficient proof that the content is of a public character.

LABOR LAWS AND THE MASS MEDIA

Laws affecting the relationships of employees and employers fall into three types. The first type is common law. Under the common law of contract, the work agreements between employers and employees have traditionally been considered "at-will" contracts, terminable by either party at any time. A second type is federal or state law specifically designed to change the bargaining positions of the two sides. The National Labor Relations Act (NLRA) and the Fair Labor Standards Act (FLSA) are the two best-known laws of this type. A third type of law aims to improve the working conditions or status of particular categories of employees. A classic law of this type is a civil rights or other antidiscrimination law, such as the federal Civil Rights Act of 1964 or the Americans with Disabilities Act (ADA).

Common Law

The notion that an employment contract is freely entered into by both sides and that each side has relatively equal bargaining power seems quaint in the late twentieth century when most of us work for large corporations or institutions. But that is exactly what the courts argued during the 1800s in establishing the "employment at will" doctrine as part of the common law of contracts. As applied by the courts early in this century, the doctrine usually meant that either an employee or an employer could cancel an employment agreement at any time. Any other rule, the courts argued, would unreasonably limit the ability of individuals to control their own behavior.

Unless there is a statute or a written contract that supersedes the common law, the hiring of an employee will be considered at will. The only significant limitation on the employment at will doctrine in its early form was that a written agreement would prevail over an oral agreement. It is little wonder that the doctrine was popular with employers, who could fire any employees for any or no reason, no matter how long or diligently they had worked.

Over the course of the century, the courts have softened the harsh effects of the employment at will doctrine by adding some commonsense exceptions. The most important exception recognizes that employee manuals or policy statements will be binding against employers. When the discharge of an employee is inconsistent with the company's written rules, the employee may pursue a contract action.[89] Another exception that has been widely accepted prevents employers from firing employees when the firing would violate public policy. For example, if a reporter was fired for reporting that her newspaper was dumping noxious chemicals into the local river, the public policy exception might prevent firing—or at least lead to reinstatement.[90]

Employment contract law usually assumes that employees are fairly interchangeable. But when an employee is considered unique or indispensable, an employer might seek a signed **personal services contract.** These contracts limit the employee's ability to quit early or to move to a competitor. Unless an employer tries to impose excessive time limits or defines competing markets too broadly, the courts will likely uphold such a contract.[91] Personal services

● **Employment at will**
Common law doctrine that assumes that employers and employees are both free agents and that either may terminate the relationship at any time.

● **Personal services contract**
A type of employment agreement used when the employer believes that the employee's skills are unique and the employer wishes to prevent the employee from being lured away to work for competitors.

contracts are most commonly used to bind television news anchors, newspaper columnists, and other high-profile employees.

The majority of news media employees are at-will employees, covered neither by a collective bargaining agreement negotiated by a union nor by a personal services contract. Their primary protection against unfair actions by employers can be found only in the company's policies.

Federal Labor Law

The National Labor Relations Act (NLRA)[92] of 1935 was passed to reduce strife between manufacturing companies and organized labor by guaranteeing employees the right to unionize and to engage in collective bargaining. The key to securing employee rights was prohibition of "unfair labor practices" by employers. Under the statute, an employer is required to recognize and bargain with a union organized by its employees. The statute specifies that contract provisions affecting pay or terms and conditions of employment must always be negotiated; these are called "mandatory subjects" for bargaining. Most other subjects for bargaining must be agreed upon by the parties. The act is administered and interpreted by the National Labor Relations Board (NLRB). Most labor disputes are resolved by the NLRB without judicial review.

Application of the NLRA to journalism was immediately challenged by media companies on the ground that direct governmental oversight of labor relations of the press violated the First Amendment. In *Associated Press v. NLRB*,[93] an employee filed a complaint, claiming he had been fired for trying to organize a union. The U.S. Supreme Court had little trouble upholding the law as it applied to the press:

> The publisher of a newspaper has no special immunity from the application of general laws. . . . The regulation in question here has no relation whatever to the impartial distribution of news.

In journalism, the most important unions affecting editorial employees have been the Newspaper Guild and the American Federation of Television and Radio Artists. The NLRA does not always match well with journalism because reporters and editors are not engaged in "manufacturing" in the normal sense of that word. For example, unionized reporters have often complained that employer-imposed codes of ethics amounted to unfair labor practices. The courts have usually agreed that penalties for violating ethics codes must be bargained, but have said that the codes themselves concern standards for the employer's product and are therefore up to management to determine.[94]

The NLRA also fits uneasily when it comes to defining what types of employees are covered. In general, managerial employees are not covered by the act. Employers have sought to have their reporters and other editorial employees declared managers. For news media, the general rule that has developed is that employees will be considered part of management when they exercise independent judgment and engage in policy making for the company. The rule emerged from *Wichita Eagle & Beacon Publishing Co. v. NLRB,* in which a federal court of appeals said that two editorial writers were so closely associated with company policy that they were managers.[95]

Media companies also deal with many other unions, but those usually represent employees in manufacturing or distribution, precisely the sorts of work the NLRA was meant to cover. As a result, there have been few disputes related to the news or advertising content of media.

The Fair Labor Standards Act (FLSA)[96] established rules for minimum wages and maximum work hours, including the requirement that work beyond maximum hours must be paid at higher overtime rates. In the news business, where hours can be long and unpredictable and stories seldom fit neatly into work schedules, the FLSA has been unpopular with employers.

Upon passage, the publishers argued that the FLSA violated the First Amendment when applied to the press. Just as with the NLRA, the Supreme Court easily found the FLSA was a law of general application that did not violate press rights.[97] The Court said that a preference in the FLSA exempting small newspapers also did not violate the First Amendment.[98] It is doubtful the Court would uphold even this "favorable" discrimination today on either constitutional or statutory grounds. In 1994, when a chain of community newspapers argued that the circulation of its publications fit the FLSA small newspaper exemption, a federal court of appeals said that the circulation figures should be added together.[99]

The FLSA exempts professional and artistic employees from the wage and overtime provisions. Media companies have argued for years that reporters, print or broadcast, are both professional and creative employees, but with little success.[100] If a reporter is taking orders, covering a regular beat, and preparing traditional "hard news" or community stories, the FLSA will likely apply.[101] Only those who are allowed to determine their own reporting assignments are likely to be within the exemption. In *Sherwood v. The Washington Post,*[102] a star reporter at the *Post* who for the most part determined his own asssignments and how to complete them was declared a professional under the FLSA.

Civil Rights Laws

The key antidiscrimination statute is Title VII of the federal Civil Rights Act of 1964,[103] usually referred to in brief as Title VII. It prohibits discrimination based on race, color, religion, sex, and national origin. Complaints are filed with the Equal Employment Opportunity Commission (EEOC). Most states have statutes that parallel the federal law and agencies that parallel the EEOC. The EEOC also acts as the interpretive and enforcement body for the federal Age Discrimination in Employment Act[104] and Americans with Disabilities Act.[105]

In general, Title VII and related laws prohibit discrimination in hiring, firing, compensation, and promotions. Title VII itself also specifically prohibits discrimination that results in sexual harassment or creation of a hostile work environment.

Complaints against employers are brought either by individual employees or by groups of employees. When the claim is individual, the plaintiff must show that an employment decision was made for an impermissible reason. When the claim is on behalf of a group of employees, there must be proof of a pattern or practice of discrimination by the employer. Proving a pattern of discrimination usually requires statistical evidence strong enough to create a presumption that employment decisions were based on prohibited factors. That sort of statistical evidence is so difficult to produce that group actions are rare—and even more rarely are they successful.

In *Hausch v. Donrey of Nevada, Inc.,*[106] a former managing editor at a daily newspaper argued that her "promotion" to the newly created position of associate editor was actually a demotion. In reality, her responsibilities decreased while, at the same time, a newly hired, male managing editor received more duties and a higher salary. The case is apparently the only court decision where a media defendant argued that federal antidiscrimination laws violate the First Amendment when applied to the press. The federal district judge treated Title VII as a law of general application, then emphasized that "[T]his court will not recognize an expanded First Amendment right to discriminate in the hiring and firing of editorial employees."

Few of the cases involving civil rights statutes involve media organizations. Since these laws have general application, however, the rules developed in nonmedia cases will normally apply in media cases. The court in *Hausch* suggested that a First Amendment argument would succeed only if it could be shown that the statute or an EEOC regulation directly affected news content.

The new ADA has not fostered cases involving media as yet, but the act broadens federal antidiscrimination protection to assure that disability will not be a basis for employment decisions. Job applicants cannot be rejected or candidates for promotion denied just because they have a disability as defined by the statute. Lack of physical access is not an excuse—employers are expected to make modifications to the workplace. Decisions must be made on an impartial assessment of merit or performance. It should be noted that this is true for the employment protections of all the civil rights statutes.

Labor Laws in Summary

Federal and state labor and employment laws are classic examples of rules that apply to all businesses. For that reason, media companies have failed to persuade the courts that they need special protection from complying. In the case of civil rights laws and wage laws, the courts apparently found the chutzpah of the media, claiming a First Amendment right to discriminate or to pay less, annoying and probably unethical.

The most important aspects of labor and employment law remain the collective bargaining guarantees under the National Labor Relations Act and the common law employment at will doctrine.

KEY TERMS

Intellectual property	Exclusive rights
Copyright	Distinctiveness
Fair use	Generic mark
Unfair competition	Descriptive mark
Trademark	Likelihood of confusion
Service mark	Dilution
Statute of Anne	Comparison advertising
Originality	Misappropriation
Injunction	Lottery
First-sale doctrine	Prize
Nature and purpose of the use	Consideration
Nature of the work	Contest
Amount and substantiality	Chance
Effect of the use	Indian gaming
Actual damages	Equal protection
Specific damages	Sales tax
Striking similarity	Rational basis
Access	Tax-exempt status
Berne Convention	Unconstitutional conditions
Performing rights societies	Paid subscriber
Compulsory license	Public character
Lanham Act	Employment at will
Secondary meaning	Personal services contract

CASE PROBLEMS

1. A student claims to have a wonderful idea for a new magazine. What can he do to gain some protection under intellectual property law for this idea that he wants to exploit?

2. A writer for a book review magazine writes a review of a mystery novel. The review quotes only about sixty words from the novel, but they are the solution to the mystery. When sued, the writer argues that her use was a fair use. Applying the four criteria of fair use, build the most convincing argument possible that this was a fair use. Then build the most convincing argument from the book publisher's side that it was not.

3. A researcher downloads the internal phonebook of a major aerospace company. Noting that the phonebook lists the colleges from which all the engineers in the company graduated, the researcher extracts that information, sorts the names by undergraduate institution, and then attempts to sell the list to those colleges for fund-raising purposes. Do you believe this is a fair use or not? Why?

4. During a strike at the *Daily Star*, a reporter decides to write articles about automobile restoration, a favorite pastime. He contacts car magazines and outlines his plans. Although none of the magazines offers an advance, they express an interest in the articles and promise to pay upon publication if they like his work. He writes at home, on a self-defined schedule, on his personal computer, and does not seek fringe benefits from the magazines when he submits his articles. When the articles are published, who most likely holds the copyright? Why?

5. Lillian Songbird files a copyright infringement lawsuit when the grunge group, CRASS, becomes a huge success with its performance of what they claim is their original song, "Kiss my Ass." Lillian sues because the basic melody line, which is repeated several times on CRASS's album, seems, to her, to be the same as a melody she write more than thirty years ago, "Coming on Fast." Although her song was never published or performed, a copy of the first page of the score was printed near her picture in her high school yearbook. She graduated in

Florida, but now lives in California, where CRASS began. What must Songbird prove in order to win her copyright infringement lawsuit? Do you think she will win? Why or why not?

6. Frank's Shoe Store erects a large wheel of fortune near its cash registers. Once patrons have made a purchase at the store, they can spin the wheel of fortune. Numbers on the wheel indicate various discounts from 5 percent to 100 percent, which are immediately refunded to customers. Is Frank's Shoe Store running a lottery? Why or why not?

7. A major national filling station company—the kind of company that seems to have a gas station on every street corner—runs a national promotion. Persons over eighteen years of age can stop by the stations and, without charge, receive a scratch-off card. Prizes on the card range from small discounts on the next gas purchase to a year's supply of free gas (on one card somewhere in the country). Is this a lottery? Why or why not?

8. A company that sells magazine subscriptions by phone runs the following contest. Persons are called and asked to name the last three presidents of the United States. People who cannot do that are immediately offered the opportunity to buy magazines. The names of persons who answer the question correctly are entered in a computer. At the end of each month, the computer randomly selects names from those who have both answered the question correctly and ordered a magazine. The persons the computer selects receive one free magazine subscription. Is this a lottery? Why or why not?

9. The city council passes an ordinance to regulate the placement of newspaper vending boxes. It requires that no more than two boxes will be allowed on any street corner. Most of the busiest corners in the city currently have up to seven boxes. The ordinance provides that those newspapers that have the largest local circulation will be given a preference. In addition, newspapers that are circulated free will not be allowed to place news boxes on any public sidewalks in the city. The council based its decision on the two-box limit on pedestrian traffic studies, which showed that limited space on crowded street corners slowed people down. The ban on free newspapers was designed to "prevent the litter that typically accompanies free-distribution publications." Will the ordinance hold up? Why or why not?

10. The National Endowment for the Arts (NEA) is funded by appropriations from Congress. Recently, Congress passed a statute mandating that "no NEA funds shall be used for the creation of materials containing or representing indecency." One project recently funded by NEA is a series of one-hour documentary films on the harmful effects of pornography, produced by the Feminist Film Cooperative. Because the films contain both extensive nudity and much swearing, the NEA withdraws its funding partway through the project. The NEA offers the cooperative the chance to resubmit the project for further funding, but insists on screening the films in progress. The cooperative rejects the offer and instead hires a local lawyer to challenge the withdrawal of funding. You're the lawyer. Challenge it.

11. Joan Taylor is a reporter for local TV station WART. She has worked at the station three years, primarily as the environmental affairs reporter. During that time she has won several state and regional awards for her work, and her salary has risen accordingly. Last Friday the news director told her she was fired, effective the following Monday. The news director said that ratings for the local newscasts had been dropping and that, like many stations, WART was forced to trim its workforce. According to the company's personnel manual, "it will be the usual practice of the station to provide employees with two weeks' notice of termination of employment." The news director told Taylor that the two-week rule did not apply because the station is in deep financial trouble. The next week Taylor watches the WART news and sees a new male reporter fresh out of college covering the environmental beat. She calls the news director and is told, "that reporter costs us less than half your salary." Taylor wants to sue both for violation of her employment contract and for sex discrimination. Can she succeed? Why or why not?

12. The state has never imposed a sales tax on the sale of services, only on the sales of tangible goods. Now the state legislature is considering a proposal that would extend the sales tax to services. Traditionally, advertising purchases have been treated as a sale of services. Under the new plan, ads would be subject to sales tax. Since advertising is a primary revenue source for both newspapers and magazines, publishers in the state have actively opposed the proposal. They claim that imposition of a sales tax on advertising would have a differential impact on

publications and would therefore violate the First Amendment. Are they right? Why or why not?

13. *Mud Wrestling Monthly* is a new magazine. It consists of roughly equal portions of editorial material—stories and photos—and of advertising. At present it has only 3,412 subscribers. The publisher of the magazine filed for second-class postal status so that it could send its copies by mail more cheaply.

The local postmaster rejected the application on the grounds that the editorial material was "not of a public character," but instead appealed only to a very narrow range of the public. The postmaster also noted that the magazine contains material that would be "considered indecent" under current constitutional definitions. If the magazine publisher appeals the decision in court, which side will win? Why?

ENDNOTES

1. Current copyright law is found at 17 U.S.C.A. § 101 *et seq.* Another area of intellectual property law, patent law, gives up to 20 years of exclusive rights to the inventors of machines, processes, manufactured products, and designs.

2. An Act for the Encouragement of Learning, 8 Anne, Ch. 19.

3. Constitution of the United States, Article I, Sec. 8 (8).

4. 3 Stat. 124.

5. 17 U.S.C.A. § 102(a).

6. 499 U.S. 340, 111 S.Ct. 1282 (1991).

7. *Georgia Television Co. v. TV News Clips of Atlanta, Inc.,* 718 F. Supp. 939 (N.D. Ga. 1989).

8. *CNN v. Video Monitoring Services,* 940 F.2d 1471, 19 Med.L.Rptr. 1289 (11th Cir. 1991).

9. 17 U.S.C.A. § 102.

10. 17 U.S.C.A. §§ 201 *et seq.*

11. *Community for Creative Non-Violence v. Reid,* 490 U.S. 730, 109 S.Ct. 2166 (1989).

12. See 17 U.S.C.A. §§ 109, 202.

13. Congress has decided that records (and CDs) are somehow different, and the "first-sale" doctrine doesn't apply to them. Thus, we no longer have record or CD "rental" stores.

14. 17 U.S.C.A. §§ 301 *et seq.*

15. 17 U.S.C.A. § 106. In 1990, Congress added several additional rights for authors of works of visual art: (1) the right to claim authorship in a work and prevent use of one's name as author

of a work one did not create and (2) the right to prevent use of one's name as author of a work if the work was distorted, mutilated, or modified in a way harmful to the author's honor or reputation. Works of visual art are defined as paintings, drawings, prints, sculpture, and photographs created for exhibition only—provided that there are only from 1 to 200 copies of such works. These changes brought the United States more in line with international intellectual property, which traditionally protects "artist's rights." 17 U.S.C.A. § 106A.

16. 17 U.S.C.A. §§ 401 *et seq.*

17. 17 U.S.C.A. § 107.

18. The U.S. Supreme Court's most recent discussion of how fair use works is found in *Campbell v. Acuff-Rose,* _____ U.S. _____, 114 S.Ct. 1164 (1994).

19. Id.

20. *Salinger v. Random House, Inc.,* 811 F.2d 90 (2d Cir.), *cert. denied* 484 U.S. 890, 108 S.Ct. 213, (1987).

21. *Harper and Row Publishers, Inc. v. Nation Enterprises,* 471 U.S. 539, 105 S.Ct. 2218 (1985).

22. 465 U.S. 1112, 104 S.Ct. 1619 (1984).

23. 17 U.S.C.A. §§ 501 *et seq.*

24. *Warner Brothers, Inc. v. American Broadcasting Co.,* 523 F.Supp. 611 (S.D.N.Y. 1981).

25. Berne Convention Implementation Act of 1988, P.L. 100–568, 102 Stat. 2853.

26. 17 U.S.C.A. § 111(c), (d).

27. Copyright Royalty Tribunal Act of 1993, 107 Stat. 2304 (1993).

28. 47 U.S.C.A. §§ 534(a), 534(b).

29. 17 U.S.C.A. §§ 1001 *et seq.*

30. 15 U.S.C.A. §§ 151–1127.

31. Jerome Gilson, *Trademark Protection and Practice* (New York: Matthew Bender, 1982), § 2.01.

32. Ibid., § 2.09.

33. Arthur R. Miller and Michael H. Davis, *Intellectual Property,* 2d ed. (St. Paul, Minn.: West, 1990), pp. 146–49.

34. See, for example, "Trademarks and the Press" (Special Pullout Section), *Editor and Publisher,* December 10, 1994.

35. 15 U.S.C.A. § 1127.

36. 15 U.S.C.A. § 1072.

37. *Dallas Cowboys Cheerleaders, Inc. v. Pussycat Cinema, Ltd.,* 604 F.2d 200 (2d Cir. 1979).

38. 28 F.3d 769 (8th Cir. 1994).

39. Robert C. Denicola, "Trademarks as Speech: Constitutional Implications of the Emerging Rationales for the Protection of Trade Symbols," *Wisconsin Law Review* 158 (1982).

40. "News Notes," Med.L.Rptr., Vol. 23, No. 5, January 31, 1995.

41. 811 F.2d 26 (1st Cir.), *cert. denied and appeal dismissed,* 483 U.S. 1013, 107 S.Ct. 3254 (1987).

42. 836 F.2d 397 (8th Cir. 1987), *cert. denied,* 488 U.S. 933, 109 S.Ct. 326 (1988).

43. *Carson v. Here's Johnny Portable Toilets, Inc.,* 698 F.2d 831 (6th Cir. 1983).

44. *Taylor v. NBC,* 22 Med.L.Rptr. 2433 (Cal. Sup. Ct. 1994).

45. Miller and Davis, *Intellectual Property,* p. 154.

46. *U-Haul International, Inc. v. Jartran, Inc.,* 793 F.2d 1034 (9th Cir. 1986); *Truck Components, Inc. v. K-H Corp.,* 776 F.Supp. 405 (N.D.Ill. 1991); see, generally, Kazumi Hasegawa, "Meeting the Public and Private Interest in Comparative Commercial Speech," unpublished paper presented to the Law Division, Association for Education in Journalism and Mass Communication, Montreal, August 1992.

47. 248 U.S. 215, 39 S.Ct. 68 (1918).

48. Broadcast and cable-related statutes are found at 18 U.S.C.A. §§ 1304 and 1307.

49. For postal statutes, see 39 U.S.C.A. § 3005.

50. *Seattle Times v. Tielsch,* 80 Wash.2d 502, 495 P.2d 1366 (1972).

51. See, e.g., *Marco Sales Co. v. FTC,* 453 F.2d 1 (2d Cir. 1971).

52. *New York State Broadcasters Association v. United States,* 414 F.2d 990 (2d Cir. 1969).

53. 18 U.S.C.A. § 1307.

54. _____ U.S. _____, 113 S.Ct. 2696 (1993).

55. 677 F.Supp. 1400 (D.Minn. 1987).

56. *Frank v. Minnesota Newspaper Ass'n, Inc.,* 490 U.S. 225, 109 S.Ct. 1734 (1989).

57. 73 CFR § 12.1700.

58. *Minneapolis Star & Tribune Co. v. Minnesota Commissioner of Revenue,* 460 U.S. 575, 103 S.Ct. 1365 (1983).

59. Chris W. Ogbondah and Monica O. Ogbondah, "Does Independence Mean Anything? A Critical Analysis of Continuity in British Colonial Press Laws in Africa," paper presented to the International Communication Division, Association for Education in Journalism and Mass Communication, Atlanta, Ga., August 1994; Kyu Ho Youm, "Freedom of the Press: A Legal and Ethical Perspective," paper presented to the International Communication Division, Association for Education in Journalism and Mass Communication, Atlanta, Ga., August 1994.

60. Stephen Lacy and Todd F. Simon, *The Economics and Regulation of United States Newspapers* (Norwood, N.J.: Ablex Publishing, 1993), pp. 238–246, 256–260.

61. *Leathers v. Medlock,* 499 U.S. 439, 111 S.Ct. 1438 (1991).

62. 297 U.S. 233, 56 S.Ct. 444 (1936).

63. 297 U.S. at 251, 56 S.Ct. at 449.

64. *Minneapolis Star & Tribune Co. v. Minnesota Commissioner of Revenue,* 460 U.S. at 585, 103 S.Ct. at 1371.

65. 323 Md. 697, 594 A.2d 1142 (App. 1991).

66. 234 Cal.App.3d 232, 286 Cal.Rptr. 470 (1991).

67. 499 U.S. 439, 111 S.Ct. 1438 (1991).

68. *Reuters America, Inc. v. Sharp,* 889 S.W.2d 646, 23 Med.L.Rptr. 1129 (Tex.App. 1994).

69. 481 U.S. 221, 107 S.Ct. 1722 (1987).

70. 489 U.S. 1, 109 S.Ct. 890 (1989).

71. 631 F.2d 1030 (D.C.Cir. 1980).

72. 710 F.2d 868 (D.C.Cir. 1983).

73. 468 U.S. 364, 104 S.Ct. 3106 (1984).

74. *Finley v. National Endowment for the Arts,* 795 F.Supp. 1457 (C.D.Cal. 1992); Amy Sabrin, "Thinking about Content: Can It Play an Appropriate Role in Government Funding of the Arts?" *Yale Law Journal* 102:1209–1233 (1993).

75. 500 U.S. 173, 111 S.Ct. 1759 (1991).

76. *Times Mirror Co. v. Los Angeles,* 192 Cal.App.3d 170, 237 Cal.Rptr. 346 (1987).

77. 486 U.S. 750, 108 S.Ct. 2138 (1988).

78. _____ U.S. _____, 113 S.Ct. 1505 (1993).

79. *Graff v. City of Chicago,* 986 F.2d 1055 (7th Cir. 1993).

80. 929 F.2d 325 (7th Cir. 1991).

81. *Sentinel Communications Co. v. Watt,* 936 F.2d 1189 (11th Cir. 1991).

82. *Phoenix Newspapers, Inc. v. Tucson Airport Authority,* 842 F.Supp. 381, 22 Med.L.Rptr. 1504 (D.Ariz. 1993).

83. *Ad World, Inc. v. Township of Doylestown,* 672 F.2d 1136 (3d Cir. 1982).

84. *Miller v. Laramie,* 880 P.2d 594, 22 Med.L.Rptr. 2302 (Wyo. 1994).

85. Richard Burket Kielbowicz, "Origins of the Second-Class Mail Category and the Business of Policymaking, 1863–1879," *Journalism Monographs* 96 (April 1986).

86. *Direct Marketing Association v. Postal Service,* 778 F.2d 96 (2d Cir. 1985).

87. 833 F.2d 1216 (6th Cir. 1987).

88. *Hannegan v. Esquire,* 327 U.S. 146, 66 S.Ct. 456 (1946).

89. *Minnesota v. Knight-Ridder,* 5 Med.L.Rptr. 1705 (Minn. Dist. 1979).

90. Annette Taylor, "Newspaper Ethics Codes and the Employment-at-Will Doctrine," paper presented to the Law Division, Association for Education in Journalism and Mass Communication, Portland, Oregon, July 1988.

91. *Capital Cities Communications v. Sheehan,* 9 Med.L.Rptr. 2172 (Conn. Super. 1983).

92. 29 U.S.C.A. §§ 151 *et seq.*

93. 301 U.S. 103, 57 S.Ct. 650 (1937).

94. *Newspaper Guild v. NLRB,* 636 F.2d 550 (D.C.Cir. 1980); *Capital Times Co. v. Newspaper Guild of Madison, Local 64,* 223 NLRB 87 (1976).

95. 480 F.2d 52 (10th Cir. 1973), *cert. denied* 416 U.S. 982, 94 S.Ct. 2383 (1974).

96. 29 U.S.C.A. §§ 201 *et seq.*

97. *Mabee v. White Plains Publishing Co.,* 327 U.S. 178, 66 S.Ct. 511 (1946).

98. *Oklahoma Press Publishing Co. v. Walling,* 327 U.S. 186, 66 S.Ct. 494 (1946).

99. *Reich v. Gateway Press, Inc.,* 13 F.3d 685 (3d Cir. 1994).

100. *Id.; Dalheim v. KDFW-TV,* 918 F.2d 1220 (5th Cir. 1990).

101. *Reich v. Newspapers of New England, Inc.,* 44 F.3d 1060, 23 Med.L.Rptr. 1257 (1st Cir. 1995).

102. 871 F.Supp. 1471, 23 Med.L.Rptr. 1273 (D.D.C. 1994).

103. 42 U.S.C.A. §§ 2000e *et seq.* Broadcasters and cable television companies face additional regulation of employment practices by the Federal Communications Commission as described in Chapter 12.

104. 29 U.S.C.A. §§ 621 *et seq.*

105. 42 U.S.C.A. §§ 12112 *et seq.*

106. 833 F.Supp. 822 (D.Nev. 1993).

Appendix

UNDERSTANDING THE AMERICAN LEGAL SYSTEM

A basic understanding of the law governing the press is essential for any journalist. No journalist is, or should be, expected to play the role of lawyer in deciding whether or not to publish. However, a basic understanding of the law and the legal system may enable a journalist to spot a potential problem, something that may skirt the line between hard-hitting journalism and libel, for instance. For example, a story may involve a charge of wrongdoing against a prominent public official. Although the story sounds plausible, it cannot be substantiated. Once a journalist spots such an issue, a lawyer should be consulted to see whether the story should run as it is or be modified. In some circumstances, it may be concluded that a story simply poses too great a litigation risk and should be pulled. A journalist who fails to seek legal assistance with such an issue risks a costly and destructive lawsuit for her employer as well as for herself.

WHO MAKES THE LAW?

Under the federal system established by the U.S. Constitution, both the U.S. Congress and the state legislatures have power to enact laws. Under the Constitution, the states and the federal government each have spheres of power that both overlap and maintain some exclusivity. The Supremacy Clause makes federal laws made "in Pursuance" of the Constitution supreme over conflicting state laws. The Supremacy Clause, which is found in Article VI, Section 2 of the U.S. Constitution, provides for the supremacy of federal law:

This Constitution, and the Laws of the United States which shall be made in Pursuance thereof; and all Treaties made, or which shall be made, under the Authority of the United States, shall be the supreme Law of the Land; and the Judges in every State shall be bound thereby, any Thing in the Constitution or Laws of any State to the Contrary notwithstanding.

An example of federal legislative power that has often been cited in this book is the Federal Communications Act of 1934. Under its power to regulate interstate commerce, Congress may regulate broadcasting. The Commerce Clause, Article I, Section 8, U.S. Constitution, is the constitutional basis for the Federal Communications Act of 1934, which, as amended, governs broadcasting to this day. Pursuant to the Commerce Clause, Congress enacted the Federal Communications Act and established the Federal Communications Commission as the agency to administer that law.

States have authority to legislate concerning the police power within their jurisdictions. This means that they may legislate in matters concerning the health, welfare, and morals of their people. Thus, states may legislate to secure the public order and safety. Crimes such as murder and robbery are prosecuted under state law. In some contexts, however, Congress has enacted legislation that allows the federal authorities to prosecute murder and robbery if such actions cross state lines. The formation and operation of corporations is largely governed by state law.

In addition to the division of legislative authority between the state and the federal government, the constitutional scheme is predicated on the separation of powers within the federal government. Article I deals with the power of the legislature, Article II with the executive, and Article III with the judiciary. The federal legislature or Congress, consisting of the House of Representatives and the Senate, is charged with making the laws. The executive—the president and the federal bureaucracy—has the responsibility of executing these laws. Increasingly, through executive orders and other actions, the executive itself has come to have a lawmaking function. The federal judiciary, through the Supreme Court and the lower federal courts, has the responsibility of interpreting the law. Under the doctrine of judicial review, the federal courts—and the state courts as well—also determine whether the actions of government are consistent with the Constitution. If they are not, such actions may be set aside.

Although the courts have the formal responsibility of interpreting the law, in truth, the courts themselves make law. Judicial lawmaking occurs in numerous ways. For example, when interpreting statutes and administrative orders, it often becomes necessary for courts to fill in the gaps caused by statutory omissions and ambiguities. In the final analysis, it is often very difficult to separate the process of interpretation from the process of lawmaking.

The foregoing account does not exhaust the sources of lawmaking in the United States. Administrative agencies must also be mentioned. For example, the Federal Communications Commission, like other administrative agencies both federal and state, "makes law." By way of illustration, the Federal Communications Act says that broadcast licenses should be granted only if it is in the public interest. The FCC has on occasion issued regulations and decisions that set forth the criteria that should inform a determination of whether a grant of a license is in the public interest. These administrative regulations and decisions themselves have the force of law. Clearly, then, administrative agencies like legislatures make law.

THE VARIOUS SOURCES OF LAW

Constitutions

There are various sources of law, including constitutional law, statutory law, and case law. As we have seen, the U.S. Constitution, where applicable, is the supreme law of the land. But each of the states has its own constitution as well. State constitutions operate like the federal constitution in the sense that they establish the essential structure of government.

The state legislatures cannot make laws that conflict with their constitutions. Many of the rights guaranteed in the federal Bill of Rights are secured in state constitutions as well. Indeed, sometimes, but not always, these individual rights and liberties are more broadly stated and interpreted than in the federal constitution.

But the journalist should note that the state constitutions do not parallel the federal in every respect. There are major differences as well. Most state constitutions are much longer than the federal constitution and deal with matters that could be covered as well by statutes. State constitutions are amended much more often than the federal constitution. A state government need not follow the principle of separation of powers unless its state constitution so provides. Some state supreme courts are permitted to give advisory opinions to the state legislature on the constitutional validity of proposed legislation. The federal courts are precluded from giving such advisory opinions because they may only decide cases that involve an actual case or controversy.

Still another difference between the federal constitution and the state constitutions is that the latter often provide for the initiative and the referendum—mechanisms that allow voters to pass directly on issues. These devices for direct participation by the electorate in government are not provided by the federal constitution.

Statutes

The federal and state constitutions set forth the structure of government and confer rights on individuals to protect them from abuse by government. Statutes are usually more prosaic. Statutes, the laws passed by legislatures, govern much of our economic and daily life. Everything from eligibility for a driver's license to the taxes a citizen is obliged to pay to the state are governed by statutes or legislation. Statutes determine what records businesses must keep, what one may do or not do with one's property, the length of the fishing and hunting season, and what conduct is criminal.

Statutes are often enacted to address specific situations. Unlike the broad and sometimes sonorous phrases found in constitutions, statutory language is precise, detailed, and complicated. In the case of constitutions, the very breadth of the language used renders it susceptible to many different interpretations. In the case of statutes, sometimes even the most carefully drawn legislation is open to varying interpretations. Sometimes it is advisable to get legal advice on the meaning of statutory or constitutional language. But the imprecision of much constitutional or statutory language is a reality that journalists must live with. Lawyers may argue for one interpretation or another. The outcome of that argument may mean the loss or gain of millions of dollars, or even jail time, for a client. Appellate courts, of course, sometimes resolve these controversies by providing a definitive interpretation of disputed statutory language.

Administrative Regulations and Decisions

Administrative agencies such as the Federal Communications Commission (FCC) and the National Labor Relations Board (NLRB) have been established by Congress to regulate communications and labor relations, respectively. These agencies interpret the legislation that Congress has enacted to regulate these fields. Decisions by federal agencies such as the FCC and NLRB are an important source of law. These agencies have administrative law judges who issue decisions just as judges do who sit on courts. In addition, these agencies issue orders, regulations, and policy statements that have the force of law. But final decisions and orders of these agencies can be appealed to the federal courts. Final orders of the FCC, for example, can be appealed to the U.S. courts of appeal.

State and local administrative agencies also issue decisions, rules, and regulations in the same manner federal agencies do. These state administrative law determinations are subject to review by the state court system according to the law of that particular state. The law generated by administrative agencies is referred to as administrative law. As we all know, we live in the age of the regulatory state. More and more aspects of daily life are governed by regulations issued by government agencies. Increasingly, these agencies are being required to index, publicize, and distribute the law they generate and the activities they undertake. Journalists must be informed about these developments so that they may better inform the public.

Common Law

The common law came to America from England and was adopted specifically in many state constitutions. The common law is the body of case law that has been generated by Anglo-American courts over many centuries. When a court is presented with an issue where past case law or precedent is clear, then the court will usually adhere to a prior decision. This adherence to precedent is a distinguishing characteristic of the common law. It is predicated on the doctrine of *stare decisis.* Literally translated, this Latin phrase means "let the decision stand."

The doctrine of *stare decisis* brings a measure of order and predictability to judicial decisions. The applications of *stare decisis* to a case means that the rulings of prior cases involving similar facts and legal issues should govern the matter. If the issue has been decided in a particular way under prior case law or precedent, it should be decided the same way again. Common law maintains itself as a coherent body of law rather than simply a compendium of cases by relying upon precedent and the doctrine of *stare decisis*. Of course, in this century statutory law has become far more important than case law. Prior precedent will only be adhered to in situations where the statutory law does not otherwise command.

Sometimes a court will be presented with a novel issue that has not been addressed by either a statute or a prior case. In that instance, the court's decision on this issue becomes a new precedent that may stand for many years as the controlling law on the point. In this way the common law continues to grow and develop.

The obligation to follow *stare decisis* will depend upon the origin of the precedent that is pressed upon the court. If the precedent, or past case law, is from the same jurisdiction in which the court sits, then the prior case law will have great force. If, on the other hand, the only precedent that is urged upon the court is from other jurisdictions, the court will feel less obliged to follow the precedent. For example, a decision on an issue of law by a lower state court in Alaska might have some precedential effect upon the decision of a state court in Florida that is confronted with the same issue. However, the Alaska state court decision would not have the same authoritative force on the Florida state court as a Florida state supreme court decision.

The common law has grown and developed incrementally. Common law courts have historically displayed a preference for the particular over the general. Common law courts usually prefer to resolve only the specific issues actually presented to them. Therefore, all aspects of a rule of law are not necessarily enunciated in a decision. Typically, a court will decide only those aspects that are raised by the actual controversy between the parties. A common law court does not decide more than it has to. Finally, it should be emphasized that the doctrine of *stare decisis* is a general principle to which, in the main, American courts attempt to adhere. But if changing social *mores* or new scientific or technical information suggests that a precedent is based on obsolete or erroneous assumptions, a court will depart from precedent. *Stare decisis* is a guide to decision. It is not an inexorable command.

FOLLOWING A CASE THROUGH THE FEDERAL COURT SYSTEM

Since journalists must report on litigation, they need to understand how a case winds its way through the judicial system. To aid in that understanding, we will follow the progress of a case through the federal court system. A case begins with the *complaint* of the plaintiff in a civil suit or the state in a criminal case. In the case of a civil complaint, the plaintiff, the party bringing the suit, states her reasons for wishing to obtain some kind of relief from the defendant, the party being sued. The complaint states the plaintiff's story; it tells why the plaintiff believes that the defendant had done her some injury. The complaint then asks for relief. This relief might be for money. Lawyers call this type of relief damages. But there are other kinds of relief as well.

The plaintiff may seek relief in the form of a court order. Injunctions and temporary restraining orders are examples of court orders. If the plaintiff so requests, a court order may direct the defendant either to do something or stop doing it.

The case we have chosen centers around a libel claim. A libel action involves a plaintiff's claim that his reputation has been harmed, i.e., he has been defamed by a writing, picture, or printing put out by another party. Libel is addressed in detail elsewhere in this book. But for now the content of the claim is not important. What is important is to acquire an understanding of the litigation process by seeing how a case progresses through the judicial system from the beginning of the suit—the filing of a complaint—to the case's final resolution by a court.

Jon Simmons's Libel Suit against the *Mainland Gazette*

Jon Simmons, a stockbroker, works in Mainland City, State of Mainland. The town newspaper, the *Mainland Gazette,* has run an article about Simmons that says that he has made a practice of selling utilities stocks to his customers. The articles states that these stocks have continuously declined in value since the time Simmons's customers purchased them.

On the advice of his lawyer, Simmons has decided to file suit against the *Gazette* for libel. In his complaint, Simmons alleges that the paper libeled him by printing an article that contained false and defamatory statements harmful to his reputation. Simmons states that these statements were made about him at the malicious instigation of the paper's owner and editor, Billy Buster. As a result of the article, Simmons alleges that he feels the disapproving stares of his formerly friendly neighbors whenever he leaves his home. Moreover, he alleges that his securities business is suffering. In this suit, known as *Simmons v. Mainland Gazette,* the plaintiff, Simmons, demands damages from the defendant, the *Gazette*, a corporation, in the amount of $500,000, which Simmons says, is the amount of business he has lost as a result of the *Gazette*'s article about him.

Simmons Files Suit in a Federal District Court

Simmons lives in Outland, a state adjacent to the State of Mainland. Thus, he can gain access to federal district court on the basis of diversity jurisdiction. When two citizens who live in different states have a dispute involving more than $50,000, the suit may be heard in a federal district court. In this case, the *Gazette* is incorporated in the State of Mainland; it is, therefore, a citizen of that state.

Now that Simmons is in court and seems to be serious about pursuing his claim, lawyers for the *Gazette* have been instructed by Billy Buster to talk to Simmons about settling the case. Buster is not sure that the paper will win in court. Buster knows that in the United States, unlike England, for example, the loser does not pay the winner's attorneys' fees. Buster is concerned about the legal costs of defending Simmons's suit against the *Gazette*. Another benefit from settling the case is that the *Gazette* would avoid the negative publicity that would flow from the lawsuit if the paper is found to be in error. But Simmons does not want to settle. He thinks the paper's offer of settlement is too low. Besides, Simmons wants to rehabilitate his reputation by winning in court.

As for the *Gazette,* it can make a number of responses to Simmons's complaint. The paper could simply *answer* the complaint. The answer is the name given to the pleading by which the defendant responds to the plaintiff's complaint. In the answer, the defendant states its side of the story. Another alternative is to make a motion to dismiss. This motion simply states that there is no basis in law to the plaintiff's complaint and, therefore, the complaint should be dismissed.

One step that both parties will take once the lawsuit is commenced involves what is called *discovery.* Through discovery the parties educate themselves about each other's case. During the process of discovery, they may, through their lawyers, ask questions of each other and of other witnesses. The parties and witnesses are sworn to tell the truth in such proceedings. A transcript is made of these proceedings, which are called *depositions.* There are other discovery mechanisms as well. Although valuable in litigation, discovery is both expensive and time-consuming. On the basis of the discovery materials, the nature of the case is disclosed to the parties and, if necessary, to the court.

Instead of making a motion to dismiss, the *Gazette* has decided to make a motion to the court for *summary judgment.* By this motion the defendant asserts that even assuming that the facts are as the plaintiff alleges them to be, the defendant is still entitled to win on the law. If the newspaper were to be successful in its motion, judgment would be for the paper and the case would be over. A motion for summary judgment is heard by the judge alone without a jury. Therefore an advantage for the newspaper, if it wins the motion for summary judgment, is that it avoids the time and expense of a trial.

In this situation, the defendant newspaper vigorously contends that the motion for summary judgment should be granted. The newspaper says it simply stated facts. Simmons *did* sell his customers utilities stocks, and the stocks *did* decline in value after the customers purchased them. The defendant newspaper says that these statements were true and, moreover, that they are not legally defamatory. In addition, the *Gazette* argues on summary judgment that if the article were held to be defamatory, this would violate the First Amendment.

The judge, however, refuses to grant the *Gazette*'s motion because the newspaper said that Simmons has made a "practice" of selling such stocks, implying that he routinely tries to sell stocks of poor value to his customers simply to get commissions. The judge says it is not clear whether the newspaper defamed Simmons or not and that a jury should decide. Moreover, the judge holds that the paper's First Amendment rights would not be violated if the jury were to find the publication to be defamatory. Therefore, the judge set the case for trial. Since Simmons has so requested, the matter will be decided by a jury trial.

At the end of the trial, the jury finds for plaintiff Jon Simmons and proceeds to award $100,000 damages to him. This was less than the amount Simmons asked for. But the jury has the power to grant less than the damages requested. The jury usually determines damages in civil suits, but the amount it recommends is subject to alteration by the judge. The judge in this case does not set the damages aside. The judge says that these damages reflect losses that Simmons—on the basis of evidence introduced at the trial—has actually suffered due to loss of business occasioned by the article.

The *Gazette* Appeals to a Federal Court of Appeals

The *Gazette* decides to appeal the federal district court's decision. When a party appeals from a federal district court, it appeals (asks for a reversal of a lower decision) to the federal court of appeals for the circuit in which the district court sits. The party bringing the appeal is called the *appellant.* Here the appellant is the *Gazette.* The appellant must submit a written brief of its arguments and then present that brief to the judges of the court of appeals. The *appellee,* here Jon Simmons, the party who must respond to this attack on the judgment below, files a reply brief. Appeals before the federal courts of appeals are usually, but not always, scheduled for oral argument. During these oral arguments, the judges can ask the lawyers for the parties questions about the case, and the lawyers have the opportunity to present their most compelling arguments to the court.

Among its contentions on appeal, the *Gazette* asserts in its brief that the federal district court was wrong in denying the paper's motion for summary judgment. The court of appeals, like all appellate courts, is concerned primarily with questions of law. Here it must decide whether the district court judge was correct in his denial of the motion for summary judgment. If the court of appeals were approaching a factual dispute, it could only reverse the district court's decision if it found the decision to be *clearly erroneous,* a difficult standard to meet. Since the First Amendment issue decided by the lower court involved issues of law and fact that were inextricably related, the court of appeals can make its own independent assessment of the First Amendment issue, including the factual bases upon which it is premised.

In this case, the court of appeals agrees with the district court in its denial of the summary judgment motion, and thus affirms its decision. Furthermore, the court of appeals affirms the judgment below including the award of damages. The court of appeals concludes that under the law the jury could reasonably conclude that Jon Simmons had been defamed by the *Gazette* and that awarding a judgment to the plaintiff implicated no First Amendment concerns. If the court of appeals were to disagree with the decision below, it could reverse the decision. The court of appeals could also remand, or send back, the case to the district court with directions to follow the appellate court's decision regarding the law. In this case, to reverse and remand would be to grant the defendant/appellant's motion for summary judgment and end the suit favorably for the defendant.

The decision to affirm by the court of appeals has precedential effect. Federal district courts within the circuit will look to the holding as binding authority. Courts in other circuits, district and appellate, will look to it as persuasive authority.

The U.S. Supreme Court—The Court of Last Resort

The *Gazette* refuses to accept defeat and decides to petition for a *writ of certiorari* from the U.S. Supreme Court. A writ of certiorari is the means by which cases are brought to the Supreme Court for review. Prospects for getting certiorari granted are not high. The Court now receives approximately seven thousand petitions for certiorari each year but grants less than a hundred of them.

If four of the nine Supreme Court justices feel that the issue presented is important enough and vote to grant the writ, the Court will hear the case. A denial of certiorari does not mean that the Court agrees with the judgment below. It just means that the Court chose not to review it.

The Court decides to grant the *Gazette*'s petition for certiorari. The lawyers for the *Gazette* contend in their petition for certiorari that the lower federal courts in this case were too ready to find that defamation was present. They contend that this readiness to find defamation in a doubtful case raises important First Amendment considerations. Perhaps the novelty of this point caused the Court to grant *cert.*, as the lawyers and journalists call it.

Once *cert.* is granted, the lawyers for the parties must submit briefs to the Court just as they did at the court of appeals level. Other interested parties may be allowed to participate by filing *amicus* briefs. After oral argument in the Supreme Court, the justices meet in conference to discuss the case and indicate to each other how they expect to vote. These conferences are not open to the public. If the chief justice appears to be in the tentative majority, he assigns himself or another member of the Court the responsibility to draft an opinion. If the chief justice is in the minority, the most senior justice in the majority assigns the writing of the Court's opinion. This draft opinion is then circulated among the justices. If the draft opinion attracts the support of a majority of the nine-member Court—five justices—the draft opinion will be published as the opinion of the Court. Often no opinion commands majority support; in that event, only the Court's judgment carries majority support. Other members of the Court, of course, may choose to publish concurring opinions indicating that although they agree with the result of the majority, they do so for different reasons. Still other members of the Court may choose to dissent because they think the result reached by the Court is wrong.

Though the *Gazette* has overcome the substantial hurdle posed by the writ of certiorari, it has not won the final battle. The Supreme Court affirms the court of appeals's holding, thus sounding the final death knell for the paper, for the Supreme Court is indeed the court of last resort. Jon Simmons is vindicated and can walk through Mainland City with his head up again.

FINDING THE LAW

One of the first, and most useful, skills that law students master is that of legal research. With this skill, law students can find the cases, statutes, treaties, and other sources of law that they will encounter in their study of the law. Since journalists must often report law-related matters, they should also have a basic understanding of legal materials and legal research.

To find a case or statute, you have to know its *citation* as well as what the citation signifies. The citation is a set form that allows legal researchers to find the case or statute in whatever form it is collected. The citation for *Red Lion Broadcasting,* an important case in mass communication law, is as follows:

Red Lion Broadcasting Co. v. FCC, 395 U.S. 367 (1969).

The citation gives you first the name of the case and at least some of the parties involved, *Red Lion Broadcasting Co. v. FCC.* The order of the parties does not tell you who was the original plaintiff or defendant, however, because the order is often switched in the appellate process. Next, "395 U.S. 367" tells you that the case can be found in volume 395 of the *United States Reports,* and that it starts on page 367 of that volume. The *United States Reports* is the official publication for the U.S. Supreme Court.

Reports of Supreme Court cases are also published in West Publishing Company's *Supreme Court Reporter* and the Lawyers Cooperative's *Lawyer's Edition.* Although these sources are unofficial, they are published long before cases appear in the *United States Reports.* These unofficial reports are abbreviated as "S.Ct." and "L.Ed.," respectively. The number "1969" in parentheses is the year in which the case was decided by the Supreme Court.

Decisions of the U.S. courts of appeals are found in the *Federal Reporter,* which is also published by West Publishing Company. The *Federal Reporter* has now gone into a third edition. A sample citation would be *Poole v. Wood,* 45 F.3d 246 (8th Cir. 1995). The "8th Cir." in the parentheses refers to the circuit in which the court of appeals sits, here the Eighth Circuit. Federal district court decisions are reported in a publication called the *Federal Supplement.* A sample citation would be *Bellsouth Corp. v. U.S.,* 868 F.Supp. 1335 (N.D.Ala. 1994). The reference to "F.Supp." indicates that the case is a federal district court decision. The reference to "N.D.Ala." in the parentheses refers to the fact that the decision is from the federal district court for the northern district of Alabama.

State court decisions cite to an official state reporter. An example of a state supreme decision reported in the official state reporter is the following Vermont state supreme court decision: *Greenmoss Builders, Inc. v. Dun & Bradstreet,* 143 Vt. 66 (1983). Besides the official state reporters, state decisions can also be found in West Publishing Company's regional reporters. The various regional reporters publish the decisions of the state courts in a particular region. The *Atlantic Reporter,* for example, publishes the state court decisions for Connecticut, Delaware, District of Columbia, Maine, Maryland, Massachusetts, New Hampshire, New Jersey, Pennsylvania, Rhode Island, and Vermont. An example of a regional reporter citation would be *Greenmoss Builders, Inc. v. Dun & Bradstreet,* 461 A.2d 414 (Vt. 1983). The "A.2d" refers to the second series of the *Atlantic Reporter* published by West. The reference to "Vt. 1983" indicates that this particular decision is a Vermont state court decision and that the case was decided in 1983.

U.S. statutes are officially cited to the *United States Code* (U.S.C.). An example of a citation to a federal statute would be 47 U.S.C. § 315. The number in front of the "U.S.C." citation refers to the title or volume in which the statute is found. Different federal laws are collected under separate titles of the United States Code. Thus, Title 47 U.S.C. contains the Federal Communications Act of 1934 and its amendments. The reference to Sec. 315 refers to a particular provision of the Federal Communications Act. Sec. 315, for example, is the "equal time" rule discussed earlier in this book.

Laws of the United States are eventually codified in the United States Code. The *United States Code Annotated* (U.S.C.A.), West's unofficial version of the United States Code, includes explanatory notes and citations to cases. The most recent amendments to a title can be found in the pocket parts at the end of the volume or title. When one researches a federal statute, therefore, it is important not only to read the statute in the hardbound volume but to check the pocket parts to see if the statute has been repeated or amended. Regulations adopted by federal administrative agencies such as the Federal Communications Commission are published in the *Code of Federal Regulations* (C.F.R.).

State statutes are published for each state. Amendments and new laws can be found in the pocket parts of the volumes containing these laws. A sample citation of a state statute or law that is discussed in this book is the citation for the Florida right of reply law struck down in *Miami Herald Publishing Co. v. Tornillo*, 418 U.S. 241 (1974). The citation for the Florida right of reply law was as follows: West's F.S.A. § 104.38. The citation "F.S.A." stands for Florida Statutes Annotated. "Annotated" means that short summaries of the cases interpreting the various statutory provisions appear under each provision. The reference to Sec. 104.38 indicates the specific provision of the Florida Electoral Code that contained the Florida right of reply law.

Lexis and *Westlaw* are electronic services that have made conducting legal research considerably quicker and provided access to legal researchers in even the most remote locations. They are subscriber online services that have a vast store of state and federal cases and statutes along with numerous other legal and nonlegal sources. Law students and practitioners refer to these services often. Although these services can be expensive, they offer instant access to a wealth of current information. The availability of these online up-to-date legal databases has made electronic research indispensable to anyone undertaking substantial legal research.

THE COURTS

The charts and maps which follow are reprinted from Gillmor, Barron, Simon and Terry, *Mass Communication Law: Cases and Comment* (West Pub. Co. 5th ed. 1990).

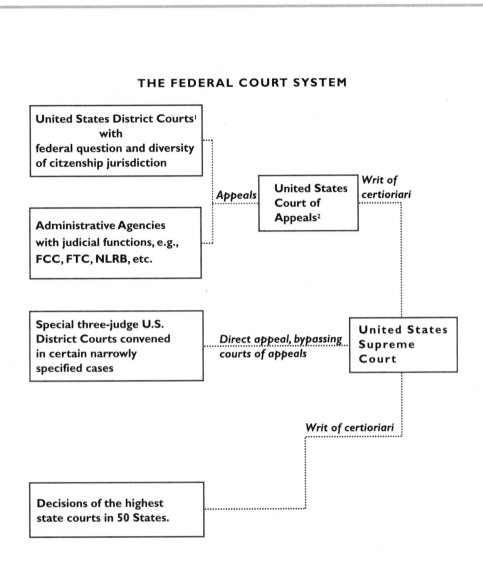

THE FEDERAL COURT SYSTEM

1. There is at least one federal district court in every state.

2. The United States is divided into eleven numbered federal judicial circuits, plus the U.S. Court of Appeals for the District of Columbia. In addition, there is the U.S. Courts of Appeals for the Federal Circuit, which was established by the Congress in 1982. This court succeeded to the appellate jurisdiction of the U.S. Court of Claims and the U.S. Court of Customs and Patent Appeals, both of which were abolished.

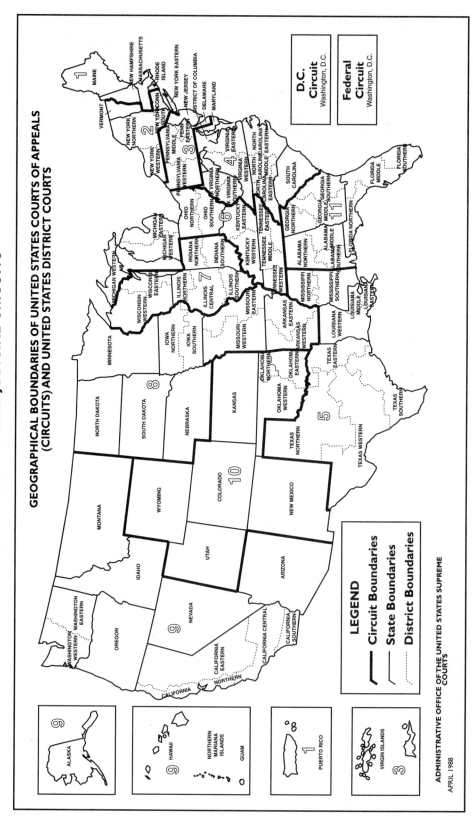

THE THIRTEEN FEDERAL JUDICIAL CIRCUITS

GEOGRAPHICAL BOUNDARIES OF UNITED STATES COURTS OF APPEALS
(CIRCUITS) AND UNITED STATES DISTRICT COURTS

LEGEND
Circuit Boundaries
State Boundaries
District Boundaries

ADMINISTRATIVE OFFICE OF THE UNITED STATES SUPREME
COURTS
APRIL 1988

A STATE COURT SYSTEM

The state court system outlined below is an example of one state court system. It is intended to provide a guide to the state judicial process for the student who is unfamiliar with the organization of state courts. There is substantial variation from state to state. The following figure illustrates the California court system.

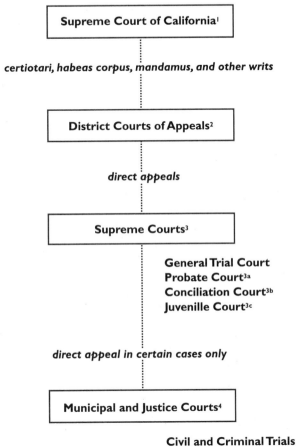

Supreme Court of California¹

certiotari, habeas corpus, mandamus, and other writs

District Courts of Appeals²

direct appeals

Supreme Courts³

General Trial Court
Probate Court³ᵃ
Conciliation Court³ᵇ
Juvenille Court³ᶜ

direct appeal in certain cases only

Municipal and Justice Courts⁴

Civil and Criminal Trials
Small Claims Court⁴ᵃ

1. Has no obligatory appellate jurisdiction; that is, it reviews cases by granting petitions for writs of certiorari and thus retains complete discretionary control of its jurisdiction.

2. Consequently the great bulk of cases reach final decision in these five District Courts of Appeals.

3. The Superior Court, the trial court of general jurisdiction, also has three special divisions: the General Trial Court, Probate Court, Conciliation Court and Juvenile Court.

3a. This court has jurisdiction over the administration of estates, wills, and related matters.

3b. The Conciliation Court is a rather unique institution that takes jurisdiction over family disputes that could lead to the dissolution of a marriage to the detriment of a minor child.

3c. The Juvenile Court considers certain types of cases involving persons under 18 years of age.

4. There is one Superior Court in each county. The Municipal and Justice Courts represent subdivisoins of each country by population. These courts are trial courts with limited jurisdiction. They also have original and exclusive criminal jurisdiction for violations of local ordinances within their districts.

4a. The Small Claims Court is the familiar forum used to settle small disputes using informal procedure and prohibiting lawyers for the disputing parties.

Note: Superior Court is usually the last state court to which a decision of these lowest courts can be appealed. It is possible that a case from one of these courts be ineligible for further state review and could have further review only in the U.S. Supreme Court.

NATIONAL REPORTER SYSTEM MAP

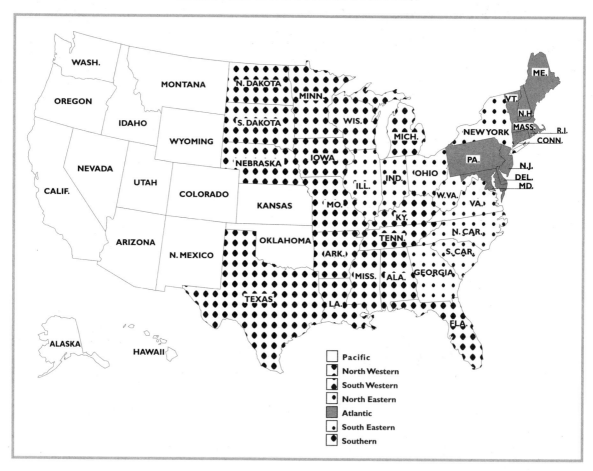

Glossary

Access To prove infringement, a copyright owner must show that the defendant had access to the original work. Proof that the original was widely available to the public will usually be sufficient.

Actual damages Compensation for demonstrated injury, whatever form that injury might take. Sometimes referred to as general damages.

Actual malice Knowing falsehood or reckless disregard as to whether a statement is true or false. The level of fault that has to be met by a public official or public figure suing for libel.

Affirmative action Federal and state laws and policies that require organizations, usually employers, to take steps to make sure that opportunities are known by and available to "protected groups" such as women and members of ethnic minorities.

Affirmative disclosure A request from the FTC that an advertiser admit to a deception or a falsehood before ordering a corrective ad.

Amount and substantiality A factor to be considered in fair use claims. In general, small amounts of copying are more likely to be considered fair uses, while use of entire works or chapters will likely be considered unfair.

Andrea Dworkin A feminist author who with Catharine MacKinnon drafted an ordinance in both Minneapolis and Indianapolis that would make obscenity an attack on the civil rights of women.

Appropriation An action to compensate private figures whose names or pictures have been used without consent in advertising or promotional materials.

Arraignment A hearing to examine evidence to determine if formal charges of criminal wrongdoing will be made against a suspect.

Associated Press v. United States The 1945 Supreme Court holding that the antitrust law did apply to newspapers and that they were not immune under the First Amendment.

Balancing test Courts using the balancing test weigh the strength of the government interest in curbing expression against the First Amendment interest in allowing it.

Bar-press guidelines Voluntary statements, adopted in many states, that have been developed by journalists, lawyers, and judges regarding kinds of information that are appropriate for news coverage of criminal cases.

Berne Convention The most important international treaty on intellectual property. It calls for member nations to generally recognize the copyright protections from an owner's home country.

Better Business Bureau An organization founded in 1912 to keep on file complaints brought against businesses by those who have used their products or services.

***Brandenburg* approach to the clear and present danger doctrine** The approach currently in force was set forth in *Brandenburg v. Ohio* (1969): Advocacy of illegal action can only be prohibited "where such advocacy is directed to inciting or producing imminent lawless action and is likely to incite or produce such action."

Cable Television Consumer Protection and Competition Act of 1992 Legislation adopted by the U.S. Congress that, in part, increased federal, state, and local regulation of cable television especially of rates cable systems could charge subscribers.

Categorical approach Expression is divided among various categories. Some like political speech receive full First Amendment protection. Others like commercial speech receive different levels of protection. False and misleading commercial speech, for example, receives no protection. Other kinds of commercial speech are evaluated under the *Central Hudson* test.

Catharine MacKinnon A University of Michigan law professor and leading opponent in articles, books, and speeches of obscenity and its consequences.

Caveat emptor Let the buyer beware, the state of being victimized by a seller.

Cease-and-desist order An order from an administrative agency such as the FTC, similar to a court injunction.

Central Hudson Gas & Electric Corp. v. Public Service Commission The 1980 case that set down the four-part test for the First Amendment protection of commercial speech.

Central Hudson test Commercial speech may be regulated only if (1) the speech at issue is not misleading or illegal, (2) the government interest served by the regulation is substantial, (3) the regulation directly advances the governmental interest, and (4) the regulation is no more extensive than necessary to advance the governmental interest being served.

Chance Exists when the odds of winning are set randomly and the participant has no way of affecting the outcome.

Checking function Theory that the contemporary role of the press is to check or curb abuses by government. In this view, press scrutiny of government is likely to be more effective than anything individual citizens can provide.

Clayton Act A 1914 federal law that prohibits anticompetitive practices such as corporate mergers and predatory pricing.

Clear and convincing evidence A standard of proof between "a preponderance of evidence" and "beyond a reasonable doubt," required in proving actual malice in a libel suit.

Colloquium A plea that, although a plaintiff is not named in a publication, facts in the context of the publication, often called extrinsic facts, serve to identify that person.

Combat zone In the context of obscenity law, an area in which "sin" businesses such as adult bookstores are clustered or concentrated.

Commercial speech Defined in *Virginia Pharmacy* as speech that does nothing more than propose a commercial transaction. Defined more broadly in *Central Hudson* as expression that relates entirely to the economic interests of the speaker and the audience.

Common carrier standard The legal approach used to describe the obligation of public utilities such as phone companies to their subscribers. As a common carrier, the phone company must transmit the messages of all subscribers without regard to the message.

Common law The body of law, originating in England and continued in the United States, whereby principles of law are shaped by judges in decisions. It is judge-made law, in contrast to statutory law, which is enacted by legislatures.

Common law malice Ill will, spite, hostility, a desire for revenge. An older, common law form of malice; still required to be shown in some states to support a claim of punitive damages.

Communications Act of 1934 The major federal statute that still governs wired and wireless interstate electronic media. Has been amended many times since 1934.

Comparative advertising Advertising messages that attempt to compare, usually negatively, or distinguish similar products from one another.

Compelling interest Regulation that infringes upon fundamental constitutional rights such as freedom of expression must further a compelling governmental interest and be narrowly tailored to do so. The governmental interest must be so compelling that the free expression interest should be subordinated.

Complicity rule In some states, an employer may not be responsible for the statements of an employee, at least not for punitive damages.

Compulsory license Statutory permission to use a copyrighted work without consent of the owner. License fees are set by formula.

Computer tapes May be records under the FOIA, but the software needed to retrieve them may not be.

Conglomerate merger The joining together of different kinds of businesses, for example, a defense contractor and a television network.

Consent Implicit or explicit consent to publication. Those talking to reporters, unless there is an agreement to the contrary, ought to assume they are speaking for publication. A secondary defense against libel. In privacy law, consent generally refers to an explicit agreement between an individual and a representative of the media. Consent is occasionally inferred when public officials or public figures have been interviewed for news stories.

Consent agreement A voluntary yielding to the will of another; the act or result of coming into harmony or accord.

Consent decree agreement An FTC agreement with an advertiser not to run certain ads in the future, but with no admission of fault on the part of the advertiser.

Consideration In a lottery, the price the consumer pays to seek the prize.

Constitution The fundamental law of the United States. Under Article VI, the Supremacy Clause, state or federal laws that conflict with the Constitution are invalid. Since *Marbury v. Madison* (1803), state and federal courts exercise judicial review—the power to set aside government action that is inconsistent with the Constitution.

Contempt of court A type of punishment for violation of a court order. It will typically include fines, but may also include jail time.

Content-based Regulation that limits expression on the basis of harm flowing from its content. Such laws are subjected to strict scrutiny by courts.

Content-neutral Regulation that is content-neutral limits expression regardless of its content. Such regulation is usually evaluated by a standard of review less demanding than strict scrutiny.

Contest Usually refers to a game in which some sort of skill or ability is used to determine a winner.

Continuance A delay in the time a trial is scheduled to begin. It is occasionally sought in hopes that news coverage will diminish over time.

Convergence The merging or melding of previously distinct communications media, making business, technical and legal distinctions among forms of electronic media less meaningful.

Copyright An intangible property interest in literary or artistic creations. The Copyright Act gives creators or owners specific exclusive rights to control sales and uses of their creations.

Counteradvertising Advertising that directly rebuts a message already presented.

Criminal libel A suit in which the state is the plaintiff. Also called seditious libel, now generally discouraged in American jurisdictions.

Critique of protection for commercial speech Commercial speech should not merit First Amendment protection since it does not contribute to self-government or to individual self-fulfillment or autonomy.

Crossmedia ownership Ownership of different media by the same party—for example, combined ownership of broadcast stations and daily newspapers.

De novo New, over again from the beginning.

Declaratory judgment A declaration by a court of the rights of the parties to a lawsuit without ordering anything to be done. A suit would end at that point.

Defamation An attack on a person's reputation or character by false, malicious, or negligent statements.

Demonstration Showing in an advertisement how to use a product or what that product can do.

Demonstration permit requirements Permit requirements for access to public forums are permissible as long as standards for awarding permits are clear and do not allow content and viewpoint discrimination by administrative officials.

Descriptive mark A trademark that on its face tells consumers what the product is. It is difficult to make a descriptive mark distinctive.

Dilution Can occur where a noncompetitor uses the mark for commentary or other purposes, such as parody. The trademark owner argues that the use will mislead consumers into thinking the use was approved, thereby diluting the mark.

Disclosure (unreasonable) of private facts An action based upon the publication of embarrassing, sensitive personal information; sometimes called "pure privacy."

Discovery A pretrial phase in which parties seek information from each other.

Distinctiveness Exists when a trademark or service mark uses a fanciful or imaginary term or symbol to set it apart.

Diversity suit A lawsuit in which plaintiff and defendant reside in different states. In such situations a federal court will generally take jurisdiction.

Downward spiral A newspaper in economic stress. Circulation falls, advertising linage follows, first-issue costs increase under what is called the economies of scale, profitability falls, and the only remedy is to raise prices or cut costs, and thereby quality, further reducing circulation. So the spiral continues downward.

Due process The requirement that courts must follow specified procedures when making decisions that affect a person's rights.

Duopolies Common ownership of two electronic media of the same type in the same community for example, owning two TV stations in the same town.

Economies of scale In the case of a newspaper, a large part of production costs for labor, paper, and ink are spent in producing the first copy. Thereafter cost per unit decreases as circulation increases.

Editorial advertising Advertising in which the primary purpose is to promote a social, political, or cultural idea.

Effect of the use A factor to be considered in fair use claims; refers to the economic effects of copying. If the economic impact is great, a use is less likely to be considered fair.

Electronic yellow pages The video services offered by telephone companies (telcos) such as sports results, news services, financial market quotations, and entertainment advertising.

Employment at will Common law doctrine that assumes that employers and employees are both free agents and that either may terminate the relationship at any time.

Equal employment opportunity (EEO) Laws and policies that require employers to select employees without regard to gender or ethnic background except where those characteristics can be shown to be truly relevant to the performance of a job.

Equal protection Under the Fourteenth Amendment of the U.S. Constitution, all similarly situated persons are entitled to nondiscriminatory treatment so far as the guarantees of the Bill of Rights are concerned.

"Equal time" Section 315 of the Federal Communications Act obliges broadcasters to give equal opportunities to political candidates. If a broadcaster sells time to a candidate, the station must sell time to the opponent. Broadcasters are immunized against libel suits resulting from this use of their facilities.

Evidentiary privilege The right to refuse to testify in court about certain confidential relationships. Attorney-client and physician-patient relationships are covered by evidentiary privilege.

Exclusive rights In both copyright and trademark law, include the rights to use material, to license uses of material, and to allow derivative uses of materials.

Executive privilege In one sense the right of an executive agency to protect its deliberative process.

Fair comment A traditional or common law defense in libel suits, now more generally referred to as the "opinion" defense. It is qualified by the requirement that opinions not be based on demonstrably false facts. It is meant to protect those who criticize persons, such as actors and authors, who seek public approval for their work. The more disconnected to fact, or the more outrageous, incredible, or unverifiable, the less the chance of a successful suit.

Fair trial A right guaranteed by the Sixth Amendment. It requires that a defendant be tried by an unbiased jury.

Fair use A doctrine in copyright law that provides a limited legal right for others to use copyrighted materials without the owner's consent, especially where news, criticism or scholarship are involved. The fair use defense has had influence in right of publicity and trademark infringement cases.

Fairness doctrine The fairness doctrine was abolished by the FCC in 1987 as part of President Reagan's deregulation program and out of First Amendment concerns. It required broadcasters to (1) present some programming about controversial issues of public importance and (2) reasonably present opposing viewpoints on those issues.

False light A privacy action based upon inaccurate representation rather than assertion of fact, regardless of whether or not the information is defamatory.

Family Education Rights and Privacy Act Also referred to as the Buckley Amendment, a 1974 federal law that gives students the right to examine their own academic files. Parents need the consent of their children to see the files after the children reach age eighteen.

Fault In tort law, fault usually refers to some type of negligence. When proof of fault is required, a plaintiff must show at least negligence on the part of a defendant.

FCC v. Pacifica Foundation The U.S. Supreme Court decision upholding FCC regulation of broadcast indecency.

Federal candidates Candidates for offices of the federal government: president, vice president, senator, and representative.

Federal Communications Commission (FCC) An administrative agency based in Washington, D.C., that is run by five commissioners. The FCC enforces the Federal Communications Act of 1934, which generally governs the U.S. electronic media.

Federal Espionage Act Legislation enacted by Congress in 1917 during World War I under which many anti-war and pro–Russian Revolution dissidents were prosecuted. The Supreme Court opinions considering these prosecutions laid the foundation for modern First Amendment law and the clear and present danger doctrine.

Federal Privacy Act A 1974 law that is meant to protect the privacy of information held in federal government files. People named in those files have access to them, subject to the act's exemptions and the requirements of the FOIA. An FOIA for the individual.

Federal Radio Commission (FRC) Predecessor to the Federal Communications Commission. Governed interstate uses of radio (but not wired services like telephones and telegraphs) from 1927 until the FCC was created in 1934.

Federal Register The first place to look for the rules and regulations of U.S. administrative agencies such as the Federal Communications Commission and the Federal Trade Commission.

Federal Trade Commission (FTC) The federal agency largely responsible for the regulation of advertising.

Fee shifting The losing party in a suit pays the winner's attorney costs.

Fighting words Words that have a direct tendency to cause acts of violence by the individuals to whom they are addressed. Traditionally considered an unprotected category of expression and, therefore, subject to sanction. The rationale for regulation is that fighting words do not contribute to the life of ideas.

First Amendment bedrock principle Government may not prohibit the expression of an idea simply because society finds the idea to be offensive.

First Amendment standard for telcos The question of whether telcos offering video programming should be held to a common carrier standard or have the editorial autonomy enjoyed by newspapers.

First-sale doctrine Guarantees that the person who buys a copy of a copyrighted work is entitled to exercise complete ownership over that copy, including the right to resell or rent the copy.

Florida right of reply law Enacted in 1913, the law, struck down in *Miami Herald Publishing Co. v. Tornillo* (1974), required a newspaper to publish without cost a reply by a political candidate attacked by the newspaper during a political campaign.

Fourteenth Amendment Provides that no state shall "deprive any person of life, liberty or property without due process of law." Liberty has been interpreted to include freedom of expression, so the Fourteenth Amendment protects against state restraints on freedom of expression in the same manner as the First Amendment protects against restraints by the federal government.

Fox limitation on *Central Hudson* test *Board of Trustees of State University of New York v. Fox* (1989), softened the fourth part of the *Central Hudson* test. Even though a regulation is not the least restrictive way of dealing with a problem, it may still satisfy the no more extensive than necessary requirement. The fit between legislative objectives and the means to accomplish those objectives needs only to be reasonable, not perfect.

Fox's Libel Act A statute enacted by Parliament in 1792 that made truth a defense in seditious libel actions and allowed the jury rather than the judge to decide whether a challenged publication constituted seditious libel.

Franchise Authorization from one party to another authorizing the second party to engage in a specific activity. Cable operators usually obtain franchises from local government.

Franchisee The party that holds a franchise.

Franchisor The party that grants a franchise (in cable television, usually cities or counties).

Frederick Schauer A Harvard law professor who assisted in the writing of the Meese Report.

Freedom of Information Act (FOIA) The 1967 federal law making government documents available to the public unless they fit one or more of nine exemptions.

FTC Act The 1911 federal law that established the Federal Trade Commission and made unfair methods of competition in commerce unlawful.

Future of hate speech regulation Although *R.A.V.,* a Supreme Court ruling, presents problems for future hate speech regulation unless *all* fighting words are regulated, enhanced penalties for bias-motivated crimes are valid. Such laws are directed to conduct rather than expression and are not protected by the First Amendment.

Gag orders Court orders to journalists prohibiting dissemination of court proceedings to protect the defendant from prejudicial publicity. Gag orders are prior restraints and are presumptively invalid unless there is a clear and present danger to the administration of justice and no less drastic alternatives are available.

Generic mark A trademark that has lost both its secondary meaning and its distinctiveness. It has instead become the everyday word used to describe a product.

Glomarization A term invented out of the Glomar case that has come to represent the right of a government agency neither to deny nor to confirm the existence of a document.

Government-in-Sunshine Act The 1977 federal open meetings law.

Grand jury An investigative body that reviews information and accusations in criminal cases to determine if there is sufficient evidence to bring an indictment.

Hate speech Expression that denigrates a racial, ethnic, or religious group. Some have contended that it should be treated as unprotected low-value speech, but so far, the Court has not made it a new, unprotected category of expression.

Horizontal merger The addition of similar outlets to a corporation, such as newspaper chains.

Hostile audience The fact that a speaker arouses a hostile reaction does not justify the speaker's arrest, unless the speaker intentionally incites to violence. One of the purposes of the First Amendment is to invite dispute and stimulate unrest.

Housekeeping The right of a governmental agency generally to manage its own affairs.

In camera An examination of material in a judge's chambers, out of sight and hearing of the courtroom.

Indecency Something less offensive than obscenity and the standard government generally applies to broadcasters in regulating content; defined by the U.S.

Supreme Court in 1978 as "nonconformance with accepted standards of morality." May involve patently offensive depictions of sexual or excretory activities or organs when children are likely to be in the audience.

Idemnification clause A statement, usually in a contract for the purchase of time or space, in which the seller indicates that he or she is not responsible for any damage or injury or lawsuits resulting from the use of the advertised product or service.

Independent state grounds A privilege based on a state constitution or state statute cannot be reconsidered by the federal courts.

Indian gaming Gaming and gambling activities lawfully conducted by Native American tribes, usually on reservations. An increasing source of income for many tribes. Refers to casinos, keno parlors, and other gambling businesses.

Individual autonomy theory Sometimes called the individual liberty model of the First Amendment. Holds that freedom of expression is protected because of its relationship to the protection of individual autonomy and individual self-fulfillment.

Industry Guides Guidelines as to standards of advertising across an industry based on the FTC's interpretation of federal laws.

Injunction A judicial order that prevents a party from doing something or orders it to perform a specific act. In copyright, an injunction is used to stop additional distribution of infringing materials.

Intellectual property Intellectual property is the product of creativity or invention, and intellectual property law regarding copyrights, trademarks and patents is designed to encourage its creation.

Intelligence Identities Protection Act A 1982 federal law making it a crime to expose covert American agents.

Intentional infliction of emotional distress Occurs when a defendant, through a pattern of behavior aimed directly at an identified third party, intends to cause anguish or distress.

Intrusion upon seclusion An action designed to protect the privacy of individuals in their homes and other spaces by preventing the press from unauthorized entry when gathering news.

Intrusiveness In broadcast law, the idea that radio and television signals come uninvited into the homes, cars, and offices of listeners and viewers and, as a result, can be regulated by the federal government.

Invasion of privacy Interference with any legally recognized interest in protecting personal information or behavior, based on constitutional, common law, statutory, or data grounds. For the mass media, common law invasion of privacy is the greatest concern.

Involuntary public figure A person who becomes newsworthy but would just as soon remain anonymous. Most criminals and accident victims would fit this definition.

Kid-Vid The name given to hearings before the Federal Trade Commission intended to explore how to protect children from the advertising of certain products such as toys and sugared cereals.

Laissez faire Letting people do what they choose to do, especially in the world of business and economics.

Lanham Act The federal statute protecting trademarks used in interstate commerce. The act also prohibits types of unfair competition.

Lanham Trademark Law Revision Act A 1989 federal law that provides remedies for those hurt by false advertising, as well as protecting competitors from one another.

Leased access channels The Cable Communications Policy Act of 1984 required that cable systems with a specified channel capacity reserve some channels for leased commercial use by entities not affiliated with the cable system. This requirement was designed to prevent a cable operator from dominating programming.

Legal advertising The means by which government communicates formally with the citizenry. Also called public notice advertising.

Legally qualified candidate A candidate for a public elected office who, if elected, could hold the office. Qualifications typically include age and residence.

Letter of compliance An advertiser's agreement with the FTC not to repeat advertising that has resulted in complaints from consumers or competitors.

Libel *per quod* Indirect libel. A libel by innuendo, implication, or inference.

Libel *per se* Libel on its face. An obvious libel.

Libel-proof A reputation so tarnished that it cannot be further impaired by a fresh accusation.

Likelihood of confusion Exists when a competitor uses a close copy of another's trademark and consumers are either misled or will likely be misled into mistaking the copy for the original.

Limited public forum A public area that, while it may be used for expression of ideas, was not opened or dedicated for that purpose. The government can eliminate all expressive activity in a limited public forum if it wishes. A content-based restriction on expression will be subject to strict scrutiny.

Limited rights of access to the broadcast media Although there is no general right of access to the media, limited rights of access to the broadcast media such as the reasonable access provision for federal political candidates properly balance the First Amendment rights of federal candidates, the public, and broadcasters.

Lockhart Commission The first Presidential Commission on Obscenity (1970), headed by then University of Minnesota Law School Dean William Lockhart.

Lottery A scheme involving the three elements of prize, chance, and consideration, the third element requiring a player or participant to give up something of value such as time or money.

Mandatory PEG channels The Cable Communications Policy Act of 1984 authorized municipalities to require the dedication of some cable channels for public, educational, and governmental programming.

Market failure theory Argues that the marketplace of ideas does not work because even if entry to the marketplace is not restricted by government, entry is still restricted because the marketplace is dominated by large business interests.

Marketplace of ideas theory Ideas should be allowed to compete freely without government censorship or intervention. Proponents contend that out of this competition the best or truest ideas will emerge.

Meese Commission The second Presidential Commission on Obscenity (1986), chaired by then Attorney General Edwin Meese.

Meiklejohn critique of clear and present danger Meiklejohn criticized the clear and present danger doctrine for offering less protection than the Framers intended. In his view, the First Amendment provides absolute protection for core political speech.

Misappropriation Occurs when one takes another's product or work and peddles it as one's own.

Monopoly power The exercise of market power to control prices or exclude competitors.

Multimedia market A market in which all media compete for advertisers and audience.

Multiple system operators (MSOs) Cable companies that operate many cable systems throughout the country.

Must-carry provisions To preserve over-the-air free broadcasting, the Cable Television Consumer Protection and Competition Act of 1992 required cable operators to carry local over-the-air broadcast signals.

National Advertising Division (NAD) Staff of the Council of Better Business Bureaus screen complaints before they move on to the NARB. A query from

NAD can lead to modification of an unsubstantiated advertising claim.

National Advertising Review Board (NARB) Part of a self-regulatory system in advertising that acts upon complaints from industry about truth and accuracy in national advertising.

National Broadcasting Company v. United States The 1943 Supreme Court ruling that upheld the constitutionality of the broadcast regulatory system.

Natural monopoly A situation in which economics dictate a single newspaper or cable company in a particular community. Competitors could not survive.

Nature of the work A factor to be considered in fair use claims; refers to the type of work that has been copied. Unpublished works are especially protected.

Nature and purpose of the use A factor to be considered in fair use claims. The statute specifies criticism, news reporting, comment, teaching, and research as uses that are likely to be thought fair.

Nature of First Amendment protection The First Amendment protects freedom of speech and press, but this does not mean that it protects every spoken utterance or every printed word. Unprotected categories of expression may be regulated.

Negligence A level of fault below actual malice that private or nonpublic plaintiffs have to prove in libel suits. Injury or harm resulting from a failure by a defendant to behave as a reasonable person would have behaved under similar circumstances.

Negligent infliction of emotional distress Occurs where a reasonable person should have anticipated that his or her actions would cause anguish or distress to an identifiable third person.

Network nonduplication rules Laws requiring cable systems to block out network signals from distant TV stations if the same programs are being aired by local network affiliates. Protects the local network affiliates from losing viewers to nonlocal stations.

Neutral reportage A secondary libel defense based on the argument that the reporter, without malice or bias, is simply reporting both sides of a controversial issue of public importance. Courts are divided on its acceptability.

New York v. Ferber The 1982 Supreme Court ruling that, in effect, upheld the constitutionality of laws in forty-seven states that seek to protect children from viewing obscenity or being involved in its making.

New York Times v. Sullivan The landmark 1964 case that constitutionalized the law of libel by making it a First Amendment matter and by shifting the burden of proof for showing fault from defendant to plaintiff.

Newspaper Preservation Act A 1970 federal law that permits the business merger of competing daily newspapers, if one is failing; editorial departments remain separate. Such mergers are called joint operating agreements (JOAs) and, in effect, give newspapers in these situations immunity from such antitrust violations as profit pooling and price fixing.

Newsworthiness A defense that prevents privacy plaintiffs from winning cases when traditional standards of journalistic judgment have been used in publishing.

No-censorship requirement Part of Section 315 of the Communications Act of 1934 that prohibits broadcasters from editing the uses candidates for public office make of broadcast stations under that law.

No First Amendment right of access to the electronic media There is no enforceable First Amendment–based right of access to the broadcast media. Recognition of such a right would involve the FCC too closely in the day-to-day editorial decisions of broadcast journalists.

No general theory of the First Amendment Different tests, doctrines, and standards of review are applied in different contexts in First Amendment law.

Nonpublic forum Public areas such as airports that are not intended to be used as sites for expressive activity. Government may subject expressive activity in such forums to reasonable regulation. A place traditionally not thought to be suitable for speech activities, unless by invitation, e.g., a private home.

O'Brien test If regulation of conduct incidentally restricts expression, the regulation will be upheld only if (1) there was constitutional authority to enact the regulation, (2) the regulation furthers a substantial governmental interest, (3) the governmental interest is unrelated to the suppression of free expression, and (4) the restriction on free expression is no greater than necessary to further the governmental interest.

Obscenity Sexual content that may be banned by the government. Specifically defined by the U.S. Supreme Court. If content meets the definition, it is not protected under the First Amendment to the U.S. Constitution.

Offensive speech Speech that provokes reactions of disgust or distaste. It is protected speech and is not subject to regulation absent some compelling governmental interest.

Oliver Wendell Holmes Supreme Court justice from 1902 to 1932; appointed by President Theodore Roosevelt. Holmes's influence on First Amendment law was considerable both because of the power of his thought and the quotability of his decisions.

On its face Refers to the actual words set forth in a law.

Open records and open meetings laws All states now have their own open meetings and open records laws.

Originality A requirement for a work to qualify for copyright protection. A work is original if it represents the actual creative effort, no matter how little, of its author.

Overbreadth A law that proscribes both protected and unprotected expressive activity is overbroad and, therefore, invalid. The problem is that an individual may forego protected expression for fear of being sanctioned for engaging in unprotected expression.

Paid subscriber In postal law, a rule that requires a publication to have a list of genuine subscribers amounting to at least half its circulation to qualify for the subsidized second-class postal rate.

Participatory media Call-in radio and television talk shows whereby members of the public are invited to participate actively in the show and voice their views on issues.

Patently offensive As defined by the U.S. Supreme Court: "ultimate sexual acts, normal or perverted, actual or simulated," as well as "masturbation, excretory functions, and lewd exhibition of the genitals."

PEG access Channels on cable television systems reserved for use by public, educational, or governmental cablecasters.

Pentagon Papers Classified papers that a former Department of Defense (Pentagon) employee made available to the press and whose publication government sought unsuccessfully to prevent.

Performing rights societies Clearinghouses created to pool royalties for authors of musical and other works that are played on radio or elsewhere.

Personal attack rules Permit a person whose honesty, character, or integrity is attacked on broadcasting during the discussion of a controversial issue of public importance to respond without cost through the provision of equivalent time.

Personal services contract A type of employment agreement used when the employer believes that the employee's skills are unique and the employer wishes to prevent the employee from being lured away to work for competitors.

Pervasive or all-purpose public figure A person who is constantly in the public eye or has gained the status of celebrity or what some courts call a "public personality."

Pervasiveness Similar to intrusiveness in indecency law. Electronic media are presumed to be different than print media because they are thought to influence everyone's life.

Petitions to deny Paperwork filed with the FCC asking the commission not to grant a license sought by a broadcaster.

Plain view A privacy defense that provides that anything that could have been seen or heard from a public place, or a private place with consent, may be freely reported on.

Political editorializing rules Rules issued by the FCC that provide that when a broadcaster editorializes against a political candidate, the candidate or a spokesperson must be afforded an opportunity to respond. Would also apply to opponents of candidates the broadcaster has supported.

Pornoviolence A mixture of pornography and violence in visual communications.

Prejudicial publicity News coverage of a criminal case that due to its style, amount, or prominence has the capacity to influence potential jurors in the case.

Preliminary hearing An examination of a person charged with a crime and a review of the evidence against that person. It is conducted by a judge or magistrate.

Prior restraint Censorship, prohibition of publication by government or a requirement that a publication be presented to an official for review and approval before it is disseminated to the public. At common law, freedom of the press was understood to mean freedom from prior restraint.

Prize For lottery purposes, anything of value for which a ticket or chance must be bought.

Procedural due process The idea that government should at a minimum afford notice and hearing to people before it attempts to affect their interests adversely.

Promissory estoppel The doctrine that requires a promise to be enforced when someone has relied upon and acted (or refrained from acting) upon it and injustice can be avoided only by enforcement of the promise.

Prudent publisher test One of a number of variations of the definition of *actual malice*; here "a showing of highly unreasonable conduct constituting an extreme departure from the standards of investigation ordinarily adhered to by responsible publishers."

Public record Any record generated by a government body. The term includes but is not limited to records specified in freedom of information statutes.

Public access channels Franchise agreements between a municipality and a cable system sometimes require the cable system to dedicate one or more channels to the public on a first come–first served basis. These are referred to as public access channels.

Public character Periodicals of a public character are given second-class mailing permits. The courts have concluded that having subscribers is sufficient proof that the content is of a public character.

Public figure A person who has either achieved general fame or who has actively sought notoriety; the definition is the same in privacy law as in libel law.

Public interest, convenience, and necessity The standard by which all actions of the FCC must be justified. If challenged, the FCC must be able to prove that what it has done advances the public interest, convenience, and (sometimes or) necessity. Vague language in the Federal Communications Act that sets the standard for the granting and renewal of broadcast licenses.

Public meeting A gathering of a quorum of a public body, such as a city council, at which government business may be conducted.

Public offices Governmental offices where public elections—rather than appointment—determine who serves.

Public press The press that is funded by the state, such as college newspapers at state-supported colleges. In some circumstances, the access obligations of the public press may be greater than is the case with the private press.

Public rights of way Physical spaces (roads, sidewalks, areas where power poles are located) that are owned by the public and dedicated to providing services that all citizens enjoy.

Puffery In advertising, exaggeration for effect, sensationalizing, phantasizing.

Punitive damages Payment of money to an aggrieved party designed to punish or make an example of so as to discourage similar behavior in the future. Sometimes called exemplary damages.

Qualified privilege A traditional or common law defense in libel suits that protects the reporting of governmental proceedings in any form, if that reporting is reasonably accurate. Negligence will defeat a defense of qualified or conditional privilege. Sometimes called the fair report or public eye defense. More generally a privilege that can be overcome by a stronger interest. For example, a journalist's privilege not to identify a source is qualified in that it can be overcome by greater constitutional interests.

Quash To vacate or nullify.

R.A.V. limitation on fighting words doctrine In *R.A.V. v. St. Paul* (1992), the Court held that even fighting words are not invisible to the First Amendment. Fighting words may be regulated for their proscribable content but may not be used as vehicles for content discrimination.

Radio Act of 1927 Federal statute regulating users of the spectrum from 1927 until 1934 when the Communications Act of 1934 was adopted. Broadcast portions of the 1927 act were nearly identical to those of the 1934 act.

Rational basis In federal constitutional law, a test used to uphold government regulation when no constitutional rights, such as freedom of speech, are involved.

Rationale for protection of commercial speech In a free enterprise society, the free flow of commercial information and democratic decision-making are　· directly related. Although commercial speech does not receive full First Amendment protection, it is entitled to some protection.

Rationale for hate speech regulation The argument that toleration of hate speech serves to reinforce the general powerlessness and subordinate status of minority groups. Protecting hate speech tends to strengthen existing patterns of inequality.

Reasonable access Broadcast stations must allow candidates for federal public office to purchase reasonable amounts of time during campaigns. The Federal Communications Act of 1934 provides in § 312 (a) (7) that the FCC can revoke a broadcaster's license for willful or repeated failure to provide reasonable access for federal political candidates.

Reasonable person A standard of culpability that is just, proper, ordinary, usual, or reasonable, or based on the views of a person with those characteristics.

Red Lion Broadcasting v. FCC The U.S. Supreme Court decision upholding the FCC's fairness doctrine because it advanced the First Amendment rights of listeners and viewers to receive information even though doing so required some government supervision of content.

Red Lion standard *Red Lion Broadcasting Co. v. FCC* (1969) upheld the fairness doctrine as reasonable regulation of the broadcast media that served the public interest, implemented the First Amendment, and was justified by the scarcity rationale. The Red Lion standard is shorthand for a First Amendment approach that permits reasonable regulation of the media.

Reporters Committee for Freedom of the Press A Washington-based watchdog organization that is especially sensitive to freedom of information and access to government records and meetings claims.

Respondeat superior An employer in most states is responsible for defamatory statements made, written, published, or broadcast by an employee.

Retraction statutes Typically provide that a defendant can mitigate damages in a libel suit by publishing a retraction. One difference between retraction and a right of reply is that the newspaper prepares the retraction whereas the person attacked writes the reply.

Retraction A full and fair correction and apology for a defamatory publication. A majority of states provide for retraction by statute, that is, by a retraction law.

Reverse FOIA suit A suit to require an agency to keep information secret.

Richmond Newspapers v. Virginia The 1980 case that first made traditional access of press and public to criminal trial courts a First Amendment right.

RICO The Racketeer Influenced Corrupt Organization law, a 1984 amendment to the federal Organized Crime Control Act of 1978, which allows the forfeiture of all assets acquired or maintained through a violation of law.

Right of access There is no general right of access to the media, but limited rights of access do exist in the electronic media. A right of access enables individuals and groups to present ideas through the media. The right would not be dependent on the media first attacking those seeking access.

Right of access to advertising Although there is no First Amendment right of access to advertise in a daily newspaper, a newspaper's refusal to accept advertising may in some circumstances violate the antitrust laws.

Right of publicity An action designed to protect the ability of celebrities and other famous people to profit from and control the use of their names, photos, or attributes in advertising and promotional materials.

Right to refuse Advertising media have an absolute right to refuse any ad submitted to them, except in some antitrust situations or where there has been a breach of contract.

Right of reply No general right of reply exists in either the electronic media or the print media, but rights of reply are available in specialized contexts in the electronic media. A right of reply would provide space equivalent to the original attack in the print media and equivalent time in the electronic media. Persons attacked would respond in their own words.

Role of judge in clear and present danger Courts and not the legislature have the task of deciding whether the clear and present danger test is met.

Sable Communications of California v. FCC A 1990 Supreme Court case invalidating legislation outlawing telephone indecency or dial-a-porn.

Sales tax A tax applied to purchase transactions, usually as a percentage of the total value of the sale. Most state sales tax laws apply to all sales of tangible products.

Scarcity theory The idea that broadcast media must be regulated by the government because only a limited number of broadcasters can use the spectrum at the same time.

Scarcity rationale Refers to the fact that the electromagnetic spectrum is finite. Since it is not possible for all who might wish to use the spectrum to broadcast to do so, government is justified in regulating broadcasting in the public interest.

Secondary meaning In trademark law, refers to the ability of a mark to instantly invoke the source of a product or service in the mind of a consumer.

Section 312(a)(7) Provision of the Communications Act of 1934 that requires broadcasters to provide "reasonable access" to their stations to federal candidates for campaigning.

Section 315 Provision of the Communications Act of 1934 that requires broadcasters to treat opposing candidates for the same public office "equally" except in a number of news-related contexts.

Sedition Act One of the Alien and Sedition Laws enacted by congress in 1798, which made criticism of the president, congress, or government a crime. The act was never tested by the Supreme Court and simply expired.

Seditious libel Laws originating in England that made criticism of government officials criminal offenses.

Self-predation Where a newspaper sells advertising and subscriptions below costs in order to be seen as failing and therefore eligible for a Joint Operating Agreement or JOA.

Self regulation Systems and standards that individuals and groups develop for themselves to guide their conduct. Often created to head off regulation by government.

Sequestration The practice of isolating members of a jury from the potential of outside influences; it may result in jurors living in hotels and having limited access to the news media.

Service mark Similar to a trademark but used to identify a service rather than a product.

Sherman Act An 1890 act of Congress that prohibits contracts, combinations, trusts, and conspiracies that restrain trade or encourage monopoly.

Shield laws State statutes that protect journalists from being forced to disclose information or materials in court.

Sine qua non A thing or condition that is indispensable.

Single publication rule Only one suit can be maintained for one libel, regardless of how many individual newspapers have been printed and circulated.

Special damages In libel compensation for out-of-pocket money losses. Damages defined by statute and provided automatically when copyright infringement is proven. The amounts vary depending on the behavior of the defendant and on the size of the copying and market.

Standard of review for must-carry rules In *Turner Broadcasting System, Inc. v. FCC* (1994), the Court deemed the must-carry rules to be content-neutral and reviewed them under the mid-level standard of review set forth in *United States v. O'Brien* (1968). The *O'Brien* standard is not as hostile to government regulation as the *Tornillo* standard nor as lenient to government regulation as the *Red Lion* standard.

Statute of Anne The first copyright law enacted in England. It established the modern principle that a primary purpose of copyright protection is encouragement of writers and artists.

Statute of limitations A statute that specifies a limited period of time in which a plaintiff may file an action. In libel one, two, or three years, depending upon the state.

Strict scrutiny The most demanding standard of review applied by courts to regulation infringing fundamental rights such as freedom of expression. Thus, these rights are not absolute, but regulations that limit them must both serve a compelling governmental interest and be narrowly tailored to do so.

Striking similarity Must be shown to prove copyright infringement. It is usually enough to show that the original work and the infringing work are substantially identical in whole or in part.

Subpoena An order requiring someone to appear in court as a witness or provide materials to the court.

Subsequent punishment Differs from prior restraint in that although subsequent punishment may befall an editor who publishes what has been prohibited, nonetheless, the publication has been disseminated. The idea has been communicated.

Summary judgment A motion designed to prevent a case from going to trial, there being no dispute as to facts and the law being clearly on the side of the defendant.

Symbolic speech Expressive activity that is not verbal or written, e.g., burning the flag to express hostility to the government. The purpose of describing such expressive activity as symbolic speech is to try to elevate it to the status of protected speech.

Syndicated exclusivity rules FCC rules that require cable systems to "block out" syndicated programming coming from a nonlocal TV station if a local TV station has the right to broadcast that program in a community.

Tax-exempt status Qualifying organizations are not required to pay the taxes a business might, although they are required to file informational returns. Available for certain types of charities, trade associations, and other groups.

Telco entry into video programming There is a controversy about whether the regional Bell telephone companies (telcos) should be allowed to originate and disseminate video programming. The newspaper and the cable industry have in the main opposed such entry, but existing legal barriers are increasingly being successfully challenged on First Amendment grounds.

Temporary restraining order (TRO) A judge's order prohibiting certain action prior to a hearing on the matter.

Testimonial Celebrity endorsement of a product or service.

Three branches of the federal government The legislative, executive, and judicial branches. The legislative branch makes laws and appropriates funds. The executive branch enforces and administers the laws. The judicial branch interprets the laws in the course of deciding particular cases.

Tornillo standard *Miami Herald Publishing Co. v. Tornillo* (1969) invalidated a state law requiring a right of reply for political candidates in newspapers attacking them as an impermissible intrusion on editorial autonomy. The *Tornillo* standard is shorthand for a First Amendment approach that is hostile to government regulation of the media.

Tort A legal action providing redress for wrongs between individuals. Tort law includes fraud, trespass, negligence, libel, and invasion of privacy.

Trade libel Disparagement of someone's product or services. Generally, special damages have to be proven in such cases.

Trade Regulation Rules Rules developed by the Federal Trade Commission to protect consumers against false and deceptive advertising and marketing practices by defining the outer boundaries of behavior for specific goods and services.

Trademark A symbol, name, logo, or other device that is used to identify the source of a product for consumers. The best trademarks are immediately recognizable.

Traditional public forum Public areas such as parks and streets that have long been opened or dedicated for expressive activity by government. Discussion and protest are available in such areas as a matter of right, subject to reasonable regulation.

Trespass Entering onto or affecting the property of another person without permission.

Truth A traditional or common law defense in libel suits. Where it is used as a separate defense, the burden of proving truth would be on the defendant.

Turner Broadcasting v. FCC Decision of the U.S. Supreme Court upholding federal statutes requiring cable systems to carry local broadcast TV stations ("must-carry" rules).

Unconstitutional conditions A doctrine used to void rules that require that the recipient of a government benefit or subsidy give up a constitutional right to get the benefit.

Unfair competition Occurs when a competing business attempts to "pass off" its product or service as if it were the product or service of a competitor.

Unprotected speech If expression is unprotected by the First Amendment, legislatures and government officials may more easily regulate it. Usually includes obscenity, fighting words, child pornography, and illegal incitement to lawless action, among other categories.

Use In broadcast law, occurs when one legally qualified candidate for a public office appears on a radio or TV station during a campaign (with certain exceptions). Broadcasters must allow opposing candidates equal opportunities to use the station.

Vaughn Index A motion for a Vaughn Index is a motion asking a court to order a government agency to provide a complete accounting of all the documents in its possession that it is withholding and its reasons for withholding each piece that has been requested.

Venue The geographic location where a trial is held. The Sixth Amendment calls for criminal trials to be held in the state and district where the crime was committed.

Vertical merger The merging of program production and distribution systems.

Void for vagueness doctrine A law that does not provide notice to people as to the conduct that they must take or not take to avoid the sanction of the law is void for vagueness.

Voir dire The portion of a trial in which a jury is selected.

Voluntary access to the press mechanisms Although the *Tornillo* case held that the press was not required to provide access, voluntary responses to the problem of access include the op-ed page and the establishment of a press *ombudsman*.

Vortex or limited-purpose public figure A person who momentarily or for a limited period becomes visible, controversial, or newsworthy.

Wire service defense An argument in mitigation of damages that your publication had a usually reliable source.

Table of Cases

Principal cases are in italic type. Non-principal cases are in roman type. References are to pages.

Index

Page numbers in italic refer to definitions.